INDIA

INDIA
A SACRED GEOGRAPHY

DIANA L. ECK

THREE RIVERS PRESS
NEW YORK

THREE RIVERS PRESS and the Tugboat design are registered trademarks of
Random House, Inc.

Originally published in hardcover in the United States by Harmony Books,
an imprint of the Crown Publishing Group, a division of Random House, Inc.,
New York, in 2012.

Library of Congress Cataloging-in-Publication Data

Eck, Diana L.
   India : a sacred geography / by Diana L. Eck.—1st ed.
       p. cm.
   Includes bibliographical references.
   1. India—Religion. 2. Sacred space—India. 3. Hinduism—India. I. Title.
BL2001.3.E25 2011
294.50954—dc22   2011009237

ISBN 978-0-385-53192-4
eISBN 978-0-385-53191-7

Printed in the United States of America

All photos courtesy of the author, except p. 113, courtesy of Asian Art Archives,
Univ. Michigan (AAAUM), and p. 357, *Krishna Lifting Mount Govardhan*,
attributed to Mola Ram (1760–1833).

Book design by Lauren Dong
Maps by C. Scott Walker, Digital Cartography Specialist, Harvard Map Collection;
map, p. 106, by Michael Gellatly
Cover design by Nupoor Gordon
Cover painting: Detail of Radha and Krishna Walking in a Flowering Grove
© *The Metropolitan Museum of Art, Image source: Art Resource, NY*

10 9 8 7 6 5 4 3 2 1

First Paperback Edition

To Dorothy Eck and Dorothy Austin
The two Dorothys, both gifts of God

CONTENTS

Note on Transliteration and Pronunciation

While Sanskrit is said to be the "perfectly made" and polished speech of the gods, those of us who are mortal and write in English have to simplify the transliteration for ease of reading. In this book, I have kept diacritical marks to a bare minimum, using only the long mark, or macron, important for the proper pronunciation of short and long vowels.

a (as allow: Shiva)	ā (as in father: Kāshī)
i (as in it: *linga*)	ī (as in magazine: *devī*)
u (as in put: Upanishad)	ū (as in rude: Chitrakūt)

For consonants, I have written both the retroflex "s" (with a dot under it as in Viṣnu) and the palatal "s" (with an accent mark as in Śiva) as "sh," since this is basically how they are pronounced. Other distinctions in this precisely articulated language have also been lost here.

Aspirated consonants (those followed by an "h") are pronounced as follows: "bh" as in clubhouse, *Bhagavad Gītā;* "dh" as in roundhouse, *dharma;* "th" as in hothouse *(tīrtha)*. Two-syllable words are usually accented on the first syllable: **Shi**va, **Vish**nu, *dharma*. In words of more than two syllables, the penultimate syllable is accented if it contains a long vowel (Vishva**nā**tha, Pu**rā**na) or a dipthong (Kuru**kshe**tra). Otherwise, the accent is on the antepenultimate (third from last) syllable, as in Ra**mā**yana, Maha**bhā**rata, Amara**kan**taka, **Rā**vana, **Laksh**mana.

Another issue is that of Sanskrit and Hindi transliteration. The most noticeable difference between Sanskrit and Hindi words is the presence of the final short "a" in Sanskrit and its absence in Hindi. For example, *darshana* ("seeing" the divine image) becomes *darshan* in Hindi, Ganesha becomes Ganesh, Prayāga becomes Prayāg. I have not chosen one form exclusively over the other, but have tried to be consistent to the context. For example, if the reference is to a Sanskrit text, I might use Somanātha, but on the whole I have kept the form in which these words are most easily recognizable today, which would be Somnāth. (Similarly, Badrīnāth rather than Badarīnātha, Hardvār, rather than Haridvāra, Chitrakūt rather than Chitrakūta.) Even when I switch back and forth, the reader will soon adjust to the fact that this is simply the complexity of an ancient, yet modern, culture.

Finally, we should note that so many of the major cities of British India have now claimed official Indian names: Mumbai rather than Bombay; Chennai rather than Madras; Kolkata rather than Calcutta; Thiruvananthapuram, rather than Trivandrum. I have used both forms, since both are still in common parlance. I have not used diacritical marks on cities, states, common mountain ranges, or other geographical features, with the exception of rivers.

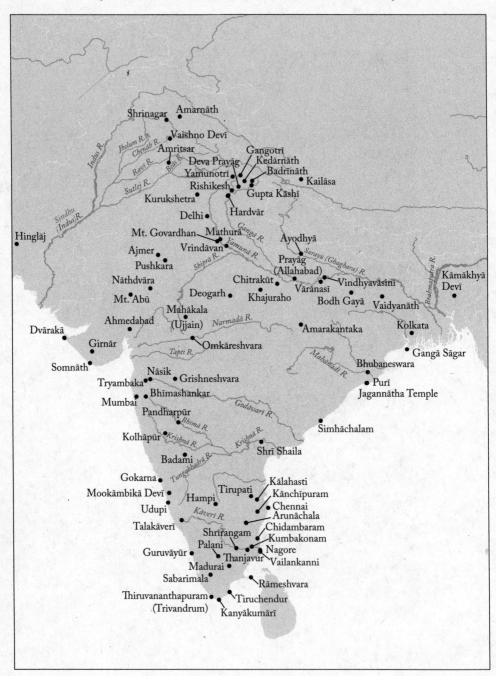

A Sacred Geography,
An Imagined Landscape

I began thinking about this book in the city of Banāras on the River Gangā in north India more than twenty-five years ago. I was then writing a book about that great city, a place I presumed to be the most important sacred city of India. Over the centuries, many visitors to Banāras, or Vārānasī, have compared this city in sanctity and preeminence to Mecca, Jerusalem, and Rome, as the holiest center of Hindu pilgrimage. For example, in the 1860s, a British civil servant, Norman Macleod, wrote effusively, "Benares is to the Hindoos what Mecca is to the Mohammedans, and what Jerusalem was to the Jews of old. It is the 'holy' city of Hindostan. I have never seen anything approaching to it as a visible embodiment of religion; nor does anything like it exist on earth."[1] The singling out of a center toward which an entire religious community turns in collective memory or in prayer made sense to Macleod, as it does for many who have been schooled in the habits of thought shaped by Western monotheistic consciousness. Even in India, there have been many who would agree on the central and supreme significance of Banāras, which Hindus also called Kāshī, the Luminous, the City of Light.[2] This is a powerful and ancient city, its dense maze of alleyways as dark as its riverfront is radiant. Its morning bathing rites facing the rising sun and its smoking cremation grounds right there along the riverfront are the heartbeat of a city that never fails to leave a lasting imprint on the visitor or pilgrim.

I lived off and on for years in Banāras. Even as I investigated the legends and temples of this city, however, I began gradually to understand what most Hindus who visit the city already know—that Banāras does not stand alone as the great center of pilgrimage for Hindus, but is part of an extensive network of pilgrimage places stretching throughout the

The bathing ghāts of Kāshī's great riverfront

length and breadth of India. The very names of the temples, the *ghāts*, and the bathing tanks of the city are derived from this broader landscape, just as the names of Kāshī and its great Shiva temple of Vishvanātha are to be found in pilgrimage places all over India. I began to realize that the entire land of India is a great network of pilgrimage places—referential, inter-referential, ancient and modern, complex and ever-changing. As a whole, it constitutes what would have to be called a "sacred geography," as vast and complex as the whole of the subcontinent. In this wider network of pilgrimage, nothing, not even the great city of Banāras, stands alone, but rather everything is part of a living, storied, and intricately connected landscape.

At first, I resisted the complexities of this peripheral vision, still interested as I was in establishing what makes this one place special, different from the rest. It became clear to me, however, that I could understand Banāras only in the context of a much wider system of meanings in which significance is marked not by uniqueness, but by multiplicity, even in the great city of Kāshī. Everything about *the* holy city seemed to be duplicated elsewhere, set amid a pattern of symbolic signification that made Banāras not unique, but inextricably part of a wider landscape shaped by the repetition and linking of its features. I began to realize that Kāshī was not *the* center, but one of multiple centers in a fascinating and poly-centric landscape, linked with the tracks of pilgrimage.

The most important of the religious claims of this sacred city is that Kāshī, the City of Light, is a place of spiritual liberation, which is called *moksha* or *mukti*. *Kashyām maranam muktih*, they say. "Death in Kāshī is liberation." Pilgrims come to Kāshī from all over India to live out their old age and die a good death there. In this, Kāshī is special, famous for death, some would say preeminent. And yet Kāshī is also said to be one of seven cities that bestow *moksha*, including Ayodhyā, Mathurā, Hardvār, Kānchī, Ujjain, and Dvārakā. These seven are all called *mokshadāyaka*, the givers of spiritual freedom. Kāshī is also said to be the earthly mani-festation of Shiva's luminous sacred emblem, the *linga* of light, where Shiva's infinite shaft of light pierced the earth. And yet so are at least eleven other places, all renowned throughout India, the whole group known as the twelve *lingas* of light. As I studied Banāras years ago, their names were just names to me, although each of these renowned sites of Shiva was represented by a temple within the sacred structure of Kāshī, as well. I began to realize that the famous goddesses of Kāshī are also linked to hundreds of goddesses in a network of association called the *shākta pīthas*, or "power seats," of the Goddess. The River Gangā, skirt-ing the city, with its famous bathing *ghāts*, is one of the "seven Gangās" of India, including the Narmadā, Godāvarī, and Kāverī Rivers, each of which lays claim to the heavenly origin and gracious power of the Gangā that flows past Banāras in north India. This whole sacred zone of Kāshī is said to have a radius of five *kroshas*, about ten miles, and this zone is circled by a famous five-day pilgrimage called the *panchakroshī*, with five stops along the way. Gradually, I discovered that the *panchakroshī* is not a unique pilgrimage, but a type of fivefold pilgrimage that is also found in Ayodhyā, in Omkāreshvara on the Narmadā River, on Mount Brahmāgiri in Maha-rashtra, and in dozens of other places. And, to top it off, Kāshī itself is duplicated, with cities and temples all over India called the "Kāshī of the South," the "Kāshī of the North," or the "Hidden Kāshī" of the Himalayas.

One afternoon on an early trip into the Himalayas, I stopped at one of these other Kāshīs: Gupta Kāshī, the "Hidden Kāshī," high in the valley of the Mandākinī River, one of the tributaries of the Gangā. Here, in this small village, I found a stout Kāshī Vishvanātha temple. In front of the temple there was a finely built *kund*, a bathing tank, called Manikarnikā after the bathing tank at Manikarnikā, the great cremation ground, in Kāshī. The bathing tank was fed by cold springs, the waters of which were said to come directly from Gangotrī and Yamunotrī, the Himalayan headwaters of the Gangā and Yamunā Rivers. Gomukh, the Cow's Mouth, as we shall see, is the name of the place high above Gangotrī where the first trickle of the Gangā emerges from the edge of a glacier. I recalled that in the great Kāshī down on the plains, Manikarnikā Kund is also fed, so they say, by an underground spring flowing directly from Gomukh. The clear connections that linked this small village, its temple, and its bathing tank with Kāshī and the larger sacred geography of India made real for me the notions I had read in the texts for many years. I found that Gupta Kāshī is also linked to the great stories of the *Mahābhārata,* as are many places in the Himalayas. The Pāndava brothers and Draupadī came this way as they climbed into the mountains on their last earthly journey, they say. Here the five Pāndavas left their war clubs, which they would need no more, and the clubs are there today, in the small temple of Shiva's manifestation Bhairava.[3]

During these subsequent years, I have traveled many thousands of miles on the pilgrim tracks of this wider sacred geography, trying to understand from the ground up the ways in which India has been composed through the centuries as a sacred landscape. I took careful notes of the duplication of sacred places, the networks of sacred rivers, the systematizing of *lingas* of light, the proliferation of seats of the Goddess. I visited the headwaters of four of the seven sacred rivers—the Gangā, the Narmadā, the Godāvarī, and the Kāverī. I traveled down the Western Ghāts, along the narrow stretch of land between the mountains and the sea called Parashurāma Kshetra, the land said to have been retrieved from the sea by one of the *avatāras* of Vishnu, Parashurāma. I discovered time and again how intricately and elaborately storied each part of the land of India really is. I sought out the places associated with Krishna's life and lore—from the birthplace of Krishna in Mathurā to the place he is said to have died in peninsular Gujarat. I came upon countless places said to have been visited by the heroes of the *Mahābhārata* as they roamed the forests of ancient India in exile, or by Rāma, Sītā, and Lakshmana in the forest journey described in the *Rāmāyana.* It became increasingly clear to me that anywhere one goes in India, one finds a living landscape in which mountains, rivers, forests, and villages are elaborately linked to the stories of the gods and heroes. The land bears the traces of the gods and the footprints of the heroes. Every place has its story, and conversely, every story in the vast storehouse of myth and legend has its place.

This landscape not only connects places to the lore of gods, heroes, and saints, but it connects places to one another through local, regional, and transregional practices of pilgrimage. Even more, these tracks of connection stretch from this world toward the horizon of the infinite, linking this world with the world beyond. The pilgrim's India is a vividly imagined landscape that has been created not by homing in on the singular importance of one place, but by the linking, duplication, and multiplication of places so as to constitute an entire world. The critical rule of thumb is this: Those things that are deeply important are to be widely repeated. The repetition of places, the creation of clusters and circles of sacred places, the articulation of groups of four, five, seven, or twelve sites—all this constitutes a vivid symbolic landscape characterized not by exclusivity and uniqueness, but by polycentricity, pluralism, and duplication. Most important, this "imagined landscape" has been constituted not by priests and their literature, though there is plenty of literature to be sure, but by countless millions of pilgrims who have generated a powerful sense of land, location, and belonging through journeys to their hearts' destinations.

In the early 1990s, the political dimensions of this sacred geography burst into flame with the contestation over the Rāmjanmabhūmi, the Birthplace of Rāma, in Ayodhyā, a site said to have been destroyed in the sixteenth century by one of the generals of the Mughal emperor Babur and forever sealed by building a mosque right on top of it. A strident new form of Hindu nationalism vowed to rebuild Rāma's temple. The throngs of activists voiced the slogan *Hum mandir vahīn banāyenge.* ("We'll build the temple at that very place.") The sustained controversy over the exact locus of Rāma's birth raised sharply the very meaning of uniqueness in the symbolization of Hindu sacred geography. Even in Ayodhyā, there had been many places that claimed Rāma's birth as part of their sacred lore. How very dissonant the pledge to reclaim "this very place" sounded, given India's long history of multiplying the sacred in a complex landscape, rich with a sense of plenitude. Of course, the traditional religious advertisements and praises of Hindu India's hundreds of sacred places do indeed extol "this very place." They even employ the poetic license of exaggeration to amplify the greatness and glory of "this very place."[4]

But such praises are always set in the context of a wider peripheral vision in which the places praised are not unique, but ultimately numberless, limited not by the capacity of the divine to be present at any one of them, but by the capacity of human beings to discover and to apprehend the divine presence at all of them. The dissonance, of course, arises from a discourse of exclusivity and uniqueness, more typical of the monotheistic traditions of the West, now arising in a Hindu context in which patterns of religious meaning have traditionally been constructed on the mythic presuppositions of divine plurality and plenitude.

This is a book about India, the pilgrim's India. For a time, I was discouraged about the writing of it, fearing that somehow the image of a sacred geography enlivened by the presence of the gods and interlinked through the circulation of pilgrims would further feed the fervor of an exclusive new Hindu nationalism. But the reality I describe and interpret here is clearly one not of religious exclusivity, but rather of complexity, mobility, and plurality. This is a book about the ways in which networks of pilgrimage places have composed a sense of location and belonging— locally, regionally, and transregionally. I do not say "nationally," for this way of articulating a land and landscape is far older than the modern nation-state. The pilgrim's India reaches back many hundreds of years and brings to us an astonishing picture of a land linked not by the power of kings and governments, but by the footsteps of pilgrims.

This narrative way of construing the land is germane, however, to understanding the communities of emotion and ritual practice that give power and depth to the Hindu nationalism of today. While some of the scholarly analyses of Indian nationalism and, more recently, Hindu nationalism have recognized this living landscape, most pay little heed to the pilgrimage practices that have long generated a relationship to the land we call India. In his book *The Felt Community,* Indian intellectual historian Rajat Kanta Ray makes a strong case for looking at what he refers to as "communities of emotion," drawing on Weber's "communities of sentiment." He looks carefully and appreciatively at the forms of cultural belonging that are deeply rooted in the Hindu and Indo-Muslim past. He writes, "The prehistory of every national movement lies in emotions, identities, and notions. These constitute the mentality and culture of the body of people who are or have been seized by the idea of becoming a sovereign national state. That idea may be new, but the mentality and emotions are rooted in the past."[5] As Sheldon Pollock has so masterfully demonstrated, this is also a literary world, in which the use of Sanskrit for royal inscriptions and praise poetry created a geographical sphere, a "Sanskrit cosmopolis," that stretched across what we call "India."[6]

There is no question that the "pilgrim's India" provides an important perspective for understanding India, not simply in the past, but in the present. As arcane as *lingas* of light, shrines linked by the body of the Goddess, and sacred rivers falling from heaven may seem to those who wish to get on with the real politics of today's world, these very patterns of sanctification continue to anchor millions of people in the imagined landscape of their country.

TĪRTHAS: SACRED CROSSINGS

The places pilgrims seek out are called *tīrthas*, literally "fords" or "crossings," coming from a verbal root meaning "to cross over." It is the first word we need to know in exploring the sacred geography of India. In ancient times, the *tīrtha* was literally a place to ford the river, and many of India's religious *tīrthas* are, to be sure, on the banks and at the confluence of its great rivers. More broadly, however, the *tīrtha* is a place of spiritual crossing, where the gods are close and the benefits of worship generous. At a spiritual crossing place, one's prayers are amplified, one's rites are more efficacious, one's vows more readily fulfilled. *Tīrtha*, with its many associations, is a word of passage and, in some ways, a word of transcendence.[7]

In the early Vedas and Upanishads, there are many spiritual uses of the term *tīrtha* and its notions of crossing.[8] In the Vedas, the fire altar in its many forms is constructed as a place of crossing and communication between this world and the beyond, the aniconic sacred fire itself being the vehicle of crossing. The gods descend to take their place in the ritual arena of the sacrifice, and the prayers of the priests on behalf of the sponsor of the sacrifice ascend to the heavens. Indeed, the sponsor of the ritual is assured ascent to the heavens as well. In the wisdom traditions of the Upanishads, "crossing over" often refers to the soul's spiritual transition and transformation from this world to what is called the world of Brahman, the Supreme, the world illumined by the light of knowledge. Here, it is a crossing made not by the elaborate Vedic rituals, but by spiritual knowledge, a crossing that must be made with the aid of a guide, a guru, and the knowledge he imparts. The *Prashna Upanishad*, for instance, ends with the student's praise of the guru: "You truly are our father—you who lead us across to the shore beyond ignorance." In the *Isha Upanishad*, a person crossing over death gains immortality by virtue of knowledge. In the *Mundaka Upanishad*, sorrow and sin are crossed over to reach immortality. The knower of Brahman, it is said, becomes Brahman. "He crosses over [*tarati*] sorrow. He crosses over [*tarati*] sin. Liberated from the knots of the heart, he becomes immortal."[9]

In the *Mahābhārata* and the popular literature of the Purānas, the term *tīrtha* comes to common use as the spiritual ford that is the destination of pilgrims. During the first millennium C.E., pilgrim journeys, called *tīrthayātrās*, were increasingly prominent in religious life and literature. The term *tīrtha* continued to bear all the symbolic meanings of the river, the ford, the crossing, and the far shore that had been developed with great subtlety and richness in the Upanishads. But alas, this age of ours, the Kali Age, is one in which the great Vedic rites of sacrifice and the pursuit of illumining wisdom are hard to come by. Nonetheless, pilgrimage to the *tīrthas* is still a viable spiritual path, and *tīrthayātrā* has become an important substitute for the more difficult and expensive rites and sacrifices. It is the path for our time. Not surprisingly, the benefits of pilgrimage to this place or that are often compared to the benefits one would gain from a powerful rite of sacrifice. For example, the famous Dasāshvamedha *tīrtha* in Banāras is the place where ritual bathing bestows the fruits of "ten *ashvamedha*" sacrifices. There are thousands of such equivalences articulated in sacred lore as the benefits of pilgrimage.

At the outset of the section of the *Mahābhārata* dealing with *tīrthayātrā*, we find a passage that makes clear the equation of pilgrimage with sacrifice:

> The fruits of sacrifices, completely and accurately expounded in due order by the sages in the Vedas, cannot be obtained by the poor man, O King. Sacrifices, with their many implements and their many various requisites, are the province of princes, or sometimes very rich men, but not of single individuals who are deficient in means and implements and who do not have the help of others. But hear, O King, of that practice which is accessible even to the poor,

equal to the holy fruits of sacrifice. This is the supreme secret of the sages, O King: the holy practice of pilgrimage [*tīrthayātrā*] excels even the sacrifice![10]

The *māhātmyas*, the texts of praise that sing the hymns and tell the stories of how the *tīrthas* became sacred and enumerate the benefits of pilgrimage, constitute a large body of Sanskrit literature. Over the centuries, they have been rendered into the vernacular literatures of India's regions, condensed into penny-pamphlets as part of local lore. If one were to judge from the sheer volume of literature of this type, pilgrimage, over the course of the past two thousand years, became one of the most extensive forms of religious practice in India.

One might go on pilgrimage to fulfill a vow, called a *vrata*, for prayers that have been answered, or one might make a vow to undertake the journey when one's prayers *are* answered. Particular places, like Tirupati in Andhra Pradesh, seem to specialize in *vratas* made for healing, for family well-being, for financial recovery or success. Or one might go on pilgrimage to bring the ashes of the beloved dead to a nearby river or even to one of the great *tīrthas* that specialize in rites for the dead—Gayā, Kāshī, or Prayāga. One might go for a sense of spiritual purification, for the praises of *tīrthas* constantly elaborate the ways in which sins and sorrows burn like puffs of cotton on entering the *tīrtha*. One might go simply to behold the place itself, for the *darshan* of a sacred place, a mountain, a river, an image of the divine that confers spiritual benefit. One might go to be in the presence of the ascetics and sages, who often reside at the *tīrthas* and amplify the power of the place.

In many ways, the pilgrim becomes an ascetic of sorts, leaving the household behind and taking up the privations and hardships of the road. There is a very real sense in which it is the pilgrims themselves who make the *tīrthas*. As the *Mahābhārata* hero Yudhisthira once said to the wise Vidura, who had returned from a long pilgrimage, "Devotees like you, who have become *tīrthas* themselves, are the ones who make the *tīrthas* into *tīrthas* by embodying the presence of God there."[11] Through many years, with their increasing numbers and the power of their cumulative devotion, India's pilgrims have continually made their *tīrthas* into *tīrthas*.

The *tīrtha māhātmyas* also make clear that going to a *tīrtha* is not only a matter of the feet, but also a matter of the heart. The "*tīrtha*s of the heart" (*mānasatīrthas*) are as important as the geographical *tīrthas*. These *tīrthas*, too, are enumerated, first in the *Mahābhārata* and then in many of the Purānas: truth, charity, patience, self-control, celibacy, and wisdom—these are the *tīrthas* in which one must bathe to become truly clean.[12] If water alone were enough to purify, they say, then the fishes of the Gangā would all be transported to heaven. It is by bathing in the *tīrthas* of the heart, as well, that one may truly cross over. "The one who always bathes in earthly *tīrthas* as well as in the *tīrthas* of the heart goes to the supreme goal!"[13]

In India today, the word *tīrtha* is primarily associated with those crossing places that bring the traditions of the gods and goddesses, heroes, heroines, and sages to living embodiment in India's geography. The most famous *tīrthas* attract pilgrims across linguistic, sectarian, and regional boundaries. In addition, there are the countless local and regional *tīrthas* visited by pilgrims from their immediate vicinity. No place is too small to be counted a *tīrtha* by its local visitors. In a sense, each temple is a *tīrtha*, especially consecrated as a crossing place between earth and heaven.

For at least two thousand years, pilgrimage to the *tīrthas* has been one of the most widespread of the many streams of religious practice that have come to be called "Hindu." The modern world has not seen the waning of pilgrimage traditions but has made transportation more readily available for a burgeoning pilgrim traffic. The high Himalayan shrines are no longer accessible to the hearty few alone but may be reached by pilgrimage bus lines that puff up the roads to the shrines of Badrīnāth and Kedārnāth, to the source of the River Gangā at Gangotrī, and the source of the Yamunā at Yamunotrī. Package tours to these four holy abodes, the four *dhāms* of the Himalayas, are advertised on the Internet. For those who want the full circuit of India, there are video coaches to take them on the four-*dhām* pilgrimage around India to Badrīnāth in the north, Purī in the east, Rāmeshvara in the far south, and Dvārakā in the far west. India is a land of ten thousand *tīrthas*, and on any given day, literally millions of pilgrims are on the road.

The *tīrthas* are intricately related to a vast corpus of stories, ancient and modern. These *tīrtha māhātmyas* and *sthala purānas* tell how each place became holy and what benefits one might gain from visiting it. Looking at both pilgrimage literature and pilgrimage sites, what are some of the ways in which holiness is articulated? How does the language of pilgrimage, with what I have called its "grammar of sanctification," create a landscape out of this vast corpus of places and their stories? As I have noted, myths literally "take place" as their mighty events are linked to landscape, and throughout this book we will look in some detail at just how the great rivers, mountains, and hillocks of India are linked to the myths of the gods and heroes.

Wendy Doniger observes in her book *Other Peoples' Myths*, "A myth cannot function as a myth in isolation; it shares its themes, its cast of characters, even some of its events with other myths. This supporting corpus glosses any particular myth, frames it with invisible supplementary meanings, and provides partially repetitious multiforms that reinforce it in the memory of the group."[14] Her observations about Hindu myth are equally true of Hindu sacred places—the places called *tīrthas* or "crossings," *pīthas* or "seats of the divine," or *dhāms*, "divine abodes." They do not stand in isolation. Even those in the most remote places, in the farthest mountain reaches of the Himalayas, where the rivers rise and the shrines are snowbound half the year, are not singular, but part of a complex fabric of reference and signification, a cumulative landscape replete with its own "invisible supplementary meanings." To paraphrase Doniger, this supporting corpus of *tīrthas* glosses every particular *tīrtha*, framing it with wider meanings and linking it to other places that amplify its significance from the local to the translocal.

SACRED LANDSCAPE AND REGIONS

In its simplest terms, geography is the description, study, and classification of the earth and its features. While many branches of geography are scientific in perspective and method, what is clear from the study of Hindu India is that its geographical features—its rivers, mountains, hills, and coastlands—no matter how precisely rendered, mapped, or measured, are also charged with stories of gods and heroes. It is a resonant, sacred geography. But it is also a landscape, in that these features are connected, linked to a wider whole. While I use the term "imagined landscape," it is far from imaginary. It is lived landscape that may focus on a particular temple, hillock, or shrine but sets it in a wider frame. Landscape is relational, and it evokes emotion and attachment. In his brilliant study of the mythic subsoil of Western landscapes, Simon Schama writes, "For although we are accustomed to separate nature and human perception into two realms, they are, in fact, indivisible. Before it can ever be a repose for the senses, landscape is the work of the mind. Its scenery is built up as much from the strata of memory as from layers of rock."[15] Here, of course, Schama refers to the painted landscape, but if we translate this to our context in India, we see that the scenery of the sacred landscape, while not painted, is also built up with the strata of myth, memory, and association that shape the human perception of nature.

The footsteps of pilgrims are the point of departure in creating the lived landscape. Pilgrims leave home, and the tracks of their journeys create a circuit of meaning and connection. Individual pilgrimage is not easy to document in India, for there is little tradition of personal pilgrimage memoir, such as the fifteenth-century *Book of the Wanderings of Friar Felix Fabri*, an exuberant record by Friar Felix himself of his journeys to the Holy Land. In India, we have very few such records. We do have, of course, the advertisements recorded in the voluminous *tīrtha māhātmyas*, exhorting pilgrims to visit this place, that place, every place. And we have the places themselves, which give their own form of evidence over the centuries of countless journeys. The footsteps of pilgrims converge, drawn by the magnetism of a particular place. Many of the "catchment areas" of India's pilgrimage landscape are very extensive; others are more local and create a sense of regional identity.

Among the great examples of this regional magnetism is the pilgrimage to Pandharpūr in Maharashtra, the site of the manifestation of the deity Vithobā, said to be a form of Krishna. Every year, the Marathi songster saints—from thirteenth-century Jnāneshvar to seventeenth-century Tukārām—make their pilgrimage to Pandharpūr for his *darshan*. Traveling in company with these saints are today's pilgrims, who sing the well-known songs of the saints all along the way. As they travel, they carry with them palanquins bearing the saints' silver footprints. There are twenty-eight such processions, originating in cities and towns all around Maharashtra, some more than one hundred miles away. These palanquins, called *palkhis,* and the processions of pilgrims that travel with them converge, day by day, on the town of Pandharpūr. In the end, they meet just outside town to form one great procession to the temple of

Vithobā. At the largest of the four times of Pandharpūr pilgrimage, this is today a convergence of some half a million people.

The Marathi anthropologist Iravati Karve, who went on the pilgrimage in the late 1940s, famously wrote in her account of the journey, "I found a new definition of Maharashtra: the land whose people go to Pandharpūr for pilgrimage."[16] Anne Feldhaus has amplified and complicated this picture through her rich and textured research in Maharashtra. She demonstrates the many different ways in which "religious imagery and pilgrimage traditions enable people in Maharashtra to experience and conceptualize regions." There is not a single geographical imagery, but more "an overlapping, ragged, unfinished patchwork of regions."[17] Pandharpūr comes closest to gathering in the whole of Maharashtra, but very likely the pilgrims to Pandharpūr themselves are not really thinking about "experiencing Maharashtra." As Feldhaus puts it succinctly, drawing on her long on-the-ground experience, "Most of them are intent on the goal of Pandharpūr and joyful at having reached it. They are worried about where to spend the night, how to evade the pickpockets, and how long they will have to wait in line for the bus back home. The unity they experience is mostly that of the *immediate* group of pilgrims with whom they have been traveling for many days, rather than some imagined Maharashtrian whole."[18] Even so, their travels on the many spokes leading to Pandharpūr have given them an experienced cultural knowledge of Maharashtra.

The pilgrimage to Pandharpūr is not an easy journey, and so, too, is another great pilgrimage: to the mountain shrine of Lord Ayyappa at Sabarimala in Kerala. This, too, is largely a regional pilgrimage, but one that now draws pilgrims not only from Malayalam-speaking Kerala, but from Tamil Nadu and throughout south India. The discipline undertaken on this pilgrimage is extraordinary. Each pilgrim must take a forty-one-day vow of vegetarianism; abstinence from sexual relations; discipline; and humility. Having been initiated to the vow, the pilgrims will take the name of Ayyappa and call one another by the single name Swami. The pilgrimage is open to all, regardless of caste, class, or religion, but only to men and to women who are either prepubescent or past the age of childbearing. After all, Ayyappa is the celibate mountain deity, who is present both at the destination and in the company of pilgrims.

The pilgrims travel barefoot, taking only a bundle wrapped up on their heads—half of it the offerings they bring to Lord Ayyappa and half of it the provisions they bring for the journey. They trek together in groups through the forests and hills of Kerala. The longest of the routes is nearly sixty miles, although the most popular is the short route of only about four miles. Especially for those who undertake the longer journey, the barefoot pilgrimage is demanding. For weeks in the high pilgrimage season, from November to January, these pilgrim ascetics, wearing black clothing and carrying their distinctive bundles, press toward Sabarimala chanting *Swamiye Sharanam Ayyappa!* "I take refuge in Lord Ayyappa." The pain, the thirst, the blisters of the journey are constant. Anthropologist E. Valentine Daniel, who made the trek with Tamil pilgrims from a village in Tamil Nadu, describes his own experience and also records the experience of those in his small party of seven. He writes, "In the words of one pilgrim, who reflected on this stage of the climb, 'there is nothing else I knew, heard, or felt. I was too tired to feel tired. All I heard was my voice calling out, "Ayyappo, Ayyappo, Ayyappo." Nothing else existed except my call and I. This was when I began to know my Lord in the true sense.'"[19] The final ascent up the famous eighteen steps to the temple is considered the climax of the pilgrimage. Indeed, only those who have observed the forty-one-day vow can set foot on the steps. It is an ascent that brings them face-to-face with Lord Ayyappa.

On the whole, the landscape created by the pilgrimage routes is the landscape of Kerala, enlivened with the story of Lord Ayyappa, clearly a local hero-deity. It is the tale of an abandoned child, found and adopted by a childless king and raised to succeed him. But a jealous queen, wanting her own son to become king, asked the boy to fetch some tigress milk to help cure a dangerous illness from which she was suffering. The boy boldly took the challenge and successfully brought home the milk of a tigress—riding on a tamed tiger! This local Dravidian hunter god of the south also became known as the incarnation of Shiva and Vishnu together in one form, thus taking on a much wider Hindu pedigree. Even so, this is very much a regional pilgrimage and one that attracts more and more pilgrims each year. In 2007, it was estimated that well over ten million pilgrims visited the shrine, with as many as 5,000 an hour having *darshan* of Ayyappa during the high season.[20]

PILGRIMAGE AND MAPPING THE NATION

Many of India's great places of pilgrimage have a transregional magnetism, and the circulation of pilgrims to these *tīrthas* creates a broader
arc of experience for people all over India. Some *tīrthas* that today have
a pan-Indian magnetism were once more-regional sites of pilgrimage,
like the mountain shrine of Tirupati in what is today southern Andhra
Pradesh and the seaside shrine of Jagannātha Purī on the coast of
Orissa. In the far north on the trail to Kedārnāth or on the beach of
Rāmeshvara in the south, pilgrims will find themselves in multilingual
crowds with fellow pilgrims from many parts of India. Many Indian
scholars have noted the significance of the network of pilgrimage places
in constructing a sense of Indian "nationhood," not as a nation-state in
the modern usage of the term, but as a shared, living landscape, with all
its cultural and regional complexity. For example, K. V. Rangaswami
Aiyangar, introducing the Sanskrit text of the *Tīrthavivecana Kānda*,
Lakshmīdhara's twelfth-century digest of pilgrimage places, writes:
"Long before wise statesmanship attempted or accomplished Indian
unification, *Akhand Hindusthān* [One Hindusthān] had sprung from

Pilgrims on the trail to Kedārnāth

the wanderings of pilgrims."[21] Aiyangar wrote in the early 1940s, the last years of the Indian independence movement and several decades before new forms of political Hindu nationalism made scholars more aware of the political resonance of such expressions. He was writing of a twelfth-century context, but as a scholar he also participated in a twentieth-century context in which pilgrimage to the *tīrthas* had scarcely diminished in importance but had grown considerably with the expansion of mass transportation.

The very idea that the imagined landscape cast by the network of India's *tīrthas* has contributed immensely to an indigenous Indian sense of "nationhood" is articulated today in a political context charged with the contemporary disputation about Hindu nationalism. Thus, it is difficult, but all the more important, to investigate what it has meant historically and what it still means today in the context of Hindu pilgrimage. It is indisputable that an Indian imaginative landscape has been constructed in Hindu mythic and ritual contexts, most significantly in the practice of pilgrimage. The vast body of Hindu mythic and epic literature is not simply literature of devotional interest to the Hindu and of scholarly interest to the structuralist, comparativist, or psychoanalytically minded interpreter. Hindu mythology is profusely linked to India's geography—its mountains, rivers, forests, shores, villages, and cities. It "takes place," so to speak, in thousands of shrines and in the culturally created mental "map" of Bhārata.

But mapping the land of India was not the domain of pilgrims alone. With the British East India Company in the eighteenth century came the British surveyors and cartographers, with a very different eye and purpose. Scientific mapping was integral to the imperial project. In introducing his book *Mapping an Empire*, Matthew Edney writes, "Imperialism and mapmaking intersect in the most basic manner. Both are fundamentally concerned with territory and knowledge. . . . To govern territories, one must know them."[22] But the knowledge was of a particular kind. In this mapping enterprise, Edney writes, "At one uniform scale, all portions of Indian space became directly comparable and normalized. Knowledge of India was homogenized; particular variations and contingencies were subsumed within a 'house of certainty.' Each town and district was identified and assigned its own particular location within the fixed and immobile mesh of meridians and parallels." Mapmaking became what

Edney has described as "a technology of vision and control, which was integral to British authority in South Asia."[23] Thus, Bombay, Banāras, and Rāmeshvara are equally dots on a graphic map. While useful for the purposes of commerce and control, this homogenization of space was stripped of cultural meaning and memory.

This kind of representational map was not part of the culture we are describing here. Nonetheless, Hindu literary and ritual culture had deep traditions of geographical awareness. In a range of Hindu traditions, imaginative "mapmaking" became the domain of both cosmologists and mythmakers. It is arguable that the imagined landscape they created is far more culturally powerful than that displayed on today's most geographically precise digital map of India. The imagined landscape bears imprints of meaning: the self-manifest eruptions of the gods, the footprints of the heroes, the divine origins of the rivers, the body of the Goddess. In this mental map, geography is overlaid with layer upon layer of story and connected in a storied landscape. In a broad sense, each village, river, and hillock has a story. Some of these stories are local, but some places are linked through their stories to several other regional shrines, and some are linked through their stories to a network of shrines all over India.

THE GRAMMAR OF SANCTIFICATION

What, then, are the systematic elements that constitute this landscape? What are those elements that are repeated, duplicated, and classified into networks so as to construe a wider landscape? What are the "sets" of the system—some ancient, others more recent—that participate in creating a landscape knit together by its repetitions and homologies? Throughout this book, my examples are drawn deliberately from a wide variety of sources—textual and ritual, ancient and modern, from the *Rig Veda* to the popular Purānas to the ephemeral pamphlets of today's *tīrthas*, from so-called classics of literature to folk art and wall paintings, and from countless hours on the road in dozens of India's *tīrthas*. In this book, we will begin to see some of the ways in which a sacred landscape is constructed and inhabited.

There are many strategies through which the sacred features of India's landscape are established and the divine presence experienced, named, and storied. Pilgrims may ask, "How did this place come to be sacred?" The stories to be told are, in many instances, part of the implicit cultural knowledge they bring with them. Perhaps the place descended from heaven to earth like the rivers, or it was retrieved from the sea by the gods, like the coastlands. Perhaps the divine erupted from the earth here, like the many *jyotirlingas* of Shiva. Or perhaps this divine image was once put down here and then clung spontaneously to the earth and could not be moved by human hands. Perhaps this place is part of the body of the divine Goddess, distributed throughout the land. Perhaps this hill is a piece of the Himalayas transported to Gujarat; this river is the Gangā gushing up from underground in Orissa; this temple is Kāshī Vishvanāth, re-created in the south. All these ways of speaking of divine presence begin to constitute a linked landscape, patterned with sacred places.

This systematic structuring of the landscape of India is, of course, based on the cosmology in which the entire universe is construed as a system, with its multiple ring-shaped islands and ring-shaped seas, each with its own rivers and mountains. As we will see in Chapter 3, these texts often begin with the story of creation and then proceed to explain the structure of the entire universe. This cosmology is instructive for us in that it establishes a "systematic geography" in which geographical features are noteworthy not for their uniqueness, but for their repetition in the ordered, systemic whole.

AVATARANA, Divine Descent

It fell from heaven to earth, and so it is sacred. There could be no better pedigree of the sacred here on earth. Divine descent from heaven to earth is certainly one way in which this world is connected to the heavens. The words *avatarana*, *avatāra*, and *tīrtha* all come from that same Sanskrit root meaning "to cross over." The language of crossing creates a world of descending and ascending, linking heaven and earth, this world and yonder. The most famous of the divine descents are the *avatāras* of Lord Vishnu, but the notion of "descending," *avatarana*, is common to many gods and to great *tīrthas*, too, such as Krishna's capital city of

Dvāravatī, said to have been the heavenly city of Amarāvatī descended to earth. As *avatāras* descend "downward," *tīrthas* are those fords where one crosses the other way—from this shore to the far shore of a river, or to the far shore of the heavens. This language of crossing has a wide symbolic reference, from the descending and ascending flow of life between this world here below and the worlds of heaven above, to the ultimate crossing of the "river" of birth and death to the "far shore" of liberation. *Tīrthas* are fords because they facilitate such crossings.

The rivers, of course, are the great descenders. Many of India's rivers, the Gaṅgā foremost among them, are said to have crossed over from heaven to earth. The story of the descent of the Gaṅgā is told in many of the Purānas and at the very outset of the *Rāmāyana*.[24] Gaṅgā was originally a divine river, streaming across the heavens. As we shall see in Chapter 4, through the asceticism and prayers of the sage-king Bhagīratha, she agreed to descend from heaven to earth to raise the dead ancestors of the solar kings of Ayodhyā. To break the force of her fall, Gaṅgā fell first upon the head of Lord Shiva in the Himalayas and then flowed across the plains of north India. Other sacred rivers, such as the Godāvarī and the Narmadā, repeat this pattern of divine descent. The Narmadā flows from the body of Shiva at Amarakantaka, in the hills of eastern Madhya Pradesh. The Godāvarī was brought to earth by the prayers of the sage Gautama and descended on the top of Brahmāgiri in the Western Ghāts of what is today Maharashtra. The priests of the Godāvarī area claim, "South of the Vindhya Mountains the Gaṅgā is called Gautamī (after the sage Gautama), while north of the Vindhyas she is called Bhāgīrathī (after the sage Bhagīratha)." The two rivers are symbolically the same river—descended from heaven and repeated, duplicated, in two geographical settings.

In investigating how systems of geographical meaning are constructed, India's rivers are important, for they are not simply individual rivers, but part of a system of rivers. They are linked together in groups—in this case, the seven Gaṅgās. They commonly issue from the "same" place—the "Cow's Mouth," Gomukh, calling to mind the image of heavenly waters released by Indra from Vritra's blockade, running out upon the earth as mother cows might be freed from the pen to nourish their young, evoking what has become a well-known homology: that of rivers and cows, waters and milk.[25] The rivers are especially sacred where they join in a *sangam,* a confluence. But three rivers joining are even better. The three are knotted together in braids—like the many *trivenīs,* or "triple braids," where a confluence of two rivers is joined by a third, understood to be the deep, symbolic waters of the underground Sarasvatī, which long ago vanished from her visible, earthly riverbed. The best-known *trivenī* is at Prayāga, today's Allahabad, but there are other *trivenīs* all over India that express the triple confluence of rivers. In sum, India's rivers are joined by the inter-referential symbolic language of their heavenly origins, their sources, confluences, and mouths. Indeed, wherever waters drip from a pot above a *linga* of Shiva in the sanctum of a temple or are poured lavishly upon the shaft of the *linga,* the *avatarana* of the Gangā is ritually repeated.

SVAYAMBHŪ: SELF-MANIFEST DIVINITY

Here, they say, the divine presence erupted from the earth and was manifested of its own accord! Innumerable places are said to be *tīrthas* because the divine burst forth in that very place. A particularly powerful example of this form of sanctification is the hill called Dawn Mountain, Arunāchala, rising from the flatlands of Tamil Nadu in south India. There is a temple at the base of the hill, the very old temple of Tiruvannamalai, its inscriptions indicating a recorded history some thirteen hundred years long. It is composed of several large, rectangular enclosures with a tall *gopura,* or tower, in each of the four directions. Inside is the *linga* of Shiva as Arunāchaleshvara, in a sanctum aglow with row upon row of oil lamps. But here, the most powerful presence of Shiva is said to be the mountain itself. It is said to have erupted from the earth at the very dawn of creation, flaming as the pillar of Shiva's fire. Brahmā and Vishnu could not fathom it. They tried but could not find its top or bottom; they exhausted themselves seeking the measure of this refulgence. Lord Shiva showed his face to them and granted them a boon. And what did they choose? That Shiva's eruptive brilliance would become a mountain and remain here on earth. Shiva said, "Since this *linga* rose up, looking like a mountain of fire, it shall be known as Dawn Mountain, Arunāchala." In those days, it was a mountain of flame; today, in this Kali Age, it is a mountain of bare volcanic rock, carpeted with green in the rainy season. It is some twenty-six hundred feet high and circumambulated on a well-worn path more than eight miles long. One climbs on the hill itself only barefoot.

One of the great festival days of the year, Krittikā Dīpa, in the lunar month of November–December, recalls this luminous eruption of Shiva. Thousands of people converge on the town of Tiruvannamalai to have *darshan* in the temple, to witness the lighting of the special oil lamps, or *dīpas,* and above all, as night falls, to witness the kindling of a huge fire at the top of the hill. For weeks, the devout have carried ghee and wicks to the summit, and on this day they stream barefoot toward it to touch the great ghee lamps before they are lit. They return to the temple below to stand and cheer as the huge fire erupts from the hilltop. They circle the hill and its many wayside shrines just as they would circle the sanctum of the temple. The blaze at the summit will last for many days, a testimony to Shiva's words, "Here I stand as Arunāchala."

The language of the divine as "self-manifest" in the natural environment is very much part of the symbolic grammar of sanctification. Holy as it is, Arunāchala is but one of hundreds of such places. The term *svayambhū,* "self-existent," is used to describe these places and images where God is said to have appeared miraculously, or some would say naturally: without human intervention or supplication. *Apne āp prakat hui,* they say in Hindi. "It appeared here of its own accord." Here the agency is completely that of the holy. This is the very meaning of hierophany, the "showing forth" of the holy. These natural manifestations are not established by human hands or by royal patronage but are said to be the spontaneous eruptions of the divine, whether as Shiva, Vishnu, Devī, or a local divinity. As we will see, one of the most prominent myths of divine hierophany is that of the appearance of Shiva's *linga* of light, the *jyotirlinga,* appearing from below and spanning earth, the sky, and the heavens above.[26] While there are said to be twelve *jyotirlingas* in India—from the northernmost at Kedārnāth to the southernmost at Rāmeshvara—it is clear that many local temples understand the sanctity of their own image of Shiva to be *svayambhū,* self-manifest.

The notion that aspects of nature are "self-manifestations" of the divine is widespread, both in Shaiva and Vaishnava traditions. Special stones are called *svarūpas,* literally God's "own form," not the divine images humans create, but God's own. Keep in mind that in consecrated temple images, *mūrtis,* made by the hands of the artisan, divine presence is established and the *prāna,* the breath of life, imparted to the image in the rites of *prāna pratishthā,* literally "establishing the breath." A *svayambhū* image or a *svarūpa,* however, has no need of *prāna pratishthā.* Symbolically speaking, the divine breath is already there and has been there from time immemorial. The *shālagrāma* stones found in the Gandakī River in Nepal are *svarūpas,* natural manifestations of Vishnu, sacred without so much as a mantra of invocation. And so are the stones found along the beaches of Dvārakā, called Dvārakā *chakras,* the "wheels of Dvārakā," pure white stones imprinted with intricate wheels, the emblems of Vishnu. Likewise, *bāna lingas,* the smooth stones found in the bed of the Narmadā River, are natural embodiments of Shiva.

Beyond these natural manifestations, there are countless local stones, rocks, outcroppings, and *mūrtis* that are called *svarūpa* by the acclamation of those who worship them. For example, the small, jet-black image of Krishna as Rādhāraman in one of the temples of Vrindāvan is a *shālagrāma* stone, now in anthropomorphic shape. The smooth stone form of Kāmākhyā Devī in Assam or Vaishno Devī in Kashmir, or the local folk image of Draupadī at the cult center of Gingee in Tamil Nadu, are all spoken of as *svayambhū.*[27] Self-manifest images are considered especially powerful in attracting pilgrims, whether locally, regionally, or nationally. Our point here, however, is not to enumerate the multitude of such divine manifestations, but to call attention to the grammar of sanctification through which a landscape is created: The sacred appeared here, spontaneously, unbidden, self-manifest.

PRATISHTHĀ: SANCTIFICATION BY ADHESION

The *linga* called Vaidyanāth in what is now rural Bihar is one of Shiva's self-born *lingas* of light. It is to be found in a sturdy stone temple set in an impressive complex, all within a spacious compound. Spacious, of course, except on great festival days, like Shivarātrī, or virtually every day during the summer month of Shrāvana, when this temple is filled to bursting with pilgrims. In Shrāvana, pilgrims converge on the temple carrying pots of Gangā water on either end of a shoulder pole. These pilgrims, called *kanwarias,* "pole-bearers," have made a vow, perhaps for the health or well-being of a spouse or child, and have walked the distance from the Gangā at Sultānganj sixty-five miles away. For a month, the road is a steady stream of saffron-clad figures, both men and women, undertaking a pilgrim's discipline that most try to accomplish within the course of twenty-four hours. Shiva as Vaidyanāth is, after all, the great physician.

According to the Vaidyanāth legend, Shiva once gave this great *linga* to the powerful *asura* king Rāvana who ruled in Lanka. Rāvana had meditated long at the feet of Shiva in the Himalayas and had accumulated the powerful energy called *tapas,* the energy of asceticism. Even demons like Rāvana accumulate such power by virtue of spiritual discipline.[28] In giving him this *linga,* however, Shiva told Rāvana that he must not put it down on the way from the Himalayas to Lanka. The gods of the heavens were understandably fearful that if Rāvana established such a powerful *linga* in Lanka, his *asura* kingdom would become even stronger. As a result, they conspired to have him put the *linga* down on the way. Varuna, the deity associated with water, entered into Rāvana, who then experienced the acute feeling of having to relieve himself. He set the *linga* down to attend nature's call. When he returned to pick it up again, it would not budge. And there it remains to this day.

When I visited Vaidyanāth and first heard this well-known myth, I thought it was a very odd story: an immovable divine image that stuck to the earth under such peculiar circumstances? The point of the myth, of course, is precisely this immovability, the creation of a bond so strong it cannot be broken. Here a sacred place was created not by falling from heaven or erupting from the earth, but by spontaneous adhesion. When an image of the divine is established in a temple, the rites of consecration include not only *prāna pratishthā,* but also the attachment of the image to its pedestal in the *garbha griha,* binding stone upon stone with the strongest of adhesives. This, too, is called *pratishthā.* But certain powerful images, we are told, adhere spontaneously to the earth. Here is yet another symbolic device through which a divine landscape is construed.

Months later I visited the famous shrine of Gokarna, along the coast of Karnataka, one of the few landmark *tīrthas* old enough to be well known even in the time of the *Mahābhārata.* There, in a temple not far from the palm-fringed beach, was the famous Gokarna *linga,* a piece of solid reddish rock, twisted like an old stump. Here, too, Rāvana had made the mistake of putting down a sacred icon. Evening had come in his journey, so they say, and he had to perform his ritual duties, for he was a piously observant *asura*. Therefore he gave the *linga* to a boy—actually Ganesha in disguise—to hold while he bathed in the ocean and performed the evening rites. But the image proved too heavy, at least that was the excuse, and Ganesha put it down. When Rāvana returned, he could not pick it up again. He tried so hard to remove the *linga* forcibly from the place where it stuck that he twisted it. Even so, it held to the earth right there.[29]

All over India, I discovered, there are *mūrtis* and *lingas* said to have adhered fast to this place or that by spontaneous natural fusion. Someone put the image down, and it could not be moved again by any amount of muscle. As we will see, such is the story of the temporary sand *linga* fashioned by Sītā on the seashore at Rāmeshvara, a sand image that became immovable stone. And such is the story of the image of Krishna whose cart got stuck in the mud and simply would not move from a place in the Aravalli Hills of Rajasthan. Clearly Krishna Shrināth-jī wanted to stay right there—and that is where the temple town of Nāthdvāra is located today. Hundreds of miles to the south is Shrīrangam, the island shrine of Vishnu at Tiruchirapalli in Tamil Nadu, where Vishnu's image stuck to the earth. Rāma had given this ancestral image, called Ranganātha, to Vibhīshana, Rāvana's brother and Rāma's great ally, and, yes, told him not to put the image down until he reached Lanka. Even so, when Vibhīshana came to the beautiful Kāverī River, he was overwhelmed with the desire to bathe. He gave the image to a Brahman boy, again Ganesha in disguise, and the boy agreed to hold it for him, under the condition that Vibhīshana come promptly if he called for him three times. When Vibhīshana was underwater, taking his dips in the Kāverī River, the boy called out. Of course, Vibhīshana could not hear him. The boy put down the image of Ranganātha, and so it is that the image has been worshipped on the island of Shrīrangam ever since.

The multitude of such stories suggests a kind of chosen-ness, a divine selection that powerfully creates a local sense of "place." Whereas many of the *svayambhū* images of the self-born divine are held to have been manifested in response to the unstinting devotion of *bhaktas,* here the principle of selection is ascribed to the affinities of the god. It is a divine reversal of the *ishtadevatā* principle, the notion that in our human diversity we each have a "chosen deity," that form of the divine that speaks especially to us. Even in a single family, members may have different *ishtadevatās*—whether Shiva, Rāma, Ganesha, or Devī. Here, however, it seems that the divine does the choosing, selecting this place or that for a home. In many of these stories it seems that the fusion of god and earth could, in principle, take place anywhere. If twilight had come a few minutes later, Rāvana might not have stopped at Gokarna for his evening rituals, but farther south along the coast of Kerala. But once the contact with earth was made, the god was there to stay.

BODY LANGUAGE: THE BODY OF GOD

No image is as evocative as the body in suggesting the systemic whole—interrelated, with distinctive differences, and yet an organic unity. Yi-Fu Tuan, theorist of space and the human experience, sees the human body as providing one of the primary schemas for understanding and ordering space. It is our primary environment, our microcosm, and it provides an intimately indigenous pattern for viewing the wider cosmos.[30] It is not surprising that the body-cosmos schema is widely employed in the patterning of India's sacred landscape. The bards of the *Mahābhārata*, introducing the subject of *tīrthas*, allude to the very diversity of the body and its hierarchies: "As special attributes of the body have been said to be sacred, so there are particular spots on Earth as well, and particular waters, which are considered sacred."[31] This world, like the body, has its eyes and ears, its heart and head. But every part of it is interdependent, related as are the limbs and functions of the body.

As we shall see in Chapter 3, the world created in the imaginative vision of the Vedas, Upanishads, and Purānas is construed as whole, emerging from the unitary *garbha*, or egg, in some cases imaged as a cosmic body. It is what we might call an "organic ontology" in which the symbolism of the body is employed to create an entire worldview.[32] The Vedic image is of Purusha—the cosmic person sacrificed at the time of creation into the time, space, and order of this world. From the cosmic being's eye, the sun was born; from his mind, the moon; from his ears, the directions. And so, all that is in the world we know is related to the body-cosmos of the divine. This image is profusely employed throughout Hindu religious literature, in hundreds of mythic transformations. The most vivid of these transformations is that of the great god Vishnu, stretched out upon the serpent called Endless, floating as the one form in a sea of formlessness. Everything that will be is within the body of Vishnu, waiting to emerge and be expressed in the myriad phenomena of creation.

In the religious landscape of India, the image of the body is frequently utilized to suggest the wholeness and interrelatedness of the land. Elsewhere, it is not so unusual to invoke the land as "mother" or "father," but here symbolic personification of the land is amplified in a detailed body-cosmos. One need only recall the Vedic homologies of sun-eye, mind-moon, veins-rivers, hair-trees, and so forth, to imagine how naturally the earth's *tīrthas* would have a place in this body. The most striking instance of relation of sacred place to body-cosmos is the system of *pīthas,* the "seats" of the Goddess said to be the various parts of the body of the Goddess, distributed throughout India. We will look carefully at the creation of these *shākta pīthas* in Chapter 6, but for now let us take an overview of this body-cosmos.

On a wall on the temple in Kankhal, near where the River Gangā enters the plains of north India, there is a painted image of Shiva, striding across a field, across a stream, carrying in his arms the limp and beautiful body of the goddess Satī. The temple is called Daksheshvara and is said to be the very site of the great sacrifice rite performed by Daksha, one of the sons of Brahmā who were subcontractors in the process of creation and also, in his case, the father of the goddess Satī. Everyone in the universe was invited to the rite, except her beloved husband, the mountain god Shiva. The enraged Satī stormed down the mountain to Kankhal and committed suicide in the sacrificial arena, furious at the insult to Shiva, whom she knows to be the lord of the universe. In many tellings of the tale, the grieving Shiva then carried Satī's body all around India, overcome with his loss.[33] Eventually, all the parts of her body fell, one by one. Where they fell, sacred sites of the *devī* were manifest. Indeed, the whole of India became, as it were, the dismembered body of the Goddess: Hridaya *tīrtha* in Bihar is her heart; Bhadrakālī in Nāsik is her chin; Kurukshetra is her ankle; Vārānasī is her left earring; in the far northeast, in Kāmākhyā, is her *yoni;* and at Kanyākumārī in the far south is her back.

In some listings of the *pīthas*, there are 51, in others 108. The eminent scholar D. C. Sircar has documented the groupings of *pīthas* in some of the earliest Tantric texts of the eighth or ninth centuries, reaching their most elaborate form with the *Pīthanirnaya* in the seventeenth century.[34] On the ground, however, it is clear that this system is open to a multitude of "subscribers," who would identify their local *devī* with Mahādevī through the body-cosmos of the *shākta pīthas*, creating as many Hindu claimants to the body of the Goddess as claimants to fragments of the true cross in medieval Europe. Just which *pīthas* are "really" part of the group is far less significant than the fact that there is a grouping in which, ultimately, every goddess may be said to participate.

In this perspective, the whole of India adds up to the body of the Goddess, for dismemberment and distribution are, from another perspective, universalization. Satī, distributed in the landscape, is not dead but alive; not fragmented but whole. As one Hindu nationalist writer put it in the 1920s, "India is not a mere congeries of geographical fragments, but a single, though immense organism, filled with the tide of one strong pulsating life from end to end."[35] Some historians, political scientists, and interpreters of the modern period in India have traced the popularization of the idea of Bhārat Mātā, or "Mother India," to the rise of Indian nationalism in the late nineteenth century, and to Bankim Chandra Chatterjee's *"Vande Mātaram,"* "I Bow to Thee, Mother," a hymn of praise to the motherland first raised in the opposition to the British partition of the province of Bengal in 1905.[36] But such a view lacks a longer historical perspective, for clearly the identification of *devīs* with the land has much older roots in the symbolization of the body-cosmos as inscribed in the system of *devī* shrines. A considerable history of pilgrimage to the multitude of India's hilltop, cave, and cliffside *devīs* preceded the use of the rhetoric of the motherland in twentieth-century Hindu nationalism.

What is true, however, is that not only did the cartographic surveying of India yield a map of imperial mastery, but that that familiar triangular shape also became a powerful icon of territorial India, especially when joined with the image of the Goddess as Bhārat Mātā. This map-goddess emblem became a pictorial representative of the idea of India, popularized and deployed in nationalist, and later explicitly Hindu nationalist, contexts.

The twentieth-century Bhārat Mātā Temple in Hardvār displays in concrete form the imaginative vision implicit in the body-cosmos: A bountiful Bhārat Mātā stands upon the map of India, holding a handful of grain and a pot of water. In New Delhi, at the headquarters of the Vishva Hindu Parishad, the World Hindu Organization, a niche in the courtyard displays a different version of the image: the goddess Durgā superimposed on a relief map of India. Such images, which so clearly display the relation of land and *devī,* are disquieting in the context of the politicization of Hindu symbolism in today's India, but it is important to recognize that this body-cosmos is not a new image, despite the seeming novelty of its nineteenth- and twentieth-century renderings. It is, rather, a very old and pervasive one, which is precisely why its power can be so effectively deployed.

THE FOUR *DHĀMS*—A FOURFOLD DWELLING

"This is a *dhām,* not a *tīrtha,*" insisted a young man, a self-appointed guide to the holy places of Krishna near Mathurā. "A *dhām* is the home of God." The point he made as we sat together in a baked-clay home-

Krishna's temple at Dvārakā, the western dhām, on the seacoast of Gujarat

stead in Gokul, the village where Krishna is said to have lived as a baby, seemed very important to him. I wanted to be clear just what he meant. The word *tīrtha,* of course, conveys a sense of "crossing," for a *tīrtha* is a ford, the spiritual ford that enables us to cross from "here" to "there." But the term *dhām* (Sanskrit *dhāman*) conveys the sense of "dwelling." A *dhām* does not necessarily transport us to the world beyond, but rather gives us a clearing in which to dwell right here. A *dhām* suggests not so much that we "cross over" to the divine, but that the divine dwells among us now. Jan Gonda, who has studied in detail the uses of this term in the ancient Vedic literature, writes that a *dhāman* may be described as both the location and the refraction of the divine, a place where it manifests its power and where one experiences its presence.[37] The very notion of a *dhāman,* a divine abode, conveys to us that the sacred takes form, is located, and is apprehended. In the Vedic ritual context this meant, for example, that the fire god Agni's *dhāman* was the fire altar, the place where the *tejas,* or luminous power, of Agni was manifest.[38]

As the term comes to use in the systematizing of sacred geography, there are four famous *dhāms* in India, sited at the four compass points of the land. Ritual enactment of the pilgrimage of the *chār dhām* is one of the most extensive ways in which a systematic geography has been construed. The standard four claim virtually unanimous agreement. In the north is Badrīnāth, the Himalayan shrine now associated with Vishnu, sitting on the banks of the Alakanandā River, one of Gangā's tributaries, within a few miles of the Tibetan border. In the east is Purī, the abode of Krishna Jagannātha, whose temple complex on the Bay of Bengal is one of the largest in all of India. In the south is Rāmeshvara, the Shiva *linga* said to have been dedicated by Rāma on the shore of the southern sea.[39] In the west is Dvārakā, the latter-day capital of Lord Krishna, where Krishna dwells as Dvārakādhīsha.

The *chār dhām* pilgrimage is one of the most popular in India, for it takes pilgrims on a circumambulation of the whole country.[40] There are still Hindu pilgrims—ascetics, widows, householders, and others—who have walked the *chār dhām* pilgrimage on foot, but today it is most commonly undertaken by chartered bus, even by "video-coach." The circling of India can be glimpsed in the pilgrimage routes described to the Pāndava heroes by the sages Pulastya and Dhaumya in the epic *Mahābhārata,* some two thousand years ago. Although their account of the *tīrthas* to be visited in the south is extremely sketchy, the shape of the pilgrimage they describe sweeps around the whole land. In the literature of the Purānas, the four directional *dhāms* have been visible for at least a thousand years and the traffic of the devout—north, south, east, and west—is certainly present. Even so, the particular name—the *chār dhām*—is not commonly known in the Purānas. Nonetheless, today's pilgrimage tracts speak of the *chār dhām* as "established during pre-historical ages."[41] For those in the Hindi-speaking regions in particular, this is a very popular pilgrimage, as can be affirmed from the presence of Hindi language publications in the extreme south of Tamil Nadu, at Rāmeshvara.

One of the myriad Hindi booklets on the *chār dhām* pilgrimage begins with a discourse on the religious nature of the land of Bhārata, with its great sages who filled the world with peace and its unbroken tradition of reverence for *tīrthas,* even in times of subjugation. It understands the four-*dhām* pilgrimage to be an expression of this Indian religiousness. The guidebook tells us, "Some people come to Badrīnāth after having already visited the three other *dhāms*. And some, at the time of their pilgrimage to Badrīnāth, set their minds on taking water from Shrī Gangotrī to offer in the temple at Rāmeshvara."[42] As is usually the case with pilgrimage in India, there is little orthodoxy about the precise form the circuit takes. It depends on one's own *bhāvana*, the disposition of one's own heart. Badrīnāth is the hardest of the *dhāms* to get to, since the others are easily accessible by train and Badrīnāth requires a journey into the mountains. Until recently it was a long and arduous journey by foot, but now there is a road all the way. Even so, it is not an easy journey. At one point, the author of this pilgrim tract reveals a schema for thinking about the *chār dhām:* Badrīnāth is the *dhām* of the Satya Yuga, the perfect age of the beginnings. Rāmeshvara is the *dhām* of the Treta Yuga, when Rāma reigned on earth. Dvārakā is the *dhām* of the Dvāpara, when Krishna held forth. With the *Mahābhārata* war and the death of Krishna began the Kali Yuga, a difficult age for human religiousness. Purī is the *dhām* of the Kali Yuga.

As we have come to expect, the *chār dhām yātrā* is a complete pilgrimage—fourfold, as signaled by the four directions—and is widely duplicated in local and regional pilgrimages. Many of the same Hindi pamphlets published in Hardvār that celebrate the four *dhāms* of India also praise the growing popularity of the four *dhāms* of the Himalayas: Badrīnāth, Kedārnāth, Gangotrī, Yamunotrī. In rural Chitrakūt, where

Rāma, Sītā, and Lakshmana are said to have halted in a forest ashram, there are also four *dhāms* to be visited. A modern temple in Ujjain is called the Chār Dhām Temple and boasts that it contains replicas of all four *dhāms* under one roof. Ann Gold's research in the rural village of Ghatiyali in Rajasthan cites a local *chār dhām yātrā* in a village where very few people aspired to visit the four *dhāms* of India. In Ghatiyali, the exact four may vary. "More important than who are named," writes Gold, "is the popularity of the concept."[43]

THREES, FOURS, FIVES, SIXES, SEVENS, AND EIGHTS

The grouping of *tīrthas* in numbered sets creates a landscape, linking place to place and thereby spanning the land between. Some groups, like the four *dhāms,* the seven liberation-giving cities, the twelve *lingas* of light, and the fifty-one seats of the Goddess, cast their imaginative net across virtually the whole of India. Other groupings identify a cluster of places related to one another in a region or a set of places in our own town. In this textured landscape, nothing stands isolated. Rivers, as we have seen, are often gathered together in threes, creating *trivenīs* where they meet. Goddesses, too, tend to appear in clusters of three, either within the sanctum or in separate shrines. Near Shrinagar in Kashmir, the great rocky slab covered with orange *sindūr* called Shārikā Devī, massive as it is, is not singular, but joined with two smaller shrines: Kālī, covered with *sindūr* and silver paper, in a nearby cave, and Lakshmī, also orange with *sindūr,* jutting forth at the top of the hill. The triplicate goddess not only demarcates a wider locale, but also indicates the complexity of the faces of the Goddess.

Sets of four, like the four *dhāms,* often mark a territory, with an implication of directionality, even if they are not exactly in the four cardinal directions, and with an implication of completeness. Five adds a center to that sense of completeness. Among the sets of five are the many places that have five-*krosha* pilgrimages, places that group a whole microcosm of shrines into a schematic plan that encircles them all. As we have seen, one of the most famous is the *panchakroshī yātrā* around Banāras, the five-day circumambulatory pilgrimage that takes one quite outside the congested streets of the ancient city and swings through the surrounding

Tiruchendur temple, one of the six abodes of Murugan in Tamil Nadu

countryside, creating a vast schematic circle said to have a radius of five *kroshas*, with shrines and temples all along the way and a rest house for each of the four nights on the road. A *krosha* or *kos* is a measurement of about two miles, and the whole of the land included in the circle is understood to be an embodiment of Shiva's *linga*. The circle is far from perfect, but the symbolic circle of the *panchakroshī* gathers a world of sacred places together. Among the other places with notable *panchakroshī* pilgrimages are the cities of Ujjain and Ayodhyā, where the dimensions are quite different from the circle of Banāras, but the *panchakroshī* pilgrimage winds around the whole of the sacred zone and embraces all that is within. Five is also the traditional number of the primary elements, and the landscape of south India includes a set of the five elemental *lingas*, where Shiva is understood to be manifest respectively as earth, air, fire, water, and space.

The most prominent set of six is the group of Murugan shrines located across the various landscapes of Tamil Nadu, from the hilltop temple at Pālani to the seacoast temple at Tiruchendur. These six constitute, again, a distinctively regional set of pilgrimage places that focus a Tamil loyalty. Murugan, popularly known as the son of Shiva, born of the ascetic Shiva to slay the demon Tāraka, is a complex deity. At least six divinities compete for his parentage, so it is no wonder that he is a deity with six faces.

His names are many: Kumāra (the Prince), Kārttikeya (son of the Krittikās or Pleiades), Shanmuga (Six-Faced), Guha, Skanda, Subrahmanya, Murugan. His temple *tīrtha*s are among the most popular and powerful in the Tamil south. Fred Clothey, who has studied Murugan and these sites, writes, "The six sites, like the god's six faces, connote the totality of divinity. They suggest that divinity in its fullness has been enshrined in Tamilnadu, and that Tamilnadu has become the sacred domain of the god."[44] He also sees the number six as symbolizing the fullness of the three-dimensional cosmos—the four directions, up, and down. At Swamimalai, one of the six not far from Kumbhakonam, a map depicting Tamil Nadu as a region linked by these six temples, is painted prominently on one of the walls leading to the entry. Some pilgrims may visit all six, but the point is not really to visit them all, but rather to live in a Tamil world linked and protected by these shrines.

And then there are the sevens, especially the seven sacred rivers, of which we will learn more, and the seven cities of liberation—Ayodhyā, Mathurā, Hardvār, Kāshī, Kānchī, Ujjain, and Dvārakā. Regions, like Maharashtra, have their own set of seven, such as the seven shrines for goddesses who are related to one another as sisters. Farther south, in coastal Karnataka, the Mookāmbikā Devī Temple sits on the Western Ghāts, slightly inland from the sea. She is one of the great *devīs* of the south, but is she alone? Not at all. She is related to the goddess Lakshmī in Kolhāpūr in southern Maharashtra, and her domain is one of the seven *mukti-sthalas*, liberating sacred places, established by Parashurāma when he forced the sea to retreat.[45]

There are many circles of eight Ganeshas arrayed to perform the task for which this deity, also called Vināyaka, is famous: guarding the threshold and removing obstacles. In Vārānasī, there is a circle of eight Ganeshas around the center of the old city. Beyond the center, there is an imaginative set of seven concentric circles of eight Ganeshas each, creating an entire grid of protective Ganeshas around the holy city. These fifty-six Ganeshas are said to be situated at the cardinal and intermediary directions. Amazingly, most of those mentioned in the texts can actually be found, somewhere. They are not arranged in a truly circular or concentric way at all, but they are there. The surrounding circles of eight Ganeshas embrace and protect the whole. In her work on Maharashtra, Anne Feldhaus tells us of the Ashtavināyakas, the Eight Ganeshas, located in the general vicinity of Pune. She tells us that pilgrims make an outing to the eight in cars and buses, in organized tours, on weekends or anytime they can spare a day or two to make the journey. The eight Ganeshas are not particularly arranged in a circle, and nobody visits them in order, for there is no systematic order. And there are hundreds of other Ganesha temples in the same area. So, she asks, what is it that brings these eight together? It is simply the number eight and the region they comprise. She says, "The Pune region is the region within which the circumscribed set of Ashtavināyak temples is located."[46] It is not even that people visit them on pilgrimage that makes them important in this way, she writes:

> Many more people in the Pune region are aware of the Ashtavināyak than have ever been to any of these places. Even most of those who have gone on pilgrimage to one or more of the Ashtavināyak temples have not, or not yet, managed to travel to all of them. Nevertheless, the existence of the Ashtavināyak as a numbered set makes possible a sense of their area as a region. Even without traveling to all of them, residents of this region can think of the eight of them as a unit by saying the name "Ashtavināyak" or by looking at the combined holy picture that is multiplied many times over on living room walls, on refrigerator doors, and in household shrines throughout the region.[47]

The grouping of places in numbered sets brings them together in the mind's eye, whether or not they are visited by pilgrims.

CLIMBING GIRNĀR

A dramatic series of peaks known today as Girnār rises from the rolling agricultural land of Gujarat's Saurashtra peninsula. While Girnār is largely a regional pilgrimage center for Gujarat, this is one of many places where I meditated upon the interconnectedness of India's broader pilgrimage landscape. There is plenty of time to do so, for the pilgrim journey begins at four in the morning and includes many hours of climbing up what are said to be ten thousand steps to the needle peaks of the

Girnār range. Girnār, sometimes called Raivataka Hill in the Sanskrit Purāṇas, is a mountain shrine including both Jain and Hindu temples, though most of the Gujarati pilgrims would find the either-or distinction of "Jain" or "Hindu" an unfamiliar way of designating identity. The Nemināth Temple, dedicated to the twenty-second *tirthankara*, or spiritual pioneer, of the Jain tradition, was built in the twelfth century and is the largest and most elegant building complex on the mountain. Nemināth is said to have renounced the world for the life of an ascetic when, as his wedding approached, he observed the penned animals that would be slain for the wedding feast. Unable to countenance this suffering, he renounced the life of society, and eventually, so did his intended spouse. It is here, years later, they say, that he finally left his earthly body. His footprints are here in marble.

The Hindu temples, one on each peak, are not so grand. The largest is dedicated to the goddess Ambā, and there are other shrines to Gorakhnāth, Dattātreya, and Mahākālī.[48] Girnār is one of countless hilltop and mountaintop shrines all over India, many dedicated prominently to forms of Devī, like the many Ambās scattered through the hill country of Gujarat and Rajasthan. The pilgrim trail up the peaks is so well established that it has long been made into a giant steep, winding staircase, cut into the rock itself. Near the base of the mountain is an inscription of fourteen rock edicts of the Mauryan Emperor Ashoka, warning against large festivals and the animal sacrifices they entail and enjoining respect for parents and devotion to the moral principles of the Buddhist Dhamma. This inscription at Girnār, one of five places in India carved with these fourteen edicts, indicates to us the significance of this place some three centuries B.C.E., in the time of Ashoka.[49]

In the textual and ritual language of Girnār, we see the use of a number of motifs that are widely employed in the description of Hindu sacred geography, including some that we have just surveyed. But first, the story, as told by a local penny-paperback *māhātmya:*

Girnār or Girinārāyana was the brother of Pārvatī, the wife of Lord Shiva. Both Pārvatī and Girinārāyana were the children of Himālaya, the mountains personified. Both of their names derive from the mountains—*giri* and *parvat* mean "mountain peaks." Like other mountains of Hindu myth, Girnār originally had wings and moved about the heavens like the clouds, creating a good deal of instability here below. Only after Lord Brahmā commissioned the god Indra to stabilize the earth by cutting off the wings of the mountains did they become known as *achala*, literally "the immoveable ones." As the local story goes, when Indra came after Girnār to cut off his wings, Girnār got permission from his father to hide in the sea, and he did. But his sister Pārvatī yearned for him and implored the gods to find him. Vishnu, Shiva, and the other gods discerned Girnār's hiding place and sang praises to the sea. For their praises, they received a boon, and as their boon, they asked the sea to retreat a certain distance. So it is, according to the *māhātmya*, that Girnār, a piece of the Himalayas, now rises abruptly from the farming land of Saurashtra, some distance from the seacoast. In order to protect her brother, Pārvatī herself came from the Himalayas to dwell on Girnār as Ambā, the mother of all the earth.

I thought about this rendition of the story as I climbed Girnār, stopping frequently to observe the life of a wayside shrine, to catch my breath, and to enjoy the sweeping view of the plains below. What struck me was the way in which those who speak of this place utilize the many motifs of sanctification as they express its significance.

This is part of the Himalayas, they say. The Himalayas are not only the "abode of snows," but are also *devālaya*, the "abode of the gods," filled with the lore of the gods, and with temples and *tīrthas*. The transposition of Himalayan peaks from the north to other parts of India is a widespread motif, creating a landscape dotted with mountains transported from the snowy north. Girnār is not the only piece of the Himalayas to be found elsewhere in India and thus to partake of this symbolic transposition. Govardhan, the sacred hill of Krishna's homeland, is said to be part of the Himalayas, brought to that place by Hanumān. In Tamil Nadu, the two hills of Pālani were carried from the Himalayas by the *asura* Idumban, who bore them on either end of a long shoulder pole. On top of the larger of the two hills is one of the six famous shrines of Murugan, or Skanda. The hills of Tirumala bearing the shrine of Shrī Ventakeshvara are also acclaimed as transposed Himalayan peaks. Ganesha Rock at Tiruchirapalli in Tamil Nadu is called Dakshina Kailāsa, the Kailāsa of the South, and one of the three hills at Kālahasti in southern Andhra

Pradesh is also called Kailāsa. Mount Gandhamādana, the Himalayan peak in the Badrīnāth area of the far north, has a duplicate the full span of India to the south, at Rāmeshvara. Clearly the currency of the Himalayas has value across the length and breadth of the land.

The sea retreated and left this place on dry ground, they say. The sacred land that emerged from the sea is another motif with wide resonance in Hindu sacred geography. All along the coasts of India are stretches of land said to have once been lost in the waters. Most extensive is the long west coast of India, from present-day Goa to Trivandrum, a coastland said to have been retrieved from the sea by Parashurāma, one of the *avatāras* of Vishnu. When the waters of the Gangā descended from heaven, they understandably filled the seas to overflowing and submerged part of the seacoast, especially the west coast with its lush, green, low-lying lands and its myriad holy places. In ancient times, they say, the sages propitiated Parashurāma to help rescue the land from the sea again.[50] There are many tellings of the tale. In most, Parashurāma stood on the hills of the Western Ghāts and drew back his bow. Threatened with Parashurāma's great arrow, the sea god Varuna recoiled in fear and agreed to withdraw from the coastlands. In other tellings, Parashurāma actually shot the arrow, or hurled his battle-ax, or threw a sacrificial ladle—and in so doing claimed from the sea the distance he was able to measure with the strength of his mighty arm.

However the tale is told, people along the western coast speak of the land as Parashurāma Kshetra, the "Land of Parashurāma." Some say Parashurāma Kshetra is Kerala; others say that it extends from Kanyākumārī to Gokarna in what is today northern Karnataka, or that it extends farther still up the Konkan Coast. In any case, there are countless temples that link themselves to this story: the hill in present-day Mangalore where Parashurāma performed austerities; the place at the top of the *ghāts* near Udupi where he stood to shoot the arrow; or the *linga* at Gokarna that was reclaimed after he forced the sea to retreat.

The sacred images, or *mūrtis*, of many shrines are also said to have come from the sea. As we will discover, this is a major part of the mythology of Dvārakā, or Dvārāvatī, the westernmost *tīrtha* in India today, sitting on the seacoast of the Saurashtra peninsula of Gujarat. At the time the city of Dvārāvatī was built for Krishna as his capital, the architect of the gods asked the sea to retreat a distance in order to accommodate the plan he had drawn up. So it happened. But the ancient Dvāravatī is said to have been submerged again by the sea as soon as Krishna died. Not surprisingly, as we shall see, many other important shrines in India are linked to the disappearance of the ancient image of Krishna at Dvārakā and claim to have found the image that was submerged. Today, Dvārakā is a busy pilgrimage town dominated by the great temple of Krishna, and other shrines that link their sanctity to this place include Udupi on the coast of Karnataka and Guruvāyūr on the coast of Kerala—both with images from Dvārakā that were rescued from the sea.

The Gangā descended to earth right here, they say. The descent of the Gangā from heaven to earth is also recapitulated here at Girnār. Partway up the steep path of stairs to the summit of Girnār's first peak is an ashram and a spring called Gomukhī Gangā. Of course, the Gangā as a whole is duplicated throughout India, but here at Girnār, one particular facet of the river's course is duplicated: Gomukh, the Cow's Mouth, referring to the place high in the Himalayas where the first trickle of the river emerges from the edge of a glacier. As we have already glimpsed, Gomukh also has numerous duplications. For instance, on the cliffs of Brahmāgiri in Maharashtra, the Godāvarī River has its own Gomukh where the source waters of the river come forth. In many temple tanks, the spring filling the tank will issue from a Gomukh spout in the shape of a cow's head, as it does at Gomukh Kund on the steep slope of Mount Abu or at Manikarnikā Kund in the Himalayan town of Gupta Kāshī, for example. And, of course, the spout that carries the waters of the *abhisheka* out of the inner sanctum of a Shiva temple is often called Gomukh, signaling the sanctity of these waters.

Four dhāms are to be visited here, they say. Puffing with pilgrims up the steep Girnār steps and stopping to talk at Gomukhī Gangā while we viewed the vast flatlands below, I became aware that pilgrims here also refer to the *chār dhām*, the four divine "abodes" of the Girnār journey. The first is the *dhām* we were then visiting—Gomukhī Gangā. Farther ahead on the trail was the goddess Ambājī, then the shrine of the great yogi Gorakhnāth, who is said to have lived in these parts, and the shrine of Lord Dattātreya, the powerful offspring of Brahmā, Shiva, and Vishnu, all three. At each of these stations on the pinnacle hills of Girnār, pilgrims receive a *sindūr* stamp on their hands or arms, the signet of having reached each *dhām*. As we have seen, the term *dhām* means "divine abode," and the term "four *dhāms*" is widely used to signify a pilgrimage of the completed whole, here a fourfold pilgrimage that is widely patterned into India's Hindu landscape.

Girnār is very much a regional pilgrimage place, but even here we begin to glimpse something of the vast systematizing of India's pilgrimage geography through the use of powerful and widely shared symbols and stories. Nothing stands isolated, but each place, each *tīrtha*, participates in the references and resonances of a wider system of meanings. Observing the ways in which this singular set of peaks in Gujarat participates in a complex grammar of sanctification, we begin to see the patterning of the landscape. There is duplication and transposition—of the Gangā, the Himalayas, the four *dhāms*. There is disappearance and discovery—of Girnār itself, the coastlands of Gujarat, and the whole coast of western India. And beginning at Girnār, we encounter yet another great fact of Indian sacred geography: that there are many overlapping worlds, like the Hindu and Jain shrines on the mountainside—virtually identical arduous mountain pilgrimages, visiting some of the "same" places, and yet calling them by distinctive names and bringing distinctive meanings to them. And, of course, the fact that Ashoka's major rock edicts are here speaks to the antiquity and layering of traditions that can be found at pilgrimage sites the world over.

Myth on Earth

In this book, we will explore in greater detail the ways in which patterns of sanctification have created a strong sense of the imagined landscape— locally, regionally, and transregionally. Whether the divine is present on earth by divine descent, divine eruption, or divine adhesion, these forms of sanctification participate in the creation of a landscape of polycentricity and duplication, no matter how deeply the heart's devotion may be attached to a particular place or manifestation of the divine.

As we have seen, both mythology and topography provide for people and cultures the "maps" of the world. Again, let us recognize that to speak of an "imagined landscape" is not to speak of something fanciful, for the imagined landscape is the most powerful landscape in which we live. No one really lives in the India displayed on a digitally accurate map, or in any other two-dimensional graph of the world. Such a map can locate our hometown, or the road that took us from Rishikesh to Gangotrī, or the rail line from Rāmeshvara to Madurai. There is no question of the utility of such a map. But all of us, individually and culturally, live in the mappings of our imagined landscape, with its charged centers and its dim peripheries, with its mountaintops and its terrae incognitae, with its powerful sentimental and emotional three-dimensionality, with its bordered terrain and the loyalty it inspires, with its holy places, both private and communally shared.

The extent to which mythology and topography overlap or diverge in the shaping of an imagined landscape is a critically important question for students of religion, culture, and politics today. As we shall see, in India, the inscribing of the land with the prolixity of Hindu myth is so vast and complex that it has created a radically locative worldview. The profusion of divine manifestation is played in multiple keys as the natural counterpart of divine infinity, incapable of being limited to any name or form, and therefore expressible only through multiplication and plurality. The land-god homologies create a multitude of imagined landscapes, lived-in maps, among the many peoples who might speak of themselves as Hindus. What they have in common is an imagined landscape constituted of such homologies, whether personal, local, regional, or national. The challenges of diaspora have not loosened that locative quality. As Hindus have moved around the world, they have taken their places with them. Among the Indian diaspora—whether the older diaspora in Thailand, Cambodia, and Indonesia or the recent diaspora communities of the West—many of India's most important sacred sites are replicated. In North America today, Hindus have built upon the patterns of duplication and sanctification found in India. They have built Kāshī's Vishvanāth Temple in Flint, Michigan; Tirupati's Shrī Venkateshvara Temple in Pittsburgh; Madurai's Shrī Meenākshī Temple in Houston. In Lanham, Maryland, they have re-created the whole of south India's sacred geography within the complex of the Shiva-Vishnu Temple. Whether in Delhi or Detroit, Hindus invoke the waters of the Gangā and the Yamunā Rivers into the waters with which they consecrate Hindu images and temples.

How does all this relate to the modern notion of "nation"? The imagined landscape may coincide with the kind of "imagined community" the political theorist Benedict Anderson speaks of as a "nation," or it may not. Many of the tensions described as "communal" in modern India arise from the challenges of bringing into being a multireligious, secular nation-state in the context of multiple, though overlapping, imagined landscapes. The Indian national anthem, "Jana Gana Mana," names an imagined landscape, reciting the evocative names of the regions of India, circling from the Punjab, to the south, and back to Bengal, and reciting the names of mountains and rivers—the Vindhyas and Himalayas, the Yamunā and Gaṅgā. Even as the mind's eye circles India, people of multiple communities will imagine different, but overlapping, landscapes. "Vindhya, Himāchala, Yamunā, Gaṅgā . . ." will be evocative in very different ways to those of the north and south, to Hindus, Muslims, and secular environmentalists. This book will be an attempt to illumine some of the particular ways in which that lyric is evocative for Hindus because of the elaborate patterns of inscribing myth on earth.

A Circuit of India in the Mahābhārata*

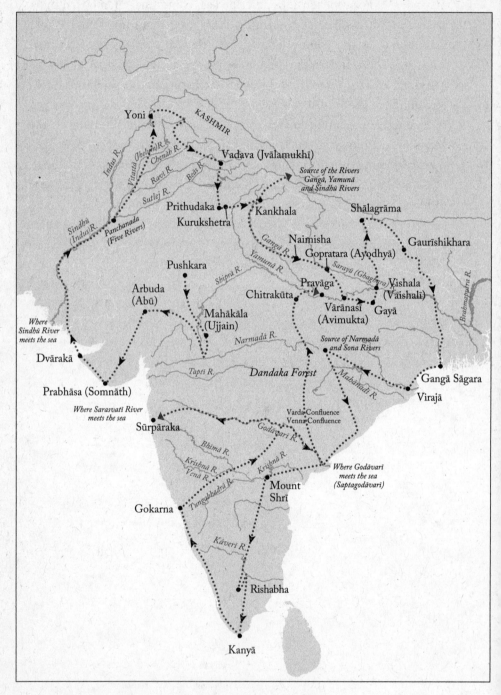

Yoni

KASHMIR

Indus R.

Vitastā (Jhelum) R.

Chenāb R.

Rāvī R.

Beās R.

Sutlej R.

Vadava (Jvālamukhī)

Source of the Rivers
Gaṅgā, Yamunā
and Sindhū Rivers

Sindhū (Indus) R.

Panchanada
(Five Rivers)

Prithudaka

Kankhala

Śhālagrāma

Kurukshetra

Naimisha

Gopratara (Ayodhyā)

Gaurīshikhara

Pushkara

Shiprā R.

Gaṅgā R.

Yamunā R.

Sarayū (Ghaghra) R.

Vishala
(Vaishalī)

Brahmaputra R.

Arbuda
(Abū)

Chitrakūta

Prayāga

Vārānasī
(Avimukta)

Gayā

Where
Sindhū River
meets the sea

Mahākāla
(Ujjain)

Source of Narmadā
and Sona Rivers

Dvārakā

Narmadā R.

Dandaka Forest

Mahānadī R.

Gaṅgā Sāgara

Taptī R.

Prabhāsa (Somnāth)

Virajā

Where Sarasvatī River
meets the sea

Sūrpāraka

Godāvarī R.

Varda Confluence
Venna Confluence

Bhīmā R.

Krishnā R.

Veṇā R.

Krishnā R.

Where Godāvarī
meets the sea
(Saptagodāvarī)

Mount
Shrī

Gokarna

Tungabhadrā R.

Kāverī R.

Rishabha

Kanyā

*Following S. M. Bhardwaj, *Hindu Places of Pilgrimage in India.*

2

"What Is India?"

The Earth, bearing upon her many different peoples, speaking many languages, following different dharmas as suit their particular regions. Pour upon us a thousand-fold streams of bountiful treasures to enrich us, like a constant cow that never faileth.

ATHARVA VEDA XII.1.45

The diversity of India's cultures, peoples, religious traditions, and languages is legendary. As the "Hymn to the Earth," found in the *Atharva Veda* early in the first millennium B.C.E., reveals, India's own recognition of this multiplicity of cultures is not new. Over the centuries, the philosophers, pilgrims, and peoples of India have explored the meanings of this celebrated diversity as intently and extensively as any culture on earth. "Unity in Diversity" is the theme, sometimes seen as a cliché, sometimes seen as an ideal betrayed by countless historical realities, sometimes seen as the hegemonic invention of India's elites to keep the diversity in its proper place. Nonetheless, it is a theme that has been sounded in many keys for well over two thousand years. One verse of the ancient *Rig Veda* has become the signature line of this theme: *Ekam sat vipraha bahudhā vadanti.* "Truth is one. The wise speak of it in many ways." The Vedic phrase crops up repeatedly in the rhetorical traditions of India: one truth, many paths; one culture, many peoples, regions, languages, and traditions.

Today Indian Oil displays the same theme on its giant billboards, which portray Indians dancing cheerfully wearing the clothing of a diverse civilization—turbans and *dhotīs*, saris and *selvārs*, *lungīs* and business suits, all beneath the motto "Unity in Diversity." Indian cultural festivals include the visual arts, music, literature, and dance of India's many regions and of its Hindu, Sikh, Muslim, Jain, Christian, Zoroastrian, and wholly secular citizens. Identities are complex and overlapping—regional, religious, linguistic, philosophical. It is this very complexity and diversity of cultures that shapes the distinctive civilization that is India.

The diversity of India is a manifest fact, with its fourteen major language groups and hundreds of dialects, with its racial and caste diversity, its tribal, ethnic, and regional diversity, and its rich and complex religious life. It is not surprising that this surfeit of diversity has provided the fuel for conflict over the centuries, including the violence that attended the partition of India into India and Pakistan and the recurrent communal violence that has erupted repeatedly in the decades since. More significant, however, especially in an era in which identity is being minted in ever-smaller denominations, is the persistence of a complex relatedness that is a constant counterpoint to the fracturing effects of violence. Mushirul Hasan, a distinguished Muslim historian, discussing Jawaharlal Nehru's view of India's communities, writes, "A simple fact that eluded most of Nehru's comrades was that Indian society was at no stage structured around religious solidarities or polarized along 'communal' lines. Nehru's exceptionally eclectic mind grasped this reality. He believed that inter-community conflicts, as and when they occurred, were counterpoised to the quiet, commonplace routines in which communities intermingled."[1] These day-to-day interactions have persistently undercut the ideological hardening of religious boundaries and have preserved a practical everyday pluralism, though many worry that it is becoming increasingly fragile.

Traveling the length and breadth of the land in the 1930s, during the independence movement, Jawaharlal Nehru, who was to become India's first prime minister, spoke of what he called the "tremendous impress of oneness." The differences were there, to be sure, but Nehru perceived in India's diversity a complex oneness. In temporal terms, he saw in India, through the centuries, "an ancient palimpsest on which layer upon layer of thought and reverie had been inscribed, and yet no succeeding layer had completely hidden or erased what had been written previously."[2] It is this very complexity that has made India more than a culture, but rather a civilization in which cultures have mingled. Alternatively, Sunil Khilani, in his 2003 book *The Idea of India*, speaks of the subcontinent as "a contingent and fragile conjunction of interlinked, sometimes irritable

cultures."[3] So is India an age-old palimpsest, or is it contingent and fragile? What competing ideas of India inform our understanding? Is India
a complex, composite civilization? A multireligious nation? A Hindu
nation? A democratic, secular, pluralist state? A creation of modern cartography, with no inherent unity at all? All these ideas have been posed
in responding to the question "What is India?"

For many of the diverse people who might loosely be called Hindu,
the unity of India is not simply that of a nation-state, but that of geographic belonging, enacted in multiple ways. Hindu pilgrims measure
the span of India with their feet, making their way up a rocky trail in
the north to the Himalayan shrine of Shiva called Kedārnāth, speaking
Hindi and Panjabi, Tamil and Kannada, or converging to bathe in the
waters of the ocean at Kanyākumārī at the tip of southern India. Some
of them bring the sands of the beach at Rāmeshvara in the far south to
the River Gangā in the plains of the north and carry the waters of the
Gangā to pour upon the Shiva *linga* at Rāmeshvara. Increasing numbers of pilgrims crowd into buses for the *chār dhām* pilgrimage around
the four corners of India—to Badrīnāth in the north, Purī in the east,
Dvārakā in the west, and Rāmeshvara in the south. Going on pilgrimage to local, regional, and pan-Indian shrines and temples is still one of
the most common reasons for ordinary people in India to travel. As we
have seen, the places they seek out are called *tīrthas*, literally "fords" or
"crossings."

This book investigates a particular idea of India that is shaped not by
the modern notion of a nation-state, but by the extensive and intricate
interrelation of geography and mythology that has produced this vast
landscape of *tīrthas*. It is an idea that is at least two thousand years old,
and it is an idea that has been enacted in the practice of pilgrimage for
many centuries. This idea of India had its genesis long before the Mughal
Empire stretched its network of alliances across much of the subcontinent in the sixteenth century, long before the British Empire formalized
a nationwide civil service and linked the land by rail. Claiming the land by
name and story long preceded the emergence of the modern nation-state.
The fact that people of ancient India, even if they were a Sanskritic cultural elite, gave a single name to the whole of this diverse subcontinent
is itself noteworthy. The name is Bhārata, or Bhārat in modern Hindi,
dropping the final "a" of the Sanskrit name. This is an indigenous name

used since the time of the *Mahābhārata* to describe roughly the territory we call India. It is also, of course, the official name of India today. India, like Japan, China, and Greece, links its modern identity with an ancient and continuous civilization. In a sense, this is not so very remarkable. But it is astonishing to consider the multitude of India's distinctive swirl of languages and cultures, ancient, ever-changing, modern. Why should people in this land ever have imagined the land of Bhārata—then or now?

This is an inquiry into a particular understanding of the land and landscape of India, one that has developed in the complex Hindu imagination and has been elaborated in text and context, ritual and pilgrimage. For centuries the understanding of India in the West has followed primarily a Western agenda, from the land called "Indika" by the Greek scholar Megasthenes, to the "Hindustan" of the Turk and Afghan Muslim dynasties, to the India of John Stuart Mill, who, in the nineteenth century, without ever leaving England, wrote an enormous English-language history of India, to the India of postcolonial studies that still sees India through the lens of Western interventions. In the past three centuries, India has been seen by traders as a source of riches, by rulers as a part of empire, by missionaries as a mission field for winning souls, by romantics and seekers as the source of something missing in the

Hindu pilgrims measure the span of India with their feet

heart and soul of the West. As a modern secular nation-state, India has been seen in the strategic and geopolitical terms of the West. As a rising economy, the "new India" has been viewed with an eye to its markets.

The idea that "India" is somehow the creation of the West has a significant and continuing intellectual history. After all, wasn't "India" really brought into being through the systems of administration, transportation, and law that imposed a semblance of unity on otherwise disparate regions? More than a century ago, many British administrators followed the 1880s lead of Sir John Strachey, who would introduce his classes of civil servants–in–training for their posts in India by saying, "The first and most important thing to learn about India is that there is not and never was an India."[4] The resistance to ideas of India's unity is embedded in colonial thought and often in postcolonial thinking as well. Even the many books that address the idea of India in recent times seem to acquiesce to largely Western constructs. For example, in introducing the volume *Contesting the Nation*, historian David Ludden writes, "Ironically, therefore, the territory that we use to describe the landscape of Indian civilization was defined politically by the British Empire. India was never what it is today in a geographical, demographic, or cultural sense, before 1947."[5]

Our inquiry, however, approaches India from the other side. What are some of the ways in which India has seen itself and enacted its regional and pan-regional identities? Political analyses do not touch this question. Postcolonial studies do not reach very deeply into the premodern subsoil of India to inquire whether there have been alternative ways of imagining the complex collectivity of India in a distinctively Indian idiom. What is the mythic and ritual language in which the land that Hindus have called "Bhārata" has been construed and expressed? Bhārata is not merely a convenient designation for a conglomerate of cultures, such as Europe has been for so much of its history or such as Indonesia has become in modern times. Nor was Bhārata ever the name of a political entity like a nation-state, at least until 1947, when it became the proper name of independent India. And yet it is arresting to consider a "sense of unity" construed in and through the diverse imagined landscape we described in the opening chapter, a sense of connectedness that seems to have flourished for many centuries without the need for overarching political expression or embodiment.

The English word "religion" comes from the Latin root *ligare,* to bind. Indeed it is the set of foundational ideas and practices that bind people together in a cosmos, an ordered world, and that link them in community. In some religious traditions, such as Christianity and Islam, this sense of belonging is ecumenical, transcending culture and land. In some traditions, such as Judaism and Hinduism, this sense of being bound together is highly locative, generating a complex rootedness in the land. Of course, the distinction is oversimplified. All religiousness is, in many ways, both locative and ecumenical. Religious lives have both roots in the earth and wings for the skies. But the distinction nonetheless helps us to see something important: Hindu narrative and mythology are richly interwoven with the geography of India—its mountains and rivers, its lakes and forests, its cities and seacoasts. In this sense, despite its strong transcendental spirituality, Hinduism is a highly locative tradition in which place matters.

The *tīrthas* stretch across India, creating a vast web of sacred sites, with roads and stories linking them to one another. This land of Bhārata has been described mythically and enacted ritually in the footsteps of pilgrims for many hundreds of years. Walking the road to a *tīrtha*—whether it be a nearby hilltop or a far-off mountain shrine—is part of what it has meant to be Hindu. And in their diverse ways, Muslims and Sikhs, Buddhists, Jains, and Christians have also come to share this locative sensibility. They, too, have places to which they repair for blessings, and many such places attract pilgrims from across religious traditions.

Geography and Mythology

The geography of India is impressive. The many tiers of the Himalayas stretch across the north, from the foothills to the world's highest mountains. The modern names of these mountains are famous today: Nanga Parbat and K2 in the Kashmir Karakoram range in the west, Neelkanth and Nanda Devī in the Kumaon area, Annapurna and Everest in Nepal, Kanchenjunga in the east. There are other mountains in India as well, though hardly impressive by comparison: the Vindhyas form a vast stretch of hills across central India north of the Narmadā River, the Nilgiris and the Malaya Mountains form a spine through south India to the very tip of the peninsula at Kanyākumārī, the Western Ghāts rise from the Arabian Sea, and the Eastern Ghāts rise from the Bay of Bengal. South of the Vindhyas between the Eastern Ghāts and the Western Ghāts is the high plateau called the Deccan, which comes from the Sanskrit term *dakshina*, meaning simply "the south." The major river systems of India lace the land with a network of waters: the Indus in the northwest, the Brahmaputra in the northeast, the Gangā and the Yamunā flowing from the high Himalayas into the plains of northern India, the Narmadā flowing westward across central India, and to its south, the Godāvarī, the Krishnā, and the Kāverī, which rise in the hills of the west and flow eastward across the whole subcontinent.

What interests us about India's landscape, however, is not simply that it is spectacular, diverse, and dramatic, but that it is alive with myths and stories. Some of the stories are known only locally or regionally, while others are part of the epic and mythological traditions known through-out the land. In short, every story has a place and every place a story. The hills of Andhra Pradesh are said to be the serpent Ananta, come to earth to support Vishnu's shrine at Tirupati. That long fertile strip along the eastern coast of India, stretching from Goa to Kerala, between the ghāts and the Arabian Sea, is called Parashurāma's Land, said to have been reclaimed from the rising ocean by the arrow of Parashurāma, an *avatāra* of Vishnu. We begin to see that geography of this kind is more than a map. It's a three-dimensional sacred landscape, linked by its story lines.

The Himalayas, literally the "abode of snows," are also called *devālaya*, the "abode of the gods," where Shiva dwells, high on Mount Kailāsa. As we have seen, there are peaks all over India that are said to be part of the Himalayas that were transported by gods or sages to some other locale, like Girnār in Gujarat or Pālani in Tamil Nadu. And comparison to the Himalayas is inevitable. For example, the Vindhyas are not just low-lying hills in central India, but mountains that once yearned to surpass the Himalayas and rose so high that they blocked the course of the sun. As the earth suffered under scorching heat, the sage Agastya was deployed to do something about it. When the great sage left his home in the north and approached the mountains, they bowed humbly to him and, at his request, agreed to remain in this posture until he returned from his jour-ney to the south. Agastya never returned, and so the Vindhyas remain low-lying hills even today. And it was Agastya, by the way, who is said to have brought many traditions from the north to the south.

And, of course, the rivers have their sacred lore. The Gaṅgā, whose waters sluice through the Himalayas and meander through the north Indian plains, is said to have descended from heaven to earth in order to give life to the dead and bring purification to the living. The Godāvarī is said to be a duplicate of the Gaṅgā, falling to earth not in the Himalayas but on a hill called Brahmāgiri in the Western Ghāts. The Narmadā rises from the very body of Shiva in the hills of eastern India, and the Kāverī, they say, was carried to the south by Lord Brahmā in his water jug.

Some three thousand years ago, the Vedic seers sang hymns to the rivers. These river hymns of the *Rig Veda* praise the "seven rivers," or the "thrice-seven rivers," for actually there are more than twenty rivers mentioned. Most prominent are the rivers of northwest India—the Sindhu, the Gaṅgā, the Yamunā, the Sarasvatī, and the "five rivers" of the Punjab, which means "the land of the five rivers." These rivers are praised as goddess rivers, mother rivers, let loose when the great god Indra slew the demon Vritra, who had coiled around the vault of the heavenly waters. Out upon earth they came, running like milk cows, their udders rich with the nourishment of life.[6]

Nearly three thousand years after the time of these Vedic hymns, as the prayer to the rivers has come into common formulation, the list of "seven rivers" has shifted and become wider, including the Narmadā of central India, the Godāvarī and the Kāverī Rivers of the south. The mental composition of India's seven rivers in this prayer includes the whole of India, as the worshipper intones, "O Gaṅgā, Yamunā, Godāvarī, Sarasvatī, Narmadā, Sindhu, Kāverī, come and enter into this water of my offering." These are the words recited as the seven rivers are invited to be present whenever water is consecrated for ritual purposes anywhere in the Hindu world. When this invocation is recited, the land in which the rivers flow is mentally composed and located. Radhakumud Mookerji expressed this in a series of lectures he delivered in 1920 on the topic of nationalism in Hindu culture: "As the mind of the devotee calls up in succession the images of these different rivers defining the limits of his country, it naturally traverses the entire area of his native land and grasps the image of the whole as a visible unit and form."[7] He sees in the river hymns of the *Rig Veda* "the first national conception of Indian unity such as it was."[8]

Even when local rivers substitute for one or more of the seven, as they often do, the mental construction of an imagined landscape watered by divine rivers remains. The specific rivers may change, but the structure of duplication and its resonances links these rivers, however enumerated, into an ordered whole coextensive with the locale, the region, the land of Bhārata, and even the wider universe.

Myths and Maps: A Locative View

Both mythology and geography provide for people and cultures the "maps" of their world. Myths, while they may be imaginative stories, are also those deeply true stories that anchor and orient people in the reality in which they live. Myths tell the tale of our deepest and most resonant human questions about life and death, our human experience, and our glimpses of transcendence. They tell the tale of cosmic creation, the birth of the earth, and the deeds of the gods and heroes. They help us think about what really matters in an ambiguous world of good and evil, competition and compromise, desire and deception. At the most difficult times of life, myths help us find our way home.

Maps are also means of orientation, displaying how the world, with its quadrants, its borders, and its features, is laid out. Mapmaking is also a form of meaning-making and world-making, and there are many kinds of maps. Most familiar to us are the maps produced by surveyors and cartographers, meant to render a scientifically accurate grid of latitude and longitude, showing us nations, regions, states, and cities. Historically, these maps of mastery came with the spread of empires and geographical knowledge and became a way of controlling territory as well as representing it.[9] Today, our maps of mastery are digital, rendered from satellites that can provide pinpoint accuracy for military targets or for the nearest hospital. A digital satellite map can home in on Main Street in our hometown. But there are other kinds of maps that orient us in alternate and affective ways. For instance, the pictographic map produced by the chamber of commerce in our hometown is made to entice and alert the visitor to the most important features of our town. In the Indian context, the pictographic pilgrimage maps of Vārāṇasī, for example, give us a few major streets, but primarily call attention to the major temples, the bathing *ghāts* along the river, and the deities whose shrines are central. The railroad line runs across one corner of the map, while at the bottom, in the middle of the river, the goddess Gangā sits on her *makara* and Shiva's large trident reminds us that the city is lifted up out of the world of time and space. As Sumathi Ramaswamy has shown, in the twentieth century, the map of India as a whole—its simplified outline the product of British scientific cartographers—was gradually iconicized and joined with the image of the Goddess, Bhārat Mātā or, in some cases, Durgā, conflating pictographic and scientific cartography in a very powerful way.[10]

In its many forms of mapping, a culture reveals, explicitly and implicitly, the order and structure of its multiple worlds, local and translocal. Where are the centers, the power points, the peripheries? Both maps and myths give one a sense of worldview and an orientation to the world, its familiar territory and its terrae incognitae. How do mythmaking and mapmaking converge? Does the land with its rivers and mountains carry the three-dimensional animated charge of myth? Are the myths people live by linked to the land and its features? What kinds of worlds are shaped by our myths and our maps? For example, land and location have been of continuing importance in the Jewish tradition, which has a long Israel-oriented history as well as a long history of adapting to the reality of exile from the land and singing the Lord's song in a foreign land. The complex culture of China also has had a highly locative sensibility, with a clear if changing sense of center and periphery, the center being the ancient city of Peking, described as the "pivot of the four quarters" and developing a cultural life largely anchored in the Middle Kingdom. More-ecumenical traditions, like Buddhism, Christianity, and Islam, have traveled across cultural regions, developing multiple cultural forms, continually composing and recomposing a more universal map of the world. While these traditions may have center points, like Rome and Mecca, they have also developed a global spiritual life, a worldwide church or a universal *ummah*.

In ancient Greece, Eratosthenes, in the third century B.C.E., was the first to coin the word "geography." He clearly saw his work—the mapping of the known world, the *oikoumene,* and the calculation of its circumference—to be quite distinct from the kind of world description found in Greek myths or in the epics of Homer. Ernst Cassirer has distinguished the "geometric space" that concerned Eratosthenes and, a few years later, Euclid from what he calls the "space of perception" and "the space of myth." He writes, "In contrast to the homogeneity which prevails in the conceptual space of geometry every position and direction in mythical space is endowed as it were with a particular accent—and this accent always goes back to the fundamental mythical accent, the division between the sacred and the profane."[11] While Olympus and Delphi retained their mythic charge in Greece itself, the study of geography began to diverge from the image of the world composed by the great Greek mythmakers.

In India, however, mythology and geography continued to be a joint imaginative and descriptive undertaking, located largely in the same set of texts. During the course of some fifteen centuries, beginning in the early centuries of the Common Era, we see the composition and expansion of the epics and Purānas, works that constitute a massive compendium of both Hindu geography and Hindu mythic narratives.[12] The epics include the *Rāmāyana* and the *Mahābhārata* in their many forms, as well as the south Indian epics, the *Shilappadikaram* and *Manimekalai*. In addition, the eighteen Sanskrit Purānas, the "old stories," have grown and changed over the course of more than a thousand years and have been translated and interpreted in the regional languages of India. All these texts include sections describing the world, known and unknown, and mapping its features onto the landscape. Geographical knowledge continued to be grounded in the mythical apprehension of the world's meaning and order. Not only was the geography of the land expounded most prominently in Hindu mythological texts, but conversely, Hindu mythology in these texts was constantly grounded in the topography of the land of India. Here the land is imaged in a particularly imaginative way as the southern petal of the lotus-shaped central island of the universe, an island called Jambudvīpa or Rose Apple Island. But whether one imagines the land as a lotus petal or not, the topography attributed to our particular petal includes the Narmadā, the Gangā, the Yamunā, and the rest of the seven rivers, along with many other holy places.

Sanskrit literary practices are also suffused with the sense of Bhārata or Bhāratavarsha beginning in the first millennium. Primarily considering these literary dimensions of Sanskrit, Sheldon Pollock writes, "So important, in fact, was the geographical mode of thought to Sanskrit literati that space not only became an object of knowledge to be fully organized in their discourse but, as we will see, wound up organizing discourse itself by providing a basic framework for structuring cultural knowledge."[13] He gives countless examples of the ways in which the analysis of culture, from sexual behavior to literary arts, is detailed in Sanskrit literature by describing the practices of the peoples of India—north, south, east, and west. "There is of course nothing remarkable about people in premodern South Asia having a clear and accurate conception of the spatial organization of their world," he writes. "What is remarkable is that the geographical template made available in embryonic form by the Purānic text and reworked by Varāhamihira became the organizing logic of so much systematic Indian thought. To know the world in some of the most elementary aspects of its social, cultural, and political domains meant, for the intellectual who wrote in Sanskrit, to know it as an immense, if specific, spatial order upon which those practices could be mapped."[14] Pollock is concerned primarily with realms of power and literary practices. His work on the geographical awareness of South Asia does not venture into its religious practices, but his careful construction of the wider world of Sanskrit learning and its relation to the emergence of regional vernaculars is an important companion to our efforts here.

Students of Hinduism or travelers in India quickly become aware of what prolific mythmakers Hindus have been. The Hindu tradition is famous for its mythologies, and for the multitude of gods and goddesses one encounters in the temples and the public spaces of India. Less well known, however, is the fact that Hindus have been equally avid geographers who have described with considerable detail the mountains, river systems, and holy places of India. For the most part, Hindu mythology has been studied by one group of scholars, primarily historians of religion, while the geographical traditions have been studied and catalogued by another group, primarily British and Indian civil servants, historical and cultural geographers. The great geography scholar Bimala C. Law speaks for this latter group when he confesses, "One finds it tedious to read the legendary history of *tīrthas* or holy places, but to a geographer it will never be a fruitless study."[15]

Here we look at mythology and geography together, in a single view, to see what we can learn of this complex conception of the land of India.

Rather than focusing exclusively on texts, however, we begin "on the ground," with shrines, rivers, and hilltops where pilgrims have enacted the sense of connectedness that is part of pilgrimage. This intersection of mythology and geography reveals how the people who have come to be called Hindus have "mapped" their world and how they have understood the land they have called Bhārata in relation to the larger universe. There is arguably no other major culture that has sustained over so many centuries, and across such diverse regions, a fundamentally locative or place-oriented worldview.

A COMMON AND COMPLEX COSMOS

The long-dominant Sanskrit-based traditions of Buddhist, Jain, and Brahmanical Hindu culture have all promoted in various ways the locative understanding of a common cosmos in which, as we shall see, India is that southern petal of the lotus island in the middle of the universe. Mount Meru stands in the middle of the cosmos, and the River Gangā falls from heaven to the top of Meru, spreading in four directions to all the continents of earth. Within India, there is implicit a kind of geographical "Sanskritization" that has constructed a common cosmos by the local adoption of the names and qualities of India's most renowned rivers, mountains, and *tīrthas*.[16] This vision of India seemed to develop during the same centuries as the "Sanskrit cosmopolis" was created through the widening use of Sanskrit in literary works and royal inscriptions.[17]

Of course, it is true that some tribal peoples, ethnic groups, and religious movements in India never participated, either consciously or by unconscious assent, in this common cosmos of Bhārata. Their mapped worlds are primarily local or regional. Be that as it may, many others have "subscribed," so to speak, to this common cosmos, attaching the significance of the places and gods close at hand to a wider stock of mythic or epic themes. Here in our village, they say, Rāma, Sītā, and Lakshmana rested in their journey through the forest. There, on that hill, the powerful goddess slew the world-threatening demon. Here in this grove, an ascetic practiced austerities so long that an anthill developed around him and he received a boon from the gods. In addition, the toponyms of the common cosmos were transposed to local and regional geographies, which created Mount Meru, the Gaṅgā, and many other *tīrthas* in the landscape near at hand.

Above all, the past thousand years of India's history have seen the creation of Indo-Muslim culture, with its own mental composition of the land it called Hindustan, not cast as the landscape of the gods, but nonetheless a land gleaming with the heritage of kings and kingdoms, monuments of empire, and the tombs of martyrs and saints. As Ayesha Jalal and others have pointed out, Muslims have had their own forms of attachment to India's cities and regions and they, too, have developed a locative consciousness, attuned to some extent to distant Mecca, but also attuned to the beauties of the cities they have created and in which they live.[18] As we shall see, there are many places where the Hindu and Muslim landscapes overlap and intersect, where Muslims and Hindus alike have celebrated holy men and sought their blessings. There are hundreds, perhaps thousands, of such places throughout India, especially the *dargahs,* or memorial tombs, of Sufi saints. There are *dargahs* known only to one locale, such as one in the back streets of Vārāṇasī, where a Hindu caretaker is responsible for what is essentially a Muslim shrine.[19] There are others known throughout India, such as the *dargah* of the Sufi saint Mu'inuddin Chishti in Ajmer.

During the past five hundred years, the Sikh community has also grown to prominence in India. Guru Nānak and many of the early Sikh gurus scorned the very idea of sacred places, as if bathing in a river or visiting a shrine could purify the soul. In this, Nānak was a kindred spirit to other great souls of his time, such as the poet Kabīr in Vārāṇasī who insisted that it is not the place, but the heart, that matters. This rejection of a purely ritual pilgrimage is part of many antinomian spiritual movements. Despite this critical sensibility, the Sikhs nonetheless developed a sacred geography centered at a place—the Golden Temple in Amritsar where Guru Arjan enshrined the sacred text of the Sikhs, the Guru Granth Sahib, in the seventeenth century. This elegant temple, situated in the middle of a large artificial lake, has a long tradition of being visited by the devout of many faiths. Other places, too, have become part of the Sikh sacred imaginary, including the shrine of the martyrdom of Guru Tegh Bahādur in the heart of old Delhi, an important destination for the Sikh faithful.

Christians, too, developed a landscape of shrines in India, especially those associated with the Virgin Mary, such as the Church of Our Lady of Vailankanni on the coast of the Bay of Bengal in Tamil Nadu. Like its neighbor, the *dargah* of the Sufi saint Meeran Sahib in Nagore, or Nāgāppatinam, Vailankanni is a healing shrine attracting Christian pilgrims, and Hindus and Muslims as well. She is called Our Lady of Health, and pilgrims come for just that. The church museum displays the crutches and canes they have left behind as well as a long history of testimonies to miraculous healings. The steeples of her distinctively Christian basilica rise white and gleaming from the sands, while the nearby tonsure centers catering to pilgrims participate in forms of pilgrim asceticism and pilgrimage practice that are widely shared in south India. In her annual festival, an image of Our Lady is brought out into the great avenue that stretches toward the sea, in a public procession that is very much like those of the Hindu temples of Tamil Nadu.

The important point is not that there is an all-India unanimity on India's sacred geography, but rather that for well over two thousand years the landscape of India has been made three-dimensional by the power of myth, narrative, and pilgrimage. The theme of a living cosmos has been continually sounded, continually heard, continually adjusted and reframed with changing times and with new movements and peoples in the composite cultures of India. The mental map of India envisioned in the narratives of the sages, enlivened by the eruptions of the divine, and imprinted in the soil with the footsteps of millions of pilgrims is still a powerful and compelling force in India today. Of course, this means there are overlapping "Indias," constituted by the lived landscape of Hindus, Jains, Muslims, Christians, and Sikhs. The idea of India has come to include a range of powerful places of every religious tradition. Even so, its most elaborate articulation continues to be the complex Hindu landscape that is the primary focus of this study.

CIRCLING THE LAND

In India's traditions of devotion, walking around something or someone is a way of showing honor. This circumambulation, called *pradakshina*, literally "keeping the center to one's right," might show honor to a parent or a teacher as well as a temple or the inner sanctum of a temple. In some cases, an entire city is circumambulated, as in the circling pilgrimage around Vārānasī. A mountain or hill might be circumambulated, as is the holy hill Govardhan in the land of Krishna. Even a river might be circumambulated, as in the famous circumambulation of the Narmadā River that streams westward across central India. In that case, the pilgrim might undertake a stretch of the river each year for many years until the circuit of the entire river—from the source at Amarakantaka to the Arabian Sea—has been completed. So it should not surprise us to find that the whole land of India was—and is—circumambulated by the especially devout or intrepid pilgrim.

Circumambulation was also part of the ritual of kingship. A king who claimed to be a "world conqueror" would circle the "four directions" to indicate his sovereignty over the territory of his kingdom. While circling the land was, no doubt, important in practice, it was also important as an idea of territorial encompassment. During the reign of the Buddhist emperor Ashoka in the third century B.C.E., the circumambulatory tour, called the *digvijaya,* literally "victory over the four directions," became, in effect, the military circumambulation of the kingdom, and in Ashoka's case this kingdom was extensive. The Mauryan Empire, founded by his grandfather Chandragupta Maurya in the fourth century B.C.E., was extended by his father, Bindusara, to include much of north and central India. However, Ashoka eventually altered the victory tour in a significant way: His was a *digvijaya* of dharma, the teachings of righteousness. Following a military victory over the Kalingas in what is today Orissa in eastern India, Ashoka is said to have been sickened by the carnage of war. He became a follower of the teachings of the Buddha—the Dharma, or Dhamma in Pali—and he took it as his mission to spread Buddhist moral teachings throughout his kingdom. His rock-cut edicts and pillar edicts are found from the Himalayan foothills in the north, to coastal Orissa near Purī in the east, to Karnataka in the south, to the Saurashtra peninsula in the west, and to Kandahar in the northwest. At the base of Girnār, the mountain shrine we have visited in Gujarat, the series of edicts called for a halt to the slaughter of animals to make food for the great festivals and announced medical provisions during the festival for both humans and animals. In part, the inscription reads, "In the past, for many hundreds of years, killing or harming living beings and improper behavior towards relatives, and improper behavior towards Brahmans and ascetics has increased. But now due to Beloved-of-the-Gods, King Piyadasi's Dhamma practice, the sound of the drum has been replaced by the sound of the Dhamma."[20]

It seems that the land the *Mahābhārata* described as stretching "from the Himalayas to the southern sea" was not only an abstract idea, but also an idea that was acted out, so to speak, in itineraries of travel. In the narrative of the *Mahābhārata*, for example, at the coronation of the eldest, Yudhisthira, the four brothers are sent to the four directions to subdue the peoples—Arjuna to the north, Bhīma to the east, Sahadeva to the south, and Nakula to the west. Later, when the Pāndava brothers have lost their kingdom in a rigged gambling match and have been sentenced to years of forest exile by their jealous cousins, the brothers conquer the directions once again as pilgrims, making a clockwise pilgrimage, a *pradakshina*, of India. They travel from the Gangetic Plain in the north as far south as Shrī Mountain and as far west as Gokarna on the coast of the Arabian Sea. Likewise, the epic *Rāmāyana* is cast, by tradition, on an all-India stage. As Rāma, Sītā, and Lakshmana submit to a period of forest exile from their kingdom in Ayodhyā, their adventures take them from Ayodhyā in the north, to today's Nāsik in central west India, all the way to Rāmeshvara in the south. There Rāma is said to have built the bridge that enabled his army of monkeys and bears to cross over to Lankā and rescue Sītā, who had been abducted by Rāvana, the *rākshasa* ruler of Lankā. In the fourth-century literary version of the tale, the poet Kālidāsa attributes such a *digvijaya* of conquest to King Rāma in the fourth chapter of the *Raghuvamsa*, which tells the story of Rāma setting off from Ayodhyā down the Gangā to plant victory pillars at the mouth of the river, then down the coast of Orissa, to the Kāverī River, the Malaya Mountains, and north once again.[21]

The *digvijaya* tradition extended from kings and heroes to spiritual exemplars as well. According to legend, the ninth-century philosopher Shankara made his own kind of *digvijaya*, traveling to the four directions of India, teaching Advaita Vedanta philosophy. The traditional accounts of Shankara's life are indeed called "Shankara *Digvijaya*" and they cast the life of India's greatest philosopher upon a sacred land that extends from his birthplace in Kerala in the south to Badrīnāth in the north, where he is said to have spent several years and written some of his major commentaries. In order that the wisdom of the tradition not be lost, Shankara is said to have requested his disciples to establish monastic headquarters in each of the four directions—at Sringeri in the south, Dvārakā in the west, Jyoshīmatha in the north, Purī in the east. These directional *mathas,* or monastic centers, still anchor the network of Shankara's orders of renunciants today.

All this is legendary, of course, or at least contains a strong dose of legend. But what is not legendary is the fact that pilgrims began to construct the landscape of India in terms of the four directions, the pilgrimage to the four *dhāms,* or "divine abodes," of the gods. Four great temples stand at the four compass points of India: Badrīnāth, the abode of Vishnu in the north, within a few miles of what is today the Tibetan border; Rāmeshvara, the *linga* said to have been established by Rāma in the far south; Dvārakā, or Dvārāvatī, the abode of Krishna at the tip of the Saurashtra peninsula in the far west; and Purī, also the abode of Krishna as Jagannātha, on the coast of the Bay of Bengal in the east. The *chār dhām yātrā,* as it is referred to in the countless pilgrimage pamphlets, may include a great many places along the way, but its standard components are these great directional abodes. As we have seen, there are other *chār dhāms,* linking four places as a complete pilgrimage circuit: the four *dhāms* of Girnār in Saurashtra, the four *dhāms* of Chitrakūt, and, most famously, the four *dhāms* of the Himalayas, where annually countless pilgrims visit Badrīnāth, Kedārnāth, the source of the Gangā, and the source of the Yamunā. The prototype remains the four *dhāms* at the compass points of India.

The common practice before modern times, of course, was to walk this pilgrimage route, circumambulating India on foot. Even today there are those who do so, such as the elderly widow I met in Banāras in the 1970s who had made the *chār dhām yātrā* on foot. There is no way of knowing how extensive this practice was in former times, and it is unclear exactly when these particular four *dhāms* began to be grouped as the representatives of the spiritual *digvijaya.* No doubt such wide sojourning was more common for *sannyāsīs,* or renouncers, than it was for ordinary householders. That the territory of the *sannyāsīs'* wanderings included the whole sweep of what we presently know as India is surely suggested in the legends surrounding the great teacher Shankara. It is also suggested in the imaginative sweep of the epics, in the journeys of both the Pāndavas and of Rāma in search of Sītā. And if we are to take seriously the account of the informants, presumably *sannyāsīs*, given to Alexander in the fourth century B.C.E., we set an even earlier date for a circuit pilgrimage. Alexander's historians wrote that he "caused the whole country to be described by men well acquainted with it." According to the accounts passed on to Strabo, these informants told him how far it was from the mouth of the Indus in the west to the mouth of the Gangā in the east, from the mouth of the Gangā to the tip of southern India, and from there, again, to the mouth of the Indus![22]

"WHAT IS INDIA?"

Those of us who take for granted the modern world of nation-states think readily of India as a subcontinent, a land, a nation. But given India's tremendous diversity, its many language groups, its multitude of ethnic groups and tribal peoples, its different sectarian and religious communities, it is not a fact without considerable consequence that India has seen itself as a land and, in the modern era, a nation. In the nineteenth century, many among those whom Edward Said would call "orientalists" were especially scornful of the idea that India might be thought of as a nation. It is well known that at least one school of British imperial thought in the nineteenth century firmly believed that "India" was really a meaningless notion. India might be seen as an integral geographical area, of course, but it was not a "nation" because it had none of the marks of unity that characterized a modern nation-state. India had no common language, no common racial or ethnic unity, no common religion or ideology. Only the Mughal Empire in the sixteenth century had managed to unify any substantial part of the subcontinent administratively, so this school argued. Before that, there were simply the regional and short-lived Hindu kingdoms, insignificant for the land as a whole. Indeed, they argued, the structure of nationhood was the superimposition of the British Raj, with its district officers, its railways, and its centralized imperial bureaucracy.

"What is India?" In 1888, Sir John Strachey, speaking to an audience at the University of Cambridge, put the question in a way that would be echoed by British administrators for many decades. "What does this name India really signify? The answer that has more than once been given sounds paradoxical, but it is true," he said. "There is no such country, and this is the first and most essential fact about India that can be learned. India is a name, which we give to a great region including a multitude of different countries. There is no general Indian term that corresponds to it."[23]

Strachey frequently makes the comparison with Europe, which had more of common culture, he contends, than India. "Scotland is more like Spain than Bengal is like the Punjab. . . . There are no countries in civilized Europe in which people differ so much as the Bengali differs from the Sikh, and the language of Bengal is as unintelligible in Lahore as it would be in London."[24] He reiterates what was to become one of the undergirding themes of empire: "This is the first and most essential thing to learn about India—that there is not, and never was an India, or even any country of India, possessing, according to European ideas, any sort of unity, physical, political, social and religious; no Indian nation, no 'people of India,' of which we hear so much. . . . We have never destroyed in India a national government, no national sentiment has been wounded, no national pride has been humiliated; and this not through any design or merit of our own, but because no Indian nationalities have existed."[25] At a time when the Indian National Congress, which was to become the vehicle of the independence movement, was just beginning, Strachey contends, "It is conceivable that national sympathies may arise in particular Indian countries; but that they should ever extend to India generally, that men of the Punjab, Bengal, the N.W. Provinces, and Madras, should ever feel they belong to one great nation is impossible."[26] Through the lens of the nineteenth-century West, a lens ground to bring to focus a particular political conception of the nation-state, "India" did not exist. It was a mere word, designating a piece of the map.

The word "India," of course, is a Greek word, referring to the land beyond the River Sindhu known to the Greeks as the Indus. The Greeks first knew of India through the Persians, whose empire extended across the Sindhu River into the Punjab. Greek historians such as Megasthenes, Strabo, Arrian, and Ptolemy wrote works they called Indika—naming with this very title the idea of a geographical area that could reasonably be described as a whole. The people of India did not call their own land India, however. The indigenous term was Bhārata, most often understood as a patronymic, derived from the name of an ancient clan and king, Bhārata, the famous son of King Dushyanta and the maiden Shakuntalā. The name must first have referred specifically to the area of north India where the Bhārata dynasty reigned. It was also called Bhāratavarsha, the land of Bhārata. In the next chapter, we will look at the *Mahābhārata's* vision of a world map of numerous islands radiating like petals from the world mountain called Mount Meru. This world, which included the land of India, was also called Jambudvīpa, Rose Apple Island, or Kumārīdvīpa, the Island of the Virgin Goddess.

Names such as Bhāratavarsha and Jambudvīpa are both ancient and strikingly contemporary. Consider this: every act of Hindu ritual begins with a statement of intention, called *sankalpa,* giving expression to one's religious intention in undertaking any ritual, whether a daily rite or a once-in-a-lifetime pilgrimage. Holding water or grains cupped in one's hand, one states the coordinates of time and place, making explicit one's position in the cosmos: "In Jambudvīpa, in Bhāratakhanda, in the sacred city of Vārānasī . . ." or "In Bhāratavarsha, in Kumārīkhanda, in the sacred city of Vārānasī . . ." Such a *sankalpa* has accompanied ritual

Bathing in the southern sea: sankalpa *at Kanyākumārī*

action for many centuries and continues today, as tens of thousands of *sankalpas* are uttered by worshippers who locate themselves with exactitude on the southern leaf of a lotus world.

By the time of the "Great Bhārata" war, described in the epic *Mahābhārata,* the name Bhārata referred loosely to the whole land of India insofar as it was known. But what did it mean to call this whole land "Bhārata" more than two thousand years ago? The bards of ancient India from the time of the *Mahābhārata* onward would have had a ready answer for Strachey's question "What is India?" or, more aptly, "What is Bhārata?" As the *Mahābhārata* puts it, "The land north of the seas and south of the Himalayas is called Bhārata, where the descendants of King Bhārata live."[27] This also became the standard Purānic definition of India, elaborated and repeated for many hundreds of years. It is a conceptual "definition" of Bhāratavarsha that is, as Pollock puts it, "uniform, stable, and most significant of all, subcontinental, and this limit, once achieved, marked the boundary of geographical concern."[28] As India's boundary, however, it was movable and flexible, and even areas beyond the four directions, such as kingdoms of Southeast Asia, claimed to be included, "by the very act of naming wherever they lived with the names of India."[29]

In modern times, pilgrims sum up the extent of India with similar brevity, saying India extends "from Badrīnāth to *Rāmeshvaram,*" the north-south axis of the *chār dhām.* Following this lead, the modern-day Geographical Survey of India adopted the motto *"A Setu Himāchalam,"* from the "Bridge," another name for Rāmeshvara, where Rāma built a bridge to Lanka in mythic times, to the Himalayas. The buses that carry today's tourist pilgrims to Cape Comorin at the very tip of southern India, named for the famous goddess Kanyākumārī, bear the slogan "From Kashmir to Kanyākumārī—India Is One."

This geographical "definition" of India is a powerful one. *The Cambridge History of India* put it matter-of-factly and succinctly: "The one clear unity which India has possessed throughout history has been geographical."[30] True enough, India, like Italy, has a geographical unity that is distinctive—a great peninsula, bordered by the seas and sealed in the north by a breathtaking range of towering mountains. What the British little understood, until the ferocious struggle over partition, was just how important this geography was, indeed still is, in Hindu India's sense of identity. Geography is important—from Kashmir to Kanyākumārī. As Mookerji put it in the 1920s, with a dose of rhetorical hyperbole, "In no other country of the world do we find such an elaborate network of shrines and sacred places as has been spread over this vast mother-country of ours by the religious enthusiasm of the people."[31] It is through pilgrimage, he argues, that the people of India expanded their geographical consciousness and emancipated it from parochialism or regionalism. It was also in the 1920s that V. D. Savarkar articulated his view of Hindutva, the "Hinduness" that describes "the love we bear to a common fatherland." The Hindu is not defined by a common creed, he contended, but is one who holds Bhārata as "holy land" and "fatherland," in contrast to those whose holy land is elsewhere. Controversial as that view was and has become once again with the "new Hindutva" of the 1990s, it is a view that must be understood and with which we must seriously contend. Its highly politicized polemics draw upon some of the same sources we consider in this book.

Nehru, imprisoned in the Ahmednagar Fort in 1944, wrote *The Discovery of India,* and reflected on that impression of "oneness" that he deeply felt as he traveled across India during the freedom struggle. "It was not her wide spaces that eluded me, or even her diversity, but some depth of soul which I could not fathom, though I had occasional and tantalizing glimpses of it. . . . Though outwardly there was diversity and infinite variety among our people, everywhere there was that tremendous impress of oneness, which had held all of us together for ages past, whatever political fate or misfortune had befallen us. The unity of India was no longer merely an intellectual concept for me: it was an emotional experience which overpowered me."[32] Nehru's vision of India surely included all its caste and regional communities, as well as its religious diversity. Although he espoused an ardent secularism throughout his political life, from his rising leadership of the Indian National Congress in the 1930s to his death as the first prime minister of India in 1964, it was a secularism that was somehow built on the kinds of deep, presumptively Hindu foundations we are describing.

For example, in 1963, during the border dispute with China, it was Nehru who, in an exchange of letters with Premier Chou En-lai, asserted scriptural sanction for the antiquity of India's claim to the Himalayas as a northern border. The document he sent, drawn up by the Historical Department of the Ministry of External Affairs, begins:

> India's northern frontier is a traditional one, in the sense that it has lain approximately where it now runs for nearly three thousand years. The areas along this frontier, which is nearly 2,500 miles long from the Keun Lun Mountains in the far north to the junction with Burma in the east, have always been part of India.... This northern frontier of India is for much of its length the crest of the Himalayan ranges. The Himalayas have always dominated Indian life, just as they have dominated the Indian landscape. One of the earliest Sanskrit texts, though its date is uncertain—the Vishnu Purana—makes it clear that the Himalayas formed the frontier of India. It states that the country south of the Himalayas and north of the ocean is called Bharat, and all born in it are called Bharatiyas or Indians. . . . The earliest reference to the Himalayas is in the Rig Veda, which was written about 1500 B.C. It states that the Himalayas symbolize all mountains (10th Mandala, 10th Adhyaya, Sukta 121.4). The Kena Upanishad, written sometime about 1000 B.C., speaks of Uma the daughter of the Himalayas—Umam haimavatim.[33]

The text goes on to mention the *Mahābhārata,* the *Arthashāstra* of Kautilya, and the *Raghuvamsa* and *Kumārasambhava* of the poet Kālidāsa as further evidence of the traditional validity of India's Himalayan border. Nehru was, in one sense, thoroughly secular in his orientation, yet his sensibilities were significantly grounded in the symbolic sacred geography of India. Anticipating his own death, Nehru asked in his "Last Will and Testament" that his ashes be thrown into the River Gangā at Allahabad. He insisted that this had no "religious significance," but his disclaimer made all the more real his deep love of India, especially Hindu India and the River Gangā: "I have been attached to the Ganga and the Jumna rivers in Allahabad ever since my childhood and, as I have grown older, this attachment has also grown. . . . The Ganga, especially, is the river of India, beloved of her people, round which are intertwined her racial memories, her hopes and fears, her songs of triumph, her victories and her defeats. She has been a symbol of India's age-long culture and civilization, ever-changing, ever-flowing, and yet ever the same Ganga."[34]

The Himalayas, the Gangā, and the other mountains and rivers of India, many of which are linked in their sacredness to the Himalayas and the Gangā, compose a sense of India that has considerable antiquity. It is not "religious," if one construes religion only as doctrinal. Yet, from the time of the *Rig Veda* to the time of Nehru, the imaginative casting of a sense of place inhabited not only by its peoples but by gods and goddesses, heroes and heroines, has answered with increasing clarity the question "What is India?"

ALEXANDER AND THE "DISCOVERY" OF INDIA

In 327 B.C.E., Alexander the Great forded the Indus River on a bridge of boats and led his troops into the "Land of the Five Rivers," the Punjab. He was received in the city of Taxila, so they say, by the submissive King Ambhi. In the summer of 326 he pressed on eastward toward the Jhelum River to challenge the armies of King Porus, one of Ambhi's long-standing enemies. The defeat of Porus on the east bank of the Jhelum was one of Alexander's most brilliant tactical triumphs. When Porus surrendered, Alexander pressed on still farther into the Land of the Five Rivers, despite the heavy rains of the monsoon season. He forded the Chenab River, then the Rāvī River. Alexander had certainly heard of the great empire of Magadha with its capital at Pataliputra, which the Greeks had called Palibothra. It was much farther east on the Ganges plain, and beyond Palibothra, he was told, was the Eastern Sea. No doubt the irrepressible Alexander intended to go that far.

But something happened in the Punjab, before Alexander's army could cross the Beas and then the Sutlej River, the last of the five, and set out down the Ganges Plain along the great trade route to Pataliputra. In Alexander's camp on the west bank of the flooded Beas, his officers, with a groundswell of support from the troops, persuaded Alexander to turn around. The historians write of the difficulty of the monsoon rains, the numerous snakes of the rainy season, and the immense war elephants of the opposing armies. But it is difficult to believe that rains and snakes daunted the men who had fought their way across Asia for seven years. Speculating on what happened in the tents along the Beas River, one can more readily believe that it had become apparent to Alexander's officers, the historian Nearchus among them, and then to Alexander himself, just where they were. One writer notes that the victories of Alexander and his men in the Hindu Kush, the Kabul Valley, and the Upper Indus were won by an army that was badly lost.[35] Alexander himself is said to have believed the Land of the Five Rivers to be Upper Egypt, leading eventually to the Nile and back to the familiar Mediterranean. But in the Punjab, Alexander's officers encountered informants who knew otherwise.

As we have mentioned above, according to the historian Strabo, Alexander "caused the whole country to be described by men well acquainted with it."[36] What the Greeks learned from them, as it comes to us in the writings of Strabo, Arrian, and Eratosthenes, was the extent and dimensions of the land into which they were venturing. It was clearly not Upper Egypt, and they were a long way from the Aegean. Might it have been such descriptions of India, elicited from Alexander's informants in the Punjab, that daunted the army and officers of Alexander? According to these Greek historians, the land described as India was a rhomboid, an "unequal quadrilateral, in shape, with the Indus on the west, the mountains on the north, and the sea on the east and south."[37] It was sixteen thousand *stadia* (1,838 miles) from the Indus in the west to the mouth of the Ganges in the east. From the mouth of the Ganges, along the eastern coast, it was another sixteen thousand *stadia* to the southern tip of India. It was said to be 19,000 *stadia* (2,183 miles) along the western coast from the tip or cape to the mouth of the Indus. The western border along the course of the Indus from its mouth to its headwaters was estimated to be 13,000 *stadia* (1,496 miles).[38] The land was clearly vast. As Megasthenes put it a generation later, "India forms the largest of the four parts into which Southern Asia is divided, while the smallest part is that region which is included between the Euphrates and our own sea. The two remaining parts, which are separated from the others by the Euphrates and the Indus, and lie between these rivers, are scarcely of sufficient size to be compared with India, even should they be taken both together."[39] From this perspective, it is no wonder that Alexander had twelve altars built to the Olympian gods along the Beas River and turned around.

It is striking that in 326 B.C.E., before the rise of the Mauryan Empire, there were informants, found apparently without much trouble, who could describe a land corresponding to what we call "India" to Alexander and, twenty years later, to Megasthenes, the ambassador of Seleucus I Nicator to the court of Chandragupta Maurya at Pataliputra. They also attested that India was roughly quadrilateral in shape, with the Indus River forming the western boundary, the Himalayas and the Hindu Kush stretched along the north, and the seas skirting the other two sides. They even cited its measurements: the length of the River Indus; the distance from the Indus to Pataliputra and from there to the mouth of the Ganges; the distances along the eastern and western coasts. Megasthenes also tells us that pillars have been set up at intervals to show the byroads and distances. More than two thousand years later, in 1871, Alexander Cunningham, then major-general of the Royal Engineers and, later, director of the Archaeological Survey of India, wrote what seems to be a footnote to Megasthenes: "The close agreement of these dimensions, given by Alexander's informants, with the actual size of the country is very remarkable, and shows that the Indians, even at that early date in their history, had a very accurate knowledge of the form and extent of their native land."[40]

Ancient India's sense of geography is indeed remarkable. For historians, who have long complained that Hindus had no sense of "history," it is remarkable to discover that they had a detailed sense of geography. For students of religion, impressed with the lavish Hindu mythic imagination, it is remarkable to discover that when the focus moves from the fabled Mount Meru and the encircling seas of milk, wine, and yoghurt to the features of the land of India, mythology becomes grounded in what one would have to call "real" geography. It is remarkable that, even in a time when travel throughout the length and breadth of the land must have been very difficult, there were traditions of geographical knowledge to suggest that such travel was indeed undertaken. And it is remarkable that even in a time when the subcontinent had no political unity whatsoever, those who described this territory to Alexander's company thought of it and described it as a single land.

The Land of the *Mahābhārata*

About the same time as Alexander's foray into northwest India, the traditions and stories of the great Hindu epic the *Mahābhārata* were in the process of becoming compiled. The epic, which contains ancient bardic stories, is generally regarded as having taken shape between the third century B.C.E. and the third century C.E. Here we can glimpse the traditions of geographical knowledge upon which the likes of Alexander's informants might have drawn for their descriptions of India. There are two kinds of *Mahābhārata* sources that give us a sense of ancient Indian geography. First, there are those cosmological texts that attempt to describe the whole universe, including India. In the *Mahābhārata*, these cosmological traditions are generally called the *bhuvana kosha*, the "dictionary of the world," which may include the geography of the wider mythic world with its seven ring-shaped islands and its seven ring-seas, along with the geography of India, with its mountain ranges, river systems, and peoples. In Chapter 3, we will explore in greater detail this mythic cosmos and the systematic worldview it contains. Second, there are those texts more specifically associated with the *tīrthas*.[41] These *tīrtha* traditions are found primarily in the *Mahābhārata*'s Vana Parva (The Book of the Forest) and specifically in its subsection called the "Tīrtha Yātrā Parvā." They are also found in almost all the subsequent Purānas.

The extensive "Tīrtha Yātrā Parvā" comes from a relatively late part of the *Mahābhārata*. It confirms and fills in our sense of what the term "Bhārata" included in the early centuries C.E.[42] This section of the epic is set during the forest exile of the noble princes, the Pāndavas. One of the princes, Arjuna, has gone to the Himalayas to secure heavenly weapons for the ominous oncoming war against their cousins, the Kauravas. While Arjuna is gone, the other Pāndava brothers and their wife Draupadī decide to undertake a pilgrimage (*tīrtha yātrā*), visiting holy places all around India. Yudhisthira and his brothers ask what reward might come to the one who makes a tour of the *tīrthas*.[43] Two great sages, named Pulastya and Dhaumya, enumerate the *tīrthas* for these would-be pilgrims and describe the benefits of pilgrimage.

First, Pulastya describes a great circuit of *tīrthas,* beginning in central north India at Pushkara, the Lotus Pond, in today's Rajasthan, praised as "the beginning of the *tīrthas*."[44] It is a place famous still today as the only major *tīrtha* of the creator god, Lord Brahmā, in all of India. It is appropriate that the pilgrimage route Pulastya describes begins at the beginning, with the Lotus Pond of the creator. From there he takes us on something of a spiraling clockwise circle of India, starting out toward the south to Mahākāla, then the Narmadā River, then west to Arbuda, or Abu, Dvārakā in Saurashtra, the westernmost point of India, then to the confluence of the Indus with the sea. Subsequently, he describes a route north to Kurukshetra and the Himalayas. Clearly Kurukshetra was known for its holiness long before the calamitous battle that takes place there at the end of the long epic. Pulastya also mentions Kanakhala, which even today attracts pilgrims along the banks of the Gangā near Hardvār. He speaks of the respective sources of the Gangā and Yamunā Rivers. From the North Country, Pulastya's description moves south through the plain of the Gangā, to Gopratāra on the Sarayū River, where Rāma attained heaven. Then he moves past Vārānasī and Gayā, and east to the Bay of Bengal, to Gangā Sāgara, where the Ganges meets the sea and where, even today, pilgrims converge to bathe. As he moves south along the seacoast, his description of the geography becomes thinner. He mentions Shrī Parvata, a mountain along the Krishnā River still famous today for its Shaivite shrine, Shrī Shaila. He speaks of the Kāverī River, which flows through Tamil Nadu, and Kanyā Tīrtha, presumably Kanyākumārī, the Virgin Goddess, whose seat is at the southernmost tip of India. Coming up the west coast, he mentions Gokarna, a *tīrtha* long associated with Shiva, in what is today coastal Karnataka. He mentions the Krishnā and Yamunā Rivers. Finally, he moves back into the heartland of the north, mentioning Chitrakūta, associated with the legend of Rāma, and, as a last stop, Prayāga, at the confluence of the Gangā and Yamunā Rivers.[45]

The sage Dhaumya's description repeats many of the same *tīrthas*, but he enumerates them not by a circuit journey, but by region—east, south, west, and north.[46] These two accounts give us not only a sense of the places known to be *tīrthas* in the early centuries c.e., but also how they are praised and storied. It is clear that there is a "sense of the whole," even though it is far more fully articulated in the region of India that lies north of the Narmadā River.

At last, with such a thorough briefing, the Pāndavas begin their journey. Following the general circuit pattern described, they set off from the land of the Kurus in the north and travel east through the Gangetic heartland to the Bay of Bengal. They are accompanied by many brahmins and forest-dwellers who see this as their opportunity to visit the *tīrthas* safely, in the protective company of these *kshatriya* warriors. They bathe in the estuary where the Gangā meets the sea. They follow the coast of Orissa into the Mahendra Mountains of the Eastern Ghāts, finally crossing the Narmadā River into the Dravida country of the south. No mention is made of how far south they go. Perhaps, indeed, they follow the Narmadā west, for their next stop is "holy Sūrpāraka," said to be on the west coast not far from the mouth of the Narmadā. Turning north, they travel to Saurashtra and the famous *tīrtha* of Prabhāsa on the coast of the Western Sea, the place known in later times as Somnāth. Here they meet the Vrishnis, the clan of Krishna that will help them in the great war. From Prabhāsa they turn back to central India, to the River Payoshnī, the River Narmadā, and on north to the River Yamunā. All along, there is elaborate mention made of the sacred mountains, the rivers, and the fords or *tīrthas*.

Finally, the Pāndavas and Draupadī come to Gangādvāra, where the River Gangā emerges from the mountains. At Kanakhala, near Gangādvāra, they prepare to go up into the mountains and meet Arjuna, on his return from Indra's heaven with the divine weapons. After a difficult journey, they reach Badarī Vishāla, the *tīrtha* famous today as Badrīnāth, in the high Himalayas. It is described as a place where the gods honor Nārāyana, or Vishnu.[47]

There is no doubt that the bards of the *Mahābhārata* knew the plains of north India and the mountains of the Himalayas far better than they knew India south of the Narmadā River. Indeed, until the Pāndavas reach the mountains, the tale of their pilgrimage has a rather artificial quality. The passages describing their journey are very lean, moving hundreds of miles in the space of a single verse.[48] At times, this Pāndava pilgrimage narrative seems to be but a literary device for threading together the tales of sages and heroes who live in the various forests and rivers along the way. Even so, the fact that the journey is described as circumambulatory, including within its mental frame the whole land, is very significant in our exploration of this idea of India.

Back north once again at the foot of the Himalayas, both the landscape and the rigors of the journey become more vivid. Now the text describes woodlands, with tender-leafed trees and flowers and cascading waterfalls, thickets of trees and creepers that make passage difficult, chill winds that make the hair stand on end, and mountains with exposed mineral patches, golden, black, and silver as if the mountain had been painted with fingers. Any traveler into the deep Himalayas today would recognize the familiarity with the landscape, heaped into the dense descriptions of the text. It is clear that the *Mahābhārata*'s knowledge of Badarī Vishāla on the slopes of Mount Gandhamādana is as immediate as its knowledge of Kanyā Tīrtha at the far southern end of India is dim. Nevertheless, these two places, then as now, constitute the far compass points of what is claimed as the land of Bhārata. Today the buses that chug and belch exhaust up the last stretch of the steep road to Badrīnāth bear the exclamation *"Jaya Badarī Vishāl!"* The famous shrine clings to the rocks high above the Alakanandā River. From there the footpath leads toward the high snows and the place called Svargarohinī, the "ladder to heaven," where, at the very end of the long epic, the last of the Pāndavas, Yudhisthira, finally left the earth.

THE INDIA OF THE OLD STORIES

The Purānas are India's "old stories," filled with the legends of kings and the myths of the gods. They also contain sections that correspond to the *bhuvana kosha* of the *Mahābhārata*—descriptions of the world, beginning with the creation of the universe, proceeding to a description of its component parts, and finally detailing the mountains and river systems of India and the *tīrthas* where one goes on pilgrimage to reap great benefits. The *tīrtha māhātmyas* of the Purānas often follow on immediately after the cosmological discussions. The writers of these texts have plunged into the enumeration and praise of the *tīrthas* with energy and enthusiasm. The *māhātmyas* constitute a distinctive genre of literature: They are praise texts that articulate in detail the places of pilgrimage and the benefits of visiting them. As the term *māhātmya* suggests, they tell what is "great" about the place. Indeed, they usually exaggerate what is "great" about the place, for that is part of the genre of praise. There are *māhātmyas* of the Gangā and the Narmadā, of Kāshī and Ujjain, and of

each and every *tīrtha*, river, and shrine. Each ends with its own statement of merit called a *phalashruti*, the "fruit" or *phala* that will be gained
from the pilgrimage and even the fruit that will be reaped from listening to the *māhātmya* itself! As we have seen, the fruits of pilgrimage are
often cited in sets of equivalences that advertise the power of the place:
Bathing at Dasāshvamedha Tīrtha in Kāshī will bring the benefits of
ten royal horse sacrifices! Even one look at the Narmadā will bring the
benefits of bathing in the Gangā! Honoring Shiva in Ujjain is equal to a
thousand years of prayerful austerities! Bathing in the hot springs called
Agni Tīrtha at Badrīnāth, one reaps the merit of three years of austerities drinking only the water that falls from a blade of *kusha* grass![49]

Tīrtha *māhātmyas* are voluminous, indeed far too extensive and,
indeed, too exhausting, to survey in detail. But the very extent of this
literature underlines the attention Hindus have paid to the intersections
of geography and mythology. The consideration of *tīrthas* and pilgrimage
claims more attention in the Purānas than virtually any other single
aspect of *dharmashāstra*.[50] When the makers of the great compendia
(*nibandhas*) of Hindu rite and custom began gathering together the
tīrtha māhātmyas to make them more readily accessible by topic, they
produced works of considerable size, enumerating *tīrthas* one by one and
gathering stories and praise texts in encyclopedic fashion from many
sources.

Each Purāna has areas of special emphasis. The *Matsya Purāna*, for
example, praises Prayāga and Avimukta (Banāras, Vārānasī, Kāshī) and
enumerates more than a hundred *tīrthas* up and down the length of
the Narmadā River. The *Vāmana Purāna* details the *tīrthas* of Kurukshetra. The *Vāyu Purāna* has an extensive *māhātmya* of Gayā. The *Padma
Purāna* has a special place for the ancient Pushkara in Rajasthan. Most
impressive of all is the *Skanda Purāna,* the mother lode of sacred geography, massive in size and structured entirely around the *tīrthas*. This
Purāna, at least in one version, comprises seven sections or Khandas. The
first, the Maheshvara Khanda, focuses on the praises of three important
areas sacred to Shiva: Kedāra in the Himalayas; Mahīsāgara Sangama,
where the Mahī River meets the sea in the west; and Arunāchala, Dawn
Mountain, located at the place known today as Tiruvannamalai in the
Tamil south. The second, the Vaishnava Khanda, contains major sections
praising Venkatāchala (Vishnu at Tirupati) in the south, Purushottama

(Vishnu at Purī, called Jagannātha) in the east, and Badarīkāshrama, or Badrīnāth, in the north. It also contains a *māhātmya* of Mathurā, the birthplace of Krishna, and Ayodhyā, the birthplace and capital of Rāma. The Brahmā Khanda contains, among other things, the praises of Rāmeshvara, called Setubandha, in the far south, where Rāma is said to have crossed the sea to retrieve the kidnapped Sītā from Lanka. The Kāshī Khanda stands on its own as the fourth major section of the *Skanda Purāna*, enumerating the many myths, the temples, and the praises of Kāshī, or Vārānasī, as well as containing an extensive *māhātmya* of the River Gangā. The Avantī Khanda praises the area around Ujjain called Avantī, with its eighty-four Shiva *lingas*, the most famous of which is Mahākāla. It also includes an extensive *māhātmya* of the Narmadā River that flows just to the south of Ujjain, here called by its ancient name, the Revā River. Finally, the Prabhāsa Khanda details the *tīrthas* of western India on the Saurashtra peninsula of what is today Gujarat—the great Shaiva *tīrtha* called Prabhāsa or Somnāth; the sacred hill called Vastra-patha and now known more prominently by its other name, Girnār; and the westernmost *tīrtha* in India, Dvārakā, the ancient latter-day capital of Lord Krishna.

The rivers are important features in the casting of this sacred geography, rivers that have been praised since the second millennium B.C.E., when the *Rig Veda* extolled them as the "mother-rivers" of northwest India. Gradually, the rivers praised come to include the rivers of central and south India. There is the Gangā and the seven sacred rivers, including the Indus, the Yamunā, the Sarasvatī, the Narmadā, the Godāvarī, and the Kāverī. Their waters are said to be purifying, and on their banks are some of the greatest of India's sacred "crossings"—Prayāga and Kāshī on the banks of the Gangā, Amarakantaka and Tryambaka at the headwaters of the Narmadā and the Godāvarī respectively, and Shrīrangam on an island in the Kāverī. So closely associated are *tīrthas* with pure, running river water that in south India the word *tīrtha* has come to mean, simply, "sacred water."

Mountains are *tīrthas* as well, the most important range being the Himalayas, literally the "abode of snows," and also the "abode of the gods." Throughout India, mountains and hilltops become the abode of particular gods—Mount Abu (Arbuda) in Rajasthan, Girnār in Saurashtra, Venkatāchala in the south. And some *tīrthas* are forests and caves, especially those associated with the *rishis,* or seers, whose presence has sanctified the places they live. While the sea is not ordinarily seen as auspicious for bathing, indeed quite the contrary, there are nonetheless specific places along the seacoast that are important *tīrthas*—like Gangā Sāgara, where the Gangā meets the sea; and Purī, along the coast of the Bay of Bengal, where Krishna dwells on the Blue Mountain next to the coast; Tiruchendur, where the southern god Murugan, also known as Skanda, defeated the forces of the netherworld with his mighty spear; and Gokarna, where Shiva's *linga* is established on the western seacoast. And of course there are cities, where the gods dwell among the people, including the famous "seven cities" known for bestowing the blessing of liberation—Ayodhyā, where Rāma reigned; Mathurā, where Krishna was born; Hardvār, where the Ganges enters the plains; Kāshī, where Shiva's *linga* of light is established; Kānchī, where Shiva and Vishnu share a city; Ujjain, where Shiva dwells as Mahākāla; and Dvārakā, where Krishna's kingdom came to an end at his death.

To summarize what must seem a very lengthy litany, there are so many *tīrthas* in the sacred geography of India that the whole notion of "sacred space" as somehow set apart from the profane is cast into question. In Hindu India, sacred space is so vastly multiplied that there is little left untouched by the presence of the sacred, reminding us that ultimately what is at stake is not the capacity of the gods to be present in the world, but rather the human capacity to apprehend that presence. In Vārānasī, they say, there is not a place as big as a sesame seed that is not a *tīrtha,* and the same is said of many of India's other great *tīrthas,* and perhaps of India itself. For the eyes of faith, this world is saturated with the sacred.

As if the *tīrthas* afforded by divine hierophany were not enough, bridges to the worlds of the gods were also built by men. Among the most important developments over the thousand years during which the *māhātmyas* of the *tīrthas* came to prominence was the emergence of the constructed *tīrtha*—the temple, built with the durability of stone. In most *tīrthas,* the temple itself is not what is important; it is the place, the power, the manifestation of the divine. The great *tīrthas* were there long before elaborate temples were constructed, and we will come across many instances where it serves us well to remember this. A *tīrtha* does not need to have a temple, and when temples are destroyed or fall into ruin, the *tīrtha* remains.

Even so, the construction of temple *tīrthas* was important. Indeed, beginning with the Gupta period, from the fifth century C.E. onward, the patronage of temple-building became a salient feature of kingship. The temple did not, of course, replace the portable altar of the sacred fire, which then, as now, is the focus of countless domestic and life-cycle rituals. Nor did the temple replace the natural features of the landscape deemed sacred—the pools, the hills, the mountains, the rocky outcroppings. But the temple did provide a congregational space and a site for the rites that linked the king with the people and the gods. The spiritual science of architecture found in the *Vāstu Shāstras* developed canons of spatial proportionality and design, and temples, like cities, were built on a sacred diagram, called a *mandala*. The temple, designed to link this world and the world beyond, became a man-made *tīrtha*, a place of crossing over.

Of course, there have always been wayside temples that are little more than shelters for an image, but with the creation of great temples, there is a new and cosmic symbolism. These temples are designed and consecrated as embodiments of the divine. In other words, the temple is not simply the place where a deity is housed, but a form of divine presence itself and, more broadly, a microcosm of the world. The great temples of north India are oriented with the guardians of the four directions and the four intermediary directions posted at eight points around the perimeter. Circling the temple is, indeed, a symbolic circling of the world.[51] The tower rising above the sanctum sanctorum is called a *shikhara*, a "mountain peak," and the styles of such *shikharas* bear the names of great mountains, such as Kailāsa or Meru.

In south India, temples are styled as virtual cities, with a central sanctum and a series of surrounding enclosing walls. A worshipper enters through tall gateway towers called *gopuras* and approaches the sanctum sanctorum through a series of circumambulatory and processional streets. One of the largest of these city-temples, the Shrīrangam Temple on an island in the middle of the Kāverī River at Tiruchirapalli, is said to have a population of some fifty thousand people. Entering the temple complex through the tallest gateway *gopura*, pilgrims find themselves on a busy commercial street with its sari shops and tea stalls. The subsequent gateway towers lead closer to the ritual center of the temple complex, and finally, the last one rises over the gateway to the inner sanctum of the temple. By the Chola period in the tenth and eleventh centuries, such great temple-city complexes extended their influence over larger regions, referred to with the term *mandala:* Kānchīpuram anchored Tondaiman-dalam, Thanjavur was at the center of Cholamandalam, and Madurai anchored Pandyamandalam. The *māhātmyas* of the Tamil south, called *sthala purānas,* refer not only to the natural features of the land and the manifestations of the gods in the landscape, but also to these great temple complexes built to house the deities.

The View from the South

The imagined landscape of India—from Badrīnāth to Rāmeshvara, from Kashmir to Kanyākumārī—as important as it is, is not the only construction of territory through the authority of myth and legend. The various regions of India have their own sense of sacred landscape, shaped by their particular history, culture, and geography. The rise of vernacular poetic and devotional traditions beginning in the thirteenth and fourteenth centuries stimulated a sense of regional culture and identity in Kashmir, Bengal, Maharashtra, and Orissa, all with strong regional traditions of landscape linked to the lore of the gods. One powerful example is Maharashtra. In the Old Marathi literature of the Mahānubhāva sect in the thirteenth century, Maharashtra is described as a holy land, its rivers enumerated, and its importance as the "great (*mahā*) land (*rāshtra*)" articulated. One popular aphorism puts it succinctly: "Stay in Maharashtra!"[52] In her extensive explorations of Maharashtra, Anne Feldhaus speaks of the "geographical awareness" that comprises a sense of regional identity, where pilgrimage expresses the connectedness of people, their deities, their villages, and their rivers. Indeed, the very definition of a region, as she puts it, is "a set of places that are connected to one another."[53] In some cases, they are connected because a river flows from one place to another; alternatively, people in a hundred villages might bring their deities to the same river on the same day, thus establishing a link between and among them all. Or perhaps they are connected because their respective village goddesses are understood to be sisters, so the connections are those of kinship. What Feldhaus has studied so carefully and meticulously in Maharashtra has many implications for the "connected places" of other regions and, indeed, of India as a whole.

The Tamil south presents perhaps the oldest construction of regional identity and one that is still in tension with the India-wide Sanskritic culture. The *Mahābhārata* is not the only ancient epic to have been built around journey narratives, filled with the mythic and divine significance of landscape. The fifth-century Tamil epic, the *Shilappadikaram*, the "Ankle Bracelet," is said to have been written by a Jain prince turned monk. Here, the heroine Kannagi and her husband Kovalan travel together through the Tamil country. The descriptions of the landscape are vivid, beginning with the city of Puhar, which must be near where the Kāverī River meets the sea. The Kāverī, which rises in the Coorg Hills of the Western Ghāts, flows eastward across Karnakata and Tamil Nadu, and becomes closely identified with the religious and cultural life of the region. In the *Shilappadikaram*, the Kāverī is praised elaborately as it flows through the Chola Kingdom:

> You gambol along the fields in the plains
> listening to the song of the peasants
> and the sweet wiles of waterfalls in eastern hills
> and the clamour of festive crowds on your banks.
> May the River Cauveri run eternally through Chola land!
> May you bring prosperity to all the Chola land![54]

While the Kāverī is the symbolic "wife" of the Chola ruler, the poet also speaks of the ruler's dalliance with the rival Gangā in the north and the sacred virgin Kanyākumārī at the tip of Tamil Nadu, but he assures the Kāverī that she need not be jealous.

The Tamil country is also delimited and defined in the *Shilappadikaram*: "The land of the Tamils, bounded on the north by the Venkatava hill of Mahāvishnu and on the south by the Virgin Cape of Kumārī and on the other two sides by the sea, is a land of rivers and traditionally ruled by the three Kings."[55] The specific enumeration of its holy places is remarkable for such an early text. Venkatava, of course, is Shrī Venkateshvara, the famous image of Vishnu who dwells in the hilltop shrine called Tirupati in what is today southern Andhra Pradesh. Even today, Shrī Venkateshvara is said to mark the northern "boundary," so to speak, of the Tamil country. Kanyākumārī is at the far tip of the peninsula. Other places are mentioned—the Podiyil Hills, where the sage Agastya dwells, and the Hill of Neduvel, where Lord Murugan pierced the demons of the sea with his spear. And cities are mentioned: "Madurai city of tall mansions, Uranthai that is luxurious, Vanchi that is strong, and Puhar of the flower gardens are the four chief cities of this land."[56] When Kannagi and Kovalan leave Puhar to journey to the city of Madurai, they go first to the famous island shrine of Shrīrangam farther upstream along the Kāverī, and then they turn south toward Madurai, where the critical events of the epic transpire. The author describes Madurai: "The city is full of temples—to three-eyed Shiva, to Vishnu who displays a bird with spread wings on his flag, to ploughwielding Balarama, to Muruga who bears a cock on his flag."[57] In addition, the goddess of Madurai is described as one who protects Tamil Nadu all the way down to Kanyākumārī.

The epic tells a powerful tale based in Madurai, where the faithful wife Kannagi sees her husband Kovalan executed unjustly, having been falsely accused of stealing the queen's anklet. Kannagi's cry for justice destroys this city of the gods, and she herself becomes an embodiment of divine energy. She circles Madurai in her righteous rage, tearing off her breast and hurling it into the city, where it explodes, burning down the city of the unjust king. It is fascinating, however, that when the king of Vanchi decides to make a shrine dedicated to the powerful Kannagi, he deliberates whether to make it from the stone of Podiyil Hill, washed by the waters of the Kāverī, or from the stone of the Himalayas, washed by the waters of the Gangā. He decides to have the image made of Himalayan stone and sets out on a journey north to quarry the stone and wash it in the Gangā. He explains that by marching through territory ruled by Aryan kings he will, in defeating them, call attention to the glory of Kannagi, in whose honor he is journeying to the Himalayas. Vanchi's exploits are glorious. He crosses the River Gangā on a flotilla of boats and defeats all who come in his way, establishing the glory of the south. "Brave Aryan soldiers of the confederate army were massacred as it were, putting to a stop the myth of Aryan superiority in battle. The captured elephants of the Aryan Kings were yoked like bulls to a plough to the enemy chariots, which were then sent into the Aryan ranks creating havoc."[58]

Just as the *Mahābhārata's* descriptions of south India are vague, even cursory, so are the descriptions of north India in the *Shilappadikaram*. The king marches to the Gangā in no time, crosses it, and proceeds to the Himalayas, as if it were a day's march. Still, the very fact that this epic journey is undertaken in order to quarry Himalayan stone and bathe it in the Gangā embeds in the very heart of the Tamil epic the spiritual currency of the north and a wider vision of India's sacred geography.

As south Indian literature develops, it includes Tamil translations of Sanskrit Purānas, some of which are in the genre of the *sthala purāna*: the praise of the sacred places.[59] It also comes to include a magnificent repertoire of devotional poems, both Vaishnava and Shaiva, that link the praises of the divine to the particular places in which God is especially manifest. The *Tevaram*, which contains songs of the Shaivite saints from between the sixth and eighth centuries, gives ample evidence of a fundamentally locative worldview in which villages, fords, seacoasts, rivers, and hills are identified with their particular deity. Shiva is addressed as "the god of Tonipuram where the sea has many beaches." He is called "the coral-hued Lord who dwells in Kanur of the fragrant groves."[60] The river estuary at Tiruvaiyaru, where the long-legged white cranes shake their feathers, that is Shiva's place:

> *The shrine of the*
> *skull-bearer, dweller in*
> *Kailasa's hill and in Kanappar,*
> *the trident-holder, bull-rider who shares*
> *his body with our Lady*
> *is Tiruvaiyaru where*
> *the red-legged white sand-crane*
> *with sharp beak ruffles its*
> *feathers to shake*
> *them dry of the water's cold*
> *and looks for prey*
> *in the fresh waters*
> *of a honeyed grove.*[61]

INDIA OF TRAVELERS, WRITERS, EDITORS, AND KINGS

One of the rarest gifts to those who study the vast corpus of epic and mythological literature in India is a date. The Purānas can often be dated only in terms of a span of centuries. As a whole, this corpus of literature covers more than a thousand years, and individual Purānas seem to shift their contents, their sectarian emphasis, even their names, expanding to include new material and appendices. But moving into the wider range of Indian literature, there is much that has a more precise date, giving us a general sense of geographical knowledge as conceived at various points in the long course of India's history. It is impossible to do more than survey a sample of this literature here, but even this gives us a glimpse of how the question "What is India?" might have been answered.

First, let us stop in the fifth century, when the poet Kālidāsa lived, at the height of the Gupta Empire. He likely lived in central India, in the city that is today Ujjain. Both his plays and his long poems, called *kāvya*, reveal a wide knowledge of Indian geography, with its associated mythological penumbra. Kālidāsa describes the Himalayas, for example: "There is, in the northern quarter, the deity-souled lord of mountains, by the name of Himalaya, who stands, like the measuring-rod of the earth, spanning the Eastern and the Western oceans."[62] He speaks of the specific mythic peaks of the Himalayas—Kailāsa, Mandara, and Meru. He describes the plains, interrupted by hills such as Govardhana, the Vindhyas, Amarakantaka where the Narmadā begins, and Chitrakūta where Rāma dwelt during his exile, and the Malaya Mountains of the far south, praised for cool breezes and the scent of sandalwood.[63] The rivers he mentions include not only the many rivers of north India, but the Tamraparnī and the Kāverī of the south as well. In the *Raghuvamsa*, based on the lineage of Rāma, the king establishes his hegemony by a circuit of the coastland of India, the classic *digvijaya*, the "conquest of the four-directions." In the *Meghadūta*, the "Cloud Messenger," Kālidāsa describes the fabulous aerial journey of a cloud taking a message of love from a banished young lover to his wife in the Himalayas. He surveys from the air the land of India, and renders a beautiful description of his native Ujjain in the land called Avantī, a place the cloud should not miss on its way north:

When you come to Avantī
where the villagers know the stories of Udayana,
you must pay a visit
to the broad and royal city of Ujjain.
Those who built it must have come from heaven where,
as their merit lessened, they garnered what was left,
and left the sky to build this heaven on earth.

Here the breeze at dawn,
rising from the Shiprā with its opening lotuses,
carries over the city
the sharp and liquid calling of the paddy birds;
touching the body softly,
soothing the weariness of ladies from their night of love,
it whispers like a skillful lover who would ask for more.[64]

In the works of Kālidāsa, especially the *Raghuvamsa*, many holy places of Shiva are mentioned, such as Tryambaka in Maharashtra, Vishvesh-vara in Banāras, Gokarna on the west coast, and Mahākāla at Ujjain.[65] These he also refers to as *jyotirlingas*, "*lingas* of light." Kālidāsa mentions the practice of pilgrimage to the *tīrthas* and gives us a clear indication of specific *tīrthas* that are celebrated in his day, such as Prayāga at the confluence of the Yamunā and the Gangā, Somnāth or Prabhāsa, Gokarna on the west coast, and Pushkara on the plains of what is today Rajasthan.[66] And what are the benefits of such pilgrimage practice? The poet tells us that freedom from rebirth or at least reaching the likeness of the gods is one of the fruits of pilgrimage.[67]

About the same time, beginning in the fifth century, Buddhist travelers from China began coming to India to find texts and to visit the places where the Buddha lived, walked, and taught.[68] First, the intrepid Fa-Hien gives us an account of the land and its sacred places and practices during the late Gupta period in the fifth and sixth centuries. The Chinese traveler describes a country triangular in shape, broad in the north and narrow in the south, and he goes on to observe that "people's faces are of the same shape as the country!"[69] He takes note of the ways in which the land is imbued with the presence and life of the Buddha.[70] Shortly after crossing the Indus River into northwest India, he finds the imprint of the Buddha's foot. He writes, "There is a tradition that when Buddha came to North India, he came at once to this country, and that here he left a print of his foot, which is long or short according to the ideas of the beholder [on the subject]. It exists, and the same thing is true about it, at the present day. Here also are still to be seen the rock on which he dried his clothes, and the place where he converted the wicked dragon."[71]

Pressing farther into the plains of north India, Fa-Hien finally came to the site near Gayā where the Buddha attained enlightenment. He writes, "Half a *yojana* from this place to the north-east there was a cavern in the rocks, into which the Bodhisattva entered, and sat cross-legged with his face to the west. (As he did so,) he said to himself, 'If I am to attain to perfect wisdom (and become Buddha), let there be a super-natural attestation of it.' On the wall of the rock there appeared imme-diately the shadow of a Buddha, rather more than three feet in length, which is still bright at the present day."[72] The intensive and imaginative correlation of the mighty happenings of the life of the Buddha with the features of the land is very much consonant with the widespread linkage of myth and earth that comes to characterize the landscape of Hindu India, here transposed in a Buddhist key.

Two centuries after Fa-Hien, in the early seventh century, during the reign of King Harsha, Hsuan Tsang also made his way from China to India and took careful note of all that he saw. By the 630s, Harsha had his capital at Kannauj, and Hsuan Tsang is said to have stayed in that city for some seven years. In his journals, Hsuan Tsang describes India as having five divisions, "the five Indies"—north, south, east, west, and central.[73] He traveled around India extensively, including visits to some of the places that figure prominently in the sacred map of north India—Mathurā, Kurukshetra, Ayodhyā, Vārānasī, and Ujjain. He studied at the Buddhist university at Nālandā and visited Buddhist monasteries at Amarāvatī and Ajanta, then lively with activity. He also made a tour into south India and describes the large area called Dravida and its capi-tal at Kānchīpura, where he notes that some ten thousand Mahayana Buddhist monks lived. He visited Madurai, farther south still, before returning north through what is now Karnataka, where he stopped at the Tungabhadrā River, with Anagundi on the northern bank, a site to which we will return in connection with the *Rāmāyana*.[74] He also traveled along the Western Ghāts of the Konkan coast. The record of these Buddhist travelers could be much more extensively plumbed for their display of the geographical power points of the land through which the Buddhists traveled. But even an overview indicates to us the ways in which the land was religiously figured some fourteen hundred years ago.

During the period from the seventh century, when Hsuan Tsang saw India at the time of King Harsha, to the eleventh century, when the first Afghan incursions into India began, the practice of pilgrimage must have become fairly extensive. The *tīrtha māhātmyas* were still in process of compilation and multiplication. Granted, they were in Sanskrit, but they functioned as the literary advertisements, so to speak, for the popular practice of Hindu pilgrimage. In the twelfth century we have the first of what was to become an important genre of ritual literature—the *nibandhas,* or "digests," that brought together information from the whole range of epic and Purānic texts and rearranged it by topic in a more user-friendly fashion. The first great digest-maker was Lakshmīdhara, who lived as a scholar in the court of the Gāhadavālas in north India. His digest is called the *Krityakalpataru,* the "Wishing Tree of Rites," the name itself indicating that ritual practice, *kritya,* yields marvelous benefits and blessings like those of the mythical "wishing tree," the *kalpataru.*[75]

Lakshmīdhara was chief minister to Govindachandra, who ruled in the first half of the twelfth century from the Gāhadavāla capital at Kannauj, one of the great cities of north India and the former capital of King Harsha as well. A formidable authority on dharma, Lakshmīdara set out to organize the vast library of Purānic and epic texts dealing with rites and duties into topical handbooks on such subjects as *rājadharma* (the duties of kings), *dāna* (ritual gift-giving), *samskāra* (sacraments of the life cycle), *vrata* (vows), *tīrthayātrā* (pilgrimage), and *shrāddha* (death rites). The effort would be comparable to those efforts to extract from the stories of the biblical literature and commentary a compendium of topical passages on marriage, property rights, prayer, initiation, death, and the afterlife. Lakshmīdhara's volume on pilgrimage is an exciting benchmark, complete with a date, giving us a clear indication of what were the most important *tīrthas* in the area he knew best in northern India. Vārānasī, which he calls Avimukta—the "Never-Forsaken" city of Shiva—is clearly the place with which Lakshmīdhara was most

intimately familiar, for he cites nearly 350 temples and *tīrthas* within
the sacred precincts of Vārānasī alone. Contemporaneous Gāhadavāla
inscriptions indicate the prominence of Vārānasī for the Gāhadavālas,
recording the many times the king bathed at one of the great bathing
ghāts on the River Gangā and then made a ritual donation of land or
money. In addition, sections of Lakshmīdhara's work deal with bathing
rites at Prayāga, at the confluence of the Gangā and Yamunā Rivers,
and *shrāddha* rites for the dead at Gayā. The praises of the Gangā are
gathered together, as are those of the Narmadā River. Among the many
tīrthas he catalogues are Ujjain in central India, Somnāth and Dvārakā
in the west, and Badrīnāth in the north. Lakshmīdhara does little more
than mention the *tīrthas* of the south, and this is true of some of the
later digest-makers of the fourteenth and fifteenth centuries as well.[76]
Through these digests, however, we get a sense of the range and scope
of sacred landscape as construed by the scholarly editors of the day, from
roughly the twelfth to the seventeenth centuries. Despite the fact that
the Purānas themselves are still very fluid and mention a multitude of
places that are difficult to locate precisely, the digests provide a window
into the most important *tīrthas* of their time.

  These scholars not only create compendia of the *tīrthas*, but they
are also concerned to emphasize the inner meaning of pilgrimage.
Lakshmīdhara and his fellow digest-makers all quote those famous
passages from the *Mahābhārata* that speak of the "fruits of *tīrthas*" and
the "*tīrthas* of the heart." The ritual journey alone is not efficacious if
there is not the inner disposition of devotion that accompanies the pilgrim. Indeed, the real *tīrthas* are virtues like patience, generosity, and
self-control. The theory of pilgrimage evoked by Lakshmīdhara gives
due importance to the practice of fasting, tonsure, and the performance
of *shrāddha* death rites as part of pilgrimage, but he simplifies them and
makes them optional. On a pilgrimage journey there is no pollution from
the touch of others. On a pilgrimage, every day is an auspicious day for
rites, bathing, or *shrāddha*. Purity of mind and devout intention, not all
the rules of practice, are critical to the journey.[77]

  Lakshmīdhara was among the first and most important of these
scholars to speak to the meaning of pilgrimage. By the twelfth century,
the Purānas were filled with *māhātmyas* of pilgrimage. They praised to
the skies the benefits of the *tīrthas* for the absolution of every manner of

sin, but the inner meaning of the pilgrim journey needed new emphasis. As K. V. Rangaswami Aiyangar, Lakshmīdhara's mid-twentieth-century editor, writes:

> Pilgrimage had come to stay. Its popularity was on the increase. Its advantages to state and society were undeniable. In ages of political fission and the multiplication of kingdoms with unstable borders and foundations, the stream of pilgrims which meandered unhindered through the length and breadth of India, helped to bring about economic and social interdependence, unification of culture, and a way to political co-operation, especially when Indian society and religion were threatened by enemies of an alien race and a hostile faith. To leave pilgrimage to develop into a soul-killing, mechanical device for giving harassed men and women a mental anodyne, was not right. The concept of *tīrthayātrā* had to be sublimated, and its ethical and spiritual tone raised.[78]

Lakshmīdhara addressed himself to this task—to enunciate pilgrimage as part of a comprehensive view of dharma and to interpret its spiritual importance. In the centuries to come, the flexibility of *tīrthayātrā* that Lakshmīdhara emphasized would be important, especially as some of the traditional places of Hindu pilgrimage came under pressure from the expanding Muslim kingdoms in much of north India.

By the time Lakshmīdhara lived and wrote in the twelfth century, Kannauj must have been a shadow of its former glory, and the Gāhadavālas moved their center of gravity farther east, to Vārānasī.

AL-HIND, HINDUSTAN

The Turks and Afghans who came to India and eventually stretched their kingdoms across much of north India called the land "al-Hind" and, eventually, "Hindustan." Beginning in the eleventh century, the expansion of Islam into India brought a new and even more complex reality to the geographical world we have been describing. Kannauj had been the epicenter of what was called Madhyadesha, the "middle land" or heartland of north India through which the Gangā and Yamunā Rivers flowed. In the eleventh century, it was a great capital of the Pratihāra kings and a center of Hindu life and brahmanical learning. In 1018–19, this city, perhaps the wealthiest in India at the time, was sacked by Mahmud of Ghazni, the first powerful ruler of the Central Asian Ghaznavid Empire, based in what is now Afghanistan, to make incursions into north India.

Historian Andre Wink, who has studied contemporaneous Muslim historians, insists that the invaders "were certainly familiar with Hindu sacred geography. The main religious sites were easily identified and taken out serially in the first quarter of the eleventh century."[79] On the list were Mathurā, Ujjain, and Banāras in the heartland of north India, and so was Somnāth, the fabled shrine of Shiva on the coast of the sea in Gujarat. Kannauj, too, was among these sites. It was "a very large city, consisting of seven fortresses, with a total of 10,000 'idolhouses,' in which enormous treasure was collected." It sat on the banks of the River Gangā, where "kings and brahmans from far away came to seek religious liberation and do worship in the tradition of their ancestors."[80] According to the historians, it took but a day for the Muslim armies to take control of Kannauj and its treasure. "The 'idols' were destroyed; the 'infidels,' 'worshippers of the sun and fire,' fleeing, were pursued by the Muslims, and great numbers of them were killed."[81] Mahmud of Ghazni took the spoils of his devastating raids, but did not stay to rule. Nonetheless, Kannauj lay in ruins. By the time of Lakshmīdhara, in the first half of the twelfth century, Kannauj had come under the rule of the Gāhadavāla kings and perhaps enjoyed a period of some stability, but it never regained its former vibrancy. In the last years of the twelfth century, Kannauj was conquered by the forces of Qutb ud-Din Aibak as the period of the Delhi Sultanate began.

From the eleventh to the thirteenth century, temples were destroyed, to be sure. In some cases, the "portable wealth" was taken off as plunder. In some cases, images of the gods were broken or smashed. Some were hauled away to be used as doorsteps in mosques and "trodden underfoot by believers." As Wink puts it, "Comprehensive destruction, clearly, was not always the aim. It was essential to render the images powerless, to remove them from their consecrated contexts. Selective dilapidation could be sufficient to that purpose. It is hard to gauge the depth of religious convictions here. Did fear play a role in the iconoclastic destruction of the early Muslim conquerors in India? Were the images destroyed, desecrated, or mutilated because they were potent or impotent?"[82]

Richard Eaton has offered a significant word of caution in his landmark article "Temple Desecration and Indo-Muslim States," where he asks, "What temples were in fact desecrated in India's pre-modern history? When, and by whom? How, and for what purpose?" He argues here that temple desecration was, on the whole, selective, undertaken for political purposes, "to delegitimize and extirpate defeated Indian ruling houses."[83] Thus, it was the relationship of a local king to a particular geographical site and temple complex that made the temple a target. There were many temples linked directly to royal patronage, of course, and Eaton records the circumstances of the destruction of each, but he does not see this as part of a religious campaign under the banner of a theology of iconoclasm.[84] The destruction of temples and images was undertaken not just to "render the images powerless," but to undermine the power of their patrons. In addition, it is clear from Eaton and other scholars that the vivid accounts of temples demolished were often embellished by both Hindus and Muslims for their own purposes.

As consequential as the destruction of temples was, the conquest of Hindu kingdoms had a more sustained impact, disrupting the whole process of temple patronage, building, and repair. Andre Wink perhaps overstates the case, but in his extensive history of al-Hind he writes, "If the temples were not destroyed, patronage dried up, and few great temples were built in North India after the thirteenth century. Even without conversion, India's sacred geography was uprooted by the Islamic conquest, and the newly evolving Indo-Islamic policy transcended it in the name of the new universal religion."[85] The imposition of a tax upon Hindu pilgrims became a persistent issue in the centuries that followed, but we know, of course, that Hindu pilgrimage did not cease. The sense of sacred geography could not really be uprooted. After all, the *tīrthas* were only secondarily temples that could be destroyed. Many of the most important *tīrthas* were not grand temple complexes of royal patronage at all, but very ordinary shrines marking places, sacred crossings, that were quite invulnerable to destruction—a hilltop, the confluence of two rivers, the place where a cow had spontaneously released her milk and revealed a long-buried image of the Lord. Stories of the recovery of hidden or long-lost images began to take their place alongside stories of divine revelation.

During the same centuries that saw the temple destruction and the disruption of the temple-based piety of India's sacred landscape, the spirit of Sufi devotion began to create new networks of holy places—the tombs (*maqbara*) and shrines (*dargah*) of martyrs and saints. In the thirteenth and fourteenth centuries, Sufi mendicants, teachers, and songsters moved into north India and became, in a very real way, the most important "missionaries" of the Islamic faith. A certain commonality of spirit linking Sufi to Hindu *bhakti* piety enabled Islam to flourish in India. In general, the Sufis, like the *bhaktas*, stressed the inner life of devotion and love, not the outer world of ritual and practice. Some were more ascetic in their language, displaying some of the austerity of the seekers of the ancient Upanishads. Others yearned for the taste and realization of a more personal God. They used the language of drunkenness and erotic love to express the expansiveness and intensity of relationship with the divine. Sufis were also diverse; there were mystics, missionaries, ascetics, and poets. On the whole, these were men of devotion whose religious spirit was not confined by doctrine.

The first Sufis in India were those of the Chishti order, and the sites where India's famous Chishti saints lived and died have become renowned places of pilgrimage. From the beginning of the Delhi Sultanate in the thirteenth century through the end of the Mughal Empire in the seventeenth century, dynastic patronage of Sufi shrines played an important role in legitimizing Indo-Muslim rulers as both Indian and Islamic.[86] The *dargah* of Nizammudin Auliya in Delhi (d. 1325) has been called "the most important Chishti shrine in South Asia" and has attracted both Muslim and Hindu worshippers for many centuries, as it does even today in the quarter of Delhi that bears his name.[87] The first Mughal emperor, Babur, prayed at the shrine of Qutbuddin Bakhtiyar Kaki (d. 1235), whose shrine on the outskirts of Delhi was visited by Gandhi as a gesture of solidarity shortly before his assassination. Today Bakhtiyar Kaki is visited day in and day out by supplicants seeking his blessings for health and family, for mental and material well-being. His compound is surrounded by the graves of those who wished to be near him in death. The *dargah* of Mu'inuddin Chishti in Ajmer (d. 1235), on

the trade route between Delhi and Gujarat, inspired both popular pilgrimage and the honor of kings, including the Emperor Akbar, who is
said to have made fourteen pilgrimages to Ajmer, some of them on foot.
The *Urs*, or death anniversary, of Mu'inuddin is still one of India's most
popular pilgrimages. Hundreds of buses ply the roads from Delhi and
elsewhere in India to be in Ajmer for this festive and holy time. A recent
Urs recorded more than three hundred thousand pilgrims.[88]

While Bakhtiyar Kaki and Nizammudin Auliya received the homage of the court, living as they did in the first century of the kings of
the Delhi Sultanate, their style of Islam was most likely disparaged by
the more orthodox ulema of their time. Bakhtiyar Kaki was said to love
sama, the devotional music on which the ulema frowned, and he is said
to have listened to it in secret. Nizammudin Auliya was antinomian in
spirit, rejecting any official association with the kingdoms and kings,
announcing that if the king were coming to the front door, he himself
would be leaving by the back door. While the popularity of the shrines
may have been enhanced by the devotions of kings, the reverse is also
true: the popularity of the kings was enhanced by their devotion to the
dargahs.

It is impossible to generalize about the diversity and extent of Sufi
shrines, the tombs of saints and the tombs of martyrs. They are surprising in their multitude and extent, most of them highly local and known
only within their own neighborhood or town. Those that attained wide
repute did so because of their remarkable powers to heal the heart and
body and to minister to the diverse afflictions that beset the human condition. One of these great shrines is the *dargah* of Sayyid Salar Mas'ud
Ghazi in Bahraich in central north India, between Lucknow and Faizabad, a shrine mentioned in the time of the Mughal Emperor Akbar in
the sixteenth century and even today filled with as many as a million
pilgrims on the *Urs* of the young spiritually minded soldier named Ghazi
Miyan. According to one version of the tale, he yearned to be a peace-
maker but was dragged into battle and died on the battlefield in 1033.
While his *Urs* attracts larger numbers of Muslim pilgrims, his two other
major annual festivals—the Basant Mela and the Jyeshth Mela—are far
larger and attract both Hindu and Muslim farmers and villagers.[89]

In this overview of the sacred geography of Hindu India, the most
important thing for us to recognize is the way in which the *dargahs*

became sites of supplication for both Muslims and Hindus, and for those somewhere in between. Throughout India, the *dargahs* came to constitute a vast web of holy lives remembered. Pilgrims flock to the annual festivals of the saints, the *Urs*. Even in a largely Hindu city such as Vārānasī, worshippers throng in procession to one or another of the dozens of *dargahs* scattered throughout the city. These *dargahs* developed much of the ritual idiom of Hindu shrines. People bring flowers—more roses than marigolds—tinseled cloth, and a multitude of other offerings. They tie threads of gold and silver wires on the enclosing rail of the grave or the branches of nearby trees. They have the *darshan,* the sacred sight of the saint, and they return home with a kind of *prasād*, which Muslims called *barakah,* the "blessings" of the saint. For many Hindus, whether new or partial converts or not, the cloth-and-tinsel-covered grave of the saint or martyr is a place where they bring their offerings, vows, and prayers.[90] Some Hindus may, indeed, have become Muslim when their prayers were answered, and scholars have often remarked that the shrine itself might have been a stronger cause of conversion to Islam than the saint was in his lifetime.

We certainly know from contemporaneous sources that Hindus and Muslims alike paid visits to the *dargahs* in centuries past, just as they do today. For example, an eighteenth-century historian writes of the shrine of Nasiruddin Chiragh, a disciple of Nizammudin Auliya, "The Shaikh [lying buried] is not the lamp of Delhi but of the entire country. People turn up there in crowds, particularly on Sunday. In the month of Diwali the entire population of Delhi visits it and stays in tents around the spring tank for days. They take baths to obtain cures from chronic diseases. Muslims and Hindus pay visits in the same spirit."[91] One of the verses famously attributed to Nizammudin is "Each nation has its right road of faith and its shrine." His disciple, the poet Amir Khusrau, is said to have responded with the second part of the couplet: "I've set my shrine in the direction of him with the cocked cap."[92] That was Nizammudin, who had put his cap on akimbo that day. More significant is the term for "the direction." It is *qibla,* which ordinarily refers to the direction of Mecca. Here among the Chishtis, however, no pilgrimage to Mecca was made. The focus of pilgrimage was right here, in Hindustan. And for some, the *qibla* was the shrine of Nizammudin.

Finally, it is important to see that attachment to the land of India, while different in nature among those who came to identify as Muslim, was nonetheless profound. Hindustan was the homeland, *watan*. Its cities, many of which were built by Muslim dynasties, evoked a sense of pride, belonging, and even passion. Al-Hind, the land Akbar was to rule, was described not as a fragmentary northern empire, but as a whole: "The land of Hindustan, from Kandahar to the sea of the south, and from Kambhayit to the sea of Bengal, will own his sway."[93] Kandahar, from the old Gandhara, is today in Afghanistan and was then referred to as "northwest India," while Kambhayit is Cambay on the Arabian Sea. This sense of just what "Hindustan" meant as the empire ruled from north India is said to have persisted, even when the empire did not.

The Indo-Muslim experience cannot be comprehended by seeing Indian Muslims as yearning for a pan-Muslim world, centered in Mecca. Rather, as Ayesha Jalal puts it, "A Muslim's identification with a non-territorial community of Islam and the sense of belonging to a territorially located community means that space is both infinite and finite at the same time. It is this dialectic inherent in their religiously informed cultural identity that has lent historical complexity and depth to the Muslims' relationship with the *watan* or homeland."[94] This included the love of its cities, like Delhi, Lahore, and Surat, the love of the soil of its *dargahs,* and even the love of its Gangā waters, which Muhammad bin Tughlaq had carried south for his use when he moved his capital from Delhi to Daulatabad, a distance of a thousand miles.

From Landscape to Nation

It is against the background of this long history, with its multiple layers of locative religiousness, that the question "What is India?" must be posed. During the century of rule by the British East India Company and, after 1858, during the near century of rule by the British crown, there were many who agreed with Strachey's assessment: "There is not and never was an India." At least not until they, the British, had come. Perhaps they would have agreed because it was convenient to do so in the justification of empire. Or perhaps they would have agreed because the particular notions of "nation" that emerged in the West did not match the reality of India. But Indians, Hindu and Muslim alike, had a very clear, if not entirely congruent, sense of "India." For the heirs of Indo-Muslim culture, the sense of "Hindustan" was vivid in history and was at least six centuries old.[95] For those in the loose family that might be called "Hindu," the three-dimensional mental map of Bhārata had long-accumulated rhetorical and ritual meanings, some of which were by now over twenty-five hundred years old.

Even so, from a British standpoint, India was literally "put on the map" by the cartographers who compiled the first scientific maps of the subcontinent. The first map to be widely disseminated was that of the surveyor general of Bengal, James Rennell, in 1782. As Matthew Edney puts it, "Rennell's maps provided the definitive image of India for the British and European public. It is in his highly influential maps that we find the establishment of India as a meaningful, if still ambiguous geographical entity."[96]

As that "ambiguous geographical entity" began to move slowly toward nationhood in the late nineteenth century, its history and conception were increasingly enmeshed with that of the West. Political interpreters of India's more recent past are concerned primarily with the modern rise of nationalism and the idea of civil society, both of which have their origins in the histories of Europe. The Indian National Congress, beginning in 1885, drew primarily on those European roots as it moved toward an independent national identity. As Rajat Kanta Ray puts it, "Indian nationalism derived from the idea of civil society imported from Europe. However, as in Europe and elsewhere, the sentiments behind it derived from a longer history, rooted, as these emotions were, in a culture of great antiquity. As emotions are as strong as, if not stronger than, ideas, the history of nationalism in India must begin with its prehistory."[97] For the story unfolding here, that "prehistory" includes the sense of "belonging" that was generated over many centuries by a shared and varied landscape, and by a shared and varied religiousness. For many centuries, the emotions that linked people to the land had been strong enough to carry them on pilgrim journeys many hundreds of miles long.

In the late nineteenth century, Swami Vivekananda, recently returned from his international triumph at the Chicago World's Parliament of Religions of 1893, barnstormed the length and breadth of India giving impassioned speeches on the ancient and continuing unity of the cultures

of India. Having seen an adolescent and materialistic America, Vivekananda described India in terms of her ancient and spiritual traditions:

> The one common ground we have is our sacred tradition, our reli-
> gion. . . . and upon that we shall have to build. In Europe, politi-
> cal ideas form the national unity. In Asia, religious ideas form the
> national unity. The unity in religion, therefore, is absolutely neces-
> sary as the first condition of the future of India. There must be the
> recognition of one religion throughout the length and breadth of
> this land.[98]

About the same time, the Maharashtrian B. G. Tilak affirmed that
despite India's differences, "the common factor in Indian society is the
feeling of Hindutva, Hinduness. I do not speak of Muslims and Christians at present because everywhere the majority of our society consists
of Hindus. We say the Hindus of the Panjab, Bengal, Maharashtra,
Telengana, and Dravida are one, and the reason for this is only Hindu
Dharma."[99] His use of the term "Hindutva" in relation to Indian society
predates the exposition of V. D. Savarkar on Hinduness by at least two
decades. The use of normative Hindu discourse in a national context
became a critical issue, and it continues to be one.

In 1905, the colonial government's misbegotten partition of Bengal
into two administrative units drew a virulent response from Bengalis,
Hindu and Muslim alike. The sense of Bengal as a "motherland" was
captured by Bankim Chandra Chatterjee in his famous hymn *"Vande
Mataram," "I Bow to Thee, Mother,"* which he had written in the
1870s and which he incorporated into his novel *Anandamath* in 1881,
a novel that breathes rebellion and Hindu revivalism. In 1905, *"Vande
Mataram"* became the marching song of the resistance to the partition of Bengal, and eventually it became the marching song of the
much broader Indian nationalist movement, as well. "I Bow to Thee,
Mother" gave emotional expression to nationalists who found in this
geographical-cultural-religious language the answer to the challenge of
Strachey, "What is India?"

I bow to thee, Mother
richly-watered, richly-fruited,

cool with the crops of the harvests,
the Mother!
Her nights rejoicing in the glory of the moonlight,
Her lands clothed beautifully with her trees in flowering bloom,
Sweet of laughter, sweet of speech,
The Mother, giver of boons, giver of bliss.
Terrible with the clamourous shout of seventy million throats,
And the sharpness of swords raised in twice seventy million hands,
Who sayeth to thee, Mother, that thou art weak?
Holder of multitudinous strength,
I bow to her who saves,
To her who drives from her the armies of her foemen,
The Mother!

These two verses hearken in so many ways to the great "Hymn to the Earth" of the *Atharva Veda* and have a kind of universal quality, despite the invocation of the Mother. But as the next verses reveal, the Hindu specificity of the Mother is not merely implied:

Thou art knowledge, thou art conduct,
Thou our heart, thou our soul,
For thou art the life in our body,
In the arm thou art might, O Mother,
In the heart, O Mother, thou art love and faith,
It is thy image we raise in every temple.

For thou art Durgā holding her ten weapons of war,
Kamalā at play in the lotuses
And Speech, the goddess, giver of all lore,
To thee I bow!
I bow to thee, goddess of wealth,
Pure and peerless,
Richly-watered, richly-fruited,
The Mother!
I bow to thee, Mother,
Dark-hued, candid,
Sweetly-smiling, jeweled and adorned,

The holder of wealth, the lady of plenty,
The Mother! [100]

Many of India's Muslim leaders certainly heard with apprehension the normative, majoritarian consciousness vocalized by the likes of Vivekananda and Tilak in their efforts to define the "nation," and emotionally articulated in *"Vande Mātaram."* During these same years in the first decade of the twentieth century, those Muslim leaders formed the Muslim League to make sure that Muslims were not lost in the move toward Indian home rule, and they successfully petitioned the British government for separate electorates and reserved seats in the legislative councils that were initiated, for the first time, by the Indian Councils Act of 1909. The question of the basis for Muslim participation in the move toward home rule and in any democratic electoral system was enormously difficult, and it continued to be contested right up to the time of the partition of India into India and Pakistan. By 1915, Hindus had launched their own organization, the Hindu Mahāsabha.

The rhetoric of the motherland, evoked so strongly by Bankim Chandra Chatterjee, was amplified by B. C. Pal in his 1911 book, *The Soul of India*. Here he evokes the power of land as Mother, writing, "Our highest ideal of love and devotion to our country is to be found in our conception of our land as Mother. . . . The imagination that clothed our conception of our country was . . . not poetical but essentially religious. We addressed our land not merely as . . . mother country, but simply as Mother. I do not know of any other people who ever did so." [101] Pal links this notion of the mother country to the Hindu conception of *prakriti,* living nature, and to the Hindu conception of the "Motherhood of God." [102] He refers to her as "this complex Being, at once physical and spiritual, geographical and social, which we call and tenderly worship as Mother in our motherland." [103]

This Mother is the Spirit of India. This geographical habitat of ours is only the outer body of the Mother. The earth that we tread on is not a mere bit of geological structure. It is the physical embodiment of the Mother. . . . These mountains, these rivers, these extensive plains and lofty plateaus, are all witnesses unto the life and love of our race, in and through which the very life and love of the Mother have sought and found uninterrupted and progressive expression. Our history is the sacred biography of the Mother.[104]

Looking deeper into the past than many modern historians often do, it is not difficult to see the strands of ritual and reverence from which Pal's interpretation is woven. These strands were grasped and utilized powerfully by V. D. Savarkar when he wrote his tract called *Hindutva*, "Hinduness," first published in 1923. Even in using the language of "Fatherland," he draws upon these same symbolic resources. He refers to "the love we bear to a common Fatherland" as the first element of Hinduness. His famous couplet defines a Hindu: "A Hindu is a person who regards this land of Bhārata, extending from the River to the Sea as Fatherland and Holyland." The "river" here is Sindhu, the ancient name of the Indus, and Savarkar waxes lyrical about the name Saptasindhu, the Seven Rivers, as the most ancient name of India, an epithet that "calls up the image of the whole Motherland."[105] From Sindhu to Sindhu, from river to river, evokes the peninsula between the Indus in the west and the Brahmaputra in the east; since Sindhu can also mean "sea," the phrase evokes the land from the Indus to the Bay of Bengal.

On the whole, Savarkar used the virile image of "Fatherland," though such a usage is not historically widespread. He also blamed the pervasion of the noble, but weakening, Buddhist traditions of nonviolence, tolerance, and monasticism for leaving the land open to the invasions of Muslim generals and the rise of Islamic empire. Even so, India's strength and identity, he believed, was to be found in its sense of inhabiting a common land, described by the term "Hindusthan." He writes:

> The most important factor that contributes to the cohesion, strength and the sense of unity of a people is that they should possess an internally well-connected and externally well-demarcated "local habitation," and a "name" that could by its very mention, rouse the cherished image of their motherland as well as the loved memories of their past. We are happily blessed with both these important requisites for a strong and united nation. Our land is so vast and yet so well-knit, so well demarcated from others and yet so strongly entrenched that no country in the world is more closely marked out by the fingers of nature as a geographical unit beyond cavil or

criticism, as also is the name Hindusthan or Hindu that it has come to bear. The first image that it rouses in the mind is unmistakably of our motherland and by an express appeal to its geographical and physical form it vivifies it into a living Being. Hindusthan meaning the land of Hindus, the first essential of Hindutva must necessarily be this geographical one.[106]

Hindutva must not be confused with "Hinduism," a term as contested in Savarkar's time as in ours. Indeed Hindutva is "not to be determined by any theological tests," he writes.[107] What is essential is to "love the land that stretches from Sindhu to Sindhu, from the Indus to the Seas."[108] Savarkar does not speak at all of pilgrimage, for he is not interested in ritual expressions or popular religiosity. Savarkar's *Hindutva* was not built up through attention to the local, regional, and transregional places where countless Hindus travel on pilgrimage. He does not name them or even mention them, and we may be certain he did not visit them. However, he does articulate a landscape through the language of primordial identity, going back to the Vedas. His vision was more political, less poetic; more rhetorical, less ritualistic; more oriented to the language of communal identity than the reality of religious practice.

The way he speaks of the land in *Hindutva* is as a living organism. The waters of her rivers flow like a "system of nerve threads" that run through the land. There is "common blood" flowing through the veins of the land. From "vein to vein, heart to heart," this living organism of Bhārata is animate, as a mother, life-giving and energizing. Her "vital spine" is the word "Hindutva."[109] In his concluding pages, Savarkar speaks of the Motherland in highly animated terms, reminiscent of the *Atharva Veda*'s "Hymn to the Earth":

> Her gardens are green and shady, her granaries well-stocked, her waters crystal, her flowers scented, her fruits juicy, and her herbs healing. Her brush is dipped in the colours of Dawn and her flute resonant with the music of Gokul. Verily, Hind is the richly endowed daughter of God.[110]

Savarkar was something of an atheist and he did not model his encomium here on the rise of the Devī and her slaughter of the *asuras*, but rather on the more land-oriented hymnody of the Veda. While it is an organic vision, it is almost romantic in tone. In the years following the publication of *Hindutva,* Savarkar became increasingly exclusionary in his articulation of God's daughter, the Hindu Rāshtra, the Hindu nation, which included not only geography, but culture (*samskriti*). It was a nation of which Muslim Indians could never truly be a part. The uses made of Savarkar's thought and rhetoric in the subsequent decades, which saw the growth of the Rāshtriya Swayamsevak Sangh and other virulent, even militarist, Hindu nationalisms, is a subject that has received full scholarly scrutiny. It would be fair to say, however, that Savarkar, though he is most closely associated with today's rendering of Hindutva as a basis of national identity, is but one articulate voice in the stream of writers, teachers, and activists throughout the nineteenth and twentieth centuries who responded, in one way or another, to the question "What is India?"

BHĀRAT MĀTĀ

In the city of Banāras there is an unusual and relatively recent temple called the Bhārat Mātā Temple, dedicated in 1936 as communal tensions were beginning to take serious hold of India's freedom movement. M. K. Gandhi, who spoke at its inauguration, addressed these growing tensions directly, as he said, "I hope this temple, which will serve as a cosmopolitan platform for people of all religions, castes and creeds including Harijans, will go a great way in promoting religious unity, peace and love in the country."[111] The temple has a sanctum consisting of one spacious room surrounded by a circumambulatory walkway. This room contains no ordinary icon, but rather an immense marble relief map of India, with its rivers and mountains and its various sacred places, the *tīrthas* that are well known to Hindu pilgrims. Making a *pradakshina* around the map is, in a sense, a circumambulatory pilgrimage to the four *dhāms* of India. The pilgrim visitors throw their offerings of bright marigolds onto the map of Mother India. Although they are discouraged from making offerings of flowers or fruits to the "image," there is no other natural place for the garlands they may have brought with them. An especially large heap of marigolds lies upon the site of Rāmeshvara on the southern seacoast, stretching out toward Sri Lanka. Perhaps its popularity is due to the pilgrims' devotion to Rāma, who established a Shiva *linga* there, or perhaps it is the realization that this far corner of the four *dhāms* of India is one they are unlikely to visit in person.

The great marble map has hardly been the "cosmopolitan platform" Gandhi hoped for. It is largely visited by tourist groups and by relatively few Hindu pilgrims. Even though it has gained a place in the tourist and pilgrimage guidebooks and on the pilgrim "maps" of Kāshī, it has not broken into the lively pilgrimage traffic in Banāras, perhaps because it has no *mūrti*. It is certainly an educational venture, to walk around the sanctuary and see the course of the Gangā and Yamunā through the mountains and the course of the Kāverī across south India, but there is little ritual weight here. It is difficult for the marble map to stand alone, for one does not really worship a map. It is, rather, what Sumati Ramaswamy describes as the "dense relationship between Mother India's anthropomorphic form and the map form of India" that has entered powerfully into the national symbolic repertoire.[112] Here the anthropomorphic form is absent, although in one corner of the temple, the corner next to the display of postcards, pamphlets, and books, hangs a large painting, not at all cosmopolitan, that supplies the yearned-for image: the Goddess Durgā on a lion, riding forth out of the map of India, the signature image of the new Hindu nationalism.

In 1983, another Bhārat Mātā Temple, even more elaborate and certainly more ritually effective, was opened in the sacred city of Hardvār, where the River Gangā leaves the Himalayas and enters the plains of north India. This white marble temple of seven floors is a kind of religio-cultural museum, not at all cosmopolitan, but very distinctively Hindu. One floor honors national heroes, from Gandhi to Subhas Chandra Bose; another honors faithful women, called *satīs;* another pays tribute to the *sants,* or saints of India, those mystics and poets renowned for their lyrical love of God. The fifth floor contains images of the various goddesses or *shaktis;* the sixth is dedicated to Vishnu and the *avatāras* of Vishnu. The top floor houses the forms of Shiva and is called Kailasa after the mountain where Shiva is said to reside. The ground floor, however, is dedicated to Bhārat Mātā, who is represented there in the form of both a map and a white marble image. This connection, implicit but not imaged in the Banāras temple, is here made clear at the entrance

to the temple. The map is laced with networks of tiny lights to indicate the groups of pilgrimage places that link the whole land of India: the
seven sacred rivers, the four directional abodes, the seven sacred cities,
the twelve *lingas* of light, the many *pīthas* of the goddess, and even the
state capitals of secular India. The image of Mother India, Bhārat Mātā,
stands above the map holding a pot of water in one hand and shafts
of grain in the other. Above her are inscribed the words "*Vande Bhārat
Mātaram*," "Praise to Mother India," recalling the praise poem of Bankim Chandra Chatterjee.

The Hardvār temple extends the symbolism of the map to the *darshan*
of the devī, the goddess. This ensemble of what Ramaswamy describes as
the scientific-geographic and the anthropomorphic-sacred renderings of
India became increasingly popular in the image-making of the twentieth
century and has served in a powerful way "to make the nation palpable
through pictures."[113] It is little wonder that this dual image—map and
Devī—was adopted by the new Hindu nationalism, a multi-pronged
movement that overtly renders religious images in political contexts.
One will see a relief of this body-map of Durgā on her lion emerging
from the map of India, for instance, at the headquarters of the Vishva
Hindu Parishad in New Delhi. One will see it in a poster advertising
an event sponsored by the Rāshtriya Svayamsevak Sangh, the R.S.S., on
which this text supplements the image:

> I am India. The Indian nation is my body. Kanyākumārī is my foot
> and the Himalayas my head. The Ganges flow from my thighs. My
> left leg is the Coromandel Coast, my right is the Coast of Malabar.
> I am this entire land. East and West are my arms. How wondrous
> is my form! When I walk I sense all India moves with me. When
> I speak, India speaks with me. I am India. I am Truth, I am God, I
> am Beauty.[114]

HYMN TO THE EARTH, REVISITED

There is a wider vision, however, that seems often to be submerged in the
new late-twentieth-century ideology of Hindu nationalism. The nationalists of the early twentieth century often drew upon the sentiment of

the famous Prithivī Sukta, the "Hymn to the Earth" of the *Atharva Veda* with which we began, a hymn that dates deep into the first or even second millennium B.C.E.[115] Even Savarkar seems to engage this image, as we have seen. However, the "Hymn to the Earth" is obviously not about nation, but expresses an open and generous conception of the whole earth as mother. "The Earth is the Mother, and I am the son of the earth," writes the ancient poet. It is the earth, wide and divine in origin, that is lauded and whose blessings are sought. It is a universal vision as well as one that informs the imagination of India:

> *May Earth on which men offer to the Gods*
> *the sacrifice and decorous oblations,*
> *where dwells the human race on nourishment*
> *proper to the requirements of its nature—*
> *may this great Earth assure us life and breath,*
> *permitting us to come to ripe old age. (22)*
>
> *Instill in me abundantly that fragrance,*
> *O Mother Earth, which emanates from you*
> *and from your plants and waters, that sweet perfume*
> *that all celestial beings are wont to emit,*
> *and let no enemy ever wish us ill! (23)*
>
> *As wide a vista of you as my eye*
> *may scan, O Earth, with the kindly help of Sun,*
> *so widely may my sight be never dimmed*
> *in all the long parade of years to come! (33)*
>
> *Whether, when I repose on you, O Earth,*
> *I turn upon my right side or my left,*
> *or whether, extended flat upon my back,*
> *I meet your pressure from head to foot,*
> *be gentle, Earth! You are the couch of all! (34)*

At times, the hymn seems to presage the importance of caring for the earth, and it is no wonder that it has been enlisted in the service of modern Indian environmentalism:

Whatever I dig up of you, O Earth,
may you of that have quick replenishment!
O Purifying One, may my thrust never
reach right unto your vital points, your heart! (35)

Your circling seasons, nights succeeding days,
your summer, O Earth, your splashing rains, our autumn,
your winter and frosty season yielding to spring—
may each and all produce for us their milk! (36)

And the hymn seems to recognize the ways in which the diversity of peoples inhabit the earth:

May Earth who bears mankind, each different grouping
maintaining its own customs and its speech,
yield up for me a thousand streams of treasure,
like a placid cow that never resists the hand. (45)

In village or forest, in all the places
where man meets man, in market or forum,
may we always say that which is pleasing to you! (56)

V. S. Agrawal, a scholar of Hindu culture, refers to the *Prithvī Sukta* when he writes, "Our conception of the Motherland embraces the whole world."[116] And so it seems, even as we stretch our imagination back nearly three millennia to the context in which the hymn was composed. Even so, according to Agrawal, here in India, the great hymn had the effect of enabling ordinary men and women "to regard the land as holy." He goes on to say, "India's religious leaders preached the doctrine of the apotheosis of the Motherland by distributing the holy places throughout the length and breadth of the country."[117] The fact that ancient literature such as the Vedas speaks religiously of its seven sacred rivers and that the epics and Purānas systematize India's sacred geography into the seven sacred cities, the twelve *lingas* of light, the numerous *shāktā pīthas* is clear evidence, according to Agrawal, "that the early inhabitants of the country had a perception and a consciousness of the geographical unity of the land, which they had made their own."[118]

Radhakumud Mookerji, writing on *Nationalism in Hindu Culture* in 1921, also recognizes both the universal and particular sentiments of the hymn. The *Prithvī Sukta,* in his view, generates "an absorbing passion for the place of one's birth."[119] For India, it was the practice of pilgrimage that enabled this passion for the land to develop and flourish. Based on this hymn, Mookerji sees India's very diversity of peoples, languages, and customs as a blessing, the "source of national strength." But nationalism is not an end in itself; it is rather "the preliminary stage in the progress of the various peoples of the world towards cosmopolitanism, internationalism, a sense of universal brotherhood, of the essential unity of mankind, toward world-federation or the parliament of man."[120]

Many of India's most forward-looking thinkers have wrestled with the problem of nationalism in the past century, for this has been a time in which new and virulent forms of nationalism have come on the scene, based on a fearful exclusiveness of race, religion, ideology, or the soil itself. Geo-piety has become too often geo-idolatry. Writing in 1917 in his book-length essay *Nationalism,* Rabindranāth Tagore sees India's task to be negotiating "the social regulation of differences, on the one hand, and the spiritual recognition of unity on the other."[121] As he looked toward an independent India, he believed that, at all costs, India must avoid the competitive, retributive, and destructive form of nation-state that created such devastation in the wake of World War I. Because of its great diversity, he believed that India had to find "a basis of unity which is not political." It would be in solving this problem that India could, in Tagore's view, make a great contribution to the major issues of the world. He foresaw a time when geographical boundaries would become almost imaginary and when our ethics "will comprehend the whole world of men and not merely the fractional groups of nationality."[122] Today, even as globalization has made the "whole world" a reality as never before, Tagore's vision of a moral world transcending nationality is still distant.

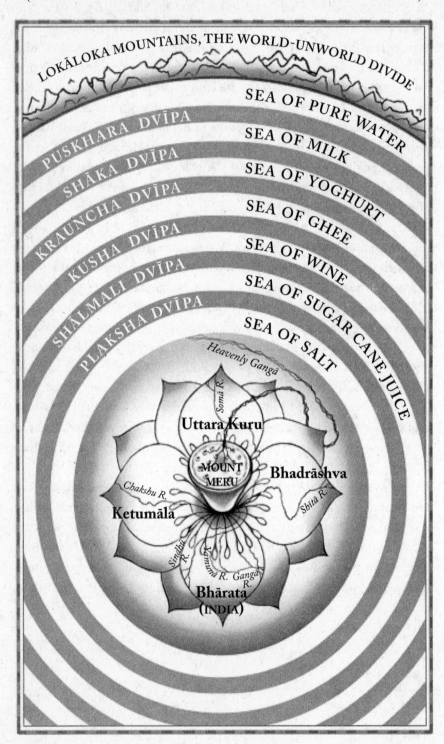

LOKĀLOKA MOUNTAINS, THE WORLD-UNWORLD DIVIDE

SEA OF PURE WATER

PUSKHARA DVĪPA

SEA OF MILK

SHĀKA DVĪPA

SEA OF YOGHURT

KRAUNCHA DVĪPA

SEA OF GHEE

KUSHA DVĪPA

SEA OF WINE

SHĀLMALI DVĪPA

SEA OF SUGAR CANE JUICE

PLAKSHA DVĪPA

SEA OF SALT

Heavenly Gangā

Somā R.

Uttara Kuru

MOUNT MERU

Bhadrāshva

Chakshu R.

Ketumāla

Shītā R.

Sindhu R.

Yamunā R. Gangā R.

Bhārata
(INDIA)

3

ROSE APPLE ISLAND:

INDIA IN THE LOTUS OF THE WORLD

In the *Mahābhārata,* as the great battle at Kurukshetra is about to begin, the blind king Dhritarāshtra learns from a host of omens that this battle will turn the earth to a river of blood and will usher in the Kali Yuga—the age of darkness and degeneracy, the last of the world's four ages. The battle is a family feud between estranged cousins—the noble Pāndavas, the nephews of Dhritarāshtra, cheated and exiled from their rightful kingdom, and the self-righteous Kauravas, the king's own sons, lined up against them. We can imagine the old king, filled with sorrow, looking down at the battlefield from a hill, with his attendants. His father, the ancient sage Vyāsa, offers to bestow sight upon him so that he can see the battle. But Dhritarāshshtra does not wish to see the slaughter with his own eyes, so instead Vyāsa bestows the gift of panoptic sight upon his bard Sanjaya, who will report everything that happens on the battlefield, day and night. Vyāsa then tells them of the signs and omens he sees, which fill them all with fear and foreboding. There are black clouds with red linings in the sky. There are showers of dust by day and showers of blood by night. Donkeys are born of cows and a horse gives birth to a calf. A bird with one wing, one leg, one eye, screams through the sky. Rivers flow backward and their waters have turned to blood.[1]

Seeing both sides of the battlefield filled with the rulers and armies of all the kingdoms of the earth, Dhritarāshtra asks Sanjaya to tell him where they have all come from, which regions and cities, and he asks his bard to repeat to him the story of the earth with its rivers and mountains, its regions and its inhabitants.[2] It is a moving reminiscence at the outset of what will be a calamitous war. It will be a battle in which even the winners will not win. In this ominous space, as the end is about to begin, the bard Sanjaya describes the order of the universe to Dhritarāshtra. His account is called the *bhuvana kosha,* the "atlas of the world."

Sanjaya first recounts to the king the layout of the whole world and the place within it of the land called Bhārata and its peoples. He describes a circular world here called Sudarshana, with six mountain ranges stretching from east to west, separating the seven regions, or *varshas,* of the earth. The southernmost is Bhāratavarsha, shaped "like a bow" with the curvature of the bottom of the circle. In the middle of the earth is the great Mount Meru, a golden mountain watered by the heavenly Gangā that falls to earth on top of the mountain and becomes seven streams, one for each of the *varshas.* Sanjaya describes four lands or islands, *dvīpas,* one in each direction from Meru, lands with their jeweled peaks and magical wishing trees. The southern island is Jambudvīpa, Rose Apple Island, named after the *jambu* tree that grows to a very tall height on the flank of the mountain.[3]

Finally he comes to this land, called Bhārata, where these armies have now drawn up to fight. The king asks Sanjaya, "Tell me about this land about which the kings, especially Duryodhana, are so covetous, and being covetous have come to fight with each other." Now, having described the slopes of Meru with its jeweled peaks, Sanjaya goes on to name the seven great mountain ranges of Bhārata, and he lists *seriatum*— one after another—a virtual torrent of rivers, 160 rivers in all, flowing from the mountains. And, at the end, he lists the clans and peoples of Bhārata, those who are gathered here on the verge of this terrible battle. Sanjaya renders an account of the world as it is known, a good thing to call to mind as it is about to undergo such a catastrophic upheaval.

From this and other passages in the epic, it is clear that the *Mahābhārata*'s vision of the land of Bhārata extends from the Himalaya Mountains that stretch across the north to the Malaya Mountains that provide the backbone of the peninsular south and fall into the sea at Kanyākumārī. The land extends from the Sahyādri Mountains of the Western Ghāts to the Mahendra Mountains of the Eastern Ghāts. It includes not only the great rivers of north India and the Deccan—the Gangā, the Sindhu, the Narmadā, and the Godāvarī—but also the Kāverī and Tamraparnī of the south. Here, as in the pilgrimage section of the *Mahābhārata,* there is no doubt that the north is better known to the bards than the south, but there is also no doubt that the term "Bhārata" gestures toward the whole subcontinent.

The "Atlas of the World" accounts, all generally similar, are found not only in the *Mahābhārata,* but in most of the Purānas. As we shall see, these accounts contain many elements of the imagined cosmos that seem quite fanciful—jeweled mountains, guardian elephants, seas of milk and sugarcane juice—and yet these same accounts move almost seamlessly into a more conventionally geographical description of the landscape of India, with its various regions, rivers, and hills. Often, these Atlas of the World accounts are followed by praises of the various *tīrthas.* What is most striking and most relevant for our purposes as we think about the "sacred geography" of India, however, is the fact that it all comprises a worldview that is highly systematized. The wider universe, even in its most extravagant mythic dimensions, has its own patterns and systems, its groupings of seven mountains and seven rivers, illumining the ways in which India's landscape has been conceived. And one other important thing: the universe imagined here is organic—a living whole—sprung from the very body of the divine. This, too, just might help us understand the ways in which the places of this earth have come to bear so many resonances for the pilgrims who have long sought them out.

ORGANIC COSMOLOGY: THE GOLDEN EGG, THE PRIMAL BODY, THE LOTUS WORLD

How a world is imagined and lived in begins with "maps" far more profoundly ingrained than those of the cartographer. It includes a deep sense of home and the familiar places likened to it. It also includes a sense of the distant and unfamiliar. Mapping the known world has always included, at its periphery, the unknown world, terra incognita, which the imagination may conceive as shadowy and frightful or as golden and glorious. Hindus, while they have long known the geography of India, have not rested content with the knowledge of their own subcontinent, nor have they imagined their own land to be the center or heartland of the entire universe. In that sense, Hindu geographical thinking as we see it in the Purānas has been somewhat modest about the place of Bhārata in the larger scheme of things. India, the known world, was but one petal of the earth, which they likened to a lotus flower. Hindu cosmology extended the imagination beyond India to the other petals of the lotus—China, northern Asia, western Asia—and even beyond our lotus-flower world to the other worlds that encircle it like water rings in a lotus pond, extending outward in larger and larger circles to the very threshold of infinity.

The whole universe is seen to consist of seven concentric ring-shaped islands and ring-shaped seas, together with the heavens above and the netherworlds beneath. All this the ancients called Brahmānda, the Egg (*anda*) of Brahman. Its farthest limit was an infinitely distant mountain range called Lokāloka, the "World-Unworld" Mountains, beyond which there was no light at all. Beyond that was the shell of the egg, if you will. Thus, the Universe, including all that the mind can know and imagine, even to the outer limit of thought, is a closed ecosystem, an organic whole.

While the word "Brahmānda" is commonly translated as "universe" in both Sanskrit and Hindi, it is a word that evokes a particular understanding of creation in which the whole universe evolves, like a living thing, from an egg or a seed. Hiranyagarbha, the "golden egg," is one of the most important recurring themes of Hindu cosmogonic myths. The word *garbha* means not only egg, but also embryo, seed, germ, and womb. It is the generative source of creation. All particular forms of life—human, animal, and plant—emerged, in the beginning, from *garbha*, in its widest sense. So too this whole universe was born from this nucleus of heat, fire, and energy. As one cosmogonic hymn of the *Rig Veda* begins:

> *Hiranyagarbha arose in the beginning.*
> *He was born, the One Lord of all that is.*[4]

Another hymn, this one from the *Atharva Veda*, evokes the image of embryo upon the waters of creation:

> *In the beginning generating offspring,*
> *The waters brought an embryo into being;*
> *And even as it sprang to life,*
> *It had a covering of gold.*[5]

The image of the golden egg or embryo appears often in the ancient Vedic hymns. So far, it is not much of a story as myths go, but it is certainly a powerful symbolic image: the incubation and splitting open of an organic whole from which the entire contents of creation pour forth. In the *Shatapatha Brāhmana*, this originary symbol begins to generate a story, a myth: The primal waters labor in asceticism, *tapas*, with the desire to create. They engender an egg (*anda*), which incubates for a year, hatches, and produces from it the creator god called Prajāpati, the "Lord of Offspring," who, in turn, creates the earth, the sky, and heaven with his speech, creates day and night, and creates the gods with his upward breath and the anti-gods, the *asuras*, with his downward breath.[6]

The egg contains within its seamless unity the whole contents of creation. The extension of correspondences from the contents of the egg to the structure of the universe is widely explored in the Brāhmanas and Upanishads. The Chandogya Upanishad, for instance, contains a succinct statement of the connective strands of correspondences from the microcosm of the egg to the macrocosm of the universe:

> *In the beginning this world was merely non-being.*
> *It was existent. It developed. It turned into an egg [anda].*
> *It lay for the period of a year. It was was split asunder.*
> *One of the two eggshell parts became silver, one gold.*
> *That which was of silver is this earth.*
> *That which was of gold is the sky.*
> *What was the outer membrane is the mountains.*
> *What was the inner membrane is cloud and mist.*
> *What were the veins are the rivers.*
> *What was the fluid within is the ocean.*[7]

The body, like the embryo or egg, also serves as an originary symbol of genesis and creation. The world with its diversity and organic unity, they say, is like the human body. The most famous myth of bodily creation is the dismemberment of the primal person, Purusha, as told in *Rig Veda* X.90. There, Purusha is the oblation offered by the gods in sacrifice. From this cosmic being, time and the seasons are born; from his various parts the Vedas are born. Horses, cattle, goats, and sheep are born. The social order is generated: from his head, the *brahmin;* from his arms, the *kshatriya;* from his thighs, the *vaishya;* and from his feet, the *shudra.* From his mind, the moon was born; from his eye, the sun; from his mouth, the gods Indra and Agni; from his breath, Vāyu, the wind. In essence, the whole universe is formed from and adds up to the very body of Purusha. But who or what is this Purusha? In the widest sense, Purusha is Being itself, not just a being. In this hymn, we are told that only a quarter of Purusha is manifest to become the various parts of the known universe. Three-quarters, so they say, is transcendent, beyond our human ken.

The Aitareya Upanishad makes clear the symbolic similarity of the egg and the body of Purusha as manifest in creation, for here the Spirit, *atman,* gathers together the primeval waters and shapes Purusha, upon whom he broods, "like an egg [*anda*]." A whole fabric of correspondences is woven, linking the seed of creation to the elements of creation and, by extension, to the human body.

> *And from that* purusha, *brooded upon like an egg,*
> *A mouth broke open. From the mouth came speech, from speech, fire.*
> *Nostrils broke open. From the nostrils came breath, from breath, the*
> *   wind.*
> *Eyes broke open. From the eyes came sight; from sight, the Sun.*
> *Ears broke open. From the ears came hearing; from hearing, the*
> *   quarters of heaven.*
> *Skin broke forth. From skin came hairs; from the hairs, plants and*
> *   trees.*
> *A heart broke forth. From the heart came mind; from mind, the moon.*
> *A navel broke forth. From the navel came the out-breath; from the*
> *   out-breath—death.*
> *A penis broke forth. From the penis came semen; and from the semen,*
> *   the waters.*[8]

In later Purānic mythology, the Hiranyagarbha, containing the full potential and diversity of life, also appears in bodily form as Vishnu, floating on the vast waters, having withdrawn the whole of the universe into his body during the period of universal dissolution called the *pralaya.* When the new creation is about to begin, a lotus springs from the navel of the sleeping Vishnu. Its stem rises; its bud is closed, containing, like the egg, the full potential of creation. When the lotus flower opens, there sits Brahmā, the creator, ready to fashion the particulars of the universe.[9] Everything that is will be manifest in creation from the nucleus, the world within.

Vishnu resting on the Endless Serpent, Deogarh 6th century

In the Purānas, we find the compelling story of the sage Mārkandeya. While Vishnu is asleep during the time of the *pralaya,* between eons of creation, Mārkandeya wanders through the condensed cosmos of the interior world within the sleeping Lord, visiting all the mountains, rivers, and holy *tīrthas* contained therein. He does not realize that he is within the body of God until, one day, he falls out of the mouth of Vishnu and into the vast sea. Mārkandeya finds, to his astonishment, that he has literally fallen out of what he had thought was the world. There in the primal sea, he is confronted by an unimaginable immensity. He is overwhelmed with another view of what is real, and he is relieved to be snatched up and swallowed again by Vishnu and to find himself once again in the familiar "real" world he knew. Many years later, he falls out of Vishnu's mouth again, and the memory of encounter with the unimaginable immensity begins to awaken him to this vast reality.[10]

In imagining the emergence of life and the world of form out of the formless waters of the deep, Hindus have envisioned that form as the Hiranyagarbha or the body of the recumbent Vishnu. How natural also to see the lotus as the seat of the Creator, the place where creation begins to take shape. After all, the lotus is the plant that rises from the muddy depths of the waters below to float and flower on the surface. Anyone who has seen the lotus in flower on a pond can well see how readily this natural form would serve the Hindu imagination. The lotus came to be seen as the first place of living form on the waters of creation. Brahmā emerges from the lotus bud to begin the work of creation as we know it. We must remember, however, that Brahmā, the Creator in this view, is not the Supreme Reality in any sense, but merely instrumental in the process of creation.

"Creation" in this Hindu view of things is designated by the word *srishthi*, literally the "pouring forth" of the universe from the source. As a complex plant or tree grows, bursting forth and developing from the simple unitary seed, or as a complex creature emerges and grows from an embryo, so is this whole and diverse universe poured forth from the Hiranyagarbha, from Purusha, or from the very body of the divine. There is no God who stands apart from it and creates it. Indeed, everything there is, as far as thought can reach, is within the unitary systemic whole of the Brahmānda. One could say that everything is a manifestation that has poured forth from the living body of the Whole, what some would call God.

The notion that the universe is a systemic whole is foundational in the Hindu imagination. Whether it is the egg or the seed or the body—all of which are important originary symbols—the system is complete. Nothing is left out. Nothing is set apart. The whole universe is a vast ecological system in which the primary life process is one of bursting forth, pouring forth, growing, flourishing, dying, decaying, withdrawing into seed form, and coming to life again. Within this systemic whole, everything is alive and interrelated. Of this organic universe, the German scholar Betty Heimann has written, "Nothing stands isolated. Everything has its repercussions in a wider sphere of time and space beyond its immediate present."[11] These "repercussions" or connotations mean that everything situated within the systemic web of meaning is a symbol. In Mircea Eliade's terms, a symbol reveals the continuity between the human, or the earthly, and the cosmic. He writes, "Religious symbols are capable of revealing a modality of the real or a structure of the world that is not evident on the level of immediate experience."[12] Symbols break open the interlocking meanings of the cosmos. They "reveal a multitude of structurally coherent meanings."[13] In India, the coherence of meanings revealed by symbols is like the coherence of the body or a living plant: a dynamic system, an interrelated whole, in which everything has symbolic resonances.

ROSE APPLE ISLAND AND THE ENCOMPASSING
RING ISLANDS

There is considerable agreement in the epics and Purānas that the Brahmānda, the Egg of Brahman, this whole universe, consists of seven islands.[14] In the middle of the universe is our own circular or lotus-shaped island called Jambudvīpa, Rose Apple Island, named for its special tree, the *jambu*, or rose apple. Rose Apple Island is what might be called "the world," or at least the known world from the Indian perspective. It is the lotus island of which Bhārata, India, is the southern petal. Sometimes the term "Rose Apple Island" is used more specifically to refer to that southern petal and becomes the ancient name of Bhārata itself. In either case, at the center of the lotus-shaped continent of the world is Mount Meru. And encircling Rose Apple Island are six other "islands," all shaped like rings and all separated by ring-shaped seas of exotic waters.

This is a fascinating view of the universe. Our little lotus island of human habitation is seen to float in the middle of a universe of vast extent. That seems natural enough to the human imagination. What is arresting in this view, however, is that the other "islands" beyond the horizon of the known world are not islands of land mass, as we normally imagine islands to be, scattered here and there through the infinite seas. They are islands of encompassment. They are ring-shaped, and these ring-islands surround their ring-seas, "like a rim surrounds a wheel."[15] Rose Apple Island is safely encompassed by one ring after another. The universe is one concentric and unitary whole.

Rose Apple Island floats "like a boat" in the middle of the Salt Sea, at the center of the universe.[16] As the *Vishnu Purāna* puts it, the Salt Sea, one hundred thousand leagues wide, encircles Rose Apple Island "like a bracelet."[17] Rose Apple Island is said to have seven zones, one of which is India. It has seven ranges of mountains, one of which is the Himalayas, and it has seven rivers, all flowing from the celestial Gangā. It is anchored at the center by Mount Meru. As we will see, this sevenfold schema is duplicated on the islands of the wider universe and within the land of India itself.

The *Bhāgavata Purāna* begins its account of the ring-islands by saying that just as Mount Meru is surrounded by Rose Apple Island, and

Rose Apple Island is, in turn, encircled by the Salt Sea, so is the Salt Sea encircled by the island of Plaksha.[18] The second of the ring-islands, named for the golden *plaksha,* or fig tree, also has seven zones, seven principal mountain ranges, and seven great rivers, all of which are named, but that need not detain us here. Encircling Plaksha is the Sea of Sugar-Cane Juice, which is twice as wide as the Salt Sea and extends up to the shores of the third ring-island, Shālmali, named for the *shālmali,* or silk-cotton tree. Just as Plaksha is twice as large as Jambudvīpa, so is Shālmali twice as large as Plaksha. And so it is, we are told, with each of the ring-islands. The islands are progressively bigger and the seas that stretch between them progressively more extensive. Beyond Shālmali is the Sea of Wine, which reaches to the fourth ring-island, Kusha, named for its sacred *kusha* grass. Beyond Kusha is the Sea of Ghee or Clarified Butter, extending to the fifth ring-island, Krauncha, named for its greatest mountain. Then comes the Sea of Yoghurt, reaching as far as the island of Shāka, named for the great teak tree. It is encircled at its outer rim by the Sea of Milk. Finally, beyond the Sea of Milk is the sixth of the ring-islands, Pushkara, named for its lotuses. It does not have seven mountains, but only one high, circular mountain range. There are no other mountains and no rivers. And beyond Pushkara, the seventh sea is the Sea of Pure Water, which reaches to the very edge of the world and the ring of mountains called Lokāloka, "World-Unworld," at the very boundary of the infinite.[19]

The mountains of Lokāloka are at the limit of the worlds that comprise the universe. The word *loka* means "world," but not just world in a geographical or spatial sense. It includes the meanings of both "space" and "light" and is, therefore, the world that shines forth. *Loka* does not simply exist; *loka* must be gained and won. It is a safe world, an ample and open place to live. It is the world, divinely illumined.[20] Not surprisingly, Lokāloka is the boundary where light is divided from darkness. These mountains are the imaginative embodiment of the very notion of "limit." The rays of the sun that circles Mount Meru and the light of the brightest star, the Pole Star, which stands high above Meru, can reach to the slopes of Lokāloka and no farther. The World-Unworld mountain range is not only as far as light can reach, but as far as thought can reach. The far slopes of Lokāloka are in darkness. And beyond, the darkness is encompassed by the shell of the Egg of Brahman. As one Purāna puts it, "Beyond it [Lokāloka] perpetual darkness invests the mountain all around, which darkness is again encompassed by the shell of egg."[21]

These concentric ring-islands, with Jambudvīpa at the center, are structurally the same: Each has its seven zones, seven mountains, and seven rivers, and each has its distinctive trees and plants. As one moves outward, each is twice as extensive as its predecessor. It is a strikingly secure and benign worldview. Looking outward from Rose Apple Island into the terrae incognitae of the outer islands, the world is *not* imagined to be shadowy and dangerous; on the contrary, it is imagined to be more and more sublime. These outer islands are not thought of as heavens, however, since the heavens rise in the vertical dimension of Brahmānda. Still, life is idealized beyond the horizon, not viewed with suspicion, as is so often the case in ethnocentric worldviews. Here, fewer and fewer of the human hardships of life in Bhārata are thought to exist as one moves outward across the seas of sugarcane juice and wine, through the various ring-islands. Increasingly, people live a very long time, as long as one thousand years. There are no heavy rains and flooding streams; no heat of summer or cold of winter; no fear from the movements of the stars and planets. There is no jealousy, hatred, or anxiety.[22]

As one moves outward through the islands, the four castes have different names and function in interrelation with each other in increasing harmony, but the social system of the terrae incognitae is nonetheless imagined to be structurally like that of Bhārata in that four castes do exist. The one exception is the outermost ring-island, Pushkara, where it is said that there is no caste (*varna*) or stage-of-life (*āshrama*) at all. There on the outer rim of the universe, people are all healthy, powerful, happy, long-lived, and equal. "There is no distinction of caste or order; there are no fixed institutes; nor are rites performed for the sake of advantage. The three Vedas, the Purānas, ethics, and polity, and the laws of service are unknown. Pushkara is in fact, in both its divisions, a terrestrial paradise, where time yields happiness to all its inhabitants, who are exempt from sickness and decay."[23]

Varnāshrama dharma is the undergirding value system of Hindu social and religious life in which one's appropriate dharma is generally determined by caste (*varna*) and stage of life (*āshrama*). It is not surprising that Hindus would imagine the terrae incognitae to have such a system too, with different names but the same basic categories, just as nineteenth-century Christian scholars and missionaries expected the terrae incognitae to have "religions," "scriptures," and "beliefs," the contents different, no doubt inferior, but the categories the same. What is remarkable and counterintuitive in this Hindu worldview is the generous presupposition that those people of the terrae incognitae, beyond the horizon, are not inferior, but even more observant and pious than we. Still more remarkable is the absence of the basic social structures of caste in imagining the most remote of the ring-islands. In India, *varnāshrama dharma* is transcended only by the *sannyāsīs*, who have figuratively "cast off" from this shore, from this way of life, for a life of freedom in which caste and station are left behind. *Varnāshrama dharma* is also transcended in the time dimension—in the first of the four ages, the perfect Krita Yuga, before time begins its downward slide through the ages. Here in the vision of the ring-islands, *varnāshrama dharma* is transcended in the spatial dimension. In imagining the ideal world on the outer rim of the universe, circled on its inner bank by the Sea of Milk and on its outer bank by the Sea of Pure Water, Hindus have overturned even their own most deep-rooted cultural assumptions, such as hierarchy and its social expressions, and imagined a world of perfect equality.

These places of the imagination are as important in the mapping of a worldview as the places that are immediately known. What characteristics does a culture attribute to the lands beyond the horizon? Are they dark and dangerous? Are they greener and richer, the desired objects of conquest? Are they virgin, wild lands? Are they frontiers to be tamed? Are they dark and pagan lands to be converted? Here Hindus have envisioned a universe that neither threatens them nor invites conquest. The abundant islands of the unknown worlds are comfortably separated by exotic oceans. Rose Apple Island is safely encircled and encompassed by islands of increasing perfection and piety, even up to the very end of the world, where the earth is made of gold dust and where "whatever is placed is not taken back."[24]

ROSE APPLE ISLAND AS A FOUR-PETALED LOTUS

Rose Apple Island, in the middle of all the rings of continents and seas, is imagined in two distinctive but not contradictory ways in the world-atlas literature. The one that appeals most to the poetic mind's eye is that of a lotus-flower world, in which the four continents spread out like the petals of a lotus from the great Mount Meru, which stands at the center, as the seed cup of the lotus of the world. As we have seen, this is basically a fourfold worldview, with four petal-continents, the southern continent being Bhārata. In addition, there is a sevenfold imaginative vision of the world, in which Jambudvīpa is circular, with seven horizontal zones. This is the view described by Sanjaya in the *Mahābhārata* and in most of the Purānas.[25] This is an expression of the system of cosmic geography in which each of the islands is seen to have seven zones. In the case of Jambudvīpa, the southernmost zone, bow-shaped, is Bhārata. We will look briefly at each of the fourfold and sevenfold conceptions and then turn to the great mountain that centers not only Rose Apple Island, but the entire universe, Mount Meru.

The fourfold worldview is mapped onto the four cardinal directions: Rose Apple Island, they say, floats like a lotus in the Salt Sea.

The four famous great continents are stationed on the petals,
The powerful Meru is stationed on the pericarp.[26]

There is unanimity in the literature on the names of the four petals, which leaf out to become the earth's four continents: Ketumāla in the west, Uttarakuru in the north, Bhadrāshva in the east, and Bhārata in the south. In the center is Meru. The heavenly River Gangā lands on top of this great mountain on her course from heaven to earth, and she, too, splits into four branches and flows out upon each of the petal continents: the Chakshu River to the west, the Soma or Bhadra River to the north, the Sītā River to the east, and finally, the Alakanandā, India's own Gangā, to the south.[27]

This is clearly a mythological view in which the universe we know is oriented to the four directions with a massive, centering mountain. So widespread is this worldview in Indic cosmology that Japanese pilgrimage maps of India show Mount Meru prominently, with a swirl of rivers circling it, one spinning off in each cardinal direction.[28] Those with a geographical bent have struggled to pinpoint the various petals of the world-lotus, and they do see it having some relation to Asian topography. Meru itself, they say, is the Pamir knot, where the mountains of Asia swirl together—the Hindu Kush from the west, the Himalayas and the Karakoram Range from the southeast, the Kunlun Mountains from the east, and the Tien Shan Mountains from the northeast.[29] From the vantage point of the Pamir knot, Ketumāla is the Central Asian plateau stretching west toward the Caspian Sea, watered by the Amu Darya River, formerly called the Oxus and identified with the Chakshu, which rises in the Pamirs and empties into the southern end of the Aral Sea. Uttarakuru is the north country, reaching today into Central Asia and watered by the Syr Darya River, the ancient Bhadra River, which empties into the northern end of the Aral Sea. Bhadrāshva is the Tarim Basin or Chinese Turkestan, north of the high Tibetan tableland and reaching toward China in the east. It is watered by the Yarkand River, known as the Sītā in the Purānas. Bhārata, of course, stretches to the south, watered by the Gangā.

From the standpoint of the deep structures of the imagination, however, the important thing is that this is a fourfold world in which the other petals are more or less like ours, spreading forth from Mount Meru in the other three directions. Indeed, the entire world order is fourfold as it spreads out in a three-dimensional geographical mandala. Mount Meru has four sides, each a distinct color (varna) and each identified with one of the four castes (also varna). Flanking Meru at the base of each petal, in each of the four directions, is a mountain that serves as a buttress (vishkambha) to this world axis.[30] These buttress mountains provide the setting for further elaboration of the fourfold scheme. On the very top of each mountain is an enormous tree, and these four trees are called the "flagstaffs" of the universe. On Mount Gandhamādana, India's buttress mountain, is the rose apple tree with fruits as large as elephants, so they say, and when they fall to the ground, they splatter to produce the delicious rivers of Bhārata to the south![31] Each mountain, further, has special forests and groves, and each sends forth seven rivers into its particular petal. According to some sources, each petal is identified with a particular theriomorphic deity, a form of Vishnu, as its support. Bhārata, for instance, is supported by Vishnu as Kūrma, the tortoise, who bears the land upon his back. There are many variations in the particular details of this fourfold world mandala, but the pattern and the intent are clear enough: The world, with its topographical features, its social order, and its gods, is four-quartered and centered at Mount

Meru. Indeed, the fourfold nature of the world extends all the way out to the far slopes of Lokāloka, where four huge elephants stand guard at the four directions.[32]

Side by side with the fourfold view of the world lotus is the numerology of the "sevens" associated with each of the petals and each of the islands.[33] Our island of Jambudvīpa, here meaning the entire lotus-island we have been describing, is also sevenfold. Just as there are seven islands in the Brahmānda, each with seven zones, seven primary mountain ranges, and seven river systems, so Rose Apple Island has this sevenfold structure as well. Its seven divisions are seen as horizontal sections of a huge circle, having as their boundaries the six long mountain ranges stretching from the Western to the Eastern Sea. In the center of the central belt of this circle-world is Mount Meru. The southernmost range of mountains is the Himalayas. The land of Bhārata and land of Uttarakuru lie respectively at the southern and northern ends of the circle, and each is said to be shaped like a bow.

This imaginative vision of a world divided into zones by one lateral range of mountains after another is certainly understandable from the perspective of India, where, to the north, stretching across the earth, are mountains, mountain valleys, and more mountains—for almost as far as one could travel, or as one could imagine. India's great Himalayas, the "abode of snows," span the subcontinent from shore to shore like the "earth's measuring rod," as the poet Kālidāsa put it. Magnificent as they are, the Himalayas are still the most earthly range of mountains in view, for they are, after all, *himavān,* "made of snow." Farther north and more distant are mountains said to be made of gold, or made of blue lapis lazuli, or the shimmering color of peacocks' feathers.[34] Just as there are seven mountain ranges in this worldview, so also there are seven rivers that branch out from the celestial Gangā to water the whole earth; three streams carry the waters of the Gangā eastward; three streams carry its waters westward; and one—the Bhāgīrathī, India's Gangā—carries its waters southward.[35]

MOUNT MERU, SEED CUP OF THE LOTUS OF THE WORLD

Jambudvīpa is symbolically centered on Mount Meru, sometimes called Sumeru. This mountain is the center not only of Rose Apple Island, but of the concentric ring-islands as well. As the cosmic mountain, Meru is imitated and repeated architecturally in Hindu temples, with their *shikharas*, or "mountain peaks," rising toward the heavens. It is repeated as the center post of Buddhist stūpas, the outer convex dome shape of which is called the *anda*, the egg, and the central axis of which, rising above the *anda*, is Meru.[36] It is repeated in the multitiered, ascending roofs of pagodas in Southeast Asia, China, and Japan. In Bali, these tall multitiered shrines that duplicate the sacred mountain are actually called *merus*, and the great volcanic mountain of Bali, Gunung Agung, is said to be a piece of Meru itself, fallen into the South Pacific. Mount Meru is the *axis mundi*, the mountain in the center of the world, joining the earth to the heavens above. But Meru not only rises toward the heavens, it is also rooted deep in the earth, joining the earth to the netherworlds beneath as well. One hundred thousand leagues high, they say, is Meru. It extends eighty-four thousand leagues into the sky and sixteen thousand leagues into the earth.[37]

Directly over Meru stands the Pole Star, Dhruva. The world-atlas literature describing the earth is often found in tandem with those sections of the Purāṇas that describe the heavens, with the movements of the sun and the moon, the stars and the planets.[38] Dhruva is the fixed point, the "star-supporting pillar," connected to Meru by an invisible but firm post. Around it, the heavenly bodies move, as if fastened by a cord. One Purāṇa compares the movement of the heavenly bodies around Dhruva's invisible post to the movement of oxen around the post in the center of the threshing floor.[39] Thus the planets move, on shorter and longer tethers, propelled by the force of the wind. And so does the sun move around Meru, creating day and night in the world below.[40] On the top of Meru, however, directly below the Pole Star, it is always day.

Meru is said to be a mountain of pure gold. As the Purāṇas commonly put it, "In the middle of Ilāvrita, Meru rises up, golden."[41] It is so brilliant that it is commonly said to be a "smokeless fire," glowing with incandescence so pure that it emits no smoke. The mountain is said to be golden because it is touched by Shiva himself.[42] And, of course, it is golden because the sun always shines upon it. Indeed, the constant light of the sun on Meru is used in Sanskrit classical literature as a common simile for constancy. When the Pāndavas enter the forest to embark on their years of exile, the bard of the *Mahābhārata* says of their good wife Draupadī, "Draupadī does not leave the Pāndavas as the light of the sun does not leave Meru."

Mount Meru is commonly described as "four-sided" (*chaturasra*), and we might perhaps think of the "sides" as its slopes. As we have seen, the four-sided Meru gives orientation and directionality to the four quarters of the world. Meru is also said to have four *varnas*, "colors," and by extension this word came to mean "caste," in its most general sense. When Meru is called the four-*varna* mountain, both color and caste are included. Indeed, the relation of color to caste is made explicit. The east slope of Meru is white, with the properties of the *brahmin* caste; the southern slope is yellow, with the properties of the *vaishya* caste; the western slope is "black as a bee's wing" and has the properties of the *shudras;* and the northern slope is red, with the properties of the *kshatriyas.*[43]

The measurements of Meru are given with consistency in all our sources. We have mentioned that its height is said to be eighty-four thousand leagues and its depth in the earth sixteen thousand leagues. The astonishing dimension, however, is the diameter of the great mountain: At its base, Mount Meru is said to be sixteen thousand leagues across; and at its summit, Meru is said to be thirty-two thousand leagues across. Here the common image of the mountain peak is turned upside down: Meru is smaller at the bottom than it is on top! Meru reverses the pyramidal image of the mountain to which the imagination is accustomed, the broad-based mountain ascending to a single peak. While such a peak may suffice for the divine abode in a monotheistic worldview, it is clearly inadequate for the gods of India. At the broad summit of Meru there is plenty of room for all. Here the center of the lotus generates the imaginative vision, spreading outward with many stems and seed pods.

Since Meru is king of the mountains in a confluence of mountain ranges that is the most awesome on earth, it is all the more arresting that Hindus do not derive their symbolic image of Meru from the great granite and ice peaks of the Himalayas. Rather, it comes from the living, organic world of flowers. Meru is the "seed cup [*karnikā*] of the lotus of the world."[44] Virtually everywhere Meru is described in the world-atlas literature, this image of the seed cup of the lotus is used. The central part of the lotus flares out distinctively at the top, supporting a flat surface with little bumps for each seed. Similarly, Mount Meru spreads out at the top, supporting a broad plain where the various gods have their citadels. The four continents leaf out like petals. And Meru is encircled not only by its four buttress mountains, but by twenty smaller mountains, said to be arrayed like filaments around the seed cup of the lotus. These are called the *kesarāchala,* the "filament mountains."[45]

Most accounts tell us that on top of Mount Meru is the city of Brahmā, the world creator. Around Brahmā's city is a circle of eight subsidiary citadels, one in each direction, the capitals of the eight *lokapālas,* the "world guardians" assigned to the cardinal and intermediate directions.[46] Despite the ecumenical nature of the mountaintop, Meru nonetheless lends itself particularly to Shaiva mythology, since Shiva is the mountain god par excellence, and since Vishnu's dwelling place is well known to be in Vaikuntha, at the zenith of the heavens. The *Linga Purāna* says that all three gods—Brahmā, Vishnu, and Shiva—have abodes on Meru. Shiva's abode is described in most detail, however, and is said to be a seven-storied palace.[47] The *Kūrma Purāna* tells us, "In front of the abode of Brahmā there stands the sacred, white, and resplendent mansion of Shambhu (Shiva), the suzerain of gods, possessed of unlimited energy."[48]

On the top of Meru, the River Gangā first touches the earth, having descended from heaven through the path of the Milky Way, from Vishnu's foot according to some sources. The Gangā circles the city of Brahmā and then flows down from the mountain in four, or in seven, streams. The *Vishnu Purāna* puts it beautifully:

The capital of Brahmā is enclosed by the River Gangā, which,
issuing from the foot of Vishnu and washing the lunar orb, falls here
from the skies and after encircling the city, divides into four mighty
rivers, flowing in opposite directions. These rivers are the Shītā, the
Alakanandā, the Chakshu, and the Bhadrā.[49]

FROM THE HIMALAYAS TO THE SEA

What is north of the sea and south of the Himalaya,
That land is called Bhārata, where the descendants
of King Bharata live.[50]

All of this cosmology, from the Brahmānda with its ring-islands to the
many zones and petals of Rose Apple Island, is finally but the wider
context for the geographical description of Bhārata, the land of India. It
is a "bow-shaped" land, according to the Purānic cosmologies, which see
it as the southern cross-section of the disc of the world. The *Mārkandeya
Purāna* pushes toward greater accuracy: It is more like a rectangle, with
the Himalayas stretched back on two sides like the string of a drawn
bow.[51] The Purānas describe its extent. It is a thousand leagues, they say,
from north to south, and from Kanyākumārī at the southern tip, the land
gradually broadens out as one goes north to the source of the River Gangā.[52]

In moving from the descriptions of the seas of sugarcane juice and
yoghurt, and the lands where trees yield fruit as big as elephants, out
onto the southern petal of the lotus, the authors of the Purānas begin to
describe a land whose topographical features are more or less the bona
fide components of a modern atlas.[53] As the British geographer B. C.
Law says of the Purānic accounts, "The fabulous element as pointed out
by Cunningham is confined, as a rule, to outside lands, and their allu-
sions to purely Indian topography are generally sober."[54] Like the other
world-islands and petals, however, it is a land with systematic features.
The descriptions invariably include an enumeration of the sets of mountains, the systems of rivers, and the respective peoples of India.

The seven mountain ranges of Bhārata are the *kulaparvatas,* the "clan
mountains," so called because each was related in ancient times to a particular clan or tribe: the Mahendra Mountains of Orissa to the Kalingas, the Malaya Mountains of the south to the Pāndyas, and so forth.
Along with the Himalayas, these seven mountain ranges compose the
very bones of India: There are the Mahendra Mountains of the Eastern Ghāts between the Godāvarī and Mahānadī Rivers; the Malaya
Mountains of the south, including the Nilgiri Hills and the southern
spine of mountains called the Cardamom Hills, which extends to the tip

of India; the Sahyādri Mountains of the Western Ghāts, running along
the coast of the Arabian Sea; the Vindhya Mountains extending across
central India, along the course of the Narmadā River; the Suktiman and
Riksha Mountains in central east India; and the Pariyatra Mountains in
central west India, including the Aravalli Hills of Rajasthan.[55]

The rivers, too, are named, and in most of the *bhuvana kosha* accounts
they are listed according to the mountain range in which they have
their headwaters. First, there are those that rise in the Himalayas—the
Gangā, Sindhu, Sarasvatī, Yamunā, Gomatī, and others. From the Pariyatra Mountains flows the Mahī River, which empties into the Gulf
of Cambay, and numerous north-flowing rivers that empty into the
Yamunā, including the Shiprā or Kshiprā River, which flows through the
central Indian city of Ujjain. From the Riksha and Suktiman Mountains
flow many rivers, the most famous being the west-flowing Narmadā,
which rises at Amarakantaka, and the east-flowing Mahānadī, which
empties into the Bay of Bengal. The Vindhyas are the source of many
rivers, including the Payoshnī and Tapi, which parallel the Narmadā to
the south. From the Sahya Mountains of the eastern coast come the great
Godāvarī and the other rivers that rise in what is today Maharashtra.
These mountains are also the source of the Krishnā and Krishnāvenī
Rivers of Karnataka and Andhra Pradesh. The Kāverī River rises in the
Coorg country of the southern Sahyas and flows eastward through southern Karnataka and Tamil Nadu. Finally, from the Malaya Mountains
flow such rivers as the Vaigāi and Tamraparnī of Tamil Nadu. In all, the
list includes more than 150 rivers and tributaries. The Purānas conclude,
"All these rivers are holy; all are Gangās that run to the sea; all are mothers of the world; and all are known to be destroyers of the world's sins."[56]

In addition to the mountains and rivers, a standard element of the
world-atlas descriptions is the account of India's regions and the enumeration of its peoples. The regions of India are five: the Middle Country (Madhyadesha) of the Gangetic Plain, the North Country or the
Northern Road (Uttarāpatha) extending into the hills and mountains;
the South or the Southern Road (Dakshināpatha), the East (Prāchya),
and the West (Aparānta). The Purānas list all of the *janapadas,* the kingdoms of the regions of Bhārata, each with its various clans and peoples. In
addition, it is commonly noted that the margins or borderlands are inhabited by the Kirata tribesmen in the east and by the Yavanas or Greeks in

the west. Between east and west, however, there is the homeland of the *brahmins, kshatriyas, vaishyas,* and *shudras* of Bhārata.[57]

There is a remarkable geographical awareness built into this worldview, a remarkable sense of "this land," its extent and features, its people, and its relation to other lands and the wider universe. In the Purānas, all this schematic exposition of the world atlas immediately precedes the extensive *tīrtha māhātmyas* that celebrate the sacred places of India. Here we see the geographical articulation of Bhārata profusely expressed as the Purānas locate and praise innumerable *tīrthas.* The *māhātmyas* go into extensive detail, in some cases enumerating hundreds of *tīrthas* up and down the course of the Narmadā River or in cities like Mathurā and Vārānasī. In our journey through India's *tīrthas,* we will see, again and again, the ways in which they are grouped in threes, fours, fives, sixes, tens, and twelves, in systems of seven rivers and seven cities, in patterns that create a complex and variegated landscape, patterns that participate in the schema of a larger patterned universe.

KARMA BHŪMI, LAND OF ACTION

Bhārata is the southernmost land of this lotus world. India's imaginative world map does not place India directly in the center of the world, as did Anaximander when he drew the first world map with Greece in the center, or the medieval cartographers when they placed Jerusalem and the Holy Land in the center, with the continents spreading forth like petals. Rather, Bhārata is but one of the petal continents. In many ways, it is the least glorious. Far from the usual cosmological ethnocentrism in which one's own world is described as civilized, while the surrounding lands, vaguely known, are thought to be less so, even barbarian, the Indian visionaries who described the world actually idealized the other petals of the world, the lands beyond, just as they idealized the outer ring-islands of the universe.

In the other lands—Ketumāla, Uttarakuru, and Bhadrāshva—people are said to have golden complexions, their skin as lustrous as seashells. They live lifetimes of one thousand or ten thousand years. They suffer no sickness or selfishness, no old age or decay. All are equal in strength and stature. Their lands are filled with rivers of cold, clear water and ponds of white lilies. The list of blessings goes on. In these other lands, people enjoy a perfection as natural as the perfection of nature. Indeed the wish-granting trees and the delicate waters seem to bestow their own perfection upon the inhabitants of these lands.[58] These lands are called *bhoga bhūmis,* "lands of enjoyment," where those who have reaped the rewards of their good deeds are born again to live long, long lives of enjoyment.

Bhārata is different. Here people are not uniformly beautiful, golden, and lustrous, but are of many races and types. Here people are generally small in stature and live relatively short lives of no more than one hundred years. They are subject to the usual rounds of sickness and misfortune, flood and catastrophe, old age and death. And yet, without exception or hesitation, Bhārata is said to be the best place to live in this wide universe, despite the abundant blessings of the other petal continents and the distant ring-islands. They may be *bhoga bhūmis,* but Bhārata is *karma bhūmi,* the "land of action."[59]

> Thus I have told thee of that four-leafed lotus-flower which is the earth; its leaves are Bhadrāshva, Bhārata, and the other countries on the four sides. The country named Bhārata, which I have told thee of on the south, is the land of action; nowhere else is merit and sin acquired; this must be known to be the chief country, wherein everything is fixedly established. And from it a man gains Svarga [heaven] and final emancipation from existence, or the human world and hell, or yet again the brute condition, O brahmin.[60]

In a worldview that places ultimate value, not upon enjoyment, but upon freedom from rebirth, the land of action is the only place where one can work to attain such freedom. Here alone through action, or karma, can one shape one's destiny toward freedom, all the while running the risk, of course, of shaping one's destiny toward further bondage as well. Life in *karma bhūmi* may result in rebirth as a human or an animal; it may lead to the enjoyment of heaven, or the punishment of hell, or it may, with practice and discipline, lead to the freedom of *moksha.* But here in *karma bhūmi,* change is possible and action matters.

One might say the Hindu vision of the other continents that skirt Meru is a utopian vision, for they are, in the true sense of "utopia," "no place," at least no place that is real. The perfection ascribed to them is generous, but when compared to the land of Bhārata, the praises of the lands of enjoyment have a hollow ring. Here in Bhārata there is sorrow and anxiety, along with joy and peace; here there is sickness and death, along with health and longevity. And yet a human birth here in Bhārata is very rare, and very precious, coveted even by the gods in heaven, so they say. For only in the hurly-burly of the land of action is the attainment of freedom, *moksha*, possible.

> *Therefore this Bhārata is the most excellent land in the*
> *Rose-Apple Island, O sage. For the others may be lands*
> *of enjoyment, but this is the land of action.*[61]

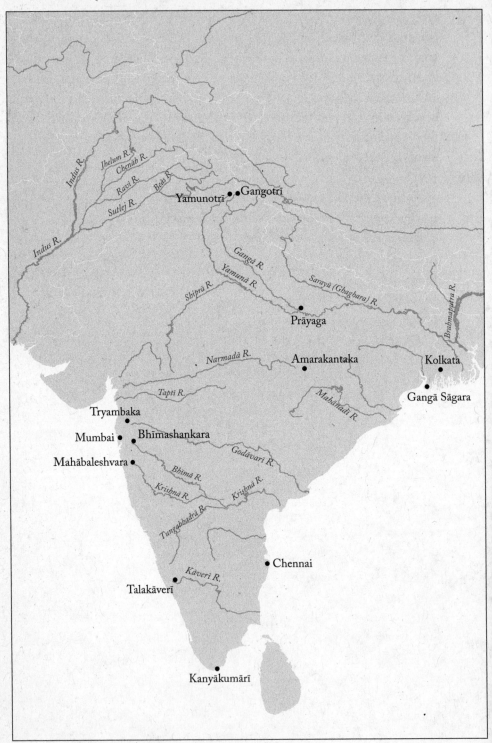

4

The Gangā and the Rivers of India

The Gangā is the river of India—a single river flowing from the Himalayas, gathering tributaries, and streaming across the fertile plains of north India. At the same time, the Gangā is the source of all sacred waters everywhere in India. The Gangā is also a goddess—Gangā Mātā, "Mother Gangā," and Gangā Devī, "Goddess Gangā." Her true headwaters are not really in the highest Himalayas, but are said to be in the highest heaven, emerging from the very foot of Vishnu. She was carried in the water pot of Lord Brahmā, and when she plummeted from heaven to earth, her cascades fell first on the head of Lord Shiva. It is no wonder the most famous hymn to the river calls her the "embodied goodness of the gods."[1]

The Gangā is mentioned in the *Rig Veda*, along with the Sarasvatī, the Parushnī, the Shatudri, and the Yamunā, more than a thousand years before the Common Era.[2] Within a few hundred years, however, the heartland of the Aryans, called Aryavarta, had moved from northwest India into the Gangetic Plain, the rich land through which the Gangā flows across north India. Today, this river basin with its many tributaries supports 8 percent of the world's population. It draws not only millions of people, but also their ills, their woes, their prayers, and their pollution. The Gangā has been dammed and distributed through canals. It has been the recipient of industrial and human waste. And even as governments and foundations tackle the pollution of the river and the silting of its dams, the enormous spiritual pull of its waters continues to draw pilgrims by the millions each and every day. The health and vibrancy of the Gangā and India's other rivers is both an environmental and a theological issue, as we shall see.

Hindus bathe everywhere along the Gangā and especially at important *tīrthas*, taking the waters cupped in their hands and pouring them back into the river as offerings to the *pitrs* and the *devas*, the departed ancestors and the gods. They present offerings of flowers and oil lamps in the river, as they would in the sanctum of a temple. On great occasions, they ford the river in boats, trailing garlands of flowers or ropes of saris hundreds of feet long to adorn the goddess river, chanting "*Gangā Mātā kī Jai!*" "Victory to Mother Gangā!"[3] Finally, pilgrims will come from all over India bringing the ashes of their beloved dead to commit ritually to the Gangā's waters. When they return to their homes, perhaps hundreds of miles away, they carry vessels of Gangā water to, one day, moisten the lips of the dying. The Gangā is holy all along its course, from its source to the sea.

THE SOURCE

At Gangotrī, the temple town at the source of the Gangā in the Garhwal area of the Himalayas, pilgrims bathe in the icy river that rises in the glaciers high above the town. They wade out knee-deep into the current, their feet seeking the sandy bottom amid the slippery stones. They plunge into the water, dipping three times, cupping their hands with offerings of water, emerging breathless and ecstatic. Having dried and dressed again, clean with the waters of the source, the pilgrims make their way to the stone temple that sits above the river. There they will present offerings to the goddess Gangā in her image form—a small golden image of the goddess on a silver throne embossed with a relief image of her *makara*, the Gangetic "crocodile" that is her vehicle, bearing in her hands auspicious emblems of her generosity—a water pot and a lotus.

The temple also houses attendant images in the sanctum: Gangesha Shiva, the Gangā's Lord; Bhagīratha Rāja, the king whose penance brought the Gangā to earth; Sarasvatī and Yamunā, her sister rivers; and the goddesses Durgā and Annapurnā. During the winter months, the image of Gangā, along with that of Sarasvatī and Annapurnā, is transported down the mountain for residence at a village called Mukhimath.

The pilgrims have purchased platters of offerings in the bazaar—a piece of pink net with a glittering gold border, a small comb, a tiny mirror, some red powder called *kumkum*, incense, sweet sugar candy, rice, and a coconut. Sitting before the door of Gangā Mātā, they employ a pilgrimage priest called a *pandā* to make their offerings and chant the requisite verses. They rinse their mouths and hands with water offered by the priest; they listen to the recitation of *sankalpa,* a statement of their religious intention with their own names chanted as sponsors of this worship there, in the presence of the goddess. They pitch pinches of green Gangā *tulsī* in the direction of her image, wave incense toward her, and flick moistened *kumkum* toward her with the tips of their fingers. Each item is offered to please the goddess, and finally, representative articles of the whole platter of offerings are tied up in the pink net and returned by the *pandā* to the pilgrims as *prasād,* the gifts of her grace.

In the evening, these pilgrims return to the temple for the *āratī,* the "lamp offering." The mountains rise steep on both sides of Gangotrī and evening comes early. The priest emerges on the porch of the temple and blows a long blast on the conch shell. Attendants beat the drum and ring the temple bells with vigor. Now, at the climax of the *āratī,* it is not the image of Gangā Devī in the temple that is the primary focus of worship, but the river itself. The priest or *pujārī* standing upon the porch of the temple, faces the river, and lifts the great multiwicked lamp, circling its light to the flowing waters of the Gangā. Only then does he return to the temple door and offer the lamps of the *āratī* to the image of Gangā within. Gangā water, now doubly sanctified having been offered to Gangā Devī, is distributed to the assembled worshippers, who receive and sip the water in cupped hands, rubbing the last drop in the palms of their hands onto their heads. They also receive the light of the *āratī,* passing the tips of their fingers through the flame, then touching their foreheads with its blessing.

The *āratī* concludes with singing the long and beautiful Sanskrit hymn to Gangā, the *Gangā Laharī,* composed in the sixteenth century by the poet Jagannātha.

> *Samriddhim saugbhāgyam sakala vasudhāya kim api tan . . .*
> *O Mother Gangā, may your water,*
>   *abundant blessing of the world,*
>   *treasure of Lord Shiva, playful Lord of all the world,*
>   *essence of the scriptures and*
>   *embodied goodness of the gods,*
> *May your water, sublime wine of immortality,*
> *Soothe our troubled souls.*[4]

This temple is closed in the winter months, as are other high Himala-yan shrines, and the image of Gaṅgā is transported in great procession to a lower altitude for her six months of residence at the village of Mukhi-math. This takes place at the time of the festival of Divālī in late October or early November, and the return journey arrives at Gangotrī on the auspicious day of Akshaya Tritīya in late April or early May. Whether going or coming, the journey takes two days, with a night halt along the way. Commenting on the yearly ritual, one priestly *pujārī* put it all in perspective when he said, "The true *mūrti*, of course, is the river. She stays here all year around."

The juxtaposition of river and image is a constant and repeated theme in the worship of India's rivers. In Hardvār, where the Gaṅgā enters the plains of India, the nightly *āratī*, or lamp offering, to the Gaṅgā is the central attraction. While there are dozens of small shrines at the water's edge, each with a decorated *mūrti* of the Goddess Gaṅgā, the main focus of the evening *āratī* is no image, but simply the flowing river. In Vārānasī, on the plains, where the river turns north, arcing toward her Himalayan home, a regiment of a dozen priests stands by the water's edge every night to honor the Gaṅgā, lifting tall multiwicked oil lamps into the night sky and dipping them toward the river in perfect syn-chronized movements. And so, too, at the temple of Yamunā Devī at Yamunotrī, across the mountains from Gangotrī, the Yamunā River is honored at her rising. At dawn, hundreds of miles downstream, along the bank of the Yamunā River in Vrindāvan, the priest turns from the riverside shrine of Yamunā Devī to offer his lamps to the river herself.

Here in this narrow valley, the River Gaṅgā has shaped the most extraordinary riverbed, running its strong streams of rushing waters through solid rock, now smoothed, sculpted, and slotted by the force of the water. At the place called Gaurī Kund it rushes in powerful tor-rents through silk-smooth channels, tumbling over a high cliff, its cata-racts throwing up a cloud of spray in the pool far below. In these rocks, and in high caves, and in forest groves, sit the yogis, ascetics, sages, and *sannyāsīs* who are the most faithful residents of this country. This is the terrain of the spiritually serious. Some come yearly to Gangotrī, arriving as the shrine opens in April or May, and some stay on right through the winter months when the high valley is frozen with snow. A *sannyāsī* from Dandi Kshetra Ashram who had been born here and grown up in one of the priestly families serving the temple of the Gaṅgā explained to me the importance of these religious adepts: "When the Gaṅgā was asked to come from heaven to earth, she was afraid that she would become choked and burdened with the weight of sin left in her waters by those who came to bathe. Brahmā made a promise to her: that sages and saints would live along her banks, and their bathing would purify her waters just as quickly as sinners could taint them."[5]

By the time the Gaṅgā reaches Gangotrī, it is already a broad stream. For the purpose of pilgrims, priests, and temple rituals, this *is* the source of the Gaṅgā, but it is not the actual headwaters. Some fifteen kilometers up the trail from Gangotrī is the glacier that releases the stream of water that begins to flow as the Gaṅgā. The place is called Gomukh, the "Cow's Mouth," reminding us that the waters of the sacred river are often poetically likened to cows, and to the nourishing milk of cows. Once pilgrims to Gangotrī get used to the fourteen-thousand-foot altitude, some of them will make the hike to Gomukh, to reach the icy waters of the source. At our visit in early May, however, few pilgrims had yet arrived, and those who had ventured to Gomukh reported the presence of a frozen ascetic, a holy man who had perished and attained his reward during the subzero winter.

Given this news, I did not venture to Gomukh, but was content to contemplate the many ways in which the Cow's Mouth is repeated symbolically throughout the whole land of India, stretching southward into the plains. In this patterned landscape, Gomukh is clearly not that glacial place alone, but has come to signify a particular kind of place where holy waters spring forth. On that very day, throughout India, people would be sipping and bathing in the waters of countless Gomukhs, all of which refer in holiness to this Himalayan place, and all of which are deemed too difficult to reach for most pilgrims. I recalled, for example, a place described as "the headwaters of the Sarasvatī River," on a steep forested hillside of Mount Abu in Rajasthan, thick with ferns, moss, and fan palms. There, Gomukh Kund, a square, stone bathing tank, is filled with water that flows through the mouth of a white marble cow's head protruding from one side, fresh marigolds tucked behind its ears. The Hindi sign posted reads THE PLACE WHERE THE SARASVATĪ RIVER RISES, and the inscription goes on to say, "This is the Cow's Mouth *tīrtha* of the Sarasvatī River. Here, doing *pūjā* and making the gift of a cow will secure imperishable merit."[6] In western Gujarat, there is the Gomukh *tīrtha* on the first of the several peaks of Mount Girnār, where a trickle of water runs from a brass cow's mouth, affixed to the rock of the mountainside, and fills a tank called Gomukhī Gangā. Along the Narmadā River, at the great shrine of Omkāreshvara, a rivulet enters the main course of the river at Gomukh, flowing through the mouth of a brass cow's head and splashing over a *linga* on its way. In Mangalore in coastal Karnataka, worshippers bathe in the Gomukh Bhāgīrathī *tīrtha* of the Kadri Temple. Most common of all, of course, is the feature called a *gomukh* in Shaiva temples: the opening, often shaped as a cow's head faucet, through which water, sanctified in the temple by being poured over the Shiva *linga*, runs out of the temple into the hands of pilgrims and worshippers. At the temple of Tryambaka in Maharashtra, for example, at the foot of the hill where the Godāvarī rises, such a brass cow's head carries water from the inner sanctum to the outside of the temple, to be distributed to those who circumambulate the temple. All these *gomukhas* and countless more are linked by common reference to this Himalayan place. This is the source. And yet, as every Hindu knows, the real source of the Gangā is in heaven.

Avatarana, The Descent of the Gangā

At Gangotrī, in the vestibule of the squat temple of rock masonry honoring the Gangā, the walls are inscribed with hymns in praise of the Gangā. The hymns refer, of course, to the well-known story of her descent from heaven.

> Om jaya gange māī, shrī jaya gange māī
> *Om, victory to Mother Gangā, praise to Beloved Mother Gangā!*
> *To redeem the sons of Sagara, you came to this place.*
> *Flowing from Vishnu's foot, pure light, savior of the world.*
> *Shiva put you on his head, you who give bliss to gods, and men,*
> *and sages.*

Each year as the hot and dry season reaches its peak in May and early June, in anticipation of the monsoon rains to come, Hindus all along the riverbank celebrate the descent of the Gangā from heaven to earth. The ten-day festival is called Dashaharā and it culminates on the tenth day of the bright fortnight of the summer month of Jyeshthā. This is one of those days when the faithful ply the river in boats, garlanding her with long ropes of marigolds. It is called the "birthday" of the Gangā, and the riverbanks are crowded with bathers, for a dip in the Gangā on that day "destroys ten sins" (*dashaharā*) or, some say, ten lifetimes of sins. Ideally one should bathe in the Gangā, but festival manuals confirm that a person far from the actual Gangā may bathe in whatever Gangā is near at hand.[7]

The story of the Gangā's divine descent from heaven to earth is known throughout India and is shared with other rivers. The descent of heavenly waters to earth is an ancient theme with many variants, beginning with one of the great Vedic myths, in which Indra, who had pillared apart heaven and earth and established the sky between them, engaged in combat with the great serpent Vritra, who coiled around the vault of heaven and closed up the celestial waters within.[8] The waters stored in the vault of heaven are often identified with *soma*, the nectar of the gods and the strengthening elixir of immortality. In defeating Vritra, Indra set free these divine waters for the nourishment of the earth. The seers of the *Rig Veda* praise the life-giving waters set free by Indra:

Forth from the midst of the flood they flow,
Purifying, never-sleeping, their leader, the sea.
Indra, the Thunderer, the Bull, dug out their channels.
Here may these goddess waters bless me!

Waters which flow from heaven,
Or which spring from the dug earth, or which meander freely,
All of which, bright and pure, head for the ocean,
Here may these goddess waters bless me!

In whose midst King Varuna moves,
Observing men's truth and falsehood,
Nectar they are, and bright and pure,
Here may these goddess waters bless me![9]

The waters are identified here as goddesses, set free from their heavenly home by Indra, who dug their channels. They are rivers of blessing and purification, and they are also referred to as "mothers." Their waters are not only the *soma* of the gods, but the milk of mothers. According to the Vedic seers, when Indra released the waters of heaven, they ran out upon the earth like mother cows released from a pen, burgeoning with milk and yearning to suckle their young.[10] The poets beg of the rivers, "Like longing mothers give to us here on earth the most blessed nectar that you have!"[11]

In the epics and Purānas, the various myths of the descent of the Gangā repeat some of the elements of the Vedic myth of descent. They make clear that this river, whose honeyed waters are said to contain *soma* or *amrita,* the nectar of immortality, has its source and counterpart in heaven. In the many Vaishnava versions of the myth, the river is called Vishnupadī after its origin in Vishnupada, meaning both the "highest heaven of Vishnu" and the "foot of Vishnu." Vishnu, who in the *Rig Veda* was Indra's helper in releasing nectar waters, is here the one who first instigates their descent to earth. In taking his famous three strides, Vishnu, the dwarf-turned-giant, strode through the earth, sky, and heavens, thus taking possession of the threefold universe. With his third stride he is said to have pierced the upper limit of heaven with his toe and released the heavenly waters.[12] Through this opening, the Gangā flowed into the heavens, landing first in Indra's heaven, where the river was caught by the steady Pole Star, Dhruva. From there she ran down the sky to the moon as the Milky Way, and from the moon to the realm of Brahmā, situated just above Mount Meru. From Meru, the story is the familiar one we have already encountered: The river split into four parts and ran out upon the four lotus-petal continents. One branch, the Alakanandā, flowed into Bhārata as the Gangā.[13]

In the most celebrated myth of the Gangā's descent into earth, however, it is Shiva whose role and relationship to Gangā is predominant. The story—told in the *Rāmāyana,* the *Mahābhārata,* and in many Purānas— is well known throughout India: The Gangā fell from heaven to earth in order to restore the bodies of the sixty thousand sons of King Sagara who had all been burned to ashes by the fierce gaze of the sage Kapila. Only the waters of the Gangā could save them.[14]

Long ago King Sagara of the Sun Dynasty wanted to perform the most magnificent of all kingly rites, the *ashvamedha,* or "horse sacrifice," a ritual of sovereignty in which a horse was let loose to wander for one

year. Everywhere the horse went, local rulers would implicitly acknowledge the sponsoring king as suzerain. So King Sagara's horse wandered
through lands and kingdoms in this way until, one day, it mysteriously
disappeared. What had happened? It seems that the emissaries of Indra,
who feared the power the king might gain from a successful *ashvamedha*,
had surreptitiously stolen the horse. The distraught king sent his host of
sons, sixty thousand of them, to search the land and find the horse. They
scoured the earth, they dug deep into the netherworlds, they left chaos
in their wake, but they did not find the horse. Finally they found the
sacrificial animal, tethered by the miscreant thieves at the ashram of the
renowned sage Kapila. Thinking Kapila had stolen the horse, Sagara's
sons approached accusingly.

Kapila was deep in meditation when they burst in upon him.
Annoyed by the intrusion of the royal search party, he opened his
eyes and burned the sixty thousand sons of King Sagara to ash with
the blazing power of his ascetic's gaze. The king was completely overwhelmed with grief. He had only one son left, the misbehaving son of
his second wife. But he also had one grandson, Anshumān, whom he
sent to propitiate Kapila. With prayer and asceticism, Anshumān won
a boon from the old sage: Yes, the sons of Sagara could be brought
back to life, but only by the waters of the River Gangā, which at that
time streamed across the heavens. Looking into the future, Kapila told
Anshumān that his grandson would be able to bring the Gangā from
heaven to earth.

It was indeed Anshumān's grandson, Bhagīratha, who undertook
fierce ascetic practice in the high Himalayas with the sole purpose
of winning the favor of the gods. He finally won a boon from Lord
Brahmā, who agreed to release Gangā to come to earth. Because the
earth would surely shatter under the force of her descent from heaven,
Bhagīratha would need to enlist Lord Shiva to catch her when she fell.
Again, through his asceticism, Bhagīratha won the boon from Shiva.
The Gangā plunged to earth, full of fish and raging whirlpools, covered
with a froth of foam. The lord caught Gangā on his head and tamed her
torrents in the thicket of his ascetic's hair, before releasing her to flow
upon the earth, dividing her into three streams.

Thus did the Gangā come to earth. She wound her way through
Shiva's hair and then Bhagīratha led her through the gorges of the

mountains, into the foothills, out into the plains of India, and finally to the sea, where she became the saving waters for the sons of Sagara.

The Gangā, having made the crossing from heaven to earth, has become a place of crossing from earth to heaven, both for the living and the dead. As the river quickened the ashes of the sons of Sagara, she will quicken the ashes of all the dead. So it is that the story of the Gangā's "descent," or *avatarana*, is read in *shrāddha* rites for the dead, that Gangā water is used in *shrāddha* and *tarpana*, or commemorative rites, and that the place where the Gangā skirts the Mahāshmashāna, the "Great Cremation Ground" of Banāras, has made it the best place to die in all of India. For the dead, the Gangā has the epithet *svarga-sopana-saranī*, the "flowing staircase to heaven." There is no theme more pervasive in Gangā hymnody than the yearning for the lap of the Gangā at the time of death. The popular "Gangāshtakam," for instance, begins:

> O Mother! I ask that I may take leave of this body on your banks,
> drinking your water,
> rolling in your waves, remembering your name, bestowing my gaze
> upon you![15]

As we shall see, the divine descent of the Gangā is repeated with all the rivers of India. Because they are seen as having fallen from heaven, they, in turn, become spiritual ladders to heaven. The very term for the place of pilgrimage—the *tīrtha*, or "ford"—is part of the symbolic language of rivers. Crossing the river became an evocative term for the heavenward spiritual crossings that are involved in life's pilgrim journey.

The Gangā's fall from heaven to the head of Shiva is also repeated countless times daily in the simple ritual act of pouring water upon the Shiva *linga*. Sometimes a pot of Gangā water with a hole in the bottom hangs perpetually above the Shiva *linga*, dripping drop after drop of Gangā water. Sometimes a worshipper will bring a pot of water into the sanctum to pour out upon the *linga*. In this ritual form, the incandescence of the *linga* of fire is joined with the energy of the living waters. Without the Gangā, Shiva would remain the scorching, brilliant *linga* of fire; without Shiva, the torrential force of the heavenly Gangā's fall would have shattered the earth.[16] The two are conjoined as Shiva and Shakti.

THE GATE OF THE GANGĀ

From Gangotrī, Bhagīratha is said to have cut a channel for the Gangā. Indeed, as far as Uttarkāshī, the deep canyon through which the Gangā flows seems as if it must have been pried open with great effort! Here and there other rivulets join the Gangā, and the volume of the river grows at each confluence. By the time the Gangā reaches Rishikesh and, a few miles farther, Hardvār, it is a broad and fast-flowing river. Here, the Gangā leaves the mountains and enters the plains of India.

One of the most repeated of Purānic verses tells us, "The Gangā is easy to reach, all along its banks. But it is hard to reach in three places: Gangādvāra, Prayāga, and Gangā Sāgara. Those who bathe in these places go straight to heaven and are never born again."[17] The term "hard to reach," *durlabha*, is commonly used to describe important *tīrthas*. For some, it means they are literally remote and difficult of access. But it is also spiritual access that is at stake here, for powerful *tīrthas* yielding

THE TRIBUTARIES OF THE GANGĀ, THE PRAYĀGS OF THE UPPER GANGĀ, AND THE FOUR DHĀMS OF THE HIMALAYAS

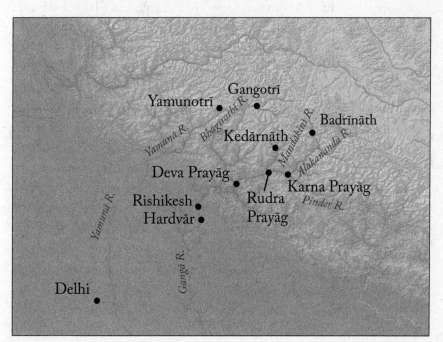

the fruits of heaven are not easy to come by. Gangādvāra, "Gate of the Gangā," is the modern temple town of Hardvār. Prayāga, where the Gangā meets the Yamunā River, is said to get its name from the ancient "sacrificial ground," or *prayāga*, of Lord Brahmā. It is today the modern city of Allahabad. And Gangā Sāgara is where the Gangā meets the sea in the Bay of Bengal. Of course, there are many other holy places along the Gangā, most notably the renowned city of Vārānasī, or Kāshī, said to have been famous as the dwelling of Shiva and the bestower of *moksha* even before Bhagīratha led the Gangā past her towering temples.

The old name Gangādvāra, "Gate of the Gangā," is still known, but the town is more commonly referred to as Hardvār—"Gate of Hari" for those bound for the shrine of Vishnu at Badrīnāth and "Gate of Hara" for those headed into the mountains for Shiva's shrine at Kedārnāth. Most pilgrims who leave from Hardvār for the four *dhāms* of the Himalayas visit both Kedārnāth and Badrīnāth, along with Gangotrī and Yamunotrī, the source of the Yamunā. Like all gates, the Gate of the Gangā takes one in and out, providing the primary access point to the Himalayan *chār dhām* shrines and providing the first great entrance of the Gangā as she makes her appearance on the plains. Hardvār is eclectic, associated not only with Gangā, Shiva, and Vishnu, but also with *devīs* such as the ancient "founding goddess," Mahādevī, and the ever-popular Manasā Devī, whose temple sits on a hilltop towering over the town and is accessible either by foot or by cable car.

The Gangā flows swiftly here and its currents are strong. It lives up to the epithets, the "Mover" and the "Swift One." Over the years, Government of India engineers have attempted to control the channel of the river with concrete embankments on both sides. Those who wish to bathe at the many fine cement *ghāts* along its course find iron chains sunk in the steps, rings to grasp, and railings providing a safely fenced area in which to enter the water. Even so, most pilgrims here prefer the bathing area created by diverting and slowing some of the water into a broad pool called Hari-ki-Pairi, the Feet of Hari or Vishnu. Here the steps rise like a great amphitheater from the small shrines at the water's edge. There are countless Gangā shrines, all boasting of being old, the oldest, the original. They beckon with bold signs painted on the walls or over the doorways: OLD SHRĪ GANGĀ MĀ, ANCIENT SHRĪ GANGĀ MANDIR, or

Hari-ki-Pairi Ghāt in Hardvār, where the swift-flowing Gangā
is diverted for bathing

COME AND SEE THE OLDEST TEMPLE OF GANGĀ-JĪ. This is a city of many
Gangā *devīs* and of one magnificent Gangā *devī*, the river herself.

The Purānas proclaim the fruit of pilgrimage to Hardvār, calculat-
ing its value in the currency of expensive and exclusive Vedic rituals—as
much merit as a king's horse sacrifice, as much as seven royal sacrifices.
The walls of the bathing houses rising above Hari-ki-Pairi also tout the
benefits of Hardvār's Gangā in carefully lettered Sanskrit:

> Whoever says "Gangā, Gangā," even from a hundred miles away, is
> released from all sins and attains the world of Vishnu.
> Haridvāra is the Door of Heaven, without a doubt. Therefore who-
> ever bathes here bathes, as it were, in a million *tīrthas*.

In the evening, the *ghāt* steps at Hari-ki-Pairi are packed with people
who have come for the Gangā *āratī*. Some have been there since the late
afternoon, like the women I saw who had gathered to hear the reading
of the *Rāmāyana* and its exposition by a traditional teacher. Many crowd
into the amphitheater of the *ghāt* steps as night falls, and the police are

on hand for crowd control. The man-made island across the bathing area is called "Tower Island" for its clock tower. There is a bridge connecting the island to the *ghāts*. Both island and bridge are also crowded with worshippers, eager to behold the famous *āratī* that takes place here. The *pūjārīs* of the many temples come to the water's edge with their five-layered brass oil lamps, laid thick with oil-soaked wicks and ready for the lighting. When the appointed time arrives, the bells begin to ring, the *pūjārīs* light the huge candelabra of oil lamps and step to the water's edge, where they raise the mountains of flame into the air, dip them in a deep arc toward the water, and raise them high, circling the flaming lamps to the water again and again. Here as at Gangotrī the blazing oil lamps, *dīpas*, are offered not before the temple images of the Gangā, but before the flowing river herself, the liquid goddess.

The great festivals of Hardvār also focus on the river. As we shall see, this is one of the four places for the great Kumbha Melā that takes place on twelve-year cycles. The most recent *melā* was in 2010, when the bathing festival ran from January 14 to April 28.[18] Authorities estimated that more than ten million people came to bathe in the Gangā.[19] Every year, however, there are also water-carrying festivals, like those described by Anne Feldhaus in her work on Maharashtra and like those common along rivers throughout the country. In the summer month of Shrāvana and the winter month of Phālguna, the town of Hardvār is inundated with pilgrims carrying *kavads*—poles slung over the shoulder with water pots on each end. They arrive in Hardvār from throughout the region, fill their water pots, and return to their towns and villages with Gangā water to pour upon the images of Shiva in their own locale.

Gangādvāra is also a repeated feature of the course of sacred rivers. It is not the source, but the gateway of accessibility. In Maharashtra, for example, just below the hilltop where the Godāvarī River rises, a trickle of Godāvarī water seeps from the rock. This place, too, is called Gangādvāra, and a priest ladles out the water to all who stop here on their pilgrimage. It is one of the five *tīrthas* to be visited by those who make the trek to Tryambakeshvara, the temple of Shiva at the base of the mountain, and then climb the hill behind to the source of the Godāvarī.

The Meeting Rivers: Triveni

All over India, the meeting rivers amplify the holiness of the *tīrtha*. Two rivers are better than one; three even more auspicious. The great site of the meeting rivers in north India is the *sangam*, the confluence, of the Gangā and Yamunā at Prayāga, where the city now called Allahabad stands. The Gangā has long been seen as the "white" river, bearing the mica-laden waters of her Himalayan course, and the Yamunā the "blue" river. This description of the confluence of the Gangā and Yamunā seems to be referred to in one of the latest sections of the *Rig Veda*, which says, "Those who bathe at the place where the two rivers, white and dark, flow together, rise up to heaven."[20] More than a thousand years later, the classical Sanskrit poet Kālidāsa describes the confluence of the "white" waters of the Gangā with the "blue" waters of the Yamunā as if they were a string of pearls and sapphires combined, or a garland of white and blue lotuses intertwined.[21]

According to the Purāṇas there is also a third river, the Sarasvatī, that joins the confluence at Prayāga, flowing in from underground. The Sarasvatī was clearly one of the great rivers of Vedic India, so impressive that it is mentioned some fifty times in the Vedic hymns. The Sarasvatī is known as the best of rivers, the goddess of river waters, and eventually her name became that of the goddess of arts and learning. The Sarasvatī River disappeared, however, leaving a powerful legacy and leaving, as well, the great mystery of her whereabouts. Many think the river once flowed east of the Indus, anchoring an entire civilization before the riverbed lost its main tributary waters and dried up, some three thousand years ago. Some have identified her riverbed with that of the Ghaggar River, a small river flowing today through the desert of Rajasthan, a river that is puny compared to the width of its dry riverbed. Scientists and geologists are drilling, looking for a great river that is no more. For today's India, however, the power and significance of the Sarasvatī is far more than that of any single river: It is in the persistent symbolic presence of the Sarasvatī waters at the confluence of rivers all over India.

In Allahabad, a long, flat plain of clay and sand extends toward the wedge where the rivers meet. In the hot season, it is a plain of baking sand, shimmering with heat. In the monsoon, when the wind blows, it sweeps the sand up and flings it horizontally across the plain before the clouds break with monsoon rains and the rivers rise to inundate the sands. In the winter, this is the scene of an encampment of thousands, at times hundreds of thousands, who gather for Māgha Melā, the religious fair that takes place here every January and that becomes the largest city on earth during the Kumbha Melā every twelve years.

The name Allahabad is said to have been bestowed by the Indo-Muslim emperor Akbar, but for well over a thousand years before the coming of Islam to India, this ancient *tīrtha* was famous as Prayāga, the King of Tīrthas, Tīrtharāja. The name Prayāga is from the sacrifice, the *yajna,* or *yāga,* said to have been performed here by Lord Brahmā himself. As the *Mahābhārata* puts it, "O hero, this meeting of the Gangā and Yamunā where Brahmā our Grandfather, the soul of all beings, performed sacrifice long ago, is world-famous. For this reason, O best of the Bharatas, it is known as Prayāga."[22] In the description of the sacred precincts offered by the *māhātmya* of the *Matsya Purāna,* the sacrificial post of Lord Brahmā, is at the center of the largest holy circle of Prayāga, called Prayāga-mandala. Within this circle is a square, comprising a smaller precinct of holy places, and finally there is the Venīkshetra, the sacred area right around the confluence of the rivers.[23]

Despite the Vedic heritage ascribed to Prayāga as a place of sacrifice, its primary fame and attraction is as a bathing place at the holy confluence of rivers. As we have seen, the rising popularity of visiting the *tīrthas,* evident by the time the dharma sections of the *Mahābhārata* were composed, explicitly attaches the benefits of *yajna,* the elaborate rites of sacrifice, to pilgrimage, *tīrthayātrā.* This is said to be the greatest of *tīrthas* for bathing, and its power is praised in the *Matsya Purāna.* The scene is after the great war of the *Mahābhārata,* when King Yudhisthira is stricken with despair, having slain so many of his kinsmen. "I have killed so many who were brave warriors, kings, and heroes. What is the good of my life now? How should I rule a kingdom, won in this way?" Oppressed with his thoughts and grief, Yudhisthira asks, weeping, where he might go to be relieved of his burden of sin and grief. The sage Mārkandeya comes to the weeping king and commends to him a pilgrimage to Prayāga.[24] Its many bathing places and *tīrthas* drive away all sins. And not only bathing there, but merely entering the boundary of Prayāga, or seeing the Gangā at Prayāga, or even thinking of Prayāga from a distance, melts away one's sins. "People who bathe there go to heaven. People who die there are liberated from the cycle of birth. Those who live there are guarded by the gods."[25]

The *Padma Purāna* proclaims, "One who bathes and drinks there where the Gangā, Yamunā, and Sarasvatī join enjoys liberation. Of this there is no doubt."[26] This is not only the King of Tīrthas for human pilgrims, but many verses in the Purānas describe how other rivers and other *tīrthas,* even the gods themselves, having collected the sins of countless multitudes of pilgrims, come here to bathe in order to become pure again. It is the *tīrtha* of *tīrthas.*

Long before the Gangā reaches Prayāga, pilgrims into the Himalayas will find multiple Prayāgas today, places where the headwater tributaries of the Gangā meet in the Himalayan highlands of Uttarkhand, "the North Country." These *sangams,* or confluences, where rivers meet in the Himalayas also have the name of the famous *sangam* at Prayāga on the plains. There are five "Prayāgs" in the Himalayas. At Vishnuprayāg two streams, the Vishnu Gangā and the Dhauli Gangā, join to form the Alakanandā, the river sparkling and milky with mica that flows past the high shrine of Badrināth. At Nandaprayāg, the Alakanandā is joined by the Nandākinī, which has its source in the high sanctuary of the

Rudraprayāg, where the Mandākinī River meets the Alakanandā River

mountain Nanda Devī. The Pindar River flowing from farther east in
Kumaon joins the swelling Alakanandā at Karnaprayāg. At Rudraprayāg,
the blue-green waters of the Mandākinī, which rises in the glacial valley of
Kedārnāth, join with the whitish, mica-laden waters of the Alakanandā.
There at Rudraprayāg, the *sangam* is accessible only by a steep, rocky
staircase descending into the white waters from the village above.

Finally, at Devaprayāg, all these waters join the principal stream of
the Gangā, the Bhāgīrathī, named for the princely ascetic who escorted
her from heaven. The Bhāgīrathī is the tributary that takes its rise near
Gangotrī. The picturesque village of Devaprayāg, like Rudraprayāg, is
wedged on a sharp point of land between the meeting rivers, its two- and
three-story buildings planted on foundations claimed inch by inch from
the steep slopes. Here, where the rivers meet below the cliff-hanging village, there is a small bathing *ghāt*. Our pilgrim party descends the steep
stairs leading to the river's edge. We grasp iron chains anchored in the
cement and let ourselves be swept into the swift current of the *sangam*.
Here the river is called Gangā for the first time.

Just as the name "Prayāg" has multiple referents, so does the name
"Trivenī," the "Triple-Braid," which refers to the confluence of the
three rivers, the Sarasvatī being the third, which joins the Gangā and
the Yamunā, so they say, from below. Originally the most celebrated
of the seven Vedic rivers, the Sarasvatī, though materially missing, has
maintained a strong reputation. She is the third river, who emerges here
and there to join in the meeting of rivers, thereby making the waters
triply holy. This three-stranded river, or the three-river confluence, is an
important repeated pattern in India's river lore.

Where are other places where the triple-river motif is identified
explicitly as a "*trivenī*"? As the Kāverī River enters Tamil Nadu in the
south, for example, the River Bhavānī joins the Kāverī mainstream.
There, too, so they say, is an underground stream, making this confluence a *trivenī*.[27] Similarly, just south of Ujjain in Madhya Pradesh is the
trivenī where the Kshiprā River, said to be sprung from Vishnu's body, is
joined by the Khyata River and another invisible river, identified in the
Purānas as the Blue Gangā.[28] Near the Shiva Temple at Somnāth in Saurashtra, there is a *trivenī* where the Rivers Hiranya and Kapila join with
yet another mysterious appearance of the Sarasvatī.[29] I have also found
trivenīs at Mahābaleshvara in Maharashtra, on the River Krishnā below

the temple of Shrī Shaila in Andhra Pradesh, and along the riverfront of Kāshī in north India.

Clearly "Trivenī" is more than the name of the famous *trivenī* at Prayāga, but is a *tīrtha* where two rivers are joined by a subtle, mysterious, underground "third" that eludes our human vision but is said to be there braiding its benevolence into the whole. It is well known that this *trivenī* also becomes part of the structure of the interior symbolic geography of the yogi, where the two vertical channels of vitality running up the spine—the *idā* and the *pingalā*—are entwined with a third, the *sushumnā*, which is subtle and completes the braid of energy channels that yogis seek to raise from the base of the spine through the crown of the head in the process of awakening.[30]

The Trivenī at Prayāga also is linked to the symbolism of the Gangā as a triple river, flowing in the three realms—in the heavens, on the earth, and in the netherworlds. She is well known as Tripathagā, the Triple-Pathed River. The Trivenī also seems to express what one might call the "ecumenical" nature of the Gangā, whose mythology associates her with all three of the major gods—flowing from Vishnu's foot in heaven, falling upon Shiva's hair as his liquid Shakti, and carried in Brahmā's water pot as his beloved as well.[31] This triple divinity is clearly present in the famous Trivenī at Prayāga. The white Gangā is associated with Shiva's Gaurī. The dark Yamunā is also called Kālindī, the wife of Krishna. And Sarasvatī, the wife of Brahmā, mysteriously meets the two from beneath the earth.[32] Similarly, at the headwaters of the Narmadā River at Amarakantaka, the symbolism of the triple river is also present. In the *māhātmya* of the Narmadā it is said that a pure river goddess issued forth from the body of Rudra. Out of her compassion, she split into three rivers: the Gangā, the Narmadā, and the Sarasvatī. The *Skanda Purāna* explains, "The Gangā has the form of Vaisnavī, the destroyer of all sins. The Narmadā is sprung from the very body of Rudra. And the Sarasvatī has the form of Brahmī, famous in the three realms."[33] The passage concludes, "As is the Gangā, so is the Narmadā, and so too the Sarasvatī. They bestow the same fruit—whether from bathing in their waters, seeing them, or just thinking about them."[34] In one of the final hymns to the Narmadā in the long section of the *Skanda Purāna* devoted to her praises, she is called Maheshvarī Gangā, and is also said surely to be Vaishnavī, Brahmī, and Sarasvatī.[35]

Aside from Prayāga, India's greatest *trivenī* is the great confluence of oceans at the southern tip of the subcontinent, at Kanyākumārī, where the Virgin Goddess stands as protector of the whole land. There, on a perfectly triangular spit of beach, waves roll in from three directions—from the Indian Ocean to the south, from the Bay of Bengal to the east, and from the Arabian Sea to the west. The waters that come from east and west bring with them the gathered waters of all India. Just to the side of this beach is a somewhat protected pool where pilgrims stand in the early morning, waist-deep in the ocean waters. As they make their *sankalpa,* holding waters of the three oceans in their cupped hands, the priest intones, "Here I bathe, in the *trivenī,* in the ocean at Kanyākumārī."

MEETING THE SEA: GANGĀ SĀGARA

The delta of the Gangā as it approaches the Bay of Bengal is vast, its distributary rivers covering some twenty-two thousand square miles and stretching through the coastlands of both Bengal in India and Bangladesh. The place Hindus call Gangā Sāgara is about eighty miles south of Calcutta in the sprawling delta of one of these rivers, the Hooghly, which runs past Calcutta, collects the waters of the Damodar and Rupnarayan Rivers, and creates an island, Sāgara Island, at its mouth.

It is there, so they say, that Kapila Muni, the sage, sat deep in meditation when King Sagara's sons rudely accused him of stealing the sacrificial horse. It was there that he burned them to ash with the fire of his gaze, promising to restore them to life only when the River of Heaven would flow upon the earth. When King Bhagīratha brought the Gangā to earth, he led her across the plains of north India, blowing his conch all the way, finally reaching the sea here at Gangā Sāgara.

Every year a great bathing *melā* takes place here. For a month, from mid-December to mid-January, this shape-shifting island at the mouth of what is, by now, a giant river becomes a virtual city of shelters and shops, sādhus and pilgrims. At the most auspicious time for bathing, on the day called Makar Samkrānti in mid-January, this will be a city of close to a million people. They come on a multitude of ferries, steamers, and launches, from river ports along the sprawling river on both sides of the island. They come especially from the closest port of Namkhana, reachable by bus from Calcutta. From the jetties where the boats dock, pilgrims walk about five miles to the *sangam* to bathe. The city on this sea island is a seasonal one. The *melā* is Gangā Sāgara's most important season. But there are other days as well when bathing here in the sea is popular, including that day in the hot summer month of Jyeshtha that marks the Gangā's descent from heaven to earth.[36]

The bathing area extends along the broad beach of Sāgara Island for a mile, and just back from the beach sits the temple of Kapila Muni. Bathing in these *sangam* waters where the Gangā reaches the sea and honoring the sage Kapila in his temple are the two most important acts of pilgrimage to Gangā Sāgara. While bathing, some will perform the special rite of holding the tail of a cow as the priest chants the words necessary to cross safely over the River Vaitaraṇī, the river that runs to the netherworlds of death. This reminds us that the Gangā is truly Tripathagā, the one who flows in the three worlds—in heaven for the gods, on earth for humanity, and in the netherworlds for the dead. At Gangā Sāgara, the Gangā had to enter into the netherworlds, called Pātāla, to raise the sons of King Sagara to life again.

The temple of Kapila has shifted repeatedly, with the storms of the sea and the erosion of soil. Today's pilgrims will find a new temple of concrete and a corrugated metal roof, built in 1974. It replaced structures that had collapsed or been swallowed by the sea at least four times in recent memory. Inside the temple sits the image of the bearded sage Kapila in a swirl of flower garlands and broken coconuts. He is now, as then, sitting deep in meditation, his head sheltered with the umbrella hood of a five-headed *nāga*. To one side is a *mūrti* of the goddess Gangā on her *makara* mount. To the other sits the image of King Sagara. "*Jaya Bāba Kapila Nātha*" and "*Gangā Māyī kī Jaya!*" are the exclamations on the lips of pilgrims here.

The sea is often described as the "lord" or "husband" of the rivers. The rivers are, on the whole, female, and Gangā describes the "womanly character of rivers" in the *Rāmāyana,* in response to Pārvatī's question to her as to how women ought to behave.[37] The rushing of a river toward the sea is often described as the rushing of a woman in love toward her lover. The meeting of the rivers and the sea is, therefore, like an auspicious marriage.

While Gangā Sāgara is the most renowned meeting of river and sea, there are well-known *tīrthas* at other river mouths as well. Mahīsāgara Sangama, a *tīrtha* at the mouth of the Mahī River in the Gulf of Cambay, is so famous that its praises fill many chapters of the *Skanda Purāna*. River mouths are complex *tīrthas,* however. The mouths of many of India's rivers sprawl into vast deltas as the rivers split into many channels. In some cases, the river is said to divide into its seven parts, evoking once again the sense that there are seven great rivers of India and that each river, somehow, contains the waters of the whole.

The Great River Melās

At Gangā Sāgara, pilgrims are advised to spend three days and three nights to reap the merit, the *punya,* of pilgrimage. Amid the makeshift canteens and shops, pilgrims mingle from all over India. One modern writer puts it this way: "The purpose of the *melā* is mixing—and the purpose of the *melā* is *mukti.*" This combination of the great cultural fair with the most lofty religious purposes is distinctive to India's great *melās,* often described as "religious fairs." "This *melā* is a small mirror of the whole society," the writer continues, "in which its energy and force, its beauty and its bad qualities as well, are reflected."[38] He describes *bhakti,* or devotion, as the thread binding people together at the Gangā Sāgara Melā—people from Bombay and Kerala, Ayodhyā and Shrīrangapattanam. Our writer insists, "One must understand the *melā* really to know India."

The *melās* that take place along India's rivers are among the most striking forms of Hindu pilgrimage. Prayāga, the King of Tīrthas, also is host to the greatest of all *melās.* Once a year, during the winter month of Māgha, in January and February, the great sandy flood plain of the Trivenī becomes a huge encampment of pilgrims. This is called Māgha Melā, a monthlong festival that brings in a steady flow of pilgrims from all over India. It is also a great convocation of gurus and pandits, saints and sādhus. They pitch huge tents, hold discussions, and offer lectures and teachings. There is the attendant bustle of commerce, both secular and sacred. "What attracts them as a magnet, all at one time, to the same place, is the still vital strength of religious tradition," writes scholar D. P. Dubey. "A miniature spiritual India is represented on the dry flood plain between the Gangā and the Yamunā during the shivering cold month of Māgha."[39]

The Māgha Melā is mentioned as early as the *Mahābhārata*, which takes us back to the early centuries of the Common Era. "The one who observes firm vows, having bathed at Prayāga during Māgha, O best of the Bharatas, becomes spotless and reaches heaven."[40] Hsuan Tsang, the Chinese Buddhist pilgrim who traveled in India during the reign of King Harsha in the seventh century C.E., seems to have visited Prayāga during the Māgha Melā and writes of it as an "age-long festival" held on the sands of the confluence of the rivers. Having looked at the evidence, D. P. Dubey claims, "There is a continuous history of the fair from at least the Gupta period to the present."[41] The *māhātmyas* claim that this is the month when all the *tīrthas* come here to bathe, for they, too, need to deposit their load of sins taken on from innumerable bathers. The mountains and rivers of India, along with the gods themselves, come to Prayāga during the month of Māgha, joining the vast assembly of pilgrims, sages, and saints. Bathing there in Māgha is said to free one from rebirth, and so it is that even the gods yearn to come to Prayāga during Māgha.[42] The *Matsya Purāna* tells us, "During the month of Māgha, sixty thousand *tīrthas* and six hundred million sacred streams are to be found at the confluence of the Gangā and the Yamunā."[43] One particularly exuberant *māhātmya* from the *Padma Purāna* claims that although Kāshī bestows liberation by the illumining knowledge imparted by the *tāraka mantra* given to all who die there, Prayāga bestows liberation even without knowledge! So it is that this place, they say, is the most sacred on the surface of the earth.[44]

While the whole month of Māgha is holy, there are three days when an especially large influx of pilgrims comes for the auspicious bath at Prayāga—the day of Makar Sankrānti, when the sun enters the sign of Capricorn, the *amāvasyā* day, when there is no moon, and the *pūrnimā* day, when the moon is full. Most auspicious of all, however, is to spend the whole month there, a tradition that is called *kalpāvāsa*, said to bring the merit accumulated by Lord Brahmā during his full lifetime, which lasts a *kalpā*—432 million years.[45]

Every twelve years, this Māgha Melā becomes the Kumbha Melā, the world's largest mass pilgrimage. We may imagine that the annual Māgha Melā became the great Kumbha Melā by the acclamation of pilgrims' feet over the centuries. During this month millions of pilgrims stream into Prayāga for a bath in the Triveṇī, chanting *"Bolo Gaṅgā maī kī jaī!"* ("Victory to the Gaṅgā!") The Kumbha Melā is rightly famous throughout the world for its incredible size, its sprawling encampments of followers of every sect and strand of Hinduism, its processions of sādhus—naked, ash-covered, eccentric—who seem to appear from a multitude of monasteries, *mathas,* and caves for the occasion.

At the Kumbha in 1977, the bathing crowd was estimated at fifteen million. By 1989, estimates were at eighteen million. In 2001, some thirty million people visited the site and bathed in the confluence during the *melā.* On the chief bathing days, the crowd was large enough to be visible from space satellites, and the *melā* was reported to comprise a city as large as New York, London, and Paris combined. For the Kumbha today, the government of Uttar Pradesh and the central government collaborate in massive civil arrangements. According to the Kumbha Melā Project, some 5,000 gallons of purified drinking water per minute are pumped in, 6,500 buses provide transportation, 6,000 electrical poles provide service, 6,000 sanitation workers are employed, and there are 13,500 latrines. Nine pontoon bridges are put in place across the Gaṅgā and 400 boats ply the river. There are 22 fire stations, 20,000 policemen and National Guard present, along with 300 lifeguards, 100 doctors and nurses, and a multitude of Indian Boy Scouts.

Such a massive, voluntary pilgrimage that draws millions to a common spiritual experience—bathing in the *sangam* of the rivers—must have a world-shaping influence for those who come from the far reaches of India. The *melā* experience, however, is not only about bathing, but also about spectacle, commerce, and education. During this monthlong encampment, the streets of the temporary city built on the *sangam* flats are lined with the temporary tent-houses that give shelter to pilgrims and provide large halls for the discourses of religious leaders. Their loudspeakers hang from the light poles, and throughout the day and night the din of *bhajans* and the soaring discourses of swamis fill the air. In her book *Pilgrimage and Power,* Kama Maclean investigates the ways in which the Kumbha Melā had unavoidable implications for those who were concerned about power and governance. Her work is framed largely through the eyes of nonparticipants, especially British administrators, and their concern to regulate such a massive gathering. She focuses primarily on the history of the *melā* from 1765 to 1964, but clearly its political implications extend to the present as well. She writes, "The Kumbh captures the attention and the imagination of masses of Hindus, and those seeking to capture them have sought to inject themselves into the *melā*."[46]

The term *kumbha* means water pot, here specifically the water pot containing the nectar of immortality (*amrita*) over which the gods and demons battled in the time of beginnings. As the gods whisked the pot away to heaven, it is said that four drops of it splashed upon the earth. Thus, there are four *melās* associated with the *kumbha*. Of course, Prayāga's is the most famous, but there are also *melās* at Hardvār, Ujjain in central India, and Nāsik in central western India. The traditional story told at all the sites has to do with that pot full of *amrita* brought up from the sea when the *devas* and *asuras,* the gods and anti-gods, churned the sea of milk, as one might churn milk for butter, using Mount Mandara as a churning stick and the serpent Vāsuki as a rope. Through this churning, which involved both the cooperation and competition of the gods and anti-gods, all the special treasures of heaven and earth rose from the sea—the elephant mount of Indra, the chariot of the Sun, the goddess Lakshmī, and the first physician, Dhanvantarī. Eventually, the churning produced the much-desired pot of immortal nectar, and the gods and demons struggled to possess it for themselves. The gods finally swept it off to heaven, but not before four drops of the *amrita* had fallen on the earth—at Prayāga, Hardvār, Ujjain, and Nāsik. These splashes of the nectar of immortality, according to legend, became the places of the great Kumbha Melās.[47]

Pandits at Prayāga today cite verses from the ancient *Atharva Veda* to claim the antiquity of the Kumbha Melā tradition. "I give four *kumbhas* in four places," the verse goes; the four places are interpreted to be those of the present *melās*. The verse is taken somewhat out of context, however, and seems scant textual evidence for the *melā*'s Vedic antiquity. Nonetheless, the connection of the Gangā with the *amrita,* the drink of immortality, is common. As the *Mahābhārata* puts it, "What *amrita* is to gods . . . so to humans is Gangā water."[48] For those who bathe in and drink the Gangā, this is *amrita*. The pot brim-full becomes a common symbol of both the goddess and the Gangā. Both the Shiprā River at Ujjain and the Godāvarī River at Nāsik are said to become pure Gangā water during their respective *melās,* underlining the connection of these huge *melās* with the Gangā.[49]

All four *melās* have been firmly fixed in the popular imagination, and even before modern communications, they attracted untold crowds, without the least bit of publicity. Each takes place every twelve years, though the seasons in which the *melās* take place are different.[50] For example, the Kumbha Melā at Hardvār is sometimes called the Ardha Kumbha Melā because its twelve-year cycle falls halfway between the *melās* at Prayāga. It takes place not in the winter month of Māgha, but in the spring month of Chaitra. At Ujjain, the Kumbha festival called Simhastha takes place in the springtime month of Vaishākha, also at the full moon. And in Nāsik, the festival, also called Simhastha, takes place every twelve years during the late-summer month of Bhādrapada.[51]

Quite outside this group of four *melās,* but related in its symbolism, is the Mahāmaham, every twelve years at Kumbhakonam in Tamil Nadu. The temple city is not far from the banks of the Kāverī River, but the festival does not take place on the Kāverī. Rather, here in the town of Kumbhakonam there is a great square tank some twenty acres in extent to which nine sacred rivers are said to come at the time of the Kumbha festival in the winter month of Māgha. The temple gate near the great *kund* depicts Lord Shiva with nine maidens, representing the rivers. The inscription reads, "Lord Shiva taking the nine maidens for a dip at Mahāmaham Tīrtha." The nine are listed there as Gangā, Yamunā, Sarasvatī, Narmadā, Godāvarī, Kāverī, Tungabhadrā, Krishnā, and Sarayū—adding two more rivers of the south to the seven.

At Kumbhakonam, Shiva's role as creator is hailed. The story, apparently taken from the *Perīya Purāna,* is told in bold painted English prose on the inner walls of the Kumbheshvara Temple:

During the Mahapralaya (Great Floods) after Dwapara Yuga the Kumbam (pot) full of amirtham and seeds of creation was set afloat by Siva. The said Kumbam had its rest in this place. Hence this ancient place is named as Kumbakonam after that kumbam. Immediately after its rest Lord Siva appeared in the guise of a hunter and broke the said kumbam full of amirtham with his arrow. The spilt amirtham pooled together in a place now known as Mahamaham Tank where millions of pilgrims have their holy Bath during Mahamaham. Then Lord Siva gathered the sand wet with the remaining amirtham, spread in the place and shaped it into the present Mahalingam which is known as Sri Adhikumbeswara. This mahalingam unlike other lingams found in almost all other temples is not made of granite stone and as such abhishekams cannot be performed with watery substances lest they should dissolve the shape of the lingam. This idol "Kirathamoorthy" is a special feature in the temple and it is a standing monument to commemorate the incident that Lord Siva Himself has created the present Mahalingam.

Also painted on the wall here is a pictorial explanation of the local lore, with captions in Tamil and English: Lord Brahmā wants to preserve the seeds of creation when the earth is engulfed with the flood called the *pralaya*. Shiva instructs Brahmā to place some earth, some water, the seeds of creation, and the nectar of immortality called *amrita* into a *kumbha*, an earthen pot, and to place the pot on top of Mount Meru. The floods of the *pralaya* come and the pot is preserved on top of Meru. As the waters subside, the *kumbha* floats south until it comes to rest on dry land right here in Tamil Nadu. The bilva leaves, the mango leaves, and the coconut that had decked the top of the *kumbha* fall off and become Shiva *lingas*. Then Lord Shiva, in the form of a hunter, shoots his arrow at the pot and splits it open, spilling the contents of creation, including the *amrita*, onto the earth. Shiva, mixing the immortal nectar with the sands, shapes a *linga* that becomes known as Kumbheshvara, honors it, and merges into it. It is also called "Kiratamoorthy," after Shiva the hunter, *kirata*. As for the nectar, it spreads out to an extent of five *kroshas*, or ten miles, in each direction, sanctifying the whole. The water gathers in a pool at the Mahāmaham Tīrtha, which becomes a sacred bathing tank.

The Kumbhakonam bathing festival, as we have seen, participates in the associative linking of the Gangā, the *kumbha,* and the nectar of immortality. It is Shiva as Kāshī Vishvanātha who brings the nine river goddesses here. It is said that at the time of this great *melā* the tank gets its water directly from the Gangā and that its waters are as pure and holy as those of the Gangā. Here, the rivers come to bathe, just as they come to Prayāga during Māgha Melā, bearing the sins they have absorbed throughout the year from the pilgrims who have bathed in their waters.

The rivers, thus, become pure again by bathing in the pool filled with the *amrita* of the Gaṅgā.[52]

In Praise of Gaṅgā: the *Māhātmyas*

Over the centuries the hymns, praises, and stories of this river have multiplied into what is today a rich body of *māhātmyas*. Indeed, in one of her many *māhātmyas*, her thousand names are sung.[53] She is called Gaṅgā, so they say, because she has "gone to earth" (*gamgatā*) from heaven. She is Mandākinī, because she is the River of Heaven, flowing through the heavens like the Milky Way. She is Vishnupadī, because she flowed forth from the foot of Vishnu. She is called Bhāgīrathī, because the sage Bhagīratha brought her from heaven to earth. She is called Jāhnavī, because she was swallowed and then released by the sage Jahnu, whose ashram she traversed on her way to the sea. The Gaṅgā, it is said, is supreme among rivers, as Kāshī is supreme among holy cities and as the Himalayas are supreme among mountains.

The *māhātmyas* extol the benefits of bathing in these waters. Purification, lifting the burden of sins, the cleansing of the heart—all are the fruits of bathing in the Gaṅgā. Indeed, *moksha*, or spiritual freedom, is said to result from bathing in the waters of the Gaṅgā, dying by her shores, or being cremated on her banks.[54] This is especially the case in this era, the Kali Yuga, when the traditional means of gaining spiritual freedom are too difficult for ordinary people. In earlier ages and better times, liberation could be had only by means of meditation (*dhyāna*), austerities (*tapas*), or rites of sacrifice (*yajna*). But now, in the corruption of this Kali Age, these practices are too difficult for ordinary people. Only the Gaṅgā can bring the blessings of salvation.[55]

The duplication of the Gaṅgā is a signal of her importance, for in this religious world the marker of significance is not the supremacy of one feature as unique in relation to the whole, but rather its infusion into the very veins of the whole. As we have seen, the symbolism of the Gaṅgā has become part of the symbolism of rivers and *tīrthas* throughout India, lending its structure and power to the rivers of the rest of India. All seven rivers and many more besides are actually called "Gaṅgā," such as the Godāvarī Gaṅgā of Maharashtra or the Kāverī, the Dakshina

Gangā, of the south. Indeed, in some of the world-atlas accounts more than 150 rivers and tributaries might be listed and placed in their respective regions of India, and after a detailed and often dry geographical exposition, the Brahmin scholars will conclude by giving the sweeping imprimatur of the Gangā to them all:

> All these rivers are holy; all are Gangās that run to the sea; all are mothers of the world; and all are known to be the destroyers of the world's sins.[56]

Gangā is the gold standard. But clearly, the Gangā is more than a single river and is not confined to the course she takes across the plains of north India. This river is the archetype of sacred waters and participates in that spatial transposition that is so typical of Hindu sacred topography, pervading the sacred waters of all of India's great rivers.[57] If a person cannot go to the Gangā, going to another of the seven rivers may be tantamount to the same thing. If one of the seven is out of reach, one might go to whatever river is nearest. In south India, virtually every temple tank is referred to as Shiva Gangā and sacred lore connects these temple tanks with the Gangā of north India through what seems to be a vast underground canal system. On the far southern seacoast at Rāmeshvara, for example, Rāma is said to have dug into the earth with the end of his bow and released a spring of Gangā water at the place today called Dhanushkoti, the "Bow Tip." On the rocky hill behind the Murugan temple at Tiruparankunram, near the city of Madurai, rises a spring of Gangā water, and incidentally, the adjoining temple contains a *linga* of Kāshī Vishvanātha from the banks of the Gangā in the north. In eastern India, at Biraja in Orissa, a well is said to connect through an underground channel to the Gangā at Kāshī.[58] The Gangā has even appeared in Mumbai, in the famous bathing tank called Bāna Gangā.

In temples and homes throughout India, Gangā is called to be present in the waters used in ritual, either by mixing those waters with a few drops of Gangā water or by uttering the name and mantras of the Gangā to invoke her presence. Thus, the Gangā is the quintessence and source of all sacred waters, indeed of all waters, everywhere. The Gangā permeates other rivers, and others are also present in her. Bathing in this one river, they say, one truly bathes in all rivers. A contemporary Indian author puts it this way: "When a pilgrim dives into the sacred waters of the Gaṅgā, he feels the thrill of plunging into the waters of all the rivers of India."[59] The *māhātmyas* claim that the Gaṅgā concentrates in her waters some thirty-five million *tīrthas*. Indeed, it is said that every wave of the river is a *tīrtha*.[60]

Liquid *Shakti*

While the Gaṅgā is associated with Vishnu and Brahmā, it is Shiva whose relation with Gaṅgā is most sustained and intimate. Shiva is Gaṅgādhāra, "Bearer of the Gaṅgā," commonly depicted bearing Gaṅgā in the tangled mass of his ascetic's hair, either as the nymph who clings to the crescent moon in his topknot or as the stream of water spurting like a spring from his hair.[61] The Gaṅgā in this form is Shiva's constant companion, making his ascetic's locks her way station on her perpetual fall from heaven to earth. Bear in mind that her descending is a continuing process, not a single event, so each wave of the Gaṅgā falls upon Shiva before touching the earth. In bearing the Gaṅgā, Shiva got himself into a relationship rather than a one-time project.

Gaṅgā is said to be the liquid form of Shiva's *shakti*, his active and creative energy. *Shakti*, as we shall see, is that life energy, conceived as female, through which the utterly transcendent Shiva manifests himself in the world. It becomes a proper name of the great goddess herself. Glimpses of Shiva as Supreme Lord may be hard to come by, but Shakti can be seen and touched, praised and loved. One can even immerse one's body in her liquid form, as countless pilgrims do every day. Shiva-in-action is *shakti*, the energy that creates and nourishes the manifest universe. Without this energy, the Supreme Lord is an abstraction, unseen and beyond human naming. As liquid *shakti*, Gaṅgā is, in more familiar terms, God's incarnation, God's divine descent, freely flowing for all. Just as Shiva became the vehicle for the Gaṅgā's fall to earth, Gaṅgā became the vehicle for Shiva's merciful work of salvation. It is through her that Shiva enters into the world as the active agent of salvation. As Skanda explains to the sage Agastya, "O Agastya, you should be amazed at the notion that Gaṅgā is really Shakti, for is she not the supreme energy of the eternal Shiva, taken the form of water?"[62]

Here, Agastya speaks of the "Eternal Shiva," Sadā Shiva, an even more expansive name that includes and transcends the three gods spoken of as Brahmā, Vishnu, and Shiva. Gangā as the liquid *shakti* of this Supreme Shiva embodies the energy of all these gods. A contemporary Hindi religious writer speaks of the Gangā as the "liquid" (*drava*) form of the Supreme Brahman.[63]

As the opening stanza of the *Gangā Laharī* puts it, she is the "essence of the scriptures and embodied goodness of the gods."[64] While the power of Shakti can often be ambiguous and dangerous, hers is an energy said to work only for the good. Despite floods and dangerous currents, her destructive force is utterly calmed in the hair of Shiva. That is her *māhātmya*.

MOTHER WATERS

The river is most universally known to Hindus as "Mother Gangā." She is embracing, nourishing, and forgiving, without a trace of anger. In India, where many goddesses combine the gentle with the ferocious, we could certainly imagine that Gangā, with the potency of both nourishment and rampaging flood, would participate in this paradigm of divine ambiguity. Thus it is all the more significant that this river, with such potential for destruction, is acclaimed in such unambiguous terms. She is not depicted with the lotus in one hand and a weapon in another, as are many other goddesses. She bears the lotus and the *kumbha,* the water pot—both symbols of auspicious blessing.

In many stories, Gangā's role as mother is specifically exalted, recalling the ancient Vedic references to Gangā and the other rivers as "mothers." In the course of mythic events, we know that Shiva and the mountain's daughter, Pārvatī, marry and engage in prolonged lovemaking. But Shiva's seed is too hot for Pārvatī to bear in her womb. The fire god Agni carries the seed to the reeds of the Gangā, where, in due time, the Seven Sisters called the Krittikās nurture the embryo and the heroic Skanda is born. Skanda is the promised son of Shiva, born to save the worlds from the power of the *asura* named Tāraka.[65] He then becomes known as Kārttikeya because of his Krittikā mothers. But Gangā also lays claim to being one of the mothers of Skanda. In another story, Gangā, as the wife of King Shantanu, becomes the mother of the hero-sage Bhīshma. Bhīshma is, in a sense, her beloved child, whom she raises herself, and when the great hero finally dies in the battle of the *Mahābhārata,* Gangā rises in human form from the river, weeping as bitterly as any mother.[66] On the whole, however, Gangā is not simply the mother of Skanda or Bhīshma, but the mother of all. Her waters, like milk, are said to be the drink of life itself. As the gods drink *soma* for life, so do humans drink Gangā water. It is as nourishing as mother's milk, and indeed the *Mahābhārata* compares human thirst for the river's waters to that of hungry children thirsting for mother's milk.[67]

Even those utterly unfit for salvation by the standards of dharma will be embraced and saved by the Gangā, so they say. The *Padma Purāna* tells us that while sons may abandon their fathers, wives their husbands, and friends their dearest friends when they discover their ugliest sins, the Gangā will abandon no one.[68] Such is the testimony of Jagannātha, the Gangā's great seventeenth-century brahmin poet, who is said to have been outcast for having a love affair with a Muslim woman. According to legend, Jagannātha went to Banāras to try to restore his status by proving himself acceptable to the brahmins there, but he was unsuccessful. He sat with his beloved atop the fifty-two steps of Panchgangā Ghāt, so they say, and as he composed each of the fifty-two verses of the *Gangā Laharī,* "The Gangā's Waves," the river rose one step. At the conclusion of the hymn, the waters touched the feet of the poet and his beloved, purified them, embraced them, and carried them away.[69]

In the *Gangā Laharī,* Jagannātha addresses the river as Mother, the one who will love and claim the child rejected by everyone else. He has been shunned, even by outcasts. He has been criticized, even by madmen. He has been rejected, even by the *tīrthas.* Indeed, they hang their heads in shame at their inability to cleanse him. There are plenty of gods who will care for the good, he writes, but who will care for the sinner, except Gangā?[70]

> I come to you as a child to his mother.
> I come as an orphan
>   to you, moist with love.
> I come without refuge
>   to you, giver of sacred rest.

I come a fallen man
    to you, uplifter of all.
I come undone by disease
    to you, the perfect physician.
I come, my heart dry with thirst,
    to you, ocean of sweet wine.
Do with me whatever you will.[71]

Above all, it is mercy and compassion that flows out from the foot of Vishnu or from the hair of Shiva in the form of this mothering river. She nourishes the land and all its creatures, living and dying. The hymns repeatedly confirm that this river is intended as a vehicle of mercy:

This Gangā was sent out for the salvation of the world by Shiva, Lord
    of lords, filled with the sweet wine of compassion.
Shiva, having squeezed out the essence of Yoga and the Upanishads,
    created this excellent river because of his mercy for all creatures.[72]

DEATH ALONG THE GANGĀ

Those who come to the Gangā today often come to perform rites for the dead. There are three holy places that came to be known as the *tristhalī*, simply the "three places"—Prayāga, Kāshī, and Gayā—where rites of *shrāddha* for the dead and *visarjana*, the committal of ashes to the river, are especially performed.

Gayā is the least popular these days, as the River Phalgu has all but dried up, leaving most of the famous bathing places a sandbar. Even so, its linkage to death rites remains. According to some legends, the city is named after the *asura* Gaya whose austerities won him a boon: that whoever touched his body would attain heaven. Vishnu spread him out upon the land and placed his own foot on the stone that held Gaya down. Therefore, they say, if *shrāddha* rites are performed at that stone bearing Vishnu's footprint, the beloved departed ones attain liberation. Today, Gayā has become of secondary importance, although many pilgrims still come en route to Bodh Gayā, the place of the Buddha's enlightenment, about an hour away.

Prayāga today still receives many pilgrims who come for death rites. Even on an ordinary day at Prayāga, when there is no sign of the multitudes that attend its winter *melās,* pilgrims still come bearing the ashes of the beloved dead. Approaching the broad sandbar of the *sangam,* they will encounter rows of *tīrtha purohits,* the special priests and record keepers who display their large trunks of record books, making evident to the approaching pilgrims their function as keepers of history and family rites. One of them, to be sure, will know or claim to know the pilgrim's very village in Andhra Pradesh, his family and ancestors there, and the rites they themselves performed here generations ago. They will tell the pilgrims of the great and famous whose rites were performed here in modern times—Mahatma Gandhi, Jawaharlal Nehru, and Lal Bahadur Shastri.

The pilgrim from Andhra Pradesh whom I accompanied as he performed these rites arrived with the ashes of his father carefully packed in a plastic bag. He and his wife came by train and met others along the way who came with the same purpose. There are three parts to the rite he performs here: the *asthi praksepana,* in which he honors the bones and ashes of the deceased, the *asthi visarjana,* in which he goes out in a boat and sinks the ashes in the river, and the *pinda pradāna,* in which he offers rice balls, called *pindas,* to the deceased and ritually unites the deceased with the lineage of ancestors in heaven. This is the rite that sons or male heirs perform as a sacred duty to their fathers. Here at Prayāga, all the mourners take their seats on the sand, cross-legged, in rows before the priest. With the others, the pilgrim from Andhra Pradesh is bare-chested, wearing only the sacred thread of the upper three castes. He now puts it on backward, hanging from the right shoulder, for such ritual reversals are common in death rites in India as elsewhere. He sips water with the right hand, a twist of sacred *darbha* grass round his fingers, purifying the mouth for the words that will be uttered. Before him is a leaf plate containing the yellow, red, and brown powders, the rice and flowers, the pot of water—all of which are necessary for rites. Before him is a clay pot in which the ashes have now been placed. He pours the waters of the meeting rivers into the ashes, stating after the priest the precise place on earth where they are located and the business for which he has come, *Prayāg Trivenyām Mahātīrthe.* . . . "Here in the great *tīrtha* of Prayāga, at the Trivenī . . ." Gradually, into the pot go all the powders, the flowers, the water. He follows the priest in stating the purpose of this rite on behalf of his father, "in order that he might reach the world of heaven."

Following this vow of intention, the pilgrim and the small band of bare-chested men get into a boat, each with his clay pot. They take the ashes out into the Triveni for the *visarjana,* the immersion or "release" of the ashes. When they return to shore, they bathe in the river and then take their places once again for the *pinda pradāna.* It is a complex rite in which the Andhra pilgrim and his companions each lay out a checkerboard grid of small white rice balls on the ground before them. Each rice ball serves ritually to constitute part of a new, subtle, spiritual body for the pilgrim's deceased father. Finally, he gathers these rice balls into one and joins this large *pinda* with two other large *pindas*—one representing his grandfather and the other his great-grandfather. Wading out into the river, he places this symbolic, now reunited, family lineage into the sacred waters of the Triveni. Now the death rites are over and he performs the ritual bathing that follows these rites. "I bathe here in the Gangā, Yamunā, Sarasvatī," he says. His prayer concludes with the exclamation *Tīrtharāja Namostute!* "All praise to the king of *tīrthas!*"

These death rites are important at Prayāga because, as in Kāshī, death itself is said to lead to the greatest of spiritual rewards—the freedom of *moksha.* Here death has a positive religious value, and it is not surprising that those suffering from serious illness or those deep into old age might seek death in such a place. Many centuries ago, this was apparently a common practice. Pilgrims would undertake a pilgrimage called "the great going forth" (*mahāprasthānaka*), meaning the journey to one's death. They would intend to die or commit suicide at Prayāga. This must have been a practice of enough concern to provoke considerable discussion in the Purānas and the digests of dharma, the conclusion on the whole being that Tīrtharāja should not be sought as a place to deliberately end one's life.[73]

Kāshi, of course, is famous for death, with its renowned acclamation "Death in Kāshī is *mukti!*" Even today, many will come to the city to live out their old age until death comes. They are called Kāshīvāsīs, those who have made the vow to live in Kāshī until they die. There are regional hostels, or *dharmashālās,* as well as shops and restaurants there, catering to Bengalis, Tamils, and Gujaratis. There are teachers and teachings

all year round, enabling those who are Kāshīvasīs to hear the Bhagavad
Gītā or the *Rāmāyana*. For some, it is the place where they take the vows
of *sannyāsa,* becoming ascetic renouncers. For some, it is a protracted
retirement. For those who are critically ill, there are hospices where family members might bring them when the end is near. One of these, the
Kāshī Lābh Mukti Bhavan, operated by the Dalmia Charitable Trust,
provides the privacy of a simple room and perhaps a second room for the
family. They provide sacred tulsi leaves, Gangā water, and the sound of
kirtan, the singing of religious chants. It is an uncommon hospice, right
in the heart of a busy city, catering to a good death.[74]

In Kāshī, as elsewhere, it is important to die in a religious atmosphere,
hearing the name of God, or being reminded of the critical teachings of
the Gītā—that the eternal soul does not die when the body dies. But in
Kāshī there is the additional confidence that Shiva himself is present at
the time of death, teaching the clear wisdom that enables one to "cross
over" to the far shore of immortality. In Kāshī, it is never too late to learn
what is necessary for liberation.

The Seven Sacred Rivers

Because they traverse the land, rivers are the great connectors. The mind's
eye imagines the river's course and the places along the riverbank, all
linked through the river's flow. In her extensive investigation of the rivers of Maharashtra in western India, Anne Feldhaus demonstrates how
"Maharashtrians use rivers to conceptualize and experience regions."[75]
They bring their local deities from many villages to bathe them together
in the Krishnā River at Karad, for example. Or they carry waters from
the Godāvarī River to offer in the Shiva temples of their own villages
during the summer month of Shrāvana. In these river rites, people conceptualize, visualize, and enact their sense of the region. And, of course,
because rivers traverse regions, one to another, they also call to mind a
larger transregional reality.

By now it should be clear that India's rivers are not simply individual rivers, but are part of river systems, both topological and symbolic.
They are linked together in groups—the seven sacred rivers, the seven
sources of the Gangā, the seven mouths of the Godāvarī where it meets

the sea. They mingle in threes in the many *trivenīs*, or "triple-braids," where the waters of three rivers join in confluence. They are joined by the inter-referential symbolic language of their sources, confluences, and mouths. In mythic terms, rivers make a pilgrimage to one another's waters to relieve themselves of the burdens they have accumulated from pilgrims. In the systematic geography of India, natural emblems of divinity, like the rivers, are important not so much for their unique features as for their repeated features, which form an intricate, systemic whole.

One of the oldest groupings of Indian rivers is, surely, the five rivers of ancient India that eventually join the Indus—the Jhelum, the Chenab, the Ravi, the Beas, and the Sutlej. The Punjab in northwest India is, literally, the Land of the Five Rivers, though the courses of the five rivers are, today, primarily in Pakistan, as is the Indus itself. In the hymnody of the *Rig Veda*, we begin to see not only five rivers, but seven. There are seven "mother-rivers," or seven Sindhus, all called by the name of the mightiest, the Sindhu, also called the Indus.[76] The seven rivers in the Vedic world are identified with the "five rivers" of the Punjab, plus the Sindhu and the Sarasvatī. These rivers of northwest India flowed through the first land in which the Aryan singers of hymns lived. Before long the Gangā and the Yamunā Rivers of the great plains of central north India were incorporated into this group of seven. When Gangā mythology was elaborated, the notion of the seven divine rivers continued in the popular myth of her descent from heaven, in which the Gangā herself split into seven branches—three flowing east, three flowing west, and one, the Bhāgīrathī, flowing south into India. There were seven Gangās, watering not only India, but, in this vision of things, the whole inhabited earth.

As we have seen, the pattern of seven rivers is further developed in the world-atlas sections of the *Mahābhārata* and the Purānas; each island of the universe is imagined to have its seven sacred rivers. And so it is in Bhārata as well. The rivers are said to take their rise in the seven mountain ranges. Many rise in the Himalayas, the mountains described in the *Mahābhārata* and the *Mārkandeya Purāna* as having been stretched from sea to sea like the string of a bow.[77] Several have their mythic source in Lake Mānasa, a lake nestled at the foot of Mount Kailāsa, Shiva's mountain home in what is today Tibet. Two of these rivers, the Sindhu, or Indus, and the Brahmaputra, form the borders of ancient India, flowing respectively west and east from this plateau on the "rooftop of the world." Farther south, there are other mountains and other rivers. For example, the west-flowing Narmadā rises in what are called the Rik-sha Mountains; the east-flowing Godāvarī and Krishnā Rivers originate in the Sahya Mountains of the Western Ghāts. In the deep south, the Kāverī River rises in the southern Sahyas, or the Malaya Mountains, flowing eastward through Tamil country.[78]

The mountain-river pairing surely forms the basis of the particular group of rivers today called the *saptanadī*, the "seven rivers," which span India from north to south. These sacred rivers, today's heirs of the Vedic rivers, are sometimes called the seven Gangās: Gangā, Yamunā, Sindhu, Narmadā, Godāvarī, Krishnā, Kāverī.[79] It is this group of seven rivers that is invoked into ritual waters of Hindu worship all over India and, today, all over the world in the temples and homes of the Hindu diaspora. When a new temple or image is consecrated, whether in Chennai or in Chicago, the mantras containing the names of these seven rivers will be chanted and the cumulative waters of India poured out in sanctification.

The seven are not neatly related to the seven mountains, but that does not matter in the least. They are components of a living system, the specific parts of which have changed repeatedly and perhaps will change again, but the structure of which remains the same, and the purpose of which is to link the parts with an ordered whole coextensive with the universe itself. Indeed, many of the individual rivers of India are said to have been constituted by seven tributaries or to split into seven streams. Just as the Gangā is said to have seven tributaries, representing the waters that were dispersed as the heavenly river flowed through the tangled mass of Shiva's hair, so the Godāvarī River and, farther south, the Kāverī River are said to be sevenfold and to split into seven mouths as their deltas deliver their fresh waters into the Bay of Bengal. Indeed, the delta of the Indus as it meets the Arabian Sea is still called Sapta Sindhu, the seven Sindhus.

Indic civilization has long been river-conscious, and while we cannot explore all seven of the great rivers of India today, we can amplify our sense of the patterning of river lore by looking at the Yamunā, the Narmadā, the Godāvarī, and the Kāverī. Along with the Gangā, they are household names across India and deep resources for Hindu spirituality.

YAMUNĀ

The Yamunā River rises at Yamunotrī, "Source of the Yamunā," just over a range of mountains from Gangotrī.[80] Like the Gangā, the Yamunā is seen as a river of heaven, indeed the daughter of the Sun. She was brought to earth by the devoted penance of the Seven Sages, a legendary group of ancient seers. She fell atop a mountain called Kalinda, and today the river's true source is a glacier on Kalinda's mountain face. Thus, one of her names is Kālindī.

The first pool of Yamunā waters is a high and icy lake called Saptarishi Kund, named for the Seven Sages. From there, the mountain river tumbles toward Yamunotrī, where the cold stream mixes with the waters of a hot spring created, so they say, by the scorching rays of the Sun himself. The pools of the hot springs here, as at Badrīnāth across the Himalayas, vary in temperature. The Sun's Pool (Sūrya Kund) is said to be hot enough to boil rice. The Hot Pool (Tapta Kund) is perfect for the high-mountain bathing of weary pilgrims. Here at Yamunotrī, the goddess is worshipped in image form, both at the famous rock called Divya Shīla, the Divine Stone, and in the temple of Mā Yamunā. Like the Gangā, she is known as Mother. As at Gangotrī, her *mūrti* is taken down the mountain at the time of Divālī in the fall to be honored there during the snowy months. And, as with the Gangā, the living *mūrti* of the goddess—the Yamunā River herself—remains. The Yamunā, like the Gangā, is seen as a liquid goddess.

The Yamunā River flows out of the mountains at Dakpathar, where today a great dam halts the free-flowing water. In much-diminished form, the river eventually skirts the modern city of Delhi and then flows through the land sacred to the followers of Krishna, the land they call Braj. In Mathurā, on the night of Krishna's birth, according to myth, his father Vasudeva carried baby Krishna across the flood-swollen waters of the Yamunā River and entrusted him to foster parents in a village on the far shore. Krishna, now safe from immediate harm at the hands of a threatening king, grew up in the village lands bordering the Yamunā. Mathurā, Gokul, and Vrindāvan became holy lands, sanctified both by the waves of the Yamunā and the footsteps of young Krishna. As a boy, Krishna roamed with his cowherd friends by the banks of the Yamunā.

As a youth, Krishna played his flute and called the milkmaid girls to dance by night, and in the waters of the Yamunā, they bathed together by moonlight.

The river becomes, here, the emblem of divine love, mutually shared. Just as Lord Krishna is said to be naturally present in the very stones of Mount Govardhan and in the very dust of Vrindāvan, so his beloved is said to be present here as the Yamunā River. Nature itself—land and river—are the icons of Krishna's presence. Krishna is himself the very mountain, and his beloved is herself the very river coursing through the land. The hymn of eight verses in praise of the Yamunā sung by devotees and pilgrims compares Yamunā to the Gangā. Like the Gangā, she carries the waters of purification. But the Yamunā carries something else that is quite distinctive: the waters of love. Only after the Gangā merges with Yamunā at Prayāga does Gangā come to enjoy the love of Lord Krishna, so they say.

NARMADĀ

Walking through the small town of Amarakantaka at the headwaters of the River Narmadā early in the morning, pilgrims hail one another with the greeting *Narmade!* "Praise to the Narmadā!" The Narmadā, like the Gangā, is both goddess and river, and her praises are extensive in the Purānas. Several verses are so well known they will be found in virtually every source:

> *The Gangā is sacred at Kankhala, the Sarasvatī at Kurukshetra,*
> *But the Narmadā is sacred all along her banks, in the forests as well as*
> *　　in the places of habitation.*
> *The waters of the Sarasvatī purify one in the course of five days, those*
> *　　of the Yamunā in seven days, of the Gangā instantaneously, and of*
> *　　the Narmadā at the mere sight of it.*[81]

The Narmadā is one of India's most beautiful, fascinating, and, today, controversial rivers. Because it is considered sacred all along its banks, the Narmadā is the one river in India with a prescribed pilgrimage of *pari-*

krama or *pradakshina*, circumambulation. The source is at Amarakantaka in the green and forested Maikala Hills of east central India. The river then flows westward across the whole breadth of India, emptying into the Gulf of Cambay in the Arabian Sea. This is the pilgrimage route—the circumambulation of the entire river! The eighteen-hundred-mile pilgrimage can begin anywhere, but pilgrims walk the entire length of the river, almost nine hundred miles, keeping the water to their right side. They walk westward, the direction of the Narmadā's flow, on the south bank all the way to the mouth of the river and then eastward toward the source at Amarakantaka on the north bank. The entire pilgrimage journey takes more than three years on foot, and many pilgrims today take the journey in sections, returning each year to the place they left off the previous year.[82] The Narmadā *parikrama* pilgrimage is one of the many casualties of the ongoing Narmadā Valley Development Project of dam building, sponsored initially by the World Bank and then by the Government of India. If most of the thirty dams of the project are completed, the course of the river and its multitude of temples and *tīrthas* will be changed forever, some of them submerged and some two hundred thousand people displaced. The intense controversy over thus project has been ongoing for more than two decades now.[83]

Perhaps because of the Narmadā River pilgrimage, the *tīrthas* along the river are numerous and the detail that is lavished upon them in the *māhātmyas* is extraordinary. No other river, not even the Gangā, has such a detailed accounting of all the holy places along its banks. "One hundred million *tīrthas* are said to lie between the confluence of the Narmadā (with the sea) and Amarakantaka (the source), and *rishis* reside in each of them."[84] The pilgrimage is also detailed in today's publications, like the *Shrī Narmadā Pradakshina* of Swami Omkārānanda Giri.[85] His Hindi guidebook of more than one hundred pages includes section maps of the route, hymns and songs of praise to the Narmadā, stories from the popular scriptural tradition, and a sequential narrative of all the places along the river. He begins at the most important *tīrtha* along the river, Omkāreshvara, the island shrine of Shiva about halfway along the river's course, then travels eastward along the northern bank to the source at Amarakantaka, all along the south bank to the *sangam* with the sea, and then back to Omkāreshvara. A sample of the account reads like many of the geographical sections of the Purānas: "From Kunar Sangam about six miles on is Sītābātika Tīrtha, also called Mother Sītā. It is said that here the great Rishi Vālmīki did *tapas*. When Sītā came to live here along with her boys, Kusha and Lava, the Sage Vasishtha and his wife Arundhatī came too, seeing that they were here. Then, in order to protect Mother Sītā, sixty-four *yoginīs* and fifty-two *bhairavas* came. In order to meet Sītā, the goddess Narmadā herself came. This is a very beautiful place, with waterfalls, with pools named for Sītā, Lakshmana, and Rāma. Here by doing *tapas,* big and difficult diseases are made well."[86] And so it continues, every three or four miles a *tīrtha,* a story, a benefit. There are 123 *tīrthas* before reaching Amarakantaka, and 481 on the whole circuit.

Like the Gangā, the Narmadā is said to be divine in origin. The local *māhātmyas* describe Narmadā's *avatarana* as she tumbles from the head of Lord Shiva to earth.[87] The Narmadā, like the Gangā, is intimately associated with Shiva and is often said to flow from his divine body. According to one myth, Shiva himself performed *tapas* on Mount Riksha, and his perspiration washed the face of the mountain, forming a holy river.[88] In popular parlance today, the Narmadā is said to come from *Shankar ke pasina,* the "sweat of Shiva." So created, the Narmadā is referred to as the daughter of Shiva, just as Gangā is known as his co-wife.[89] Narmadā is said to be a *brahmachārinī,* a celibate and pure woman.

Popular *māhātmyas* today elaborate the story: The sweat that fell from Lord Shiva was a great cascading waterfall; and the waterfall became the beautiful lady Narmadā. She immediately began to worship Shiva. When he offered her a boon, she said, "I ask a boon for all creatures: that I may remain immortal to destroy the sins of the world, even in the time when you destroy the earth with your *tāndava* dance. Give the greatness that Gangā has in the north to me in the south. Let there be no difference between me and Gangā. Thus, whoever bathes in my waters on Makara Sankrānti will receive the benefit of bathing in all the *tīrthas* of India. And whoever dies on my banks, having worshipped you, will receive *moksha.*"[90] Shiva grants her this boon and sends her on her way, leaping and flowing toward the places we now know as Jabalpur, Omkāreshvara, and Bharuch, and to the sea at Revā Sāgara Sangama.

In another story, King Pururava asked the brahmins in his court how people could be freed of sin in the absence of elaborate sacrificial rites, too expensive and complex for today's world. The brahmins told him that the

Narmadā destroyed sins and if she were to come from heaven to earth it would be a blessing for all people. So the king performed severe asceticism and eventually won the favor of Shiva. As a boon, the king asked for the Narmadā River to come to earth. Shiva gained Narmadā's assent and then got the support of eight mountains, sons of the Vindhya, who agreed to hold her. The myth obviously gestures toward the tale of Gangā's descent in the Himalayas. So it was that Narmadā came to earth to relieve people of their sins in this era of darkness. Everything she touched, everywhere she ran, became pure—the mountains, the villages, the jungles, and the ashrams all along her banks, all the way to the sea.[91]

In another popular tale of the Narmadā, the gods complained to Vishnu that they themselves were loaded down with the burden of people's sins. Vishnu took the matter to Shiva, who mercifully removed the crescent moon from his hair and shook from it a drop of *amrita*, the nectar of immortality, which fell down upon the earth. From that drop appeared a beautiful maiden, blue as a lotus leaf. She bowed to Shiva and praised him, asking what she might do for him. He sent her out to flow upon the earth, to lift the burden of sins borne by the gods. Even more, he promised that in her waters there would be stones to be worshipped for one's heart's desires.[92] This is but one of a multitude of stories told about the famous *bāna lingas* found at certain places in the waters of the Narmadā. These smooth, elliptical, river-polished stones are said to be natural manifestations (*svarūpas*) of Shiva and are the most prized of Shiva *lingas*. They do not need to be consecrated for worship, for they are already sacred. As the saying goes, "Narmadā's stones (*kankar*) are Shiva Shankar." These *bāna lingas,* in their various sizes, colorations, and markings, may be found in markets selling religious goods all along the Narmadā and, indeed, all over India.

Today in the hill country of the Maikala range, the home of the tribal Gonds, Amarakantaka is a popular pilgrimage place. There in the thick forest is the grove called Maī kī Bagīya, "Mother's Garden," where a small well is said to be the actual source of the Narmadā. From there, the rivulet is said to go underground. A short distance away is the official Narmadā Udgam, the "Rise of the Narmadā," a temple compound and tank. This is the commonly visited and acknowledged source. The temple is called Narmadā Mandir and the tank Koti Tīrtha, the "Ten Million Tīrthas."

The shrine of Shrī Narmadā is to the right as one enters the temple. She is of black stone with a silver crown on her head, standing on a lotus, wearing a blue printed sari, with garlands of red flowers and gold tinsel. Worshippers offer her a split coconut, white candy *prasād,* and incense, pouring a pot of water on the steps just inside her sanctum. They honor Shiva and Pārvatī across the entry in a facing shrine, and then proceed to pour lustrations of water on all the other subsidiary shrines of the temple—the *linga* of Shiva as Amarakanta Mahādeva, a white marble image of Pārvatī, and images of Rāma, Sītā, and Lakshmana. In the tank holding the springwaters of the Narmadā is another Shiva *linga,* this one called Narmadeshvara, located underwater in the tank itself and reachable only by wading out into the waters. Here also is Gomukh Kund, a gesture toward the high Himalayan source, and just across the road is Trivenī Kund, where three rivers, here the Narmadā, Gāyatrī, and Sāvitrī, are said to join.

Another river that rises within a mile of the Narmadā's source is the Sone River, one of two important "male" rivers in India, the other being the Brahmaputra. The Narmadā and the Sone flow in opposite directions, while a smaller stream, the Jvālā, also begins here, joining the Narmadā not far from her source. The source of these two rivers is mentioned in the account of the *tīrthas* of India as given in the *Mahābhārata.*[93] In the Purānas, a legend is told about the two rivers, a story linked to Narmadā's life as a *brahmachārinī.* Hear it in the words of Geoffrey Maw, an English Quaker, who lived by the Narmadā for forty years:

A marriage, it is said, had been arranged between Son and Narmadā, but Narmadā, a traditional Indian bride, had never seen the groom. Being curious, she sent her little friend Jwālā, the barber's daughter, to find out what he looked like. Son saw the beautiful little girl approaching, supposed her to be the bride, and gave orders for the marriage ceremonies to begin. The goddess Narmadā was deeply offended, and turning her back on Son she dashed away over rocks and precipices, north and then west, forming rapids and waterfalls which still resound with her displeasure. Son, the rejected suitor, flung himself over a high cliff, and flowed east and north east to join the Gangā on her way to the Bay of Bengal.[94]

At pilgrimage places all along the river, the goddess Narmadā is honored—as both river and *mūrti*. At Chandod in Gujarat, for example, hundreds of miles seaward, the river is wide and deep, with a sweep of broad steps descending to the river's edge. There a temple of Narmadā Devī sits at the top of the *ghāt* steps, with a white marble image of Narmadā Devī inside, elaborately dressed and flanked by two images of Shiva—Narmadeshvara and Omkāreshvara, the latter being the most famous of the Shiva shrines along the riverbank upstream, in central Madhya Pradesh. We will return to Omkāreshvara, the famous island shrine in the Narmadā, in our discussion of the great sanctuaries of Shiva.

GODĀVARĪ

The Godāvarī rises in the Western Ghāts of Maharashtra not far from the city of Nāsik and flows eastward across the whole of India, emptying into the Bay of Bengal. The source of the Godāvarī is high in the dry hills above the *jyotirlinga* of Tryambaka. The hike up the hillside is steep, and a group of brightly turbaned Rajasthani pilgrims, walking sticks in hand, struggles under the baking sun of midmorning. On top of the hill, there is a grove of trees and a well said to be the first rising of Godāvarī Devī. Here, too, as in the Himalayas, the Gaṅgā is said to have descended from heaven to earth, this time at the request of the sage Gautama. The river is called Gaṅgā Godāvarī and Dakshinā Gaṅgā, the "Gaṅgā of the South," although we have just learned that the Narmadā made a bid to be the Gaṅgā for the people of the south when she agreed to come to earth. At the source of the Godāvarī, however, we are told that south of the Vindhya Mountains, the Gaṅgā is called Gautamī, while north of the Vindhyas she is called Bhāgīrathī.[95] Whereas Bhāgīrathī Gaṅgā's descent was to bring life to the dead ancestors of Bhagīratha, Godāvarī's mission was to expunge the worst of sins, specifically the killing of a cow. Because she came to aid the sage Gautama, she is also called Gautamī, and sometimes Gautamī Gaṅgā.[96]

According to the story, the other sages were envious of Gautama's prosperity during a time of drought. After all, Gautama had a deep well, seemingly inexhaustible, from which to water his fields. The sages decided to get rid of Gautama by inducing him to commit a serious sin. They placed a cow in his ashram, and as the cow nibbled its way into the granary, Gautama tried to turn it aside by striking it with a rod made of *kusha* grass, a gentle rod to be sure. Even so, the cow died from the blows of Gautama. Now, cow-killing is among the worst of sins in India, so Gautama undertook severe austerities in penance and then received a boon from Lord Shiva: The Gangā would flow into his ashram in order to purify him. So here in western Maharashtra, the Gangā descended to earth, taking the form of the Godāvarī River, also called the Gautamī.[97]

In another version of the story, when the Gangā came to earth and Lord Shiva held her in his hair and kept her there, Pārvatī became jealous and thought up a ruse to get the river out of Shiva's hair. She sent her servant Jayā to earth as a cow and sent her into Gautama's ashram. He chased away the cow with a fistful of sacred grass, but it died of the blows. Pārvatī's emissary Ganesha told Gautama that only the waters of the Gangā would provide absolution from the sin of killing a cow. So Gautama went to the top of Brahmāgiri Mountain and practiced severe penance. Shiva was pleased and offered him a boon. Of course, Gautama chose to have the waters of the Gangā come to his ashram. She did not really want to go, but Shiva loosed his tangled hair to fall upon the mountain, separated the Gangā from his hair, and left her there.

Today pilgrims climb to the top of Brahmāgiri, the steep, broad-topped hill where the Godāvarī is said to have landed upon earth. There a deep well contains the first springs of Godāvarī Gangā's presence. A short distance away is a shrine housing nothing more than a long, rippling outcropping of rock, said to be the very hair of Shiva, upon which the Godāvarī fell. Down the hill in a cliff-side cave shrine is Gangādvāra, the "Door of the Gangā," where the springs are accessible to pilgrims. At the base of the cliff is Chakra Tīrtha, where the water pools into a tank where pilgrims can bathe in Godāvarī waters for the first time.

According to the local legend, Gangā was very displeased to find herself separated from her Lord. She disappeared, they say, and went underground to the netherworlds, Pātāla. Again, Gautama performed fierce penance and won a boon, this time from Vishnu. Vishnu struck a blow with his discus, and created a *tīrtha* into which he brought the Gangā back from Pātāla. This is today's Chakra Tīrtha, a popular place for ritual bathing. From this great tank, the Godāvarī flows on her way.[98]

Gangādvāra, the "Door of the Gangā" in Maharashtra

The first stop of the Godāvarī on her eastward journey across India is Nāsik, only ten miles away, where the river flows through what was called the Dandaka Forest in the *Rāmāyana*. Nāsik was then called Panchavatī, famous for its ashrams. And it was to Panchavatī that Rāma, Sītā, and Lakshmana came on their forest sojourn, settling here on the advice of the sage Agastya. According to popular lore, the place came to be called Nāsik, "the Nose," because it was here that Lakshmana cut off the nose of the hag Shūrpanakhā, who tried to get Lakshmana to marry her. That, of course, was not the end of it, since Shūrpanakhā's brother was the *asura* Rāvana, who took revenge for the insult to his sister by kidnapping Sītā from the forest hut in which the three exiles were living. Everyone knows the story of how Rāvana created the illusion of a golden spotted deer, how Rāma gave chase with his bow, how Lakshmana and

Sītā heard what seemed to be his cry for help, and how Lakshmana ran into the forest after Rāma. Then, while Sītā was alone, Rāvana came and abducted her.

In Nāsik, the Godāvarī River is diverted into a series of tanks and pools, connected by cement and stone walkways and embankments. The river is effectively tamed and brought to the people. Stories linking the place to the *Rāmāyana* abound. The pools are variously called Rāma Kund, Lakshmana Kund, and the sweeping Dhanusha Kund, named for Rāma's bow. Pools are also named for Sītā and Hanumān. Here along the river, they say, Rāma, Sītā, and Lakshmana used to bathe. And here, at Rāma Kund, so the legend goes, Rāma performed his father's rites. It is an important place for the *asthi visarjana* rites even today, as pilgrims come to place the bones and ashes of the deceased into the waters.

It is at Rāma Kund that the Simhastha bathing *melā* takes place every twelve years, the most recent beginning in late July of 2003 and continuing for one year. Millions of pilgrims crowd into Nāsik for this "Half-Kumbha." Every evening in quieter times, the waters of Rāma Kund are honored with the lighted lamps of *āratī*. Small leaf boats containing a stiff cotton wick rolled in ghee are floated out upon the waters. As the sky becomes dark, the pool is covered with bobbing lights. At the edge of Rāma Kund there are temples to the goddess waters in image form, such as the Shrī Gangā Godāvarī Temple housing the image and footprints of Gangā. Everyone will attest that Godāvarī here *is* Gangā, and the story of Gautama's penance to bring the river here to Brahmāgiri is well known.

In the course of her journey 650 miles eastward, the Godāvarī is said to divide into seven streams, like the Gangā. When the river approaches the eastern coast of India, it forms an expansive delta, and each of the seven rivers is named for one of the seven sages of ancient India.

KĀVERĪ

In Coorg country, near Mercara in the hills of western Karnataka, rises the Kāverī River. Coorg is a green, green fertile land, famous for its honey, cardamom, coffee, pepper, bananas, and papayas. The source of the Kāverī is called Talakāverī and demonstrates, as we have come to expect, that the headwaters of India's rivers are not simply beautiful destinations for the hiker or tourist, but shrines for the pilgrim. The high road to the Kāverī's headwaters, completed only in the 1950s, climbs past a glistening wall of stone, flowers, and mosses wet with the seepage of springwaters. The site of the source itself is a finely made stone masonry tank, some thirty feet long, with a long flight of steps leading down to the water on two sides. The first water of the wellspring deep below rises in this bathing tank. At the water's edge is a small shrine of the goddess river at the very place from which the waters of the Kāverī come forth, marked BIRTHPLACE OF KĀVERĪ.

While the birth of the Kāverī is celebrated at this deep mountain well, the stories of her arrival participate in the wider river-goddess mythology. According to the legend of the Purānas, this river is a liquid form of the goddess Vishnumayā, who was asked by Vishnu to become a river of blessing as well as the wife of the sage Agastya. This goddess, compliant, took form as the virtuous woman Lopamudrā, Agastya's wife, and when the sage learned of a severe drought in south India, she assumed the form of water and he brought her here to the south in his small brass water pot. Remember that Agastya is often credited with bringing the riches of the north to the south. In this case, his liquefied wife, a river. Here on this high hill, Agastya set down the water pot and it was overturned by the wind, or perhaps by a crow, or perhaps by Ganesha. In any case, Kāverī ran rapidly down the hills, watering the land as she went.

In a related account, it is said that Agastya practiced spiritual austerities in the Himalayas and Lord Shiva granted him a boon—that the pure waters of Kailāsa would accompany him in his water pot wherever he went. Then Shiva asked Agastya a favor—to travel south and tame the pride of the Vindhya Mountains, which had grown up incredibly high in order to challenge the height of the Himalayas. So high were the Vindhyas that they had blocked the course of the sun, and the sun was scorching the earth. Agastya obediently took off toward the Vindhya Mountains. Seeing the renowned sage coming, the mountains bowed deeply at his feet and asked how they could serve him. Agastya asked them to do one thing: remain in that posture until he returned from the south, which he never did. Agastya traveled on south to the high reaches of the Sahya Mountains. There, while he practiced his austerities, the gods, worried about the drought, knocked over his water pot and released the waters from Kailāsa to run upon the parched south.

The Kāverī rises very near the western coast of India. Indeed from the high hill above its source, one has a vista of the entire Coorg range and, on a good day, the sea. But from Coorg, the river flows all the way across southern India eastward. As it descends through the hills of Coorg and begins the long journey across Karnataka and Tamil Nadu, the first town it reaches is Bhagamandala, just at the base of the mountain. The first *sangams* of the river are near Bhagamandala, in bright green meadowlands brilliant with paddies, where the newborn Kāverī joins with the Hemavatī and the Kanakavatī Rivers, said to be her two childhood friends joining her for the journey eastward to her husband, the sea. The Kāverī flows on eastward for 475 miles and, in the course of this run, encircles three major islands, each of which houses a great shrine of Lord Vishnu sleeping on the serpent Shesha. There is Adirangam, east of Mysore, where the temple of Shrīrangapattanam stands; Madhyarangam with the temple of Shivasamudram; and finally, the famous island of Shrīrangam where one of south India's most renowned temples of Vishnu stands.

THE MULTIPLE DESCENT OF RIVERS

We cannot begin to explore the multitude of India's rivers, but it is clear that in every region the rivers share much of the implicit and often explicit symbolic and narrative structure we have described. In Gujarat, for instance, it is said that just as Bhagīratha's *tapas* brought the Gangā to the Himalayas, the *tapas* of a sage named Satyadhama brought the Gangā to Mount Girnār. In Rajasthan, the Sabarmati River flowing from the Aravalli Hills is said to have had its origin when the ascetic Kāshyapa performed *tapas* on Mount Arbuda, known today as Mount Abu. Lord Shiva was pleased with his asceticism and gave him the River Gangā, which fell from his tangled hair down upon Arbuda and then became the Sabarmati, which like the Gangā is said to have split into seven streams.

Anne Feldhaus's extensive work on the rivers of Maharashtra provides evidence of the ways in which rivers create a cultural and regional landscape. Five rivers radiate into the region from the Mahābaleshvara Temple on top of the Sahyādri Mountains. Two of these rivers flow westward down the steep hills into the sea, three flow east and southeast into the Deccan and toward the Bay of Bengal. The Krishnā is the largest and most renowned of these rivers, but the Gangā is said to come here too, once every twelve years. The whole Mahābaleshvara Temple complex also has the name Panchagangā, the "Five Gangās." Here in Maharashtra, the five rivers create a sense of the region.

Throughout Maharashtra, Feldhaus demonstrates the relation between the mountain shrines of Shiva and the origin of the divine rivers. For example, at Bhīmashankara, another of the great Shiva *lingas,* the Bhīma River rises, said to have sprung from the perspiration of Lord Shiva as he took rest, having destroyed the Triple City of Tripurāsura. Most of the regional rivers are said to originate on hilltops identified with Shiva and a Shiva *linga.* Pouring water upon the Shiva *linga* recapitulates ritually the falling of the rivers from heaven. The associations of rivers and mountains, goddess waters and Shiva *lingas,* do not belong only to those who have access to Sanskrit texts or their popular Marathi *māhātmyas;* they are also embedded in local culture. Feldhaus writes, "The associations and images also belong to people whose prestige is purely local and whose learning is based on traditions not found in Sanskrit texts."[99] In their water-carrying rituals, for example, people of countless villages converge at Paithan on the bank of the Godāvarī River and carry the sacred waters home in pots slung over their shoulders at the ends of long poles, to pour it over their own Shiva *lingas.* "The water carrying rituals dramatize that the river serves to unite the scattered villages and to make them into a region, a discrete area defined by the river that runs through it. By fetching and pouring water onto the gods of their villages throughout the region, the men who carry the water make the region itself imaginatively visible."[100]

THE USES AND ABUSES OF THE GANGĀ

In the fall of 1983, three great truck caravans bearing enormous eight-foot-high vessels of water from Gangotrī, crisscrossed India from north to south and from east to west. These three great journeys were called *yātrās*, and carried with them the symbolic freight of pilgrimages. There were, simultaneously, eighty-nine *upayātrās*, or subsidiary journeys. All in all, they brought the waters of the sacred Gaṅgā to millions of people in villages all over India. People from every village and district joined in the *yātrā* processions, walking for a few miles or for a few days behind the trucks bearing Gaṅgā water. And, of course, people gathered in each halting place, coming from the surrounding villages to fill their small bottles with Gaṅgā water to carry home. And each village added its own local water to the vessels of Gaṅgā water, for any water mixed with the Gaṅgā becomes the Gaṅgā.

These *yātrās*, like the famous *chār dhām yātrā*, the "pilgrimage of the four directions," linked the directional compass points of India—north, south, east, and west. One truck moved southward through India from Pashupatināth in Nepal to Rāmeshvara in the Tamil south; another carried its huge vessel of sacred water from Hardvār on the fringes of the Himalayas in the north to Kanyākumārī at land's end in the south; the third crossed India from Gaṅgā Sāgara at the mouth of the Gaṅgā in Bengal to Somnāth, the famous Shiva temple on the coast of Gujarat in Saurashtra. Along the way the procession moved to the tape-recorded chant of *Hara Hara Gange!* "Victory to Mother Gaṅgā!" The entire rite of pan-Indian solidarity was called the Ekātmatā Yagna—the "Rite of Unity."[101]

The sponsor of this "rite of integration" as they called it, the Vishva Hindu Parishad, had shrewdly taken as its symbol the one unifying image to which all Hindus and, in some ways, all Indians of every tradition, could respond: the River Gaṅgā.[102] This was the opening action of a movement that would launch a new form of Hindu nationalism into the political arena. In the subsequent decade, that movement came to focus on the restoration of the site said to have been the birthplace of Lord Rāma in Ayodhyā—a site upon which there stood a mosque that had been there since the sixteenth century. The turbulence that surrounded the movement to destroy the mosque and rebuild a temple at the birthplace of Rāma is well known. But the movement began a decade earlier, and it began with the evocative use of the symbolic power of the Gaṅgā. This rite, linking the country by Gaṅgā water, made quite clear the ways in which this symbolic power might be negotiable as contemporary currency. There are few things on which Hindu India, diverse as it is, speaks with one voice as clearly as it does on Gaṅgā Mātā. The river carries an immense cultural and religious significance for Hindus, no matter what part of the subcontinent they call home, no matter what their sectarian leaning might be. As one Hindi author writes, "Even the most hardened atheist of a Hindu will find his heart full of feelings he has never before felt when for the first time he reaches the bank of the Gaṅgā."[103] Or, we might add, when the Gaṅgā reaches him. The use of Gaṅgā water to evoke sentiments of unity among people of diverse regions and multiple Hindu traditions should be wholly benign. After all, this is a symbol that bears only beneficence, only the brimming water pot and the lotus, no weapons, nothing threatening or fearsome.

And yet the movement launched by using the Gaṅgā in this way has ultimately abused the symbolic embrace of the river with a rhetoric that made the river of India a symbol of Hindu chauvinism. Perhaps more important in the long run, the Hindu nationalist movement that has used the symbolism of the Gaṅgā so effectively has scarcely addressed the *real* issue facing the Gaṅgā and India's other sacred rivers: the crisis of pollution, damming, and river degradation. As Kelly Alley, an anthropologist who has worked on issues and attitudes on river pollution in India, writes, "In the current period, movements for reclaiming sacred spaces reproduce models of religious mobilization that successfully use religious symbols for political effect, yet leaders have not transferred the dynamism of these movements into environmental programs to save or clean Gaṅgā."[104]

POLLUTION AND THE SACRED RIVERS

In this chapter, we have explored India's rivers as they are lauded and storied in Hindu literature and ritual. We have seen many ways in which the Gaṅgā and other rivers become the place where people deposit the sins and spiritual impurities they have accumulated over the years. Bathing at the water's edge as part of a daily rite of prayer is one of the most basic and widespread aspects of Hindu religiousness. The temple-side bathing tanks and the multitude of rivers all gather their load of human sins and, so they say, repair to the Gaṅgā to bathe in her waters. Even the *tīrthas* need to be purified, having taken on so many of the impurities of the prayerful faithful who bathe in them.

That rivers become impure and burdened with the load of human sin is evident today in a more material and visible way than ever before. Anyone can see that India's rivers are used, overused, and abused. The burden of sin they bear includes the enormous load of pollution that threatens to choke the life out of the great rivers. The uncontrolled flood of sewage and industrial waste pouring into the rivers, including the Gaṅgā, has created the worst environmental crises confronting India today. More than 600 million people live in the area of north India watered by the Gaṅgā and its tributaries. As the river passes through a dozen cities with populations over one hundred thousand, some 80 percent of the urban waste goes directly into the river.

Even at Hardvār, one of the first of these cities, where the river enters the plains, the Uttarākhand Environment Conservation and Pollution Control Board registered the coliform levels as completely unacceptable, even for bathing. The levels, they say, should be less than 50 for drinking purposes, below 500 for bathing, and below 5,000 even for agricultural usage, but the level at Hardvār in 2007 was 5,500.[105] The board estimated that 89 million liters of sewage poured into the Gaṅgā daily from its source to the point at which it reached Hardvār. Flowing across the plains, past industrial cities like Kanpur, the river accumulated an ever-increasing burden of human and industrial waste, including untreated chemicals and pesticides.

The Yamunā, too, is choked with pollution, and its flow is so attenuated that there is no opportunity for the river to recover. Water is extracted, and untreated waste flows into the river. An official of the Central Pollution Control Board told David Haberman, "The Yamunā is the most polluted river in India, at least the five hundred kilometer stretch from Delhi to the Chambal confluence. There is no other river in India carrying this much pollution load."[106] Sunita Narain of the Centre for Science and Environment reported in 2007, "What is happening to the Yamunā is reflective of what is happening in almost every river in India. The Yamunā is dead, we just haven't officially cremated it yet."[107] Here, too, the primary issue is sewage, tons of untreated sewage and industrial waste not only killing the rivers, but killing people who depend on the rivers for drinking water. Neither sewage treatment plants nor water treatment plants are up to the task.

The dissonance between the sacredness of India's great rivers and the pollution of human and industrial waste is one that has been explored by both scholars and activists. Religious leaders, environmental activists, and political activists have different vocabularies in which to conceptualize both the problem and the solution. Kelly Alley and David Haberman, who have studied the degradation of the Gangā and Yamunā respectively, have found, quite independently, that there is considerable resistance among the faithful, the priests, and the religious leaders to saying plainly and simply that the rivers are impure. They make a distinction between *shuddhtā* (purity) and *svacchatā* (cleanness) as well as between *pavitratā* (purity) and *gandagi* (dirtiness). In her research in the heart of Banāras, at Dasāshvamedha Ghāt, where thousands of residents and pilgrims come for ritual bathing every day, Kelly Alley found that it is hard to deny the dirtiness. "On Dasāshvamedha Ghāt, while pilgrims perform ablutions, others wash clothes with soap, a *pandā* spits, an old woman 'does latrine' on a corner of the *ghāt* (for lack of public facilities), and urban sewage flows into the river under the *ghāt* floor. *Gandagi* surrounds the people seeking purification."[108]

So how is this degeneracy understood, right in the heart of one of the greatest cities on the Gangā? According to scientific and environmental assessments, it is human and industrial waste that has led to the ecological degeneracy of the river, but for the residents and religious practitioners of Dasāshvamedha, the abuse of the river is a sign of the moral degeneracy of the age, the corruption and immoral behavior of humans. It signals the corruption of the age itself. The inability to create workable sanitation and sewage treatment facilities, the lack of public respect and engagement, the corruption of government officials—these are the issues. Scientists lace their analyses with terms like "biological oxygen demand" (BOD) and "fecal coliform count" (FCC). The religious emphasize the competition, cheating, and wholesale materialism of our time that have led people to disrespect the Gangā. They are both discourses of degeneracy, but they often talk past each other in idioms that are mutually unintelligible. For some the river crisis is about "resource management," and for others it is about the saving power and grace of the river. They see the river through different lenses, they do not trust each other's efforts or goals, and they do not have confidence in each other's bureaucracies. As Alley writes, "Eulogies to Gangā and worship of *gangājala* are central sacred symbols in pilgrimages and in *pūjā*, but they do not describe *gangājala* as a finite resource whose contours are shaped by a larger ecosystem."[109]

Among those who bridge these discourses is Virabhadra Mishra, the *mahant,* or chief priest, of Sankat Mochan Temple as well as a professor of hydrology at Banāras Hindu University. For his entire life he has lived along the Gangā at Tulsī Ghāt, the site where the great Tulsīdās himself was said to have lived in the sixteenth century. "There is a struggle and turmoil inside my heart. I want to take a holy dip. I need it to live. A day does not begin for me without the holy dip. But, at the same time, I know what is BOD and I know what is fecal coliform."[110] Mishra launched the Sankat Mochan Foundation and the Svaccha Gangā Campaign to "clean the Gangā," bringing together scientific concerns with religious discourse: respecting Mother Gangā and her purity by not fouling her waters with dirtiness, again making use of the significant conceptual difference between sacral purity and cleanness. The river is sacred and as such is considered pure, and it is on the basis of that faith and conviction that the filth of untreated sewage, drain water, industrial waste, and trash must be halted. As Mishra puts it, "The main motivation for environmental work in India is religion." If one hopes to make real progress, one cannot simply dissociate an environmental crisis from religious discourse, but rather the very language of the purity of Mother Gangā must be employed to raise the alarm and to raise consciousness. "If you go to the people who have a living relationship with Gangā and you say, 'Gangā is polluted, the water is dirty,' they will say, 'Stop saying that. Gangā is not polluted. You are abusing the river.' But if you say, 'Gangā is our mother. Come and see what is being thrown on the body of your mother—sewage and filth. Should we tolerate sewage being smeared on the body of our Mother?' you will get a very different reaction, and you can harness that energy."[111]

Harnessing that energy has been the goal not only of the Svaccha Gangā movement but also of people's movements concerned with the degradation of the Yamunā. The Friends of Vrindāvan, for instance, addresses specifically the local issues of refuse and sewage as the river flows through the holy land of Lord Krishna, past Vrindāvan, a busy pilgrimage town where Krishna is said to have lived as a child and youth, and the *ghāts* of Mathurā, where he rested after defeating the wicked king Kamsa. As we have seen, the Yamunā River is understood to be a *svarūpa*, an "embodied form" of the divine. One after another, devotees told David Haberman, "Yamunā is polluted because people see her as something ordinary. They are not aware of her as Yamunā-jī. They are not aware of her *svarūpa*."[112] However, as Haberman notes, if we look only at the transcendent aspect of the river, we undermine the urgent necessity of addressing the filth and pollution of the physical river, and if we look only at the filth and pollution, we lose the capacity to see the deepest meaning of the river. We need to have both eyes open to Yamunā, who is "concurrently a goddess and a (now polluted) river."[113] One eye must continue to be trained on the infinite, the "transcendent dimension of divinity that is beyond the contingency of everyday life." The other eye, however, must focus on "the small, the fragile, the ever-changing tangible and precious world that is right before our eyes." Both will be important for effective environmental activism in a land flowing with sacred, but choking, rivers.

This is not wishful thinking, but "deep ecology," recognizing the interrelatedness of the worlds of nature and the human. Haberman cites a boatman whose wisdom on the matter is arresting: "The power (*shakti*) of the river does not become less with pollution, but because of the pollution our access to it has become less. We can't see clearly because the filth gets in our eyes."[114]

The dissonance between the unique significance of sacred rivers and the awful reality of rivers streaming with sewage and choked with waste poses a dilemma for India that cannot be understood or solved without resorting to sophisticated religious as well as scientific understanding. There is arguably no place in the world that should have a higher standard of river quality than India, for there is no other culture in which rivers have such a central role in the daily ritual lives of countless millions. There is no other place in the world where worshippers and pilgrims repair daily to the great rivers and the river fords to bathe, sip water, and make water offerings for the departed. The web of India's rivers constitutes one of the most important religious theaters of the nation, so the crisis of environmental degradation is not only environmental. It is a cultural and theological crisis. It is not a matter of tradition that will somehow disappear with the onset of modernity. Polluted or not, India's rivers are as busy as ever.

It will surely require the best efforts of technological experts, environmentally committed activists, and religious leadership to solve this critical problem. Yet there seems to be all too little dialogue between those who make the plans for dams, hydroelectric power, and treatment plants and those who recognize the ongoing ways in which the rivers are and will continue to be utilized for religious life. Pollution is not the only issue. There is a water crisis in the Punjab, the ancient land of the Five Rivers, as subsoil water tables shrink to record levels. The building of a hydroelectric dam along the waters of the upper Indus River has added yet another dimension to the tense relations between India and Pakistan, since Pakistan's large irrigation system depends on waters that flow first through the mountains of Indian Kashmir. A treaty negotiated in 1960 divides the river waters between the two nations, but the demands for both power and water have grown on both sides over the decades. Farther south, the dams along the sacred Narmadā River have displaced thousands of people and threaten to turn the great waterway of central India into a series of long lakes if all thirty dams ever come to completion. The Himalayan dams and hydroelectric plants have created havoc with the high tributaries of the Gangā, and the Bhāgīrathī River has almost disappeared. River activism has taken a hundred forms, from the demonstrations of strictly secular environmentalists to the fasts, Gandhian campaigns, and online petitions of religious activists.

The rivers that are said to have descended to earth as sources of salvation are now, in their earthly form, in need of salvation themselves.

5

Shiva's Light in the Land of India

In the colonnade inside the temple of Mahākāla in the city of Ujjain in central India, a great map of the whole of India is painted on a wall. Highlighted on the map are the twelve places called *jyotirlingas*, the "*lingas* of light," of which Mahākāla, Shiva as the "Great Lord of Time," is one. These twelve are the places where Lord Shiva is said to have appeared as a fathomless column of light. These shafts of light are spread throughout the entire subcontinent, from Kedāra or Kedārnāth in the high Himalayas to Rāmeshvara at the tip of southern India. In another, adjacent wall-sized image, a blue, four-armed Shiva stands superimposed on a map of India, and here the sites of the great *lingas* of light are located on his body. His head is at Kedārnāth, his feet at Rāmeshvara. At about the level of his knees are Grishnesha in Maharashtra and Mallikārjuna in northern Andhra. His waist is imprinted with the temple of Omkāreshvara along the Narmadā; at his heart is Ujjain, and so forth. The body of the Lord, the map of India, and the *jyotirlingas* are superimposed on one another and symbolically joined. This image tells at a glance part of our complex story of casting a landscape.

Painted on the wall is an inscription enumerating the twelve *jyotirlingas*. Most are places known to Hindus all over India but not so widely known by others, for they are not the great architectural monuments of royal patronage built in the capitals of kings, and they do not find a place on today's tourist maps of India. This is a pilgrim's landscape. The inscription at Mahākāla reads:

In Saurashtra, Somnāth and
At Shrī Shaila, Mallikārjuna.
In Ujjain, there is Mahākāla,

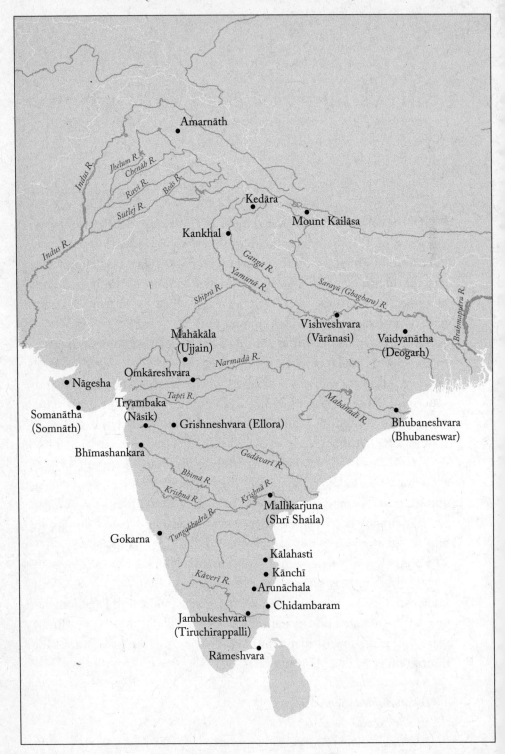

At Omkāra, Mamaleshvara.
And at Paralli, Vaidyanātha,
In the south, Bhīmashankara.
At the Bridge, there is Rāmeshvara,
And in the Pine Forest, Nāgesha.
In Vārānasī, there is Vishveshvara.
On the bank of the Gomatī, Tryambaka,
In the Himalayas, Kedāra.
At the abode of Shiva, Grishnesha.

These twelve I honor.
Whoever, on rising in the morning, may read this,
Is free from all sin,
And obtains all-powerful fruit.[1]

In speaking of these twelve places as "*lingas* of light," Hindus refer to one of the great myths of India: Shiva's awesome appearance as a column of sheer light or fire. That was the vision of Shiva that no one but the gods saw, back in the time of the beginning. It is this primary myth that will anchor our exploration of Shiva's presence in the land of India, for it is largely through this myth that the landscape of Shiva's India has been articulated. The myth is present, even when it is not told, just as Shiva is often present, deep in the subsoil of countless Hindu shrines dedicated today to other deities. Here in Ujjain, Hindi penny-pamphlets, glossy polychrome images, and a video CD advertise and reinforce the pilgrim's sense of being linked to the larger reality of twelve icons of light scattered across the land, from the Himalayas to the tip of south India. In one image, a muscular, blue Shiva, his trident gripped firmly by two hands, stands next to the Mahākāla *linga* and temple, both placed against the backdrop of the Himalayas and the Gangā. The twelve powerful *lingas* of light surround him. For the pilgrim who takes this image home, there is a scriptural affirmation somewhat like the one painted on the wall inside the temple, giving the assurance of spiritual benefit: "Remembering the names of these *lingas* morning and evening will destroy the sins of seven lifetimes."

The earliest textual references to the twelve as a group of *jyotirlingas* come from the *Shiva Purāna* in about the twelfth century. Benjamin Fleming, who has studied the textual traditions associated with the twelve, writes, "The unity of these twelve sites . . . seems to have been limited—at least at first—to the manuscripts and minds of a small group of medieval Brāhmanas. Only later was this idea absorbed and developed within a variety of vernacular traditions across the Indian subcontinent." He goes on, "In the *Jnānasamhitā* [of the *Siva Purāna*], it is clear that the rubric of the twelve *jyotirlingas* is a relatively artificial redactional device that frames what appear to be, for the most part, independent tales about the sites themselves."[2] Working largely from textual traditions, he sees this as an example of the dynamic relation between local traditions and an emerging pan-Indian consciousness. "These literary mappings of sacred geographies may reflect elite Brāhmanical efforts to integrate local and regional traditions under unifying religious rubrics. As such, the evidence of such lists may also speak to the self-conscious promotion of a developing concept of 'India' as a cultural and religious unity."[3]

In the twelfth century, and even in the twenty-first, there is little evidence of journeying to all twelve of the *jyotirlingas* being a popular pilgrimage practice. Rather, the grouping of the twelve, today articulated not merely in texts but in the traditions and images associated with each of the great sanctuaries of Shiva, affirms something wider and more comprehensive about the powerful presence of Shiva. Commanding the map of India as he does at the Mahākāla Temple, Shiva's presence stretches from the Himalayas to the southern seas. It is in the awareness of such a presence, transcending any one of these places of power, that the devotee is "released from the sins of seven lifetimes."

SHIVA IN TEXT AND LANDSCAPE

The textual traditions acquainting us with the god who is worshipped here at Mahākāleshvara are old and numerous. They begin with hymns to the Vedic god Rudra in the *Rig Veda* and the *Atharva Veda*, where Rudra is the lord of weapons, implored to come near and protect us even as he is treated with apprehension and entreated to keep his distance. He has many names, among them Bhava, "Being"; Sarva, the "All"; Pashupati, the "Lord of Creatures"; Kapardin, the "Lord of Dreadlocks"; Nīlagrīva, the "Blue-Throated"; and Sahasrāksha, the "Thousand-Eyed."

In both of India's great epics, this mountain-dwelling Shiva is often called simply the Great God, Maheshvara. It is he whom the Pāndava hero Arjuna seeks out for heavenly weapons before the great war of the *Mahābhārata*. And it is he who is honored in one holy place after another as the royal exiles Rāma, Sītā, and Lakshmana travel through India during the course of their forest journey recounted in the *Rāmāyana*. Over the centuries, Shiva becomes the focus of attention in many of the Sanskrit Purānas, especially the *Shiva Purāna* and the *Linga Purāna*, which relate countless stories of the appearances of Shiva. Another set of texts, called Āgamas, details the rituals of worshipping Shiva—in the temple and in the microcosm of the body, explicating both apparent and esoteric meanings. And then, of course, there are the poets, especially the south Indian devotional poets of the sixth to ninth centuries, whose songs praise Shiva and the many places where Shiva is to be found.

To explore the prolific texts of the brahmins and the lyrics of the poets, composed over many centuries and in many languages, would require volumes of analysis. But our approach here is different. We will begin with some of the great myths of Shiva, but our aim will be to explore those places "on the ground," where Shiva is and long has been most powerfully worshipped. Here we find one powerful and repeated vision: Lord Shiva cannot be fathomed, cannot be contained, is without beginning and end, and yet this same Shiva is the one who dwells right here in this temple, right here in this little village shrine, right here where the rivers meet, right here in the sanctum of the heart. As Appar, a seventh-century poet-saint of Tamil Nadu, attests, Shiva is beginningless and endless—and he is here in our town, right here in Shivapuram.

> *See the god!*
> *See him who is higher than the gods!*
> *See him who is Sanskrit of the North*
> *And southern Tamil and the four Vedas!*
> *See him who bathes in milk and ghee,*
> *see the Lord, see him who dances, holding fire,*
> *in the wilderness of the burning-ground,*
> *see him who blessed the hunter-saint!*
> *See him who wells up as honey*
> *in the heart-lotus of his lovers!*

See him who has the unattainable treasure!
See Shiva! See him who is our treasure
here in Shivapuram![4]

SHIVA, THE OUTSIDER

The story of Shiva in the land of India begins on the frontier, so to speak. He is the Outsider, the Mountain Dweller in the far north country. Who is Shiva? In ancient India, Shiva was certainly not the "Four Vedas," as the Tamil poet Appar put it. In fact, he is seen as outside the Vedas, *vedabāhya*. He has no share in the Vedic sacrifice. We need to begin here in our attempt to comprehend the full measure of this theological vision.

The myth of Shiva's exclusion from Daksha's sacrifice is a good place to start in our explorations. It will lead us, eventually, to the apotheosis of the Goddess as well. This story is one of the most ancient and popular of the *Mahābhārata* and the Purānas.[5]

Daksha was a demigod, a minor player in the world of affairs. As if to demonstrate his significance, he decided to hold a great ritual sacrifice, a *yajna*, right at the place where the River Gangā emerges from the Himalayas, the place called Kankhal, near Hardvār, where pilgrims can still visit the temple of Daksha Prajāpati. To this cosmic ritual, Daksha invited the entire universe—all the gods and sages, the rivers and mountains, everyone—but not Shiva. According to some versions of the myth, Daksha felt that Shiva had previously insulted him. According to others, he felt that Shiva, the ascetic mountain god, was simply not a fit guest for such a proper ritual occasion. In any case, the omission of Shiva from the guest list was deliberate.

In one of the *Mahābhārata* versions of the myth, we learn that all the gods who assembled around Shiva in the Himalayas had been invited to Daksha's sacrifice, so Devī asked Shiva why he was not invited. Shiva responded simply that it is part of the order of things, dharma, that the gods never give him a share in sacrifice. Devī was outraged, and because of her anger, Shiva went out to destroy the sacrifice. The sacrifice is often imaged as a deer, and here the destruction takes the form of a hunt. Shiva drew his bow and shot the deer with his arrow. Then, from a drop of the sweat of Shiva's brow emerged a fiery being, whom we presume to be the fierce form of Shiva called Vīrabhadra, who burned up the sacrificial grounds.

A second *Mahābhārata* version repeats and adds to the story. In this version, the *devī* is called one of her many names, Umā. She is not, incidentally, identified as Satī or the daughter of Daksha, as in other versions of the myth. Here, when Umā complains of Shiva's exclusion from the sacrifice, Shiva creates the blazing Vīrabhadra, and Umā creates Mahākālī. The two terrible surrogates with their denizens storm into the sacrifice and utterly destroy it. In the midst of the havoc, all the assembled hosts implore Shiva Mahādeva to have mercy. Even Daksha praises Shiva and asks that the sacrifice be restored. The episode ends with Daksha singing a hymn of the 1,008 names of Shiva. In these early *Mahābhārata* versions of the tale, the story is one of the exclusion and, in turn, the exaltation of Shiva.

The most extensive telling of the myth of Daksha's sacrifice in its Shiva-centered form is in the *Shiva Purāna*. It incorporates elements of the versions told in many Purānas.[6] Here Daksha is the father of Satī, and Satī herself is variously called Kālī, Kālikā, and Chandikā, all names identified with the ferocious power of the goddess. It is this goddess who was beseeched by all the gods and who eventually took birth as Satī so that she might marry Shiva.[7] As a young girl, Satī drew pictures of Shiva; as a young woman, she performed austerities in order to win him as her husband. Finally, the two were united in marriage, as Shiva and Shakti are ever destined to be united. They are the eternal pair, united "like a word and its meaning."[8] The story foreshadows that which will take place in the next aeon when Satī is born as the divine Pārvatī and again wins Shiva as her husband.

As the sacrifice began, the exclusion of Shiva did not go unnoticed. The outspoken sage Dadhichi railed against Daksha for not inviting Shiva. Shiva, he said, was literally the "auspicious one," for the name Shiva means "auspicious." It is he who makes everything holy. Without Shiva, Dadhichi said, the sacrificial ground was a cremation ground. Daksha was outraged at the comparison of his pure sacrifice to a polluted cremation ground. He took this occasion to make explicit and verbal his insult to Shiva: Shiva fit none of the categories of dharma. He had no *varna*, or caste. He was therefore outside the social order. He could not be known by his stage of life, his *āshrama*, for he was both young and old, married and celibate. He was an outsider to *varnāshrama dharma* and could not therefore expect a portion of the sacrifice.

Meanwhile, Satī found out about the great sacrifice. She saw the moon and the stars all dressed up and on their way, and asked where they were going. When she discovered they were going to Kankhal and that Shiva had not been invited, she was furious. Satī insisted on going to the sacrifice, even though Shiva warned her against going uninvited. Satī burst into the sacrificial arena at Kankhal, demanding to know why Shiva was not invited to share a portion. The dialogue that ensued between Satī and Daksha is a revealing statement of the theology of Shiva. Every insult Daksha heaped on Shiva, Satī deftly turned to Shiva's praise. Shiva may dwell in the cremation ground, she says, but the gods of heaven touch the dust of his feet to their heads. Shiva may have no lineage, clan, or *varna*, but he is the Lord of the Universe, who is literally beginningless. Finally, after this argument, Satī created from the power of her *tapas* a great blaze of fire and burned herself up. Both her faithfulness as a wife and her power as a *yoginī* gave her the capacity to set herself on fire.[9] She burned herself in the flames of her own *tapas*, right there in the midst of Daksha's guests gathered for the sacrifice.

On learning from his attendants of Satī's death, Shiva was enraged. He pulled out a clump of his ascetic's hair and dashed it on the mountaintop. From half of the clump of hair the fiery Vīrabhadra was born, and from the other half, the terrible Mahākālī. The two of them stormed down from the heights of the Himalayas, into the sacrificial arena. The participants sensed the coming destruction with a sequence of omens: jackals howled, whirlwinds whirled, and Daksha began to vomit pieces of flesh and bone. Vīrabhadra came with ten thousand lions pulling war chariots, and Mahākālī arrived with a battalion of nine Durgās and sixty-four *yoginīs*. They were accompanied by thousands of attendants called *ganas*. All seven continents, with their oceans, forests, and mountains, began to quake with fear.

Vīrabhadra and Mahākālī desecrated the sacrificial arena with their denizens of horrific ghouls and strongmen—throwing the offerings about, eating the food and drinking the drinks intended for the gods. It was a scene of sheer havoc. Everywhere there were decapitated heads, torn ears, and severed limbs of the gods and the guests. The sacrifice was completely destroyed and Daksha was beheaded. Finally, all the gods begged for mercy. Leaving the carnage of the sacrifice, the gods went to Shiva, seated under a tall cosmic tree on top of Mount Kailāsa. They asked that Daksha be restored to life and that the mutilated guests be restored to wholeness. Shiva was merciful and restored everything. Alas, Daksha's severed head was not to be found, however. So Daksha's body was fitted with the head of a goat.

The sacrifice resumed, with a proper share dedicated to Shiva. In the end, Daksha and all the gods praised Shiva as Supreme. Shiva himself offered a concluding homily on the waning efficacy of sacrifice: One cannot cross the flood of birth and death and gain salvation by rites and sacrifices alone. One must also have knowledge, and especially the knowledge of Shiva as Lord.

Here, in the *Shiva Purāna*, the emphasis is on Shiva's role as the outsider among the gods. He is the outsider who is, nonetheless, Supreme. Shiva is excluded from any share in the elaborate offerings of the Vedic liturgies.[10] And yet, outsider though he be, Shiva the Kapālin, the skull-bearer, is clearly the utterly Supreme One, who destroys and who makes whole. The entire myth culminates in the praise of Shiva.

Shiva, the Mountain God

Shiva is the yogi of the mountains. Even today in his popular depictions painted on walls or printed on posters, Shiva is shown meditating in the snowy mountains. He is the high-mountain yogi, dwelling in the far north, deep in meditation, facing south. The classic pose as rendered by the sculptors of India is called Dakshinamūrtī, the "South-Facing" Lord. He is the teacher of deep wisdom. He is also the Lord who dwells there with his beloved consort Satī. To explore the ways in which Shiva is anchored in the landscape, there is no better place to begin than in his Himalayan home. From ancient times, Shiva is the mountain god, Girīsha.

When Satī was eventually reborn, she again took birth in the mountains as Pārvatī, or Girijā ("Mountain-Born"), the daughter of the personified Himālaya and his wife Menā. In the mountains, she served Shiva, hoping to win him as her husband. But he was oblivious of her presence, so deep was he in meditation. Unable to gain his attention through service, Pārvatī decided on another strategy: She would perform penance to win Shiva as her husband. And so she did, growing somehow more beautiful with each season of severe austerities. It was in the Himalayas that their wedding took place, a great cosmic in-gathering in which the whole universe took part. It was in these same mountains that their son Kumāra, or Skanda, was born. All of this establishes Shiva's mythic homeland as mountain terrain, and the tales of the mountain days of this holy family are filled with the intrigue, humor, and dialogue that are at the heart of great stories. Artists loved these scenes as well, and when Shiva comes to be depicted in sixteenth- and seventeenth-century Rajput and Pahari miniature painting, he is shown as a family man in his high mountain abode, a tent of skins stretched near the campfire, his wife Pārvatī and their sons Ganesha and Skanda gathered round. Sometimes he might be depicted stringing a necklace of skulls, delighting the children as if they were beads.

If we stand in the special places where Shiva dwells in the Himalayas, one of the first might be an icy white mountain knifing into the sky near Badrīnāth. It is known as Nīlakantha, the "Blue-Throated One," named for Shiva, whose throat turned blue from drinking down the world-threatening poison churned up from the sea of creation. Across the high ridge from here is Kedārnāth, one of the twelve great *jyotirlingas*. Hundreds of miles to the northwest in the Kashmir Himalayas, we would find the *linga* of Amarnāth, made of sheer ice and visited by hundreds of thousands of hardy pilgrims during the month of Shrāvana each summer.[11] All over India, even in the most tropical of places where people have never seen natural ice, the image of Shiva's face superimposed on a shaft of ice is instantly recognizable as the "Eternal Lord," Amarnāth.

Above all, however, Shiva's mountain abode is identified as Kailāsa, located today inside the borders of western Tibet. Kailāsa rises to more than twenty-two thousand feet and stands virtually alone on a high plateau, a pyramidal black peak, streaked with glaciers, ice, and snow. It is the ultimate dream and goal of many a Hindu pilgrim, and in the past twenty years the land route to Kailāsa through India and Nepal has been opened to Indian pilgrims for the first time since the Chinese control of Tibet began. Hindu pilgrims come this way, converging with other pilgrims, largely Buddhists, who travel to Kailāsa by way of Lhasa. The *parikrama*, or circumambulation, of the peak takes two days of hiking at

altitudes over fifteen thousand feet. Like many sacred places, Kailāsa is
complexly layered with Hindu and Buddhist meanings, and pilgrims of
both traditions make the arduous journey to this remote mountain, circling the mountain and Lake Mānasarovar with tired feet and constant
prayers. Not surprisingly, in both traditions Kailāsa is most often identified as Mount Meru, the mythic mountain standing at the center of the
world, anchoring not only this lotus-world, but also the entire universe
beyond. For Hindu pilgrims, this world-centering mountain is the home
of Shiva. The foothills nearby are said to be Pārvatī, Skanda, Ganesha,
and Shiva's mount and guardian, the bull Nandi. Kailāsa itself is the
mountain manifestation, so they say, of Shiva's *linga* of light—the one
that pierced the earth in the very beginning of time.

As we will see, however, Shiva's presence as a mountain god is
repeated all over India. There are many mountains where Shiva dwells,
some of them understood to be parts of the Himalayas that have been
transported to other places. Shiva dwells as Bhīmashankar in Maharashtra and as Tryambak on the Sahyādri Mountains of the Western Ghāts,
as Mallikārjuna at Shrī Shaila in Andhra Pradesh. And just as Kailāsa is
a mountain manifestation of the divine light, so is Arunāchala, "Dawn
Mountain," in the Tamil south, a mountain said originally to have been
sheer fire, now turned to stone in this Kali Age.

Despite his mountain origins, we know that Shiva also takes up eternal residence on the plains—especially in the sacred city of Kāshī or
Vārānasī. According to one myth cycle, Pārvatī's parents, Himālaya and
Menā, following the grand Himalayan wedding ceremony, begin to bad-
ger Shiva to find a proper home for his bride. Menā is especially vexed,
believing that Pārvatī deserves a home somehow more permanent and
comfortable than the tent of flayed elephant hide pitched on the mountainside. So it is that Shiva comes to dwell in Vārānasī, having scanned
the entire earth for a lovely place to bring his bride. Shiva names the
city Avimukta, the "Never-Forsaken," because he vows never to leave it
and to uphold this city on the tip of his trident even when the rest of the
universe is submerged in the waters of the *pralaya* at the end of time. In
Vārānasī alone, there are countless Shiva temples, including all twelve
of the major *lingas* from elsewhere in India that have come, according to
tradition, to take up residence in this city. Vārānasī, like Kailāsa, comes
to be understood as the earthly manifestation of Shiva's *linga* of light,

a sacred zone of five *kroshas,* where the fathomless light of Shiva intersects the plane of this earth.[12] The whole sacred zone is called Kāshī, the "Luminous."

In truth, though Shiva dwells in Kailāsa and in Vārānasī, he also dwells everywhere. There is scarcely a village in India without a shrine devoted to Shiva in one of his forms, most prominently in the form of the *linga,* the rounded stone shaft that is the most pervasive symbol of his presence. The *lingas* of Shiva are to be found in the countryside, on the hilltop, along the riverbank, and where rivers meet. Each shrine claims Shiva's whole, undivided presence, even if only for one festival day a year. Shiva is known by thousands of local names. In a high valley of cedar forests called the Daruvana, in the Kumaon Hills of the Himalayas, Shiva is called Jāgeshvara, "Lord of Waking," for here, they say, while the Pāndava princes were sleeping, Shiva burst from the earth to wake them up as the rival Kauravas were getting ready to move upon them and kill them. At the headwaters of the Narmadā River, he is called Narmadeshvara, the "Lord of the Narmadā," and is said to have poured forth the river from his own body. In Krishna's city of Purī, on the east coast of India in Orissa, Shiva is present as Lokanātha, or Lokeshvara, "Lord of the World." He is housed in one of five ancient Shiva temples that are said to be among the oldest buildings in Purī, predating even the great Vaishnava temple of Jagannātha.[13] Across the whole span of India, on the westernmost coast of Gujarat, Shiva is sheltered in a tiny temple clinging to the rocks, and he is called "Lord of the Waves."

The relation of Shiva to the landscape of India is expressed prolifically in story, song, and symbol in one locale after another throughout India. We might speak of this simultaneous sense of transcendence and presence as the intimate immensity of Shiva—as vast as the cosmos, as close as the hill at the edge of town. This is the indigenous theological language of the multiform Shaiva tradition, expressed through the agency of ritual and pilgrimage, story and song. The Tamil songster Campantar asks, "What hill does he love?" It is Kālatti's hill, today known as Kālahasti in southern Andhra Pradesh.[14] Where does he love the sea? It is at the beach in Venkuru, "where, at night, waves dash against the shore, and scatter shells and oysters on the sand."[15]

Even in the midst of this wealth of particular, locative expression, the poets all insist it is our capacity to apprehend Shiva's larger presence that makes any place powerful. As the poet Appar puts it:

> Why bathe in the Ganges or the Kāverī,
> why make a pilgrimage to Kumārī's cool, fragrant beach,
> why bathe in the ocean's swelling waves?
> All this is in vain, if you do not think:
> "The Lord is everywhere."[16]

Shiva is everywhere—and that means he is right here, and the "right here" matters. This sense of Shiva's omnipresence is carried in the hearts of the pilgrims who take to the road to seek out the places of Shiva's distinctive presence. The sense of Shiva as both utterly transcendent and yet insistently local is shared throughout the length and breadth of India. Shiva is right here, and yet it is of the nature of pilgrimage that people take to the roads to visit somewhere far away, like Mahākāleshvara.

LINGAS OF LIGHT

According to the most common tradition, there are twelve great manifestations of Shiva in India. These twelve *jyotirlingas*, the *lingas* or "emblems" of holy light, are places where Shiva made himself manifest "of his own accord." They were not established by human hands, but by divine revelation. On the whole, these sacred sites are not the famous temple sites of India, established by the patronage of kings and known for their art and architecture. These cultic centers, so they say, are places where ordinary devotees, through their extraordinary acts of devotion, have evoked the blazing presence of Shiva. As shrines, they have become, over time, the creation of pilgrims who have sought out and witnessed the presence and power of Shiva. They are popular temples, glorious in their own way, but often remote and off the beaten track. Very often, they are but simple stones or rocky outcroppings said to be natural *lingas* of Shiva. In our exploration of the mythology and symbolism of Shiva, it is precisely to these places of iconic presence, empowered by the religious imagination of the people, that we must look to refine our vision of Shiva.

The myth of the appearance of the *jyotirlinga* is not only linked to these very powerful places, but is also understood as a charter myth for *linga* itself. The myth is referred to as *lingodbhava*, the "appearance of the *linga*." It is told often in Sanskrit and vernacular literature, and it is given iconographic shape in bas relief on the walls and pillars of many a temple. The myth is important enough to be told twice at the beginning of the *Shiva Purāna*.[17] The question posed is a common one: What is the relation of Shiva's transcendence to his multiple and embodied presence? The interlocutor stretches the mind back to that time before the beginning of time.[18] In this cosmology, the world evolves through age after age, then falls to destruction, then lies in formless dissolution for a period of rest before it evolves again. This time after the end and before the beginning is called the *pralaya*. It is the period of dissolution, darkness, and rest. Let us briefly summarize the myth:

In the *pralaya* there was neither day nor night. There were no elements—fire, wind, air, earth, or water. There was simply immeasurable, incomprehensible, pitch darkness, without even so much as a needle of light. Being alone existed then. It was One without a second. It was Brahman. Taking form in the beginning, that formless One became Sadā Shiva, the "Eternal Shiva." Sadā Shiva, desiring a partner, divided in half and became half-Shiva and half-goddess, called Shakti. The two of them, Shiva and Shakti, then created a place to stand in the vast darkness. They called it Kāshī, the "Luminous," for it was a spot of pure light. Kāshī is what Hindus even today call the city of Vārānasī, or Banāras.

Then Shiva and Shakti created a third being to take up and continue the process of creation. They made a golden being called Vishnu and set him to work. Vishnu entered into meditation, and with the heat, or *tapas*, of his body he generated the waters that filled the void. Weary, he floated out upon the waters to sleep the deep sleep that precedes the dawn of creation. Inside the body of the sleeping god the whole universe incubated. In time, a lotus arose from Vishnu's navel. The bud of the lotus opened, and out stepped Brahmā, the firstborn of creation, the god who creates all the particulars of the cosmos.

As far as Brahmā knew, he was the only one in the universe,

although he imagined he must have a creator somewhere. Still, when he noticed the sleeping Vishnu, his egotism got the best of him. He woke Vishnu up. "Who are you?" Brahmā asked him.

Vishnu opened a sleepy eye and said, "Welcome, welcome, dear child."

"Child?" said Brahmā. "How can you address me as a child! I am the creator of the worlds!"

"Oh no," said Vishnu. "I am the creator of the worlds. I gave rise to you from my navel, and I support you with my immortal limbs."

"How can you talk so!" retorted Brahmā angrily. "You are not the creator. I am!"

They exchanged insults. Their argument grew more heated. According to some accounts, they came to blows and fought with a fury that nearly destroyed the world before it began. Suddenly, between them, the ground of the cosmos opened and there appeared a fiery shaft of light. It rose up from the depths below and extended upward through space as far as the eye could see. This was the *jyotirlinga*—the *linga* of light. It was a column of fire too brilliant to look at, inexpressible in its glory.

Vishnu and Brahmā left off their arguing, stunned to silence by this fiery radiance. They decided to find out what it was, where it began, and where it ended. Vishnu became a boar with tusks and a long snout, and he dug deep down, through the waters, into the mud beneath, to find the root and source of this light. And Brahmā became a wild gander and flew high up into the sky to find its top. For thousands of years, they say, Vishnu plunged downward, but he could not find its root. And for thousands of years Brahmā flew upward, but he could not find its top. They returned to their starting place, exhausted, unable to fathom the *linga* of light. Then, the mass of fire opened and Shiva emerged out of the pillar in embodied form, with five faces and ten arms. The gods trembled to see the Lord emerge from the shaft of light, and they bowed down to worship him.

This is the basic myth: the emergence of Shiva from a fiery *linga* of light. Brahmā and Vishnu humbled themselves before the blazing *linga*, and the air resonated with the sound of *Om*, the most sacred mantra, said to embody the whole of the Veda in a single word. There are many variants of the story, however. In one version, for example, the disputing gods call in the four Vedas to settle their argument, and each Veda attests to the supremacy of Shiva. This, of course, is ironic because, as we have seen, Shiva is often derisively called Vedabāhya, "Outside the Vedas," one who does not participate in the Vedic rites of sacrifice. Yet here, the Vedas show up to affirm his supremacy.[19] Another version tells us that Brahmā, vain and deluded, actually lied, boasting that he saw the top of the fiery pillar.[20] Because of this lie, they say, Brahmā was condemned never to have a cult of his own worshippers. In another setting, the whole story is told by Krishna in order to explain why he, too, honors the *linga*.[21]

The world-spanning image of Shiva's emblem of fire also has multiforms in Shiva mythology. One of the most prominent is the flaming arrow that Shiva shoots from his bow to penetrate the three cities, or the three worlds—earth, space, and the heavens beyond.[22] Mythology also connects the *linga* explicitly with Shiva's phallus, fallen and then flaming. In these myths, the ascetic Shiva wanders stark naked as a beggar into the Devadāru Forest, the "Cedar Forest," in order to test the knowledge of the sages. The wives of the forest-dwelling sages are both frightened and excited by his ash-covered body. They throw themselves in lust at Shiva. Their husbands, not seeing this to be a test of their true knowledge of Shiva, are furious at his indecency and curse Shiva's *linga* to fall off. This would seem, on the face of it, to be a story of castration, for the sages think his *linga* is his sexual organ. But the instant it falls, the *linga*, Shiva's "mark" or "emblem," becomes the world-spanning, brilliant flame, the ends of which cannot be found.[23] It burns the earth, the netherworlds, and even scorches the heavens before coming to rest in the Cedar Forest.[24]

The version we have summarized from the *Shiva Purāna*, however, presents and praises the shaft of light itself. The *linga*, in the theological vision of this Purāna, is an epiphany of such transcendence that it can hardly be considered a part, much less an anatomical part, of Shiva as he appears in embodied form. Quite the contrary, Shiva in embodied form is but a part, a mere fraction, of the *linga*, standing forth in embodied form from this larger, transcendent reality.

SHIVA AS *SAKALA* AND *NISHKALA*

The *jyotirlinga* is, to use Mircea Eliade's term, an *axis mundi*, a cosmic axis, in this case a piercing pillar of light, running through the very core and center of the universe. Not surprisingly, one account of the first *linga* describes it as a giant tree called the Pillar (Sthanu), which stands in the middle of a lake that is, in turn, in the middle of the world.[25] Like the *axis mundi*, the *linga* both centers the world and transcends it. There are really two revelations of Shiva here in the *jyotirlinga*. First, there is the fiery shaft of blinding light, indescribable, limitless, so deep-rooted and high-reaching that it cannot be fathomed even by the gods. This is often referred to as Paramashiva, "Shiva the Supreme," or Sadā Shiva, "Shiva the Eternal." This is another way of naming the supreme Brahman of whom the Upanishads speak—that reality of which one can only say *neti, neti*—"not this, not this." In addition, there is the personal manifestation, the one who steps out of the *linga* and shows himself to be bodied, with a face, with multiple arms, with gestures and weapons.

The point is a powerful one theologically, and it is made explicit in the interpretive theological passages surrounding this myth in the *Linga Purāna* and the *Shiva Purāna*. Shiva, they say, is twofold. First, Shiva is utterly transcendent and is described as *nishkala*, "without parts." This is the transcendence symbolized in many traditions as sheer light. Shiva *nishkala* is Being itself, one without second, identical with the supreme Brahman, the source and essence of all. The "form" of this formless, unfractured transcendence is the *jyotirlinga*, if we can speak of this blazing pillar as a form.

But Shiva is also *sakala*, "with parts." He shows himself visibly in many forms, with many faces. As Natarāja, he is a dancer, creating and destroying the cosmos with the rhythms of his dance. As Dakshināmūrti, he is an ascetic and teacher sitting high in the Himalayas. Though ascetic, he is also Umāpati, the husband of Umā or Pārvatī, the father of Ganesha and Skanda. One moment he looks like the Lord of the Universe, Vishvanātha, wearing silk, adorned with fragrant sandal-paste, his hair decked with the crescent moon. The next moment he is the beggar, gaunt and ugly, wearing animal skins for garments, his body smeared with human ash from the cremation pyre, ornamented with skulls and snakes.

Shiva is depicted in all these poses—dancing, begging, slaying demons, and protecting devotees. In and through this complexity, he is enthroned with the goddess called Shakti, literally his "energy" or "power." Indeed, Shiva is never separate from Shakti. One cannot really speak of Shiva as "he," for "he" is Ardhanārīshvara, the Lord who is half-woman.

According to the *Shiva Purāna*, other deities have only this *sakala* aspect. "Shiva alone is known as *nishkala*, because he is indeed Brahman. Because he has an embodied form, he is also *sakala*. Thus he is both *sakala* and *nishkala*. Because he is without parts, the formless *linga* is appropriate. And because he has parts, his embodied form is appropriate."[26] When the *jyotirlinga* is depicted, as it often is, in bas relief sculpture on the exterior of temples, the image shows clearly the twofold nature of Shiva. The smooth shaft of the *linga*, Shiva's *nishkala* form, is broken open, and Shiva emerges in *sakala* form. In an oval-shaped opening in the granite shaft of the *linga*, Shiva stands forth, with four arms, gesturing both strength and benediction. Below him, on the shaft of the *linga*, is Vishnu, the boar, diving downward; above him is Brahmā, the wild gander, flying upward.

THE *LINGA* IN SHAIVA WORSHIP AND RITUAL

In the *Shiva Purāna*, the hierophany of the *jyotirlinga* is also linked to Shaiva worship and ritual.[27] In many an image, Brahmā and Vishnu stand to either side of Shiva and worship him, offering garlands of flowers and leaves, camphor and incense. The two gods are the first to worship the *linga*. Pleased with their worship, Shiva gives them two boons, both of which become foundational for the worship of Shiva. His first gift is Shivarātri. He says, "Dear ones, today on this great day I am pleased with your worship. Therefore this day will be the most auspicious of days. This lunar day, very dear to me, will be called Shivarātri."[28] Shivarātri, literally, the "Night of Shiva," recalls the manifestation of Shiva in the darkness of the uncreated cosmos. There is a monthly Shivarātri, on the darkest night of the month, just before the birth of the new moon. Once a year, during the winter months, comes the Mahāshivarātri, the "Great Shivarātri," when the faithful keep vigil and fast throughout the night. At many Shiva temples, such as the great Omkāreshvara on the Narmadā

River, this is the one night during the year when the temple is open for the entire night. At all of the great Shiva temples, this is a night of brilliant lights. Fires are kindled on the slopes of Arunāchala in Tamil Nadu. The temple tower of Shrī Shaila in Andhra Pradesh streams with a carnival of colored electrical lights and dazzling medallions.[29]

Shiva's second boon was the *linga* itself. He says, "This pillar, without beginning and end, will become small in size so that people may behold it and worship it, dear sons."[30] The myth, then, ascribes to that fiery theophany of light the origin of the symbolic *linga* to be found at the center of Shiva's worship and in all of Shiva's temples. With such splendid origin, it is no wonder that many Shiva *lingas* in temples large and small are said to be *svayambhū*, "self-born" or spontaneously manifest, rather than established by human hands.

The self-limitation of the cosmic, the shrinking of the immense to be accessible on a human scale, is a theme played on with brilliance in the mythic lore of many Hindu temples. In one sense every temple contains small images that represent a vast and unfathomable reality. This is the very meaning of the symbolic sensibility at the core of religious life everywhere. In the Padmanābhaswamy Temple in Trivandrum, for example, this intimate immensity is narrated explicitly in a Vaishnava key: Vishnu appeared to a devotee in a form so vast it stretched across most of the land of Kerala. Eventually, he had to become small in order to take his place in the sanctum of the temple at Trivandrum, as Lord Padmanābhaswamy.

Especially in Shaiva theology, the entire cosmos pulses to the rhythm of expansion and contraction, *pravritti* and *nivritti*, pouring forth and drawing back. The divine expands, evolving as if from seed, and stretching into the immense, indeed infinite reality of the cosmos, which lives and breathes. And, in turn, the divine withdraws that vast complexity into the seed of Being itself. This dynamic streams through the vivid symbolic realms of Hindu thought and image, and the *linga* in this world is the symbol par excellence. The infinite contracts and is concentrated in image and form so that the sacred may be present to human sense and vision.

It is well known that some interpreters, especially outsiders, have considered the *linga* to be overtly and overwhelmingly a "phallic symbol." One of the first to be horrified by its apparently phallic connotations was the Abbé Dubois, who, in the early nineteenth century, described it as "obscene" and found it impossible to believe that, as he put it, "in inventing this vile superstition the religious teachers of India intended that people should render direct worship to objects the very names of which among civilized nations are an insult to decency."[31] The castration cycle of myths we have noted certainly lends credence to the phallic view, except that, on the whole, the stories themselves split open that limited consciousness to reveal the world-spanning emblem. Unfortunately, even in the 1970s, the translators of the first English edition of the *Shiva Purāna* decided to translate *linga* as "phallic emblem," perpetuating this symbolic distortion. Such a translation is not completely erroneous, but it does not in the least convey what Hindus have seen and understood in this symbol. It is as inadequate as would be an interpretation of the Christian eucharist that saw the rite first and foremost as ritual cannibalism, eating the body and drinking its blood, and could not get beyond such an interpretation to any deeper and more complex understanding.

The word *linga* simply means "emblem," "mark," or "symbol." It is in one sense an emblem of gender, and as such it indicates Shiva's two kinds of power: his procreative, generative power as husband of Pārvatī and his retentive, ascetic power as yogi. It is he who pours forth the universe as its creator and who withdraws the universe as its destroyer. Shiva is both husband and ascetic, both creator and destroyer. These faces are aspects of *sakala* Shiva, the one "with parts." But the *linga*, as is clear from the myth of the *jyotirlinga*, is the symbol or emblem of *nishkala* Shiva—the fractionless, transcendent, and supreme Lord. The *linga* is the emblem of Shiva's unfathomable presence. It is to this *nishkala* Shiva that the author of the *Linga Purāna* refers when he paradoxically speaks of Shiva in *linga* form as the one who is *lingavarjita*, "without distinguishing marks or symbols."[32] The *linga* is the visible symbol of the invisible, the form of the formless. Similarly, in the *Kūrma Purāna*, we find, "[t]he *linga* is, truly, Brahman—who is One, unmanifest, and *alinga*."[33]

It is in *linga* form that Shiva dwells in the sanctuaries of India's temples and is worshipped. Only a very few temples—such as the famous temple of Shiva Natarāja, the "Lord of the Dance," in Chidambaram in Tamil Nadu—have an anthropomorphic *sakala* image of Shiva in the sanctuary.[34] Shiva may be known in art and in myths as beggar, dancer, lover, and ascetic, and in these forms he may be depicted on the walls of temples and in the subsidiary shrines. But he is worshipped in this *nishkala* form alone. The relation of the *linga* in the sanctum to the fathomless *jyotirlinga* is made explicit in the standard iconography of many south Indian temples: At that especially auspicious place on the exterior circumambulatory, on just the other side of the wall from the interior sanctum of the *linga*, is a bas relief of the *jyotirlinga*, with Brahmā and Vishnu seeking its ends and Shiva emerging from the shaft.

The *linga* of Shiva has two distinct parts, reminding us of the primordial bifurcation of the eternal Sadā Shiva into male and female, Shiva and Shakti. The shaft, or *sthambha*, the pillar of the *linga*, is Shiva, while the circular base, called a *pītha* or *yoni*, the "seat" in which it is established, is Shakti. Shiva is timeless transcendence; Shakti, the active energy of time and creation. Together, they form the whole of what is worshipped as the *linga*—both Shiva and Shakti, male and female. As the *Shiva Purāna* puts it, "What is known as the *linga* is the coming together of the symbols [*chihna*] of Shiva and Shakti."[35]

The shaft itself has three divisions, according to iconographical canons—the square Brahmābhāga at the bottom of the shaft, the octagonal Vishnubhāga in the middle, and the circular Rudrabhāga, which is the only portion visible, the other two being embedded in the base of the *linga*. This threefold division expresses Shiva's relation to and transcendence over the other gods. However, it also suggests the *nishkala* Shiva's transcendence of any partial manifestation—even that represented by his own section of the shaft, the Rudrabhāga.

In a similar symbolic way, Shiva's faces sometimes emerge from the shaft of the *linga*, as if to make fully manifest the theological point that Shiva, though transcendent, appears here on earth with a face. There may be one face coming forth from the shaft. Or there may be five—four emerging in the four directions, with expressions both fierce and benign, and the fifth face, not imaged, transcendent, the uncarved top or, perhaps, the shaft of the *linga* itself. In the *Shaiva Āgamas*, the faces of Shiva are systematized: Ishāna, the vertical shaft itself, shows forth Shiva's grace. Sadyojāta, the western direction, reveals Shiva's face of creation, emitting the worlds from himself. Vāma, the northern direction, displays Shiva as the sustainer of the world. Tatpurusha is the eastern direction, in which Shiva's mysterious, veiling presence is visible. Aghora, the southern direction, shows forth Shiva's face of destruction. All these five faces comprise Sadā Shiva. The five faces with their names and mantras are imposed with appropriate markings not only on the shaft of the *linga*, but with sandal-paste on the body of the worshipper, creating a series of identities between the microcosm and macrocosm.[36]

In many temples, the juxtaposition of the unfractured transcendence of the Supreme with the many faces of Shiva is expressed ritually by placing a four- or five-faced brass or silver cap called a *mukut*, literally a "crown," upon the *linga* during certain of the daily hours of worship. Such ritual recognition of the twofold *nishkala-sakala* nature of Shiva is a prominent aspect of the worship of Shiva in several of the temples of the *jyotirlingas*. During certain times of the day, worshippers may pour water and milk offerings directly on the *linga*, heaping there on the shaft of the *linga* the garlands of flowers they bring. They offer the oil lamps of *āratī* to the unadorned shaft that is emblematic of the *nishkala* Shiva. During the daily *shringāra*, the decoration and adornment of the *linga*, the *sakala* aspect is emphasized with sandal-paste, flower garlands, a silver face, perhaps a crown. At Kedārnāth in the Himalayas, for example, we will see this juxtaposition of *nishkala* and *sakala* Shiva enacted in the morning and evening *darshans*. In the morning, the stone of the *linga* is completely bare, and pilgrims stand in line for hours with their offerings,

Water libations, poured upon the five-faced silver crown of Lord Shiva, Nāsik

waiting their turn to go right into the sanctum itself and place their bilva leaves, wildflowers, raisins, and water offerings directly on the rock. In the evening, however, Shiva's *linga* is lavishly decorated by the temple priests, adorned with silk, garlanded with leaves, sheltered with a golden umbrella. Worshippers keep their distance at the door of the sanctum. At Kedārnāth, it is the *nishkala,* the faceless transcendent, form to which worshippers gain the most intimate access in worship. Perhaps Shiva's faces may, in fact, distance the worshipper from the Supreme Lord, while the sheer stone invites the most immediate communion.

There are many kinds of *lingas,* but the most important distinction is between those that are *svayambhū,* "self-manifest," and those that are fashioned and consecrated by human hands, *sthāpita,* literally, "established." Many temples old and new have Shiva *lingas* with a finely shaped shaft and base, placed in the sanctum and consecrated with elaborate rites to be the permanent presence of Shiva. *Svayambhū lingas* are, instead, already there. The powerful presence of Shiva is *discovered,* revealed in the earth, not established by human hands. These *lingas* are said to be spontaneous, perhaps miraculous, appearances of Shiva. All of the *jyotirlingas* are *svayambhū,* "self-born."

In some cases, human creation and divine revealing are present together. Shiva appears in response to the simple, focused adoration of a devotee who makes and honors a simple *linga* of earth. These are called *pārthiva lingas,* "earthen *lingas,*" from the noun *prithivī,* "earth." With a prayer called an *āvāhana,* "invitation," Shiva is beckoned to be present in this simple earthen lump. At the end of ordinary worship, such a *linga* may be ceremonially thrown away into the Gangā, the Narmadā, or some other body of water, its use as a temporary focus of God's presence now gone. In the stories of the *svayambhū linga,* however, Shiva manifests himself right out of the clay, appearing to his devotee and promising to remain forever in that very place.

In the *Shiva Purāna* account, ten of India's twelve great *jyotirlingas* are said to have been fashioned originally as *pārthiva lingas* in just this way.[37] For example, in one account a devout king has been imprisoned by a demon, a nephew of the infamous Rāvana. The king fashions a clay *linga* and prays fervently to Lord Shiva. When the demon comes to harass the king and he hurls his sword in fury at the *linga,* Shiva emerges from the *linga* and destroys him. Such is the origin, they say, of the Bhīmashankar *jyotirlinga* in Maharashtra.[38] Though the *pārthiva lingas* are simple, even crude, they provide an occasion of devotion for Shiva to step forth into the world in his full presence. In most of these stories, Shiva then agrees, at the request of his devotee, to be forever present right there, and the humble *pārthiva linga,* a simple pinch of clay, is transformed from the most transient to the most eternal of images.

The term *svayambhū* is used characteristically to describe the *jyotirlingas,* but many other *lingas* also partake of this language of self-manifestation. Indeed, there are probably thousands of *lingas* in India considered by their local worshippers to be *svayambhū*. Of these, the twelve most famous and powerful have come to have the name *jyotir-linga* after that first fiery eruption of the supreme Shiva. But even as the twelve are enumerated and praised in their particularity, Shiva is affirmed to be the one who saturates the entire cosmos with his presence. As the interlocutor puts it in the *Shiva Purāna,* "O sage, there is no limit to the number of *lingas.* The entire earth, the entire universe, is in the form of a *linga.* . . . In order to bless the worlds, Lord Shiva assumes the form of different *lingas* here in the holy centers as well as in other places. Shiva incarnates in those places wherever he is devoutly remembered by the devotees. After carrying out their task he stations himself there."[39]

The *Jyotirlingas* of India's Sacred Geography

A pilgrimage pamphlet from the streets of Omkāreshvara, the dusty island sanctuary on the Narmadā River, gives a brief introduction to the importance of Shiva's holy places: "Devotion to Shiva has been an unbro-ken tradition in our country since ancient times. . . . At the holy places (*punya sthalī*) of Bhārat many of these devotees did such powerful ascetic practice that Lord Shiva appeared to them and these devotees saw him directly. These places became famous as *jyotirlingas.*"[40]

If *tīrthas* are those sacred crossings that link this world and the beyond, then the *jyotirlingas* are *tīrthas* par excellence. Indeed, the eruption of the *linga* of light, piercing earth and heaven, creates a natural bridge of light, spanning the space between the world and the heavens. In defining a "sacred place," no mythic theme could be more powerful. Here, they say, Shiva broke open the earth and stood as a fathomless shaft of light.

Places great and small link their sanctity directly to this story. Even when they do not tell the story as such, the story of the hierophany of the fathomless light is present in the very name *jyotirlinga*. There are many *jyotirlingas* in India—some that are part of the group of twelve, such as those linked with the body of Lord Shiva in the Mahākāla Temple in Ujjain, some that stake claim to be one of the twelve and are contested, and some that are simply called *jyotirlinga* by their devotees. There well may be hundreds of places called *jyotirlingas* in India, but over the centuries a cycle of twelve has come to be recognized.[41]

The *Shiva Purāna* lists these twelve great *jyotirlingas:* Somanātha in Saurashtra; Mallikārjuna in Shrī Shaila; Mahākāla in Ujjain; Parameshvara in Omkāra; Kedāra in the Himalayas; Bhīmashankara in the Deccan; Vishvesha in Vārānasī; Tryambaka on the bank of the Gautamī River; Vaidyanātha in the cremation ground; Nāgesha in the Daruka Forest; Rāmesha at Setubandha; and Ghushmesha, also called Grishnesha, at Shivālaya.[42] These are the twelve best known in India today, although the sites of Nāgesha and Vaidyanātha have several claimants. The text then goes on to list what it calls *upalingas*, the "subsidiary *lingas*" of each of the twelve. In its subsequent chapters, the *Shiva Purāna* discusses a great number of other *lingas* according to their location in India—east, south, west, and north.[43]

Geographically, the famous twelve are located throughout the length and breadth of India. In introducing them, the author of a popular Hindi tract on the *jyotirlingas* writes, "From all over India these twelve *jyotirlingas* have come to be especially important, and in this our symbolic, religious, and national sense of unity is vested."[44] The writer imagines the spread of these shrines on a map of India: In the Himalayan north is Kedāra. In the Gangetic Plain is Kāshī Vishvesha, and farther east in Bihar, Vaidyanātha. In central India are Mahākāla and Omkāreshvara. At the headwaters of the Godāvarī is Tryambaka. Nearby in the Deccan and along the Western Ghāts are Ghushmeshvara and Bhīmashankara. In the far west in Saurashtra are Somanātha and Nāgesha. In the east, along the River Krishnā, is Mallikārjuna at Shrī Shaila. And in the far south along the seacoast is Rāmeshvara.

Many popular polychrome images, like those we saw painted on the wall and printed in the little shops at the Mahākāla Temple in Ujjain, are mass-produced for devotion, for calendars, or simply for souvenirs. They depict the twelve *jyotirlingas* as a group, linking them together as Shiva's manifestations. They form a border or a circle, and Shiva is depicted in the middle of them. They are clustered in the high mountains, and the Gangā, spurting from Shiva's hair, falls upon each of the twelve. But even though they are linked in map, image, and myth, the *jyotirlingas* are not at all the same. Each gives us a special insight into the worship and theology of Shiva that is embedded in the landscape where he is most powerfully present. We cannot look at them all here, but we will look at six of them, standing in their sanctuaries and reflecting on what it means to speak of myth on earth in the presence of these *jyotirlingas*.

BEGINNING WITH KĀSHĪ VISHVESHA

Despite the fact that Somnāth or Somanātha comes first in the ordering, the most famous of the twelve *lingas* of light is surely Vishvesha, popularly called Vishvanātha, the Lord of the Universe, located in the city of Vārānasī on the River Gangā in north India. Indeed, the city is known to Hindus as Kāshī, the Luminous, the City of Light. Here, according to the myth, the *linga* of light split the cosmos during the argument between Brahmā and Vishnu.[45] Here Shiva stood forth from the unfathomable shaft of light. This Kāshī was the first spot of light from which the whole cosmos expanded and was manifest, the first "place" to be created by Shiva and Shakti at the dawn of creation. This was the very place where Shiva and Shakti stood as they decided to create the world we know, a task they initiated and then turned over to Vishnu, who would carry it out. So Kāshī is seen to be the source of creation. Shiva stands on this ground at the time of creation and then holds it high on his trident above the floodwaters of destruction at the time of dissolution, the *pralaya*. It is said to be a place beyond the reach of the cycles of time. Shiva's *linga* of light here has the ancient name Avimukteshvara, because it is never-forsaken (*Avimukta*) by Lord Shiva, even at the end of time.[46]

Pilgrims have come to Kāshī, year after year, for many centuries. They come from all over India, and there are *dharmashālās*, or pilgrim rest houses, that cater to the needs of those from different regions. In the neighborhoods and shops around these regional *dharmashālās* one might hear more Tamil or Bengali than Hindi. Some come for what they call

Kāshīvāsa, "living in Kāshī," or, more accurately, living out their lives to the end, in the faith that the City of Light is a good place to die. Others come from Tamil Nadu or Bengal simply as pilgrims, and they do what all pilgrims do here: bathe in the River Gangā and worship Lord Shiva.

Kāshī was here, they say, even before the Gangā plunged from heaven to earth. But when she fell from heaven upon the head of Shiva, and when King Bhagīratha led her out onto the plains and across north India, he brought her past the sacred Kāshī, making this place doubly sacred. Here, the fire of Shiva and the cooling waters of the Gangā, considered to be a liquid form of Shakti, are inextricably linked together. As we will see, all the great *jyotirlingas* are associated, in some way, with divine waters. There are springs, streams, and wells that bring the heavenly Gangā to the *lingas* of Shiva, wherever they may be located.

Here in Kāshī, there are hundreds of Shiva temples, large and small, where pilgrims and local worshippers make their prayers and offerings. As the saying goes, *Kāshī ke kankar Shiva Shankar.* "The very stones of Kāshī are Shiva." And so it seems. At every corner, at every turn in the dense heart of the city lanes, there is a tiny shrine, a Shiva *linga,* its stone worn with the water and worship of the ages. Some *lingas* are arrayed under the shelter of a tree; others are ensconced in a maze of doorways, leading to courtyards, leading to temples. And there are many Shiva *lingas* right on the riverbank itself, excavated annually from the mud and silt residue of the monsoon as the Gangā subsides after the rainy season. True enough, some of Kāshī's major temples, including the famous temple of Vishvesha, or Vishvanātha, have been repeatedly looted and destroyed. They have been shifted from one place to another, rebuilt, and reconsecrated. Yet nothing seems to have been erased from the multilayered landscape of this city.[47] Here, the worship of Shiva has stubbornly persisted, proliferated, even flourished through the centuries.

Vishvanātha, called the Golden Temple, is certainly considered the central Shiva temple today, the *jyotirlinga* where Shiva's light pierced the earth. Tucked into the labyrinth of thread-narrow lanes in the inner city, Vishvanātha is housed in a modest, but very fine, temple complex, built in the eighteenth century by the patronage of Ahalyābāi Holkar of Indore. The stones of the inner sanctum are worn smooth with the feet of millions of pilgrims, as is the tiny alleyway that takes them by a knee-high window opening just to one side of the sunken square pit containing the *linga*, affording *darshan* to all who stoop to gaze inside. Daily, pilgrims bathe in the River Gaṅgā at the nearby *ghāts* and make their way up the steep steps and into lanes of the city, following a pilgrim guide to Vishveshvara. This is the core of Kāshī pilgrimage.

And yet here in Kāshī, as we will also see at the sites of other *jyotir-lingas*, the *real linga* of light is not contained in this particular temple or in any temple, but is said to be the place itself, in this case the whole of the sacred zone called Kāshī, a circle with a radius of about ten miles. This *jyotirlinga* extends beyond the limits of the city and out into the countryside. The whole *kshetra*, or field, is called Kāshī, they say, because here the light, the *jyoti*, shines forth.[48] And here, as at other *jyotirlingas*, pilgrims circumambulate the entire sacred *kshetra*—a journey called the *panchakroshī yātrā*, which takes five days on foot. Keeping the city on their right, pilgrims walk a circle around Kāshī, stopping each night at a pilgrim rest house. Along the way, there are protective shrines, including a circle of eight Ganeshas, standing guardian at the perimeter of this large, earthly *jyotirlinga*.[49]

All twelve *jyotirlingas* are said to be present within the sacred zone of Kāshī. The temple of Kedāreshvara anchors the southern third of the city with its popular bathing *ghāt*. Omkāreshvara is located on a hill in a somewhat forlorn area of the northern part of the city, a small temple well kept today but clearly a representative of what was once a more impressive temple complex. And so it is with the others—a temple and *linga*, each duplicating and representing a great *jyotirlinga* in some far-flung part of India. The persevering pilgrim can visit them all, but as with the all-India *jyotirlingas*, few really do. But let us note that even before the all-India *jyotirlinga* tradition seems to have caught hold, there was a cycle of twelve *lingas* praised as constitutive of Shiva's presence in Kāshī, not these particular twelve, not *jyotirlingas* per se, but twelve nonetheless, perhaps providing a key to the emergence of this particular framework for casting the presence of Shiva.[50]

Finally, there is one temple in Kāshī that today makes clear the patterns of duplication and condensation that have served to map a sacred geography. A single *tīrtha* is duplicated so that its presence is found in multiple places. And multiple *tīrthas* are condensed into a single place. This is the Panchakroshī Temple, located in the narrow lanes of the heart of the city, where one may visit all the holy sites of the circumambulatory *panchakroshī yātrā*, indeed all the holy sites of Kāshī, in a single place. This temple, impressively documented in detail by anthropologist and architect Niels Gutschow, was probably built in the nineteenth century, as a three-dimensional "built map" of the whole sacred zone.[51] In the rows of niches around its perimeter are some 273 individual shrines, each providing a symbolic duplicate of one of the stations along the Panchakroshī Road or one of the other sacred sites in the zone of Kāshī. At this temple, the condensation of a universe of *tīrthas* into a single place is illustrated in brick and stone. Here we visit the Kedāreshvara *linga,* there the Durgā temple, the ancient Lolārka Kund, the shrine of Tilabhāndeshvara, a large *linga* said to grow by the size of a sesame seed each day. Around the perimeter of the temple are niches displaying specific shrines to Ganesha and Bhairava, particular temple images of Vishnu and Krishna, *sancta* of the goddesses, and, of course, the many Shiva *lingas.* Fittingly, in the central sanctum is a very special *linga*: the Dvādasheshvara "Twelve Lord" *linga,* a single linga representing all twelve of the *jyotirlingas* in one place. The shaft of the *linga* anchors the mandala, while crystal stones representing the other eleven *jyotirlingas* are arrayed around the *pītha,* or base.

This temple was built about the time that several Kāshī scholars were developing two-dimensional "maps" of the whole of Kāshī, such as the 1876 map of Kailāsanātha Sukul, *Kāshī Darpana,* the "Mirror of Kāshī." I was fortunate to obtain this map from his son, the distinguished Kāshī scholar Kubernāth Sukul. Printed on cloth, it includes the many little shrines of the *panchakroshī* perimeter as a circle surrounding the city. Within the circle, the map enumerates, in tiny but legible hand, the multitude of Kāshī's temples. The fact that the map is schematically shown as a circle indicates that this is a symbolic mandala, meant to gather up the whole. Just as this map and the Panchakroshī Temple gather all that is sacred within the symbolic circumference of Kāshī, so Kāshī gathers up the whole of sacred India. In addition to the twelve *jyotirlingas,* there are also symbolic duplicates of the four *dhāms,* the seven sacred cities, the seven sacred rivers, and individual *tīrthas* of note throughout the land, such as the seaside shrine of Gokarna in Karnataka. The point is not really to visit all these places on a pilgrimage to Kāshī, but to emphasize that this one place includes them all, gathers them into its sanctity. This intensification of the whole into a single point is one of the ways in which the symbolic imagination operates in this religious world.

The play of light and illumination is certainly part of the daily religious life of Kāshī. Standing on the riverbank at dawn, facing east as the sun rises and spreads its rays across the river to illumine the sandstone steps of the *ghāts* and the walls of the city's temples, the faithful give ritual expression to the great prayer of the Gāyatrī mantra, "I worship the light of the divine sun. May it illumine my mind." The sun also adds radiance to the faces of those early-morning bathers, who raise the water in their cupped hands and pour it out for the gods and for their ancestors. By night, a relatively new Vārānasī ritual brings people once again to the river. It is an elaborate *pūjā* to Shiva and the Gangā, conducted by a synchronized team of *pūjārīs*, offering the incense, flowers, and oil lamps of the *āratī* to the river. They, and the crowd of many hundreds, chant, *Hara Hara Mahādeva Shambho! Kāshī Vishvanātha Gange!* "Praise to Shiva, the Great Lord, Kāshī Vishvanātha, and the Gangā!" With their muscular arms, these *pūjārīs* raise the blazing fire of huge, multitiered oil lamps to the night sky.

Those who gather for the beautiful *āratī* inevitably see the fires of the cremation ground at Manikarnikā, burning round the clock a short distance down the river. Contemplating this conjunction of the worship of the living and the cremation of the dead, we, as they, are reminded that life and death are not presented in Kāshī as in conflict. Living and dying are what this city of Shiva is all about. "Death in Kāshī is liberation," as the saying goes. *Kāshyām maranam muktih.* The key to the spiritual freedom of liberation is wisdom, the enlightening wisdom of deep self-knowledge. Here, so they say, that wisdom and that freedom is to be gained merely by breathing one's last. Dying in Kāshī leads directly to liberation, according to tradition, for here Shiva himself becomes the guru and imparts the enlightening wisdom to the dying. Flooded with the light of wisdom, one's soul can make the final crossing to the "far shore." It is this, we are to understand, that is going on there in the cremation grounds where the fire of funeral pyres illumines the dark riverbank.

Vārānasī is a very worldly city, lavishly displaying both life and death. Its market streets today are more densely crowded than ever, packed with merchants and street stalls, pilgrims and local customers. Entrepreneurs competing for tourists have painted its ancient buildings with sometimes garish advertisements for lodging, food, and services. The population of people and pilgrims has grown, but the old streets of the inner city are still the sidewalk-narrow lanes, twisting and turning, filled with shops and temples, now marked with arrows and signs directing one through the maze to a restaurant or a silk factory. The pulse of the inner city is intense, accented with the chants of funeral processions making their way toward Manikarnikā bearing the body of a deceased relative on a bamboo litter. Yet the cramped lanes of this dense city eventually open onto the spacious steps leading to the river, like clutched hands releasing their offerings of flowers into the stream. The intensity and the calm, the business of life and of death, go together.

With the 1990s and the rise of new strains of Hindu nationalism, Vārānasī has also made its accommodations to the politics of communal identity. When trouble flares up, the Indian Army is posted in the heart of the city, guarding against what is perceived by some to be a tinderbox of potential violence. It is common knowledge that right at the center of Vārānasī a temple and a mosque stand side by side. Today's "Golden Temple" of Kāshī Vishvanātha replaced a much grander sixteenth-century Vishvanātha temple built by Nārāyana Bhatta at the time of the Mughal Emperor Akbar. That temple was partially destroyed in the seventeenth century, under the rule of the deeply conservative Aurangzeb. It was turned into a mosque, and another Vishvanātha Temple was built a short distance away. The mosque today bears the popular name Jnāna Vāpi Mosque, so called because of the sacred Well of Wisdom, the Jnāna Vāpi, located in a pillared arcade between today's mosque and temple. For more than three hundred years, they have sat side by side, temple and mosque. Whether or not the mosque is built of a ruined temple is hardly contested, as it is in Ayodhyā. One side of the old temple still stands, ornamented and broken, the rest having been incorporated into the mosque. While the site has provided the venue for sporadic communal tension during the past two hundred years, the city is far too focused on the exigencies of life, death, and commerce to be fertile soil for Hindu nationalism, even though the Vishva Hindu Parishad has often demanded that the mosque be surrendered to Hindus.[52] In the City of Shiva, where the very stones are said to be Shiva *lingas* and where temples have shifted and readjusted their footing century after century, the boisterous claim to a particular plot of land makes little sense.

In the Far West: Someshvara, or Somnāth, the Moon's Lord

The first-listed of the *jyotirlingas* is always Somnāth, or Somanātha, or Someshvara, the "Moon's Lord," located in a great temple that sits on the seacoast of Gujarat, right above the sandy beach and the roar of the waves. Standing on the seacoast at Somnāth, we can see ships in the harbor of the nearby port of Veraval. Were we to sail due west, we would come to the Arabian Peninsula and the Gulf of Oman. Indeed, historians have documented the seafaring trade that has flourished here for well over a thousand years, linking this western peninsula of India to points in west Asia and Africa. Archaeologists have found evidence of human settlement here as early as the third millennium B.C.E. Somnāth is important to our exploration of the *jyotirlingas* both because of its primacy on the list and because its lore is heaped high with both myth and history, with episodes of destruction, with periods of reclamation, with emotion, devotion, and politics. Yet, through all of this, there is the enduring attraction of the place itself, in good times and bad. While temples may be *tīrthas, tīrthas* are not necessarily temples. *Tīrthas* endure, while temples come and go.

At this *tīrtha*, a river meets the sea. Actually, it is a *trivenī*, a triple-confluence, where the Hiran and Kapila Rivers join with a third, the mystical underground Sarasvatī, just before they flow into the sea. As we know by now, this is one of the multitude of *trivenīs* in India where two visible rivers are joined by the Sarasvatī, the river that always brings her unseen waters to amplify the blessings of the confluence. Pilgrims to Somnāth bathe in the rivers and they also bathe in the ocean itself, this being one of those special shrines along India's seacoast where the fear and taboo of the sea fall away and ocean bathing is part of sacred ritual.[53]

The oldest name of this *tīrtha* was Prabhāsa, the "Glorious," and it was famous as a *tīrtha* even in the time of the *Mahābhārata*. Prabhāsa is mentioned as one of the places visited by the Pāndavas as they traveled in clockwise pilgrimage through the *tīrthas* of India. It was here, according to the *Mahābhārata*, that Arjuna sought out Krishna, who agreed to serve him as charioteer during the impending battle. And it was here, so they say, that after the world-shattering battle was over, another awful battle took place, this time among Krishna's own clan, the Yādavas. Finally, at the close of the age, Krishna died just a short distance from here, shot in the heel by a hunter.

The lore of the *Mahābhārata* and the Purānas associates Prabhāsa not only with Krishna, but more prominently with Shiva, the "Moon's Lord." As the story goes, Soma, the Moon, married twenty-seven wives, but neglected all of them in favor of one, the beautiful Rohinī. Daksha, the father of all these women, implored Soma to be fair-minded in his treatment of them, but the poor Moon was helplessly in love with Rohinī. So Daksha cursed Soma to waste away with consumption, a terrible curse. The Moon waned to almost nothing, and all the gods and sages were miserable because of the unremitting darkness of the night sky. Finally, the gods and sages took matters in hand and brought the Moon to Prabhāsa to worship Shiva. Soma worshipped an earthen *linga* for many months, until Shiva was pleased with him and granted him a boon to alleviate his curse. The boon was this: Soma would wane day by day during one half of the month and then would wax to his full glory, day by day, during the other. And so it is with the waning and waxing of the moon.[54]

Shiva also pledged to dwell there forever in Prabhāsa, in the form of Somnāth or Someshvara, the "Moon's Lord." As we know, the moon became an important part of the iconography of Shiva, who is depicted with the crescent moon adorning his ascetic's hair as a jewel. The very notion of Shiva as both *sakala,* "with parts," and *nishkala,* "undivided, without parts," draws its meaning from the waxing and waning of the moon. One translation of *kala* is a "fraction or digit of the moon," which is always whole, fractionless, and yet is rendered visible in its parts. So it is with Shiva—fractionless, but variously visible in his parts. Here, at the edge of the sea, where the high tides bring the water to the very foot of the temple, the story of the Moon's Lord, Someshvara, is especially resonant. Indeed, some traditions held that the ocean would, at high tide, rise into the very sanctum of the temple and submerge the Shiva *linga.* The Moon's Day, Monday, or Somavāra, is also associated with Shiva, as is the fourteenth day of every waning fortnight—the day preceding the new moon. On the new-moon day, so they say, the Moon himself bathes there where the Sarasvatī meets the sea, and so do countless pilgrims.

Some historians contend that the worship of Shiva may have been in place as early as the second century, when Prabhāsa was a central site of the Pashupata sect of Shaivas. This was, of course, several centuries before the great era of temple construction. Since then, it seems there have been many temples dedicated to Shiva as Someshvara here. Evidence of a thriving temple culture at Prabhāsa begins in the ninth and tenth centuries. It was this temple that was destroyed in 1026 during the raid into Gujarat by the Afghan king Mahmud of Ghazni. This temple was said to be famous far and wide, its glory no doubt amplified by the fate that befell it. Persian chronicles of Mahmud's looting and burning of Somnāth constitute their own kind of glorification of the temple, describing its beauty and its treasures, its columns of teak from Africa, studded as they were with jewels, emphasizing the antiquity of the temple, lauding its supreme importance for Hindus. These chronicles also describe the fierce defense of the temple, in which fifty thousand Hindus were killed. Mahmud, so they say, broke the *linga* of Somnāth into pieces, burned down the temple, and hauled away its riches. In the eyes of the Persian historians, of course, all this was evidence of the conqueror's glory.[55] Al-Biruni, writing four years after the sack of Somnāth, summarized the exploits of Mahmud of Ghazni this way: "Mahmud utterly ruined the prosperity of the country and performed there wonderful exploits by which Hindus became like atoms of dust scattered in all directions and like a tale of old in the mouth of the people. Their scattered remains cherish, of course, the most inveterate aversion towards all Muslims."[56]

The sack of Somnāth in the eleventh century begins a narrative of temple looting and destruction, followed by rebuilding and resistance, followed by looting and destruction once again. This is a narrative that continues to be part of the lore of Somnāth deep into the twentieth century. The representation of these events and their historiography has become a matter of vivid public and scholarly debate in modern India, especially in the fifty years since Indian independence.[57] No doubt the story of Hindu-Muslim animosity generated by the razing of Somnāth was exaggerated by both Muslim dynastic historians and also by Hindus who looked back on the glory of Somnāth through the lens of its repeated destruction and its repeated rising, "like a phoenix from its own ashes."[58] It was surely hyperbole when K. M. Munshi wrote that the destruction of Somnāth "has been burnt into the collective sub-conscious of the race as an unforgettable national disaster."[59] In fact, it seems clear from all sides that pilgrimage to Somnāth actually continued through the centuries following Mahmud. Even within a few decades after the raid of Mahmud of Ghazni, Sanskrit inscriptions begin to give evidence of continued pilgrimage. The Chalukya kings patronized the temple in the eleventh and twelfth centuries, supporting its priests and protecting its many pilgrims. One long twelfth-century inscription tells of a Shaiva priest and visionary, one Bhava Brihaspati, who was sent by Shiva himself to persuade King Kumārapāla to renovate the temple, which was suffering from deterioration, mismanagement, and lack of care. No mention is made of the looting of Mahmud.[60] Kumārapāla's grand temple was renovated again in the late thirteenth century by yet another Shaiva leader, the renowned Tripurāntaka. From inscriptions, we know not only of his fame in Somnāth, but of his pilgrimage to other *jyotirlingas*—to Kedārnāth in the Himalayan north, to Tryambaka on the Godāvarī River, and to Rāmeshvara in the far south.[61] While the temple was plundered in the fourteenth century, and again in the fifteenth converted briefly into a mosque, it was not until the early eighteenth century that Somnāth was destroyed once again, this time by the forces of the Mughal Emperor Aurangzeb. Kumārapāla's twelfth-century temple now lay in ruins.

At the end of the eighteenth century, the great temple-building Queen Ahalyābāi Holkar of Indore wanted to rebuild a temple at Somnāth. She found, however, that it was impossible to build upon the old ruins, so she built a temple a short distance away. For 150 years, the site of the old Somnāth was silent. In 1922, Gujarati writer and political leader K. M. Munshi visited Somnāth for the first time. He had already written a trilogy of novels set in what he saw as the golden age of Gujarat, before the Delhi Sultanate extended its control into western India in the thirteenth century. Standing in the ruins of Somnāth, he mourned for this place as a symbol of that glory, now gone. Reflecting upon what he saw, Munshi wrote, "Desecrated, burnt, and battered, it still stood firm—a monument to our humiliation and ingratitude. I can scarcely describe the shame which I felt on that early morning as I walked the broken floor of the once-hallowed *sabhamandapa,* littered with broken pillars and scattered stones. Lizards slipped in and out of their holes at the sound of my unfamiliar steps and—Oh! The shame of it—an inspector's horse, tied there, neighed at my approach with sacrilegious impertinence."[62]

Munshi's popular novel *Jaya Somanātha*, published in 1937, brought the glory, the romance, the intrigue, and the poignancy of Somnāth to a Gujarati audience, and its success surely heightened awareness of this important old shrine. Somnāth was not simply the site of ancient ruins when India gained independence in 1947, but was a place charged with feeling. In the months following independence, K. M. Munshi and Sardar Vallabhai Patel, both Gujarat natives, became vocally and publicly committed to the reconstruction of Somnāth. They established the Somnāth Trust for the project and began to raise support and money. Prime Minister Nehru was at pains to dissociate the government of India from this undertaking, writing to all the state chief ministers in 1951, as the opening ceremonies of the temple approached:

> You must have read about the coming ceremonies at Somnāth temple. Many people have been attracted to this and some of my colleagues are even associated with it in their individual capacities. But it should be clearly understood that this function is not governmental and the Government of India as such has nothing to do with it. While it is easy to understand a certain measure of public support to this venture, we have to remember that we must not do anything which comes in the way of our State being secular. . . . It is important that Governments should keep the secular and non-communal ideal always before them.[63]

The opening ceremonies did take place, with public officials present from throughout India, perhaps in their "individual" capacities, and with substantial support from the government of Gujarat. Trust officials argued that the government of India does indeed take an interest in concerns for security and public health whenever there are large religious observances, including the massive Kumbha Melā at Allahabad, the smaller *melās* at Nāsik and Hardvār, or the *Urs* at the Sufi shrine in Ajmer. So it was that the president of India, Rajendra Prasād, presided at the Somnāth opening ceremonies. He insisted, over Nehru's objection, that he would also preside over the opening of a mosque or a church. The new temple, built in the Chalukya style with its magnificent pillared halls and open porticos, was dedicated in 1951, although work on the temple and the surrounding site continued into the 1990s.

The *linga* of Somnāth is a huge black stone some three feet high, worshipped with both the distance and intimacy of Shaiva rites that we see in Ujjain's Mahākāla and in the Himalayas at Kedārnāth. This new temple, while not partaking of the stone-worn antiquity of some of the other *jyotirlingas,* has taken its place once again as first in the list of the twelve *jyotirlingas* and attracts thousands of pilgrims each week. On great festival days, the crowd in the sanctum sanctorum is as dense as at any of the great Shiva temples, allowing for no more than a moment's worship and meditation before one is moved on by its force.

Today's Somnāth participates, to be sure, in the resonances of Hindu nationalism that have come with the rebuilding of this temple and the presumed normative Hindu idiom that has so often infused public affairs, even in a constitutionally secular state. In October of 1990, the Vishva Hindu Parishad launched a *yātrā* from Somnāth to Ayodhyā, drawing attention to its demand to reconstruct a Hindu temple on the presumed site of Lord Rāma's birthplace by beginning at India's most well-known temple restoration in Somnāth. Bear in mind that pilgrimages are rituals of connection, and as the truck decked out to be Rāma's chariot wound its way from place to place all across central and north India, its point of origin and its destination were linked together in the "spirit of Somnāth." In this vision of India, the iconoclasm of the past would be set aright in the ritual and religious constructions of the present. The movement launched by that now-famous chariot-*yātrā* has created its own fresh round of suspicion, polarization, and violence. Entering the great gate into the grounds of the Somnāth Temple today, one passes through a security gateway of metal detectors unknown at other great Shaiva temples.

The "spirit of Somnāth" is certainly complex, and the scholars who have written about it in the present context of communal contestation in India—Romila Thapar, Richard Davis, and Peter van der Veer—have explored the ways in which history and memory have made Somnāth a place that has come to stand for the repeated enactment of religiously based division. Another scholar, the Gujarati historian of religion Neelima Shukla-Bhatt, offers a different perspective, drawing on her own work in Gujarat. She recalls the observation of the anthropologist William Sax that many interpreters who write out of textual materials "bypass local contexts and understandings altogether."[64]

So how does all this look from the local standpoint of Somnāth?

Shukla-Bhatt argues that in the local context of today's pilgrimage life in Somnāth, "conversations with pilgrims clearly indicate that a large number of them do not know or care about the history of the shrine's destructions or reconstructions."[65] Munshi's dream of a Somnāth Temple attracting crowds of pilgrims once again has certainly come to fruition, but from the pilgrim's standpoint, it is not laden with a load of poignancy and politics. Somnāth is fully incorporated into the Saurashtra pilgrimage circuit of those who visit the great Krishna temple at Dvāraka to the west and the mountain shrines of Girnār to the north, and Somnāth is fully a living part of the twelve *jyotirlingas*. Its *māhātmya* comprises the first band on the video CD *Dvādash Jyotirlinga,* which displays them all in song and sights. Interestingly, this video *māhātmya* is not all infused with the narrative of destruction and resurrection that informs Hindu nationalist discourse. Pilgrimage to Somnāth is, once again, about the Moon's Lord, Someshvara, and the abundant blessings of bathing and prayer in this place.

IN THE NORTH COUNTRY: KEDĀRNĀTH

The most ancient mythology of Shiva associates him with the mountains, the Himalayas, the "abode of snows," also called *devālaya,* the "abode of the gods." They are also the terrain of yogis, ascetics, and renouncers who make this mountain land their home. The most rigorous of them stay here all year, even through the snows of winter, while others head for the Himalayas every summer. Pilgrims who make their way up the trail on the final steep haul to Kedārnāth, the northernmost of the *jyotirlingas,* will encounter these mountain ascetics, either as fellow travelers or as cross-legged, ash-covered practitioners who sit by the trail to seek the beneficence of the pilgrims.

The pilgrimage to Kedāra used to take many weeks of hiking through terrain imprinted with the mythic presence of Shiva. Today most pilgrims come by bus to Gaurī Kund, a small village with a natural hot springs where Pārvatī, also called Gaurī, is said to have practiced severe spiritual austerities to win Shiva for her husband. The penance of Pārvatī is a story pilgrims will invariably know. It is a tale that begins as so many do, with the well-being of the cosmos threatened by a powerful demon.

Tāraka's special boon was that he could be slain only by a son of Shiva. In Tāraka's view, this made him almost invulnerable, since Shiva was an ascetic, unlikely to father a son. But Pārvatī, the Mountain's Daughter, was determined to win Shiva as her husband. She served the ash-covered Lord in his austerities, hoping to attract his attention. She was as lovely as a woman could be. Even Kāma, the divine Cupid of passion, brought his full energy to the effort. As he entered the grove where Shiva sat in meditation, he brought the fragrances and blossoms of springtime with him. Slowly he drew his bowstring of buzzing bees, set his arrow of flowers, and aimed at Shiva's heart. But that very moment, as Kāma let loose his flower-power arrow, Shiva opened his third eye and released a bolt of fire, burning Kāma to ash.

Pārvatī, undaunted, resolved that if she could not win Shiva's heart with the service of love, she would win him by her own asceticism. And so she did, standing for hours on one leg, sitting in meditation day and night, season after season, sitting between blazing fires in the heat of summer, sitting through ice and snow in the Himalayan winter. Remarkably, her austerities made her lovelier than ever. At last, Shiva came to her, in disguise at first, to test her understanding. He asked why on earth she would ever want Shiva as a husband. Could she imagine their wedding, with her bridal silks and his garments of hides? Did she know he had no proper lineage or clan? Pārvatī responded, "Don't you know that Shiva is Brahman? He is unchanging, indescribable, eternal, though he assumes shapes and forms for the welfare of his devotees. He does not make a show of worldly lordship, as do those who are deluded by the superficial wealth of the world. But I swear to you, if Shiva does not marry me, I shall remain forever a virgin." With this, Shiva, satisfied that she understood what she was getting in for, revealed himself to Pārvatī and asked her to be his bride.[66]

In this mountain town, a small but well-kept temple of Gaurī is marked with a red Hindi inscription proclaiming, "This is the place of Mother Pārvatī's *tapas*." To one side of the temple door is a fine stone bas-relief image of Pārvatī at her austerities, standing on one foot in the middle of five fires. Not far away is a much smaller temple of Shiva

Kedārnāth temple in the high Himalayas

Mahādeva, and its painted inscription includes the listing of twelve *jyotirlingas.*

Most pilgrims arrive in the evening for a morning departure on the trail to Kedārnāth. They will perhaps visit the temples here in Gaurī Kund, but Kedārnāth is foremost on their minds. Those who need porters or ponies will make arrangements for the journey, and many pilgrims will take advantage of a "holy dip" in the bathing tank. The deep, square tank at Gaurī Kund is fed by hot springs and includes a special section for ladies. As at Badrīnāth and Yamunotrī, these mountain hot springs are a welcome respite for ritual bathing and the relaxation of weary limbs. Pilgrims will surely look forward to a dip in the hot springs after their return trip from Kedārnāth.

Pilgrims strike out early in the morning to walk the steep trail over ten miles to Kedāra. Finding their own pace, they stretch out along the trail—ponies in the lead, followed by pedestrian pilgrims both with and without shoes, and four-man *dhoolies* carrying the elderly or infirm. There are white-clad widows in tennis shoes, their walking sticks an absolute necessity, some making their way slowly with one stick in each hand. There are Rajasthani women in bright skirts and thick silver anklets, walking barefoot. There are robust old men wearing jackets and woolen mufflers, with porters carrying their gear; and there are scantily clad *sannyāsīs* carrying nothing but a water pot and a bowl. Parties of pilgrims from Gujarat and Karnataka mingle with families from Maharashtra and schoolgirls from Bengal. They cross high snowfields and marvel at the snow. For most, it is the first snow they have ever seen. They sing, *Jaya ho, Kedārnāth barfānī! Bhukhe ko rotī, pyāse ko pānī.* "Hail to the snows of Kedārnāth! To the hungry, they are bread. To the thirsty, they are water!"

The last pull up the trail to Kedāra is especially steep, but by then pilgrims are drawn forward by the sight of the snowy peaks, fully in view ahead. Finally, from the place called Deva Darshan, they stop to behold the temple in the distance where it first comes into view. The small village ahead is inhabited only six months a year and covered with as much as twenty feet of snow for the other six months. Climbing the steps to the stone temple of Kedāra, pilgrims look around with awe at the towering mountains that rise on three sides, the rocky scree slopes and avalanche falls, the high snowfields and glaciers. The energetic among them might use the last hours of late afternoon to climb to the lofty promontory over the valley of Kedāra, where Shiva's guardians keep watch. There, more than twelve thousand feet above sea level, is a cluster of *bhairavas*, Shiva's fearsome manifestations, with prominent and fearsome faces carved in stone. Bhairava is known in these parts as Bhukund Bhairava or Bhairavnāth. Tridents brought here by intrepid ascetics are stuck firmly into the ground, and flags of orange, red, and white are posted on this lookout. From here, both the pilgrims and Bhairavnāth have a commanding view of the grassy glacial cirque below where Shiva's temple stands.

Across the high mountains in another stretch of high country only thirty miles away as the crow flies is Badrīnāth, the other great shrine in this part of the Himalayas. Badrīnāth and Kedārnāth are two of the four *dhāms* of the Himalayan North Country called Uttarakhand. As we will see in our survey of the landscape of Vishnu, Badrināth is famous for the temple and presence of Vishnu and yet has many strong links to Shiva in its own lore and legend. In one such story, Lord Vishnu usurped Shiva's own seat there, and then asked Shiva to move over the mountains to another location, and Shiva gladly complied. From the Shaiva perspective of accounts in the *Shiva Purāna*, we learn that the two legendary sages—Nara and Nārāyana, considered by some to be *avatāras* of Vishnu—performed spiritual austerities in the high mountains where Badrīnāth is today.[67] Like so many others, they made an earthen *linga* of Shiva to focus their devotion, and in response to their spiritual effort, Shiva appeared to them and gave them a boon. They asked Shiva to be present as eternal light, for the good of all humanity. Shiva agreed, and pledged to dwell in these mountains as a *jyotirlinga*.

The sturdy stone temple of Kedāra is open for only a few months each year. It houses a natural *svayambhū linga*, a rock outcropping said originally to be the earthen *linga* made by Nara and Nārāyana. When Shiva appeared to them, the *linga* took the form of sheer light, although we now see it in the form of a stone. The light-turned-stone theme is not uncommon in the mythology of Shiva. This is the story of Kailāsa, the archetypal *jyotirlinga*, which became the massive world-centering mountain. This too is the story of Arunāchala, "Dawn Mountain," in Tamil Nadu—a mass of brilliant fire that now, in this Kali Age, is visible as a mountain.

Each October at Kedārnāth, a *jyoti*, an oil lamp, is kindled in the sanctuary, and the priests close the temple and retreat down the mountain to the village of Okhi Math for the season of snows. In their procession, they carry the *mukut* of Shiva, the golden coils and hood of the *nāga* that sits like a crown on top of the *linga*. It is to this crown that they offer substitute worship during the winter. According to the account of the faithful, when they return to open the temple in May, the light is still burning, even after all the intervening winter months. The miraculous lamp is brought forth from the sanctuary for the public *jyotidarshan*, the "beholding of the light."

During the summer months, there are two major times for *darshan* at Kedārnāth, evening and morning. All of the polychrome glossy images of Kedārnāth display the two: the adorned *ārati darshan* of evening and the naked *nirvāna darshan* of the morning. The rhythm and juxtaposition of these two evoke in ritual the Shaiva theology of a god who is both describable and indescribable, both apprehensible and utterly transcendent. In the evening, the irregular, pyramidal stone *linga* is decorated for *ārati darshan*. It is covered with silken cloth, and the golden coils and hood of the *mukut* are placed on its "head." It is garlanded with leaves and flowers. A golden umbrella is mounted above it, as might shelter the head of a king. Pilgrims press forward to stand for but a moment at the doorway of the sanctum and behold this beautifully adorned "face" of Shiva. In the morning, however, quite a different procedure is followed. The stone is left unadorned and the rock itself is wholly visible. The sanctum door is open and pilgrims are bearing their own offerings— platters of white crystallized sugar, *chana dal*, dried fruits, nuts, coconut, sandalwood powder, red *kumkum*, and wildflowers. They wait in a long line that winds around the temple in the warm sun. But this time, when they enter the temple and reach the door of the inner sanctum, they will be able to enter right into Shiva's sanctum, touching the stone with their own hands, touching their foreheads to it, rubbing it with ghee, placing their offerings upon it. They pour water on the *linga*, sprinkle their raisins, nuts, and flowers, or place an offering of silken cloths upon the sides of the stone. All this is part of *nirvāna darshan*, and the intimacy it permits between worshipper and deity is very powerful indeed.

Leaving Kedārnāth, a few of the most hardy pilgrims undertake a pilgrimage to what are called the Five Kedārs, all in the Uttarakhand area of the Himalayas. The same section of the *Shiva Purāna* alludes to another popularly told story about the manifestations of Shiva here in the mountains. Following the great war of the *Mahābhārata*, which had left the world of warriors covered with blood and submerged in grief, the Pāndavas sought out Shiva to expunge the sins of battle. They went first to Kāshī, but Shiva eluded them and headed for the Himalayas, where he hid at the place now called Gupta Kāshī. When the Pāndavas found him there, Shiva transformed himself into a bull and dove into the earth. They caught him by his tail and begged him to stay. The great hump of the bull remains there in the rocky outcropping of Kedārnāth. Tunganāth, Rudranāth, Kalpeshvar, and Madhyameshvar are the other parts of Shiva in the landscape of the North Country. According to some legends, his head emerged from the earth at Pashupatināth in Nepal. The versions of this popular story are many.

The memory of the Pāndavas here, as elsewhere in the mountains, is strong. The Pāndavas are carved in stone around the inside of the anterior chamber of the Kedārnāth Temple. There, a popular image shows the five, standing with Draupadī to one side of the exposed stone outcropping of the Kedārnāth *linga*, their hands pressed together in prayer. Although Shiva is said to have changed his form and disappeared into the earth itself when they approached, the Pāndavas were nonetheless the first to have his *darshan* here, in this form.

As we know by now, Shiva's fivefold nature is a common way of speaking of his presence. He is present in the five elements—earth, air, fire, water, and ether. He has five faces—creating, sustaining, destroying, surprising, and transcending the universe. His mantra of praise is fivefold: "*na-ma-shi-va-ya*." His mystical sound *Om* is composed of five sounds—*a, u, ma*, the nasal sound, and silence. Similarly, this mountainous abode of Shiva is itself said to be fivefold. Here in Uttarakhand, those in the know point out the parts of the bull form of Shiva in the landscape. These five spread the divine embodiment of Shiva throughout the high mountain country of the Himalayas. Shiva is not merely the one who dwells in the mountains, or the one who dwells in a great temple in the mountains, but the one who is present in the mountain landscape itself.

Tunganāth, one of the Five Kedārs, is the highest temple in this part of the Himalayas. From Chopta Chatti, where the path to Tunganāth begins, pilgrims can see a vast range of peaks—the Kedārnāth Peaks, the Badrināth Peaks, and even Nanda Devī to the south. The trail to Tunganāth climbs through forests of rhododendrons and emerges, finally, into wide meadows. The Tunganāth Temple sits just below a high summit at more than twelve thousand feet. The temple and the small settlement around it are made of stone, with slate roofs. Only the hardiest pilgrims come here, and very few ever stay overnight. This rocky fastness, high above the timberline, is bitterly cold. The *linga* of Shiva in the temple here is flanked by an image of the Panchavaktra—the "five faces" of Shiva as the Lord of Kedāra. But looking around the mountain peaks that stretch out in every direction from Tunganāth, one is clearly aware that the "five faces" of Shiva's light here shine forth not only in the temple images, but in the very land of Uttarakhand.

The priests of Kedārnāth interviewed by Luke Whitmore expressed in their own words the view that "here, Bhagavān (God) and place (sthān) are the same," as one priest put it. Another said, "Inside the temple there is a mountain. It is the Himalaya mountain inside the temple. And the Bhagavān (god) there means the mountain. But if you say to someone worship a mountain, he won't do it, will he? Worship the mountain, brother no one will do it. What we old people did is we put the mountain inside the temple. We took that very mountain and built an impressive temple there, where now people come and exclaim, 'Vah, vah, what an enormous *linga*!' That's whose *puja* we do. We are doing the *puja* of the Himalaya. We do the *puja* of that lap of the Himalaya in which we live."[68]

The *Shiva Purāna* closes its praise of Kedāra by saying that while Shiva is Lord of the whole universe, he is especially present in this North Country of Bhārata, for here Shiva is worshipped directly, face-to-face, by the people of India.[69] Indeed, those who may die on their way into this mountain country will not be born again.

IN THE FAR SOUTH: RĀMESHVARA, KING RĀMA'S LORD

Far from the Himalayan Kedāra, at the distant southern end of India, on the flat coastlands of the Bay of Bengal is Rāmeshvara. Casting an image of the land, Kedārnāth and Rāmeshvara are the antipodes. The Rāmeshvara Temple compound is located on the offshore island that stretches out from the coast of Tamil Nadu toward Sri Lanka. Rāmeshvara is sometimes called Setu, the "Bridge," for here, according to the *Rāmāyana*, Lord Rāma, with the help of his monkey armies, built a bridge to the island called Lanka to rescue his wife Sītā, who had been kidnapped by Lanka's king, the demon Rāvana. The land of India has often been described with the words *A Setu Himāchalam*— "From the Himalayas to the Bridge." Indeed, as we have seen, this phrase became the motto of the Geographical Survey of India, describing the whole span of the land.

Just as pilgrims make the trek to Kedārnāth from the Tamil-speaking south, so pilgrims come to Rāmeshvara from the Hindi-speaking north.

In contrast to many places of pilgrimage in Tamil Nadu, where Tamil is almost exclusively the language of temple culture, here at Rāmeshvara pamphlets and guides cater to the needs of Hindi-speaking pilgrims.[70] Some pilgrims enact the symbolic coherence of their journey by bringing water from the Gangā in the north to sprinkle upon the *jyotirlinga* of Rāmeshvara in the distant south, and then returning with the sands of Rāmeshvara to place them in the River Gangā, a practice that has mention in the *Skanda Purāna*.[71] There is a popular tradition of uncertain antiquity that a pilgrimage to Kāshī on the Gangā in the north is not truly complete without a pilgrimage to Rāmeshvara. How many pilgrims take this to heart, I do not know. Even today, however, there are temple protocols for those who bring Gangā water along with them and for those who send Gangā water to the temple by rail. An online temple guide specifies:

> Gangā water to be accepted for Abhishekam should be brought in brass, copper or bronze vessels and such vessels will be accepted on payment of the prescribed fees per vessel to Peishkar. Vessels made of tin or iron will not be accepted; but those who bring such vessels should pay for copper or brass vessels available in the temple and the peishkar will have the Gangā water transferred to temple vessels after satisfying himself about the genuineness of the water. Gangā water can also be sent by post or rail with prescribed fee per vessel and an additional one rupee.[72]

The *linga* of Rāmeshvara is said to have been established by Lord Rāma himself, a scene popular in the glossy depictions of today's calendar artists. We see him kneeling in the sand, honoring Shiva, with Lakshmana and Hanumān reverently to one side. In one account, Rāma established an earthen *pārthiva linga* here and invoked Shiva to be present, making sixteen offerings of worship. "Victory! Victory!" he prayed, as he danced before the image of Lord Shiva. Pleased with Rāma's devotion, Shiva took the form of sheer light and gave Rāma a boon. Rāma's first request was not for himself, but rather for the whole earth. He implored Shiva, "Stay here in this place, O Lord, to purify the worlds." And so it was that Lord Shiva agreed to remain in the *linga* now famous as Rāmeshvara. And Shiva blessed Rāma, saying, "May you be victori-

ous, O great king." And so it was that Rāma crossed the ocean to defeat
Rāvana.[73] In the Vālmīkī *Rāmāyana*, Rāma, Sītā, and their entourage
take an airborne chariot from Lanka back to Ayodhyā, and as they lift
off into the sky they look down at Rāmeshvara, the sacred shrine so holy
it destroys all sins.

Other myths link the *linga* at Rāmeshvara to the time right *after*
Rāma's victory over Rāvana, when he returned to Setu with Sītā, Lakshmana, Hanumān, and the rest of his entourage. Here he wanted to establish a *linga* to worship Shiva in expiation for the sin of killing Rāvana.
After all, Rāvana was a brahmin, even though he was a demon-king. By
slaying him, Rāma incurred the sin of brahmin-murder.[74] And Rāvana
was also, we recall, a great devotee of Shiva. This, then, is the scene
depicted most commonly in the polychrome images sold to pilgrims:
Rāma worships Shiva, surrounded by his whole entourage, including
Hanumān, Lakshmana, Sītā, and even Rāvana's brother Vibhīshana.
Such devotion must also include Rāma's gratitude for victory.

Procuring the stone for the Rāmeshvara *linga* generates another set
of stories. According to one, Rāma sent Hanumān, swift as the wind,
to the far Himalayas to bring an appropriate stone from Mount Kailāsa.
Bringing a *linga* from the Himalayas to honor Shiva on the seashore
of the south again underlines the strong symbolic links forged by this
north-south axis. However, as the astrologically determined auspicious hour for establishing the *linga* approached, Hanumān had not yet
returned with the stone. So Sītā fashioned a makeshift *linga* of sand and
Rāma consecrated it at the sacred hour. In their worship, Shiva became
fully present to them there. When Hanumān returned from the Himalayas, they thought they would replace the temporary sand *linga* with the
special Himalayan stone. But Sītā's sand *linga* could not be moved, no
matter how hard they tried. Even when Hanumān tried to pull the sand
linga up with the strength of his tail, it would not budge. The *linga* of
sand had become hard as rock. Thus, at Rāmeshvara there are really two
lingas: the Himalayan stone, called the Vishvanātha *linga*, brought from
the north by Hanumān, and the pile of sand established by Sītā, called
the Rāmanātha *linga*. In keeping with the traditions of natural hierophany associated with *jyotirlingas*, the latter has pride of place in the temple
of Rāmeshvara.[75]

Today, pilgrims make their vows of intent, *sankalpa*, on the ocean beach at the place called Agni Tīrtha, fashioning *lingas* of sand here, as did Rāma and Sītā. Then, committing their makeshift *lingas* to the ocean, they bathe and enter the Rāmanātha Temple to honor Rāma's Lord, Shiva. It is a spacious temple, with many circumambulatory corridors. Near here, they say, Rāma dug a well with the tip of his bow, and the waters of the Gangā miraculously became present in the well, so in fact everyone is able to honor Shiva here with Gangā water, even those pilgrims who have not come from the north. The Rāmanātha Temple is famous for its sacred waters. It contains twenty-two *tīrthas,* or wells, whose waters bestow various blessings and benefits. Among them, of course, are wells containing the waters of the Gangā and the Yamunā. Pilgrims make their circuit through the temple with a bucket, drawing water from all twenty-two *tīrthas,* before entering the sanctum with their libations for Lord Shiva.

Rāmeshvara gives us insight into the convergence of the Rāma cycle of *tīrthas* with the major shrines of Shiva. As we shall see in following Rāma's journey from Ayodhyā, through the forests of India, to Rāmeshvara and back to Ayodhyā, the hero Rāma, long before he comes to be seen as the Divine Lord, is truly the devotee of Shiva.[76]

AT THE CENTER OF INDIA: MAHĀKĀLESHVARA

About midway between Rāmeshvara and Kedāra is the *jyotirlinga* of Mahākāla, located in the city of Ujjain. This old city reaches back to the time of the Buddha, when it was known as the capital of the kingdom of Avantī. In the era of India's epics, beginning in the third century B.C.E., it was known as the City Victorious, Avantikā or Ujjayinī. It flourished in the golden age of the Gupta kings, from the third to the sixth centuries C.E., and in the fifth century was described by its great poet Kālidāsa as a city that must have been built by those who came from heaven "and left the sky to build this heaven on earth."[77] This was Kālidāsa's hometown, and the poet's special temple-image of the goddess Kālī is still worshipped today in the small temple called Garha Kālikā, literally "Kālī's House." The poet also offers his homage to Mahākāla, the principal deity of Ujjain then, as now: Shiva as the great destroyer, the Lord of time and death. The praises of Ujjain are found in many of the Purānas, especially the long Avantikā Khanda of the *Skanda Purāna,* devoted entirely to the sacred world of Ujjain. We remember, of course, that in mythic terms, the antiquity of this place goes back to the very beginning, when the gods and *asuras* were churning the sea for the precious *amrita,* the nectar of immortality. When the vessel of immortal nectar appeared and the gods whisked it away to heaven, four drops fell upon the earth. One of them fell here, at Ujjain.[78]

Today, Ujjain is a small city of fewer than 400,000 people in western Madhya Pradesh, though it has grown in the past decades with the expansion of industry and business and with the spiritual commerce of its periodic *melā* called the Simhastha, which brings millions of pilgrims here for a month every twelve years. Indeed, some estimates of the size of the crowd for the 2004 Simhastha ran as high as twenty million. As at the other sites of such high-density pilgrimage, Ujjain's Simhastha required a burst of road building, bridge construction, water treatment, and infrastructure improvements to accommodate such a vast encampment. Most of it was undertaken at government expense, with projects carried out by the Ujjain development authority, the state public works department, and the national bodies concerned with the environment, rivers, and public health.

Literature ancient and modern speaks of Ujjain as the city at the very center of India. It is the navel, the *nābhi.* Today, almost any Ujjain resident will confirm this part of the city's lore. As one local informant put it in a riverside conversation, "Madhya Pradesh is the center of India, and Ujjain is in the center of Madhya Pradesh. Mahākāla, or Mahākāleshvara, is in the center of Ujjain and is the navel of the earth." The *tīrtha purohits* here all know and recite the Purānic verse that places Mahākāla not only in the center of this world, but on the vertical axis of the three worlds, identifying Shiva's form here with *lingas* in both the heavens above and the netherworlds below:

> *In the heavens is the Tāraka linga,*
> *In the netherworlds is Hatakeshvara,*
> *And here in this mortal world is Mahākāla.*
> *Praise be to thee, O Triple Linga!*

As one of the "seven cities" that bestow liberation, the city of Ujjain, like Kāshī, is filled with temples. In addition to its celebrated temple of Mahākāla Shiva, the city hosts a select realm of other gods who are part of Ujjain pilgrimage. Harasiddhi Devī is one of the fifty-one *pīthas*, or "benches," of the goddess. Her quiet, well-maintained compound across the Shiprā River from Mahākāla attracts a steady flow of local devotees and pilgrims. Bare Ganesha, "Big Ganesha," huge and brightly painted, is posted at the threshold of the western entrance to Mahākāla's compound. The temple of Kāla Bhairava is one of the important sites in the motorized rickshaw pilgrimages that ferry pilgrims around the city today. He anchors a small and ancient temple set just outside the city, on a high bank overlooking the Shiprā River, and those who visit him there will have *darshan* of a face so layered with centuries of vermilion that his eyes are, by now, deeply set into his extraordinary countenance. Even today, he is called the "chief" of ancient Avantikā and one whose jurisdiction as the general (*senapati*) of the town is still affirmed. Sacred Ujjain has also been famous for its sages. Not far from Kāla Bhairava, our rickshaw pilgrims might visit Bhartrihari Gufā, the cave of the wise poet Bhartrihari, or they might stop at the ashram of the sage Sandīpinī, the very place where he is said to have instructed Krishna and Balarāma in the Vedas. Coming back into the city, pilgrims will surely visit Garha Kālikā for the *darshan* of Kālī, here an electric, orange-painted and silver-tinseled image, her limbs smooth with the vermilion of the ages. Finally, they must come to the river's edge, to the *ghāts* of the "swift-flowing" Shiprā, flowing north here, just as the Gangā flows north at Kāshī. Rounding out the cumulative sanctity of Ujjain is the blessing bestowed on the place by those drops of the nectar of immortality, splashed upon this place as the gods wrestled it away from the clutches of the demons and sped off to heaven.[79]

Even with all its other deities and credentials, Ujjain is most famous as the place of Shiva's *jyotirlinga* of Mahākāla. The *Shiva Purāna* tells two stories about the manifestation and power of Shiva in this place, both of which are good examples of *māhātmya* legend. The first concerns a pious brahmin of Ujjain named Vedapriya, "Veda-Lover," and his four equally exemplary sons. Long ago they were persecuted by an *asura* named Dusana, who had gained power through a boon and had vowed to eliminate Vedic rites and devotion to Shiva. The brahmins had no weapons to protect themselves from the threats of the *asuras,* but they established an earthen *pārthiva linga* of Shiva and devoted themselves to the worship of the Lord. When they were attacked by the *asuras,* Shiva rose up from the earthen *linga* as Mahākāla and burned the attackers to ash in a second.[80] Another story takes place during a somewhat later mythic time, when Ujjain was under seige. As the attacking armies assaulted the four gates of the city, King Chandrasena took refuge in the temple of Mahākāleshvara and devoutly worshipped the Lord day and night, fasting and focusing his mind completely on Shiva. At that time, a cowherd woman and her five-year-old son also went to the temple, and they observed the king at his worship. The little boy was so impressed with the king's devotion that he went back to the fields near his home, found a pebble, and imitated the king's worship with great fervor. So absorbed was the boy that his mother scolded him and pulled him away from the place where he had created his play world of worship. In his grief, the little boy fell unconscious, and when he awakened, the whole area where he had worshipped the pebble had become a brilliant, golden, bejeweled temple of Mahākāla. The cowherd woman called the king to see the amazing sight, and the king, overcome with joy, burst into song in the praises of Shiva. Even the hostile attackers laying siege to the city saw the refulgence of this beautiful place and came with humility to worship Shiva, saying, "Here, even a child worships Shiva, so let us abandon our enmity lest we offend the Lord." Even though he was but a cowherd, the little boy was initiated into the company of the king and brahmins and joined with them in the sacred rites of Shiva.[81]

Mahākāla means "Great Lord of Time." It was, perhaps, the name of an ancient deity, drawn into the entourage of Shiva as a *gana,* one of his attendants, and then identified with Shiva himself. The word *kāla* ranges through a span of concomitant and related meanings—time, death, and black, all of which fall within the compass of the Supreme Lord. The temple of Mahākāla today sits on a low hill a short distance from the River Shiprā. It is an elegant temple, with three sets of porches and three stories surmounted by a tall *shikhara.* Immediately adjacent to the temple is a temple tank called Koti Tīrtha, where the waters of "ten million" *tīrthas* are said to be present. Surrounding the tank is a multitude of smaller shrines, including those dedicated to Vishnu and Ganesha, along with dozens of subsidiary *lingas.* There is also an old shrine to

The jyotirlinga *of Mahākāleshvara, Ujjain*

the "founding goddess" (*adhishthātrī devī*) of the place, Avantikā Devī. Today, however, she is almost invisible if one does not know she is there, for a relatively new shrine of Rāma, Sītā, and Lakshmana stands immediately in front of her, suggesting that the ancient *devī* has been displaced in the popular imagination. We know, however, that the "founding" deities of many places in the sacred geography of India are, in the beginning, goddesses like Avantikā Devī.

In the spacious temple of Mahākāla, the sanctum sanctorum is in what we might call the basement, the bottom level of the three-story temple, reached with a steep set of stairs. Above Mahākāla, in the ground-level sanctum, is the *linga* of Omkāreshvara, and above it on an upper floor is yet a third *linga,* called Nāgachandreshvara, an image of Shiva worshipped primarily on the Nāga Panchamī day in the monsoon month of Shrāvana. The center of gravity here, however, is the sanctum of Mahākāla at the bottom of this axis of *lingas*. In its newest renovation, the entire area under the temple has been further excavated to create a large underground hall next to the sanctum sanctorum, where hundreds of pilgrims can wait for the opportunity for *darshan*.

The sanctum of Mahākāla is small, and priests struggle to keep order while a human throng surrounds the *linga*, the dense air resounding with

Namah Shivāya, "Praise to Shiva." The *linga* of Mahākāla, when it is fully visible, is a two-foot-high smooth stone set in a solid silver *pītha* in the floor of the sanctum. Shiva's *nāga* swims up the silver channel of the *pītha*. The scene is a colorful human swirl of devotion—a dozen arms reaching out toward the *linga*, circling brass trays heaped with red *kumkum*, gray ash, and small oil lamps, hands stretched toward Mahākāla clutching bilva leaves and flowers to heap on the top of the *linga*, hands holding pots of water to pour upon the *linga*, hands touching the red *kumkum* to the forehead. In the morning, when the pilgrims have coursed through this small chamber with their offerings, the whole enclosure of the *pītha* is filled with green leaves and flowers. This is one time during the day, as at Kedārnāth, when pilgrims come into the sanctum, touch the *linga* with their hands, and place their offerings directly on the tall stone shaft. For the evening *āratī*, the *linga* is elaborately adorned and the priests are the strict intermediaries of offerings.

As at Kedārnāth, the rites of Mahākāleshvara's temple juxtapose the faceless *nishkala* Shiva with the more apprehensible *sakala* Shiva. Here Shiva shows his face on the stone shaft in a remarkable variety of ways. There is, of course, the standard four-faced silver cap, set over the top of the stone during certain periods of worship. And there is the silver, coiled *nāga* that curls around the stone like a crown. Both of these are used as processional stand-ins for the *linga* itself during the great festivals, such as Shivarātrī. Most unusual here at Ujjain are the distinctive faces called *jhankis*, "glimpses," of Shiva rendered upon the smooth stone shaft by artist-priests, with the eye and hand of a Picasso. They use ash, sandalwood, and *kumkum* to paint the expressive faces of Shiva's presence. Half cashews outline the face and add emphasis. In the famous *bhasma shringāra*, the entire stone is covered with gray ash and the face of Shiva, with yellow eyes and red pupils, gazes forth. In another *shringāra*, the face is half-black and half-orange, half-male and half-female, the black half of the forehead streaked with Shiva's horizontal markings, and the orange half decorated with the ornaments of the goddess. The eyes are of silver, and a silver crown with the spreading hood of a cobra adorns his head. At the festival of Holi, the *jhanki* is of Shiva strewn with red powder, and on Ganesha Chaturthi, the face of Ganesha is outlined with cashews on the shaft of the *linga*. These glimpses of the divine vary with the sacred times of the temple ritual calendar, but they all remind the worshipper that we human beings may indeed glimpse the multiple faces of Shiva, even in the shaft of the world-spanning, transcendent *linga*.

In Ujjain, as in Kāshī and at Kedāra, we are constantly pointed beyond the stone *linga*, beyond the temple itself, to a larger reality. The real *linga* of light here is not so much a single icon, not even the magnificent Mahākāleshvara, but a whole area, a *kshetra*, or field. The Purānic *māhātmyas* tell us that when Shiva appeared here, he expanded one *krosha* (two miles) in each direction, filling a wide *kshetra* of power with his presence.[82] At the center of the *kshetra* is the particular *linga* of Mahākāla, but there are eighty-four *lingas* listed in the *kshetra*, their tales recited in the *Skanda Purāna*. One might imagine that such a number of *lingas* would simply be acknowledged as a group, but in Ujjain today the penny-*māhātmyas* locate each individually. On many temples the specific name of the *linga* is given with a notation painted on the temple wall, stating which one of the eighty-four *lingas* is within. On the bathing *ghāts* of the Shiprā River is one single stone slab in which all eighty-four are represented as small *lingas*, gathering the whole of the sacred precinct into one. This symbolic strategy of condensation goes hand in hand with the symbolic tendency to expand, proliferate, and duplicate the one into the many. The eighty-four matter, and are named in their separate locations, and yet again the eighty-four can be honored all at once, right here.

OMKĀRESHVARA, SHIVA AS THE COSMIC SOUND

Some sixty miles south of Ujjain is the *jyotirlinga* of Omkāra, or Omkāreshvara, an island *tīrtha* in the middle of the Narmadā River. Pilgrims are likely to come by road, winding into the mountains from the flatlands of the city of Indore. They actually "descend" into these mountains here, for they are the steep, rugged lands that tumble down toward the Narmadā. Enormous stones are littered through the forests of *kadamba* and teak trees. The road cuts hairpin turns back and forth down a landscape sliced with rock cliffs and gorges, dry in summer, a sluiceway of rivers in the rainy season. Winding through this terrain, the pilgrims finally reach the valley of the river. After they cross the bridge to the far side, a narrow road lined with ancient trees then leads them eastward through the fields of yellow flowering mustard to the little town

The temple of Omkāreshvara on the Narmadā

of Mandhātta, named after one of India's legendary kings, who left his kingdom to become a sage. Here they behold for the first time the steep, copper-colored cliffs, the fortresslike walls, and multiple *shikharas* of the Omkāreshvara Temple. As they look north across the Narmadā, it might seem to them that this massive temple is located on the far side of the river, but in fact Omkāreshvara is on an island shaped like a half circle. A six-hundred-foot-long footbridge stretches across from the village of Mandhātta to the island of Omkāreshvara, and a second suspension bridge is under construction. Until 1971, when the first footbridge was built, pilgrims would have made the journey to the temple by boat, and many still take advantage of the boatmen who ply the river.

We remember here that this great river, one of India's seven sacred rivers, is said to flow from the very body of Shiva, beginning at Amarakantaka in the green hills, some five hundred miles to the east. This is the river circumambulated by the most devout of pilgrims, even today. Its banks are famous for hundreds of small temples and dozens of confluences. Even now at Omkāreshvara there are encampments of pilgrims making the *parikrama*. The Narmadā is broad and majestic here, even though it has been constricted, expanded, and manipulated elsewhere along its course by the controversial series of dams of the Narmadā

Valley Development Plan, projected to build thirty large dams and hundreds of medium and small dams on the Narmadā and its tributaries.
The two dams closest to Omkāreshvara are the Maheshwar Dam and the
Omkāreshwar Dam, both contested and both being slowly constructed
amid the start-and-stop of controversy. The displacement of local villagers and tribals will be severe, as at the other big dam projects. For
now, here at Omkāreshvara, in the midst of the winter season, the river
is still broad and deep, its flow seemingly unaffected by the taming and
flooding of dams, but a dark cloud hangs over the fate of the Narmadā's
riverside temples, large and small.[83]

At Omkāreshvara, the Narmadā is joined by the River Kāverī, which
shares a name with one of the sacred rivers of south India.[84] The Kāverī
flows in toward the back of the island and splits, cupping around the
island sanctuary and joining the Narmadā with two *sangams,* one at the
eastern and one at the western end of the island. Today the boatmen who
make their living on the river ferry pilgrims both upstream and downstream to bathe in the two *sangams.* In addition, pilgrims will bathe at
the *ghāt* called, like so many others, Koti Tīrtha, "Ten Million Tīrthas,"
just below the citadel temple of Omkāreshvara.

This *jyotirlinga,* they say, was established as a mere lump of earth, a
pārthiva linga, set here by the Vindhya Mountains. We have encountered
the Vindhya story before:

> Vindhya, the mountain range of central India, was humiliated to
> learn from the sage Nārada that Mount Meru was taller and more
> splendid than he. So Vindhya established a *linga* here and wor-
> shipped Shiva with fervent asceticism. At last, Shiva appeared to
> him in person and agreed to dwell forever in the earthen *linga,*
> bestowing both *bhukti* (enjoyment of worldly blessings) and *mukti*
> (liberation).[85]
>
> He also received a boon from Shiva: Vindhya asked to be the
> tallest mountain in the world. His boon granted, Vindhya stretched
> so high into the sky that he blocked the daily course of the sun. As
> the earth was scorched, the gods begged Shiva to do something. He
> sent the sage Agastya, who reached the Vindhyas on his way south.
> Vindhya bowed deeply to honor Agastya and asked what he could
> do to serve him. Agastya asked that Vindhya remain bowed down

until he returned from his journey. Agastya went on his way, and never returned from the south. So the humbled Vindhya remains a low-bowing mountain range, even today.

The whole precinct of Omkāreshvara is divided into three parts—Brahmāpurī, Vishnupurī, and Shivapurī. Sometimes it is called Omkāra Tripurī, the Triple-City of Omkāra. We have seen that the theology of the *linga* and, indeed, its iconic structure, comprises Brahmā, Vishnu, and Shiva, all three. All are sectors of the shaft of the *linga*. The word "Omkāra" is all-inclusive too. It means simply the "Syllable Om," the sound that contains and transcends all sound, the holy mantra that resonated from the flaming pillar of light in the beginning. The three primary sounds—"a," "u," and "m"—are said to correspond to the gods Brahmā, Vishnu, and Shiva, all of whom are present here at Omkāreshvara. But there are two other "sounds" that are part of the fivefold *Om:* the nasalization and the final silence. The esoteric symbolic connections of the fivefold Shiva with the fivefold mantra *Om* are many, but the essence is this: *Om* is the sound-symbol of all reality.

Omkāreshvara is one of the many places that describe the sanctity of their wider precincts with the term *panchakroshī*. The most famous *panchakroshī* is, of course, that circuit around Kāshī, but much smaller sacred precincts, or *kshetras,* also have a circle pilgrimage known by this name. Here it is clear that *panchakroshī* does not have to do with any unit of measurement, but rather with a form of symbolic wholeness. To speak of five *kroshas* is to embrace the totality, the comprehensiveness of Omkāreshvara as a *tīrtha.* Here the symbolism of the *Om* is present not only in the temple, but in the landscape as well. The fivefold pilgrimage inscribes in the earth the fivefold *Om.* In following this "circumambulatory" trail, worshippers trace out the syllable *"Om"* with their feet. The pilgrim maps of the island for sale in the markets that line the steep lanes toward the Omkāreshvara Temple depict the shape of *Om* superimposed on the island, with the stations of pilgrimage positioned along the traceries of the sacred syllable.

This comprehensiveness of Omkāra as a sacred precinct is underlined by its *māhātmya:* "Shrī Omkāreshvara's most important excellence is that here all of the eleven other *jyotirlingas* are present in symbolic form (*pratīk rūp me*)."[86] In the island temple itself are three floors, just as there are in the temple of Mahākāla to the north. Pilgrims first make their offerings in the sanctum of the Omkāreshvara *linga,* a stone outcropping that is surrounded by a silver *pīṭha.* They pour plastic packets of milk upon the *linga* and sprinkle trefoil bilva leaves and flowers, and with their prayers, they receive the assurances of fulfillment from their ritual guides. In addition to Omkāreshvara there are representatives of two other *jyotirlingas* here—Mahākāleshvara and Vaidyanātha. The rest of the twelve are apparently located in the immediate surrounding area, both on the island and across the river in Mandhātta, where the old temple of Kāshī Vishvanātha stands.[87]

Pilgrims to Omkāreshvara will soon discover just how profuse the temples here are: the circuit of temples on the island, the *tīrthas* up and down the river from one *sangam* to the next, the holy sites in the town of Mandhātta, with old temples claiming hoary antiquity vying for attention with new temples rising from the riverfront. In the midst of it all, pilgrims might well participate in a form of worship that sums up the nature and intent of the worship of Shiva here. In the pillared arcade outside the old temple of Mamalleshvara, a group of pilgrims sit in the midafternoon, protected from the hot sun while they watch five men create hundreds of *pārthiva lingas.* Each of the men has a wooden board with row upon row of marble-sized indentations to each hold a small clay *linga.* They roll bits of clay into cones, each about the size of a Hershey chocolate Kiss, and place them one by one into the indentations, crowning each with a single grain of rice. By early evening, their boards full of clay *lingas* are complete. With a priest, they begin a brief ritual, inviting Shiva to be present here in these *pārthiva lingas.* They offer a cascade of flowers and prayers. Finally, they clamber down the bank to the water's edge and wade into the Narmadā, submerging the *pārthiva lingas* in the current of the river. In a moment, they are all gone, swirling downstream with the lazy current of the Narmadā. It is a perfect biodegradable liturgy. This, of course, is the origin of so many *lingas,* as told in the sacred lore: An earthen pinch of clay focuses the heart's devotion, and the worship of this ephemeral symbol gives rise to the mighty and eternal presence of Lord Shiva.

Mountain, Earth, River, and Light

Each of the twelve *jyotirlingas* has its special qualities and its own story, and we will not repeat them all in this context. They are not such unusual stories, but are like the thousands of tales told about the manifestation of Shiva in one locale or another all over India. They give evidence of some of the same themes that constitute the landscape of Shiva everywhere. At Tryambakeshvara in Maharashtra, near Nāsik, for example, the "Three-Eyed" Shiva, Tryambaka, is worshipped within a massive stone temple at the base of a great range of bluffs, the northernmost spur of the Sahyādri Mountains, also called the Western Ghāts. The hills here are high, abrupt, and bare, and it is here that the Godāvarī River has its rise. By now, we are not surprised to learn that from the temple of Tryambaka, pilgrims climb up these hills to the top of the five-peaked mountain called Brahmāgiri. Like the symbolic structure of Kedāra in the Himalayas and Omkāra on the Narmadā, these five peaks are said to be the five faces of Shiva, and the whole mountain is called Shiva *svarūpa*—Shiva himself. Here, too, the presence of Shiva is inscribed in the landscape itself.[88]

The manifestation of light-in-earth is, as we have seen, a common theme of many of these *jyotirlinga* tales. At Bhīmashankara in the mountains of Maharashtra, the *jyotirlinga* was also, originally, an earthen *linga*, established by a captive king who made an earthen *linga* in his prison cell. At Nāgeshvara in western Gujarat, the *kshatriya* Vīrasena established an earthen *linga* and worshipped it until Shiva became manifest. At Ghrishneshvara, near Aurangabad in Maharashtra, it was a woman, the devout Ghushma, who made the *pārthiva lingas*. This temple—variously called Ghrishneshvara or Ghushmeshvar—is located just half a mile from the cliffs of Ellora, the site of the fifth- to seventh-century rock-cut Buddhist cave sanctuaries and the great seventh-century Hindu temple called Kailāsanātha. Hindus may come to these admirable old ruins, which are an ever-popular tourist destination, but the real destination of pilgrims is the living temple of Ghrishneshvara, quiet as it is. The official polychrome pictures provided for sale at the temple office show a *linga*, light radiating from its base, with a man kneeling before it. This man, we are told, is the devout Sudharma, the wonderful son of a woman named Ghushmā, a faithful woman whose daily practice was to make 108 *pārthiva lingas* for her Shiva *pūjā* and, after worship, deposit them in the pond. According to the story, young Sudharma was murdered, cut up in pieces, and thrown into the pond by Ghushmā's jealous elder co-wife Sudehā. On the fateful day she discovered her son's grisly murder, the grief-stricken Ghushmā resolutely completed her *pūjā*. And when she cast the earthen *lingas* in the pond, she saw her son standing there once again, whole in body. In recognition of her intense devotion, Shiva pledged to stay there forever as Ghushmeshvara, Ghushmā's Lord.

The *jyotirlinga* farthest to the northeast is Vaidyanātha or Vaidyanāth. It is today in Bihar, not far from the border of Bengal. The first thing to be said is that this one is contested by other claimants to the position of Vaidyanāth, the Lord of Physicians.[89] Distinctive to this temple's ritual life are the water-carrying rituals that are popular here during the season of Shivarātrī, usually in February/March, and during Shiva's special summer month of Shrāvana, usually in July/August. These rites link this Shiva temple to the River Gangā, some eighty miles away. Many pilgrims who undertake this difficult form of pilgrimage practice arrive at Vaidyanāth bearing water jugs in baskets at either end of a bamboo shoulder pole, having carried this water all the way from Sultanganj on the Gangā, a journey that takes at least three days. It is both an offering of devotion and a severe form of asceticism. For some, a shortened and considerably easier version of this ritual takes place in the compound itself, where pilgrims circumambulate the temple carrying the pole with its burden of water at either end. All the water carriers, however, will circle the temple court, where there are some twenty-two subsidiary shrines, and, at last, enter into the heavyset stone temple at the center.[90] The Vaidyanāth Temple has but a single door for exit and entry, and the inner sanctum is crowded and streaming with the hundreds of worshippers who press forward to pour the Gangā water and present their offerings.

These rites at Vaidyanāth serve also to remind us of the close connection between Shiva and the Gangā, the river that, in one sense, continues to cascade down from heaven upon the head of Shiva, who catches the divine water in his hair before releasing her to flow upon the earth. The water-carrying rituals that link the Gangā to Shiva temples may be found all over India. Twice a year, for example, pilgrims converge

on Hardvār where the Gangā enters the plains of north India, fill their
water pots with Gangā water, and return home to their local Shiva temples to pour the water upon the Shiva *linga*.[91] As at Vaidyanāth, many
carry two pots of water balanced in baskets on either end of a bamboo
pole, vowing not to let the water pots touch the ground on the journey
home. Another regional example of these water-carrying rites is the pilgrimage to Maharashtra's Shingnapur, a hill described as Kailāsa, where
Shiva and Pārvatī dwell. There, some half a million people come from
villages across the region, villages referred to as the *panchakrosī* villages,
carrying their local water, slung on bamboo poles. Here, too, they not
only carry the water from their villages to the mountain, but valiantly
carry it to the top of the mountain, where they pour it on Lord Shiva.[92]
And here too, Shiva is not only in the temple in the form of the Shiva
linga, but is the mountain itself, the peak upon which the Gangā fell in
her cascade from heaven to earth.

One final word about the distinctiveness of Vaidyanāth. Remember
that this *jyotirlinga* is said to have been established unwittingly by the
demon king Rāvana, who was well known to be a devotee of Shiva. The
ten-headed Rāvana had gone to Kailāsa and had put in many years of
severe penance, hoping to gain Shiva's favor and to procure a powerful *linga* to take with him to his island home of Lanka. Eventually, his
religious discipline was so firm that Shiva gave him one of the twelve
jyotirlingas as a boon, but with the proviso that he could not put it down
until he got back to Lanka. Seeing their enemy Rāvana in possession of
such a powerful *jyotirlinga* made the gods uneasy. Scheming to make
him put it down along the way, Varuna, the Lord of Waters, entered into
Rāvana's body so that he had to relieve himself. Rāvana gave the *linga*
to a cowherd to hold while he went to do so, but as the cowherd stood
holding the *linga,* it became immensely heavy. He had to put it down.
When Rāvana returned from relieving himself, he could not lift it again,
try as he did with his enormous strength. In his ardent devotion, Rāvana
cut off nine of his ten heads as offerings to Shiva. Even so, the *jyotirlinga*
would not move. Shiva miraculously restored Rāvana's heads, thus giving
this place the name Vaidyanātha, the "Lord of Physicians."[93]

As we have seen, this form of sanctification by adhesion is one of the
repeated themes, told in multiple stories, throughout the sacred landscape. The famous Shiva *linga* at Gokarna, on the coast of Karnataka, is

also linked to this very story of Rāvana's penance and his great misfortune in setting down the precious *linga*. There, when he tried heroically to pick up the *linga,* he pulled and twisted so that the stone itself looked like a cow's ear, thus the name Gokarna, literally "Cow's Ear." Even so, it remained stuck to its place in the earth, unmoving. We have seen the story of Sītā's sand *linga* at Rāmeshvara, meant to be temporary, just until Hanumān arrived with the proper Himalayan stone *linga.* But when Hanumān arrived, it could not be moved. This theme is widely present in the construction of India's sacred geography: a place sanctified by the seemingly magnetic force joining the divine image to the earth itself.

Finally, we must mention Shrī Shaila in northern Andhra Pradesh, the home of the Mallikārjuna *jyotirlinga.* It, too, is distinctive among the twelve, its first distinction being the extraordinary beauty of the site, set above the Krishnā River, at some considerable distance from any major town. Its relative remoteness has also given this place a long, continuous history. The mountain Shrī Shaila, or Shrī Parvata, is likely the one mentioned in the *Mahābhārata,* but we know little of this place in early centuries. The outer *prakāra* wall, or enclosure wall, of the temple compound is one of the most detailed and impressive in all India, covered with bas reliefs dating to at least the twelfth century and displaying narratives from the whole epic and mythic repertoire of India. The spacious temple campus within is anchored by the temple of Mallikārjuna, a freestanding temple with tall south Indian *gopurams,* the roof rimmed with life-sized stone cows lying down and keeping a watchful eye over the compound.

Shrī Shaila is, in a sense, where north meets the south—both in story and in style. Most important, it is linked with Kailāsa and Kāshī through its storied connection with Skanda. Shiva is shown on the great bronze doors of the temple compound, flanked by his two sons Ganesha and Skanda, and it is with their story that the *māhātmya* of Shrī Shaila begins:

Shiva and Pārvatī set a contest for the two sons to see which one could circle the earth more swiftly—the portly elephant-headed Ganesha or the strong and youthful Skanda. Ganesha's animal mount was the mouse, while Skanda's was the peacock. The two set off on the race around the earth, but Ganesha realized immediately that he, portly and riding a mouse, stood no chance at all to win. So he reined his little mouse in a circle around his own parents, Shiva and Pārvatī. In doing so, he proclaimed that one's parents *are* the whole earth for a devoted son. When Skanda returned, Ganesha had already won the race.

Skanda, returning on his peacock mount, was clearly annoyed by the outcome of the race. Skanda left Kailāsa and the family residence of Shiva and headed south. He came to live on Mount Krauncha, which is right here at Shrī Shaila. Shiva and Pārvatī decided to visit him here, but as they arrived, Skanda snubbed their affection and moved a short distance away. So Shiva and Pārvatī took up residence here—Shiva in his fiery form—to be near their son.[94]

Many stories are linked to Skanda's prideful abandonment of the family nest.[95] Elsewhere in the south, the mountain called Pālani in Tamil Nadu claims to be the very place where Skanda took up residence in his exile, and indeed it is one of the six great shrines of Skanda in Tamil country today. At Mallikārjuna, however, the story is really about Shiva, who resides at Shrī Shaila to be near Skanda, who had decamped from home. Vague as the story may be, this is suggestive of one of the great mysteries of Hindu theology: that sometime after the Gupta period, the worship of Skanda gradually ceased in north India. Today there are scarcely any major temples of Skanda north of the Godāvarī River. The most prominent Skanda temples are all in the south, mostly in Tamil Nadu, where the six famous shrines to the six-headed god attract millions of pilgrims. He is known in the south as Murugan, as well as Kārttikeya, Kumāra, and Kumāraswami. Here at Shrī Shaila, however, where Skanda is said to have gone on voluntary exile and where he became the major interlocutor of the *Skanda Purāna,* there is no Skanda shrine of significance at all. This is a place dominated by Shiva and the goddess, who is known here as Bhramarāmbā.

The temple of Shrī Shaila is also linked to a set of shrines in Andhra Pradesh, all of which are said to lie along the back of the serpent Ananta, whose very body has become the Andhra Hills. At his tail is Shrī Shaila and on his hood is Tirupati, while on his back is the Narasimha shrine of Ahobilam and at his mouth is the Shiva temple of Kālahasti. It is also one of the five sites where one of the great Shaiva monastic orders, the Virashaivas, have a *matha,* or monastic compound, and, as such, is one of the five great pilgrimage sites of the Virashaiva, or Lingāyat, tradition. While they acknowledge Mallikārjuna to be a great *linga* of light, the Lingāyats are distinctive in that they fasten small *lingas* around their necks, personal emblems of a deep monotheism, and many of these *lingas* come from the Krishnā River here at Shrī Shaila.

Inside the Mallikārjuna Temple, their hands folded in prayer, pilgrims line up two and three deep along the two railings that extend out from the door of the inner sanctum. Many are shaven headed, having come to Shrī Shaila on a pilgrimage circuit that includes Tirupati farther south in Andhra Pradesh. As the doors to the sanctum open, the crowd at the railing is on tiptoe, necks craning for *darshan,* hundreds of arms then stretching forward at once to touch the flame of the *ārati* lamp as it is passed and to convey the touch to the forehead, the eyes, the heart. Then pilgrims line up to approach the sanctum individually. One by one they kneel at the doorway of the small sanctum containing the *jyotirlinga,* making their offerings. As her turn comes, an English-speaking woman from nearby Hyderabad quickly hands her purse to the woman behind her, falls to her knees, touches the *linga* with both hands, pouring upon it the water she has brought from her bathing rites in the Krishnavenī River earlier in the day, and rubbing the water all over the *linga.* A constant line of pilgrims follows, each with some variation of this brief but intimate ritual—a handful of flowers offered, spilled in a flower cascade over the *linga,* a potful of water. Entering into the sanctum and touching the *linga* in this way is, on the whole, prohibited in the temples of south India, but it is permissible, at least during certain hours of worship, in many of the great temples of the north. Here at Shrī Shaila, we are at the juncture of these ritual idioms, and the permission to touch the image itself certainly suggests a ritual form more like that of Vishvanātha and Omkāreshvara than that of Rāmeshvara.

The famous twelve *jyotirlingas* are recognized widely. Their images and locations are arrayed on polychrome posters sold in temple bazaars across India. Most important, these twelve also become a framework for seeing the manifestation of Shiva in hundreds of other places. Temples that have not even a nominal relation to the twelve and are not vying for a slot in the list nonetheless refer to the *linga* in their sanctum as a *jyotirlinga.* Even the great ice *linga* at Amarnāth in Kashmir is, significantly, called a *linga* of fire. There is virtually no distinction between a self-manifest *svayambhū linga* and a *jyotirlinga*. Both are revelations. Both are manifestations of Shiva on his own terms and by his own grace.

SHIVA IN THE FIVE ELEMENTS:
THE *PANCHABHŪTA MAHĀLINGAS*

The *jyotirlinga* is a common theme in the iconography of temples of Tamil Nadu and the south, and it is here that some of the most elegant bas reliefs of the revelation of the *linga* (*lingodbhava*) are found. They are often located on the first circumambulatory that takes pilgrims around the inner sanctum of the temple, and they are often on the exterior wall directly behind the *linga*. There, crafted in stone relief, Brahmā flies upward, Vishnu searches downward, both looking for the ends of the fathomless column of light. The stone shaft of the *linga* opens to reveal the embodied Shiva.

Although the myth of the *linga* of light is widely told in the Tamil south, only Rāmeshvara and Mallikārjuna are southern temples. The group of twelve *jyotirlingas* is less significant here than another set of five: the *panchabhūta mahālingas*, the "great *lingas* of the five elements." In each, Shiva is present as one of the constituent elements—earth, air, ether, fire, and water. Given our familiarity, by now, with the ways in which Shiva's presence extends quite beyond the sanctum of any temple, this sense of Shiva as manifest in the primary elements seems fitting.

In Indian cosmology, five elements both comprise and pervade the entire universe: earth, water, fire, air, and space. As Abhinavagupta boldly proclaims: "The earth, the water, the fire, the air, and the void— these indeed are the five principles by which the entire universe is pervaded."[96] They are connected symbolically with a complex set of linking resonances—the five faces of Shiva, the five activities of Shiva, the five syllable mantras of *Om* and *Namah Shivāya*. When offerings are made, the five are represented: sandal paste represents the earth, food represents the water, a lamp offers fire, incense signifies air, and flowers represent space. There is totality in this fivefold vision. Not surprisingly, then, the five are also connected to five great manifestations of Shiva. All of them are in south India, in Tamil Nadu and Andhra Pradesh, and the vision of Shiva they represent is grounded in the elements that comprise all creation.

The great temple of Chidambaram in Tamil Nadu is a good place to begin this exploration, for here Shiva comes into being as space itself. The temple of Chidambaram is perhaps most famous for its Dancing Shiva. Here at Chidambaram, Shiva is the cosmic dancer, pounding the earth with the tempo of his step, flinging his arms in the four directions, his hair flowing wild. Here Nataraja occupies the central sanctum of the temple, but to one side is the Ākāsh Linga, the *linga* of space or ether. It is invisible to the natural eye, its place marked only by oil lamp stands to either side. We see nothing at all, so to speak. But the priest makes the offerings, circles his five-wicked lamp and the incense before this "nothing" at the time of worship.

In the famous city of Kānchīpuram, one of the great seven "*moksha-giving cities*," Shiva is said to become present as a *linga* of earth, reminding us of the multitude of *pārthiva lingas* shaped from a pinch of clay. In Kānchī, according to legend, it was the goddess Pārvatī herself who fashioned a *linga* from the earth. When Shiva tested her devotion to him by sending a torrential flood, she clung confidently to the *linga*. The marks of her breasts and bangles are indented upon the earth *linga* even today, they say. At Jambukeshvara, located on an island in the middle of the Kāverī River, in the city of Tiruchirapalli, Shiva became manifest as a *linga* of water, and every year during the rains the subsoil water rises through the floor of the sanctum to inundate the *linga*.[97] And air? It is at Kālahasti in southern Andhra Pradesh that Shiva is present as a *linga* of air, moving so slightly as the breeze, which makes the lamps flicker even in the deep inner sanctum of the temple.

Shiva is manifest in all the elements, and not in light or fire alone. Yet light has had a special place at the heart of religious symbolism the world over, and it is no surprise that light or fire has become preeminent among the elements where Shiva appears. In the group of Lingas of the Five Elements, Shiva's manifestation at Arunāchala is as fire. Everyone speaks of this as a *jyotirlinga* and a very important one at that. Arunāchala, "Dawn Mountain," is today a bare volcanic hill of igneous rock. In ages past, they say, it was a mountain of fire.

In several scriptural accounts of the Purānas this hill is the primal *jyotirlinga*.[98] It was here that the *linga* of light split the earth between the disputing Brahmā and Vishnu. It was here that the two, having exhausted themselves seeking the ends of the effulgence, bowed low to Shiva. It was here that the Lord gave them a boon, and they asked that Shiva's *jyotirlinga* become a mountain and remain as such on earth. Shiva said, "Since this *linga* rose up, looking like a mountain of fire, it shall be known as the Dawn Mountain, Arunāchala."[99]

Today the busy temple town of Tiruvannamalai is at the base of Arunāchala, and the temple itself covers many acres in a series of increasingly smaller concentric rectangles. Entering the temple through one great ornamented gate after another, past one enclosing wall after another, one comes at last to the sanctum sanctorum in the dark, windowless interior. Appropriately, the sanctum is splendidly aglow with row upon row of tiny oil lamps. A tall cone-shaped lamp stand holds hundreds more oil lamps. The sanctum of the temple seems, indeed, to be on fire. On the wall of the circumambulatory behind the sanctum is a grand relief of Shiva emerging from the pillar of fire. Shiva stands forth from the *linga*, splitting the pillar of brilliance and appearing in embodied form before the two gods.

And yet the *linga* here in the great temple of Tiruvannamalai is, like the other *jyotirlingas*, but a representative of the natural *jyotirlinga*, which is the mountain itself. "I stand here by the name of Arunāchala, the Dawn Mountain," says Shiva.[100] "Those men who devoutly bow to this fiery form named Arunāchala become superior, even to the immortal gods."[101] Back in the perfect age, according to tradition, it was a mountain of flame. In the next age, it became a mountain of jewels; in the next, a mountain of gold; and now, in this Kali Age, it is but a mountain of stone.[102] Still, it is Shiva himself. And on great festival days, a huge fire is lighted on top of the mountain as a representation of the fire of Shiva.

The sixth- to eighth-century Tamil poets praise Annamalai, or Tiruvannamalai, as a hill more than a mere temple:

The Highest Lord who destroys
for his devotees who meditate on him,
the bondage of past karma
as well as the fruit of future deeds,
lives in the shrine of Annamalai,
on whose ancient rocky slopes

echoing with the best of drums
the evening moon rests.

The Lord of the gods,
whom Tirumāl and Vishnu could not find,
so that they might end their long search,
is the Lord of Annamalai,
on whose slopes
bands of gypsy women wander,
hawking piles of pearls
gathered from tall old bamboos.[103]

In the twentieth century, Arunāchala also became famous as the hermitage of the great mystic Shrī Rāmana Maharshi, who took up residence here when he renounced the world. He lived an ascetic life in the mountainside caves for many years and finally built an ashram here. Every day he is said to have circumambulated the mountain itself, just as worshippers might circumambulate the sanctum of a temple. Those who stay at the ashram follow his path around the mountain daily. Usually they go barefoot, and anyone setting foot on the hill itself is advised to go barefoot. Thus the traditions of revering the hill as Shiva himself continue strong in the twenty-first century. One of Rāmana Maharshi's followers speaks of Arunāchala as "the heart-center of the earth" and writes, "Unlike other hills which have become holy because the Lord dwells in them, this hill is itself Lord Shiva. Just as we identify ourselves with our body, He identifies himself as this Hill."[104] Among the hymns Rāmana Maharshi composed to Arunāchala, written for the most part in 1914, there is frequent reference to the *linga* of light: "Silent you stand, O Shiva, as the hill Arunāchala, shining from heaven to earth."[105] In the verses of this twentieth-century sage, the hill Arunāchala, an ordinary hill to the secular traveler, is clearly the symbol and presence of the Supreme Brahman, as Shiva, in both his transcendent and immanent forms.

6

SHAKTI, THE DISTRIBUTION OF THE
BODY OF THE GODDESS

In the hills near the town of Mirzapur in the state of Uttar Pradesh in north India is a busy pilgrimage site called Vindhyāchala, which means the "Vindhya mountain," although only by an imaginative sense of geography could this hilly area be called a part of the Vindhya range, which is farther west and south. Here dwells one of India's greatest goddesses, Vindhyavāsinī Devī, the Vindhya-Dwelling Goddess. Like many goddesses, especially the strong ones who wield weapons, she lives in the hills. Like many goddesses, she is not one here, but is threefold.[1]

First, there is Vindhyavāsinī herself. There is nothing special in the architecture of her spacious temple compound, but even on an average day the temple is crowded with thousands of worshippers who stand in line for hours to enter into the small, airless sanctuary, where they will make offerings of flowers and red cloth and crack coconuts as sacrifices before the goddess. For a moment, they will gaze into the big silver eyes of Vindhyavāsinī and utter their heartfelt prayers, before being pushed on by the crowd. Beneath the great heap of marigold garlands they can see no "image" of the goddess at all—only her eyes. For the *darshan*, the "sacred sight," of the divine, the eyes of the goddess are enough. The image beneath all the flowers is said to be *svaymbhū*, "self-manifest," like some of the natural stone *lingas* of Shiva.

A short distance away, on their own small hillocks, are two other *devīs*—Asthabhujā, the "Eight-Armed One," and Kālī, the "Black One." Their inner sanctuaries are but caves in the rock, so low that the pilgrims cannot stand erect but must crouch and work their way through the darkness toward the oil lamps on the rock ledge, to the place in the cavern wall where the silver face of the goddess shines. The "three-cornered"

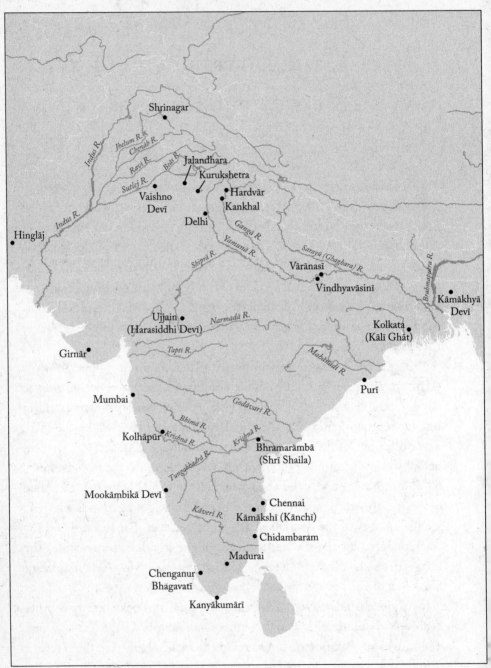

Shrinagar

Indus R.
Jhelum R.
Chenab R.
Ravi R.
Beas R.

Jalandhara
Kurukshetra
Sutlej R.
Vaishno
Devī
Hardvār
Kankhal
Delhi
Gangā R.
Yamunā R.
Shiprā R.
Sarayū (Ghaghara) R.
Brahmaputra R.
Hinglāj
Indus R.
Vārānasī
Vindhyavāsinī
Kāmākhyā
Devī
Ujjain
(Harasiddhi Devī)
Narmadā R.
Kolkata
(Kālī Ghāt)
Girnār
Tapti R.
Mahānadī R.
Purī
Mumbai
Godāvarī R.
Bhimā R.
Kolhāpūr
Krishnā R.
Krishnā R.
Tungabhadrā R.
Bhramarāmbā
(Shrī Shaila)
Mookāmbikā Devī
Kāveri R.
Chennai
Kāmākshī (Kānchī)
Chidambaram
Madurai
Chenganur
Bhagavatī
Kanyākumārī

trip to Vindhyavāsinī and the two others is one of the common forms of pilgrimage here.

Some claim this triple goddess of the Vindhyas is the most powerful in all India. It was she, they say, who slew the great world-threatening bull demon Mahisha. When the gods were helpless against him, she took their weapons, one in each of her many hands, and killed and beheaded her foe.[2] It was she, they say, whom the Pāndava heroes asked for protection during the critical final year of their long exile before the *Mahābhārata* war began.[3] And it was she, they say, who took birth as a baby girl and traded places with Krishna the night he was born. His father, Vasudeva, carried baby Krishna to safety on the other side of the flooding waters of the River Yamunā, entrusting him to foster parents Nanda and Yashodā. Then he returned to the dungeon with the baby girl who had been born to Yashodā that same night. When the wicked King Kamsa came to kill the infant Krishna, who was destined to challenge his throne, he found a newborn baby girl. He seized the infant and dashed her against the stones. The great goddess emerged from this baby, laughing at the futile rage of the king. She came here to Vindhyāchala to dwell, so they say.[4] With such a rich heritage, it is no wonder that today's pilgrims say Vindhyavāsinī Devī can do anything. "Whatever prayer is in your heart when you stand before Vindhyavāsinī," claimed one of the temple priests on my visit, "that will be fulfilled by the goddess. One hundred percent guaranteed!"

SHAKTI, THE POWER OF THE GODDESS

Vindhyavāsinī is a good place to begin our exploration of the Goddess in the landscape of India. Crouching in the womblike cave sanctum, gazing at the face of the Goddess, and listening to the devout address her—*Mā! Mā!* they say, "Mother! Mother!"—we cannot help but wonder about the nature of the Goddess power that is so palpable, so powerful, and so mysterious here. This power is called *shakti,* a word that simply means "power" or "energy." It is not female power or energy in particular. More accurately, *shakti* is all power and energy, and it is the attribute of the Goddess. In Sanskrit and Hindi, the root of *shakti* (*shaknoti* in Sanskrit; *sakna* in Hindi) is the helping verb that means "to be able." In a broad sense, the can-do capacity for any activity is *shakti*. The *Devī Bhāgavata Purāna* describes *shakti* as the strong life force that animates all creation: "A very weak man is declared to be without any strength (*shakti*). He is not said to be without Rudra, or without Vishnu. Nobody says this. Everyone says he is without strength, without Shakti."[5] The famous hymn to the goddess, the *Saundaryalaharī*, begins, "If Shiva, the Auspicious One, is united with Shakti, He is able to create. If He is not, He is not even capable of stirring."[6] It is well known, as the saying goes, that "without Shakti, Shiva is *shava*." The word *shava* means "corpse," and the goddess is sometimes depicted dancing on the inert, corpse-like body of Shiva, wielding the weapons and emblems of her power and putting on full display the energy that is hers. Some see this energy as spinning out of control, and only by standing or dancing on Shiva does she balance that energy, with his stability.

Even the gods, it seems, are powerless without the kinetic energy of Shakti. A story in the *Devī Bhāgavata Purāna* tells of a time when both Gaurī and Lakshmī left their husbands because they saw them as braggarts, boasting of their feats in defeating their foes. But when their consorts left, Shiva and Vishnu became powerless and lusterless, unable to fight, unable to fulfill their duties. Only when the gods persuaded the goddesses to rejoin their husbands was order restored to the world.[7] Such is the power of *shakti*, present as the creative energy of all life and, as the proper name Shakti, the pervasive energy of the gods themselves.

Of course, the most celebrated myth of Devī's power is that of the *Devī Māhātmya*. Here, the gods are unable, individually or collectively, to quell the mighty Mahisha, the bull demon. Helpless and distressed, they come before Devī and implore her to fight Mahisha. They give to her their *tejas*, their lustrous brilliance, and they hand over their weapons to her. Seizing all their weapons in her many hands, Devī challenges Mahisha and his armies. In a fiercely fought battle, she finally slays the bull demon, even as he tries time and again to change his shape and escape. In the end, she stands triumphant on his severed head.

Devī collects all the weapons of the gods, but it is no secret to those who know her that the many weapons signifying the power of the gods never really did belong to them. They were always hers. The famous trident, or *trishula*, of Shiva is a case in point. The trident that Shiva carries as his own seems originally to have been an emblem of the threefold

Devī as Mahishamardinī, standing upon the slain bull demon, Mahisha

goddess. Whenever one sees that three-pronged emblem standing alone, it is an emblem of Shakti. It stands throughout rural India today as her aniconic image. The fact that Shiva took the *trishula* as his weapon is but confirmation of the fact that Shakti is the source of all power, even that which is apparently the power of the gods. In the myth of the slaying of Mahisha, the gods overtly give to her what is really already hers. This power may be used to destroy as well as to protect. It is dangerous and it is beneficent. Above all, it is hers.

To the pilgrims and worshippers who visit the famous temple of Kālī at Kālī Ghāt in Calcutta, the dangerous side of Shakti, which they might but sense in the caves at Vindhyavāsinī, is dramatically visible. They crowd into the temple for the *darshan* of Kālī, the "Black One." All they can see is her great black face, her three golden eyes with jet-black pupils, her reddish-gold tongue hanging out. She is covered with garlands of marigolds and red hibiscus. Her icon is familiar to her worshippers, however, and they can imagine the rest: One fist grasps a sharp, curved cleaver; another holds a severed head; and yet another, despite the horror, gestures not to be afraid. Those who can afford it will surely stop at a shop in the busy bazaar and purchase a plaster image of Kālī, as she is known in this temple—a black goddess with jet-black eyes, a long red tongue, a necklace of heads, a skirt of severed arms.

Leaving the sanctum and circling around the back of the temple, the worshippers find a courtyard in the center of which is a small cast-iron sacrificial post. A young goat is brought forward, having been consecrated to the goddess. The goat's neck is placed in the U-shaped cup of the post. A priest steps up with a sharp cleaver, like that the goddess holds in her hand. The cleaver may be inscribed in vermilion with the mantras of Kālī. According to researcher Suchitra Sumanta, it is she who ritually holds the cleaver as "the sacrificer mentally transfers the sword to the goddess' hand, conflating the qualities of Kālī with those of the sword."[8] In one swift blow, he decapitates the goat, and in a moment, the pavement is splattered with blood. Bengali women, and a few men, line up and approach that cupped stake, one by one, placing their own foreheads on top of it. After a moment, they wet their fingers with a drop of the blood left in the cup. Perhaps the priest will mark their foreheads with a blood-red spot, the *tilaka*. Here, too, they say *"Mā! Mā!"* Mother Kālī clearly embraces both life and death, and devotees understand that even as she deals death, she brings liberation.

At the Kālī Temple, a single goat is offered daily as a sacrifice, here called *bali*, and it is cooked and offered to Kālī along with other components of a Bengali midday meal, such as rice, fish, and vegetables. After they have been presented in the sanctum, the food offerings are distributed to pilgrims and worshippers as *prasād*. Individuals also offer *bali*, often in fulfillment of a vow, at the time of a difficult life crisis, or as part of one of the great festivals of Kālī. Goats killed in this way are then butchered and a portion is symbolically offered to the goddess, while the rest is taken home for consumption. The temple management today, influenced over the generations by Bengali Vaishnavism and its more vegetarian traditions, is quick to point out that, except for one night a year, neither blood nor raw meat ever enters the sanctum.[9] The offering of the sacrificial animal is understood by some adherents to be an offering of oneself, a victory over one's own lower instincts.[10] One suspects, however, that such an appealing interpretation of the beheadings in the temple compound is not necessarily part of the spiritual disposition and intention of those who come as pilgrims. On the whole, they are seeking the favor of Kālī by making a blood sacrifice. In the late 1980s, as many as seventy goats might be offered as *bali* in the temple on an average, ordinary day, and ten times that many on a great festival day.[11]

At the opposite end of Kālī's temple from this stake is a cactuslike tree where some of the pilgrim women stop for special rites. People called it the "barren tree," and it is associated with the goddess Manasā, a goddess associated with snakes and healing. Honoring the goddess here is said to bring fertility to barren women and protection to their young children. Here, as at so many similar shrines in India, the branches are covered with bits of cloth and ribbons, twisted with pieces of hair, tied here by those who have propitiated the goddess for her blessings and protection.[12] The Manasā shrine is also associated with one for the goddess Shashthī, who is understood to have the protection of children in her portfolio. The sap, the life energy, of trees seems to symbolize the life force that surges through creation. We also see and feel this life force of Shakti, nourishing and protective, in the River Gangā, which winds its way through the nearby countryside of Bengal. As we have seen, these Gangā waters are constantly referred to as Mother and are said to be Shakti in liquid form. Even here in Bengal, where destructive monsoon floods are common, the *shakti* of the goddess is affirmed to be as lifegiving as mother's milk.

The power that is Shakti is both life-giving and death-dealing. Both the milk of the River Gangā and the blood of the goddess Kālī, different as they may seem to us, connote the presence of Shakti. Although sometimes we see one aspect more clearly than the other, in this goddess or that, ultimately they cannot be separated. While Gangā comes closest to being purely beneficent, she is part of a symbolic repertoire in which Shakti is ambiguous. Her twofold nature is the subject of many myths. In one account, for example, the goddess emerges at the beginning of time as a woman, half-black and half-white.[13] In some myths, the Black Goddess becomes white by some penance, as when Pārvatī performs penance to become golden as Gaurī.[14] In others, the White Goddess becomes black by some indiscretion, as when Pārvatī playfully covers the eyes of Shiva and the whole universe, including Pārvatī herself, is plunged into darkness.[15] Indeed, two of the most prominent names of the goddess are Kālī, the "Black One," and Gaurī, the "White One." Simply said, Pārvatī and Kālī have a complex relatedness.

The relation of these two—Kālī and Gaurī, the black goddess and the white one—has been widely studied and theorized about. Scholars have discerned the differences between "goddesses of the tooth" and "goddesses of the breast," the "tenebrous" and the "luminous," the meat-eating and the vegetarian, the virgins and the mothers, those who dwell outside the boundaries and those who dwell within the city.[16] Generally, the former, the black goddesses, like Kālī, seem to be those not closely tied to any male god, as his particular consort, or *shakti*. They are often virgin goddesses, like Kanyākumārī, who stands protective at the tip of southern India and whose vow of maidenhood is the source of her unmatched power. The fair goddesses, on the other hand, like Gaurī, are ordinarily married to their consort gods. Pārvatī, another name for Gaurī, is the consort of Shiva; Lakshmī is the consort of Vishnu, and Sarasvatī of Brahmā. All three are auspicious, as married women are in India, and more apt to be beneficent than dangerous. And yet it is not so simple. All of them are called "mother," even the virgin goddesses. And all are propitiated for kindnesses and blessings, even the ones who stand threatening with upraised cleavers. Shakti bedevils any scholarly typology that would attempt to draw too firm a line between the black goddesses and the white ones. Both aspects are important to the worship of the Devī, and in the particular temples and shrines of India both seem to be prominently present.

In south India, Shiva is often said to have two consorts. One is his bride, of the fair Gaurī type, the "marrying kind." The other is his mistress, or perhaps an unconquered virgin, of the dark and dangerous type. Often the dark goddess's shrine might be found just outside the proper enclosure of the temple household.[17] But at Chidambaram, for example, the two shrines are virtually side by side. There is the spacious temple of Shiva's fair bride Shivakumārasundarī Ambā and, next to it, a much smaller but more crowded and popular temple of Durgā Mahishamardinī, an elegant goddess standing on the severed head of a bull.

In the *Devī Māhātmya,* by far the most famous of India's hymns to the Goddess, the complicated interrelation of the goddesses is on full display. In one episode Pārvatī, the Mountain Girl and the spouse of Shiva, produces Ambikā (the Mother), also known as Kaushikī (the Glorious), from her body. Having released the motherly and luminous aspect of her divine being, she herself becomes black and is known as Kālikā. But there is a further complication: The motherly Ambikā also produces the fearsome Kālī from her forehead. Kālī kills the demons Chanda and Munda and thus becomes known by the famous name Chāmundā. Finally, seven mother goddesses appear. With Kālī in the lead, they destroy the demon armies of Shumbha and Nishumbha. Here there is no separating the black and the white, the mothers and the warriors.

As we explore the topography of Devī in India, it will become clear that the exploits of her power as sung by the hymnists of the *Devī Māhātmya* in her triumph over the demons—Chanda and Munda, Shumbha and Nishumbha, and the great bull-demon Mahisha—are inscribed profusely in the land. At Ambājī in Rajasthan, near Mount Abu, Ambikā destroys Shumbha and Nishumbha; at a shrine near Almora she appears as Kaushikī to slay Shumbha and Nishumbha; at Chāmundā Devī in the Kangra Hills of the north, she slays Chanda and Munda. At Manasī Devī in Hardvār or at our own Vindhyāchala, she manifests herself in all her power to slay Mahisha. Her presence "at this very place" throughout India links her and hundreds of local *devīs* to this series of myths.

The Triune Goddess

In addition to seeing Shakti as twofold, black and white, Hindus often describe her as threefold, the one whose emblem is the trident or, sometimes, the triangle. The high theology of Shakti is found in the fifth or sixth century in the *Devī Māhātmya* and reaches full form in the extensive *Devī Bhāgavata Purāna* nearly a thousand years later.[18] It elaborates both her utter supremacy and the three aspects or "qualities" (*gunas*) through which she shapes the cosmos. In this vision, the hymnists see the Supreme Reality, Brahman, as Devī. The Goddess is the All—indescribable and ultimately ungraspable. When she takes form, however, she is triple. Manifest as *sattva* (purity), she is Mahālakshmī; as *rajas* (power or passion), she is Mahāsarasvatī; and as *tamas* (darkness), she is Mahākālī.[19] This theology is sung in a hymn, often recited as a supplement to the *Devī Māhātmya,* called the *Rahasya Traya,* literally, the "Triple Mystery." In this theology, the goddess is not simply the *shakti* of Shiva, not even the *shakti* of all the gods together. She is not a consort goddess at all. She is the Supreme Being, the ground of all Reality.

The worship of the threefold goddess is surely much older than such theological formulations, however. Her trident is found in the backcountry all over India, and yes, the trident standing alone always belongs to Devī. Her many shrines also attest to her triune nature. At Vindhyāchala, as we have seen, they say that Vindhyavāsinī herself is Mahālakshmī; Ashtabhujā is Mahāsarasvatī; and Kālī, of course, Mahākālī. At the ancient shrine of Garha Kālikā in the city of Ujjain, we find the image of Kālī said to have been the favorite of the great poet Kālidāsa, in the sixth century. Here Kālī has a huge, bright orange face with silver eyes and a blood-red tongue, and she is flanked by two small orange stone figures of indistinguishable features, said to be Mahālakshmī and Mahāsarasvatī. The shrines of both Mookambikā Devī, in the hills of coastal Karnataka, and Mahālakshmī, at Kolhāpūr in southern Maharashtra, house

The Devī's trident, on the ghāts of the Shiprā River in Ujjain

prominent threefold *devīs* and participate in this conceptualization of the triune goddess. At Shārikā Devī's temple on the outskirts of Shrinagar in Kashmir we see yet another example of this iconography of the goddess. Here her "image" is but an immense stone outcropping, a slab in the hillside, smeared smooth with layer upon layer of orange *sindūr*. Within a short distance on this hill are three separate subsidiary shrines, each but a smaller stone smoothed with *sindūr* and decorated with bits of silver paper, representing Mahālakshmī, Mahāsarasvatī, and Mahākālī. Similarly, at the mountaintop cave shrine of Vaishno Devī in Kashmir, there are three lumps called *pindis* inside the cave of the goddess. They, too, are said to be stone manifestations of Mahālakshmī, Mahāsarasvatī, and Mahākālī. The popular pilgrimage literature of Vaishno Devī today claims that this is the only place in all India where one can worship Mahālakshmī, Mahāsarasvatī, and Mahākālī at once. Her *māhātmya* notwithstanding, this is simply not at all the case. Devī's triple presence in a single place is almost as common as the Goddess herself.

THE "BENCHES" OF THIS SHORE

In speaking of the holy places of India, we have used the word *tīrtha*, a sacred "ford" or "crossing." Many *tīrthas*, as we have seen, are actually river crossings, and yet the term resounds in the spiritual realm. At *tīrthas*, pilgrims may ford the river of *samsāra*—this earthly round of continuous birth and death—to the "far shore" of immortality.[20] As we have seen, the hierophany of Shiva's great *linga* of light certainly attests to the quest for transcendence that the word *tīrtha* implies. And certain *jyotirlingas*, such as Kedāra, Mahākāla, and, above all, Kāshī, are famous precisely because they bestow liberation, *moksha*—the freedom of the far shore.

The great goddess shrines are sometimes spoken of as *tīrthas*, but they are more prominently known by another name. They are called *pīthas*, the "seats" or "benches" of the goddess. Unlike the word *tīrtha*, which has meanings traceable deep into the Vedic tradition, the word *pītha* does not occur in the Vedic hymnic literature.[21] Perhaps this is because *pīthas*, like most of the goddesses themselves, are part of the vast, complex fabric of old and local religious traditions unsung by the Vedas. Hers was, and still is, a locative religious tradition—one focused on the places of divine power, in this locale and that. The *pītha* is not so much a place of crossing beyond this world. It suggests, rather, that the goddess takes a seat right here in this world—a firm seat, a bench really—under a tree, by the side of a pool, or at the edge of a village, as the presiding mistress of the place. She is immanent. Her supremacy is thoroughly embedded in this world of name and form, work and worry, a world that is sanctified by her presence. Her images are anointed with *sindūr*, or vermilion, a ritual substitute for the blood offerings she still sometimes receives. And the prayers and concerns that one might bring to the Goddess are not usually the otherworldly concerns of the far shore. They are the prayers and concerns of this shore, having to do with protection and blessing, birth and death, disease and health, food and water, fertility and longevity.

The word *pītha* also refers to the base of Shiva's *linga*. This is the female component of the *linga*, also called the *yoni*. It is in the stone *pītha* that the shaft of the *linga* is established. If the shaft is simply placed on the ground or is a natural stone outcropping, it is understood that the earth itself is the *pītha*. According to one articulation, the sky is the shaft of the *linga* and the earth its *pītha*.[22] But the earth, of course, is more than a place to stand and view the transcendent vastness of the sky. It is the scene of the whole course and flow of human life, and it is here—on this shore, in the cave, on the hilltop, beneath the tree—that the Goddess is vividly present. It is to these places we must go to seek the manifestations and meanings of Shakti.

We know very little about the origins of the holy places of local *devīs* that came to be called *pīthas* or of pilgrimage to them. As with many strands of the indigenous locative traditions of India, these matters are not directly recorded in the early texts of the Buddhists, Hindus, and Jains. One must read between the lines of the texts for early glimpses of the local goddesses, who do not become clearly visible in these sources until the late Gupta period, that is, the fifth or sixth century. We need not rely entirely upon texts, however. As long as three thousand years ago, people of the Indus Valley civilization shaped female images of terra-cotta. We cannot necessarily call them "goddesses," for we do not really know how they were used or understood. Even so, many centuries later, we can recognize the ample hips and breasts and the hip-line sash called the *mekhalā*, worn by these ancient sisters of the Indus, on the *yakshīs* who are present on the surrounding fences and gateways of the Buddhist stupas of Bhārhut and Sānchī.[23]

The *yakshīs* and their male *yaksha* counterparts are life-force deities. Associated with the energies of nature as *genii loci* of particular places, they are propitiated for beneficences. Although their place in Buddhist sites might be seen as more decorative than devotional, it is clear that *yakshīs* had their own cult and were honored, usually in aniconic form, on their own "benches" throughout rural north India. So it is that they have a supportive, protective, and surrounding role at the stupa sites of the Buddha. It is likely that such goddesses of local or regional significance have flourished in India for a very long time, attracting supplicants for their particular blessing and protection.

Although we have used the terms Shakti, Devī, and the Goddess as if they all referred to the same and singular goddess, it would not have been meaningful or accurate to speak of *the* Goddess throughout most of the long history of goddesses in India. In some respects, it is not meaningful or accurate to use the term even today. True enough, for the past fifteen hundred years or so, Hindu texts have spoken of Devī or Mahādevī as a singular goddess of many manifestations. But in some respects, even today, it is essential to recognize the plural and multiform reality of Mahādevī's presence. The many goddesses are known by particular names, particular locales, and particular spheres of influence. Some, like the row of lumpish orange stones with large enameled eyes found in a wayside shrine in the far west, in Saurashtra, are known only by the people of their own locale. Others are famous throughout India. Even the famous ones, however, are not simply universalized as Mahādevī in general, but are known by their particular place-names— Vindhyavāsinī Devī, Kāmākhyā Devī in Assam, Vaishno Devī in Kashmir, or Kanyākumārī at the southern tip of India.

All these goddesses are firmly linked to place—to mountaintops, rivers, caves, and villages. As the life energies, the *shaktis,* of this world, they are associated with both the nourishment and the vagaries of nature. Nature—called *prakriti*—is feminine in India, as in many cultures. Purusha and Prakriti, male and female, spirit and nature, are more general designations for the cosmic pair we know as Shiva and Shakti. Nature is not devalued in this twosome, however. Nature is alive with power. Shakti, the power that streams through this world, can be tapped and used by ordinary people, for whom the distant horizon of the far shore is not nearly as significant as the landscape of this shore. It is to the power seats of Shakti that they bring their prayers for birth and health, marriage and longevity, a good planting and a good harvest. The identification of Shakti's places of power with the various topographical features of nature is not surprising, for it is in the land itself that she has her domain. We have already seen the extensive ways in which the rivers of India have come to represent liquid Shakti, flowing with the energies of milk and motherhood. So, too, the nourishment of the earth, the life energies of vegetation, the territorial domains of village and mountain-top. All these are sites for the manifestation of Shakti.

Earth, the Original Shakti

The most basic manifestation of Shakti is the earth itself. The earth as mother and guardian of life is sometimes referred to as Ādi Shakti, the "Original Shakti." Her presence as the source of life may be seen as a leitmotif of the human religious imagination far beyond India. It is not at all surprising that some of the names by which the Goddess is widely known in India are earth names. There is Bhū, for instance, who is Vishnu's consort along with Lakshmī, and whose very name means "earth." And there is Sītā, the "furrow," whose father, Janaka, plowed her up from the earth. Sītā, the flawless woman and the devoted wife of Rāma, eventually returned to the earth at the end of her epic life.

The earth itself is considered to be female, with the cycles of fertility and production that are common to women. In Bengal, for example, the earth is said to have a yearly menstrual cycle before the time of seeding. During these days all plowing of the soil is forbidden and women undergo a rite of fasting. The Goddess is sometimes called Mahīsvarūpa, the one "whose very self is the earth."[24] Giving ritual reality to this understanding, the great shrine of the goddess Kāmākhyā in Assam is closed for the yearly observance of her menstrual period, and all plowing of the earth ceases, with the new cycle of plowing and planting beginning immediately afterward.[25] At Kāmākhyā, no image of the goddess exists, only a depression in stone, deep within a cave, said to be the *yoni* of the goddess.

While there are particular sanctuaries of the Goddess that are linked to the earth, of greater interest to us here is the suggestion that the earth as Ādi Shakti is the very ground of all sacred geography. A few verses from the *Atharva Veda* hymn called the Prithivī Sukta, the "Hymn to the Earth," will give us a sense of just how ancient these traditions of honoring the earth really are:

> Untrammeled in the midst of men, the Earth,
> adorned with heights and gentle slopes and plains,
> bears plants and herbs of various healing powers.
> May she spread wide for us, afford us joy!
>
> On whom are ocean, river, and all waters,
> on whom have sprung up food and ploughman's crops,
> on whom moves all that breathes and stirs abroad—
> Earth, may she grant to us the long first draught!
>
> To Earth belong the four directions of space.
> On her grows food; on her the ploughman toils.
> She carries likewise all that breathes and stirs.
> Earth, may she grant us cattle and food in plenty!
>
> On whom the men of olden days roamed far,
> on whom the conquering Gods smote the demons,
> the home of cattle, horses, and of birds,
> may Earth vouchsafe to us good fortune and glory!
>
> Bearer of all things, hoard of treasures rare,
> sustaining mother, Earth the golden-breasted
> who bears the Sacred Universal Fire,
> whose spouse is Indra—may she grant us wealth!
>
> Limitless Earth, whom the Gods, never sleeping,
> protect forever with unflagging care,
> may she exude for us the well-loved honey,
> shed upon us her splendor copiously![26]

Whether it is the Shakti of Mother Earth, called Prithivī Mātā, or of Mother India, called Bhārat Mātā some three thousand years later, the earth itself is the source of the inexhaustible power of creation. Beneath the temple, the shrine, the *linga,* the image, is the earth itself, the "mistress of the place." Finding the locative presence of Devī in India leads us inevitably to countless unprepossessing villages, groves, rivers, mountains, and hilltops.

SYLVAN SHAKTI

Trees and groves have long been associated with goddesses called *vanadevatās* and *vanaspati kanyās*—"forest goddesses" and "tree maidens." They were also called *yakshīs,* those nymphs of ample breasts and hips who were shown in early sculptural art entwined about trees, their limbs lithe, vine-like extensions of the life of the tree itself. These sylvan goddesses are embodiments of the life-giving energy so abundant in the growing green world of nature. Not surprisingly, people propitiate them for a share in that abundance, as we have already seen.

Evidence for the worship of tree *devīs* is literary, iconographic, and ritual. The *Mahābhārata* mentions these "*devīs* who take birth in trees" as the ones who should be worshipped by men and women who desire children.[27] In Bengal such *devīs* are known by a variety of names, among them Manasā, whom we have met, a goddess associated with snakes, who has also a tree form and an anthropomorphic form. Other *devīs,* such as the Vana-Durgās, the "Tree-Durgās," of Bengal are especially honored for the nourishment and health of small children.[28] A special form of the Goddess called the Navapatrika is made by bundling together nine leaves of various plants, each associated with a different goddess; the Navapatrika as a whole is worshipped as a representation of Durgā.[29] A distinctively sylvan form of Shakti is *tulsī,* a plant embodiment of Devī found in millions of household courtyards and gardens, and found, most especially in Krishna's holy land of Braj, in northern India, where she is honored as Vrindā Devī. In Orissa, on the east coast, the goddess Mangalā is the guardian of the forest from which trees are cut every twelve years to make the famous wooden embodiments of Jagannātha Krishna, whose huge temple in Purī is but a short distance away. At the time of this twelve-year cycle, the non-brahmin priests come to the forest to seek the right tree for the new image. Their first stop is Mangalā's temple, where they must obtain the permission of the goddess to cut the trees.

There are many trees and groves of individual fame in India. There are Panchavatī groves of "Five Trees," associated with the goddess and her worship. The most famous is in what is now the town of Nāsik in Mahārāshtra, often called by the compound name Nāsik-Panchavatī. This is the very grove, they say, where Sītā was living with Rāma when she was kidnapped by the wicked Rāvana, triggering Rāma and Lakshmana's search for Sītā and the subsequent war with Rāvana that drives the action of the last part of the *Rāmāyana*. In Prayāga, at the confluence of the Gangā and Yamunā Rivers, there is the famous Akshayavat, the "Tree Immortal," and in Ujjain the great Siddhavat, the "Success Tree," worshipped today with a mustached face painted in its ancient roots, but said to have been planted long ago by the goddess Pārvatī. It is unclear, at least to me, just why these particular trees have attained the fame they have. Even so, we should note that seemingly ordinary trees of no wide-reaching fame also receive the honor of worshippers. The primitive face of the goddess may shine forth from an old knothole. Her shrine might be at the base of the tree or on a simple benchlike platform, like the ancient seats of tree deities. Or there may be nothing distinctive at all. Still, on special days, such as Akshaya Tritīya, these trees will be circled by the devout, watered with Gangā water, and wrapped round and round with yards of the red and yellow threads of the goddess.[30]

Today, pilgrims flock to the hilltop temple of Manasī Devī, overlooking the main bathing *ghāts* of Hardvār. They make their way up the steep hill on foot or resort to the far more popular cable car. While the temple housing Manasī Devī is important, the clearest focal point of worship is actually outside of the main shrine: a tree whose branches have been wrapped so thoroughly and thickly with the red and yellow threads of pilgrims that they must be supported from beneath by posts. The sign posted at the tree reads: THE WISHES OF YOUR HEART WILL BE FULFILLED. On festival days, the hilltop is jammed with pilgrims, and on ordinary days all year long, pilgrims will come to this tree, as they do to the tree in the Kālī compound in Calcutta, bringing their prayers and vows.

Of course, there are other deities besides goddesses who make their dwellings beneath great trees. This is a favorite station for many deities. But the growing power of the tree itself, and, indeed, of the whole world of vegetation, belongs to the Goddess. This is Shakti. The vegetative deities are, in a sense, the visible manifestations of Ādi Shakti, the primordial power of the earth. In one vivid passage of the *Devī Māhātmya*, the great goddess Mahādevī describes herself as the Shākāmbarī, the "Vegetable Goddess." She says, "O Gods, I will support the whole world with life-sustaining vegetables which I shall grow from my own body during the time of heavy rain."[31]

The auspicious presence of Shakti is ritually marked by the sprouting of plants. Many rites of fertility and auspicious beginnings involve the sowing and sprouting of seeds. When a temple is to be built, for example, seeds are sown and sprouted to determine if the site is a good one. When a marriage is performed, the bride and bridegroom may plant a pot of seeds and watch for their speedy sprouting as a sign of their own anticipated fertility. And, of course, when the springtime festival of Vasanta Panchamī is at hand, the ritual sprouting of barley shoots is the lucky signal of the new season of growing.

Finally, in seeking the presence of Devī in the world of growing things, we must acknowledge the special place of the lotus, the plant that most widely connotes the auspicious blessings of this shore and this life. The lotus grows in the earth, indeed in the mud below the waters, and then rises to beautiful bloom on the surface of the waters. It is associated with the earthy, the aquatic, and the vegetative aspects of Shakti, all three. In one sense, the lotus is the base and support for the gods. We see them, in temples, shrines, and museums, sitting or standing upon the lotus. So familiar is this element of Indic art that we sometimes fail to notice it. The lotus is the firm seat, the *pītha*, par excellence—and not only for the gods and goddesses of Hindu India, but for Buddhas and *bodhisattvas, jinas* and *tīrthankaras*. The lotus is a gift to all Asia. Not only is the lotus a seat of the divine, but the lotus is also to be found as an emblem of blessing in the hands of innumerable deities. Perhaps in another hand the deity may clutch a weapon, another emblem of Shakti, but the presence of the lotus is firm assurance that the divine is not only dangerous, but also gracious and bountiful.[32]

From another perspective, we remember that the lotus is the plant that represents the whole world—a lotus-shaped world centered at Mount Meru, one petal for each continent. Women throughout India, and especially in the Tamil south, make lotus-based designs, called *kolams*, on the earth in front of the entry to their homes, tracing the intricate geometry of the world-lotus with rice powder on the ground. Especially beautiful are those created entirely of flowers during the ten-day festival of Onam in Kerala and Tamil Nadu. Like the lotus, the *kolam* becomes the focal point of worship, evanescent though it is. Wherever we see the lotus—whether in the hands or under the feet of gods and goddesses, whether in the geometric designs made on the earth, or whether in the esoteric world of Tantric mandalas—it connotes the auspicious, generative power of Shakti.

Village and City Goddesses—the Guardians of This Place

The most immediate divine presence in India's thousands of villages is a *grāma devatā*, literally the "village deity." These are place-specific, highly local deities, and most of them are goddesses. The village goddess makes the primordial association of Shakti with the earth concrete. Her domain is a particular territory—for the *grāma devatās*, a village; for the *nagara devatās*, a city. She may have her seat at the center of town or at the edge of town, depending on her temperament. Or perhaps the village goddess will have two seats, one for her benign and married form at the center of town, and one for her dangerous and virginal form at the borders.[33] She is honored both for prosperity and protection.

Not surprisingly, village deities are widely reported to receive both auspicious offerings, such as milk, honey, and flowers, as well as sacrificial blood offerings. The village deities of India may number as many as India's villages, but they have in common the fact that they are linked to the place they protect, however large or small, and they are linked to the people of that area.[34] Scholars have done significant work on the regional pilgrimage sites of Hindu goddesses. The most frequent pilgrimages and the most oft-told tales are associated with these very proximate deities. Ann Gold has studied these proximate gods in and around the village of Ghatiyali in Rajasthan, where, for example, the roadside shrine of Path

Mother is honored with the sprouting of grains in the soil.[35] In her work on Maharashtra, Anne Feldhaus has shown how these local *devīs* are often linked as sisters, village to village, establishing a kinship network and a sense of a region as well. Whether in Maharashtra or in Himachal Pradesh in the Himalayas, a married *devī* will usually be linked not only to the village of her husband, but to that of her natal family, and a pilgrimage procession will carry her back to that place for a visit, year after year.[36] The anthropologist William Sax has studied the pilgrimage, the "Royal Procession," of the goddess Nandā Devī through the mountains of Uttarakhand, one of the most complex and extensive of these journeys. During this *yātrā*, villagers escort Nandā Devī through the villages of the whole region, carrying her image in a palanquin and stopping often along the way. Eventually, they return the goddess to her high mountain home, where she lives for most of the year as the consort of Shiva. In the 1990s, this old pilgrimage took on fresh meaning as a cultural event in the region's identity as it bid for its own statehood in the Republic of India. Uttarakhand became India's twenty-seventh state in 2000.

Just as women as brides are living links between the family into which they are married and the family from which they came, so it is with many of the goddesses. And just as brides return for visits to their natal families, so, too, do the goddesses. As they are carried to and fro, they connect the places of their more stationary fathers and husbands. The goddesses are the networkers whose travels and intricate sisterly relations establish a sense of territory, large or small.

There is a complexity here, however. Even though many of the village goddesses are peripatetic, they are also considered to have primordial roots in the very soil of the places they protect. This is true not only for the thousands of local sisters who are rooted in the soil of villages all over India, but it is also true for the goddess guardians of India's most famous pilgrimage centers. Shiva's city of Kāshī, or Vārānasī, for example, is said to be protected by a ring of eight goddesses, one for each direction and intermediate direction.[37] In addition to these guardian goddesses, there is the "founding goddess" of Kāshī.[38] Some call her Kāshī Devī or Vārānasī Devī, goddesses who bear the names of the city itself. Others call her Vishālākshī, the "Wide-eyed" goddess; others say the founding goddess is Manikarnī Devī, who guards the most ancient and sacred bathing place in the city, Manikarnikā Kund, right next to the famous cremation *ghāt*. What is agreed, however, is that the most ancient deity of this city is a goddess. The term used, here and elsewhere, is *adhishthātrī devī*. Even today the goddess Annapūrnā, of "plenteous food," has a place of prominence right next to the temple of the *jyotirlinga* of Shiva. What is said in Kāshī of Annapūrnā and Vishvanātha could well summarize the theology of Shakti and Shiva. Annapūrnā, they say, provides food (*anna*) in the widest sense of the meaning of "food," that is, all that nourishes and sustains life on this shore. Shiva, they say, bestows the liberation of the far shore.

Similarly, at the famous pilgrimage temple of Krishna Jagannātha at Purī in Orissa, the goddess Vimalā is known as the ancient goddess of the place.[39] Those who have studied the folk deities of Orissa and the emergence of the Krishna cultus here say that this place, too, was a *pītha* of the goddess long before being appropriated by Lord Krishna. It was Vimalā who occupied the hillock where Jagannātha's temple now stands. Today, the temple of Krishna Jagannātha is so massive as to obscure the fact that a hillock is there at all. Yet in recognition of her ancient status, Vimalā, who still has a shrine in a corner of the sacred precincts, is the first to be offered the temple's celebrated *prasād*, the consecrated food.

Guarding the great temple city of Kānchīpuram in south India is the "Love-Eyed" goddess Kāmākshī, the establishing deity of the city. According to the mythology, it was she who fashioned the *linga* of earth there to honor Lord Shiva. And when a great flood swept the earth, it was she who clung to the *linga* and held it in place until the waters subsided. She held it so firmly that she left the imprints of her breasts and her bangles upon the *linga*.[40] Although Shiva's temple in Kānchīpuram, Ekāmranātha, is unique in that it contains no shrine for the goddess, pilgrims are well aware of the fact that it was she who established this sanctuary to begin with. Kāmākshī, the great goddess here, is also linked to two sisters elsewhere in India—Vishālākshī, the "Wide-Eyed," whose dwelling is in Kāshī, and Mīnākshī, the "Fish-Eyed," who lives farther south in Tamil Nadu, in the temple town of Madurai, forming an all-India threesome.

In Madurai, Mīnākshī has long been preeminent. According to legend, she was born from the immense effort of a king's ritual sacrifice to obtain the birth of a son and heir. He was both disappointed and astonished when the sacrifice produced a daughter—and with three breasts! As he lamented his luck, a divine voice is said to have come from the sky: "O king! Treat your daughter as though she were a son: Crown her Queen. And when this woman, whose form is golden, meets her Lord, one of her breasts will disappear."[41] So he did. He raised her as a prince, and as she grew in years and confidence, she became queen. She set out to conquer the world, leading her armies in all the eight directions and subduing all—at least until she came to the northern quarter, where Shiva, dwelling on Kailāsa, came out to survey the battle. At that moment, her third breast disappeared, and Mīnākshī stood before him, bashful and beautiful. Shiva will be her husband, and all of Madurai was sent into a spin preparing for her wedding.[42]

Originally a virgin goddess, Mīnākshī, having met her match in battle, becomes the bride of Shiva. Shiva, originally the gnarly mountain ascetic and yogi, becomes the husband of Mīnākshī, settling down in the kingdom of Madurai as Sundareshvara, the "Beautiful Lord." Even so, the vast temple compound of Madurai is still known by her name—Mīnākshī. Within the temple compound, there are separate temples for Mīnākshī and Sundareshvara. Hers occupies the preeminent position and is unquestionably the more popular. In the rites of the temple, Mīnākshī is both the powerful, independent goddess, worshipped

Devotees, come for the darshan *of Mīnākshī in Madurai*

alone by day, and the consort of Shiva, worshipped in his company by night.[43]

In the yearly round of spring festivals, the marriage of Shiva and Mīnākshī is celebrated every year during the month of Chaitra, which falls in April or early May. The goddess comes forth from her temple in an enormous chariot, a mobile replica of her temple, with tall pillars of brightly colored cloth, and is pulled by hundreds of devotees who strain together at the thick ropes. They pull the great temple-chariot around the rectangular processional streets of Madurai. Circling the temple, Mīnākshī does battle with the eight directions and symbolically conquers the whole earth. Finally, she encounters Shiva, and in the end, she herself is conquered. Then, their marriage is celebrated. Yet one cannot help but wonder who conquered whom here. For Mīnākshī is still very much the ruler of Madurai, having successfully incorporated Shiva himself into her entourage.

Finally, at the southern tip of India, there sits a goddess who seems to protect not only her own village, but the whole of India. She is Kanyākumārī, the "Virgin Goddess." According to legend, one of the great demons, named Bāna, gained a boon as a reward for his disciplined ascetic practice. He chose to be invulnerable to death, just the sort of boon the *asuras*, or demons, perpetually choose. But, as is well known, no one can really be guaranteed invulnerability to death, so every boon of this sort that is granted must have a loophole, even a preposterous one. In Bāna's case, he chose to be invulnerable to death, except at the hand of a virgin, who would be, so he thought, too rare and weak to worry about. So the gods pleaded with Shakti to become manifest as the Virgin Goddess in order to slay Bāna. She agreed and posted herself as a virgin goddess at the tip of southernmost India, right on the seashore, in order to guard the whole land, which comes to a point right there. Eventually, however, she was betrothed to marry Shiva, who lived nearby as the lord of Suchindram. Understandably, the gods conspired to prevent the marriage, fearful of losing their great protector. So, as Lord Shiva was on his way from Suchindram to the marriage, which had been set for the auspicious dawn hour, the sage Nārada took the form of a cock and crowed to announce the dawn prematurely. Dismayed at having missed the appointed hour for the wedding, Shiva turned around and went home. So it is that Kanyākumārī remained a virgin. Then, in full strength as the

Virgin Goddess, she slew Bāna. Ever since, so they say, Shakti has been present here as a virgin, keeping watch at the shore of the southern sea.[44]

Kanyākumārī stands at the place where three oceans meet, the Bay of Bengal on the east, the Indian Ocean on the south, and the Arabian Sea on the west. The waves roll in from three directions and collide with one another on the beach in front of her temple. This bathing place, as we have seen, is called a *triveṇī*, a "triple stream," and people say that here they bathe in all the *tīrthas* of India. The waters that run from the Himalayas and the other mountains of India, through the channels of many holy rivers, and into the eastern and western seas, are said to meet and mingle here at the *triveṇī*. And here, as well, the people of India meet and mingle, coming from virtually every regional and language group. On the whole, pilgrims are unfamiliar with bathing in the sea; they fall into the shallow waves on the beach, laughing with delight. They buy plastic packets of sand as souvenirs, with a small, sealed compartment for the sand of each of the three seas.

Mountain Goddesses

The goddesses of the earth, the grove, and the village live among the people, some at greater distance than others. They all fall generally within the realm of what we might call the domestic and agricultural sphere. However, many of India's most prominent and powerful goddesses live on hilltops and mountaintops more remote from the daily domestic world. Generally these goddesses command a wider realm of influence than others, for their special territory is not that of a single village. Indeed pilgrims come from all the villages round about to climb to their hilltop or mountain sanctuaries.

Pārvatī, Shiva's consort, is literally the "Mountain's Daughter." She is also called Haimavatī, "Himālaya's Girl," for her father is the Himalayas personified. Similarly the name Durgā, meaning "Difficult of Access," "Hard to Reach," may originally have referred to the association of the goddess with the high terrain of the mountains. While not all of India's mountain deities are goddesses, there are hundreds of goddesses who make the mountains their sanctuaries. Some of them are linked together like the seven sisters who claim countless devotees in the foothills of the Punjab and Himachal Pradesh.⁴⁵ In the hills of Rajasthan, there are well-known hilltop goddesses, such as Arbudā Devī and Arāsur Ambājī at Mount Abu. Nosar Mātājī sits in the barren rock hills between Ajmer and Pushkara and has a large local constituency. Across India, it seems that the strong goddess-in-arms who slew Mahisha is almost always said to live in the hills. She is Vindhyavāsinī in the Vindhya Mountains. She lives as Unnamulai on the hill called Dawn Mountain, Arunāchala, in the Tamil south, and she is Chāmundā Devī on the hilltop at the edge of Mysore City. The myth is flexible, multi-local, and timeless.

We have already visited one of India's most dramatic mountain-top Goddess shrines on top of the peaks of Girnār in the Saurashtra peninsula of India's far west, where the goddess Ambikā, the Mother, reigns. To reach her shrine and those on the adjacent needle peaks where Gorakhnāth and Dattātreya are honored, pilgrims climb ten thousand stair steps cut into the rocky face of the hill and its steep cliffs. Despite the convenience of steps, the climb is daunting, and pilgrims often leave the base of the mountain at three in the morning. Ambikā's shrine is hard won. One suspects that this entire range, with its seven dramatic peaks, was once the stronghold of the Goddess. Today, however, but three of the needle peaks are explicitly named as hers. Ambikā, the Mother, is the first destination of pilgrims, and at the far end of the range is Kālikā, the Great Destroyer. In between these mothers of birth and destruction is the peak of Renukā, the mother of Vishnu's *avatāra* Parashurāma. Girnār, according to legend, is a piece of the Himalayas and, thus, the little brother of Pārvatī. And it is Pārvatī, they say, who rules here as the goddess Ambikā. Just below the crest of Ambikā's peak, the Gaṅgā is also present, her waters issuing from the mountainside at the place called Gomukha after its Himalayan prototype.

Sometimes the strong goddesses of the mountain are found not on the mountaintop, but inside a mountain cave. Remember that two of the goddesses at Vindhyāchala are found in womblike caves. Similarly, the great Kāmākhyā Devī in Assam, one of India's most revered goddesses, is located in what was originally a cave on the "Blue Mountain," Nīlāchala, near Gauhati. The stone depression said to be the "image" of the goddess here is continually moistened by a spring. Her *māhātmya* in the *Kālikā Purāṇa* details the sacred places of Kāmākhyā's domain and the praises of her power. Across India in the far northwest, near Jammu in Kashmir, is perhaps the most famous mountain-cave shrine, Vaishno Devī, located on a hill called Trikuta, the Triple Peak. It is said that the goddess hollowed out a cave there with her trident. Pilgrims come from all over India to make the trek up her hill and then to squeeze, ten to twelve at a time, into the cave where her triple image may be seen. One by one they crawl through the passageway that leads into the chamber of the goddess. The ritual crawl has all the symbolism of gestation and birth, even though Vaishno Devī is a virgin goddess. According to local legend, Bhairava, one of the fearsome forms of Shiva, pursued her fiercely, desiring to marry her. Finally, she simply beheaded him, and his head rolled down the hill, where he is honored even today as a guardian of this powerful *devī*. But even as a virgin goddess, she clearly is a life-giving mother for those who make this initiatory journey.[46]

Finally, we should mention one of the most famous mountain goddesses of India, Hinglāj, located in Baluchistan, beyond the Indus River, in a mountain range just west of Karachi, in what is now Pakistan. Until the partition of India in 1947, Hinglāj was one of the westernmost places in the sacred geography of India. The local *māhātmya* claims that this, too, was the place where Durgā slew the bull-demon Mahisha. This also was the place where Lord Rāma came in order to gain expiation for having killed Rāvana, who was, after all, a brahmin, and killing a brahmin is one of the most dreadful of sins.[47] According to local legend, Rāma came on pilgrimage to Hinglāj with his entire army, but was stopped in a mountain pass before he could reach the goddess. He must come, she said, not as a triumphant king leading an army, but as a supplicant and worshipper. Going ahead with only Lakshmana, Sītā, Hanumān, and Ganesha, Rāma honored the goddess at Hinglāj and received expiation for his sin. As at Vaishno Devī, farther east in Kashmir, the innermost sanctuary of Hinglāj is a cave, and crawling through a narrow passage in the cave is part of the pilgrimage ritual. It is both an ordeal and a rebirth.

MAHĀDEVĪ, THE GREAT GODDESS

These goddesses of earth and village, glade and river, hilltop and mountaintop—all have been forms and manifestations of Shakti, named with thousands of special and local names. In the context of our study, it is important to note that they are place-specific in their power, from the village goddess whose domain extends around village boundaries, to Ambikā Devī, who claims the allegiance of all Saurashtra, to Kanyākumārī, who claims to protect the whole of India. Yet despite the multiple and locative nature of these goddesses, we also see evidence that they are all understood to be particular manifestations of a single goddess. In a hymn associated with the *Harivamsha*, the Great Goddess Mahādevī is extolled in ways that seem to embrace the whole range of Shakti: "O Mahādevī, you dwell on the forbidding mountaintops, in the rivers, and in the caves, in the forests and in the winds!"[48]

By the fifth century, the *Devī Māhātmya* of the *Mārkandeya Purāna* praises a goddess whose independence and supremacy are bountifully manifest as the slayer of demons—especially the earth-threatening Mahisha. This victorious one is truly a Great Goddess of multiple names and forms. The full-blown myth of Mahādevī slaying Mahisha has become a powerful meta-narrative that links local devotion to cosmic realities. The importance of the *Devī Māhātmya* is not so much the action-packed narratives that tell the tale of the Devī's fierce battles. Even more important are the well-known hymns of praise that follow each of her great victories, giving voice to an understanding of the supreme Mahādevī. After the slaying of the first pair of demons, Madhu and Kaitabha, the hymn begins:

> *By thee everything is maintained, by thee this world is created, by thee it is protected, O Goddess! And thou dost always consume it at the end. At its emanation, thou didst take the form of creation, and in protecting it, thou hast the form of permanence, and at the end of this world, thou wilt have the form of contraction, O thou who containest the world!*[49]

These are the kinds of praises most often employed in the honoring of Shiva or Vishnu, but here they are directed toward the all-powerful Goddess—creator, sustainer, destroyer of all. The pieces of a complex kaleidoscope of image, word, and praise have now fallen into place around the central vision of Mahādevī, who embraces the whole. Similarly, after slaying the bull-demon Mahisha, the greatest of her opponents, the gods join together in praise, making clear the oneness of this vision of the goddess:

Thou art Durgā, the boat to cross the difficult ocean of existence, devoid of attachments! Thou art Shrī, who has planted her dominion alone in the heart of Vishnu! Thou indeed art Gaurī, who has fixed her dwelling in the moon-crested Shiva![50]

Finally, after she has slain Chanda and Munda, the gods sing her praise at the conclusion of the cosmic battle, invoking her presence and protection as the sovereign of all:

Be gracious, O mother of the whole world!
Be gracious, O Queen of the universe! Safeguard the universe!
Thou, O goddess, art queen of all that is movable and immovable!
Thou alone hast become the support of the world, because Thou does
*   subsist in the form of the earth!*
By Thee, who exists in the form of water, all this universe is filled![51]

These are but excerpts of hymnic sections of the *Devī Māhātmya*, also called the *Saptashatī*, literally the "Seven Hundred" verses in praise of the Goddess.

And where did the Goddess slay the mighty Mahisha? We have already seen that many of the places of the victory of the Goddess are marked by mere indentations in stone, or rough images in the dark of caves, or images grown shapeless with centuries of vermilion. Of course, the Goddess does have an elegant form as well, but not usually inside the sanctuaries where she is worshipped. Rather, on the exterior panels of temples or on their circumambulatories, we may encounter the image of Mahishamardinī, Slayer of Mahisha, rendered in the finest sculptural arts. She plunges her trident into the chest of the shape-shifting demon or stands triumphant and stately upon his severed head. She is displayed prominently on some of India's great historic temples, constituting a visual historic record of her presence—at Udayagiri in Madhya Pradesh in the fifth century, at Aihole in Karnakata in the sixth century, in the Rāmeshvara Temple at Ellora in Maharashtra in the seventh century, and at Mahabalipuram in Tamil Nadu in the seventh and eighth centuries. This Mahishamardinī image is also featured on living temple complexes, like those in Kānchīpuram and Tanjore in Tamil Nadu, where we see Mahishamardinī standing on the severed head of a horned bull, her

image daubed with oil and glistening black. At the Nāgeshvara Temple
in Kumbhakonam, for instance, by far the most active subsidiary shrine
is that of Durgā, four-armed, crowned, standing in a niche entirely filled
with flowers, standing triumphant upon the silver head of Mahisha. In
northern Andhra Pradesh, at the temple of Bhramarāmbā Devī, the
Durgā Saptashatī is chanted daily and a beautiful small image of Durgā
as Mahishamardinī is framed above the door of the inner sanctum. Her
head is anointed with red *kumkum* powder and flowers are tucked into
the frame around her. Worshippers reach up to touch her before bowing at the door of the sanctum sanctorum. It would be difficult to enumerate or overestimate the number of local shrines and the countless
ritual forms in which this myth of the triumph of the Goddess has been
evoked and imaged throughout India. This is one of the great myths
of the Hindu tradition, to which countless connecting strands of local
power are fastened.

By the time of the *Devī Bhāgavata Purāna,* the conception of
Mahādevī, the Great Goddess, that "crystallized" in the *Devī Māhātmya*
has become a complete and complex Goddess theology in which all the
goddesses, under a variety of names, are seen to have issued from Prakriti
Devī, the Goddess Nature.[52] Here we have a full theological exposition
of how such a range of *devīs* belong together as divine manifestations of
the One Goddess. The Supreme Reality, Shakti, is manifest as various
Shaktis—Durgā, Lakshmī, Sarasvatī, Sāvitrī, and Rādhā. These Shaktis
are also manifest in their various parts, or *amshas.* The River Gangā is
such a partial manifestation. So are the sacred *tulsī* plant and the goddess Manasā. So are the many village goddesses. Finally, there is the
shakti that is present in qualities such as faith (*shraddhā*) and devotion
(*bhakti*), and there is the *shakti* that includes "all women everywhere in
the universe."

Yet it is not only that the Goddess gathers together all the Shaktis
in one Supreme Being, for the Goddess really *is* the Supreme Reality,
Brahman. One of the most dazzling images of this is the journey of the
great gods Vishnu, Shiva, and Brahmā to heaven itself on the divine
chariot of the Goddess. Passing one heavenly realm after another, they
actually see themselves in their respective heavens, and are filled with
puzzlement and wonder at their own identities. Finally, they come to the
Island of Jewels, where the Goddess is seated, dazzling, inconceivably

exquisite. Choked with emotion and awe, the great gods approach her, bow at her feet, and there, in her toenails, they see the whole universe. They see themselves and all the other gods. They see the heavens where they themselves dwell. They see the entire cosmos, the earth, its mountains and rivers. All this, they see in the toenails of the Goddess. They burst into praise of the Goddess, who is Being, Consciousness, and Bliss, those few words one uses to speak of the Supreme Brahman. She indeed is the One from whom the whole universe arises and into whom it again melts away.[53]

Such a vast vision of the Goddess reaches its fullness in the *Devī Bhāgavata Purāna*, but we can glimpse this vision much earlier in the *Devī Māhātmya*, and earlier still in the ways in which goddess names are often treated in many texts. J. N. Tiwari has done the most extensive study of how this vision gradually took shape.[54] At first, he tells us, the texts contain simply long lists of the names and locales of goddesses, some of them inserted for what seems to be merely the purpose of meter and rhyme. In the first five centuries of our era there are lists of this sort in the *Mahābhārata*, in Jain and Buddhist literature, and in the early Purānas. Such simple lists are remarkable theological artifacts. They are important not for their accuracy, although in them one can see the names and locations of many of the goddesses we have come to know well in later times, such as Vindhyavāsinī, Kāmākhyā Devī, and Kanyākumārī. But these goddess-place lists tell us far more than name and place: They reveal the cumulative movement of the religious imagination. The lists are important for their very existence and conception, for here local *devīs* are understood to belong together, as manifestations of Shakti. And they are important for the one consistent fact that they reveal: that every *devī* is linked to a place, and is listed as such.

THE ANKLE OF DEVĪ

On a dirt road outside Kurukshetra, north of Delhi, is the village of Thanesar, named for Sthānīshvara Shiva. Here the Pāndavas are said to have received Shiva's blessing before the great war of the *Mahābhārata*. The battleground of that war is all around these parts. We can see the field where the armies of the Pāndavas and Kauravas were arrayed against each other, the tree beneath which Krishna is said to have revealed his teachings to the warrior Arjuna as the battle was about to begin, and the deep ruts where the truthful Yudhisthira's war chariot hit the ground the moment he told a lie. And yet the old temple of Sthānīshvara, today's Sthāneswar, reminds us that Kurukshetra had been famous for a very long time, even before the great events that took place there.

While they were there, so they say, the Pāndavas also took the blessing of a fearsome and powerful manifestation of the goddess, Bhadrakālī. Her black stone image occupies the sanctum of her temple today. She is four-armed, silver-eyed, garlanded with marigolds, and dressed in a red sari with silver tinsel. The door to her sanctuary is guarded by an ancient black Bhairava as well as a mountain-bearing orange Hanumān and an orange Ganesha, both strewn with bits of silver paper—all extraordinarily striking images, elongated, of local provenance to be sure. Outside the temple, however, is a much newer image. It sits in the courtyard in front of Bhadrakālī's temple door, under an enormous banyan tree, next to a deep circular well. There, on a platform by the well, is a finely made marble ankle, with attached foot. The inscription reads, "Here at Kurukshetra fell the right anklebone of the Goddess."

What does it mean to find the ankle of the Goddess here at this temple in rural north India? Here we encounter another universalizing myth that connects one goddess to another throughout the length and breadth of India. There are countless such places in India, claiming to be sanctified by the body of the Goddess. They are said to be body parts of the goddess Satī, beloved of Shiva. When she died, so they say, Shiva carried her body in mourning throughout the land, and the parts of her body fell here and there. The myth of the dismemberment of the Goddess, more than any other, places the body of Mahādevī on the landscape of India. The places where her body fell are called pīthas, the "seats" of Devī. There are traditions that describe either 51 or 108 such pīthas.[55] In very few of these places is the body part of Devī actually represented, as it is here in the fine form of this marble ankle. On the whole, the body part is not represented, but the sense of belonging to the body of Satī is shared by pīthas far and wide, many more by far than are part of the textual lists.

The full myth of the dismemberment and distribution of Satī comes from the Kālika Purāna and the Devī Bhāgavata Purāna, both Purānas in which the Goddess is front and center.[56] However, the symbolic framework in which this story participates is as ancient as the great Vedic hymn of creation, the *Purusha Sukta*. Here, as we recall, the cosmic being, Purusha, was divided by the gods at the dawn of creation to become the entire universe. By dismembering Purusha in the cosmogonic sacrifice, the gods created an extensive series of correspondences between body and cosmos: his mind the moon, his eye the sun, his mouth Indra and fire, his breath the wind, and so forth. Purusha is the body-cosmos that unifies, even as it differentiates. Indeed, this ancient mythic image is appropriated in the *Devī Bhāgavata Purāna* to describe the whole universe as various parts of the body of the Goddess.[57] In the *Purusha Sukta*, not only is the cosmos created, but a type of symbolic thinking and ritual action is also created. This symbolic thinking, filled with correspondences between the microcosm of the body and the macrocosm of the universe, permeates the Hindu tradition from ancient times to the present.[58] In addition, we see the ways in which division and distribution are, indeed, a form of unification and universalization. This is a common theme in the ritual world of India and, indeed, in the ritual enactments of religious traditions the world over. For instance, no sooner had the Buddha given up his earthly body than it was cremated and the ashes distributed to the kings of the several great dynasties of India; at the time of Ashoka, the number of stūpa reliquaries was said to be a legendary eighty-four thousand. The relics of the saints and martyrs of the Christian world were, likewise, many in number and constituted what Peter Brown has called "those tiny fragments that condensed the solidarity of the Christian world."[59] In a ritual sense, of course, the distribution of the sacrifice of the body of Christ in the mass reconstitutes and unifies the body of Christ in the church.

The mythic dismemberment of Satī did not, however, create a reliquary cult of Devī. Nothing would more thoroughly puzzle and horrify most Hindus, even Shāktās, than the fragments of bone that are on display in sancta throughout the Catholic Christian world. Indeed, the locative worship of the goddesses of India at her many *pīthas*, or "seats," must predate the emergence of the myth of the dismemberment of the Goddess by some two thousand years. Locative forms of worship clearly take precedence. The myth of the distribution of Satī creates not a cult of Shakti, but a theology of the pervasiveness of Shakti. The ankle at Kurukshetra does not betoken a mere fragment of the Goddess, but rather signifies that the presence of the Goddess is much wider than this or any local manifestation, a sense of the Goddess that claims as her domain the whole of the land. The myth of dismemberment casts a net of unification over a vast number of place-specific goddesses.

THE DISTRIBUTION OF THE BODY OF DEVĪ

As we seek the presence of Devī in the landscape of India, the story of Daksha's sacrifice in Kankhal comes again to view. Recall how Shiva had been omitted from the guest list of the Vedic sacrifice. At Devī's insistence, Shiva decimated the whole sacrificial arena, and then was begged by the gods to restore it once again. The Supreme Lord, who was excluded from the Vedic liturgies, was embraced and given a share of the sacrifice. In the end, Daksha sang a long hymn of praise to Shiva. In many later versions of the myth, however, the grand finale is the exaltation and glorification of Satī, who is clearly the Great Goddess, Mahādevī. In the brief telling of the story in the *Matsya Purāna,* for example, Satī's death scene becomes the occasion for Daksha's repentance.[60] As she creates a fire and enters into it by her yogic power, Daksha recognizes her as Mahādevī herself. His hymn of praise is directed not to Shiva, but to her. He asks where he might worship her. The Goddess tells Daksha that she is truly in every being and in every place. She reveals the 108 places where she is especially worshipped. She mentions Vishālākshī in Kāshī, Lalitā in Prayāga, Kāmākshī in Gandhamādana, Nandā in the Himalayas, Mādhavī in Shrī Shaila, Devakī in Mathurā, Vinduvāsinī in Vindhyāchala, and so forth. Finally, she is *"shakti* in all bodies." In such a telling, we see the energy and teleology of the myth reoriented toward Devī. The destruction and restitution of the sacrifice are not even part of the narrative.

Another version of this myth, as told in the *Vāmana Purāna,* includes an additional important element: Shiva's grief.[61] In this telling of the tale, Satī does not go to the sacrificial ground of her father Daksha, but on hearing the news of Shiva's exclusion she dies of indignation straightaway. When Shiva finds her, "lying on the ground like a creeper chopped down with an axe," he creates out of his wrath the fearsome Vīrabhadra and a thousand henchmen. He goes along with them to Kankhal and participates in the utter destruction. He wrecks the sacrifice and chases the deer through the houses of the heavens before piercing it with an arrow.

Shiva does not restore the sacrifice, for that is not the point of the story here. Instead, Shiva is struck by the flowered arrow of Kāma, the Lord of Love, and is overcome with the passion of his lost love and the madness brought on by his beloved's death. He wanders through the whole of the land of India, but can find no peace.

The *Kālīkā* and *Devī Bhāgavata Purāṇas* include both the exaltation of the goddess and the grief of Shiva. Most important, they include what becomes the well-known myth of the dismemberment of Satī and the origins of the *shākta pīthas*. The story has become so widely known that it is, indeed, grafted onto the telling of the *Shiva Purāṇa* version of Daksha's sacrifice in the popular *māhātmya* on sale in the markets of Kankhal even today. In the minds of many it is simply part of the "original" tale.

In the *Devī Bhāgavata Purāṇa*, the actual account of the sacrifice and of Shiva's destruction and restoration of the sacrifice is truncated. Indeed, there is but one stanza telling us that Daksha's daughter burned herself up in the heat she created from her yoga.[62] This telling of the tale emphasizes the madness and grief of Shiva. He took her up in his arms, and bearing the body of his beloved Satī, he began to weep. He roamed about the country crying, "Oh, Satī! My Satī!" The gods became anxious about Shiva's great sorrow and his seeming neglect of the world. On their behalf, Vishnu followed along behind Shiva and cut off bits of the body of Satī with his discus. The places where her body fell became the *pīthas*, the seats of the goddess. There are 108 such places listed in the *Devī Bhāgavata Purāṇa*, and the list given is substantially the same as that found in the *Matsya Purāṇa*. The text does not reveal which body part became which *pīthā*, except to say that it was her face that fell in Kāshī and became the *pīthā* of Vishālākshī.[63]

The *Kālīkā Purāṇa* is the *locus classicus* of the Goddess-oriented myth of the *shākta pīthas*.[64] Here the story of Satī's birth and marriage follows closely the narrative of the *Shiva Purāṇa*. As in the *Vāmana Purāṇa*, Satī does not actually go to her father's sacrifice in Kankhal. Rather, immediately upon hearing of the insult to Shiva, she enters into a yogic trance and gives up her life on the spot. Here is a synopsis of the story:

When Shiva learned of Satī's death, he created the blazing Vīrabhadra and set out to destroy Daksha's sacrifice. He pulled out the eyes of one god, smashed the teeth of another, and chased the deer form, which escaped from the sacrifice. The deer ran into Satī's corpse.

When Shiva saw Satī's body, he was overcome with grief and began to weep. He wept like an ordinary mortal, and his tears of grief were so profuse that they deluged the earth. He picked up Satī's body and carried her about, in mourning and in madness. He roamed the land, weeping and dancing wildly. The gods were fearful of Shiva's extreme sorrow, and so they entered Satī's body and caused pieces of it to fall here and there.

In seven places, parts of her body fell. Her feet fell at Devīkuta, where she is called Mahābhagā; her thighs at Uddiyāna, where she is called Kātyāyanī; her *yoni* at Kāmarupa, where she is called Kāmākhyā; her shoulders and neck at Pūrnagiri, where she is Pūrnesvarī; her navel to the east of Kāmarūpa, where she is Dikkaravāsinī; her breasts at Jalandhara, where she is Chandī. And Shiva became present in each of these places as well, establishing himself as a *linga* attached to each manifestation of the *devī*.

In these accounts, the myth of Daksha's sacrifice moves from the orbit of Shaiva theology to that of Shākta theology. The theme of the exclusion and inclusion of Shiva is replaced by the theme of the division and reappearance of Shakti. In some of these myths, the sacrifice still has a central place. The whole universe gathers for the sacrifice. The sacrifice is destroyed, dismembered, and eventually reconstituted. In the Shākta myths, however, Shakti is central. She herself becomes the sacrificial victim. She *is* the sacrifice. It is she who is offered up in the fire, even in the fire of her own austerities, her *tapas* or her yoga. She becomes the symbolic home of the "deer" of the sacrifice. She is the one dismembered and scattered throughout the land. And she is the one who is ultimately reconstituted in the linked places of the *shākta pīthas*.

Even in the *Shiva Purāna* account, it is clear that Satī *is* the sacrifice. Her own sacrifice, however, is more in accord with that prescribed by the emerging Shaiva theology. It is prepared for and motivated by her unswerving devotion to Shiva. In the *Shiva Purāna* account, she sips water [*achamāna*], covers herself with a cloth [*diksha*], and enters into a trance from which she sheds her body. The whole ordered world is gathered for the sacrifice. All is prepared. And when Satī enters the sacrificial grounds, she simply consummates the true sacrifice: the one in which Shiva is the center. With her death, Satī has indeed made the sacrificial ground into a cremation ground, sacred to Shiva. The *Kālīkā Purāna*, however, reverses the flow of affection at this point. Satī's devotion to Shiva is matched by his devotion to her. Shiva is wild with grief. He takes her body, into which the deer of the sacrifice has run, and, carrying it in his arms, he roams the world. The dismemberment and distribution of Satī is the dismemberment and distribution of the sacrifice. And it is distributed all over India.

THE *SHĀKTA PĪTHAS* IN THE LAND OF INDIA

In the remote hills of northern Andhra Pradesh, high above the Krishnā River, is Shrī Shaila, an ancient and holy temple complex containing one of India's famous twelve *jyotirlingas* as well as a shrine to the Goddess, known here as Bhramarāmbā, literally the "Black Bee Goddess." The tableau on the great bronze door of her temple makes clear the wide reach of the goddess within. On the beautiful bas relief panels of the door, we see Kālī, four-armed, standing on Lord Shiva. We see Lakshmī emerging from the lotus, Sarasvatī playing the vina, Durgā riding the lion, and Annapurnā spooning out food to Shiva. On the exterior wall to the right of the door is a huge map of India on which are number-coded "18 *Shākta Pīthas*" in Telugu. Not surprisingly, there are more in central and southern India, for Shrī Shaila is linked more closely to the south. Only six of the *pīthas* are scattered across the north India plains and the Himalayan tier. Even so, the conceptualization of an India-wide network of Goddess shrines in which this Bhramarāmbā is embedded is clear.

Beyond the myth of Satī's sacrificial dismemberment, there are many textual traditions about the *shakta pīthas* of India, all enumerated in D. C. Sircar's classic work on the subject, *The Sākta Pīthas*. Several sources list four great *pīthas*. The earliest source is the eighth-century *Hevajra Tantra*, which speaks of Jālandhara (Punjab), Odiyāna (Uddiyāna in the Swat Valley), Pūrnagiri (in the south), and Kāmarūpa (in the east, in Assam).[65] This Tantra reminds us that the notion of seats of power was shared by the Buddhist tradition as well. Uddiyāna, with its goddess Pīthesvarī, for instance, was an important place of Tantric revelation for Buddhists.[66] The *Kālikā Purāna,* from the period of the eighth to eleventh centuries, also speaks of a set of four.[67] Some texts, cited by Sircar, speak of a group of seven goddesses or a group of ten. Several sources, following the *Matysa Purāna* and the *Devī Bhāgavata Purāna,* list the auspicious number 108 as the number of *devīs* that constitute the full body of *pīthas.* Taken as a whole, these texts give us a tradition of grouping the goddesses, listing the goddesses, connecting them, and ultimately linking them in a single body.

One of the most prevalent traditions is that there are fifty-one *pīthas.* These are carefully enumerated in Tantric works such as the Pīthanirnaya of the *Tantracūdāmani,* a late-seventeenth-century text that D. C. Sircar edited and drew upon in his study. This list of *pīthas* does not display much familiarity with the goddesses of the south but draws more upon the Tantric ambiance of the north. Here the *devīs* are listed not only with respect to their places, as in the *Matysa Purāna,* but with respect to the limb or portion of Satī distributed in each place. In addition, the list includes the Bhairava form of Shiva paired with the goddess at each place. The Pīthanirnaya goes even another step and identifies each of the *devīs* with one of the fifty-one letters of the Sanskrit alphabet, extending the homologies and connections so typical of Tantra symbology and making the letters themselves integral to the mantra of each goddess.

We can see the concrete reality of this imaginative conception today in the Harasiddhi Devī Temple in Ujjain, where the inner dome of the sanctum is ringed with a series of fifty-one medallions, each identified with one of the goddesses, one of the letters of the Sanskrit alphabet, and one of the *pīthas.* Each goddess is depicted in her medallion—with her animal mount, her weapons, her emblems—making the temple interior a virtual mandala of the Goddess, with all of the goddesses and, indeed, all of language condensed in the surround of the walls and ceiling. Partway around the circle, just above the clock, is a large color painting of a very muscular blue Shiva, wrapped in a leopard skin, striding across the landscape and carrying the body of Satī over his shoulder.

In the popular Hindi pilgrimage guides and manuals that enumerate the seats of the goddess today, such as *Hamare Pūjya Tīrtha,* the old story of Daksha's sacrifice is told as the context for and introduction to the list of *shākta pīthas*. The myth of Shakti's dismemberment becomes what I have called a "subscription myth," a story to which local *devī* shrines have subscribed as a way of articulating the particular sanctity of their own place and connecting it with the larger systemic reality. Our place is distinctive, they seem to say, yet our place is also related to the great, cosmic events displaying the power and presence of the Goddess. Throughout north and central India, many places claim participation in the myth of Shakti's distribution in the land.[68] Two or more places may even claim the same *devī*, the same body part, as in the case of Harasiddhi Mātā, who is present in both Ujjain and on the coast of Saurashtra in Gujarat. According to the Gujarati claimant, the goddess spends her days in one shrine and nights in the other.

The popular accounts of the *shākta pīthas* reiterate the kinds of body-land correspondences we saw in the Purānas. It was her elbow, they say, that fell in Ujjain and became Harasiddhi Devī. It was her face, or some say her earring, that fell in Kāshī and became the *pītha* of Vishālākshī. It was her heart that fell at Vaidyanātha in eastern Bihar. Then again, they say, her heart also fell at the great shrine of Ambājī, on the Rajasthan-Gujarat border. At Biraja in Orissa, her navel fell. There in the temple compound of Biraja the very navel of the Goddess is identified, where a deep well plunges into the earth. At Jālandhara in the Punjab is her left breast, and an image of that breast is said to be there in the sanctum, covered with a piece of cloth. In Kangra in the Himalayan foothills is her head, or alternately near Cannanore in Kerala. And at the far southern end of India, at Kanyākumārī, is her back.

One of the most distinctive regional manifestations of multiple goddesses is the group of seven *devīs* of the Punjab Hills.[69] To be sure, this is not the only regional group of seven sisters in India, and we have seen the ways in which Anne Feldhaus has documented the ritual connections among the sisters in her study of Maharashtra. Here in the Punjab Hills, however, we see the ways in which the seven goddesses, each with her distinctive lore, are linked not as sisters, but as a body. We have already met Vaishno Devī, whose hilltop shrine in the Jammu district of Kashmir attracts millions of pilgrims each year. It is here, they say, that Satī's arms fell. At Jvālāmukhī in the Kangra District of the Punjab, flames emerge from the earth and are said to be the tongue of the goddess. The flame is still visible today. At Kāngrevālī Devī, also in Kangra District, it is said to be the breast of Satī that fell. Both Jvālāmukhī and Kāngrevalī Devī are associated in lore with the early Tantric reference to Jālandhara—one of the four famous *pīthas*. Chintapūrnī in Himachal Pradesh is the "wish-fulfilling" goddess, often seen as the younger sister of Kāngrevalī Devī and Jvālāmukhī. According to local lore, it was here that the feet of Satī fell. At Nainā Devī, on a hilltop in Himachal Pradesh, the eye of Satī fell. At Manasā Devī in the Kalka district of Haryana, her forehead fell. Finally, Chāmundā Devī in Kangra District is one of this group of seven sisters but is not associated in popular lore with the body of the Goddess. Her wider penumbra is linked explicitly, however, to the victorious demon-conquering goddess who defeated the demons Chanda and Munda. As a group, however, these seven goddesses, through their connections, cast the imagined landscape of their domain across the foothills of the Himalayas.

Perhaps no *pītha* is as renowned throughout India as one of the most distant: Kāmākhyā Devī, in the far northeast in Assam, often called Kāmarūpa. According to the *Kālikā Purānā*, "Kāmarūpa is the sacred land of the Goddess; there is no equal to this. Elsewhere the Goddess is rare; in Kāmarūpa, she is in every house."[70] According to local tradition, it was in the hills of Assam where Kāma, the god of Love, tried to shoot the flower-arrows of love into the heart of the meditating Shiva. For his audacity, Kāma was burned to a pile of ash by Shiva's fierce third eye. The land is called Kāmarūpa, literally "having the form of Kāma." The land is famous, however, not so much for Kāma, but for the great goddess Kāmākhyā. It was here, they say, that the sexual organ, the *yoni*, of Satī fell when Shiva danced wildly around India. It became the stone, which is the "image" of the goddess Kāmākhyā even today, a depression in the stone.[71] The temple of Kāmākhyā Devī sits on a hill, called Nīlāchala (Blue Mountain) or Kāmagiri (the Hill of Kāma). Inside the temple structure, the sanctum sanctorum is actually a cave into which pilgrims enter to honor the image of Kāmākhyā. Annually, in June, the temple is closed for three days during the time believed to be the menses of the goddess. This is a great pilgrimage time, for all cultivation is halted. During the period of her menses, it is forbidden to plow the earth or even scratch it with a needle. On the fourth day the temple is again opened for what is the most auspicious *darshan* of the whole year. Immediately after this period, Assamese farmers begin a season of planting.

Many of the traditions associated with Kāmākhyā are also linked to a temple in Kerala, some two thousand miles to the south, the temple of Chengannur Bhagavatī, south of Kottayam.[72] There, in a lush land of mangos, bananas, and paddy fields, near the Pampā River, is the goddess Bhagavatī. The temple is linked with the tradition of the dispersed body of Satī, for here, too, they say, her *yoni* fell, as at Kāmākhyā, in the north. According to the tradition at Chengannur, Bhagavatī is Satī reborn as Parvatī, who came here with Shiva following their Himalayan wedding. Here Parvatī got her menstrual period and stayed for twenty-eight days. So here, as in Assam, the temple is closed for three days during the menses of the goddess. Of course, those who know Kerala realize that there are many local Bhagavatīs in Kerala. And they are, for the most part, intimately linked to the land. As Sarah Caldwell writes, having worked for years in Kerala, "Bhagavatī is important to Malayalis not only as a legendary protectress, but as a deity of the land. For communities dwelling in the hills, she is the spirit of the mountains; for lowland agriculturalists, she is the paddy and the earth from which it grows; for toddy tappers, the graceful coconut palm is her form. The idea of human embodiment, then, is natural to the concept of Bhagavatī as she permeates all living things through the energies of the soil."[73]

The myth of the dismemberment of Satī provides a context for viewing the apotheosis and distribution of the goddess. Here the symbol of the divine body unites the various parts or manifestations of the Great Goddess into one organic whole. Division is a powerful form of unification. The many goddesses of India are seen to be manifestations of Shakti, universal and yet local and particular. This conception of Shakti is not merely the work of the mythic imagination of Purānic theologians; it seems truly to reflect the place-specific way in which the Goddess has long been honored in India. There is also no doubt that the *pīthas* as seats of divine energy are much older than the body-cosmos myths that make their systemic connections explicit. These many local goddesses have occupied their particular seats for countless centuries.

From late Gupta times to the present the systematization of Goddess temples, linking them together as part of a wider sense of divine power, has been common. The tradition of the *pīthas* extends far beyond any list of 51 or 108, for there are thousands of goddesses all over India that people claim to be a part of the body of Shakti.

Standing in the caves and sanctuaries of the Goddess at Vindhyavāsinī, where we began, we can see something important about the nature and distribution of Shakti, highly local and yet translocal. Here also, we glimpse something essential about the land of India itself. The land, in this vision, is the dismembered and distributed body of Shakti, providing the soil for a strong sense of translocal belonging. Put in another way, the whole of India, taken together, is the body of Shakti.

"Mother" is the name—both powerful and affectionate—by which Hindus call Shakti, be she Kālī the frightful or Gangā the beneficent. It is hardly surprising that it is also the name by which they call the land of India—"Bhārat Mātā, Mother India." As we have seen, the hymn *"Vande Mātaram,"* "I Bow to the Mother," which became an inspiration to the Indian nationalist movement in the early twentieth century, was written in Bengal, an area of India where the worship of the Goddess is vibrant. Here Bankim Chandra Chatterjee praises the land as Mother, in language that could easily have come from the *Atharva Veda*'s "Hymn to the Earth," composed well over two thousand years earlier:

> Mother, I bow to thee!
> Rich with thy hurrying streams,
> Bright with thy orchard gleams,
> Cool with thy winds of delight,
> Dark fields waving, Mother of might, Mother free.[74]

From the partition of Bengal in the first decade of the twentieth century to the partition of India and Pakistan in the fourth, the cry of protest that arose from some Hindus was against the "vivisection" of that organic whole, which is the body of the Mother. Recall here the rhetoric of the motherland articulated by B. C. Pal in his 1911 book, *The Soul of India*. He writes that the people of India address their land not simply as "motherland," but as "Mother."[75] Seeing India as Mother is both spiritual and geographical. It is grounded in Hindu affection for the land itself—its mountains, rivers, and plains. But he cautioned, "The cult of the Mother among us is by no means a political cult. The political propaganda with which the cry of *Bande Mataram,* or Hail Mother, has recently been associated, is not in any sense an organic element of the real cult of the Mother or Motherland. . . . The real cult of the Mother among us is part of our general spiritual culture. It is organically related to our highest conceptions of Humanity."[76]

Let us call to mind, again, the modern evocation of Bhārat Mātā in the temples that have made this image of land as mother the central icon and focus of worship. At the Bhārat Mātā Temple in Vārānasī, pilgrims and tourists circumambulate the marble relief map of the whole of India, which constitutes the sanctum of the temple. This temple is not, incidentally, a place that throbs with national feeling, although a large pictorial image of the goddess Durgā riding forth on her lion from the map of India has been added, perhaps to provide the iconic focus many might be seeking here. Even so, for the most part, the Bhārat Mātā Temple in Vārānasī is one of the sleepiest places in the city. In Hardvār, however, a more recent temple steers directly into ideological Hindu nationalism, envisioned and built as it was under the guidance of Swami Satyamitranand Giri.[77] In the temple entry on the first floor, the goddess Bhārat Mātā stands prominently upon the map of India, holding a sheaf of grains in one hand and a vessel of water, the aniconic emblem of a goddess, in the other. The words of *"Vande Mātaram"* by Bankim Chandra Chatterjee are inscribed above her. From our attempts to trace the manifestations and meanings of Shakti in the landscape of India, we certainly know how such an image came to be. While this temple may not be the locus of militant motherland nationalism, even so modern India has yet to contend with the meaning, the power, and the deployment of the image it enshrines.

As we have already seen in our opening chapters, the song *"Vande Mātaram"* found a new popularity in the 1990s, with new recordings and new adherents, inspired by the agitations of a new form of Hindu nationalism. While the song had been rejected as the national anthem of newly independent India, in favor of Tagore's *"Jana Gana Mana,"* it nonetheless became the marching song of the Bhāratīya Janatā Party with their rise to greater prominence in the 1990s. Our survey of the local and yet wide-reaching presence and power of the goddesses of India—from Kanyākumārī in the far south to Vaishno Devī in the northwest and Kāmākhyā Devī in the northeast—should make clear that this symbolic language in praise of the mother has deep roots in India. Like the image of Bhārat Mātā or Durgā astride the map of India, *"Vande Mātaram"* has been able to take hold so powerfully in modern India not because it was fabricated and instrumentalized in the colonial context by Hindu nationalists old and new, but because of the widespread associative meanings that have long linked the land and the goddess.

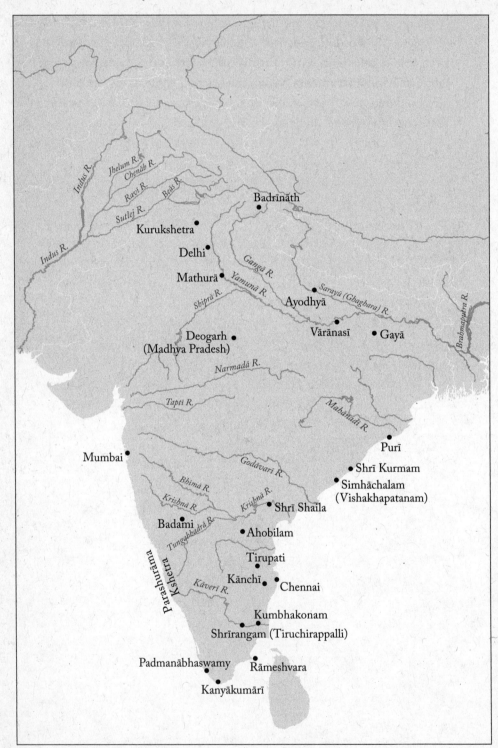

7

VISHNU: ENDLESS AND DESCENDING

Close to the southern tip of India is the city of Trivandrum, the capital of the present state of Kerala. The proper old name of the city is Tiruvanantapuram, the "City of the Holy Serpent Ananta," the serpent named Endless, who bears the reclining Vishnu upon his coils. The temple of Padmanābhaswamy, "The Lord from whose Navel the Lotus Rises," anchors the city as its most sacred shrine. During the period of the *pralaya,* when all creation has dissolved into quiescence, Vishnu rests upon Endless, containing within his body all the seeds of creation. With him is Shrī, his consort, often depicted massaging his feet. Eventually, after many millions of years, a lotus sprouts from the navel of Vishnu. From the lotus, Lord Brahmā arises with a face in each of the four directions. He will be the subsidiary agent of Vishnu in creating the particulars of the world of name and form, everything we know as the universe.

There are many places in India where we might stand to see the great images of Vishnu sleeping on the Endless Serpent, often called Vishnu Anantashayana. Any art historian would direct us first to the elegant reliefs in the exterior iconography of great Hindu temples in north and central India, such as the fifth-century brickwork sculpture from Bhitargaon and the famous sixth-century panel from Deogarh. They are beautiful temples, with beautifully rendered images of the sleeping Lord, but today they are not living temples. Like many that were built by the patronage of kings, they flourished for a century or two, but they did not permanently claim the allegiance of the people. We can visit and appreciate them as treasures of fine architecture and sculpture, but we will not get a taste of Hindu devotion there. For that, there is no better place to begin than the temple of Padmanābhaswamy right here in Trivandrum.

This is one of the most extensive, splendid, and spiritually powerful of the great south Indian temple complexes. Inside the exterior wall of the temple, the outermost processional corridor or circumambulatory is 450 feet long and 350 feet wide, with the corridors themselves measuring a breadth of 25 feet. Pilgrims and worshippers will walk around the whole perimeter of the sanctuary through a series of consecutively smaller circumambulatories, one after another, before reaching the deep center, the womb-chamber, or *garbha griha,* of the temple. From the outermost corridor, they will gaze through doorway after doorway, receding toward the distant inner chamber. Each doorway is lit with oil lamps, casting a glow upon the dark circumambulatory corridors. At the center, a twelve-tiered tree of oil lamps lights the court immediately in front of the image. The play of light and darkness so typical of the temples of south India here is profound.

Walking the corridors of the great temple, pilgrims will see painted murals, many of them from the eighteenth century, depicting the lore of gods and goddesses. The largest of these murals displays the mystery that lies at the heart of the temple, the scene of primordial creation: from the navel of the Supreme Vishnu, resting on the Endless serpent, arises a lotus, which opens to release Lord Brahmā, the creator of the world. It is this very image the pilgrims have come to see, as they finally enter the holiest sanctum: the huge eighteen-foot-long image of Vishnu, reclining on the serpent Ananta, as creation is about to begin.

The image of Vishnu they behold in the inner sanctum is so large that it is fully visible only through three sets of doors, which are opened sequentially by the priests at the time of worship. When open, they become an immense stone triptych of the Lord. At the time of the evening *āratī,* the central set of doors is flung open to reveal the midsection and navel of Vishnu; then the doors to the left are opened to reveal his head and the doors to the right are opened to reveal his feet. Devotees cannot really see the full image of Vishnu at all, but as the many multi-wicked lamps of *āratī* are lifted to honor him, they have a glimpse of his presence there, through each of the doors. It is an enormous presence, dimly seen, illumined suggestively by oil lamps and by the intermediary grace of the priest who moves the soft light along the long body of the Lord. First, he lifts the lamps toward Vishnu's face. In the center, he raises the lamps high as an offering to Lord Brahmā, coming forth from the navel of the sleeping Lord. Finally, in the last doorway, he offers the lamps to Vishnu's feet. With the quickening crescendo of bells, the *āratī* reaches its climax and the priest brings the oil lamps presented to Vishnu out of the inner sanctum to be offered now to the people as a blessing. Hundreds of hands reach for a sanctifying touch of the flame.

As the liturgies of the priest conclude, people surge up to the platform where, from the distance of a few feet, they can look through each set of doors for a closer view of each section of the image. Gazing up at Vishnu's face, they see a countenance of peaceful repose. But the image is too large to take in with the eyes. The people sense, rather, an enormous reality, like the sage Mārkandeya, who suddenly beheld the whole of Vishnu in the cosmic sea. According to this well-known story, the great sage traveled extensively through all the pilgrimage places of the world, not realizing he was traveling all the while in the worlds inside the body of Vishnu. One day, he fell out of the mouth of the sleeping god and into the vast ocean. Then he beheld Vishnu's form from the outside, a form simply too large to comprehend. He was relieved to be snatched from the deep and swallowed again and to find himself in the familiar territory of what he thought was the world!

No one is certain how old the Padmanābhaswamy Temple is. A *māhātmya* in the old palm-leaf records of the temple says the temple was established by a Tulu brahmin named Divākara Muni on the 950th day of the Kali Yuga, thus placing its origins in what one simply has to call "ancient times." In the eighth and ninth centuries, the great Vaishnava poet Nammālvār sang the praises of the Lord of this temple. Temple records indicate the temple was reconstructed in 1050, that it came under rule of the king of Travancore in the fourteenth century, and that it was renovated several times in the subsequent centuries. In the seventeenth century, a fire destroyed nearly the whole of the temple, with the exception of the main image. In the eighteenth century, the image was removed in order for a major reconstruction to be undertaken. It was then that the temple was erected on the massive scale we see today. In the sanctum itself, a new image of Vishnu was installed, said to have been made of some thousands of sacred *shālagrāma* stones, mortared and smoothed into the shape of Vishnu.[1]

According to legend, the original image of Vishnu in the Padmanābhaswamy Temple was made of wood and was a miraculous manifestation of Vishnu to Divākara Muni. The story is familiar at Padmanābhaswamy. Divākara Muni was a *bhakta*, a devotee of Vishnu. To serve his Lord, he engaged in deep meditation and austerities. One day, Vishnu appeared before him in the form of a lively two-year-old boy. Divākara Muni was charmed by the boy but did not recognize him as the Lord. He asked the child to stay, and the boy agreed, on condition that Divākara Muni treat him lovingly and never scold him. Generally, Divākara Muni tolerated the two-year-old's pranks, but one day, when he was deep in meditation, the child took the sacred *shālagrāma* stone, symbolic of Vishnu himself, and put it in his mouth. Divākara Muni could not tolerate this seeming blasphemy and chastised the boy. Immediately, the child disappeared, saying, "If you wish to see me, go to the seacoast of Kerala, to the Ananta Forest." The sage glimpsed the boy disappearing into a huge tree that immediately crashed to the ground and assumed the shape of the immense recumbent Vishnu. That divine form lay along the seacoast for eighteen miles. Divākara Muni was overwhelmed with devotion and prayed that the Lord would condense himself so that he could see this image-incarnation within his own field of vision. Vishnu complied and shrank to the eighteen-foot image that remained for many hundreds of years in the sanctum of the temple in Tiruvanantapuram.

There are many themes here that link us into the wider complex of myth and its sacred geography. First, of course, is the story of the child god, the prankster, beloved throughout India as Krishna, and here present as Vishnu. There is also the theme of divine immensity, the huge divine embodiment that becomes smaller in size so that devotees can more readily worship it. Remember the world-spanning *linga* of light so immense that it could not be fathomed or comprehended, and Shiva's gracious agreement to become small in form so that the *linga* might be worshipped. Time and again, we are reminded that, as the Vedas put it, "three-quarters" of the divine reality is beyond human comprehension, and our grasp is limited to the fraction available to us here below, in this dimension of vision.[2]

When we seek the presence of Vishnu in the land of India, it is natural to begin with those shrines of Vishnu reclining on the serpent Endless at the dawn of creation. As we shall see, they are numerous, especially in south India, in the island sanctuaries along the Kāverī

River. Of course Vishnu has drawn to himself many other forms as well, such as the numerous divine "descents," or *avatāras*, associated with him. Even if we leave aside, for the time being, the two most important of these *avatāras*, Rāma and Krishna, the many *avatāras* of Vishnu have made their imprint on the land of India. Vishnu, the wide-striding, all-pervading God, has placed his foot on the earth and claimed it for himself and then placed his foot in the highest heaven. Vishnu is the god whose footprints may be found on the earth, and most often, when one sees the presence of footprints—in a shrine or a temple—they are the feet of Vishnu in one of his many forms.

NĀRĀYANA, DWELLING UPON THE WATERS

Vishnu is forever associated with the waters of creation, which precede and support the universe, from which form arises and into which, in the end, the forms of universe we know finally dissolve. Many of India's great temple images of Vishnu show him as we saw him in Trivandrum—reclining on the waters, or perhaps seated on the coiled serpent. Vishnu is himself an embodied form of the cosmic egg, which incubated on the primordial waters and brought forth the whole creation. From ancient times, he was also known by the name Nārāyana, meaning "the one who rests upon the waters."[3] Just as the primordial ocean contains all form in potential and, when churned by the gods, yields up the life-giving contents of creation, so Vishnu, floating on the ocean, contains within himself the whole of creation. Whether manifest in the intricate, spectacular universe we know, or unmanifest inside the very body of God, this entire universe is held within the seed of the divine.

The story of the sage Mārkandeya makes this dramatically clear. When he fell out of the body of Vishnu, he was overwhelmed by the vision of the great sleeping god and was relieved to be scooped up by Vishnu and swallowed again, to find himself once again in the familiar world of the interior. The notion that Vishnu swallowed the worlds and, thus, contains within himself the whole of what we know as reality is a common one in the poetry of the saints of south India. Vishnu both holds reality within and pervades reality without. The ninth-century poet-saint Nammālvār sings to him:

Lord of Wonder!
Long ago, you ate the seven worlds,
you disgorged them and by your amazing power,
you enter them. . . .
Becoming all things
spread on open space, fire,
wind, water, and earth,
He is diffused through them all.
Hidden, he pervades,
like life in a body.
The radiant scripture [speaks]
of the divine one who ate all this.[4]

Vishnu Nārāyana rests on the aquatic serpent named Ananta, the
Endless, the Infinite. Serpents, *nāgas*, are well known to signify the
life force and the energy of the waters. Vishnu's serpent is also called
Shesha, which means literally the "Remainder," what is left of Being
itself after heaven, earth, and the netherworlds have all been created, or
have all been withdrawn. Shesha, in the philosopher Rāmānuja's terms,
is the plenitude, the overflow, the surfeit of God's being. Everything
has originated in Vishnu, who overflows and extends beyond the created
order. It is not surprising that this great serpent, who supports the sleeping Vishnu during the time of *pralaya*, also supports the whole universe
during the ages of manifest creation. The sages of the Purānas sometimes see the serpent Ananta as resting at the base of the entire universe,
supporting all its ring-islands, all its netherworlds and heavens, on his
thousand-headed and bejeweled hood.[5]

Vishnu is himself the creator, the Supreme God, who transforms
himself into the whole of the cosmic order at the time of creation. In
this theological view, Vishnu is creator, sustainer, and destroyer of the
universe—all three. In the *Nārada Purāna*, for example, we read:

The entire Universe including the mobile and the immobile beings,
from god Brahmā down to a clump of grass, is identical with Lord
Vishnu. There is nothing else other than he. He alone is god Brahmā,
the Creator of the Universe, as well as god Rudra, the destroyer of
Tripuras. He alone has assumed the forms of gods, demons, and

sacrifice. He alone constitutes this Brahmānda. There is nothing else that is separate and distinct from him. There is nothing else greater than he. There is nothing more minute or more immense than he. All this wonderful Universe is pervaded by him. One should bow down to that Lord of gods, worthy of being praised.[6]

Those who tried to express the nature of this supreme Vishnu and his pervasive presence developed the notion of *vyūha,* a term meaning the "expansions" or "expressions" of Vishnu. The term *vyūha* gathers together meanings particular to Vishnu—spreading through, traversing, pervading all that is. One enumeration speaks of Vishnu in five *vyūhas:*

- The Supreme Vishnu (*para*), the transcendent one, dwelling in that highest heaven, which is called Vishnupada or Vaikuntha. There Vishnu is eternally attended by his consorts Bhū, literally the "Earth," and Shrī, the "Auspicious."
- The emanation of Vishnu as the Lord who rests on the Endless serpent Ananta, manifesting the worlds during the period of creation and containing them within himself during the time of quiescence or *pralaya.*
- The divine "descents," the *avatāras,* also called *vibhāvas,* revealing Vishnu as the Lord who "comes into being in age after age" in order to uphold dharma and to challenge the forces of *adharma.* (*Bhagavad Gita* 4.)
- The indweller (*antaryāmin*) of each and every soul, that aspect of the divine within each living thing.
- The material forms, the images, or *mūrtis,* in the sanctuaries of Vishnu, called *archas,* the "image incarnations," like the image in the sanctum at Padmanābhaswamy, in which Vishnu graciously condescends to become present to those who seek him.

These *vyūhas* are not entirely separate aspects of Vishnu, just as the "persons" of the Christian Trinity are not separate, and certainly not separable. They are all understood as integral to the complexity of the one devotees address as Vishnu. For most people now, in the Kali Yuga, when there are no *avatāras* present and when the Supreme Vishnu as well as Vishnu on Ananta are not visible to the eyes of ordinary folk, the

"image incarnations" are the forms of Vishnu that are most vividly present here in the world. As Nammālvār's tradition puts it, Vishnu enters
the sea of milk and reclines there so that the gods may see him, and
Vishnu becomes present in pilgrimage places and temples so that human
beings may see him. Indeed, if one can see the wondrous and beautiful
Lord right here on earth, why should one go to Vaikuntha?[7]

THE BELOVED PLACES

In south India, the worshippers of Vishnu in the Shrīvaishnava tradition
speak of the many sanctuaries of Vishnu as "beloved places" and enumerate 108 of them.[8] For well over a thousand years, the relationship between
the devotee and the Lord in south India has not been an abstraction, or
even a matter of the heart alone, but a relationship situated in the land—
on the riverbank, in the field, at the seacoast, and in the city—in the particular shrines where Vishnu is to be found. As Katherine Young notes in
her study of the beloved places, "They are places graciously enjoyed and
loved by God and the devotees; the magnetic attraction to these special
places is mutual."[9] In other words, these places are beloved not only to
human seekers and pilgrims, but beloved by God as well. Indeed Vaikuntha, heaven itself, is listed among the places beloved both to the divine
and the devoted. Most of the 108, however, are seen to be both part of
and yet different from this geographical world. They are real places, but
they somehow transcend the world in which they are situated.[10] While
in a wider sense, Vishnu is omnipresent, these are felt to be the places of
his special presence. Each place among the 108 is unique, and just as the
landscape is different, the encounter with Vishnu is different. The faithful discover ever-new facets of Vishnu's presence by journeying to the
particular sanctuaries where he has graciously come to dwell. As Katherine Young observes, pilgrimage in this tradition is really the exploration of various "situational landscapes," which give the pilgrim "profound
delight in continually exploring the relation with God in new settings."[11]
Theologically speaking, every devotee knows that Vishnu is utterly transcendent, and yet the language used in this Shrīvaishnava tradition is the
language of presence and location: Vishnu is present here and partakes
of the complete simplicity of worldly dailiness. He owns the temple, he

resides there, he sleeps and he wakes there. And it is there that ordinary people may visit him and serve him. In this theology of accessibility, the temple is the place where the Lord is "easy to reach," giving us quite a contrast to the places of pilgrimage praised as "hard to reach," requiring exhaustive effort. A commentator on one of the Tamil hymns wrote that in the temple people can find something they could not even find in heaven, for here the Lord is present, "assuming visible form even for the lowest persons, more so than even in the highest heaven, like a lamp in a dark place."[12]

The most popular of the Beloved Places are Shrīrangam, Tirupati, Kānchī, and Melcote—all great sanctuaries of Vishnu.[13] The Tamil poet-saints called the *ālvārs* visited and sang of these places between the sixth and tenth centuries, often contributing to the fame of the place with the ardor of their songs. As early as the eighth century, Tirumankai, one of the *ālvārs*, sang of the temples of Tamil Nadu, arranging his pilgrimage of praise in a circumambulatory sequence, beginning in the north at Venkatam (Tirupati) and moving south to Tanjore, to Kurunkuti at the southern extreme, and then back to Kottiyur, north of Madurai.[14] Most of the 108 beloved places are in south India, although the greatest sanctuaries of the north are included as well—Dvārakā, Mathurā, Badrīnāth, Ayodhyā.[15] Tamil Nadu as a region has long been "defined" by its beloved places: It is "the good world between Venkatam in the North and Kumārī in the South."[16] The sixth-century epic the *Shilappa-dikaram* describes the land this way: "The land of the Tamils, bounded on the north by the Venkatava hill of Mahāvishnu (Tirupati) and on the south by the Virgin of Kumārī and on the other two sides by the sea."[17] Gradually, the *ālvars* began to center their poetic songs more and more on the great shrine they simply called "The Temple," Shrīrangam, the island shrine on the Kāverī River at Tiruchirapalli.[18]

THE ISLAND SHRINES OF THE KĀVERĪ

In our exploration of the legends and lands of India's rivers, we have met the beautiful Kāverī, rising in the lush, green hills of the Coorg country. The Kāverī is said to have been brought here by the sage Agastya, who carried her in his water pot from the north. The source of the river is honored at Talakāverī, where the headwaters collect in a tank for bathing. From here, the Kāverī leaps and splashes down the hills, bursting forth in springs and waterfalls, then forming a river and flowing eastward through Karnataka and Tamil Nadu, finally entering the Bay of Bengal. Along its course there are twelve "Beloved Places," a number of which are important shrines in which the primary image is Vishnu the creator, reclining on the waters. Several major shrines are situated at places where the river divides to form an island sanctuary. The island setting of these temples is appropriate, since Vishnu reclining on Shesha rests, in a sense, on a serpentine island in the middle of the cosmic sea.

As the Kāverī flows down from the Coorg hills into the plains of Karnataka, there are island temples, large and small. First, we might mention Kushalnagar, where there is a temple of Shrīranganātha, although the area is better known today for its large Tibetan refugee monastery. Then, beyond Mysore, on the road to Bangalore, is the island temple of Shrīrangapattanam, one of the most important of these island shrines. Here, within the sanctum, pilgrims will encounter the image-incarnation of Vishnu reclining on Shesha, the serpent reaching round and lifting its five-headed outspread hood to protect the Lord's head. Even the Muslim ruler Tipu Sultan is said to have made offerings at this shrine. Farther downstream on the Kāverī is the shrine called Madhya-rangam, nearly on the border of Tamil Nadu. Here the Kāverī splits once more and forms the island of Shivasamudram. The two branches also form magnificent waterfalls and, today, power a hydroelectric plant.

Shrīrangam is without doubt the foremost of these island sanctuaries of Vishnu. It is located in the modern city of Tiruchirapalli, once a site of the capital of the Chola kings, some two thousand years ago. It is mentioned in the *Shilappadikaram* in the sixth century and praised by the *ālvārs* from the sixth to tenth centuries. By the time of the philosopher Rāmānuja in the eleventh century, Shrīrangam was clearly one of the most important centers of Vaishnava thought and devotion. It was among the three most important of Vishnu's Beloved Places, the others being the Venkateshvara Temple at Tirupati and the Varadarāja Temple at Kānchī. Because of its preeminence, it was often called simply Koyil, literally "The Temple." Local lore refers to this place as a *svayamvyakta kshetra*, a "spontaneous holy place," of Vishnu, where he dwells because of his own great desire to be there and not because he has been requested to come by the sages or devotees.[19]

The sheer size of the Shrīrangam Temple complex is impressive. While it has taken many centuries to reach this size, it is today one of the largest in all India, with seven *prakāras,* or enclosing walls, with circumambulatory walkways that form progressively smaller corridors surrounding the central sanctuary. Here at Shrīrangam, the outermost wall encloses what is essentially a city of some forty thousand people. Approaching the temple, pilgrims first pass under an enormous 236-foot-high *gopura,* an immense gateway, covered with thousands of images of the gods, the kings, the poets, and the patrons of the temple. This colossal *gopura* of the seventh and outermost wall of the temple is called the *rājagopura,* the "king's gateway," and was completed and consecrated only in 1987, reminding us that even for a temple of such antiquity, the process of construction is ongoing. Its mass of relief sculpture is painted in the multitude of bright colors that was typical of earlier temples. Gazing upward as they approach, pilgrims can see directly above the gate the image of Vishnu reclining on the serpent. This is truly the gateway to a small city, for entering through this gateway, we find a street busy with stores and enterprise, sari shops, hardware stores, and tea stalls.

Gopuras of the Shrīrangam Temple, Tiruchirapalli

For those used to thinking of temples as buildings, it requires a mental readjustment to conceive of the magnitude of this temple. Here, the very precincts of the temple cover more than 156 acres. The outer avenues of approach to the temple and the outer circumambulatory streets house a population of merchants, public officials, and brāhmins who live and work in the temple complex. Twenty-one towering *gopuras* rise above the successive gateways leading to the inner temple from the four directions. Entering through the fourth gateway, worshippers remove their shoes, indicating entry to the more sacred precincts of the temple-city. In the large corridor that surrounds the temple inside the fourth gateway is a thousand-pillared public hall, where people of all sections of society gather for public festivals and great occasions, such as the annual recitation of the *Divya Prabandham,* the four thousand hymns of the *ālvārs,* often referred to as the *Tamil Veda.*

Shrīrangam has been praised in song by all twelve of the great Tamil *ālvār* poet-saints. Among the processional images housed in the temple are images of the *ālvārs* themselves, who, on festival occasions, are carried to the thousand-pillared hall of the temple for the singing of their hymns to Vishnu, praised here as Lord Ranganātha. Two of the *ālvār* songsters were especially close to Ranganātha, and their legends tell us something distinctive about this manifestation of Vishnu. The untouchable poet Tiruppan Ālvār is said to have stood every day by the bank of the Kāverī, praising Vishnu, but never entering his temple because of his low birth. One day, a brāhmin priest who came to bathe threw a stone at the untouchable, warning him to clear the way. He hit Tiruppan with that stone, and the lowly devotee bled profusely from the wound. When the Brahmin priest returned to the temple from his ablutions and entered into the sanctum, he was shocked to see the image of Lord Ranganātha bleeding in the very same spot. Vishnu told the chastened brāhmin to carry Tiruppan, his favorite songster, into the temple sanctum. And so he did, packing the untouchable poet on his back so that his feet would not touch the temple floor, carrying him into the sanctuary of Vishnu to sing and have direct *darshan* of the Lord.

Andal, the one woman among the songster *ālvārs,* was another special devotee of Lord Ranganātha. Her thirty beautiful stanzas called the *Tiruppāvai* are dedicated to Ranganātha, whom she praises as Krishna. These verses are known and loved throughout India and are sung, even today, to awaken Ranganātha in the morning. As a young girl, completely in love with the Lord, Andal insisted she would marry only him. According to the lore associated with her, she received a vision that she would indeed marry Ranganātha. On the auspicious day, she dressed confidently in bridal finery, and as her palanquin entered the temple, she leapt out in eagerness, threw herself upon the image of the Lord, and melted into it. Andal is said to have merged fully and physically with Vishnu. Even so, she is today honored in her own temple, in the southwest corner of the inner court of the Shrīrangam complex, and her image is carried in palanquin procession around the temple on her festival days.

Over the centuries, Shrīrangam has attracted not only millions of devotees, but all the major teachers and philosophers of the Shrīvaishnava tradition. Nāthamuni was the one who gathered the collection of the hymns of the *ālvārs,* called the *Tamil Veda,* to be sung in worship in Shrīrangam. He may also have had a hand in the construction of the temple in the tenth century, for he bore the title of *shrīkaryam,* "temple manager." Yamunā, his successor in the line of teachers, and Yamunā's successor, Rāmānuja, were also associated closely with both the administration and the devotional life of the great temple. Rāmānuja, surely the most famous of these teachers, wrote his commentaries on Vedānta philosophy and on the Bhagavad Gītā here in the eleventh and early twelfth centuries. Later heirs of the tradition, such as Pillai Lokachārya and Vedānta Deshika, were also attached to Shrīrangam. For more than a thousand years, then, this vast temple has been the spiritual and intellectual capital of Shrīvaishnavas. During these many centuries, kings and their dynasties—the Cholas, Pallavas, Pāndyas, and later Cholas—also lavished their attention and patronage on the temple. After a period in the fourteenth century when the temple fell into the hands of Muslim sultans in Tamil Nadu, it was again reclaimed and restored, by the Vijayanagara kings, and by the fifteenth century it was patronized by the Nayak kings of Madurai. The temple is filled with a record of inscriptions that give us a sense of its age and its significance over the course of many centuries.

Rich with history and the records to prove it, the temple is also rich with mythological association, for it is seen as the earthly link to heaven itself. The island where Shrīrangam is located, surrounded as it is by the Kāverī River, is likened to Vaikuntha, Vishnu's highest heaven, sur-

rounded by the River Viraja. The great temple is called Bhūloka Vaikuntam, literally "Heaven on Earth." As one writer put it, "Just as Lord
Vishnu reclines on His serpent couch on the island in the Kāverī, so
the Lord reclines on His serpent couch that forms an island in the
middle of the Milk Ocean."[20] The greatest festival day at Shrīrangam is
known as Vaikuntha Ekādashī, the eleventh day of the lunar month of
December-January, when the festival image of Lord Ranganātha is carried in procession through the northern *gopura* of the sanctum named
Vaikuntha, for heaven itself. It is the culmination of a twenty-one-day
festival season, and more than one hundred thousand people are on hand
for this once-a-year opening into heaven's realm. As the image of the
Lord is bathed in the great temple tank within the temple walls, called
the "Lotus Pool," women and men crowd into the pool to bathe in the
water sanctified by his presence.

The image of Vishnu at Shrīrangam is said to have come originally
from the royal family of Rāma in Ayodhyā. The story of its journey to
the south is widely known and repeated in the lore of the temple today.
Like so many stories in pilgrimage lore, it connects this place with
another famous place and with the mighty events of a renowned epic, the
Rāmāyana. Originally this sanctuary of Vishnu arose from the ocean, in
response to the austerities and meditation of Brahmā, so they say. Sūrya,
the Sun, was appointed to serve Vishnu as priest, and the descendants
of the Sun, the Ikshvaku line of kings, took this image to their capital
Ayodhyā. This was the lineage of sun kings into which Rāma was born.
After the long drama of the *Rāmāyana*—the forest exile of Rāma, Sītā,
and Lakshmana, Rāvana's kidnapping of Sītā, and the war to reclaim
Sītā from captivity—Rāma returned safely to reign in Ayodhyā. He was
accompanied by the noble Vibhīshana, the demon Rāvana's brother, who
had nonetheless rendered great service in helping Rāma defeat Rāvana.
As reward for Vibhīshana's help, Rāma gave him this ancestral family
deity, Ranganātha. Vibhīshana set off for Lanka, carrying the beautiful image of the Lord upon his head. When he reached the Kāverī
River in the south, he set the image down so that he could bathe and
worship there. That was on the island we now know as Shrīrangam.
When he tried to pick Lord Ranganātha up again, he could not move it.
Vibhīshana was disconsolate, but Ranganātha explained that he wanted
to remain here by the Kāverī River. He promised to rest here facing

south, toward Vibhīshana's kingdom in Lanka.[21] By now we have seen this story of spontaneous attachment several times. Immovable adhesion is one way of speaking in the strongest terms of the power of place itself, the magnetic power of the very ground where the divine is situated.

According to legend, it was a king named Dharma Varman who consoled Vibhīshana by agreeing to build a grand temple here. He built it according to specification: The innermost enclosure of the temple has only one open entry—a gate facing south. In the inner sanctum is the enormous relief image, some twenty-one feet long, of Vishnu reclining on Shesha, glistening black with the oils of anointing, his consorts Bhū and Shrī flanking him on either side. Vibhīshana is there too, standing in reverence at Ranganātha's feet. The sanctum image is called the *achalamūrti,* the immovable image-incarnation of the Lord. Shrīrangam, like all south Indian temples, has a smaller portable image too, here called simply *nampurumal,* "our God." Because it is especially taken in procession during the time of a festival, or *utsava,* it is also called an *utsavamūrti,* a "festival image." At Shrīrangam, the festival image is not the recumbent Vishnu, but a seated four-armed image about three feet high.

Adorning this image of Ranganātha and carrying it in procession is the signal event of some 322 festival days during the course of the year. While these processions are part of the life of many temples, Shrīrangam seems to have developed this processional life to an extraordinary extent. On these many festival days, different images of Shrīrangam's resident deities and saints, Ranganātha included, are taken in procession around the outer circumambulatory streets of the temple complex. There is a striking juxtaposition here: the huge, recumbent, all-creating Lord in the sanctum and the peripatetic festival image, moving about town and into the surrounding countryside. During one of the great festival seasons, called Adhi Brahmotsavam, in the lunar month of March-April, the image of Vishnu travels a total of nearly sixty miles, going twice a day around the temple through the processional streets and going on four separate trips, one in each of the cardinal directions, even beyond the temple walls. According to Paul Younger, who has studied this complex festival, the journeys take Vishnu through neighborhoods and villages composed of people of many different classes of society. He visits the different deities of the areas over whom he asserts sovereignty and in whose temples he accepts hospitality. The kingship and supremacy of Vishnu are expressed not only in genres of praise, song, and philosophy; they are enacted and inscribed in the surrounding land.[22]

Finally, before leaving the Kāverī River, we find one more major temple where Vishnu sleeps upon the Endless serpent. It is in the town of Kumbhakonam, about fifty miles downstream from Shrīrangam, bright green with palms, banana trees, and rice paddy. As we have seen in discussing India's great rivers and holy waters, it was here, according to myth, that the pot (*kumbha*) containing the nectar of immortality and the seeds of creation, floating on the floodwaters, came to rest as the floods subsided. It is truly a place linked to the dawn of creation. Here Shiva, so they say, shot through the pot with his arrow, releasing the waters and the contents of creation into the great temple tank of Kumbhakonam, called the Mahāmaham Tank, where, every twelve years, the great *melā* takes place, bringing countless pilgrims from all over India for a dip in the sacred waters of the tank. The last Mahāmaham bathing festival took place on March 6, 2004, with more than one million pilgrims bathing on that one day alone. No matter when they come, pilgrims will make this celebrated *tīrtha* their first stop in Kumbhakonam, for these waters are famous as the waters of creation and as waters that gather in the sacred essence of all the rivers of India.

In this town of temples, there is one important old temple of Vishnu linked to the creation of the world—the Sarangapāni Temple. As at many Tamil temples, the traditions of Sarangapāni are very old, even though the existing temple today is perhaps only eight hundred years old, dating to the thirteenth century. To be sure, its tradition was known to the *ālvārs* and to the redactor of their poems, Nāthamuni, a thousand years ago. This is one of the 108 *Divya Deshas,* the "Beloved Places," of Vishnu. Sarangapāni is one of a number of temples in which the central sanctum is built in the shape of a stone chariot, pulled by a horse and an elephant. Inside the "chariot," in the sanctum, a large sleeping Vishnu lies on his right side, crowned with a silver crown. He rests high on the coils of Ananta, so as the priest lifts an oil lamp of *āratī* to the Lord's face, he must raise it to full arm's length to begin to illumine Vishnu's serene countenance.

THE LORD OF THE SEVEN HILLS

The Vaishnava shrines along the Kāverī River comprise the most distinctive set of Vishnu embodiments in south India, but the serpent
called Endless, bearing Vishnu on his coils, is also embedded in the very
topography of the land. North of the Kāverī in what is today Andhra
Pradesh, the serpent Ananta, also called Shesha, took the form of a chain
of winding hills. Yes, the serpent is a mountain range!

At the beginning of the Kali Age, so they say, Vishnu resolved to
dwell as near as possible to his devotees, to be accessible to them and
to protect them. He asked the sage Nārada to recommend a place most
suitable for his earthly dwelling, and Nārada recommended this place
in south India, on the banks of the Svarnamukhī River. The serpent
Shesha became these hills known as Sheshāchalam, the "Hills of Shesha," or simply Tirumala, the "Holy Hill." Vishnu, then, took the form
of Venkateshvara, dwelling on top of the hill in the shrine renowned
throughout India today as Tirupati, where he was often called by the
more intimate name Bālājī.

Another legend probes deeper into the past and associates this place
with Vishnu's *avatāra* Varāha, the boar, who dove deep into the cha-
otic sea and rescued Prithivī, the Earth, setting her once again on the
surface of the waters. He placed her here, so they say, upon the back of
the mountain range formed by Shesha. And he himself dwelt here, and
the place was called Varāha Kshetra. The glorious form of Vishnu as
Varāha was also frightening, however, and Lord Brahmā requested that
the Lord take a more benign form here. So it is that he took the form of
Venkateshvara. Even now, however, Varāha has a special temple on the
other side of the sacred tank, called Swami Pushkarinī.

Shesha's supporting presence as a winding mountain range is not
limited to bearing up Vishnu's shrine at Tirupati. Indeed his serpentine
body links four of the major shrines of the region. The tail of Shesha is
at Shrī Shaila, the great Shaiva shrine to the north on the banks of the
Krishnā River. On the winding back of Shesha is Ahobilam, connected
with Vishnu's *avatāra* as Narasimha. Tirupati Venkateshvara rests on
the seven-hooded head of Shesha. Finally, the famous Shaiva sanctum at
Kālahasti, where Shiva takes the elemental form of air, is situated at She-

sha's mouth.[23] These four places, linked together by the Endless serpent, stretch through much of today's Andhra Pradesh, from north to south.

As at Shrīrangam, the manifest presence of Vishnu as Venkateshvara Bālājī is considered, in this age of ours, truly "Heaven on Earth," Bhūloka Vaikuntam. In every age, they say, the Lord has taken *avatāras*, divine descents, for the well-being of his devotees. In the Third Age, the Treta Yuga, he came as Lord Rāma. In the Dvāpara Yuga, the Second Age, he came as Lord Krishna. Now, in this Kali Yuga, the times are such that the four-legged "cow" of Dharma, who loses one leg with each passing *yuga,* has but one leg left. In this age, Vishnu came to earth as Shrī Venkateshvara and abides here, at Tirupati, close to the people who need him. Unlike Shrīrangam, however, which is strongly and clearly Shrīvaishnava, Tirupati is complex in its heritage and tradition. Vishnu is not reclining, but a standing, black, four-armed form said to be self-born. His arms are adorned with Shaiva-like cobra ornaments. He bears the conch and the discus in his upper hands, offers boons with his outstretched right hand, and his left hand is placed on his waist, his arm bent at the elbow. He stands alone in the sanctum, although the *devīs* are imprinted on his chest. There is some mystery here, more like some of the other great shrines where Vaishnava and Shaiva traditions seem to be overlaid, one on the other. Is there something of Shiva in this Vishnu? The *ālvārs,* after all, praised him as Harihara—a name combining Vishnu (Hari) and Shiva (Hara). There is a tradition associated with Rāmānuja that the great eleventh-century scholar left a flower on Bālājī's head one night, with the prayer that it would fall in one direction or other to signal his true identity. Apparently, it fell to the Vaishnava side. This is surely the consensus today, and the processional festival images of Venkateshvara include Vishnu's usual consorts, Bhū and Shrī, to either side.

There is virtually an encyclopedia of Purānic stories that constitute the mythological repertoire of Venkateshvara. These *māhātmyas* also underline the Vaishnava origins of this beloved place. In one sequence, for example, the sage Bhrigu went to each of the great gods to see which one was most worthy of receiving the *yajna.* He was disappointed by each of them. Brahmā was preoccupied with the goddess Sarasvatī, while Shiva was engaged in lovemaking with Pārvatī. And when he came to Vishnu's heaven, he found Vishnu asleep. Annoyed, he kicked Vishnu in the chest. But Vishnu responded graciously, to his surprise, even massaging Bhrigu's poor foot in one telling of the tale. But Lakshmī took umbrage at the insult, for he had kicked her Lord on the chest, the place she herself ordinarily reclined. She said she would not stay in Vaikuntha with a Lord who bore such indignities. Off she went in a huff. Some say it was then that she took up dwelling in the great city of Kolhāpūr in Maharashtra, the greatest shrine to Lakshmī in all India.[24]

Wherever she went, Vishnu followed. Down to earth he came, searching for her throughout the realms of earth, determined to find her again. From the Himalayas and the Gangā to the plains and the Vindhya Mountains he roamed. When he reached Sheshāchalam, the hills formed by his own serpent Shesha, he suddenly felt at home again. The place felt like Vaikuntha itself. And it was there, eventually, that he was reunited with Lakshmī, who, in this Kali Age, took the form of Padmāvatī, a divine child plowed up from the earth itself. It was this same Padmāvatī who, in the previous era, had served as the surrogate for Sītā when she was abducted by Rāvana. Now, in this era, she was united with Vishnu in his incarnation as Venkateshvara. Her form dwells perpetually upon Bālājī's chest.[25]

While there is mystery in Shrī Venkateshvara's deep past, the most important thing drawing people together from every part of the Hindu tradition is his wide reputation as the boon-giver of the Kali Age.[26] On this there is no disagreement whatsoever. For this reason, Tirupati is certainly the most popular single pilgrimage temple in all India. From March through September, the peak season for pilgrimage here, some twenty thousand pilgrims make their way daily up the steep road, most of them by motor vehicle. The especially devout and those who have taken a special vow to do so will take the footpath from the bottom of the hill and climb the eleven kilometers to the top, as pilgrims before them have done for hundreds of years. Having reached the pilgrimage town on the hilltop, many pilgrims will go to the large tonsure halls to have their heads shaved. While a first tonsure is a common rite of pilgrimage for a child, here at Tirupati men, women, and children all have their heads shaved as a sign of their submission to the Lord and their seriousness of purpose. For those unable to undertake a full tonsure, just a symbolic clipping of locks of hair is important.[27]

Pilgrims arrive at their destination with many prayers in their hearts, especially prayers having to do with health, the well-being of family members, the prospering of a career, or even material success. Here all such prayers are in order, and when uttered here they are said to be efficacious. The fame of Lord Ventakeshvara is enhanced by his reputation for responding to the vows and prayers of the faithful. Making an offering in the temple is also part of the pilgrimage, and large receptacles called "*Hundi*" especially for this purpose are located throughout the temple. The *Hundis* receive everything from offerings of a few rupees to offerings of tens of thousands of rupees, bank drafts, property, and gold jewelry.

The most important rite of pilgrimage, of course, is the *darshan* of Bālājī. At any hour of the day or night there are long, long lines winding back and forth in an orderly fashion through and around the temple. The temple administration organizes this *darshan,* supplying tickets and *darshan* times for more than twenty thousand people a day, with festival days bringing more than fifty thousand worshippers to the temple. Thus, for each person, the *darshan* of the Lord will be a matter of a bare second. And that moment, gazing straight at the powerful image of Shrī Venkateshvara Bālājī, adorned with golden ornaments, will mark the culmination of the pilgrimage. Understandably, the *pūjārīs* who serve in the sanctum of this great temple also require the special assistance of traffic monitors to keep the line moving. *Darshan* is free, unless,

Pilgrims at Tirupati, having come for the darshan *of Shrī Venkateshvara*

of course, one wants to avoid the long wait in the queue, in which case there is a "special *darshan*" line for which a fee is charged, and this line merges with the longer line toward the front. In addition, as at other temples, one can pay to participate in sponsoring one of the forms of "service," or *seva*, offered to the Lord, such as the morning *suprabhātam*, when Venkateshvara is awakened at about three in the morning, or the *abhishekam*, in which Venkateshvara is sprinkled with water and other sacred and fragrant substances.

Tirupati today is run by a trust called the Tirumala Tirupati Devasthānams, or T. T. Devasthānams (TTD) for short. Through its administration, pilgrims can book rooms in advance in the well-organized hilltop cottages and arrange for all kinds of pilgrimage services. Through its donations and properties, the sheer wealth of this religious institution is estimated to be second only to that of the Vatican. With this immense wealth, the TTD Trust also runs numerous charities for social work, including schools for destitute girls and boys, training centers for the handicapped, a school for the deaf, a medical school, and an institute of surgery for the disabled. Its educational work includes colleges, high schools, and elementary schools in the town of Tirupati, at the base of the hill. Its literary work includes the study and publication of the thousands of poems written to Lord Venkateshvara by the fifteenth-century poet Annamachārya, and its religious work includes training programs for *pūjārīs*, *archakas*, and other priests who serve in the temple.

Tirupati is a premier example of the growing significance of pilgrimage and its economic, social, and cultural implications in modern India. Over the years, the regulation of such a popular pilgrimage site and its many related institutions has come under the control of the state government of Andhra Pradesh, which understandably has a strong interest in its effective administration. Traditionally, the temple was in the hands of a small group of families who, since the fifteenth century, had traditional priestly rights at the temple under a system of temple administration called the Mirasi system. However, the sheer volume of pilgrims and the wealth of the temple became so great that it was eventually brought under government regulation. In 1987, the temple was placed under the control of a fourteen-member board appointed according to the provisions of the Andhra Pradesh Charitable and Hindu Religious Institutions and Endowments Act, which took control of the temple out of the hands of the traditional families. This move was challenged all the way to India's Supreme Court, but the court finally ruled in 1996 in favor of government regulation of the T. T. Devasthanams.[28]

Remember the ancient legend: that Vishnu chose to dwell here on this hilltop so that he could be accessible to people, now in the Kali Age. Clearly the demand for Vishnu's *darshan* is great, and yet providing this accessibility for the throngs of pilgrims has become a vast and complex business. The temple trust runs a bus company, transportation facilities, dozens of hotel and hostel accommodations, two large canteens able to serve twenty thousand people a day, and a huge kitchen to prepare temple *prasadam,* especially the daily output of thirty thousand or more of the *laddus* for which the temple is famous. It also runs a publications department, two marriage halls, facilities for tonsure and ear piercing, and a corps of priests able to help with countless rites. Online reservations are available and touch-screen kiosks provide up-to-date information about daily events. Today, the Shrī Venkateshvara Temple at Tirupati is not only the abode of Vishnu, but the magnet destination of millions who come to it as pilgrims. Its fame is such that even in the United States, one of the first Hindu temples to be built was the Shrī Venkateshvara Temple in Pittsburgh. Even today, Pittsburgh remains an important American pilgrimage destination, although by now there are dozens of American Hindu temples that have consecrated an image of Shrī Venkateshvara in their own town—from Los Angeles, to Chicago, to Louisville, to Boston. Never has the image of Vishnu as the one who pervades heaven and earth, yet dwells on hilltops and in suburbs, seemed more powerful.

VISHNU'S FOOTSTEPS AND FOOTPRINTS

> *I will declare the mighty deeds of Vishnu*
> *of him who measured out the earthly regions,*
> *Who propped the highest place of congregation,*
> *thrice setting down his footstep, widely striding.*[29]

This vision of Vishnu comes from the earliest religious literature of India, the *Rig Veda.* Here there is no developed mythology of Vishnu, but there is the clear and commanding image of a transcendent god who strides through the universe. Vishnu is a wide-striding God, whose three giant steps claim the "three worlds"—the earth, the atmosphere, and the heavens beyond. Much later, the three strides are repeated in the well-known story of Vāmana, the dwarf *avatāra*. The *asura* king Bali had grown so much in power and in piety that the gods were being threatened and the universe was falling out of balance. At this time, Vishnu took the form of a dwarf to attend the *yajna*, the great ceremony of sacrifice sponsored by Bali. As a guest at the *yajna*, he asked his host, the generous Bali, to give him as much land as he, a dwarf, could pace off in three steps. Bali readily agreed, for the dwarf had very short legs and the land he would require would amount to very little. As soon as Bali granted the boon, however, Vishnu rose to full universal stature and paced off all the earth with his first step, strode across the heavens with his second step, and set his foot in the highest heaven with the third step.[30]

Vishnu, the wide-strider, is the transcendent god who pervades the three realms of the universe—the earth, the atmosphere, and the heavens beyond. As one ancient text puts it, "The god deposited himself in three places: a third on earth, a third in the atmosphere, a third in the sky."[31] The very name "Vishnu" comes from a Sanskrit verbal root meaning "to spread, to pervade." The many etymologies of Vishnu play upon the language of pervading and traversing the worlds.[32] In the *Mahābhārata*, for example, Vishnu is praised with these words: "Thou hast pervaded (*vyāpta*) the sky with thine head, earth with thine feet, and the three worlds with thy steps (*vikrama*); the directions are thine arms, the sun is thine eye."[33] As the pervader, Vishnu gathered to himself much of the solar imagery of the ancient Hindu imagination. The three steps perhaps recall the daily journey of the sun through the three realms from its ascent in the morning, to its zenith in the noonday, to its touchdown in the evening. Long after Sūrya, the sun god, ceased to have a cult of his own, Vishnu retained the sun's discus as one of his principal emblems.

Vishnu leaves his footprints in each of the three realms through which he strides. They are imagined to be like the cowprints that fill with water in the swampy fields. But the footprint of the Lord is filled, rather, with honey. In the highest heaven, it is filled with the nectar of immortality. With that highest footstep, Vishnu utterly transcends the worlds, placing his foot in heaven. Indeed, the highest heaven, Vaikuntha, also comes to be called Vishnupada, Vishnu's footstep. As the Vedic hymnist put it:

A mortal man, when he beholds two steps
of him who looks upon the light,
is restless with amaze.
But his third step doth no one venture to approach,
no, nor the feathered birds of the air
who fly with wings.[34]

In later mythology, this third step of Vishnu pierces the outer egg-shell of the vast universe, letting the sweet waters of the Gangā flow into the part of the universe we know. The waters cascade through the sky as the Milky Way, fall on Mount Meru, and roll out onto the petals of this lotus earth.

Measuring earth and heaven, Vishnu also creates space for human habitation. He makes the world safe to live in, not only as territory the Lord has conquered for himself, but as land cleared, claimed, and protected for all life. The hymnist describes Vishnu as the one "within whose three wide-extended paces all living creatures have their habitation," and the one who has "measured this common dwelling place, long far-extended."[35] In a somewhat later text, the hymnist implores, "O Vishnu, stride thou widely forth, make ample room for our abode."[36]

It is little wonder that this Vishnu, whom the ancients saw as striding through the universe, should emerge as one of the great gods of the Hindu tradition, associated with an extensive and sophisticated theology and a vast number of shrines. He is a god who has placed his mighty and merciful foot in this world. Unlike Shiva and the Goddess, who do not, for the most part, make their powerful presence known by their footprints, Vishnu's presence here is indicated especially by his footprints, which may be seen in holy places throughout India. The scholar Jan Gonda reminds us that Vishnupada, the foot of Vishnu, is not only a way of speaking of "heaven," for this heaven "is often locally defined and reflected in, or represented by *tīrthas* called Vishnupadas which are sometimes described as Vishnu's perpetual residence and as an entrance into his world."[37]

Among the most famous *tīrthas* called Vishnupada is the sacred site in Gayā, in the heart of present-day Bihar, in north India.[38] One of the commentators on the three steps of Vishnu, as mentioned in the *Rig*

Veda, says that these three are to be identified as Samarohana, Vishnupada, and Gayāshiras, which all are identified by tradition as sacred sites in Gayā itself.[39] The story of the origin of Gayā is later told in the Purānas, and while it does not refer specifically to the striding of Vishnu, the *tīrtha* called Vishnupada is seen as comprising the presence of all three gods—Brahmā, Shiva, and Vishnu:

> There was an *asura* named Gaya, who was devout, pious, and strong. The gods, led by Brahmā, became fearful of Gaya's rising strength and paid a visit to Shiva on Mt. Kailāsa to ask his protection. Shiva joined the delegation and they all proceeded to call on Vishnu. All the gods thus assembled went to where Gaya was practicing austerities and Vishnu granted Gaya a boon. The *asura* requested only purity—that he might be purer than the gods, purer than the rivers, the holy pools, and the mountains. Vishnu granted his request, but the gods were not happy. After a short while, the earthly realm was virtually empty because so many people had gone straight to heaven, having seen so pure a soul as Gaya. No one was left to make the needful offerings to the gods. Vishnu suggested, then, that Lord Brahmā approach Gaya and ask a favor: might he use Gaya's pure body as a sacrificial ground? Brahmā made this request, telling Gaya that he had looked the wide world over and had not found a sacred site as pure as Gaya's body. Of course, Gaya acquiesced and lay down on the earth. Everyone assembled for the *yajna,* the sacrifice. But Gaya was still moving. Brahmā and the other gods got an enormous stone slab and placed it on his head. Still he moved. They asked Shiva and the other gods to sit on the stone. Still, Gaya moved. Ultimately Vishnu came to sit on the stone too, and Gaya was happy to lie motionless, under the rock on which Brahmā, Vishnu, and Shiva all sat. Gaya spoke, saying: "As long as the earth lasts, as long as the mountains, the Moon, the Sun and the stars remain, may Vishnu, Brahmā, and Maheshvara stand on the slab along with all other Devas. Let the holy centre be named after me. The holy centre of Gaya shall extend to five *kroshas* and Gayashiras, the stone slab, to one *krosha.* Amidst them may all the holy centres grant welfare unto all men."[40]

The whole body of Gaya, some six miles long, thus became the holy *tīrtha* where the gods congregate. While all the gods and *tīrthas* are here, it is named especially for Vishnu's foot, Vishnupada. Gayā has long remained famous as one of the *tīrthas* to which pilgrims repair to offer final rites for the dead, a role it shares with Kāshī and Prayāga. The three are called the Tristhalī, and the great *māhātmya* that collects their praises is the *Tristhalīsetu,* the "Bridge to the Three Holy Cities." Especially during the fall fortnight called *pitrpaksha,* the "fortnight of the forefathers," pilgrims come for rites of *pindadānam,* offerings to the departed.

Throughout India, Vishnu, in his various forms, has left the footprints of his presence, often marked in very material ways in stone and marble. We should remember, of course, that footprints are also among the first icons of the Buddha, and that the auspicious markings on the feet of the Buddha were among the legendary signs by which sages recognized that the newborn Prince Siddhārtha would become an awakened one, a Buddha. These also are the signs imprinted on the feet of Vishnu, and many Vaishnavas consider the Buddha to be an *avatāra,* or divine descent, of Vishnu.[41] Within a few miles of Vishnupada, at Gayā, is the famous Bodh Gayā, where the Buddha is said to have attained awakening. There, too, the image of the large granite footprints of the Buddha are touched and honored with flowers, like those of the various forms of Vishnu. Long before the first anthropomorphic images of the seated or standing Buddha were made, his footprints were the focus of reverence and an indicator of his earthly presence. Touching the feet of the Buddha while he was living would surely have been consistent with widespread traditions of reverence for great teachers and sages. These forms of reverence, so deeply practiced within all the Indic traditions, remind us of the ways in which people touch the feet of parents, honor the feet of teachers, and take refuge in the feet of the gods. Bowing to the iconic feet of the Buddha is an integral part of these traditions.

While Vishnupada at Gayā is widely known, there are nonetheless countless temples and *tīrthas* where we might find the imprint of Vishnu's foot either symbolically or iconographically present. Pilgrims circling the sanctuary at Shrīrangapattanam, one of the island shrines of the Kāverī River, for example, will pause to make offerings where the footprints of Vishnu are imprinted on an immense circular slab of stone in the circumambulatory corridor. They will offer flowers and coins, touching reverential daubs of red and orange powder to these divine feet. The image of Vishnu is also present at this small shrine, but the footprints offer themselves, so to speak, as an intimate icon of the Lord's grace. In north India, pilgrims will find the footprints of Rāma honored by the banks of the Sarayu River in Ayodhyā, where he was king; imprinted on the stones next to the Mandākinī River in Chitrakūt, where he lived in forest exile; and raised on a marble slab next to the river in Ujjain where he performed funeral rites for his father. In Vrindāvan, the homeland of Krishna, pilgrims will find marble footprints of Krishna, together with those of his beloved Rādhā, honored in the grove of Nikunjabān, where they met to dance.

Touching Vishnu's feet is both a gesture of submission to the Lord and a signal of God's grace. One "takes refuge" in these feet, which remind us of God's presence and mercy. The prayer of surrender used by the great Vaishnava theologian Rāmānuja concludes: "Thou art the friend of those that are in distress. O Nārāyana united with Shrī, refuge of those without refuge, I have no other resort. I surrender myself and seek refuge at Thy two lotus-like feet." [42] In many Vaishnava temples in south India, the feet of Vishnu are imprinted on a silver dome, just the size of a cap or hat, and the priest goes around to the assembled worshippers to touch this dome to each and every head. Thus, taking refuge in the "lotus-like feet" of Vishnu becomes part of the temple liturgies.

DESCENDING: THE *AVATĀRAS* OF VISHNU IN THE LANDSCAPE OF INDIA

North of present-day Delhi, in Kurukshetra, down a dusty road from the place where the great battle of the *Mahābhārata* war is said to have taken place, we find an especially renowned set of footprints: a marble slab bearing the imprint of Krishna's feet placed under a great tree. This gnarled old tree, we are told, was "witness" to the teachings given by Lord Krishna to the warrior Arjuna as they paused at the edge of the battlefield. Here, Krishna began to reveal to Arjuna who he is—not just Arjuna's counselor and charioteer, but the Supreme Lord, indeed Vishnu himself. In these teachings, called the Bhagavad Gītā, or the "Song of the Lord," he articulates one of the earliest Hindu expressions of *avatāra:*

the "descent" and manifestation of the divine here on earth. He *tells* Arjuna that he, Krishna, has been born many times by his own manifest power. "When *dharma* wanes and *adharma* increases, I come into being. For the protection of righteousness and the destruction of unrighteousness, I come into being in age after age."[43]

As Vishnu strides through earth and heaven, he is both the one who is transcendent and the one who descends, time and again, to earth. As we have seen in our discussion of the great rivers of India, the notion of *avatārana*, the "descending" from heaven to earth, is a well-established way of describing the presence of the divine: It came down from on high. As the rivers descend, so do the gods, especially Vishnu, rescuing, creating, reestablishing order in a world constantly threatened with imbalance and chaos. Vishnu's *avatāras* take many forms and fall eventually into a standard list of ten. First is the fish, Matsya, who rescued the "man," Manu, at the time of the flood, towing to safety Manu's boat, filled with the Vedas and the seeds of creation. Then comes the tortoise, Kūrma, who bore up the worlds from below, offering his back as the support of the churning rod when the gods and *asuras* churned the sea to create the world. Then the boar, Varāha, rescued the earth when she had been flung to the bottom of the sea; diving deep into the waters, Varāha lifted the earth up and placed her once again on the surface of the waters. As the man-lion, Narasimha, Vishnu saved his devotee, Prahlāda, from the *asura*-king Hiranyakashipu. As a dwarf, Vāmana, he saved the three worlds for the gods by securing a boon and then expanding to his cosmic form and taking his three world-spanning strides. As Parashurāma, a brahmin, Vishnu slew the *kshatriyas*, the "warriors," who had been wreaking havoc on earth. As Rāma, a *kshatriya*, Vishnu demonstrated unswerving dharma and the rule of righteousness. As Krishna, a *kshatriya* raised by cowherding *shudras*, he taught the lessons of dharma to Arjuna on the field of battle and also overturned dharma to teach the religion of sheer love and devotion, *bhakti*. As Buddha, he is said to have deluded both demons and kings and caused their downfall with teachings that rejected the authority of the Vedas. There is a future *avatāra* coming as well—Kalki, who will come when rulers have corrupted the earth with their plundering ways and who will bring in a new age once again. On the whole, the *avatāra* theme in Vishnu mythology sounds a repeated note: Heaven and earth are threatened by the rise of mighty *asuras* and the forces that undermine the order of dharma, and Vishnu comes into being to restore balance, to restore dharma, and to restore the world to the hands of the gods.

This ongoing competition of gods and *asuras* is never finally resolved, once and for all. It is what drives the action of the world in which we live. However, the great gods—Vishnu, Shiva, and Devī—are the ones who are so all-encompassing that they are not entirely captivated by the rivalries of the gods and *asuras*. The *asuras*, as we've discussed, are not necessarily evil. They are the opposite of the gods. Indeed, some *asuras* might be very righteous, like the *asura* King Bali, who ousted Indra from heaven and ruled over the worlds until Vāmana won them back by his mighty strides. Very often, *asuras* have accumulated great power by their austerities, *tapas*. The power they gain by virtue of austerities is simply raw spiritual power that can be wielded for good or for ill. When anyone, human or *asura*, amasses such power, one or another of the great gods appears to grant a boon. The *asuras* often have the same request: The boon they want is immortality. But, alas, immortality is the one boon that can never be chosen or given. The *asura* can choose conditional invulnerability and immortality, however. In the case of Rāvana, his boon was that he could not be killed by any god; he did not even consider that he might be killed by a mere human. In the end, it was the man Rāma who killed him. In the case of Hiranyakashipu, the boon he chose was to die neither by day nor by night, neither inside nor outside, neither by man nor by beast. Under these conditions, he felt fairly secure. But, in the end, he was killed at twilight, on the threshold, by a man-beast.

If we begin our investigation of *avatāra*s in the literary lore of the epics and Purānas, we may be overwhelmed with the magnitude of the exploration. But our discipline here is to begin on the ground, in the landscape of India, where there is plentiful evidence of their presence. How do these divine descents take their place in the landscape and in what ways do they take part in the creation of that landscape? Of course, Rāma and Krishna are the most widely worshipped of the *avatāras*, and we will seek out their shrines in separate chapters. Perhaps the least visible are Matysa and Kūrma. Both are foundational, and yet they seem to have little imprint on the land, primarily because they have not generated an independent following. Although there is a shrine called Shrī Kurmam near the border of Orissa and Andhra, along the coast of the Bay of Bengal, Kūrma did not gain a substantial devotional following. Even so, the *Brahmā Purāna* lists Shrī Kurmam as one of the *Divya Deshas,* the 108 Beloved Places.

Varāha has many images and even dedicated shrines. The story of Varāha's rescue of the earth from the bottom of the ocean is widely depicted in some of India's earliest sculpture, and the prayer "Raise up this earth for the habitation of living beings!" seems to have captured the religious imagination for many centuries. The huge fifth-century Gupta relief at Udayagiri, in today's Madhya Pradesh; the sixth-century rock-cut cave images at Badami in Karnataka; and the seventh-century Pallava images at Mahabalipuram, in the far south, give us a sense of the great popularity of the rescuing Lord. There are living sanctuaries, too, like the Ulagalanda Perumal Temple in Kānchī, where the great image of Varāha stands some fifteen feet tall, jet-black and glistening in a darkened sanctuary. The story of Varāha as earth-rescuer is also linked to the shrine at Shrīmushnam, also known as Bhūvarāha *kshetra,* where Varāha is said to have blessed Bhū, the Goddess Earth, after bringing her up from the sea.

As we have seen, Tirupati has its own Varāha traditions. In one of them, after Varāha rescued the earth from the depths, she begged him to stay with her. So Varāha sent Vishnu's bird-mount, Garuda, to Vaikuntha, "heaven," to bring back a shining hill. This hill, then, was holy Tirumala, and on its top he created Varāha Pushkarinī, the "Lotus Pool of Varāha." According to custom, pilgrims should honor Varāha in his temple on the hilltop before going for the *darshan* of Shrī Venkateshvara. In north central India, Varāha is imaged in multiple places in the twelfth-century Chandella temples at Khajuraho, the most unusual being the image of a boar standing on the serpent Shesha, his boar body completely covered with tiny images of the gods and goddesses. Finally, among the *tīrthas* associated with Varāha, is Mathurā's Vishrām Ghāt. Vishrām means "rest," and while it is most commonly said to be Krishna's resting place after he dispatched the wicked King Kamsa, the *ghāt* is also understood to be the place Varāha rested after lifting the earth from the bottom of the sea.[44]

In mythic terms, Varāha is an *avatāra* of times past—from the Satya Yuga, the first and best of the four ages. His temples and images in India also seem to speak of a popularity that was at its zenith in centuries past—not exactly the Satya Yuga, but before the crescendo of devotion to Rāma and Krishna that has poured forth over the past five to eight hundred years. Even still, there are places where devotion to Varāha is strong, and among them is one of the places where he is worshipped in tandem with Narasimha: the sacred hill called Simhāchalam.

THE HILL OF THE MAN-LION

In contrast to his predecessors, the *avatāra* Narasimha is much more fully present in the sacred geography of India, especially in eastern India, in the hills of Andhra Pradesh and Orissa. Indeed, in this region there are more than 160 shrines of Narasimha.[45] The most prominent is Simhāchalam, "Lion Mountain," situated ten miles north of Vishakhapatanam in coastal Andhra Pradesh. It is a beautiful wooded hill some fifteen hundred feet high, terraced with orchards of pineapple, jackfruit, bananas, and limes. Pilgrims climb up a staircase of thousands of stairs to reach the hilltop temple of Narasimha, and nowadays, of course, many come by bus up a terrifyingly narrow roadway. The temple at the top of the hill bears inscriptions dating back to the eleventh century. Its sanctum contains a remarkable image of Varāha-Narasimha deemed to be so powerful that it cannot be seen by the naked eye except on one day a year. For the rest, it is covered with layers of fragrant sandalwood paste applied so thick that it appears to be a post, perhaps like the pillar from which Narasimha is said to have burst forth. Simhāchalam is a popular pilgrimage temple all year round, but especially on Akshaya Tritīyā, the "immortal third" in the springtime month of Vaishākha, when people come for what is called Chandana Yātra, the "sandalwood pilgrimage." It is on that day alone that one can see the Lord's own image—both Varāha and Narasimha in a single body—when the sandalwood paste has been removed.

The story of Narasimha is popular in this area. It is the story of a profound devotee of Vishnu named Prahlāda, whose name has become synonymous with the power of faith and devotion. The *Vishnu Purāna* tells it this way:

The *asura* Hiranyakashipu was outraged to find that his own son, young Prahlāda, was a devotee of Lord Vishnu. Prahlāda addressed

Vishnu as his Lord and the supreme Lord of all. "He is creator and protector not of me alone," said Prahlāda, "but of the whole world, even of you, father. He pervades not only my heart, but the whole universe." When Hiranya's henchmen tried to kill Prahlāda for such blasphemy, the boy insisted that Vishnu was present even in their weapons and therefore they could not harm him. He was right. Hiranya tried a dozen ways to put his son to death, but without success. Venomous serpents could not bite him or make him afraid; fire could not burn him; poisoned food could not kill him. Finally Hiranya threw Prahlāda into the sea and ordered his armies to hurl boulders in after him and bury Prahlāda beneath their mass. If he could not kill the boy, he could at least pin him at the bottom of the ocean. But Prahlāda prayed ardently to Vishnu. The ocean convulsed, heaved, and hurled up the rocks upon the shore again, releasing Prahlāda. Finally, Vishnu, never having seen such faith, granted the boy a boon. In his filial virtue, he first chose to have his father released from his ignorance and sin. And so it was that the King finally embraced and kissed his son. Hiranyakashipu was then killed—and saved—by Vishnu, who took a form that was part man and part lion.[46]

Some of the early versions of the Narasimha story, such as those found in the *Harivamsha* (III.41–47) and the *Matsya Purāna* (161–63), scarcely mention Prahlāda at all. They expand on the conflict of gods and *asuras* and on the horrible battle that ensued when Vishnu assumed the man-lion form to destroy Hiranyakashipu, who had the protection of his famous boon. In these versions of the tale, all of Hiranya's powers and weapons were turned upon the great man-lion. The battle was fierce, but in the end, Vishnu tore open Hiranyakashipu's chest with his pointed claws. The *Bhāgavata Purāna*, however, contains both stories: the story of Prahlāda and the battle, and the full, very popular story of how Vishnu as Narasimha burst out of a pillar to kill Hiranyakashipu. It tells the tale of Narasimha's fierce power as well as Prahlāda's deep devotion:

Hiranyakasipu was furious that he could not kill Prahlāda, apparently because of the boy's ardent faith in Vishnu. "Where is this Vishnu?" the father taunted. "If Vishnu is everywhere, as you say, then is he in this post?" He slammed the stone pillar with his stick. Immediately, Vishnu emerged from the pillar as Narasimha, who grabbed the wicked king to kill him. And what of Hiranya's boon of invulnerability? At that time, it was neither day nor night, but dawn; it was neither inside nor outside, but on a threshold; and his assailant was neither man nor beast, but both, a man-lion. So it was that Vishnu laid Hiranyakashipu over his knees and tore his chest open with his lion's claws.[47]

In all the multiple variations of this popular story, the most important distinction to be made is between those emphasizing the *bhakti* of Prahlāda and those exalting the horrific appearance of Narasimha. The two, of course, go together and, in a sense, must be construed in sequence. Those who told the story of Prahlāda for its majesty of faith and devotion no doubt took for granted the horrific aspect of Narasimha as well. But they did not delight in worshipping this aspect of Vishnu. There is a softening of Narasimha's frightening violence in the devotion visible at Simhāchalam, where Narasimha is worshipped in conjunction with the powerful but more peaceful Varāha. Pilgrims circle the temple, pausing to point to exterior reliefs situated in niches on the temple wall. One shows Varāha coming up from the depths with the Goddess Earth on his arm. The second depicts the fierce Narasimha, seated with Hiranyakashipu laid out upon his lap, tearing apart the *asura*'s stomach with his claws. The pilgrims know by heart these stories of Vishnu's divine descents and recall them together as they circle the temple.

Entering into the sanctum of the temple, they are told that the image beneath all that smoothed, fragrant sandal-paste is actually an image of Narasimha joined with Varāha, and the goddess Lakshmī. The *sthala purāna* of Simhāchalam tells the familiar tale with a few changes:

Hiranyaksha and Hiranyakashipu were formerly Vishnu's gate-keepers. Because of some act of disrespect to visitors, the two were cursed to be reborn as *asuras*. And so they were, and true to their nature, they tirelessly disturbed the peace of the world. Hiranyaksha even threw the earth to the bottom of the sea, and Vishnu had to take on the Varāha *avatāra* in order to dive deep down to the mud at the bottom of the sea, slay Hiranyaksha, and bring the world

back up again. The other *asura*, Hiranyakashipu, was angry at the
death of his brother and performed fierce austerities, *tapas*, in order
to gather to himself extraordinary power. He was granted a boon:
to be invulnerable to death either by day or night, either inside or
outside, either by man or beast. The boy Prahlāda was Hiranya's son
and was a devotee of Vishnu. He was ceaselessly persecuted by his
father, who tried to kill him for his devotion to Vishnu. He tried
to have elephants trample the boy, to have fires burn him, all to no
avail. Finally, he ordered his armies to hurl Prahlāda into the sea
and to place a great mountain upon him. They were about to pick
up Simhāchalam and drop it upon Prahlāda when Vishnu himself
jumped over this mountain and rescued Prahlāda from the sea.
Prahlāda, then, was the first to establish the worship of Narasimha
here on the hill. His prayer to Vishnu was that he might be able to
see both faces of the Lord at once: Varāha and Narasimha.[48]

Here at Simhāchalam, the *bhakti*-oriented story of Narasimha is
emphasized. Having circled the temple and seen the horrific image of
Narasimha disemboweling the *asura*, worshippers enter into a sanctum
where no such image is present. In the inner sanctum of this temple,
pilgrims see a shaft of wheat-colored sandal-paste, some four feet high,
elegantly decorated with pink and white rhinestones outlining the vertical Vaishnava forehead markings. It could easily be seen as a *linga*. While
water offerings are advanced toward the image, they are not actually
poured on it, because of the delicacy of the sandal-paste and its ornamen-
tation. Over the image is raised a silver umbrella of royalty and around
it is a silver grillwork. Those who are privileged to have the "special
darshan" of Varāha-Narasimha may stand right in the sanctum itself,
within just a foot or two of the powerful image. Throughout most of
the year, however, there are substitute images that actually receive the
water and flower offerings of the devout. The one seen, worshipped, and
bathed on a regular basis is an image of Narasimha in a yoga posture,
Yoganarasimha.[49]

Like many places of pilgrimage, Simhāchalam is eclectic. Its courtyard contains the shrines of Lakshmī, the famous woman poet-saint
Andal, and the other *ālvārs*. It is, after all, a shrine in the Shrīvaishnava
tradition, and Rāmānuja himself is said to have visited here in the twelfth

century. As at other Vaishnava centers in south India, the song-poems of
the *ālvār* saints called the *Tamil Veda* and the *Tiruppāvai*, the devotional
poems of Andal, are part of the regular ritual of the temple. The connective links of the temple are very much with the south, and the ritual
idiom of shrines of healing, such as Tirupati, is in evidence here. There is
a large tonsure hall, for example, where thirty or forty barbers are working at once to shave the heads of those who come here and make their
vows. And yet, there are also ties to the north. In the area surrounding the main temple of Varāha-Narasimha there is an important temple
of Kāshī Vishveshvara and with it a shrine for the goddess of Kāshī,
Annapūrnā. There is a spring called Gangādhara, where the water of
the Gangā emerges from the rock and cascades over a Shiva *linga*. And
there is a Hanumān shrine containing the image of Hanumān, here
called Anjaneya, who is considered to be the "chamberlain" of the Lord
at Simhāchalam.

As in many shrines of India, the "real identity" of the place has a long
and probably very complex history.[50] Here at Simhāchalam, there is a
story, like that told at Tirupati, of how Rāmānuja visited the shrine in
the early twelfth century and restored it from Shaiva traditions to proper
Vaishnava worship: Having placed both the ash, or *vibhūti*, sacred to
Shiva and the *tulsī* leaves sacred to Vishnu in the sanctum at night, he
returned to find the *tulsī* had been moved to the altar.[51] Still, such a legend
underlines the contention that this hilltop shrine was originally Shaiva.
After all, the image looks like a *linga* for most of the year and is set on a
pedestal with a water spout, just like the *pītha* a *linga* would have. Some
say the image of Varāha-Narasimha was carved from the shaft of a *linga*.
In addition to the Kāshī Vishveshvara *linga* here, there is the shrine of
Shiva as Tripurāntaka, the Slayer of the Triple-City. This form of Shiva
is said to be the *kshetra pālaka*, "place-protector" of Simhāchalam. In
addition, the range of mountains on which Simhāchalam is situated is
called, even today, the Kailāsa range, after the mountain home of Lord
Shiva in the Himalayas. Finally, there is the evidence of the calendar, for
festival cycles often have a kind of tenacity that outlasts even the gods.
Here the day called Kāmadahana, the "Burning of Kāma," is celebrated
with great fervor. And what is this day? It is hardly a Vaishnava festival,
but the day on which Kāma, the god of passion, is said to have made
his assault on the ascetic Shiva. When Kāma released his flower-arrow

aimed at Shiva, Shiva opened his third eye and burned Kāma to ash, since which time Love has roamed bodiless in the worlds. This remains today one of the great festival days at Simhāchalam, celebrated on the full moon of the springtime month of Phālguna and coinciding with the festival of Holī.

We have dwelt on Narasimha here, because clearly this manifestation of Vishnu has made a significant impact on the landscape of India, if we begin on the ground, with the places where he is worshipped. There are many temples where the story of Narasimha is imprinted in the pilgrimage landscape. For example, in Maharashtra, not far from Pandharpūr, there is a Narasimhapur, where there is a spacious temple of Narasimha. In the same compound is an image of Prahlāda, for this is said to be the very birthplace of Prahlāda. As we have seen, Simhāchalam, across the breadth of India in Andhra, is said to be the place where Prahlāda was rescued by Vishnu from the sea. At Ahobilam, in Andhra Pradesh, located along the undulating mountains said to be the earthly incarnation of Shesha, Hiranyakashipu had his capital, so they say. Today Ahobilam boasts a pilgrimage complex rivaling that of Simhāchalam in its prominence as a place of devotion to Narasimha. And on a hill called Yadagiri, northwest of Hyderabad, is a shrine marking the very place where Prahlāda and Narasimha came after the death of Hiranyakashipu, in order to practice yoga.[52] There are many other Narasimha shrines, linked in one way or another to this mythology.[53]

The complexity of horrific (ugra) and peaceful (shanta) forms of Narasimha is very much part of the landscape of the Narasimha shrines today, but the fierce form of Narasimha tearing open the asura is rarely found alone as the focus of worship in the central sanctum of a temple. It is simply too harsh and dangerous for Vaishnava sensibilities.[54] At Simhāchalam, we have seen that Narasimha is joined with the far more beneficent Varāha, and flanked by images of the beneficent goddesses Bhū and Shrī. This move to soften the power of Narasimha is also seen at Ahobilam, where the image of the fierce Narasimha is set in a small and dark sanctum, barely lit with an oil lamp and positioned in such a way that it cannot be seen from any of the main temple entrances. It is also, somehow, neutralized by the adjacent images of Lakshmī, Shiva, and Pārvatī. At Dharmapurī, the ugra image of Narasimha in the central sanctum is hidden most of the time by an ordinary festival image of

Vishnu flanked with Shrī and Bhū. Next door, again, is a peaceful form of Narasimha, Yoganarasimha, the man-lion seated in the practice of yoga. It seems that when the horrific form of Narasimha is combined with Lakshmī as Lakshmīnarasimha, with Varāha as Varāha-Narasimha, or with a yogic posture as Yoganarasimha, the danger of this ferocious form of Vishnu is made more accessible to devotion.

The convergence of theological vision and ritual practice that began to produce the great "all-India" gods, such as Vishnu, Shiva, and the Goddess, was a long process that found various ways of including the tribal gods of the regions of India. The Shaivas and Shāktas had their own adaptive ways, incorporating *ganas,* local deities and *devīs,* into the entourage of Shiva and Shakti. For Vishnu, the elaboration of the *avatāras* provided a theological framework of understanding into which many deities could be incorporated, and surely the complexity of Narasimha bears witness to just this process.[55]

Jaya Badrī Vishāla!

High in the Himalayas, at an altitude of more than ten thousand feet, on a ledge between two mountains, clinging to a rocky slope over the rushing Alakanandā River, sits the shrine of Badrīnāth. It is within a few miles of the border of Tibet and is snowbound for most of the year. The buses that puff up the last leg of the steep mountainside from Jyotirmath to Badrīnāth have to observe a system of "gates," the one-way traffic that takes turns plying the narrow road up and down. The buses loaded with pilgrims are emblazoned with the words *"Jaya Badrī Vishāla!,"* Victory to the Great and Wide Badrī!, painted gaily on the front end. For many centuries, indeed from the time of the *Mahābhārata* in the early centuries of our era, the name Badrī Vishāla has referred to this high Himalayan fastness in the lap of the mythically famous Mount Gandhamādana. Reaching Badrīnāth, even by bus, is a victory for the pilgrim traveler.

Pilgrims come to Badrīnāth from all over India, for this is the northernmost of the four *dhāms* that mark the four directions of India. Especially arresting, as we consider geographical awareness of the breadth of India in pre-modern times, is the fact that the *raval,* the hereditary priest of the Badrīnāth temple, always comes from the community of Nambudiri brahmins in the far southland of Kerala. Apart from the *raval*, no one can touch the *mūrti* of Lord Vishnu.[56] This relation to the Nambudiri brahmin lineage comes perhaps from the great sage Shankara himself, who is said to have visited Badrīnāth in his circle tour of India and reinvigorated worship here in the ninth century. The Badrīnāth-Kerala connection underlines the magnetic importance of this Himalayan shrine for pilgrims from every part of India.

In addition to its place in the great four *dhāms* of India, Badrīnāth is also integral to the popular four *dhāms* of the Himalayas—Badrīnāth, Kedārnāth, Gangotrī, and Yamunotrī. These four, once almost out of reach because of their remote locations, have been vigorously promoted by today's pilgrimage package tours. As both pilgrimage and tourism become more popular, with campaigns by the government of the new state of Uttarakhand, the number of pilgrims to this Himalayan tier of *tīrthas* has continued to grow, more than doubling between 1976 and 1996, to almost half a million pilgrims every year at Badrīnāth alone.

Steep steps lead to the door of the Badrīnāth Temple, a squat temple with a small cupola, all gaily painted in hues of red, blue, gold, and orange, as are many of the tin roofs in the village, quite in contrast to the pale scrub green of the hillsides and the massive gray stones that fall to the river. The temple is the primary destination of pilgrims, to be sure, but the bathing tanks are also important here. Down the steps from the Badrīnāth Temple are the hot springs, swirling into the bathing tank called Tapta Kund and its adjoining pools. The combination of snowy peaks and steaming hot springs makes this nature's manifestation of the sacred, in need of no special *māhātmya*. The hot springs are channeled into four bathing pools, the most important of which is Tapta Kund itself. Steps on three sides enable tired pilgrims to ease into the steaming water, the *pandās* urging pilgrims on with the insistence that here the sins of many lifetimes will be absolved. Tapta Kund itself is reserved for religious bathing, while three other pools, where the hot water is mingled with cooler springs, are for more general bathing and washing.

The high-country Himalayas are famous as the retreat of ascetics, yogis, and sages. All the great sages are said to have performed austerities here, and their presence is vividly remembered in the landscape. The mountains on either side of the gorge are known as Nara and Nārāyana, for here, in the beginning, these divine ones, the foremost of ascetics, had their retreat. Both the *Mahābhārata* and the later Purānas tell us that this mystical twosome—Nara, the human soul, and Nārāyana, the divine lord—practiced austerities here in the lap of Mount Gandhamādana. If we are puzzled by the divine soul and the divine Lord practicing austerities, so was the celestial *rishi* Nārada, who is also linked to the landscape of Badrīnāth. Nārada yearned for a face-to-face vision of the Supreme and searched the heavens until he glimpsed Vishnu as the Supreme Lord. Then he was directed to this retreat where the Supreme Lord, in the form of these two ancient and luminous *rishis,* were performing their rites. Here, they explained, the Eternal Nārāyana, the Soul of the Universe, has taken birth as Nara and Nārāyana. This is a high mystery, even for this high country.[57] Here, too, the lovely goddess Urvashī, the most beautiful of all the celestial dancers, was born from Nārāyana's thigh.

So Nārada himself did *tapas* here in their company for a very long time, a thousand celestial years, so they say. The rock where he meditated is named for him, as is the bathing tank called Nārada Kund. In describing the *tīrthas* of Badrīnāth to Skanda, Shiva enumerates five rock *tīrthas* here, each with a special story underscoring the presence and power of Vishnu. The first is the rock of Nārada, whose penance and spiritual practice here won him a boon from the Lord, and for his boon he asked that Vishnu be perpetually present, right here in this rock. The rock of Mārkandeya is named for the ancient sage who also wandered through all the *tīrthas* of the earth to see Vishnu with his own eyes. It was here, seated on this rock, that Mārkandeya saw the Lord. He, too, was given a boon, and he, too, asked that Vishnu's *darshan* be available to all who sit on this rock. The rock named for Garuda is the very place, they say, where the penance of the celestial bird won him the position of serving as Vishnu's winged vehicle. The rock named for Varāha is the place Vishnu came after killing Hiranyaksha and bringing up the earth from the bottom of the sea. As the Purāna puts it, "The Lord stationed himself there in the form of a rock." Finally, the fifth rock is named for Narasimha, who was implored by the frightened gods to withdraw his blazing and fierce form. He, too, went to Badrī Vishāla, and stationed himself as a rock in the middle of the cold, fast-moving waters. The fright of the gods subsided, and they implored Vishnu to remain there forever in that form.[58]

These five rocks amplify the sense of spiritual power associated with

Badrīnāth by virtue of the sages and gods who have taken up residence here through the ages. Not surprisingly, other *tīrthas* are also said to be present here in the form of rushing streams of water. Five of the rivulets that form the Alakanandā River are named for five of the great *tīrthas* of India—Prabhāsa, Pushkara, Gayā, Naimisha Forest, and Kurukshetra. According to mythology, they all came here, staggering beneath the load of sins they had removed from pilgrims.[59] Here they were relieved of this burden of pollution. The *tīrthas* then assumed dual forms, returning to their purifying duties as *tīrthas* in their own places and yet remaining here, too, flowing as streams of *water*.[60] This condensation and localization of sacred power even gathers in the four Vedas that constitute the very blueprint of creation. The Vedas, too, are said to love the *āshrama* at Badrīnāth, and at the time of creation, when Brahmā received the Vedas from Vishnu, they begged to stay here. Finally Brahmā agreed, giving the Vedas, too, a dual nature—both as word and water. The liquid form of the Vedas remained right here in the mountains.[61]

It is said the present *mūrti* of Vishnu here is the very image of the Supreme Lord that Nārada saw face-to-face—an image of the Lord in meditation. In Buddhist times, however, this image in meditation posture was understandably worshipped as the Buddha. When the Buddhists retreated in the advance of a Hindu renewal brought by Shankara, they threw the image into the Alakanandā River, so they say. In the ninth century, the great teacher Shankara came to Badrīnāth from south India, retrieved the ancient image from the river, and reestablished it for worship. Interestingly, the story of the retrieval of the image by Shankara is found in several *māhātmyas*. In one popular pamphlet, the critical lines are spoken by Shiva himself: "When at the beginning of the Kali Age, the Lord has disappeared, then, taking the form of a *sannyāsī*—as the Shankarāchārya *avatāra* for the benefit of the world—having retrieved the *mūrti* from Nārada Tīrtha, I will establish it. And merely its *darshan* will free all people from their sins and enable them to obtain *moksha*."[62] He is said to have established the image near the hot springs tank today called Tapta Kund. It is widely acknowledged that the first shrine here was near Tapta Kund, where a natural hot springs emerges, just below the main temple.

Badrīnāth also has a prominent role in the lore of the *Mahābhārata*, where it is one of innumerable places associated with the Pāndava princes. We know that in a subsequent age, Nara and Nārāyana are said to have become Arjuna, the warrior, and Krishna, the Lord. In the *Mahābhārata*, it was Arjuna, son of Indra, who made the arduous journey into these mountains to secure divine weapons for the war to come. During his journey he climbed to Badrī Vishāla, where he did combat with a fierce mountain man, who finally revealed himself to be Shiva. Arjuna praised him, and Shiva then took him by the hand and addressed him as Nara, saying, "You were in your former life Nara, the friend of Nārāyana. You passed many thousands of years in fearful and austere asceticism."[63] Eventually, climbing to Indra's heaven, Shiva bestowed on Arjuna the world-destroying weapon called the Brahmashiras.

While Arjuna was away, the four other Pāndava brothers and Draupadī made the long journey we described earlier, circling all the *tīrthas* of the earth and, in the end, climbing high into the Himalayas, toward Badrīnāth. The climb was difficult, the woods thick, and the mountain passes snowy. Eventually the powerful Bhīma called upon his half-*rākshasa* son Ghatotkacha to help out by carrying Draupadī. So Bhīma's son became the divine porter, and engaged other *rākshasas* as transport for the whole party. They carried the Pāndava brothers and Draupadī high above the forests, to the beautiful hermitage of Badrī Vishāla. It was as sublime as heaven itself, they said, with trees in perpetual flower and fruit, with abundant grass and wildflowers, without gnats and mosquitoes, without the burning of the sun and with only a gentle touch of snow. This high mountain sanctuary dispelled the weariness of their journey. With delight, the sages greeted Yudhisthira, the Son of Dharma, and his party. Here they waited for their reunion with Arjuna, returning from heaven with the divine weapons.

The Himalayas are filled with the lore of the Pāndavas, as William Sax has so fully explored in his work as an ethnographer. For example, here in this part of the mountains we find the village of Pāndukeshvara, the place where their father, King Pāndu, lived out his last years and died. As a young man, Pāndu had shot two deer in the act of procreation, and was thus cursed to die in the act of sex. Luckily, one of his wives, Kuntī, had a boon that enabled her to bear a child simply by meditating on one of the gods. Thus, Yudhisthira was born from her meditation on Dharma, Arjuna from Indra, and Bhīma from Vāyu. She then gave her boon to her co-wife Mādrī, who meditated on the Ashvins, the heavenly twins, and produced Nakula and Sahadeva. After many years of celibacy, he was overwhelmed here in the mountains by desire for his wife Mādrī. Here, alas, in the throes of ecstasy, the great Pāndu died.[64]

During the winter months, it is here in Pāndukeshvara that the portable image of Badrīnāth comes for the winter. When the snow falls and the shrine closes, a woolen blanket, or *choli*, is presented to Badrīnāth as an offering, and the image is laid in a position of rest for the winter months, with the *choli* over it. When the temple opens again in the spring, the *choli* is removed and distributed to the faithful as part of the *prasad* of the Lord. According to tradition, the celestial sage Nārada continues to perform *pūjā* here during the winter, when the *raval* retreats down the mountain with the portable image. For six months, they say, ordinary men and women worship here, and for six months only the gods worship here.

On the approach to Badrīnāth, as the pilgrim route becomes very steep, is Hanumān Chatti. Here, according to local tradition, as the Pāndavas were on their way to Badrīnāth, they were blocked by a huge monkey, his tail stretched across the trail. Bhīma, the strongman of the brothers, asked the monkey to move, and the monkey told Bhīma just to pick up his tail and move it himself. Even with all his strength, Bhīma could not lift the monkey's tail. He discovered only then that this was the great monkey Hanumān, Son of the Wind, and Son of Shiva, as well. Here, the Pāndavas had the *darshan* of Hanumān, whose shrine continues to be a halting place on the road to Badrīnāth.

Finally, we should note that Shiva also has an important place at Badrīnāth. In the *Skanda Purāna*, Shiva is the interlocutor who tells his son Skanda about the many *tīrthas* within the precincts of Badrīnāth and their saving benefits. He begins by reviewing all the sacred *tīrthas* of India and then comes to Badri. He compares it to the best of all possible *tīrthas*, Vārānasī. Vishnu may leave other *tīrthas* during the different ages, but he never leaves Badri. It is called Vishālā because "it is the abode of all the *tīrthas*."[65]

In his teachings, Shiva describes the place in Badrīnāth most sacred to himself, Kapālamochana, "Where the Skull Fell." At the time of creation, he says, the five-headed Brahmā lusted after the daughter he himself had formed. Shiva, furious at this incestuous behavior, cut off one of Brahmā's heads. He punished Brahmā's sin, but in that act he himself incurred a sin as well—the sin of killing a brahmin. The skull of Brahmā's fifth head stuck to Shiva's hand and could not be removed. Shiva then roamed the earth, visiting its many *tīrthas* to rid himself of the skull and find expiation. Finally, taking the advice of Vishnu, he came to Badrī Vishāla. The moment he arrived, the skull began to tremble and come loose. It dropped from Shiva's hand and vanished. That place became known as Kapālamochana, "Where the Skull Fell," and ever since that time, Shiva and Pārvatī have stayed here at Badrī Vishāla, delighting the ascetics and sages.[66] We know by now that there are many places in India with their own Kapālamochana *tīrthas,* from Vārānasī in the north to Madurai in the far south. Like this *tīrtha* at Badrīnāth, the many places "Where the Skull Fell" link their sanctity to this story: Even the great Lord Shiva found expiation from even the greatest of sins by bathing right here.

The association of Badrīnāth with Shiva is legendary in this part of the mountains. After all, it is Shiva's name, Nīlakantha, the "Blue-Throated One," that is given to the mountain soaring into the sky to the west of Badrīnāth. Originally, they say, Shiva and Pārvatī lived here and Vishnu came to them as a very small child. Pārvatī happily took the boy home, not quite realizing who he was. Once there, the presumptuous child took command of the whole house. One day while Shiva and Pārvatī were bathing in the river, the child slipped in and sat upon Shiva's seat. When the couple returned, the boy asked Shiva to leave this *kshetra* and go to nearby Kedārnāth Mountain. At that time, so they say, Shiva, who knew all along that this was Vishnu, agreed to let him stay at Badrīnāth while he himself moved to the stronghold of Kedārnāth, just over the mountains, about fifty miles due west. Even so, Shiva remains here in a very old temple, Ādi Kedāreshvara, the "Original Lord of Kedār." The story could not be clearer: Shiva and Pārvatī were once here, proprietors of this place, a theme very common here in the mountains where one finds both Shiva's meditation retreats and Pārvatī's childhood home.

Today inside the gaily painted temple of Badrīnāth, fewer than one hundred people stand together in the antechamber of the temple, waiting for the *darshan* of Badrī Nārāyana. The antechamber is supported by four huge columns, carved on all four sides with the images of the *avatāras* of Vishnu. Even if Badrīnāth has Shaiva undertones, the Vaishnava message today is clear. The image of Badrī Nārāyana is said to be made of

Vishnu's sacred *shālagrāma* stone. The image is seated in meditation, so they say, but all that is visible to the worshipper is his face, since the *mūrti* is so fully swathed in garments and garlands of *tulsī* leaves. Some still say the image is the meditating Shiva, but most see it as Vishnu Nārāyana. One sidewalk commentator says that every individual, whatever way of thinking he follows—Vaishnava, Shaiva, or Shākta—receives *darshan* of his own *ishtadevatā* in this image, according to his own *bhāvana*, his inner disposition. A modern writer and Himalayan traveler reports the same sentiment. In his book on the Garhwal Himalayas, A. P. Agarwal writes, "The elasticity of the faith permits devotees to see in the idol Brahmā, Vishnu, Shiva, Kālī, Mahābīr, Guru or the Buddha."[67] Present in the sanctum, next to Badrī Nārāyana, are the two ancients Nara and Nārāyana. To the left is the brass face mask of Kubera, the Lord of Wealth and the proprietor of the Himalayan mines and minerals. Flat copper impressions of the altar array for sale in the bazaar add other important deities: the auspicious Ganesha and Lakshmī, whose shrines are around the perimeter of the temple compound; Garuda and Nārada, whose penance is remembered in the very rocks of the river.

Vishnu's footprints are here too. High on the open slope leading toward Nīlakantha is a rock called the *charana pāduka,* the holy footprints. In May, the meadows are filled with shades of blue and purple wild irises, strawberry blossoms, buttercups, and forget-me-nots. Streams rush down from the mountain glaciers, falling in long, soft cascades over the high rocks. By the time these waters fall into the Alakanandā River far below, they have joined together and are called the Rishi Gangā. But even as they climb toward the footprints of Vishnu, pilgrims are well aware that they are in the lap of Shiva's country, so dominant is the peak of Nīlakantha, the Blue-Throated Shiva, straight ahead.

In the small village surrounding the temple, the headquarters of the *raval* is marked with a large sign, HIS HOLINESS RAVAL OF SRĪ BADRĪNĀTH. In our interview, the *raval* is keen to emphasize the importance of Badrīnāth. "This place is called Jnāna Bhūmi, the Land of Wisdom, and also Tapobhūmi, the Land of Sacred Austerities. Other places, like Kāshī, Prayāg, and Gayā, are called *tīrthas*, but Badrī is a *dhām*, and a *dhām* is more important than a *tīrtha*. A *dhām* is a house, a place where God dwells."

The *raval* is well aware of the complexity of God's dwelling here, however. He describes the story of Shiva yielding his place to Vishnu, who came as a child to sit on the seat of Shiva in the old Shiva temple here, the one now called Old Kedāreshvara. He makes clear that Nīlakantha looks much like a Shiva *linga* and that on its far side is Kedārnāth, the greatest abode of Shiva in the Himalayas. And is there a *devī* here too? Yes, indeed, the goddess Urvashī, whose *pītha* is there, just below Badrīnāth, where the Rishi Gangā joins the Alakanandā. Most telling, of course, is the *samkalpa* recited for each pilgrim who has special rites performed here. As a ritual statement of intention, the *samkalpa* always includes reference to the location of the person. Here, they recite: *Nārāyana kshetre, Urvashīya pīthe, asmin Shrī Badrīshvarasya mandire, Shrīmad Nārāyana caranasannidhau* . . . "In the Land of Nārāyana, at the sacred seat of Urvashī, in this Temple of Shiva, Lord of Badrī, and at the feet of Nārāyana . . ." These are the holy and powerful coordinates of Badrīnāth.

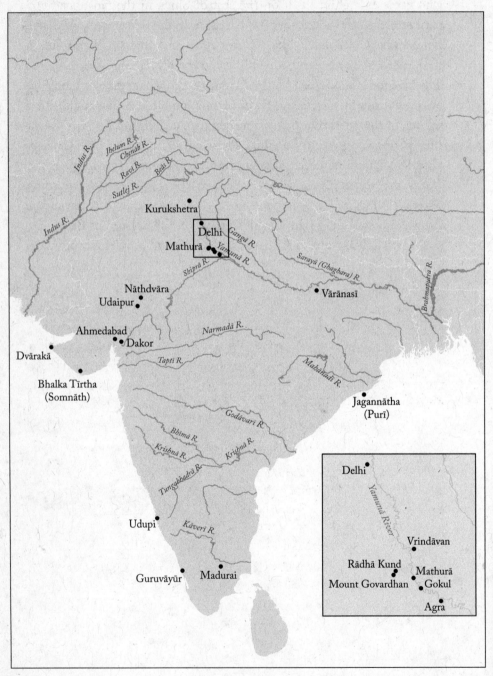

{ KRISHNA IN THE LAND OF INDIA }

8

The Land and Story of Krishna

Tens of thousands of pilgrims crowd into the little town of Vrindāvan, in central north India, to celebrate the birthday of Krishna this September. The day is called Krishna Janmāshtamī.[1] The temples of Vrindāvan, Krishna's childhood home, are filled to capacity for the liturgies that mark his birth. In each temple, the image of Krishna is bathed with profuse lustrations of milk and dressed as a royal child. Devotees gather in the temple of Rādhāraman for hours on this holy day, standing so tightly packed together that all sense of individual boundaries dissolves in a sea of devotion. They gaze at Krishna, brought forth upon a small silver altar, on the raised stage at one end of the temple courtyard. In rapt attention and with ecstatic songs and shouts, they watch as Krishna receives the ritual ministrations of the priests. The small, jet-black image of Krishna is bathed with Yamunā water brought in special procession from the river a short distance away and, of course, with milk by the gallons. Krishna is rubbed down with turmeric and sandalwood paste and is then dressed in silk, supplied with ornaments of gold and pearl and a crown of pearls. He is given a regal umbrella of gold and a tiny silver flute. The entire throne is filled with fresh flowers and the leaves of the sacred tulsī plant, a species of basil. Everyone there has come for the *darshan* of the newborn Krishna, eager to hold Krishna in his or her own gaze. The jostling, elbowing current of the crowd somehow brings each person close enough to see to each heart's satisfaction.

Ten miles away, in the city of Mathurā, Krishna's birth is celebrated in the very place, so they say, where it all happened. As the story goes, Krishna's father, Vasudeva, and his mother, Devakī, were in prison when he was born.[2] They had been confined by the evil designs of Devakī's own brother, Kamsa, who had received word that her child would oust him from the throne and kill him. Kamsa promptly put his sister Devakī and her husband, Vasudeva, in prison. He made sure that each child Devakī bore was killed at birth. Devakī and Vasudeva saw six infants killed in this way, but the seventh, Balarāma, was safely transferred from Devakī's womb to the womb of Rohiṇī, Vasudeva's sister, a miraculous embryo transplant that was considered a "miscarriage" by the prison guards. So was born the elder brother of Krishna, Balarāma.[3]

The eighth child was Krishna himself. Even at his birth, Devakī and Vasudeva recognized Krishna to be the Supreme Lord, for he filled their prison chamber with his radiance and bore the emblems and marks of the Supreme Vishnu. As Vasudeva put it in his first hymn of praise, a remarkable greeting for a child newly born:

> It is clear that you are Bhagavān, God himself, the supreme being beyond the material world. You are the knower of the minds of everyone. Your form is pure bliss and majesty. It was you, in the beginning, who created this world.... There is no inside and outside of you. You are the universal soul of everything, and the essence of the soul.[4]

Following their prayers and praises, Vasudeva and Devakī saw the Lord changed into an ordinary child before their eyes. Then, on that very night, the prison guards were overcome with sleep, Vasudeva's shackles fell from his ankles, and the locks of the prison fell open. Vasudeva was able to escape from the prison cell with baby Krishna. It was a stormy and rainy night. Shielded by the spreading hoods of the river serpent Shesha, he carried the baby across the floodwaters of the Yamunā River to the little settlement today called Gokul. There the cowherd Nanda's wife Yashodā was sound asleep, having just given birth to a baby girl. Vasudeva switched the babies, returned with Yashodā's newborn girl, and placed her in the arms of Devakī. Again, the prison guards were, by divine design, asleep. When Kamsa heard of the birth of another child, he promptly came to the prison cell to kill the baby. But when he picked up the infant girl and dashed her against the stone floor, she rose up as a mighty goddess, "bearing weapons in her eight mighty arms" and laughing at the impotence of the king. "She became known by many names on the earth in many different places," the *Bhāgavata Purāna* tells us.[5] One of those, as we have seen, is Vindhyavāsinī, whose shrine we have visited.

In the meantime, Krishna slept in safety in the rustic homestead of Yashodā and Nanda, the keepers of cows who became his foster parents. When Kamsa discovered that the divine child had escaped, he set his mind to kill all the baby boys under ten days old in the Mathurā area.[6] As the drama of Krishna's young life unfolds, it is filled with episodes pitting the demonic agents of Kamsa against the child Krishna. Eventually, as a young man, he returns to Mathurā to vanquish Kamsa himself and restore the lineage of Vasudeva to the throne.

At the heart of Krishna pilgrimage is the process of remembering and telling the tale of the places where Krishna lived and grew up in the area known as Braj or Vraja in Sanskrit, meaning "where the cows roam."[7] Here he lived as a child with his foster parents. Here he herded cows during the day with the cowherds of the village, faced and conquered innumerable foes. Here he captivated the hearts of the milkmaids of the village and lured them to dance with him in the forest groves. Here more than anywhere else in India, the story lines and pilgrimage tracks are interwoven in a continuous narrative, creating a sacred landscape in which the story is inscribed in the topography. As we shall see, the process of pilgrimage brings devotees into the world of Krishna as participants. They enter the story through the narratives linked to places and through plays called *līlās* in which the story is enacted by troupes of young boys, especially consecrated to the plays. And they participate in the story through various pilgrimages, the longest of which takes them two to three weeks and many miles on a circuit of the land of Krishna. This experience of pilgrimage is both in and out of time, connecting devotees to a transcendental reality. As Braj scholar Alan Entwistle puts it, "A fundamental concept underlying the motivation for pilgrimage to Braj is that Krishna's activities, while they once occurred on earth in historical time, are by no means over and done with. They are not remote events that nowadays serve as more than an allegory of how we should relate to god, but are being enacted eternally on a plane that transcends the world of our blinkered everyday experience."[8]

Mathurā: Center and Starting Place

Mathurā is a very old city. There are references to what we presume to be this place as early as 500 B.C.E., in the age of early Buddhist and Jain traditions. Archaeologist and historian Shiva Bajpai writes of its history, "Literary and archeological evidence reveals a phenomenal transformation in the fortunes of Mathurā and its environs from the age of the Buddha, when it suffered from bad roads, dust storms, infestations of fierce dogs and bestial *yakkhas*, and niggardliness in alms-giving, to the period between the second century B.C. and the third century A.D., when it attained the position of a leading metropolis 'rising beautiful as the crescent moon over the dark streams of the Yamunā' and celebrated for its magnificence, prosperity, munificence, and teeming population."[9] The growing city sat not only on a major waterway, but also on trade routes running from east to west and north to south across India. Not only trade, but eventually pilgrimage, made this crossroads important. Mathurā has many layers of history, but today, in this city of some three hundred thousand, the links to its role as the birthplace of Lord Krishna predominate.

In Mathurā, pilgrims gather by the thousands for Krishna Janmāshtamī in late August or early September. According to one of the Hindi pilgrim's guide available in the market today, the most important temples for the midnight *darshan* of Krishna on the night of his birth are the Krishna Janmasthān and the Dvārakādhīsh Temple. At Dvārakādhīsh, worshippers crowd into the temple for the *āratī* and *darshan* of the Lord, who links Krishna's birthplace to the great capital city of Dvārakā, in the far west of India where Krishna reigned in his later years. Here Krishna has a jet-black four-armed form, a manifestation of the Supreme Lord said to be like that glimpsed only for a moment by Devakī and Vasudeva on the night of Krishna's birth. "*Govinda Hari! Gopāla Hari!*" they sing, packed together before the altar, waiting for the curtain to be pulled back and the image of Krishna revealed. An electric sense of excitement fills the air, and when the moment comes, they raise their hands in reverence, cheering as they lean forward, craning their necks for a view of the Lord. This temple, rebuilt as recently as the early nineteenth century by patrons from Gwalior, is certainly the most popular in Mathurā today.

That very day, many of these pilgrims also visit the Janmasthān Temple, the place of Krishna's birth, where, formerly, the old Keshava Deva Temple stood, a temple said to have been built many centuries ago. This old temple must have witnessed the sack of Mathurā during the reign of Mahmud of Ghazni in 1017 and, again, during the time of Sikandar Lodi (1488–1516). It is not clear how badly it may have been damaged in those times, but a contemporaneous Muslim historian insists that they had "destroyed many places of worship of the infidels and left not a single vestige remaining of them."[10] The temple was rebuilt by the Bundela Raja Bir Singh during the time of the Mughal Emperor Jahangir, and the French traveler Bernier saw it in 1663 and described it as "an ancient and magnificent pagan temple."[11] In 1669, the Keshava Deva Temple was razed during the time of the Mughal Emperor Aurangzeb and the site used for the construction of a mosque, which remains today.[12] While new Hindu nationalists have made threats to recover this site for a Hindu temple, there has been little enthusiasm for this project from the locals, including the Krishna devotees of this area.

Today, the hand-painted sign with an arrow pointing to the Janmasthān, the "Birthplace of Lord Krishna," takes pilgrims into a chamber beneath the mosque where they can stand, palms pressed together, to pay homage to the divine child. Since Krishna is said to have been born in prison, the austerity and confinement of this subterranean site is somehow fitting. It is called simply the *garbha griha,* the "womb chamber," of the old Keshava Deva temple. *Garbha griha* is the term commonly used for the inner sanctum of a temple, here particularly appropriate for the chamber of Krishna's birth. While a new temple was built nearby in the 1950s, the darker and more confined ambiance of the prison-cell temple is still a must for those who would experience a real taste of the celebration of Krishna's birth.

According to one of the Hindi guides, it was here at the Janmasthān that "Shri Krishna appeared from Devakī's womb in his four-armed form."[13] Today, pilgrims see not the four-armed Krishna, but the baby: The raised altar of the *garbha griha* bears an image of Laddu Gopāl, the baby Krishna, crawling with a *laddu,* a round milk sweet, in one little fist. On the walls are prints of Devakī and Vasudeva pressing their palms together in prayer before the Lord, and of Vasudeva carrying the baby across the Yamunā in a basket on his head. Many times as the story of

Krishna unfolds we see the striking juxtaposition of Krishna's magnitude as the Supreme Lord and his earthly presence. He appears in infinite glory, and only then becomes a baby, so small that Vasudeva carries him in a basket.

A priest, dressed in a golden-hued *dhoti* and side-tying *bagal bandhi*, accepts the offerings of worshippers and distributes *prasād*. "Is this the real place?" asks an old woman who has come with a group of pilgrims. "Absolutely, the real place! This is it!" he answers.

Krishna is vibrantly present in many temples in Mathurā today, as well as on the *ghāts* along the Yamunā River, the most famous of which, Vishrām Ghāt, is said to be where Krishna rested years later, having defeated Kamsa. But if we survey the landscape of this old city that very much looks its age, we will find Shiva and the Goddess honored in many temples, and we will find innumerable images of Hanumān and Bhairava. Indeed, this city has such a prolixity of gods, it is no wonder that it is seen as one of the seven *moksha*-giving cities of India.[14]

Mathurā has a long, continuous history dating back more than two thousand years. The Mathurā Museum provides a provocative record of these centuries. There are images of *yakshas* and *yakshīs* dating to the first and second centuries B.C.E. Then we begin to see images of the Buddha, among the first ever made, reflecting some of the features of the *yakshas*. Beginning in the Kushāna period (first to third centuries C.E.), these seated and standing images of the Buddha are hearty, grounded, open-faced images quite distinct from the later, more graceful, fine-featured meditative Buddhas from the workshops of Gupta Sarnāth near Vārānasī, farther east. A Jaina stūpa has been excavated in Mathurā, also from this early period, and with it images of many of the Jaina spiritual "ford makers" called *tīrthankaras*.

The first substantial indications of Krishna in this art historical record are what art historian Doris Srinivasan speaks of as "kinship" sculptures from the Kushāna period, showing Krishna and his brother Balarāma flanking their sister Ekanāmsā.[15] Gradually, images of the *tīrthankaras* and the Buddha began to give way to the four-armed Krishna-Vāsudeva. After the Kushāna period, however, Srinivasan sees an extraordinary change in the number of Vaishnava images produced in the Mathurā area, with a virtual "explosion" in the number of images of the Krishna-Vāsudeva type.[16] In the Gupta period, from the fourth to sixth centuries C.E., there are more images of Krishna. Not surprisingly, they show two of the heroic poses that link Krishna to the living topography of the land: Krishna lifting Mount Govardhan to protect the people from the wrath and thunderous rain of Indra, and Krishna quelling the powerful *nāga* Kāliyā, who had brought terror to the Yamunā River and the land through which it flowed. These images display some of the continuities between the rise of Krishna and the cult of the strong *yakshas* who preceded him. Indeed, one scholar has seen Krishna as the *yaksha* of Govardhan.[17] His lore and iconography display the triumph of Krishna over older gods and the infusion of new meaning into the mountain and river that are so central to the landscape of the region. In this early period, however, we do not see the depiction of the cowherd Krishna whose life in this region has come to predominate in today's landscape.

We know that by the eleventh century there were several major temples to Krishna, but interestingly, the region was still primarily the sacred landscape of Shiva. Charlotte Vaudeville and other scholars who have studied Mathurā and its surrounding area conclude that before the sixteenth century, when the major Krishna sects were established in this area, "the Shaiva and Shākta cults were prevalent in the Braj area, as in northern India in general."[18] Shiva is the guardian and first lord of the area surrounding Mathurā, with a quartet of Shiva temples, one in each of the four directions. Bhūteshvara reigns from Mathurā, Kāmeshvara from Kamban, Chakreshvara from Govardhan, and Gopīshvara from Vrindāvan. It seems likely that despite the efflorescence of Vaishnava images, the lively religious life of the Mathurā region prior to the sixteenth century consisted largely of Shiva and Devī worship and popular forms of nature worship—ancient holy places such as Govardhan Hill, the River Yamunā, and the trees, pools, and hillocks where life-force deities like *nāgas* were honored.

In the past five hundred years the mythic landscape of Mathurā and the wider circle of Braj has become ever more elaborately and profoundly linked to the lore of Krishna. Yet even today, Vaishnava pilgrimages around the twelve forests of Krishna's Braj begin with the honoring of Shiva—at Gopīshvara in Vrindāvan and at Bhūteshvara in Mathurā. The latter is said to be the "guardian," or *kshetrapāla*, of Mathurā. On the first night of the forest pilgrimage, many pilgrims encamp at Bhūteshvara

and ask blessings for the journey: "O Shiva, Promoter of All Auspiciousness, Accomplisher of all aims, through your grace may my pilgrimage
be successful."[19]

Braj Mandal, the Sacred Circle of Braj

From the standpoint of pilgrimage, Mathurā has become the center of
the area called Braj Mandal, the sacred land of Braj. The Sanskrit term
mandala, mandal in Hindi, means both "circle" and "world." It is a circle
that symbolically maps a whole world. A mandala might be the circular
painted diagram of Tibetan Buddhists in which the entire Buddhist cosmology is inscribed, along with its cardinal and intermediate directions,
its powers and guardians. It might be the three-dimensional mandala
of a Hindu temple, with its eight horizontal directions and its vaulting
verticality, symbolically re-creating the mountain at the center of the
world. It might be the large area surrounding Kāshī, the city of light, a
city of expanding concentric circles, guarded by ranks of Ganeshas and
goddesses, and symbolically likened to a mandala.

Here in Braj, the popular map of the mandala shows us a free-form,
undulating "circle," meandering through the world of Krishna's *līlās,* the
playful and loving relationships of Krishna with the people of Braj. This
is a "circle" with a diameter of about sixty miles. In some of the imaginative "maps" of local lore, Mathurā is the center of the pericarp of a
symbolic lotus that extends its petals into the surrounding countryside,
saturated with the footsteps and the fragrance of Krishna. The lotus petals are the twelve forests, each with its many beloved places. During
the day, it is said, the whole lotus is spread forth and the places are far
apart, but during the night, when the lotus flower closes, all the sacred
places are drawn together, enfolding the landscape, the devotees, and
Lord Krishna himself in the flower's intimate enclosure.[20]

Braj embraces the villages, groves, rivers, and ponds where Krishna
spent his childhood and youth, living amid village folk whose business
was to watch their herds of cows, milk them, and churn butter from the
milk. The *Harivamsha,* a text dated to approximately the second century
and a companion, in a way, to the legend of Krishna in the *Mahābhārata,*
describes the land as a fine country of many pasturelands, with well-

nurtured people and cattle, the soil ever moist with the froth of milk. It is a land flowing with buttermilk, filled with cowherds and milkmaids, the air resonant with the sound of the sputtering churn.[21] Aside from the city of Mathurā and the growing congestion of its towns and roadways and the deforestation of its legendary forests, Braj is a rural area of villages and farmlands even today. The myth of Krishna told from Braj is not at all regal, but very earthy. While he is understood to be the Supreme Lord, he did not live among priests and kings, but among the rustic folk of the village. He is Gopāl, the cowherd, the protector of cows.

We are told in the *Bhāgavata Purāna* that the village folk loved him and put up with his pranks as a baby, chastised and admired him as a friend in his boyhood, and loved him with the passion of lovers in his youth. And they were saved—as are those who love Krishna even today—not by the wisdom of the scriptures, not by the asceticism of the renouncers, not even by the ritual ministrations of priests, but simply by their unwitting and unconditional love for Krishna, by the relationships of love called *bhakti*. This word *bhakti* and all it represents in expressing human relatedness to God is surely one of the most important words in the Hindu vocabulary. The stories of the love of Krishna and Krishna's reciprocating love explore and expand the meanings of *bhakti*. The villagers of Braj, like Devakī and Vasudeva on the night of Krishna's birth, recognize, in one sense, that Krishna who lives among them is extraordinary. They glimpse his divinity in a religious world in which divine "incarnation" is not so uncommon. They even glimpse the full majesty of Krishna as Supreme, creator and sustainer of the whole universe. But such glimpses cannot be sustained; for the whole point of the love of Krishna is to expand the spontaneous and natural love of the heart.

The legend and presence of Krishna is inscribed in the land of Braj in ways that seem somehow familiar to many who come from the Christian tradition and have visited the "holy land," as pilgrims have from the first Christian centuries. Medieval European pilgrimage was filled with the lore of the storied holy places—the very place near Bethlehem where the shepherds were guarding their flocks when the angel told them of the miraculous birth, the very place in Bethlehem where Mary nursed Jesus as a baby, the very place where she washed his clothes and, at the far end of his short life, the very place where the food was cooked that was served at the Last Supper, the very place where Jesus was scourged and the crown of thorns placed on his head, the very place where Simon of Cyrene joined Jesus to help carry the cross, the very place of Jesus's crucifixion. This kind of detailed ascription of the story to the land is not so uncommon in the human valuation of sacred places. Remember the Chinese pilgrims to India in search of texts and yearning for proximity to the life of the Buddha. They, too, found joy in innumerable specific places—the place where Siddhārtha received nourishing food from a village woman to help him regain the strength he had lost in austerities; the place he sat in meditation beneath the Bodhi Tree until he saw through to the nature of reality. Here, they said, is the place he walked up and down in meditation; here is the place his shadow fell. The lives of Jesus, the Buddha, and Krishna were larger than life, to be sure, and yet these lives are mapped on a landscape that lends itself to the memory and the pilgrimage of ordinary people.

THE *LĪLĀSTHALAS*, PLACES OF THE LORD'S PLAY

The holy places that dot the landscape of Braj are called *līlāsthalas*, literally the "places of play." They create the scene of Lord Krishna's playful and powerful relations with the villagers of this area. They are not referred to as *tīrthas*, for here the point is not to cross over the entrapments and snares of this earthly life to seek the world of the "far shore," but to taste the flavor and savor the essence of life in all its fullness, life in the presence of Lord Krishna. With its elaborate scenery of *līlāsthalas*, the land of Krishna's birth has become a living text, each and every place associated with the events of Krishna's life. Pilgrims visit the place where he was born in Mathurā, the sites of his childhood in Gokul, Nandagaon, and Vrindāban, and the multitude of groves and glades associated with his life. Their guide will show them almost innumerable places where the events of Krishna's life are remembered: This place is where Yashodā went to milk the cows for Krishna's milk; here Krishna cut the bamboo for his beloved flute; there he slid down a smooth rock with his friends; and there he blocked the road and demanded a toll from the *gopīs* before he would let them pass as they took their pots of butter to the market.

In Gokul, at the place identified as Nanda's house, pilgrims can sit on

Krishna lifting Mount Govardhan, protecting the villagers from Indra's rainstorm

the very earth where Yashodā might have sat, so they say, and pull a silver cord to swing the cradle of Krishna. This, of course, for a small fee. In an adjacent shrine, they can put a hand on Yashodā's churning stick while dedicatory prayers are recited. Gokul calls to mind and heart one of the strongest forms of devotional love: the unconditional love of parents for their children. Perhaps pilgrims to Gokul will tell one of the traditional accounts of Mother Yashodā and her love of Krishna that remind them that the baby was the Supreme Lord, and yet a baby nonetheless.

Once Yashodā was suckling Krishna, and as he looked up from her breast, she looked into his tiny mouth. The *Bhāgavata Purāna* tells the tale:

When her son had almost finished drinking, the mother began caressing his sweetly smiling mouth. As he yawned, she saw in there the sky, heaven and earth, the host of stars, space, the sun, the moon, fire, air, the oceans, the continents, the mountains and their daughters the rivers, the forests, and moving and non-moving living things. Seeing the universe so suddenly, she began to tremble.[22]

Yashodā closed her eyes, and mercifully the overwhelming vision was withdrawn. But it happened again when she scolded Krishna for eating mud and reached into his mouth with her finger, as a mother would, to remove it. Once again, she glimpsed the swirl of the whole universe. And she saw Braj there, inside his mouth, and she saw herself there in Braj. Once again, we are told, the Lord cast the veil of his divine power upon her, and she became just a mother, who bounced the child on her lap and loved him with a mother's love.[23]

In the love of baby Krishna, the utterly spontaneous, selfless, joyful love of parents for their children becomes a paradigm for the kind of love we might have for God. It is called *vātsalya*, a term our Braj pilgrims certainly know. It means, literally, the mothering love of a cow for her calf, her *vatsa*. The mother cow's milk flows spontaneously in the presence of her calf. *Vātsalya* is that kind of love. Although Yashodā glimpses Krishna in his fullness, she is mercifully enabled to forget the cosmic vision so that she can simply love Krishna, naughty and playful, with the full force of a mother's love. So it is that those who come to Gokul might buy for their home altar the most popular of all images of Krishna, the crawling baby with a ball of butter in his fist. This is the mischievous child, the butter thief, who constantly steals Yashodā's freshly churned butter, and, of course, her heart.

Throughout the villages and groves of Braj there are many *līlāsthalas* associated with the stories of Krishna as a boy, stories that evoke the companionable, admiring love between Krishna and his childhood friends, the cowherds with whom he spent his days, relatively carefree except for their responsibility for the care of the cows. These friends love Krishna with the ardent love of best friends.[24] In his boyhood years, according to legend, Krishna's life is filled with the innumerable and often subtle threats that come from Mathurā. Kamsa's emissaries are still at work, trying to find and destroy the boy born to overturn the king. Krishna inevitably rescues them from one close call after another. The tales of his scrapes with demons and danger are plentiful and they provide excitement not only for Krishna, but for his childhood friends as well. He is a hero, with strength, grace, and courage, and the places of his victories are inscribed in the land. The most famous of the heroic exploits of Krishna was his effortless lifting of Mount Govardhan, the long, low hill in the middle of Braj.

GOVARDHAN

Govardhan has a complex mythological pedigree that links it with other well-known ways of creating a landscape. In one account, it is the sacred mountain of the island of Shālmali—one of the ring-shaped islands of the universe, between the sea of sugarcane juice and the sea of wine. The sage Pulastya wanted to move Govardhan to Kāshī, but when he got as far as Braj, Govardhan refused to continue the journey: This hill chose this place, and refused to budge. Pulastya cursed Govardhan to decrease in size by one sesame seed every year, and so it is that it is not much of a mountain today.[25] In another account, Govardhan was brought from the Himalayas by Hanumān, and thus this account participates in the common theme of constructing a mountain landscape by moving a bit of the Himalayas to another part of India.[26] In Braj, however, Govardhan is intimately associated with cows and with Krishna. So significant is this site that it comes to be seen in one devotional tradition as the center post of the great *dhāms* of India: At the four corners of India are Jagannātha in the east, Ranganātha in the south, Dvārākanātha in the west, and Badrinātha in the north. "And in the middle, O Prince, the Lord of Govardhana is found. These are the five gods of gods, the Five Nāthas, in the holy Bharatavarsha."[27]

At Govardhan, as the Purānic story goes, villagers from the whole area would prepare an autumnal festival in honor of Indra, the god of rain and storm. But Krishna dissuaded them from continuing this practice and convinced them to have a festival in honor of Mount Govardhan instead. "Decorate your cows, give them grass, circle the mountain," he told them. "Don't worship gods that are far-off, but give thanks for those things that are precious right here." So they prepared a *giriyajna*, a great offering of foods and delicacies to the mountain. Krishna then transformed himself into Mount Govardhan and, in that form, received the delicious offerings of food they had prepared. Of course, Indra was furious, saying, "Just see how intoxicated the forest-dwelling cowherds are because of the wealth of the forest. They have taken refuge with Krishna, a mortal, and now they neglect the gods." So Indra unleashed the rain clouds, sending torrents of rain and daggers of lightning down upon the land. Unperturbed, Krishna, gracefully and effortlessly, lifted

Mount Govardhan with one hand, indeed with the little finger of one hand, and held it as a giant umbrella to protect all the people and cattle of Braj. The rain pounded down for a week before Indra, overwhelmed with the strength of Krishna, gave up. While everyone watched, Krishna put the mountain back in its place. So goes the most well-known version of the story, as told in the *Bhāgavata Purāna*.[28]

Govardhan, that elongated hill that Krishna lifted so effortlessly and held aloft as an umbrella during the torrential rains of Indra, has long been one of the central places for the worship of Krishna in Braj. One of the only early images of Krishna in the Mathurā Museum shows a strong *yaksha*-like, heroic Krishna with upraised arm, holding the hill on the palm of his hand. It comes from the Kushāna period (first and second centuries C.E.), but the rites of Govardhan are no doubt even older. Pilgrims who circle the hill today certainly participate in one of the most ancient forms of devotion in this Braj country. Govardhan literally means "increaser of cattle," and the hill was also called Girirāj, the "King of Hills." Here cow-herding locals, like pastoral cow-herding tribes across north India, worshipped a benevolent hill deity to whom they brought prayers for their own well-being and for the fertility of their cows.[29]

The autumn festival of Girirāj Govardhan must be very old indeed, for in the *Harivamsha*, a work more than fifteen hundred years old, Krishna urges the cow-herding folk to give up their rites to the Vedic god Indra, saying, "We are milkmen and we live in forests and hills. Hills, forests and cattle, these are our supreme benefactors. . . . From hills we derive the greatest of benefits. We should therefore start sacrifices in honor of the hills. Let cows and bulls decorated with autumnal flowers go round yonder hill."[30] In the *Vishnu Purāna* account of the autumn festival, Krishna duplicates himself and then appears on top of the hill itself, saying, "I *am* the manifestation of the hill." As such he receives and consumes the offerings of food given by the cowherds. Here Krishna also lifts the hill when the rain pelts down, as in the *Bhāgavata Purāna* account, but we also learn that he *is* the hill, as well as the chief of the cow-herding folk who worship the hill.[31]

As pilgrims make their way around the hill, a course of some eleven miles, they stop at shrines along the way, many of them containing but a simple stone of Govardhan, wrapped with yellow cloth and honored with garlands of flowers. They offer gifts and food at the "mouth" of the mountain, called the *mukhārvind*, at Mānasī Gangā or alternatively at Jatipura. For some, walking on the hill itself, they are told, is quite forbidden because of its holiness.

Many of these pilgrims have participated since childhood in a symbolic form of circumambulating Govardhan and offering food to the mountain. In the fall festival called Annakūt, literally "mountain of food," observed on the day following Divālī, families will create a blockish image of Girirāj Govardhan made out of cow dung. It might be decorated with little trees made of weeds and with tiny representations of cows, and of course, it must have a mouth. Annakūt is famous for the preparation of fifty-six kinds of food (*chappan bhog*), keeping the women of the household busy for weeks in advance. The food is heaped up in a great display and in the evening a ritual officiant—not a Brāhmin, but a member of a cow-herding caste—leads the circumambulation of the symbolic hill of Girirāj, followed by a cow and a bull, and the rest of the family or the village. They offer food to the hill and to the cows and then consume the mountains of food themselves. At Govardhan, in the heartland of pastoral Braj, Annakūt is unquestionably the great festival of the year, attracting huge crowds and, by the way, also attracting the Chaube brahmins of Mathurā, famous for their capacious ability to participate in the gastronomic riches of this festival. The feeding of brahmins is integral to ritual success, even in an age-old and clearly non-brahminical festival. Everybody stands to gain in these rites dedicated to the increase of cows, fertility, and prosperity. Pilgrims, locals, and cattle circumambulate the hill in a steady stream.

Here in the heartland of Braj, Girirāj is identified with Krishna Gopāla, the cowherd god. As we shall see, later devotees developed more-elaborate theologies and liturgies of Krishna as Govardhan's lord, but for the people of this area, the hill itself remains preeminent. As Charlotte Vaudeville writes from years of fieldwork in this area, "The villagers of Braj, up to this day, continue to worship the hill itself as they have always done, by circumambulating it, by flocking to the Mānasī Gangā at the time of the autumnal festival and by offering the *pūjā* to their 'cow-dung Shrī Girirāj' and to their cattle within the courtyards of their homes. Though nominally Vaishnava, the pastoral people of Braj never had a share in official Vaishnava rituals. Today, as in the days of yore, they remain mountain and cattle worshippers. To them, Govardhan is Krishna and Krishna is Govardhan. Their simple devotion still finds its expression in their favorite cry, *Shrī Girirāj Mahārāj kī jay*! 'Victory to the King, the Lord of the Mountain!'"

ON THE BANKS OF THE YAMUNĀ

The day after Annakūt is dedicated here in Braj to the worship of the Yamunā River, the second of the great icons of nature that pervade the religious life of Braj. Krishna is intimately associated with the Yamunā. As a river goddess, she comes to be seen as Krishna's bride, but she is also just the river, and along her banks are many of Krishna's *līlāsthalas*.

Vrindāvan is the village to which Yashodā and Nanda moved during Krishna's childhood to be somewhat farther away from the designs of King Kamsa in Mathurā. There today's pilgrims will find the famous *līlāsthala* at Kāliya Ghāt, with its red sandstone pavilion and its great kadamba tree, its branches bearing yellow blossoms in season and its old roots gripping the riverbank. Here the tale is told of how the serpent Kāliya poisoned the River Yamunā with venom so noxious that even the birds flying over the river were overcome and plunged to their death. One day, Krishna decided to deal with Kāliya. Jack Hawley, one of the great scholars of Vrindāvan, followed a group of Rajasthani pilgrims with their *pandā* pilgrim guide to this spot by the river. He writes:

> From earliest childhood aunts and grandmothers have told these Rajasthanis how as a little boy Krishna was playing ball with his friends by the banks of the Jamna when their ball bounced into the water at the swirling hole where the dread black snake Kaliya lived. Or perhaps they know the version that says the evil king of Mathurā specifically required Krishna to retrieve a thousand lotuses from the fearful place. Whatever the story, the outcome was the same. With complete unconcern Krishna climbed into the branches of the *kadamb* tree that overhangs the pool and jumped in to do battle with the great coiled monster, until he emerged victorious on the surface of the turbulent water As a sign both of his conquest and the serpent's relief that the miraculous boy would not destroy him altogether—only banish him to make the waters safe—he danced with

abandon on the snake's several plumed heads. "And this is where it happened," the *pandā* concludes, gesturing toward a fragrant green tree on the bank and to the backwater nearby, where a number of people are bathing. "Here is the *kadamb* tree and there is the hole."[32]

The scene from the *Bhāgavata Purāna* is also a favorite with Rajput court painters. They show Krishna's peacock-feathered crown, hanging in the kadamba tree, where Krishna left it before leaping into the roiling water. On the bank of the river, cowherds and cows faint from fear, but Krishna emerges from the waters victorious, dancing with shattering step on the hundred hoods of the deadly serpent. The wives of Kāliya rise from the river to beg Krishna not to kill their lord, and so Krishna lets the vanquished Kāliya go and banishes him forever from Braj.[33]

Another riverside kadamba tree not far away tells a different tale, also connected with a famous incident in Krishna's lore. This is at Chīr Ghāt, right in the heart of Vrindāvan. It was here, so they say, that the *gopīs* went to bathe daily during the winter month of austerities, praying to the goddess that they might gain Krishna for a husband. One day Krishna followed them and mischievously gathered up their clothes from the riverbank as they bathed, and climbed into this very tree at the water's edge, hanging their saris on its branches. Laughing and lovingly, he asked them to come one by one to take their clothes from him. Embarrassed, trembling, captivated, wearing nothing, they recovered their clothes from Krishna. He promised them that their vow would come to fruition, and they would indeed enjoy his company at night.

Today at Chīr Ghāt, pilgrims drape lengths of colorful cloth on the branches of the kadamba tree, making their own vows and offering prayers to Krishna. In the branches of the tree sits an image of Lord Krishna fluting. Hawley continues to follow the Rajasthani pilgrims and writes:

At every spot there is something the pilgrims can do to solidify the connection and add their own contribution to the generations of faith that have kept the story alive, and they can do so here as well. This time it is not just a coin or rupee they can offer to the image: they, like Krishna himself, can hang bits of cloth from the branches of the tree. A Brāhmin who claims his family has supervised the spot for five hundred years sits in its shade tending the recently modeled image of Krishna that rests in one of the crotches, and offers varicolored scraps of silk for sale at a rupee or two apiece. The buyers, who are almost always women, perform a memorial, but it is more than a memorial. Their ritual action recapitulates the *gopīs'* vow; they hope for Krishna's presence in their lives.[34]

Hawley notes the ways in which the *pandā* expands the narrative about offering cloth here at the kadamba tree. The priest links this story to another: the episode in the *Mahābhārata* in which the Kaurava princes, having just won the virtuous Pāndavas and their wife Draupadī in a rigged gambling match, demand that Draupadī be brought forcibly into the assembly hall. She resists, and Duhshāsana, one of the Kaurava princes, proceeds to strip her publicly, pulling the end of her sari. Draupadī prays to Krishna, and her sari is miraculously lengthened. The harder Duhshāsana pulls, the more the sari appears to keep Draupadī covered. Finally, he gives up. Here at Chīr Ghāt, according to Hawley, "the priests and the *pandas* assure the pilgrims that if they leave a bit of cloth for Krishna at this spot, they will never in their lives lack for garments. It is a simple fact, they say, it has never been falsified. Other wishes carry, by extension, the same hope of fulfillment."[35] Although both the *pandās* and the pilgrims know the two stories are quite distinct, they both involve Krishna and nicely complement each other, bringing the force of Krishna's providence in supplying Draupadī with a sari of infinite length.

Among the most famous of the *līlāsthalas* near the Yamunā bank are the forest groves where Krishna would meet the *gopīs* at night and dance the *rās* dance with each of them in a wide circle. He created a well for them when they were exhausted with the dance and too thirsty to walk to the Yamunā River. There, too, is Sevā Kunj, the very bower, so they say, where Krishna met Rādhā for lovemaking. We can see their footprints. The pilgrimage pamphlets and the Vrindāvan guides of today warn visitors that they may not stay in this place after sunset, for it is the private circle of Krishna, Rādhā, and the *gopīs*.

The heroic Krishna who lifts the mountain and conquers Kāliya elicits awe, worship, even love. But it is not quite the same love as that which Krishna elicits from Rādhā and the other milkmaids, the *gopīs*, who were roused by the sound of his flute and who yearned for his presence. Here at

Sevā Kunj, we cannot but wonder what it means to see and experience the divine with the intense love of a lover. This complex emotion is explored in the love of the *gopīs* for Krishna and in Krishna's love for them. The milkmaids are said to be entranced with the sound of Krishna's flute and irresistibly drawn to his presence. The *Bhāgavata Purāna* delights in describing the enchantment of the *gopīs* as they dropped whatever they were doing, leaving their tasks without a moment's thought and responding to the flute's call. One left the milking half done, another left the milk boiling on the stove. One was suckling a baby, another bathing, another putting mascara on her eyes. But at the sound of his flute, they left at once, their mascara half-on, their skirts and blouses inside out, their anklets on their wrists, their hair tangled, uncombed, half-braided. To their astonishment, when Krishna met them in the dark of the forest, he told them to go home and tend to their families and husbands. They were indignant and refused to go, chastising him and saying, "Oh beloved, pour the nectar of your lips on the fire dwelling in our hearts, which has been kindled by your musical harmonies, your glances, and your smiles."[36] And so Krishna frolicked and danced in the forest with the *gopīs*. Krishna, the loving, the playful, the embracing Lord.

The climax of the legend of Krishna is the *rās* dance, the great circle dance in which Krishna joined the *gopīs*, multiplying himself to dance with each one. The *Bhāgavata Purāna* describes the dance on that autumn night: "The festival of the *rāsa* dance began, featuring a circle of *gopīs*. The Lord of all yogis, Krishna, inserted himself between each pair of *gopīs*, and put his arms about their necks. Each woman thought he was at her side only."[37] The drums sounded, the bells of their anklets resounded, and Krishna and the *gopīs* danced; the gods gathered on high to behold the scene, and flower petals fell from the heavens. The love of Krishna, so cherished, made each young woman proud, and she thought herself to be the best and luckiest woman on earth to have received his undivided attention.

Krishna, seeing their pride, would suddenly vanish from their company in the forest. When he was gone, so they say, the despondent *gopīs* roamed through the woods asking each tree and plant if they had seen where Krishna had gone. The very beauty of the earth convinced them that Krishna must have passed that way. They saw his footprints everywhere and they smelled the sweet scent of his presence. The vine wrapping round the tree, the soft glistening eyes of the deer seemed to bespeak the passing presence of the Lord. They followed his footprints and interpreted his every step, imagining what he must have been doing. Nikunjabān is the leafy forest where these sublime events are called to mind.

Participating in the Krishna *Līlā*

One of the most distinctive aspects of the pilgrimage landscape of Braj is the extent to which pilgrims enter into the drama as participants. Yes, pilgrims and townspeople alike worship Krishna in the numerous temples of Vrindāvan, in much the same way that worship is offered and *darshan* received in temples all over India. But here there is also a living quality to the *līlās*. They are not just remembered episodes in the life of Krishna. They are plays that give dramatic expression to the birth and childhood stories of Krishna. For example, during the Janmāshtamī festival, a short distance from Rādhāraman Temple in Vrindāvan, devotees have been sitting for days on the floor of a great performance hall to watch the cycle of plays called *līlās*. The episodes of the sacred story are enacted by troupes of young boys specially consecrated for their divine roles and made up daily to be young Krishna, Rādhā, and the *gopas* and *gopīs*.

Hundreds of people sit in the great hall, singing and clapping, hushed and then cheering, watching the enactments of stories they know by heart. No story is more beloved than the *makan chor*, the "butter thief." As a baby, Krishna is utterly mischievous and naughty, always getting into the butter pot for a little fistful of delicious butter. When he is a young boy, Yashodā becomes more inventive, stringing the butter pot high in the rafters. Even then, Krishna manages to shinny up on the shoulders of his friends to reach the butter pot. The young actor Krishna hams it up with his pals, who are complicit in the theft of butter. In another play, Krishna is upset because his beloved flute has been stolen, and the drama revolves around finding and recovering the flute. In yet another episode, Krishna encounters, at last, the wicked king Kamsa and defeats him soundly, dragging him around the stage by the hair. Whatever story is enacted, each of the *līlās* concludes with the *rāslīlā*, the great circle dance. When the dramatic episode is complete, there is a *pūjā* right there on the stage. The *pūjārīs* circle the oil lamps of *āratī* before the face of the actors playing the roles of Krishna and Rādhā. Members of the audience, young and old, women and men, clamber up on the stage with offerings of sweets, flowers, and money to present to the young deities, in person so to speak, placing offerings of sweets right into their mouths.

Pilgrims who come to Braj for a day or a week might visit several of the *līlāsthalas* of Krishna. Depending on the season, they might also enjoy a cycle of Krishna *līlās* performed in the many *līlā* halls. Some pilgrims, however, will undertake a longer pilgrimage through the land of Braj, with the aim of participating even more fully in the realm of the Lord's play. One of the circumambulatory routes, called *parikramas,* takes pilgrims through the sacred woods, pools, and villages of Braj, associated at every step with Krishna. This annual "Forest Pilgrimage," called the Ban Yātrā, takes a group of dozens of pilgrims together through the land, walking for about three weeks, more than two hundred miles in all. Every day, they visit the places linked to Krishna's presence. In pilgrimage parties of all sizes, they depart, accompanied these days by bullock carts loaded with gear, tents, food, and personal baggage. This is not a pilgrim journey to a sacred place or a single destination, but a meandering journey through a landscape saturated with the lore and life of the divine.

The pilgrimage officially begins in Mathurā, but for many Vaishnavas, Vrindāvan is their actual starting point, beginning with a ritual bath in the Yamunā River and the worship of the goddess Vrindā, whose natural form is the sacred tulsi plant. Pilgrims begin with Nature, so to speak, and then turn to the Lord, who reminds them of their own nature. Surprisingly, at the outset of the journey, this is Lord Shiva, who is worshipped at the old Shiva temple called Gopīshvara.[38] It was here, according to tradition, that Shiva himself became a *gopī* to witness and enjoy the sacred *rās* dance of Krishna with the *gopīs*. He was drawn to Braj by the sound of Krishna's flute, but was refused entry and could not cross the Yamunā until he became a woman. So Shiva bathed in the river and emerged a *gopī*. In the sacred circle of the dance of Braj, they say, Krishna is the only male. Everyone else, all the pilgrims, even Lord Shiva himself, the he-man of the Himalayas, is a *gopī*. At Gopīshvara in the evening, Shiva is adorned by the priests with a bright sari and the silver mask of a woman wearing lipstick and eye makeup.

As the pilgrims set out for their weeks in the forests of Braj, they are all *gopīs*, like Shiva. David Haberman's *Journey Through the Twelve Forests* gives a wonderful personal account of this pilgrimage, through the eyes of a scholar-participant. Haberman writes of his own pilgrimage, beginning in Vrindāvan, and his surprise in discovering he had become a *gopī*! "My guide narrated the story of Gopīshwar as we stood before the sari-draped marble figure of Shiva. He then explained that this was the reason I had worshiped the goddesses Yamunā and Vrindā, and had bathed that morning in the waters of the Yamunā. Inadvertently, I had transformed myself into a *gopī*."[39]

The journey through the twelve forests takes place in the rainy season, beginning after Krishna Janmāshtamī, the day of Krishna's birth. It is an auspicious season, to be sure, and one that has drama and beauty as no other. Huge clouds gather and burst, to be followed by sunshine streaming in beneath them, and brilliant sunsets. It is a season of love and longing. For the pilgrim, of course, it will be muddy and occasionally beset with a deluge. While many might associate such a forest trek with a kind of asceticism, for the most part the pilgrims do not think of this pilgrimage as an ascetic practice, but rather a chance to enjoy the presence of Krishna. It is a circular journey, beginning in Mathurā, at Krishna's birthplace, and ending in Mathurā, at Vishrām Ghāt, the place where Krishna rested by the Yamunā River, having killed the wicked King Kamsa.

In the late nineteenth century, British district officer Frederic Growse described the *yātrā* in his book *Mathurā: A District Memoir:* "The number of sacred places, woods, groves, ponds, wells, hills and temples—all to be visited in fixed order—is very considerable; there are generally reckoned five hills, eleven rocks, four lakes, eighty-four ponds, and twelve wells; but the twelve, bans or woods, and the twenty-four upabans or groves are the characteristic feature of the pilgrimage, which is thence called the 'Ban-Jātra.'"[40]

One might imagine that aspects of this pilgrimage noted more than a century ago by Growse may well be very old. But it is really only in the sixteenth century that Braj becomes so thoroughly mapped and articulated with the life and lore of Krishna, as a center of devotion and pilgrimage. The *Mathurā Māhātmya* of the *Varāha Purāna* may well come from this time. The *māhātmya* details the temples, the river *tīrthas* of

the Yamunā, and the various forests and groves of Mathurā and its surrounding area. Indeed, it mentions the Ban Yātrā, the eighty-four-*kosh*,
147-mile pilgrimage through the forests and shrines of this area during
the month when Krishna was born. The sixteenth century also saw the
arrival of Vaishnava devotees of new *bhakti* movements, represented by
Vallabha and Chaitanya, whose followers were respectively to become
the Vallabhite movement (also called the Pushti Mārg) and the Gaudiya
Vaishnava movement. The journey of these pioneering pilgrims through
this countryside was one of remembering, experiencing, and mapping
the places of Krishna's earthly life, and it is this that is at the heart of the
pilgrimage through Krishna's sacred landscape even today.

BRAJ LOST AND FOUND

The process of remembering and reclaiming the old sacred places thought
to be connected to Krishna's life on earth has its own mythic trajectory. In
the Purānic legend, Krishna's destiny was to return to Mathurā and kill
the wicked Kamsa, who had usurped the throne that rightly belonged
to Krishna's uncle. The boy who grew up the foster son of a cowherd
resumed his role as a *kshatriya*. Krishna and his brother Balarāma challenged Kamsa to a wrestling match, and the boys won handily. In the
final act of this drama, Krishna, triumphant, dragged the defeated
Kamsa around the wrestling ring. Thus, after many years, Krishna was
able to bow at the feet of his real parents, Devakī and Vasudeva, and to
place his uncle Ugrasena, Devakī's brother, on the throne of Mathurā.

Even though he had slain Kamsa, Krishna did not return to the
cowherds and milkmaids of Vrindāvan. Rather, he sent Uddhava, his
good friend, to console them and to direct their spiritual lives toward
the study of Vedas and the performance of austerities. They laughed at
poor Uddhava, telling him that such austerities were not for simple village folk and keepers of cows. Their life with Krishna, they said, was
one of sheer love. Their sense of Krishna's presence was only heightened
by his absence. Now they experienced another even more intense form
of love—the longing love of lovers in separation, a longing love called
viraha. But they also experienced his presence through memory and
landscape. The forests, hills, and rivers, the movement of the cows and

the sound of the flute, are all the instruments of memory that now make Krishna present.[41]

In the story, the *gopīs* introduced Uddhava himself to the special places, the forests, the pools, the bowers where they remembered the presence of the playful Lord. Uddhava was drawn in by the emotions elicited from memory and gave up trying to teach them philosophy and meditation! Three generations later, they say, it was Krishna's own great grandson, Vajranābh, who became ruler in Mathurā and who came to Braj to find the places linked to the life of Krishna. According to tradition, Vajranābh searched for the places of Krishna's glory and found them.[42] To him are attributed eight major temples that are part of the landscape of Braj even today—four for Krishna and four for Shiva.[43] But over the centuries, time and the jungles once again left most of the sites of Krishna's life eclipsed from view.

In the sixteenth century, we move into the more recent period of the "siting" and systematizing of Krishna's land, albeit still five hundred years ago. A teacher named Vallabha (1479–1531), a devotee of Krishna and a widely traveled philosopher from south India, is said to have visited the Braj area in the late fifteenth or early sixteenth century.[44] In the village of Gokul, where baby Krishna had lived with Nanda and Yashodā, Vallabha had a vision of the child Krishna, who revealed to him the saving devotional path for the corrupt age in which we live—the Pushti Mārg, the "Path of Grace." Vallabha and his disciples communed with Krishna throughout the rural land of Braj, and especially in the twelve forests that came to constitute the Forest Pilgrimage, the Ban Yātrā. On Govardhan Hill, Vallabha identified an image, then emerging from the hill itself, as an image of Krishna.

Long ago, the villagers said, a cow had spontaneously shed her milk on this very spot. On that spot appeared what seemed to be a hand and arm. At first, they worshipped this form as a *nāga*, a serpent deity. It was, after all, on Nāga Panchamī, the one day in the year when snakes are especially honored, that the arm, or perhaps a snake, appeared. It continued to be honored on that day for many years. Some of the locals saw it, however, as the very same arm with which Krishna had lifted the mountain. They said Krishna was standing within the hill in a rock cave and would manifest himself fully in due time. The image began coming forth from the mountain, they said, in the year 1410, and according to later tradition, Krishna's face emerged in the very year Vallabha was born, 1479. According to the sectarian historians, Krishna had spoken directly to Vallabha, saying, "As you know well, I am present in a cave of Shrī Girirāj under my essential form (*svarūpa*) of Shrī Govardhanadhāra, the Bearer of Mount Govardhan. None but the Brajvāsīs who live there had a vision of Me. Now I intend to make myself manifest to all. For that purpose, I have been waiting for you. So now, you must go quickly to establish my cult (*sevā*) there."[45]

So it was, according to tradition, that Vallabha finally arrived at Govardhan and rejoiced to find this image of Krishna, an image not crafted by human hands, they say, but the self-manifestation of the Lord that had emerged over the course of nearly one hundred years. The image of the beloved Lord manifest fully from the hill became known as Shrīnāth-jī, and he gave instructions to Vallabha as to how he should be attended and worshipped. We shall shortly return to his story.

Another participant in the reclamation of the holy sites of Braj was Chaitanya (1486–1533), a Vaishnava devotee and teacher, an ecstatic saint, devoted to Krishna and devoted to overcoming the proponents of what he considered arid and loveless Advaita Vedanta philosophy. Indeed, for those in his Bengali Vaishnava movement, Chaitanya came to be seen as an *avatāra* of both Krishna and Rādhā in one body. Chaitanya also journeyed through the land of Braj in the sixteenth century with two of his disciples, Rūpa Gosvāmī and Sanātana Gosvāmī, searching out the places of Krishna's life. According to his nearly contemporaneous biographer, Krishnadās Kavirāj, when Chaitanya arrived in Braj, he visited places that made him swoon with love and devotion, and he identified the *līlās* of Lord Krishna in each place. Srivatsa Goswami, a teacher in Chaitanya's lineage today, reminds us that when Chaitanya came to Vrindāvan in 1515, he came as a divine embodiment of both Rādhā and Krishna. "The discovery act of Shrī Chaitanya is a peculiar *līlā*, since for Shrī Chaitanya it was a journey into his own past as Rādhā and Krishna."[46]

Chaitanya seems to have made his own journey through the twelve forests of Braj, and as David Haberman puts it, "he was overwhelmed in these forests, diving into ponds, hugging the trees, and marveling over the deer and the peacocks."[47] Entering into meditation, he identified the place called Rādhā Kund, where Krishna and Rādhā would play water games together. Arriving at Govardhan, "he threw himself to the ground, hugged a rock from the mountain, and became delirious."[48] According to tradition, he carried a stone from Govardhan with him throughout his pilgrimage, a stone that came to bear Chaitanya's own thumbprint.[49] Finding the *līlāsthalas,* literally the "places of Krishna's play," Chaitanya and his disciples created a set of emotional links to the land that Gaudiya Vaishnavas reenergize even today on their pilgrimage through the forests of Braj.

The major contributor to this attempt to "find" and systematize the places of Krishna's life and lore was the scholar Nārāyana Bhatta, born in Madurai, in Tamil Nadu, in 1531 and said to be an incarnation of the celestial sage Nārada. When he was still scarcely twelve, Krishna appeared to Nārāyana Bhatta, so they say, and gave him a small image of himself, directing the boy to carry this image with him to Braj. And so young Nārāyana Bhatta took off with Krishna's image. According to legend, Krishna would periodically emerge from the little stone image as a small boy and run ahead, directing Nārāyana Bhatta to the places Krishna had lived and loved. Thus, with Krishna's help, Nārāyana Bhatta identified the site of the Lord's birthplace in Mathurā, the many sites of Gokul and Vrindāvan, where he had lived as a boy, and the sites of Barsāna, Rādhā's village. In his travels, there were many places where Lord Krishna seemed to reveal himself directly to Nārāyana Bhatta. A cow would spontaneously give forth her milk, for example, and when Nārāyana Bhatta investigated, an image of Krishna would be found in the earth.[50]

The biography of Nārāyana Bhatta has the seductive quality of blending this legendary account with the historical artifacts of dates, books, and emperors.[51] He arrived in Braj in 1545. His prodigious energies seem to have come to the attention of the Mughal emperor Akbar and his Hindu treasurer Todal Mal, from whom Nārāyana Bhatta requested help in excavating ponds and building temples. By 1552, he was living at Rādhā Kund, where he is said to have written a number of books, the most famous of which is the *Vraja Bhakti Vilāsa,* a Sanskrit text detailing the sacred landscape of Braj more comprehensively than any other work, even today. Having uncovered or discovered the many sites of Krishna's *līlās,* Nārāyana Bhatta described them and mapped the basic route of the Ban Yātrā, the Forest Pilgrimage, much as it is still practiced. He has a distinctively theological view, linking the entire landscape to the body of Krishna: "The fifty-five forests, groves, and villages are the various limbs of Bhagavān Krishna. Mathurā is the heart, and the auspicious Madhu-van is the navel. Kumudvan and Talvan are the breasts, and Vrindāvan is the forehead." He goes on to detail the body-landscape of Krishna, right down to his toes.[52]

These sixteenth-century journeys of Vallabha, Chaitanya, and Nārāyana Bhatta identified and brought to life a sacred landscape. Krishna's temples in Mathurā were increasingly under pressure dur-ing the Mughal period, but now the worship of Krishna was sited quite outside the urban environment in the landscape itself. The journeys of these sixteenth-century pioneers largely cast the landscape of *līlāsthalas* that pilgrims visit today. At these many *līlāsthalas*, there are small shrines, larger temples, and images of Krishna, to be sure. Some of the images are said to "emerge" miraculously or are said to be *svayambhū*, "self-manifest," appearances of Krishna or *svarūpa*, the "very own form," of Krishna. Most striking in the accounts of these pioneer journeys, however, is the affection for the land and its features the men experience, and so it is with the experience of today's pilgrims. As the French scholar of Braj, Charlotte Vaudeville, puts it in her landmark article "Braj Lost and Found," "Images and shrines, wherever they are set up, are second-ary: in the realm of devotion, at least, *prakrti-pūjā* takes the precedence over *mūrti-pūjā*, not only in time but also in importance."[53] That is, the experience of Krishna in nature—in the woods, rivers, ponds, and hills of Braj—is the central focus of Krishna worship. It is said that the very dust of Braj, *Braj kī raj*, is sacred.

"Braj is the very form of Krishna," writes scholar David Haberman, recounting his own modern-day *yātrā* through Braj in the company of pilgrims, in his book *Journey Through the Twelve Forests*. It is "a realm where matter matters." Two aspects of nature in particular are under-stood to be *svarūpa*—Govardhan and the Yamunā River. They are, as Vaudeville writes, "the greatest and most ancient *tīrthas* of Braj-bhūmī, which were never 'lost' nor 'found' again."[54] Yamunā, as we have seen, is born a goddess in the high Himalayas and flows through the whole of the land of Braj, skirting Mathurā and Vrindāvan, providing holy water for bathing and temple worship. She comes to be seen as the bride or lover of Krishna in liquid form. And Govardhan, that long, low mountain that

Krishna lifted so effortlessly and held aloft as an umbrella during the torrential rains of Indra, was surely the site of local devotion long before its explicit affiliation with Krishna's heroic feats, and it has persisted as the site of cowherd devotion through many centuries.

Yamunā and Govardhan are central to a much wider landscape, however, in which the entire natural realm of Braj is experienced as evocative of Krishna. The very dust of Braj is considered hallowed by the presence and footprints of Krishna. As Haberman puts it, having experienced the pilgrimage for himself, "Mountains are worshiped, stones touched, trees embraced, dirt ingested, dust rolled in, water sipped, and ponds bathed in. Instead of seeking to penetrate appearances to come to some underlying essence, as does the ascetic, the Braj devotee worships forms and caresses surfaces."[55]

In Braj, pilgrims experience the landscape as infused with the presence of Krishna. It is truly Krishna's world, and the worship of Krishna is hardly a matter confined to the multitude of temples and wayside shrines, but is related at every step to a sacred geography. But, of course, Krishna's wider world extends far beyond Braj too. There are major shrines of Krishna in every part of India, and they are, in a variety of ways, linked to the story that begins here in Mathurā, Vrindāvan, and Govardhan.

SHRĪNĀTH-JĪ, THE CHILD LORD OF THE PATH OF GRACE

At a local temple in the city of Ahmedabad, an old woman in a white sari stands against the railing that separates worshippers from the small altar on which Krishna is receiving his morning ministrations. She lifts her binoculars to her eyes for the *darshan* of Nātvarlāl-jī, a tiny five-inch-high image of Krishna as a child. In point of fact, the woman in the white sari is only a few feet away from the small image of Krishna, but for the devout, a really good look at the divine child requires those binoculars, which they pass from hand to hand, smiling with satisfaction at the close-up *darshan*.

This place is not really called a temple, but rather a *havelī*, a great household, a mansion really, with courtyards and balconies, a distinctive feature of Mughal courtly architecture. In the tradition of the Pushti Mārg—the Path of Grace—it is, indeed, the home and extended household of the ritual officiant of the tradition, who is called the *mahārāj*. More broadly, it is the home of Krishna as Shrīnāth-jī. It is sometimes referred to as Nanda's house, the house where he grew up in Braj in the care of his foster parents, Nanda and Yashodā, though the *havelī* is a far cry from the simple rural homesteads of Braj.

At home here, Krishna is served and honored from morning to night. Eight times a day, Krishna is brought forth upon a small and finely decorated "seat" to meet his devotees. This early-morning *darshan* of the divine child, just as he is being wakened from sleep, is called *mangala darshan*, the "auspicious sight" of the Lord, and it is indeed auspicious to have *darshan* of Krishna first thing in the morning. An hour later, Shrīnāth-jī is dressed and has had breakfast; he receives his flute and is ready for the *sringāra darshan*. Perhaps he will also receive miniature silver tops and toys for the sheer enjoyment of play. By the next *darshan*, he has taken the cows to pasture with his friends; at midday he has his main meal and is presented with a garland of flowers; after his nap, he is awakened with the sound of the conch; in the evening he has a light meal; at the end of the day, he appears as the cows come home; finally, he is readied for the night's sleep. During each of the day's *darshans*, Shrīnāth-jī is dressed in distinctive clothing. Indeed, the wardrobe of Shrīnāth-jī is surely the most extensive of any Hindu deity, with the color, style, and weight of clothing keyed to the time of day and the seasons. At each *darshan*, musicians play music that is right for the time of day and pleasing to the Lord. This *havelī* is truly Krishna's home, where Krishna is honored as the divine child.

The full abundance of the rainy season is at hand and the day called Haryālī Amāvasyā is being celebrated.[56] It is the new-moon day of the monsoon month of Shrāvana (July/August), and the color of the day is green, bright green, like the new life that has come forth everywhere with the arrival of the rains. In the late afternoon, the child Krishna is taken outside into the courtyard for a swing. The *mahārāj*, Krishna's chief caretaker and attendant, wears a green cotton shawl, and the swing itself is intricately covered with a patterned overlay of fresh green leaves. The *mahārāj* tenderly places Krishna in the swing and honors the Lord by swinging him gently back and forth while he sings a beautiful *bhajan* in a strong, classically trained voice. Later, he carries Krishna back inside to a small chapel, where he honors him with the oil lamps of *āratī*.

Seated on his *baithak,* a "seat" or "throne," the *mahārāj* himself receives the devotion of the followers of the Path of Grace as they press forward to touch his foot.

In his own pilgrimage around the *tīrthas* of India, Vallabha established a series of *baithaks,* those seats where he taught. Today, these *baithaks* are found throughout north and central India, from Purī in the east to Junagarh in Saurashtra in the west and Hardvār in the north. They constitute a sacred landscape for this tradition. The landscape expanded as Vallabha himself had sons and heirs. According to legend, when Vallabha was at the great Maharashtrian pilgrimage site of Pandharpūr in the early sixteenth century, he was instructed to marry by Lord Vitthal, also called Vithobā, an especially celebrated form of Vishnu. So he did marry, and thus began a tradition of married teachers and priests. Vallabha's second son, Vitthalnāth (1516–1586), named for Vitthal, was his immediate successor. Vitthalnāth served the image of Krishna at Govardhan, constructing a small shrine and launching daily worship, simply called *sevā,* or "service," in this tradition. He was largely responsible for the distinctive, highly aesthetic articulation of the Pushti Mārg tradition, with its special forms of music, dress, food, and entertainments specific to every time of day and each season of the year.

Vitthalnāth had seven sons, and toward the end of his life he entrusted each of them with one of the images of Lord Krishna under his care in the vicinity of Gokul and Govardhan. Many of these images eventually migrated with the times to other parts of India. Some of them were extremely small, perhaps to render them portable and to escape the notice of Muslim authorities in unfriendly times. The household context of worship, with no distinguishing temple tower or publicly recognizable features, may also have emerged from this period. These *havelīs* were not only indistinguishable from other large households, but also proved to be a fitting environment for the familial nature of the worship of Krishna. For example, the tiny *svarūpa* of Mathuresh-jī became established in the royal court of Kotah in Rajasthan, where a tradition of painting developed depicting the Mahārāja Kishore Singh rendering service to him. From the painted images of his court at Kotah, we see a *mūrti* of Krishna so very small one would truly need binoculars for *darshan!*[57] During the last decades of his life, Vitthal devoted his attention to the sites of Gokul and the service of Shrīnāth-jī, but the many images of Shrīnāth-jī, including the little image of Nātvarlāl-jī in this Ahmedabad *havelī*, are part of an entire network of places linked to the Path of Grace, the Pushti Mārg. The *mahārāj* swinging Krishna in the green-leafed swing at the *havelī* of Nātvarlāl-jī in Ahmedabad is part of this lineage, as are those who serve at all the major *havelīs* of the tradition.

The story begins, of course, at Govardhan, with the image of Lord Krishna as Shrīnāth-jī, the one who emerged from the mountain itself and was worshipped there for many years. In time, a temple was built for him in Mathurā. In the time of the Muslim emperor Aurangzeb, in the seventeenth century, however, when iconoclasm and the destruction of temples and images was a constant threat, the image of Shrīnāth-jī was taken on a cart from its home in Braj and transported westward into Rajasthan.[58] In the Aravalli Hills, in the country just north of Udaipur, the cart got stuck and would move no farther. This was taken as a sign to stay in that place. The temple town of Nāthdvāra grew up around the image of Shrīnāth-jī. It remains the premier center of Krishna worship for the Pushti Mārg to this day, although there are six other important sites for Krishna worship connected to the tradition.[59] The town of Nāthdvāra surrounds the *havelī* of Shrīnāth-jī, here an extensive mansion of hundreds of rooms.

Nāthdvāra is surely the liturgical and artistic epicenter of this tradition today, with painters whose studios have been renowned for centuries. They produce the elegant painted *pichhavais,* which form backdrops suspended behind the image of Shrīnāth-jī in the altar of the *havelī.* One *pichhavai* might depict Shrīnāth-jī and his companions, another Krishna and the *gopīs* in the *rās* dance, and another simply a beautiful multitude of cows. In addition, the artists of the Pushti Mārg tradition here in Nāthdvāra have developed an artistic rendering of Shrīnāth-jī that is recognizable all over India. It is a stocky, black, stylized image with wide curvilinear eyes. He raises his left arm straight up, as if to lift the mountain, and his risen arm breaks through the rim of the ellipse representing the mountain. He is both lifting Govardhan and emerging from a cave within it. He is depicted wearing a very thin, almost transparent, cotton *dhoti* in May and June for the heat of summer, a golden color for the festival of Annakūt in the fall, an elegant red quilted paisley coat for winter, a vivid green for Haryālī Amāvasyā at the beginning of the monsoon season. Shrīnāth-jī is depicted in countless painted images that serve as icons of Krishna in the homes of Pushti Mārg devotees.

Through each day, and through the year, those in the household of Krishna participate in the divine play, the *līlā*, of Krishna expressed in the "domestic" liturgical arts of the tradition. At the times of *darshan*, the curtain is pulled back, and Krishna is seen. However, because he is understood to be a living *svarūpa*, Krishna's own form, his *darshan* is not quite the same as it was this morning, or last week. His familiar image is always somehow new, with a wardrobe that changes with the hour and the season. As Erik Erikson writes in his study of everyday ritualization, *Toys and Reasons*, ritual at its best is playful and yet formalized, combining repetition and surprise. "Far from being merely repetitive or familiar in the sense of habituation, any true ritualization . . . is yet pervaded with the spontaneity of surprise."[60] It depends on the interplay of surprise and recognition. It is precisely this play—being surprised by the recognition of the familiar—that is at the heart of the artistic theology of Krishna as Shrīnāth-jī.

The Pushti Mārg tradition of Krishna worship creates yet another landscape—a linked network of *havelīs*, each housing a small and powerful image of Krishna, and a network of *baithaks* where Vallabha taught. While few pilgrims undertake a systematic journey to all these places, it is clear that this connected landscape provides a mental map of the Pushti Mārg tradition. At any one of these *havelīs*, the pilgrim experience brings vicarious participation as members of the extended family in the daily life of Krishna—his waking and sleeping, his caring for the cows and coming home at dusk, his swinging and his water sports. Visiting a *havelī*, one will catch the Lord somewhere in the daily domestic cycle and enter into that very moment. Coming in the early morning, worshippers might feed one of the cows in the courtyard with a bundle of grass. Later, after breakfast, worshippers might be present for one of the eight *darshans* of the day, as the curtain is pulled back and the attendants bring little silver toys for Krishna's amusement. In the evening, there will be music. All of it is cast in the domestic sphere of the household. Thus, the extended household of Krishna is a kinship network mapped across western and central India. And now, in the twenty-first century, there are Pushti Mārg *havelīs* in the United States, as well, the most extensive being Vraj, a large multimillion-dollar temple complex on three hundred acres of land in rural Pennsylvania, with its own Yamunā River and sacred sites. This Vraj in America now anchors a large devotional community and attracts almost one hundred thousand Hindu visitors yearly.[61]

THE LORD OF DVĀRAKĀ

Mapping the legend of Krishna in the land of India takes us from the sweetness of today's Braj and the playful liturgies of the Pushti Mārg tradition to the far western edge of India and the ancient kingdom of Dvārakā, where Krishna is said to have ruled in his adult years, following the defeat of Kamsa and the restoration of the throne of Mathurā to his uncle Ugrasena. As it happened, the rivalries of north Indian kingdoms continued, and the Yādavas who ruled Mathurā were routed by the Magadha kings, led by Jarasandha. So it was that Ugrasena, Krishna, and the Yādavas fled westward. There, on the seacoast of Saurashtra, on the far-westernmost point of the peninsula, is the place where Krishna built his legendary capital of Dvārāvatī, a city said to be an earthly version of Amarāvatī, the heavenly city of the gods, laid out by the architect of the gods, Vishvakarman himself.[62] The master plan was so elaborate that Krishna needed to ask the sea to recede in order to carry it out. When it was built, Dvārāvatī brought to this earth the finest of everything—from the golden peak of Mount Meru to the gems of the ocean. It was truly heaven on earth. Peninsular Gujarat, then, is the stage on which the final chapter of Krishna's earthly life is played out.

We hear much of Krishna in his new role as king, though for Krishna's devotees this is not as central to their devotion as the circle of love in Braj. Krishna was a wise and strong king, married to Rukminī and, so they say, to sixteen thousand wives. As the clouds of war gathered in Kurukshetra, Krishna received the rival cousins, Arjuna and Duryodhana, both relations, each with a legitimate claim on his help. When offered the choice between having thousands of Krishna's soldiers and having Krishna himself as a noncombatant, Duryodhana chose the soldiers. Arjuna, then, gained Krishna to serve as his charioteer for the battle. In the Bhagavad Gītā, his famous discourse with Arjuna on the first day of the war, Krishna reveals to Arjuna that he is the Supreme Lord who has come into being as an *avatāra* to protect dharma at a time of terrible threat from the forces of disorder, *adharma*. And so does he come into being in age after age. Although this is a war between cousins, Arjuna must not turn away. During the days of battle, Krishna's help as adviser to Arjuna and the Pāndava brothers is critical. The story of the unfolding of that war is complex and elaborately recorded in the *Mahābhārata*. Although the Pāndavas win and their rivals are completely destroyed, the victory is hollow and the world stands in ruins.

As for the relationship of this great drama to the land of India, let us say simply that Kurukshetra itself is a powerful place of pilgrimage even today. Many of its sacred sites claim an antiquity that predates the great battle, and many are associated with the battle itself. One old tree—old, but not that old—is identified as the "immortal banyan tree, witness of Celestial Song, Bhagavad Gītā." Beneath it today is a small marble chariot bearing images of Krishna and Arjuna and the marble footprints of Krishna. Perhaps of most importance as we think about the landscape shaped by the *Mahābhārata*, however, are the many *tīrthas* in India where Yudhisthira, Arjuna, and the other Pāndavas went to seek relief and expiation from the burden of sin incurred by the war. Prayāga is perhaps the best-known example, but there are many others, including Shiva as Kedāreshvara in the Himalayas.

The *Mahābhārata* and the *Bhāgavata Purāna* take the story of Krishna forward after the war. He returned to Dvārakā, his incarnation to overcome the oppressive forces of *adharma* having now been accomplished. The internecine war of the *Mahābhārata* brought the age to a close, and it would soon consume his own clan, the Yādavas, as well, for the clan had fallen under a curse of brahmins who had pronounced its destruction. Krishna, foreseeing the end of the glorious city of Dvārāvatī, brought his retinue to Prabhāsa, now called Somnāth, farther east along the seacoast, in order to bathe in the sacred waters of the ocean there. The time for his departure was at hand.

And why the destruction of the Yādavas, among whom he was born? This strange denouement to the legend of Krishna requires the explanation of the Lord himself. He says, "The Yadu dynasty, which had become unrestrained through its wealth, heroism, and power, was about to devour the world. So it was checked by me, like the ocean by the shore. If I were to leave without restraining the great dynasty of the proud Yadus, this world would be destroyed by their excess."[63] So when they came to the ocean at Prabhāsa, a fight broke out. As if acting out a prescribed drama, Krishna's own people, the Yādavas, became drunken and fought there with one another. Even the blades of grass, when grasped in anger, turned to iron so that they could use them as weapons to bash and kill. Drunk with liquor, casting their friendship and kinship to the wind, they all killed one another.[64] Krishna knew the hour of catastrophic destruction had come.[65]

Taking rest in a nearby grove, manifest in his four-armed form, Krishna was shot through the foot, hand, and heart by the single arrow of a hunter named Jarā. Krishna was reclining there, so they say, and Jarā mistook his reddish foot for a deer and released his arrow. There Krishna died. Today's pilgrims may visit this very spot where Krishna sustained the fatal shot and breathed his last. It is called Bhalka Tīrtha or Dehotsarga, literally where Krishna "gave up his body." It has been restored as a place of pilgrimage by the same Somnāth Trust that rebuilt the Somnāth Temple a few miles away. Today, pilgrims visit this grove, where they will find a marble image of Krishna reclining, his blessed foot covered with the auspicious symbols of divinity. A marble image of the hunter Jarā kneels nearby, palms pressed together in reverence. The Hindi sign reads, HERE LORD SHRĪ KRISHNA GAVE UP HIS EARTHLY BODY. It is said that with the death of Krishna, the Kali Yuga began. This, too, is a *tīrtha*—even and perhaps especially this place where the Lord died and the darkness of the present age began.

As for Dvārakā, the legendary account tells us that as his death neared, Krishna sent his charioteer there to warn the people to leave the city, saying, "The ocean will submerge the city once it has been abandoned by me."[66] That's all the *Bhāgavata Purāna* tells us. The *Vishnu Purāna* confirms the legend: "On the same day that Krishna departed from the earth the powerful dark-bodied Kali Age descended. The oceans rose and submerged the whole of Dvārakā." In the *Mahābhārata*, it is Arjuna himself who describes what happened, having returned to Dvārakā to perform the lasts rites of Krishna's father Vasudeva, who died of grief, and the wives who died along with him on his pyre:

The sea, which had been beating against the shores, suddenly broke the boundary that was imposed on it by nature. The sea rushed into the city. It coursed through the streets of the beautiful city. The sea covered up everything in the city. I saw the beautiful buildings becoming submerged one by one. In a matter of a few moments it was all over. The sea had now become as placid as a lake. There was no trace of the city. Dvārakā was just a name; just a memory.[67]

No wonder the mystery of Dvārakā has elicited such interest over the centuries and is still the focus of controversy. Dvārakā is a thriving *tīrtha* today; indeed it is one of the four *dhāms,* the "abodes" of God, in the four cardinal directions. But what is the relationship between that golden Dvārāvatī that was swallowed by the sea and this Dvārakā that rises glorious on the seacoast today? No wonder major marine archaeological initiatives have taken to the exploration of the coast around Dvārakā and the offshore island called Bet Dvārakā, said to be part of the "city-state" of the legendary Dvārāvatī. Between 1985 and 1989, nine marine archaeological expeditions were mounted; there, beneath the sea, they found remains of old ramparts, buildings, and streets. Some of the remains could be dated to the age of the *Mahābhārata* in the second millennium B.C.E., according to S. R. Rao, whose book *The Lost City of Dvārakā* explores the data produced from the marine archaeological explorations.[68] Even earlier materials were also found, suggesting an ancient port with active trade at the height of the Indus Valley civilization; and later ruins were found too, suggesting that the city was submerged not once, but several times.[69] Interpreting the marine excavations has produced hot dispute—from those who see this as proving the historicity of Krishna and his city to those who do not think the ruins point to any such conclusion at all.

Fascinating as it is, what was "really there" at this ancient port is only marginally relevant to the legendary city of Lord Krishna and to today's city of pilgrimage bearing the same name. The landscape of the faithful is not shaped by archaeology, but by a faith that simply assumes the connection between Krishna of old and Krishna here today. The story of discoveries at sea may bolster those for whom the "quest of the historical Krishna" is important, but for most of the faithful who come to Dvārakā today, it is not. Their journey presumes the reality of Krishna—then and now.

The Saurashtra peninsula that juts out into the Arabian Sea is flat farming land, fertile under irrigation and producing crops of cotton, corn, wheat, ground nut, and red chilis. At the very end of the peninsula, the farthest-west point in India today, the great temple of Dvārakā soars up from the edge of the sea with its tall *shikhara* and a huge golden flag flying from the very top. The waves of the Arabian Sea wash the tip of the peninsula, roll in from two directions, splashing together before sliding up the beach. The temple is virtually on the beach itself, although on higher ground. One can well imagine how vulnerable it would be to the rages of the open sea. Along the beach, pilgrims hunt for stones called Dvārakāshīla or Dvārakāchakra, white stones imprinted with the delicate *chakra*-marks of Krishna's discus. For Vaishnavas these stones are like the *shālagrāmas* found only in the Gandakī River in Nepal or like the stones of Govardhan: Without invocation or consecration they are natural, elemental forms of Krishna himself. One can take them home just as they are, place them on the home altar, and offer daily *pūjā* to Krishna.

The image of Krishna here at Dvārakā is jet-black, four-armed, like that of his counterpart in Mathurā. Pilgrims stream into the temple through the doorway called Svargadvāra, the "Door of Heaven." The evening crowd gathers and the temple bells ring, resounding in the dark interior. Among those in the temple this evening are thirty pilgrims from Madhya Pradesh for whom this is the final stop on their *chār dhām* pilgrimage. They have come from visiting Purī and Rāmeshvara; last year they made it into the Himalayas to Badrīnāth. Tonight, they are here, at last, at Dvārakā. Krishna is decked in rose-colored silk garments with a silver brocade border. The priests are dressed in matching rose side-tying vestments and wear dark rose-colored stoles. The principal priest shows Krishna his own reflection in the mirror before undertaking the series of offerings that constitute the evening *pūjā*. He places a silver flute in Krishna's hand. He advances water offerings to the Lord and then sprinkles the water over the crowd, all hands extended for a drop of the blessed substance. Then, standing straight with the erect posture of a yogi, and with a strong arm, he circles the heavy silver candelabrum of oil lamps before the black face of Krishna, with reverence, elegance, and grace.

Krishna has departed this world. Yet here in Dvārakā, as everywhere in India, Krishna is very much present to the community of the faithful. How are we to understand this? One writer, K. R. Vaidyanāthan, asks the question plainly: "What happened to the Lord when He departed after fulfilling the purpose of His *avatāra*? That beauteous form with all the auspicious marks in which He manifested Himself in flesh and blood to the people of His time is preserved for all time in the sanctified idols of our temples."[70] This is, in a sense, the theology of the image that pervades the understanding of Krishna devotees: Krishna was among us as "flesh and blood" and now remains among us in the sanctified images of temples. Among the most precious of these images are those that are said to have come from Dvārakā itself. So captivating is the legend of the disappearance of Dvārakā that, not surprisingly, many places link their sanctity to this place.

UDUPI AND GURUVĀYŪR: THE IMAGE OF KRISHNA FROM DVĀRAKĀ

Among the finest of Dvārakā images is one said to have been created by the great artisan of the gods, Vishvakarman, for Krishna's mother Devakī. It was created to satisfy Devakī's yearning to have an image through which she could continue to behold Krishna as a child. The image the artisan created was of Krishna holding a butter churn. It was much beloved not only by Devakī, but also by Krishna's wife Rukminī, who also cherished it in Dvārakā. After the swamping of Dvārakā, Arjuna is said to have found and recovered this particular image of Krishna and hidden it in the Rukminī Forest just outside the city. Here again, we see the pattern of loss and recovery; the image was lost, covered over with a mass of sandal-paste mud called *gopī chandanam*. Eventually it was found again, but hundreds of years later and a thousand miles away, on the seacoast in southwestern India.

According to legend, after many, many centuries, the heavy image, indistinguishable as a form of Krishna, was taken on as ballast by a sea-going ship. Hundreds of miles to the south, along the Malabar coast of

Karnataka, the seas became rough and the ship was about to go down. Just then, the captain saw a holy man standing on the beach, waving his garment seaward. The seas miraculously became calm. That holy man was the thirteenth-century sage and philosopher Madhva, whose home was in the town of Udupi, a short distance from the Malpe beach where he stood. The grateful captain of the boat offered Madhva anything he wanted from the boat's cargo. To the captain's surprise, he chose this mud-covered ballast, which he knew to be an image of Krishna.[71] "The source of this legend is not known," writes Kannada scholar Bannanje Govindacharya, but he gives greater credence to a simpler version of the story, written down by the head of one of the monastic institutions of Udupi in the eighteenth century, as part of a commentary on the life of Madhva: A ship carrying the image from Dvārakā was wrecked off the Malpe coast and sunk to the bottom of the sea. Madhva found the mud-covered image at the seashore and established it in Udupi.[72]

So it was that Dvārakā's image of Krishna came to Udupi more than seven hundred years ago. This image of the young Krishna holding a churning stick and a string was cleaned and sanctified by Madhva, and a temple was built to house the image. On the wall outside the main entrance to the Krishna temple today is a painting depicting Madhva, standing on the beach, calming the storm by waving his ochre garment. Madhva, the great Dvaita, or Dualist, philosopher, was born near here, in coastal Karnataka in the early thirteenth century.[73] He traveled as a seeker and student throughout the sacred cities of India before settling in Udupi. His heart's favorite among the tīrthas was Badrīnāth in the high Himalayas, which he is said to have visited three times, the last time as he finished his life's work and prepared to die at nearly eighty years of age.

Madhva's home, however, was Udupi, the temple town still today renowned for its Krishna temple, as well as for an adjacent Shiva temple and eight mathas, or monastic institutions, established by Madhva. The swamis of these eight mathas serve the temple in a complex rotation called paryaya, each having a period of service lasting two years, serving Krishna in the temple with fourteen periods of worship each day.[74] This paryaya system also generates a set of pilgrimages. As each swami prepares to take the helm every sixteen years, he makes a tour throughout the tīrthas of India "from Kanyākumārī to Badrīnāth" obtaining bless-

The chariots of the gods at Udupi

ings for his tenure of service and collecting donations for the *paryaya* festivities. Again, we see how the linked landscape of a broader Bhārata serves as authorizing authority for brahmin priests in a local context.

In a sixteenth-century legend, we hear how Krishna made it clear that he was to be visible at Udupi to everyone, high and low, regardless of caste. A devotee named Kanakadāsa came as a pilgrim to Udupi but was unable to enter the temple because of his station in life as a shepherd. So he sang songs of devotion outside the temple, and Krishna, they say, was moved by his song. The Lord opened up a crack in the temple wall and turned 180 degrees to face west so that Kanakadāsa could have his *darshan*. Rather than patch up the crack, the temple authorities turned it into a window, which they dubbed Kanakadāsa's window, through which everyone can peep in from the outside and see Lord Krishna. Today, it is customary to peek through Kanakadāsa's silver-framed and highly ornate window before entering the temple for *darshan*.

The *darshan* of Krishna takes place not only in the temple, but in the streets as well, especially in the circumambulatory street surrounding the temple square, called Car Street. The town plan of Udupi is typical of many south Indian towns: a cluster of temples at the center and a square processional route for public *darshan*. Here, as in many great temples, the images specially consecrated for public processions are taken out of the inner sanctum and placed in a vehicle to see and be seen by the people. The gods now become pilgrims as well. Amid fireworks, holiday lights, and cheering, Krishna comes out almost every evening for a ride. The *rathas*—variously called "cars," "chariots," or "carts"—are sometimes as simple as a wagon, but here in Udupi the three temple *rathas* are huge and elaborate. The largest of the three *rathas* is at least thirty feet high, with wheels the height of a full-grown man. The superstructure of the *ratha*, corresponding to the *shikhara*, or spire, of the temple, is a thatched beehive shape. The priest carries the processional image of Krishna up a ramp into the sanctum of the cart. The *ratha* is then pulled round the processional streets by dozens of devotees, leaning forward into long, thick ropes, gathering their own share of blessings for participating in the evening's journey. For at least nine months a year, halting only in the rainy season, these *ratha* processions around the streets are almost a nightly feature, usually sponsored by the contributions of a devotee.

The grace of the town of Udupi is evident in the streets and coffee-houses today. "It is the great fortune of this land to have given birth to the Acharya Madhva and to have obtained the idol of Krishna from Dwaraka." So say the authors of *Udupi, Past and Present*.[75]

Farther south along the coast, in what is now Kerala, is another of the great images linked to Dvārakā: the image of Krishna at the temple of Guruvāyūr. This image is the four-armed image of Krishna that Devaki and Vasudeva saw on the night of his birth: carrying the conch, the discus, the mace, and the lotus. It is this image that is seen in the temple of Dvārakādhīsha in Dvārakā today, as well. Again, the story begins as Krishna approaches the time of his departure from the earth. According to tradition, Krishna told his friend and disciple Uddhava that he would become manifest in an image and that Uddhava should care for it when Dvārakā would be submerged in the ocean. He should be sure it was established at another holy place, to be determined in consultation with the guru of the gods, Brihaspati.[76]

When Dvārakā had been swept away, Guru Brihaspati came to that site with the lord of the wind, Vāyu. They implored the lord of waters, Varuna, to withdraw for a time, so that the image of Krishna could be retrieved. Vāyu retrieved the image and carried it on his head. Then the two of them, Brihaspati and Vāyu, went looking for another place to install this image of Krishna. They carried the image round about the kingdoms of north India and through the south as well, looking for a suitable place. Along the southwestern coast they met Parashurāma, one of the *avatāras* of Vishnu, who had reclaimed the whole seacoast of west India from the sea—from Gokarna to the tip of India at Kanyākumārī. In fact, Parashurāma informed them that he had been on his way to Dvārakā to look for this very image in order to bring relief to people with certain rheumatic illnesses. Guru Brihaspati and Vāyu were invited to install the image in an area called Rudratīrtha, at the edge of a lovely lake and near the seacoast in Kerala, a place already occupied by Shiva and Pārvatī. However, Shiva was happy to withdraw so that Krishna could dwell there. Indeed, it was Shiva who insisted that Brihaspati and Vāyu install the image in a temple, which then became known as Guruvāyūr. Here Krishna is known as Guruvāyūrappan, the "Lord of Guruvāyūr." Today Guruvāyūr is sometimes called the "Dvārakā of the South," and its *māhātmya* claims that this image of Krishna takes the very form Krishna took when he revealed himself to Devakī and Vasudeva on the night of his birth.

Here we have no historical anchor like Madhva to give us a sense of the times, and the story is clearly set in mythic time. It is said that Guru and Vāyu had the temple built by the architect of the gods, Vishvakarman, the same architect who had also designed Dvārāvatī. We do know, however, that Guruvāyūr became famous as a place of healing and was praised lavishly in a sixteenth-century hymn, composed by Melpathur Nārāyana Bhattathiri, a scholar and songster. This hymn, the *Nārāyanīyam*, remains, even today, the most beloved hymn of Guruvāyūr devotees. The author himself was healed of exceedingly painful arthritis by Guruvāyūr. According to the legend, Bhattathiri was moved by the suffering of his own teacher who was afflicted with the disease and he pleaded with the Lord to transfer his guru's affliction to his own body. So it happened. Bhattathiri himself took his teacher's rheumatism. But gradually, as he composed and sang the *Nārāyanīyam*, based on the *Bhāgavata Purāna*, his pain subsided. In the hundredth section, he evokes the Lord before his very eyes. *Agre pashyāmi,* "I see him before me," is the famous refrain. And in the closing verse, he prays, "May this *Nārāyanīyam* give us here in this world longevity, health, and happiness."[77] Bhattathiri's health was completely restored. To this day, the many stories of Guruvāyūr's healing touch abound.

Pilgrims arriving here find a quiet temple nineteen miles from Trichur, the nearest city of any size. Guruvāyūr is set amid tall palms, the temple grounds exuding an atmosphere of peace. Devotional songs, including the *Nārāyanīyam*, are playing on loudspeakers. It is well known that "longevity, health, and happiness" are the blessings of pilgrimage to this place. The striking beauty of the temple is made all the more dramatic by row upon row of oil lamps that protrude from the enclosing wall, surround the temple on all sides, and enhance the approach of the pilgrim. Literally thousands of flames flicker in the evening light. In 1970, the temple was devastated by fire, but today it has been rebuilt, including the surrounding regiments of oil lamps.

The "customs of the temple" are listed on the temple's literature: Worshippers are enjoined to bathe in the Rudratīrtha adjacent to the temple before entering and are encouraged to enter the temple with wet clothing; as in many south Indian temples, men are asked to enter bare-chested; no cameras or mobile phones are to be taken inside the temple; worshippers are to avoid the advances of fraudulent guides not affiliated with the temple authority.

Among the long-standing customs, however, is that "only Hindus are allowed to enter the temple." Like many temples in the south, Guruvāyūr has a long tradition of brahminical orthodoxy. The temple at Guruvāyūr was one of those targeted by a Gandhian *satyagraha* movement in the 1930s aiming for temple-entry privileges for untouchables. Eventually this battle was won, leading to the Temple Entry Proclamation of the Maharaja of Travancore, now Kerala, issued in 1936. Its preamble read, in part, "Profoundly convinced of the truth and validity of our religion, believing that it is based on divine guidance and on all-comprehending toleration, knowing that in its practice it has throughout the centuries adapted itself to the needs of changing times, solicitous that none of our Hindu subjects should, by reason of birth or caste of community, be denied the consolations and the solace of the Hindu faith. . . ." On this basis, no one who was "Hindu by birth or religion" was to be denied temple entry. Still, only Hindus were to be allowed entry at Guruvāyūr, and the temple entry controversy has continued. In 2007, the Kerala government proposed to add the words "or faith" to "Hindu by birth or religion," allowing for those with "faith" in Hinduism to enter. For many years the prime exemplar was the Christian singer Yesudās, who has made heartfelt recordings of Guruvāyūr's devotional songs popular all over Kerala. But Yesudās has never been allowed to enter the temple. He has often said that he could imbibe the presence of Krishna perfectly well from outside. But public controversy over Hindu and non-Hindu temple entry has flared for the first time in seventy years and has become embroiled with the thorny issue of just who *is* a Hindu.[78]

In the case of Udupi and Guruvāyūr, it is the image itself that has brought significance to the place. This, too, as we have seen, is a powerful way of construing a sacred geography: The divine image is lost and found again, and it is claimed by multiple temples. We could add to this group the temple of Krishna called Rinchor in Dakor, just to the west of Ahmedabad, where another series of legends links Krishna to Dvārakā. In that case, the story is of an aging devotee who used to make the trek from Dakor to Dvāraka on a regular basis to honor Krishna with *tulsī* leaves he had grown himself. Eventually, he became too old and lame to do so, and so he drove to Dvārakā in a cart intending to seize Krishna and take the image home with him to Dakor. Despite the security precautions of the Dvārakā Temple, Krishna was willingly kidnapped and spirited away in the cart to Dakor, where he is honored today as Rinchor. Here, as with the other legends, it is the powerful presence of the Krishna image and its linkage to the luster of Dvārakā that is important. The claim to have a great image of Krishna from Dvārakā does not necessarily link these places to one another, however. Each anchors its own faithful clientele.

Purī: Jagannātha, Lord of the World

The image of Krishna as Jagannātha is readily identifiable all over India: a blockish black image, virtually all head, with large saucer-disc eyes and little stumps for arms. He doesn't stand alone, but is always in the company of his brother Balarāma and sister Subhadrā. They, too, share the blockish physique and the large eyes, though Balarāma is white and Subhadrā yellow. The three of them occupy the sanctum sanctorum of one of the most prestigious temples in India, the temple of Jagannātha at Purī. How these deities came to be represented in this distinctive way poses a multitude of questions that have made the cult of Krishna Jagannātha in Orissa the focus of intense scholarly investigation.

On the beach in the early morning, a woman makes an image of these three deities, drawing it carefully with her finger in the sand. It is an ephemeral icon, made to focus her attention for her morning devotions by the seashore. When she has finished her prayers, she takes a pinch of sand from her creation, turns to the waves, and places it in the water. Within moments, on the smooth sand where the image she scratched has slipped away, others are standing, unaware of the temporary image of god once at their feet.

While Guruvāyūr and Udupi are near the beach, there is no ocean-bathing component of their regular ritual life. On the whole, Hindus rarely bathe in the ocean as a ritual matter; the running waters of rivers or the sacred waters of temple tanks are for ritual bathing. Indeed, the sea is often used as the latrine, continually flushed with the rising and retreating tides. But here at Purī, it is different. Bathers come to the ocean's edge in the morning as they do at the *ghāts* of the Gangā in Vārānasī, greeting the rising sun with their devotions and ablutions. Most pilgrims are unfamiliar with the currents of the sea and are both thrilled and frightened by the waves. There are lifeguards in pointed hats who keep watch as morning bathers duck beneath the waters in their ablutions.

Purī, too, is one of the four *dhāms*, or divine abodes, situated in eastern India, all the way across India from Dvārakā on the coast of the Bay of Bengal. It sits on a slight hill called Nīlāchala, a short distance from the beach. This twelfth-century temple is one of India's largest temple complexes, covering some four hundred thousand square feet. The series of pillared halls, called *mandapas,* that lead to the inner sanctum are progressively larger and taller, and the *shikhara* rising over the sanctum is well over two hundred feet high, capped by a large ribbed, circular sun-stone. Every day, its kitchens—said to be the largest temple kitchens in all India—make *mahāprasād* for some fifteen thousand people, with more than five hundred liters of milk and 3,200 kilograms of rice.

There is at least one tradition that also connects Purī with Dvārakā: that the body of Krishna, which could not be consumed by fire, floated all the way from the coast of Saurashtra, around Cape Comorin, and up the east coast of India, where it was discovered here on the seashore by the tribal people of Orissa. It eventually became a tree, out of which an image of the Buddha was made, the Buddha being the next *avatāra* following Krishna. This tradition is recorded by the Oriya epic writer Sarala Dāsa in the fifteenth century.[79] C. G. Tripathi, Anncharlotte Eschmann, and H. von Steitencron, authors of groundbreaking studies of Jagannātha, all agree that the cult of Jagannātha, now firmly identified with Krishna, has very complex underpinnings, with historical roots in earlier religious traditions and in the tribal cultures of Orissa.

Von Steitencron, for instance, clearly sees that Buddhism, Jainism, and Shaivism all had influence in Orissa much earlier than Vaishnavism, which, he writes, is "by far the latest major Indian religion to reach central Orissa, the area where today Jagannātha dominates the religious scene."[80] As for Buddhism, the very name Purushottama, the most ancient name of the site, is an epithet of the Buddha, as are the names Jagannātha and Lokeshvara, one of the Shiva temples in Purī. As for the Shākta and Shaiva traditions, von Steitencron notes that the low hill called Nīlāchala, on which the temple sits today, was once the domain of the goddess named Vimalā, who is "the presiding goddess of this place," the *kshetrādhīshvarī*. We have often seen the ways in which Shakti predominates in her claim to the very earth beneath any city or temple. While her prominence on Nīlāchala is obscured today by the massive Krishna temple, her shrine still is present in the sacred precincts, and she is the first to receive the *prasād*, the consecrated food offerings that only then become the *mahāprasād*, the "great grace of the Lord," to be distributed to the worshippers. Her central place is also indicated by the centrality of Krishna's sister Subhadrā in the triune Jagannātha group. In addition to the goddess, we find, at a distance around the Jagannātha temple, numerous Shiva temples of "considerable antiquity." All of this indicates, according to von Steitencron, that this was probably a Shaiva and Shākta place of worship long before it became identified with Krishna.

Anncharlotte Eschmann identifies the substrate of worship here with the tribal or aboriginal traditions in which the anthropomorphic representation of the deity is rare and aniconic symbols like posts or stones are far more common. The process she calls "Hinduization" includes the incorporation of many such deities into the broader entourage of the

great gods. In rural Orissa, the post-deity is identified with a local goddess known simply as Khambheshvarī, the "post-goddess." In addition,
however, the post-deity often represents the man-lion Narasimha who,
after all, is said to have manifested his form from a pillar. That was when
Vishnu's great devotee, Prahlāda, was taunted by the evil Hiranyakashipu to show him just where his beloved "god" might be. Striking a
pillar, he asked, "Is he in this pillar?" And there the Lord was, bursting forth from the pillar. From the perspective of iconography, Narasimha is worshipped throughout Orissa and northern Andhra Pradesh
in forms that resemble the blockish, postlike form. And remember the
image at Simhāchalam—an image with no real shape at all, covered with
sandal-paste to look more like a Shiva *linga* than an image of Narasimha.
From the perspective of temperament, the Narasimha form of Vishnu,
who tears open the chest of Hiranyakashipu, is certainly the one that
best enables the strong and sometimes fierce tribal deities to find a home
in the Vaishnava fold. It must also be said, however, that the relationship
of Narasimha and Shiva, who also emerges from the shaft of a *linga,* is
quite close here, and elsewhere in India.

At Jagannātha, Narasimha is iconographically prominent in the temple itself, his image carved many times on the outer walls and standing
prominently right at the entrance to the temple complex. Even more,
Narasimha is worshipped at the outset of temple rituals and at the times
when the Jagannātha images are said to be indisposed or ill, during the
periods of their yearly renewal. And during the month when the images
are replaced, indeed reborn, through the elaborate ritual of identifying
auspicious trees and carving new images, the mantras of Narasimha are
an important part of the ritual recitation.[81] Indeed, as we shall see, both
the goddess and Narasimha have a role in the rites of Navakalevara, the
"New Embodiment."

Local traditions and the Purushottama Māhātmya of the *Skanda
Purāna* have another story about the images of Jagannātha, Balarāma,
and Subhadrā. In brief, it is about a king named Indradyumna who had
heard of the powerful deity of Nīlāchala and set out on a pilgrimage
to pay his homage. As he approached the coast, Indradyumna learned
that the image had disappeared. When he arrived, grief-stricken, he
worshipped Narasimha and had the vision of a great world-tree rising
from the ocean. Indradyumna found the very tree of the vision, and a

divine carpenter told him to leave him alone for fifteen days, drums beating constantly, so that none could see or hear the creation of the divine image. In this version of the story, the king was overcome with eagerness to see how things were going and peeked in before the process was complete. Thus, the image-making was abruptly halted and the images were fixed as they were at that point—stubby and blockish in shape.

Here at Purī the images themselves are of primary and powerful importance. As a place of pilgrimage, Purī is not simply about "what happened there," as is often the case in the Krishna homeland of Braj. As at Udupi and Guruvāyūr, it is precisely the presence of these particular powerful images that draws pilgrims to this place. But how are wooden images preserved over the decades and centuries? Here, the story of Indradyumna and the auspicious tree comes into play again as we encounter the elaborate and revealing rituals of Navakalevara, the "New Embodiment." In these rites, the wooden forms of the Jagannātha deities are given new bodies. This takes place every twelve or nineteen years, when the intercalary month, added to the Hindu lunar calendar to align it with the solar calendar, falls in the summer month of Ashādha. Not surprisingly, many call this month Purushottama Month, after the ancient name of Jagannātha. And not surprisingly, the renewal of these deities is largely in the charge of the local tribals called Daitas.

As the process begins, three Daita chiefs, who will be in charge of the search for a new tree, are given special "garlands of authorization," flower garlands that have been worn that morning by the temple deities. The search party includes both Daitas and brahmins, the latter to be in charge of rites to be performed after the tree is identified. The group camps in a forest about thirty miles from Purī, where the shrine of the goddess Mangalā is located, and the worship of this goddess is the first order of business. She is said to offer signs for the search, pointing the direction of a likely tree through the head Daita's dream-vision or by the way the first flower falls from her head during the *pūjā*. Tradition prescribes a long list of qualities a tree should have if it is to be cut for the image of a deity, including the presence of a wheel or conch marking on the trunk. Of course, the tree must be straight and solid, and it will be a neem tree, since these are long-lasting. As each tree is identified, it is honored with the "garland of authorization" brought from its counterpart in the temple and presented with the honor-offerings of *pūjā*. At this point, the Brāhmins have a role, measuring and building a temporary *yajnashālā*, a "sacrificial arena," next to the tree. A fire altar is kindled and the rites of *vanayāga*, "sacrifice to the tree," are performed. The local deities residing in the grove are asked to give their blessing to the tree-cutting. Throughout this process, the presiding deity is Narasimha and the main mantras recited are those of Narasimha. Now the Daitas take charge. Three axes have been present in the ritual arena, and when the rites are finished, the Daitas receive the axes and cut down each tree. They measure a log of the appropriate length, about eight feet, which is then carefully wrapped in silk and placed on a cart for transport to the temple complex in Purī. The logs for Balarāma and Jagannātha are also bound with two thick branches to serve as arms. The rest of the tree is buried on site.

One by one, the carts return to Purī, where their arrival is heralded and they are greeted with music and dancing. Indeed, sometimes the king of Purī himself comes out to greet the trees. They are placed in a special shed within the temple compound, where they will receive the ritual bathing called *abhisheka* and will then be carved by Daita crafts-men wearing silken turbans, given by the king, a sign of their authorization to make the images. As in the legend of Indradyumna, no one may see the work as it proceeds and no one should even hear the sounds of the work. Musicians are set outside the craftsmen's shed to play loudly the entire time. It takes almost two weeks for them to create the images. During this same time, the priests of the temple are performing consecration rites, which they do by consecrating a piece of wood taken from one of the trees. This consecrated wood will have an important role in the midnight rites to follow.

When the logs have been carved, these basic forms are transported into the inner sanctum of the temple in the middle of the night. They stand as skeletal unfinished wooden images facing their counterparts. Soon they will be covered with the strips of cloth and layers of resin that will give them final form before they are painted. But now the most important rite takes place: The Daitas remove the cloth coverings from the old images, layer by layer. All the lights are extinguished, and in the pitch dark the critical rite is performed. One of the Daitas, wearing a blindfold, opens the hollow cavity of the old image, reaches in with a hand that has been wrapped to the elbow so that he cannot feel anything, and removes the "immortal life substance," called the *brahmapadārtha,* from the old image and places it in the inner cavity of the new image. Then, from that piece of wood consecrated by the brahmins, a plug just the right size is carved to place in the hole, sealing the new image with the immortal life substance inside.[82] Many are the speculations as to just what the *brahmapadārtha* is, but so far it remains a mystery, even to those closest to the rituals. The old images are now considered dead, and the aboriginal devotees observe rites of mourning and bury them in a graveyard near the temple.

The Daitas now apply layers of cotton cloth and resin, sandal and camphor paste to give the image "flesh," so to speak. The painters then take over and apply the distinctive brilliant colors to the images. Only then, when everything is almost finished, are the brahmin priests given their concluding responsibility: painting the pupil in the eyes of the deities. The images are ceremonially purified and then brought to the great *rathas,* the chariots, waiting outside the temple, along with tens of thousands of people.[83]

The renewal of the images occasions one of the greatest pilgrim gatherings in India. It occurs at the time of the annual Ratha Yātrā and is an amplification of what is already a huge crowd gathered for one of India's most renowned pilgrimages. Each year, during the summer month of Āshādha (June–July), Jagannātha, Subhadrā, and Balarāma are moved out of the temple to the summer residence at the garden called Chandrabhāga, where the Gundīchā Temple sits. For two miles down the wide processional street the faithful pull the huge chariots, straining together on the thick ropes that eventually start the great wheels moving. Jagannātha's chariot, the largest, is more than forty-four feet high, with sixteen huge wheels. This temple, like that in Guruvāyūr, is closed to foreigners and non-Hindus, but the public procession of the deities here is spectacular. Especially at the time of the New Embodiment, the public *darshan* of the deities is cherished. Tens of thousands of pilgrims stand on tiptoe to catch a glimpse of the gods and stretch out their arms to get a hand on the ropes that pull them through the streets.

From Purī, our journey with Krishna in the land of India comes full circle back to Braj. It was in the sixteenth century that the Bengali Chaitanya first came to Purī, and there is much in his biographical legend that connects him with this place. It is said that from seven miles away, when first he saw the temple tower, Chaitanya began to dance for joy. When he entered the temple and beheld Jagannātha, he fell completely unconscious. His biography records, "I rushed to embrace Jagannātha. What happened afterwards, I do not remember." We remember the emotion Chaitanya is said to have exhibited in Braj, when he arrived there a few years later with his disciples Rūpa and Sanāthan Gosvāmī, swooning at the places of Krishna's *līlās*, holding fast to the rocks, and hugging the trees. He certainly brought this supercharged devotional sensibility to Jagannātha, to which he returned often on his journeys. His devotion to Krishna here was profound. He is said to have swept and washed the Gundīchā Temple at the time of the Ratha Yātrā and prostrated himself before the wheels of the chariot. He was overcome with tears of emotion each time he beheld the Lord. In the year 1533, Chaitanya died in Purī. He is said to have died in the presence of Jagannātha. He is said to have vanished into the Lord's image or disappeared walking into the sea.

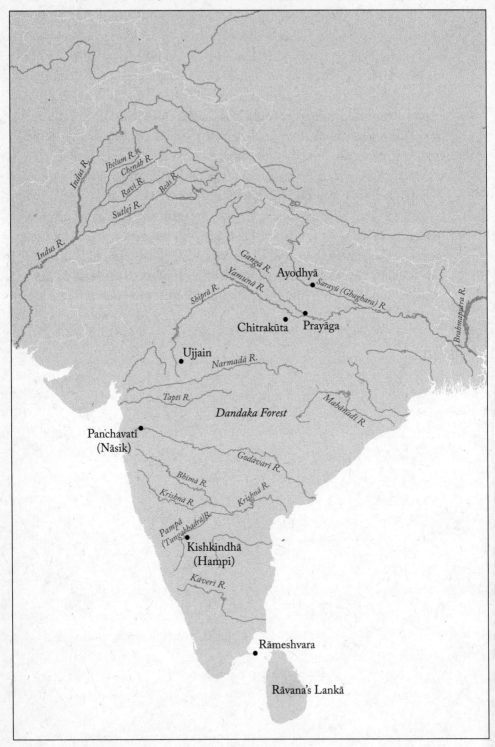

9

FOLLOWING RĀMA: THE *RĀMĀYANA* ON THE LANDSCAPE OF INDIA

The *Rāmāyana* is the most beloved epic of India. The story of Rāma, the "Journey of Rāma," penetrates Hindu consciousness and culture to the extent that it is almost universally known. In our explorations of sacred geography, we note immediately that because the legend is based on a journey, it creates a landscape and a map. The footprints of the heroes and heroines of the *Rāmāyana* are tracks that we can follow through the land of India.

The Sanskrit *Rāmāyana*, said to have been composed by the sage Vālmīki, tells a very, very old story. Indeed, it displays evidence of the world of north India prior to the rise of Buddhism, probably before the sixth century B.C.E. But, more important, it is also a living epic, told in the vernacular languages of every region of India. The most well known of these regional and vernacular versions of the *Rāmāyana* come from the past thousand years, with their surging religious devotion to Rāma as the Supreme Lord. Kamban wrote the Tamil *Rāmāyana* in the twelfth century, Krittivāsa wrote his version of the *Rāmāyana* in Bengali in the fourteenth century, and Tulsīdās composed the influential Hindi *Rāmāyana*, the *Rāmcharitmānas*, in the sixteenth century. This living epic also extends its reach beyond India and its Hindu context. The *Rāmāyana* is popular among a largely Buddhist population in Thailand and Cambodia and a largely Muslim population in Indonesia. Indeed, the Thai city of Ayutthaya, named for Ayodhyā, was for four centuries the capital of Thai kings, many of whom took the name Rāma. For many centuries throughout India and across Southeast Asia, the legend of Rāma has been represented in cultural arts, in ritual, sculpture, drama, and dance. The *Many Rāmāyanas*—regional, poetic, colloquial—described in Paula Richman's work immerse us in a cultural universe in which people have told, retold, and refashioned this legend over the course of many hundreds of years.[1] In this volume, A. K. Rāmanujan writes that the Rāma legend constitutes "almost a second language of the whole cultural area."[2]

Why does the legend of Rāma have such a tenacious hold on the hearts of so many people? In one sense, it is but one of the myriad mythic stories of a world of competition between the gods and demons, a world in which the demons are constantly gaining the upper hand and threatening the well-being of the gods and the order of dharma. Here it is Rāma who confronts and defeats the ten-headed Rāvana and establishes a kingdom where dharma reigns once again. We should remember that Rāvana had a special boon that made him utterly fearless of death at the hand of either gods or demons. He had practiced severe asceticism, accumulated the power that comes from ascetic practice, and won a boon from Lord Brahmā. His boon? Neither gods, nor *rākshasas*, nor serpents, nor other classes of supernatural beings would be able to kill him. He thinks he is safe, but he fails to even entertain the possibility that a human, not a god, might bring him down, or that his challengers in the end will be men fighting in the company of monkeys. Rāma is a human king, or as Vālmīki tells the tale, he is a partial *avatāra* of Vishnu, half-human and half-divine.[3] He is a human king, with his own frailties, and yet godlike, and he is the only hero who can slay the demon-king.

The *Rāmāyana* is also one of many stories in which a righteous prince is exiled from his kingdom and lives in the forest. Such was the story of the Pāndava princes of the *Mahābhārata* who lost their kingdom unjustly in a rigged gambling match. Their forest exile was to last twelve years, with a thirteenth year to be lived incognito in the forest before they could return to claim their kingdom. In this case, it is Rāma who is unjustly exiled for fourteen years in the forest. In the forest, of course, he encounters the denizens of the wild, defeats the wicked and defends virtue. In the forest exile, he is accompanied by his faithful brother Lakshmana and his devoted wife Sītā.

The drama that unfolds during the forest exile is simple and poignant. While they are living in the forest, Sītā is abducted by the trickery of the demon Rāvana in disguise. She is carried off through the air to his kingdom in Lankā, dropping her scarf and her ornaments along the way, hoping they will be found. Rāma, heartbroken and mad with grief, sets off with Lakshmana to search for her. Finally, they recruit allies of monkeys and bears to help them find her. When they discover she is on the island of Lankā, they first must build a bridge across the sea to get there. In the end, they challenge the powerful Rāvana and ultimately win Sītā back. The fourteen years is over, the kingdom is restored, and a reign of peace and justice begins in Rāma's capital, Ayodhyā.

The simplicity of the tale of wrenching separation, search, and triumph, however, is but the frame for a complex human drama that touches the heart, stirs the emotions, probes family jealousies and bonds, ethical dilemmas, and the meaning of human life. As the story unfolds, it is far more than a personal drama of family rivalry within the kingdom of Ayodhyā. We begin to see it as a cosmic struggle of the king of dharma with truly vast forces of disorder and evil. The exile in the forest, even the kidnapping, is necessary as part of this cosmic struggle in which Rāma has a unique role as the one able to subdue Rāvana.

EXILE AND SEPARATION

The action of the *Rāmāyana* is driven from beginning to end by the theme of exile and separation. In one sense, it is a love story filled with the emotion and poignancy of separated lovers. The epic begins as the sage Vālmīki witnesses the death of one of a pair of mating lovebirds, shot by a hunter's arrow. As the bird dies, the mate cries out in what, to Vālmīki 's ears, is a cry of utter anguish. The sage was so moved by this scene that he spontaneously composed the first line of poetry ever written. Yes, sympathetic grief (*shoka*) gave birth to poetry (*shloka*). And so was born, according to Vālmīki, the verse form in which most of the epic is composed, the *shloka*.

The connection between separated lovebirds and the themes of the *Rāmāyana* is not incidental. To begin with, it prefigures the fateful separation of King Dasharatha from his son Rāma. On the joyful eve of Rāma's coronation as successor to Dasharatha, one of the king's wives, Kaikeyī, reminds the king of a boon he had once given her to choose anything she wished. In this moment, she decides what she wishes. And what does she choose? Her own son Bhārata will be crowned king and Rāma will be sent into exile in the forest for fourteen years. The palace and the city of Ayodhyā are turned upside down with the shock of this news, for Rāma is much loved by the citizens. Bhārata is out of town, ignorant of what has happened. Rāma insists on being true to his father's promise. Rather than ascend to his father's throne, he prepares to leave for the forest and enable his anguished father to keep his word. A word of promise, after all, once given, cannot be broken without threatening the very fabric of dharma. With him go his wife, Sītā, who is the very model of the faithful wife, and his brother Lakshmana, who is strong, somewhat impetuous, but ever loyal.

In the background of the epic is another story of the pain of separation: Long ago, King Dasharatha mistakenly shot a young boy who was drawing water at the river for his aged parents. Dasharatha was a fine archer, able to shoot merely by hearing the sound of his prey at a distance. He thought he heard the sound of an elephant drinking from a nearby river and he released his arrow. Upon approaching his prey, he was horrified to find a dying boy who had been filling a water pot for his aged and infirm parents. With his dying breath, the boy told the king where his parents were waiting for him. Dasharatha found the aged parents and told them just what he had done. Grief-stricken, they asked to be carried to the place where their son's body lay. They prepared his young body for cremation and then joined him in death, entering the pyre with their son. As he was about to die, the boy's father told Dasharatha that he, too, would be separated from his own beloved son and die of grief. And so, many years later, this is just what happens. The moment the king can neither see the dust of Rāma's party leaving Ayodhyā nor hear the sound of his chariot, he collapses in grief. On the sixth day after the departure of Rāma, his eldest son and heir, Dasharatha dies.

The brothers suffer the grief of separation, too. Bhārata, shocked to find what has happened in his absence, seeks out Rāma in the forest, determined to persuade him to return to the throne. He finds Rāma at the hermitage of Chitrakūt, but is unable to change Rāma's resolve. Bhārata returns, heartbroken, to Ayodhyā to place Rāma's sandals on the throne. For the duration of the exile, he lives not in the palace, but in a hut, taking on the life of an ascetic and awaiting the return of Rāma.

Most poignant, however, is the separation of husband from wife, as Sītā is kidnapped from the Panchavatī Forest by the trickery of the demon king Rāvana. The rest of the epic is driven by the search for Sītā, as Rāma and Lakshmana pursue every clue until they reach the region of southern India called Kishkindhā. There, the rainy season begins and they have to suspend their search, making Rāma's emotional yearning for his beloved all the more intense. While there in Kishkindhā, however, they gain an unlikely set of allies—the monkey Hanumān and an army of monkeys and bears. After the rains, the search begins in earnest. Hanumān's search party finds Sītā—imprisoned in the garden of Rāvana in Lankā. Winning her back requires a long battle, but eventually Rāma and his allies defeat Rāvana. Sītā and Rāma are reunited and return to Ayodhyā.

Even then, however, the sorrow of separation is not over. In Vālmīki's *Rāmāyana*, the citizens gossip about Sītā's long captivity in the palace of Rāvana and speculate about what might have happened there in the house of another. This unseemly talk leads the dharma-conscious Rāma to send Sītā away to a hermitage in the forest so that the citizens will have no doubt about his integrity. Again, the two are separated. There in the forest she gives birth to their twin sons, Kusha and Lava. They grow up in Vālmīki's hermitage and learn to recite the whole legend of Rāma, becoming famous for their recitation of the story that we know as the *Rāmāyana*. Then, one day, they come to Rāma's own court and sing the story. Rāma is shocked to recognize that it is *his* story, and these are his sons. The story has come full circle, with Rāma's heirs. In the end, Sītā returns to the earth, whence she came, and Rāma enters into heaven, walking into the waters of the River Sarayū until they swallow him up.

The story of the *Rāmāyana* has been told and retold, sung and enacted in countless ways. This epic tale has a long and multiform life in the many cultures of India and Southeast Asia. Most important for us in our geographical explorations, however, is the remarkable fact that this great legend has been written into the landscape of India. Its stories have been made real and alive in the footsteps of pilgrims, who seek out the places where Rāma, Sītā, and Lakshmana traveled.

INDIA, THE GREAT STAGE OF THE *RĀMĀYANA*

A landscape is larger and more sweeping than any single feature. A landscape takes the measure of distances and perspectives. It links places together, evoking pleasure, emotion, and connection. It is little wonder that the *Rāmāyana* has created a landscape that has become its own "text," so to speak. Entering into this landscape tells us a great deal about the ways in which this epic has been owned by Hindus in their pilgrim journeys. The drama is cast on an all-India stage, stretching from the Himalayas in the north to the shore of the Indian Ocean at Rāmeshvara.

Some of the places linked to the epic are famous throughout India, like the capital city of Ayodhyā, where Rāma's lineage of solar kings reigned, where Rāma was born, and where he entered into heaven at the end. The exile from Ayodhyā took Rāma, Sītā, and Lakshmana to many other places, famous and widely known. First, they traveled to Prayāga at the confluence of the Yamunā and Gangā Rivers, where they stopped at the ashram of Bharadvāja. Following his advice, they journeyed southwest to the hermitage called Chitrakūt, where they stayed for some time before pressing on south to the forest of Panchavatī around the present sacred city of Nāsik. It was here, they say, that Sītā was abducted by Rāvana who came in the guise of a hermit. The search of Rāma and Lakshmana for Sītā took them farther south, to the area called Kishkindhā and the hill of Malayavat on the River Pampā, in what is today Karnataka. Here they met Hanumān and Sugrīva who, with their armies of monkeys and bears, aided Rāma in the recovery of Sītā. Finally, at the far southern shore of India, they came to the long spit of land stretching out toward Lankā, the island said to be today's Sri Lanka. They honored Shiva there and the place became famous as Rāmeshvara. From that seashore, they built the famous bridge to Lankā, with the enthusiastic help of the monkey and bear regiments of Hanumān and Sugrīva.

The *Rāmāyana* is an epic of exile, so much of the action takes place far from cities and towns. The forest sets the stage. The broad term for the forest is *vana*, the "woods" where ascetics and sages have their hermitages. The fourteen years of Rāma's exile are often referred to as the *vanavāsa*, the forest-dwelling years. The three royals, exiled from Ayodhyā, live in and around the hermitages of forest-dwelling sages. They dress in the fibers of the forest made from leaves and bark. And around the campfire, they certainly learn tales and truths from the forest sages. They live virtually as ascetics. But they are not ascetics. Rāma and Lakshmana are princes skilled in arms and kings with an obligation to protect their subjects. So the forest is also the place where they do battle with the demons, *rākshasas*, that threaten the lives of the ascetic sages who have made their retreats there. The deeper forest, the wilderness, called the *aranya*, is filled with the threats of demons and beasts. The most famous of the deep forests of Rāma's journey is the Dandakāranya, the Dandaka Forest, stretching across central India.[4] Entering into the Dandaka Forest, Rāma is welcomed by the forest sages, who call on him, as king, to protect them. Tulsīdās adds a flourish here: Rāma sees a pile of bones and asks what happened. They tell him that these are the bones of the sages who have been devoured by the demons. Here Rāma vows to rid the earth of demons, and this is his mission in the Dandaka Forest, and beyond. Eventually it is here that his beloved Sītā is snatched away by one of those demons.

No matter how much or how little the bards who told Rāma's story may have actually known about the whole of India, their tale takes place on the great stage of the land itself. Ayodhyā, Prayāga, Chitrakūt, and Rāmeshvara became well-known landmarks on the stage. But this forest journey, traversing vast stretches of India, lends itself to being claimed by countless locales, by all the in-between places not famous on the all-India map. These places are perhaps acclaimed only locally. Taken as a whole, the journey of Rāma and the search for Sītā creates a complex sacred geography. As Tulsīdās tells it, everywhere they went, whether town or forest, became sanctified by their presence. "All the towns and villages that lay on their way were the envy of the cities of the gods. The lakes and rivers of the gods lauded those lakes and rivers in which Rāma bathed. The tree of paradise gave glory to the tree in whose shade Rāma rested, and when earth touched the dust of Rāma's lotus feet, she deemed her blessedness fulfilled."[5] Obviously, this kind of journey is highly suited to local subscription. The villages and towns that claim to have been blessed with the presence of Rāma's party must be legion. Here they worshipped. Here they stopped on their journey. Here they encamped. Here Rāma performed the death rites for his father Dasharatha. Here is Sītā's kitchen where she cooked for Rāma and Lakshmana. Indeed, the multiplication of Sītā's kitchens from Ayodhyā to Chitrakūt to Nāsik and many places in between may constitute a study in itself! In sum, the possibilities for remembering the epic story are as wide as India, the great stage on which it was enacted.

It is important to note here that the very notion of the *tīrtha* as it came to be so prominently developed in the *Mahābhārata* and the Purānas is not fully present in the text of the Sanskrit *Rāmāyana*. The itinerary of the Pāndavas in the Vana Parva of the *Mahābhārata* is much later and is plotted around places already identified as *tīrthas*. This is not the case in the *Rāmāyana*, however, where the geography of the exile's time in the forest is plotted from one ashram or forest hermitage to another, identified primarily by the *rishis*, ascetics, and sages who dwell there. There is the ashram of Bharadvāja in Prayāga, of Atri in Chitrakūt, Agastya in Panchavatī, and of Shabarī in Kishkindhā. Given the later importance of the *tīrthas* in Hindu popular culture, it is quite amazing that they are very rarely spoken of in the *Rāmāyana*. We do know that by the time of the *Mahābhārata*, one of the characteristics of a *tīrtha* is the empowering presence of the ascetics and *rishis* who congregate there. It is perhaps an indication of the antiquity of the Rāma legend that the story of the journey is told without the elaborate armature of *tīrthas* that are part of the Tīrtha Yātrā Parva of the *Mahābhārata*, a section of the epic that is said to date from around the second century C.E.

As one might imagine, the alleged sites of the episodes of the *Rāmāyana* are not without dispute. Most famous is the controversy that has raged about the location of Lankā. Is Lankā really the island of Sri Lanka, as is believed by today's pilgrims? In 1914, Sardar M. V. Kibe of Indore propounded the interesting thesis that Lankā was really located at Amarakantaka, that site in the mountains of western Madhya Pradesh where the Narmadā River rises.[6] Others have held the view that Lankā was somewhere along the east coast of Andhra Pradesh. D. P. Mishra's study, *The Search for Lankā*, locates the stronghold island of Rāvana in the Godāvarī delta.[7] These theories are based in part on the peculiarity that the Narmadā River, which flows so prominently across central India north of the Godāvarī, is not mentioned in the *vanavāsa* account of the *Rāmāyana*. The only way Rāma's party could have journeyed from Chitrakūt to the Godāvarī River without fording the Narmadā would have been to travel southeastward from Chitrakūt, toward the Orissa and Andhra coast. It is not only the exact location of Lankā that is disputed, however, but also that of Chitrakūt, Kishkindhā, Panchavatī, and even Ayodhyā.

We cannot enter into the complicated and, frankly, insoluble problem of where these sites "really" were, for they are "really" part of an ancient and powerful myth that might lend itself to geographical or historical speculation, but not geographical or historical certainty. In pilgrimage traditions, however, this scholarly controversy has had little traction. If we follow the lead of pilgrims, we learn where these sites came to be located and mapped in the mythic lore and ritual enactments of the people. Today, pilgrims throng to Ayodhyā and Chitrakūt, bathe in the Godāvarī at Nāsik and deem it to be Panchavatī, and travel to Rāmeshvara and the place of the famous bridge to Lankā. For pilgrims, there is no doubt in their minds that these are the places sanctified by the life and legend of Rāma. The importance of these places is told in the countless local *māhātmyas* that praise their origins and their power. In the story of Rāma as it is known today, these are the places that are important, along with the countless local shrines of the in-between.

These are complex places, though. What we find as we follow today's pilgrims across the map of the *Rāmāyana* is not an unalloyed devotion to Rāma. On the whole, there was no cult of Rāma in which Rāma was worshipped as Supreme Lord until the last five or six centuries. Rāma is an *avatāra*, to be sure. Rāma is the king-exemplar. Rāma is the model hero and the champion of dharma. There is no question that he is regarded as "divine," for Hindu understandings of the divine span a spectrum that those in the West divide too bluntly into divine and human. Rāma

The Mandākinī riverfront in Chitrakūt

incorporated the worlds of both humans and gods. After all, Rāvana's boon from Brahmā was to ask that he be invulnerable to death, except at the hand of a human. He imagined, of course, that human beings were good for food, not for battle. To say Rāma was not "worshipped" as such in no way diminishes his great importance, for Rāma's legend had long been embraced, depicted in temple sculpture, and written into poetry, even before the apotheosis of Rāma as the Divine Lord that came with the fervor of Tulsīdās, for instance. Rāma was also a great devotee of Shiva, and as we follow the tracks of Rāma across India, we will very often find ourselves standing with pilgrims in the temples of Shiva, some of them said to have been established by Rāma. And, of course, we will also find countless shrines of Hanumān, Son of the Wind, Shiva's Son, and Rāma's devotee.

AYODHYĀ

The great city of the Rāma legend is Ayodhyā, known to the Purānas as one of the seven *moksha*-granting cities of India. Present-day Ayodhyā sits on the banks of the Sarayū River in north India, adjacent to the modern city of Faizabad. The Sarayū, spanned now by a new rail bridge, is said to flow from Lake Mānasa in the high Himalayas at the foot of sacred Mount Kailāsa. It is in some ways a dilapidated town, with the relentless problems of poor electrical service, poor roads, and poor sanitation that plague so many towns of its size. Pilgrimage is its primary business, and tens of thousands of pilgrims flock to Ayodhyā during its great pilgrimage seasons. They come especially for the *panchakroshī* pilgrimage circumambulating Ayodhyā during the Rāmnavamī festival celebrating the birth of Rāma in the spring month of Chaitra, in April–May.

The legends of Ayodhyā cast the mythic imagination back to the time of King Sagara and his grandson Bhagīratha, famous for bringing the River Gangā from heaven to earth. Like many of the old sacred places of India, Ayodhyā has a complex history, layered with Jain and Buddhist, Shaiva and Vaishnava traditions, and one that has been studied by many historians.[8] Ayodhyā is no doubt a very old place. Archaeologists have dated some of the remains of the Ramkot area of the city to the seventh century B.C.E., when this was the capital of the ancient kingdom of Koshala. The city was known in the ancient Buddhist world of north India as Saketa, a place visited by the Buddha himself in the sixth century B.C.E. Saketa was also important to the Jain tradition as the traditional birthplace of Rishabha, the first of the *tīrthankaras*, the spiritual "ford-makers" of the tradition. For Hindus, Ayodhyā was and is associated with the legendary events of its most celebrated son, Rāma, the descendant and rightful heir of the throne of the solar kings. From the time of Vālmīki's *Rāmāyana*, the name of Ayodhyā, the "Unconquered," has been linked with the saga of Rāma as hero and king. The model of the god-king, Rāma held a powerful place in the structure of Hindu kingdoms across India. But to understand Ayodhyā as a center of religious devotion to Rāma, we look to the more recent past. The careful historical and textual work of scholars has placed the beginnings of the actual worship of Lord Rāma in Ayodhyā in the eleventh or twelfth century C.E.[9]

The popularity of Ayodhyā as a place of devotion and pilgrimage may be an even more recent phenomenon. The emergence of Rāma's Ayodhyā has many parallels to the "rediscovery" of the sites of Braj associated with the legend of Krishna. This *bhakti* devotional spirit focused on Rāma began in the late fourteenth and early fifteenth centuries. The *bhakti* saint Rāmānanda popularized Rāma devotion during his lifetime, in the latter half of the sixteenth century. His influence spread with the many *bhaktas* who counted themselves as his disciples, such as Kabir and Tulsīdās. Hans Bakker, who has translated and annotated the *Ayodhyā Māhātmya*, has placed it in the context of this time. Its myths and praises render the portrait of an Ayodhyā dominated by Rāma, but with many older, established traditions, especially those of Shiva. In the *Ayodhyā Māhātmya*, for instance, the most important site associated with Rāma is the Svargadvāra, the "door to heaven," a bathing *tīrtha* along the Sarayū River where tradition holds that Rāma ascended to heaven at the end of his life. Of course, later popular *māhātmyas* also extol Rāma's birthplace, the Janmasthān, and other nearby sites associated with the Rāma legend, such as Sītā's palace called Kanaka Bhavan and the basement chamber known as Sītā's kitchen, but these are not part of the older *māhātmya* tradition.

It is important to note that many sites of Shiva are not only mentioned, but praised in the various versions of the *Ayodhyā Māhātmya*.[10] Indeed, among the most important deities of the city is Nāgeshvaranātha, Lord of the Nāgas. Even today, pilgrims who make their way down the slippery bank to bathe at Svargadvāra in Ayodhyā will find this Shiva temple right next to the bathing *ghāt*. This temple is not simply one of the many to be found adjacent to the *ghāts*. On the contrary, priests will tell the pilgrims that without the worship of Shiva Nāgeshvaranātha one will not reap the benefits of pilgrimage to Ayodhyā.[11] This *linga* is said to have been established by Rāma's own son Kusha. According to Hans Bakker, Nāgeshvaranātha "is considered the presiding deity of Ayodhyā."[12] The present temple dates to the eighteenth century, but the tradition of such a *kshetrapāla*, or "territorial protector," is clearly much older. It is well known that Shiva, like the Buddha, gathered into his entourage in ancient north India both the popular cults of the *nāgas* and the *yakshas*, the guardian deities associated with pools and groves. Bathing at Svargadvāra and honoring Shiva as *kshetrapala* is said to be the foundation of Ayodhyā pilgrimage. As Peter Van der Veer put it in his study of Ayodhyā, "The most important of the many temples on the *ghāts* are undoubtedly those dedicated to Shiv, even though Ayodhyā is the place of Ram."[13]

Going from the riverbank into the streets of the town of Ayodhyā, pilgrims quickly find that the liveliest shrine in all Ayodhyā today is that of Hanumān Garhī, the Fort of Hanumān. They climb up a long staircase to this hilltop temple, a marble temple compound at the heart of the city of Ayodhyā where, again, the primary deity in the sanctum is not Rāma. It is his chief devotee, the monkey Hanumān, who offers his *darshan* from beneath a mountain of marigold garlands and gladiolas. His image is covered with orange *sindūr,* and only his orange face is visible, with silver eyes and a silver vertical Vaishnava marking on his forehead. Around the perimeter of the temple compound are smaller shrines where pilgrims will find images of Rāma, Sītā, and Lakshmana. The walls are covered with tiles bearing the names of Rāma and Sīta. But the primary deity here is Hanumān himself. Pilgrims "vote with their feet," and by that count Hanumān Garhī is the center of Ayodhyā's religious life. As one of the contemporary *māhātmyas* of Hanumān Garhī puts it, "When Sri Rāma, the lord and master of Ayodhyā, was about to return to his eternal abode, he handed over the charge of defending Ayodhyā to

Hanumān. From then on, Hanumān was regarded as the lord and ruler of Ayodhyā."[14]

Hanumān is an important link between Rāma and Shiva, since the monkey-god is often regarded as the son of Shiva and even as a manifestation of Shiva. Indeed, Bakker notes that devotion to Hanumān was already well established among Shaiva *sannyāsīs* before the cult of Hanumān rose to popularity within Rāma *bhakti*.[15] The author of the modern Hanumān Garhī *māhātmya* links the importance of Hanumān at Ayodhyā to that of Shiva, saying, "Hanumān is regarded as the eleventh Rudra, an incarnation of Shiva. So in and around Ayodhyā, Hanumān Garhī and Nāgesvarnāth are regarded as places of prime importance. Pilgrims who come to Ayodhyā first of all bathe in the river Sarayū and pour a jug of water at Nāgesvarnāth. Then they worship Hanumān and return home. Most of these pilgrims are not aware of the importance of the birthplace of Sri Rāma or of Kanakabhavan."[16]

The *māhātmya* perhaps overstates the case. Rāma's sites are clearly very important in Ayodhyā and have been so for perhaps five hundred years. At the same time, however, the history, literature, and ritual life of Ayodhyā remind us that the importance of the city as a *tīrtha* is much broader than Rāma legend, much broader than any single temple or *ghāt*. As a *tīrtha*, it is one of the seven cities that bestow liberation, and its power is not linked to Rāma alone, but includes its presiding deity, Shiva, and its present guardian, Hanumān. We will later return to the controversies surrounding the site regarded as the birthplace of Rāma, the Janmasthān.

CROSSING THE GANGĀ, ON TO PRAYĀGA

On leaving Ayodhyā for exile in the forest, Rāma and his party traveled to the Gangā, the first river to be crossed on their journey. They described the beauty of the sacred river, with its trees and flowers, its herons and murmuring waves. It was there on the bank of the Gangā that Rāma and Lakshmana made their hair into *jata*, the mass of dreadlocks worn by ascetics, thus symbolically entering into the ascetic life of the forest. As they crossed the river, Sītā threw flowers into the Gangā as offerings. There, she made a vow to honor the river goddess with gifts of cows and a thousand and one other offerings on safe return from fourteen years of forest exile. That first night, the exiles made their bed in the forest, gathering grass and leaves and lying down under a banyan tree.

The first major stop mentioned in the *Rāmāyana* was Prayāga, where Rāma, Sītā, and Lakshmana are said to have stayed with the sage Bharadvāja at his ashram in the open land between the two rivers. The site of Bharadvāja's ashram is today still part of the pilgrim itinerary in Prayāga. Pilgrims who visit this site will find a small temple dedicated to Rāma, Sītā, and Lakshmana, along with some Hindi verses from Tulsīdās's *Rāmāyana*. For the most part, however, it is Shiva who is centrally honored in Bharadvāja's ashram. In the main temple, restored in 1968, pilgrims will place their flower garlands on a Shiva *linga* with a copper-plated *pītha* holding what appears to be an ancient stone. The sage Bharadvāja is represented to one side of the *linga*, and a fine orange Hanumān guards the door. Coming and going along the alleyway, pilgrims will see many small temples, containing many *lingas* in various states of repair. They will not be disappointed to find that this place of legendary antiquity is also home to a new goddess, Santoshī Mātā, made popular through the *māhātmya* of a 1970s film.

According to the *Rāmāyana*, Bharadvāja invited Rāma and his party to stay for some time with him, but Rāma preferred to press on and find a place somewhere farther away, where he would not be besieged with people following after him from Ayodhyā. Bharadvāja recommended the hills of Chitrakūt, a day's journey to the southwest, and so they left. The three royals would return again to Bharadvāja's ashram, at the very end of the fourteen-year exile, just before coming home to Ayodhyā.

CHITRAKŪT

Bharadvāja described Chitrakūt as a sacred hill, surrounded with groves where many saints had hermitages, devoted themselves to meditation, and attained heaven. Arriving in Chitrakūt, the three new forest-dwellers were welcomed at the hermitage of Vālmīki himself, and they built their own hut not far away. As Tulsīdās tells the tale, they were greeted by the forest dwellers, who exclaimed, "Happy that land and forest and road and hill where thou, my Lord, hast planted thy foot! Happy the birds and deer and beasts of the forests whose life has been crowned by thy sight; happy we and all our kin who have filled our eyes with thy vision! Thou hast chosen an excellent spot to dwell in; here in all seasons of the year thou wilt live at ease."[17] Rāma, Sītā, and Lakshmana did indeed come to love the hills, the deer, peacocks, and cuckoos, the flowering trees and lotus blossoms that open near the banks of the Mandākinī River. Here in the area surrounding Chitrakūt hill, they first settled in the forest. They loved the sylvan beauty of this place. Remarkably, today's Chitrakūt and surrounding area still have the restful feel of the woodlands. There is no question in the minds of today's pilgrims to this place that they are following in the footsteps of Rāma. They find the "impressions of his footprints" (charana chihna) in the very stones of the surrounding countryside and they raise the cry Bole Raja Rāma Chandra ki jai! Victory to the great King Rāma!

At dawn in Sītāpur, the central village of Chitrakūt today, the air is filled with the morning sounds of an awakening center of pilgrimage. Pilgrims splash and bathe at Rāma Ghāt or Rāghava Prayāga Ghāt, along the banks of the Mandākinī River, skirting Sītāpur. They scoop up brass vessels of water, utter their prayers, bargain for flower garlands, and then clamber up the steep steps to worship in a popular temple high above the riverbank. One by one they clang the temple bells to announce their presence—to Lord Shiva. Here in the busy center of Chitrakūt, the pilgrims and daily worshippers who converge in the early morning on this most popular of temples have come to worship Shiva, whom they here call by the name Mattagajendranāth. There is no question that along this peaceful river, where pilgrims say that Rāma once walked, it is Shiva who is preeminent in the early-morning prayers of the devout. Here, as in Ayodhyā, he is called the kshetrapāla, the "territorial guardian," of this area. The Shiva Purāna mentions this linga as having been established by Lord Brahmā himself.[18] While we might expect to find one or more prominent temples remembering Rāma's sojourn during the vanavāsa, what we find here in Chitrakūt is a ritual milieu with strong Shaiva underpinnings. At Chitrakūt, the ritual relation of Shiva and Rāma is articulated in a popular saying attributed to Tulsīdās: "Shiva's best bhakta is Rāma, and Rāma's best bhakta is Shiva."

This theme—that Rāma worshipped Shiva at this and other promi-

nent sites of his *vanavāsa*—is part of the local *māhātmya* of several of
the great sites associated with the *Rāmāyana* today. Rāma was no doubt
very devout and appealed in his own devotion, interestingly, not to
Vishnu, with whom he became linked as *avatāra*, but to Shiva. While
this theme does not appear at all in the Sanskrit *Rāmāyana* of Vālmīki,
it is articulated in later and vernacular versions of the *Rāmāyana*, such
as the *Adhyātma Rāmāyana*, the Hindi *Rāmcaritmānas*, and the Bengali
Rāmāyana of Krittivāsa, all of which date to the fifteenth and sixteenth
centuries, the period of the flowering of Rāma *bhakti*. More important,
this theme of Rāma's devotion to Shiva is articulated virtually without
question in the landscape of sacred places associated with the *Rāmāyana*
today, a landscape that has its own tale to tell.

In Rāma's time Chitrakūt is said to have been the forest dwelling of
ascetics and sages. According to its local *māhātmya*, this place has an
unbroken tradition of spiritual adepts.[19] In addition to Vālmīki's ashram,
the sage Atri and his wife Anasūyā had their ashram here. Tradition has
it that through the power of Anasūyā's service to Shiva and to her husband Atri, the River Gangā also came to this place.[20] This Gangā rises at
Anasūyā's ashram, several kilometers from the village of Sītāpur, and is
called the Mandākinī, the name of the River of Heaven. The river swings
through Sītāpur, where its fine *ghāts* are at the center of Chitrakūt's pilgrimage life. A few miles away is a transposition of the famous Godāvarī
River farther south. There, intrepid pilgrims will find a river that rises
and begins to flow inside a cave. With a pilgrim-guide, they wade in
knee-deep water into a claustrophobic series of interior cave chambers,
to bathe in a river called the Gupta Godāvarī, the "Hidden Godāvarī."

The most important of the green hills of Chitrakūt is the one called
Shrī Kamadnāth or Kamadgiri. This hill, mentioned as the "sacred
hill" by Bharadvāja, is clearly the ancient place of honor at Chitrakūt,
famous before Rāma and Sītā ever came here. Virtually every pilgrim to
Chitrakūt will circumambulate the hill, for local lore instructs pilgrims
to bathe at Rāma Ghāt, have the *darshan* of Mattagajendranāth, and
then proceed along the road to Kamadgiri.[21]

No one sets foot upon this tree- and rock-covered hillock. For the
most part, it is the domain of monkeys who perch on the boulders. By
contrast, the path pilgrims take around the mountain is well worn,
indeed mostly paved. All along the way, the loose stones of the mountain

to the pilgrims' right are daubed with red *sindūr.* Many of these stones are said now to be Rāma's footprints, the *charana chihna* of Rāma. The way they are ritually treated is readily comparable to the stones of Mount Govardhan in Braj. A stone of Kamadgiri, like the stones of Govardhan, is naturally sacred and in no need of consecration or invocation in order to be a suitable focus of worship. Such a stone is sometimes referred to as Rāmasvarūpa, the very embodiment of Rāma, or at Govardhan, Krishnasvarūpa. As at Govardhan, pilgrims circling the hill will find a *mukharvind,* literally a "lotus mouth," of the mountain, which represents the whole sacred mountain and receives offerings. Here, they will see a stone face, bearing Vaishnava markings. In fact, they will gradually find that there is not a single *mukharvind,* but four, one in each of the four directions of the hill. Locals will tell them that these "mouths" appeared of their own accord.

The whole cult of the hill, as well as the Kamadnāth Temple at the end of the circumambulation, bespeaks a popular and probably ancient practice with its roots elsewhere than in the traditions of Rāma. In local traditions today it is not clear whether this mountain is identified with Rāma, or with Shiva, or the Goddess, even though its stones are called Rāmasvarūpa. The temple contains modern, rather doll-like images of Rāma, Sītā, and Lakshmana, but its big black-faced image of Kamadnāth suggests quite another ritual and mythic idiom, perhaps linked with ancient *yaksha* traditions.

Rāma himself came to the hill of Chitrakūt because it was known to be sacred. It is fitting, therefore, that this *parikrama* of the sacred hill is filled with reminders of Rāma and the *Rāmāyana.* On the route around the hill, pilgrims stop to receive *charanāmrita,* the water that has washed the feet of Rāma. They find a small wayside plaza called Shrī Bhārat Milāp, where Bhārata is said to have met his brother Rāma, having followed his route into the forest after the death of their father Dasharatha. Bhārata's mission was to persuade Rāma to return to the throne of Ayodhyā. Rāma, of course, refused, having promised Dasharatha he would spend fourteen years in the forest. Dejected, Bhārata returned again to Ayodhyā. Tulsīdās writes that the very rocks melted with grief when the brothers parted.[22]

Continuing their circuit around the hill, pilgrims find a shrine beneath a large tree containing the wooden shoes of Hanumān. Of course, strictly speaking, Hanumān was not yet an ally of Rāma in the days Rāma spent in Chitrakūt, but such historical details matter not the least to the devotional memory of the pilgrim here. Where Rāma is, there is Hanumān. Indeed, one of the most important shrines of the entire area is Hanumān Dhārā, located across the Chitrakūt landscape several miles, on top of another hill.

In the wider area of Chitrakūt, pilgrims find many reminders of Rāma and Sītā in the form of footprints, called *charana chihnas*. Pilgrims will find and touch these traces of their feet at a place called Jānakī Kund, named for Sītā, daughter of King Janaka, on the banks of a small river. At Rāmashayya, they will see where Sītā and Rāma slept the night and Rāma laid his bow between them. Just above Hanumān Dhārā, they will find Sītā kī Rasoī, Sītā's Kitchen, where there is a hand-painted sign reading, HERE SĪTĀ MADE FOOD FOR THE *MAHĀTMAS*, meaning not only Rāma and Lakshmana, but Atri and Agastya and all the other sages for whom she cooked while she lived here. Another sign posted outside the small hexagonal building boasts, THIS IS AN ANCIENT PLACE OF RĀM'S FOREST EXILE (*Prāchīn stān banabāsī Rām*). Another instructs pilgrims who have climbed the hill, SIT DOWN, AND HAVE THE *DARSHAN* OF SĪTĀ'S KITCHEN. Sītā is flanked by Rāma and Lakshmana to either side. Here at Sītā's Kitchen, women make offerings and vows with gifts of bangles, *sindūr*, mirrors, and other feminine accoutrements.

The places associated with Rāma and Sītā in Chitrakūt are many and popular, but they are small and rustic, and the images often have a rudimentary quality. The contrast is especially striking when one compares these small Rāma shrines to the great Shiva temple on the high bank above Rāma Ghāt, buzzing with morning ritual activity. Shiva's *linga* is said to be *anādi*, "beginningless," according to informants. When Rāma came here, Shiva was already here. Even so, pilgrims come to Chitrakūt today because of its fame as a place where Rāma himself lived. Rāma is very much in their hearts and is honored throughout Chitrakūt, even though here, as in Ayodhyā, Shiva remains the preeminent ancient deity of the place.

PANCHAVATĪ

From Chitrakūt, Rāma, Sītā, and Lakshmana are said to have traveled south into the wide area called the Dandaka Forest.[23] The account of their forest sojourn includes extensive descriptions of nature and the seasons as well as tales of the various demons Rāma slew along the way for the protection of the forest-dwelling sages. Their journey from Chitrakūt to Panchavatī is said to have included many stops, to visit the various hermitages of the *rishis,* one after another, for a period of some ten years.[24] As we have said, many places along the way claim today that Rāma sojourned there. For example, pilgrims to the city of Ujjain, famous for its *jyotirlinga,* will find that at Rāma Ghāt, along the Kshiprā River, there is a set of Rāma's footprints. There, according to the lore of Ujjain, Rāma performed *tarpana,* death rites, for his deceased father Dasharatha. Nearby, they will find a temple of Rāmeshvara Mahādeva, enshrining not only a Shiva *linga,* but images of Rāma, Lakshmana, and Hanumān. According to the temple priest, Rāma established this *linga* of Shiva after the death rites, in which he offered *pindas,* or rice balls, and water to his father's spirit. At that time, they say, Shiva spoke aloud in the air, saying that Rāma should establish a *linga* there. The *linga* Rāma established is called by his name—Rāmeshvara.

Finally Rāma, Sītā, and Lakshmana reached the hermitage of Agastya, who directed them to the forest of Panchavatī on the Godāvarī River. If we go along with the consensus of the tradition, Panchavatī is represented today in the town of the same name adjoining the modern city of Nāsik in the state of Maharashtra. Nāsik is famous as one of the four places where the divine nectar of immortality, *amrita,* fell to earth. Churned up from the sea of milk, the *amrita* was at first seized by the *asuras,* but Vishnu transformed himself into the beautiful damsel Mohinī to distract the *asuras* for long enough to steal the *amrita* for the gods. When it was whisked away from the *asuras,* four drops of the divine nectar fell upon the earth—at Nāsik, Ujjain, Hardvār, and Prayāga, the four places in the cycle of Kumbha Melā festivals today. In 2003, on the primary day of the *melā,* an estimated six million people came to bathe in the waters of the Godāvarī River—both in Nāsik and in the nearby tanks at the Shaiva temple of Tryambakeshvara.

In Nāsik, the River Godāvarī is channeled into a series of *kunds*, or bathing pools, bearing the names of the epic visitors Rāma, Sītā, and Lakshmana. In one corner of Rāma Kund the Godāvarī River flows into the complex of pools. At that place, as in Ujjain, Rāma is said to have performed *tarpana* rites for his deceased father.[25] Having bathed at Rāma Ghāt, pilgrims will go for *darshan* at a substantial Rāma Temple, containing relatively new black stone images of Rāma, Sītā, and Lakshmana. Near the temple is Sītā's Cave, where, they say, Sītā was staying at the time of her abduction. The cave contains another of the numerous Sītā's Kitchens that dot the sacred geography of India. At Sītā's Cave, pilgrims find a tunnel-like staircase that takes them down to three underground chambers—one housing images of Rāma, Sītā, and Lakshmana, one containing only a cooking station, and one containing a Shiva *linga*. Pilgrims who imagined a hut in the sylvan forest might well wonder how the Panchavatī hermitage could have been this underground chamber!

The association of the Nāsik/Panchavatī area with Rāma is evident in a great variety of local legends linking places and events. Just outside the town, at the Godāvarī's *sangam* with the Kapilā River, Lakshmana is said to have cut off the nose of Shūrpanakhā, Rāvana's ogress sister. She had made advances to both Rāma and Lakshmana, and when she was rebuffed, she attacked Sītā. Rāma ordered Lakshmana to cut off her nose as punishment. It was, of course, in revenge for her mutilation that Shūrpanakhā persuaded her brother Rāvana to abduct Sītā. One of the derivations of the name Nāsik is that the nose (*nāsa*) of Shūrpanakhā was cut off here. Also on the outskirts of Nāsik is a place called Sītāharana, the very place, they say, where Sītā was seized and carried off by Rāvana.

Aside from its associations with the Rāma legend, however, Nāsik is also known to pilgrims for the nearby Shiva *jyotirlinga*, Tryambakesh-vara, just ten miles from town. This is one of the twelve great *jyotirlin-gas* of India, and as we have seen, its sanctity is not only located in the temple, but inscribed in the hills behind the temple, seen to be manifestations of Shiva. There, too, as we have seen, are the headwaters of the Godāvarī River, which rises, according to tradition, on top of Brahmāgiri Hill. Where the waters first pool for bathing, pilgrims can take a dip in another Rāma Kund and a Lakshmana Kund. There is no mention of Tryambaka in the Sanskrit *Rāmāyana,* yet the famous *jyotirlinga* and its traditions are clearly imprinted in the lore of this part of India. The great *melā* at Nāsik is known for its combination of Vaishnava and Shaiva traditions, as the regiments of *sādhus* inaugurate the Kumbha Melā in two sites—the Vaishnavas in Nāsik proper and the Shaivas at Tryambakeshvara.

KISHKINDHĀ

The old bird Jatāyū, king of the vultures, was the only witness to the kidnapping of Sītā. He tried to save her from Rāvana's clutches, but was mortally wounded. Rāma and Lakshmana found Jatāyū, barely alive. With his last words, the noble bird directed them toward the south, where Rāvana was heading with Sītā when last he saw them. There are, indeed, legends that associate Rāma and Lakshmana with the hunt for Sītā through the vast lands of the Deccan. For example, in Tuljāpūr in southern Maharashtra, it is said that the goddess Ambā appeared before Rāma, taking on Sītā's form. Rāma was not misled, however, and recognized the goddess immediately. He bowed to worship her and ask her blessing upon the search for Sītā. Two *lingas,* respectively called Rāmeshvara and Lakshmaneshvara, along with a temple to the goddess Rāmavardayanī Devī, mark the spot.[26]

Pilgrims who seek out the trail Rāma followed in his search for Sītā will inevitably find their way to the area near Hospet in central Karnataka, widely acknowledged to be the Kishkindhā of the *Rāmāyana*. There the Pampā River, today also called the Tungabhadrā, runs through an extraordinary landscape—rocky and monumental, strewn with enormous monolithic boulders. The specific site is today called Hampī, a name said to be a Kannada form of Pampā, the river flowing through this spectacular landscape. Today Hampī is most famous as the site of the great medieval capital of the Vijayanagara kingdom located here in the fourteenth to sixteenth centuries. Some five hundred temples and other structures are part of this extensive site. Archaeological work has brought numerous art historians and tourists to the site. But the ruined palaces and temples of the Vijayanagara kings are still recent compared to the traditions associating this site with the Rāma legend.

In the *Rāmāyana,* the Pampā River is a lake, described beautifully and poignantly. It was the full-blossoming springtime month of Chaitra when Rāma and Lakshmana arrived at the banks of the Pampā, and the fragrance of the breezes and blossoms made Rāma's grief and yearning almost unbearable. It was here the two of them met the monkeys Hanumān and Sugrīva and won their alliance for the battle to regain Sītā. And it was here that Rāma helped Sugrīva in his struggle with Vālī for the throne of the monkey kingdom. By this time, the rainy season had set in, making it impossible for them to mount a search for Sītā. Rāma and Lakshmana took refuge in a cave dwelling to wait out the rains.

Tulsīdās describes the rainy season at Pampākshetra with striking images: The earth became muddy as the soul, caught in illusion. The lightning flashed through the night sky as quick as the friendship of the wicked. The rivers flowed into the bosom of the ocean, like the soul that has found rest in the Lord. The green earth was so choked with grass that the paths could no longer be distinguished, like holy books obscured by the wrangling of heretics![27] Once again, the tumultuous, thundering, greening season so painful to separated lovers took its toll on Rāma. Here at Pampā, Rāma yearned for Sītā with the deep heartache of a lover. Rāma and Lakshmana stayed here for the months of the rains, waiting.

Today by the banks of the Pampā River pilgrims can visit the cave temple of Kodanda Rāma, its sanctum containing tall, angular images of Rāma and Lakshmana carved into the living stone by the river's edge. It is a good example of the vast aesthetic and architectural distance between the monumental temples of nearby Vijayanagara and the popular shrines of the Rāma legend. Taking a boat across the river to Anegundi, pilgrims will find a small town of mud stucco houses and thatched roofs, crouched amid the boulders at the base of a hill. Here pilgrims will find plenty of reminders of the sojourn of Rāma and Lakshmana. In Anegundi itself is an old Rāma temple called Shrī Ranganāthaswamy. Nearby is Shabarī ashram, a cave ashram complex where the wise woman ascetic Shabarī is said to have lived. When Rāma arrived, Shabarī told him she had long been expecting him and could now depart for heaven.[28] And so she did. Pilgrims will find Rāma's footprints, *charanapādukas*, preserved and revered in a chamber of the ashram. Next to the ashram, they will find a temple dedicated to the goddess Pampādevī, considered the ancient custodian of this area and Shiva's consort here in Pampākshetra. The head of

Shabarī ashram, a man of the Rāmānandī order, summarizes for today's pilgrims a succinct view of the places of Rāma: "Here in Pampākshetra, also called Kishkindhā, Rām spent four months. There are other places associated with Rām as well. There is Ayodhyā, of course, and Prayāga, with Bharadvāja's ashram. There is Janakpur, where Sītā was born. Then there is Nāsik and the Dandakāranya."

Not surprisingly, the Pampā River has another claimant in the south—the river that flows at the foot of Sabarimala in Kerala. One of the great rivers of Kerala, sometimes called the Dakshina Gangā, this is the river in which the pilgrims to Lord Ayyappa's mountain shrine bathe before their climb to the summit. The very name of the mountain is derived from the forest retreat of the great female sage Shabarī, who offered Rāma and Lakshmana hospitality and then lit her own funeral pyre and ascended to heaven, having fulfilled her earthly mission. In that vicinity, too, we are told there is the capital of Sugrīva, and there are footprints of Rāma, all giving this place a link to the Rāma legend in the south.

Even so, the associations of the Rāma legend with the rocky hills of Kishkindhā are perhaps more numerous. Many of them link Rāma with Hanumān. About a mile away from Shabarī ashram is the Anjanī Mountain, where, according to local tradition, Hanumān was born. On top of the hill, pilgrims will find an image of Hanumān and of Anjanī, his mother. Across the Pampāsarovar tank to the east is Vālī's Mountain, where Kishkindhā's monkey king Vālī is said to have had his fort. Across the Pampā River from Anjanādri is Rishyamukha, the mountain abode of Sugrīva, Vālī's rival brother. Hanumān, they say, took Rāma and Lakshmana on his shoulders and carried them to the top of that mountain to meet Sugrīva, who became their ally.

The birth of Hanumān, well known to be the chief servant of Rāma, is a story not found in the Sanskrit *Rāmāyana,* even though his birthplace is said to be there in Kishkindhā. Hanumān's surrogate father is the wind, Vāyu, who carried the seed of Shiva to this place, giving it to Anjanī, who dwelt on that hillock in Pampā. There she gave birth to little Hanumān. So while Hanumān is son of the wind and as fast as the wind, he is also widely known as a son or even an *avatāra* of Shiva. We know, of course, that Hanumān is famous as the *bhakta* of Rāma, and keeps both Rāma and Sītā within his heart. He is often depicted as pulling open the skin of his chest to reveal Rāma and Sītā within. Even so, if one travels the byways of central and western India, one sees that it is Hanumān who also stands to one side of the door of Shiva's shrine as gatekeeper, with Ganesha on the other side. This contextual evidence is supplemented with textual traditions, too. According to R. S. Sen, the Bengali *Rāmāyanas* depict Hanumān as the gatekeeper of Shiva and the *avatāra* of Rudra.[29] The Tamil *Rāmāyana* of Kamban also shows Hanumān not only as Rāma's devotee, but as an incarnation of Shiva, frequently comparing him to Shiva. In the sixteenth-century *Rāmcharitmānas*, the various gods are said to become incarnate as *vanaras*, monkeys, and Tulsīdās suggests that it is Shiva who becomes Hanumān. In Tulsīdās's songs, the *Dohāvalī*, for instance, he writes, "Giving up his Rudra form, Lord Shiva as Hanumān adopted a monkey figure, only in view of his affection for Rāma."[30] Obviously, the legend of Hanumān is complex, and it is for the most part not told in the *Rāmāyana*, or in the Sanskrit *māhātmyas*. It is, however, a legend that is told in shrines and images all over India. Here in Kishkindhā, the story of Hanumān's birth is a tale told not in a text, but in a hilltop shrine.

Most of what pilgrims have seen thus far in the pilgrimage shrines of Kishkindhā are rustic shrines, laden with lore. They are not beautiful *pakka* temples. For that, we turn to the ruins of the great city of Vijayanagara that bring tourists and pilgrims alike to this area. The finest and most visible site of worship among them is not a Rāma temple, or even a shrine to Hanumān, who almost never gets a proper temple, but the Shiva temple of Virupāksha, situated at the end of the main street in what is today the Hampī bazaar. It is a large temple and, according to Michell and Filliozat, the archaeologists who have studied this site, Virupāksha's temple is "the earliest nucleus in Hampi."[31] While other great temples of the Vijayanagara kings have fallen into a state of ruin over the centuries, including those of Krishna and Venkateshvara, this dominant temple of Virupāksha is an active and living temple even today. It dates only from the fourteenth or fifteenth century, but the site is likely much older. According to local tradition, the *linga* in the temple is *svayambhū*, having appeared here spontaneously, of its own accord. Here, they say, Shiva responded to the penance of Pampādevī. Here he appeared to her and married her. The *pūjārī* of the temple today does not include Virupāksha among the great twelve *jyotirlingas*, but he does insist that this manifestation of Shiva was worshipped in epic times by Rāma and Lakshmana—right here in Kishkindhā.

A synopsis of the temple's *mahātmya* is inscribed on the wall of the inner court of Virupāksha and certainly is told to the pilgrims who make their way to this temple:

> Hampi is called Pampākshetra according to the *Skanda Purāna*. Pampādevī, daughter of Brahmā, did great penance on the banks of Pampāsarovar and succeeded in winning Lord Shiva, also called Virupāksha on account of the third eye. The deity which is Udhavalingam is also popularly known as Pampāpathi. Hampi has been referred to as Kishkindhā in *Rāmāyana*. Rāma worshipped Virupāksha, and took assistance from Sugrīva and Anjaneya in redeeming Sītā from Lankā. The existence of Shabarī Ashrama, Anjanādri Hills, Sugrīva's cave, Vālībhandara etc. at Hampi are standing evidence of Kishkindhā Khānda in *Rāmāyana*.
>
> —Temple Authority.

Although the pillars of the temple courts and arcades are covered with themes that include Rāma and Lakshmana, as well as Hanumān and the other monkeys, they are assembled here around Shiva and his consort Pampādevī. The nearby caves and hills associated with Rāma's sojourn here also display a Shaiva orientation. For example, on top of nearby Malayavanta Hill is a Shiva temple called Raghunātha, Rāma's Lord. Here, according to tradition, Rāma waited for Hanumān to return from his search for Sītā. The *shikhara* of Raghunātha is built out of the living rock of the hilltop—a boulder that has been carved, layered, and shaped as a *shikhara*. All around on the crown of the rocky hilltop are some twenty-five Shiva *lingas,* also shaped from living stone. At the end of the rainy season, while monkeys and bears fanned out—north, south, east, and west—to search for Sītā, Rāma waited here for news.

In the legend of the *Rāmāyana*, Kishkindhā is a pivot, a turning point, the place from which a seemingly hopeless search began to yield success. Hanumān leapt the sea to Lankā, found Sītā there in the garden of ashoka trees, and gave her Rāma's signet ring to let her know that Rāma would soon be coming.

Rāmeshvara

At Rāmeshvara, a long spit of an island stretches out toward Lankā. It was there, according to tradition, the monkeys built the bridge of stones to cross over to Lankā. In Purāṇic literature, Rāmeshvara is often referred to simply as Setu, "the Bridge," after the bridge built by Rāma. Fascination with this bridge to Lankā was revived by the space satellite images of NASA released in 2002, showing clearly the traces of a thin and now submerged bridge of land, a chain of shoals some eighteen miles long between Rāmeshvara and Sri Lanka.

Some took the NASA photo as "proof" that Rāma built the bridge, others simply as evidence that there was once a land bridge, so long ago it surely predated even the mythic Treta Yuga in which the events of the *Rāmāyana* are said to have transpired. But when, in 2007, the government of India undertook the Sethu Samudram Shipping Canal Project to dredge and deepen the channel through these straits, in order to create a shipping lane linking the east and west coasts of India, controversy erupted throughout India and, to some extent, throughout the Hindu world. The "Save Rām Setu" campaign brought several Hindu organizations together to oppose the project. The president of a U.S.-based Hindu environmental lobbying group said, "The bridge is as holy to Hindus as the Wailing Wall is to the Jews, the Vatican to Catholics, Bodh Gaya to Buddhists and Mecca to Muslims. It is an unacceptable breach of the religious rights of over one billion Hindus to destroy such a sacred landmark without even consulting us."[32] Added to their concern was post-tsunami environmental awareness that the natural bridge had also been a protective barrier to the full impact of the waves. Rāma's Bridge was in the news. The Setu is sunken today, and it is understood that Rāma himself broke it up at the request of Vibhīshana, Rāvana's virtuous brother who became king of Lankā after Rāvana's death. Even so, the importance of the remnants of Setu, "the Bridge," create a symbolic link to a previous age and the powerful presence of Rāma.

In this area, pilgrims will find many places linked explicitly with the Rāma legend. One of the most important is Dhanushkoti, the place where Rāma, with the tip of his bow, broke up the bridge. They might also visit Mount Gandhamādana, northwest of the town of Rāmeshvara.

Like many *tīrthas* in the south, Mount Gandhamādana has its counterpart in the far north. Its very name links this place with the mountain
near Badrīnāth in the Himalayas. Here Gandhamādana is more a hillock than a mountain. Pilgrims will hear that this is the high place from
which Hanumān first surveyed the horizon and saw the island kingdom
of Lankā. At Chakra Tīrtha, Rāma first halted near the ocean. At Agni
Tīrtha, they say, Rāma had Sītā's purity tested by asking her to enter the
fire. At Sītāsarovara, Sītā bathed after her trial by fire. At Koti Tīrtha,
Rāma pressed his bow into the ground to release the waters of the Gangā.

Yet despite all its profound associations with the Rāma legend,
Rāmeshvara is also called a Shivakshetra, a land sanctified by the
presence of Shiva. The Vālmīki *Rāmāyana* makes but brief mention of
the honoring of Shiva in this place. On their journey homeward, Rāma
points out to Sītā the place called Setu, where Lord Shiva bestowed grace
upon him before the construction of the bridge. That is all that is said of
this place. However, many of the Purānas and several later *Rāmāyanas,*
such as the *Adhyātma Rāmāyana,* make explicit the claim that Rāma
established and honored the *linga* Rāmeshvara at this place.[33] Pilgrims
to Rāmeshvara today will hear these stories, as they honor Lord Shiva
there. In the *Shiva Purāna,* for example, it is said that Rāma, having

Consecrating a sand linga *on the beach at Rāmeshvara*

arrived at the seashore, was thirsty. When Hanumān brought him water, Rāma, as a devotee of Shiva, first established an earthen *linga* of Shiva and honored it before drinking. Shiva, pleased with Rāma's devotion, complied with Rāma's request that he ever remain present in this *linga* of Rāmeshvara.[34]

Recall that another popular tradition has this *linga* established not before, but after Rāma's successful battle against Rāvana. In the *Skanda Purāna*, for example, Rāma, Lakshmana, and Sītā assembled there at Setubandhu, and Rāma sent Hanumān to the north to bring an appropriate stone for the *linga*. Some say Hanumān went to the Himalayas and others to Kāshī, but even though he was as swift as the wind, Hanumān had not yet returned to Setu when the auspicious hour for consecrating the *linga* arrived. So Sītā made a *linga* with her own hands, shaping it from the sand, and they worshipped that image of Shiva. Shiva manifested his presence there, and the sand *linga* became hard as rock. When Hanumān returned bearing the stone *linga* from the north, he could not lift up the sand *linga*, even with the strength of his tail, in order to replace it with a proper stone. Hard as he pulled, he could not get the *linga* to budge. So they established two *lingas* in this place.[35] The old pillars of the temple show this scene in stone relief, as do the newest glossy polychromes available in the bazaar, telling the tale that pilgrims will surely hear: Sītā, Rāma, Lakshmana, and Hanumān all did honor to Shiva's *linga* at Rāmeshvara.

The temple of Rāmeshvara, or Rāmanāthaswami as it is known in Tamil Nadu, was built beginning in the twelfth century, around the existing *linga*. Construction and renovation of the *gopuras* and the circumambulatory walkways, the *prakāras*, has continued in virtually every century since that time. Today's temple contains twenty-two *tīrthas* within its walls, the word *tīrtha* here meaning specifically a well of holy water, and pilgrims are invited to visit and refresh themselves at the waters of each. Pilgrims take buckets through the temple to do just that, scooping up the waters of each of the holy *tīrthas*. Inside the temple there are actually two Shiva *lingas*, as one might expect. The sanctum sanctorum is said to contain the *linga* shaped by Sītā and consecrated by Rāma. North of this is the *linga* of Vishvanātha, said to have been brought from Kāshī by Hanumān. Elsewhere there are *lingas* established by Rāma's brother Bhārata and Rāvana's brother Vibhīshana. Outside the temple on the beach, priests assist pilgrims in making sand *lingas* to worship, as presumably Rāma and Sītā did. Their worship complete, they walk into the waves and deposit the sand in the sea.

As with many great *tīrthas*, the *māhātmyas* of Rāmeshvara emphasize the efficacy of penance in this place. According to the *Skanda Purāna*, Rāma established the *linga* here after the battle to atone for the sin of killing Rāvana. Other traditions associate Rāmeshvara with Krishna's atonement for killing his maternal uncle Kamsa, or with Shiva's atonement for cutting off one of Brahmā's five heads, or with Yudhisthira's atonement for lying about the death of Drona during the great battle of the *Mahābhārata*.[36] Atonement is part of pilgrimage, and here the exemplars of atonement are many.

At Rāmeshvara, we are poised to remember once again the links that knot this place into a wide web of Hindu lore and that stretch from this place in the far south of India to sacred places in the north. Pilgrims still know the traditions of bringing the waters of the Gangā to Rāmeshvara and carrying the waters of the *tīrthas* within the Rāmeshvara temple to Vishvanātha Temple in Vārānasī, where these waters are sprinkled on the *linga*. There in Vārānasī, the name "Rāma" is sometimes inscribed on the bilva leaves, sacred to Shiva, before they are presented as an offering.

VICTORY AND THE RETURN TO AYODHYĀ

Rāmeshvara seems to span the time before and after the great battle. Now let us return to Lankā. When the battle between the forces of Rāvana and the armies of Rāma was over, Rāma finally slew Rāvana with the all-powerful Brahmāstra arrow. Sītā, the beloved, was at last restored to her place at Rāma's side, but not before Rāma, ever-mindful of dharma, subjected her to a public test of her purity. How could he take her back, he said, when she had lived in another man's house? Grief-stricken, Sītā asked Lakshmana to build her funeral pyre right there, and she entered the fire, praying for the protection of Agni. Of course, the fire would not burn her, or even scorch her fresh flower garland. The fire god Agni, witness to her stainless character, brought her back to the rejoicing Rāma. The trial by fire is remembered today at the Agni Tīrtha in Rāmeshvara, even though this trial is said to have happened in Lankā itself. There is much to say about these dramatic, critical events, and many tellings of the *Rāmāyana* are clearly restless with this episode. For example, Tulsīdās creates a "phantom Sītā" who is abducted, while the real Sītā is protected by Agni. At the time of Rāma's test, the real Sītā emerges from the fire, never having been subjected to Rāvana's captivity. Interesting as these variants of the epic tale are, our focus here is primarily on the ways this epic is inscribed in the land. And for this, the journey home to Ayodhyā provides one final overview of the map of epic action.

The royal threesome traveled back to Ayodhyā on a remarkable aerial chariot named Pushpaka, a magical vehicle Rāvana won from his conquest of Kubera, the Himalayan king of the *yakshas* and lord of wealth. Now this chariot was given to Rāma by Vibhīshana, Rāvana's brother, who had repeatedly tried to dissuade Rāvana from his reckless, vainglorious ways and who had become, in the end, a staunch ally of Rāma. With Rāvana's death, Vibhīshana became the king of Lankā. The royal party entered the chariot—along with Vibhīshana, Sugrīva, Hanumān, and the rest of the monkeys, all eager to travel with Rāma to Ayodhyā. Pushpaka was a huge chariot and it accommodated them all. As it lifted off from Lankā, Rāma could see down below the entire landscape of their epic exile.

Looking down at the land below, Rāma took delight in pointing out to Sītā all the places of the epic action, marking once again the map of the land. As they rose into the sky, he pointed out the city of Lankā, sitting on Trikūta Hill, looking like Kailāsa itself. "Over there I have slain Rāvana," he says. "And there! There is Setu, the bridge, and there stands the sacred shrine of Setubandha! There is Kishkindhā, the beautiful land of Sugrīva! There is Rishyamūkha Hill and Pampā Lake, where I wept for missing you! There is the place Jatāyū fought Rāvana and died And look, there in the forest is the hut where we stayed at Panchavatī and where Rāvana abducted you. There is the sparkling Godāvarī River and the hermitage of Agastya. And look, there is the hermitage of Atri, and there is Chitrakūt Hill, where Bhārata came to persuade me to return to Ayodhyā. There is the River Yamunā and the hermitage of Bharadvāja! And look, there gleams Ayodhyā, the capital of my father's kingdom!"

The heroes stopped first at Bharadvāja's ashram in Prayāga, the place that had been one of their first stops on the outgoing forest journey.

Rāma sent Hanumān on ahead to notify Bhārata, who was living the ascetic's life in a hermitage, on the outskirts of Ayodhyā. Bhārata was overjoyed and all Ayodhyā began to prepare for the day awaited now for fourteen years.

In all its *mahātmyas*, Ayodhyā is glorious and is also personified. It is a city that bloomed with blossoms and joy at the approach of young Prince Rāma's coronation. It is a city that wept with tears of lamentation when Rāma left to enter the forest. It is a city that held itself in waiting during the long years of Rāma's exile and was electric with anticipation at the word of Rāma's return. It is a city in which the reign of Rāma, at long last, was a time of flourishing, of justice, and of peace. As Vālmīki tells the tale, "During his reign no woman became a widow. There was no fear of ferocious animals, and diseases were unheard of. The whole kingdom was free from robbers and thieves. Nobody suffered in any way during his rule, and the aged had not to perform funeral rites for the young. At that time, everybody was happy and virtuous. Nobody attempted to do violence to anybody out of their respect and love for Rāma."[37]

RĀMLĪLĀ: THE LOCAL STAGE

Across north India, there are dramatic performances of the Rāma saga called *rāmlīlās*. This performance genre re-creates on a local scale this landscape from Ayodhyā to Rāmeshvara. Throngs of local spectator devotees wait for hours to glimpse the human icons of Rāma, Sītā, and Lakshmana enact the highlights of the *Rāmāyana* drama. The maharaja of Kāshī sponsors one of the most elaborate and famous *rāmlīlās* every fall in Rāmnagar, the town across the River Gangā from Banāras, where the local maharajas have had their palace since the mid–eighteenth century. The performance lasts for a month, each day attracting as many as twenty thousand spectators. It culminates, at the time of the festival of Dasehra, with Rāma's victory over Rāvana and his glorious return to Ayodhyā.

In Rāmnagar, the symbolic landscape of India is created in the town center, in various neighborhoods, and in the outskirts of town. This local stage covers an area of nearly two square miles. Ayodhyā is in the town square. Platforms and pavilions are erected to be Chitrakūt and

Panchavatī. Local temples and temple tanks, ponds, and pools are incorporated into the landscape of Rāma's journey. Lankā is at the southern edge of town. For an entire month, the small town of Rāmnagar is transformed into an epic landscape familiar to Hindus from every corner of India.

During the *rāmlīlā*, ordinary talented citizens are consecrated to the main roles of the epic, young boys taking the key roles of Rāma, Sītā, and Lakshmana. As in the Krishna *līlās* of Braj, these young actors are called *svarūpas*, "divine embodiments," for the duration of the drama. Devotees carry them from place to place during the *līlās*, so that their feet do not touch the ground. In addition, actors of local legend take on such roles as Hanumān and Rāvana, over the years becoming quite famous for their roles. Just as townspeople become the actors, so, too, town space becomes epic space. And when the *svarūpas* appear, it truly becomes sacred space. Each of the *līlās* concludes with worship and an *āratī* to the *svarūpas*.

Anuradha Kapur, who has studied the Rāmnagar *rāmlīlā*, day by day, writes of the ways in which the spectators or the audience are not just onlookers, but participants in the play. They are also pilgrims, following the action from place to place, each place re-creating one of the great sites of the epic. When there is a downpour and roads are muddy, they slog through the mud to reach the venue of the next episode. Kapur writes, "The very act of following the gods from location to location as they enact their history on a sacred map gives the spectators a role. Here Rāma rested, here he crossed the Gangā, here he battled with Rāvana. In visiting places sanctified by divinity, the spectator does what countless pilgrims do, for her/his worship, like theirs, consists in visiting holy places. And her/his journey becomes at once physical, metaphorical, and spiritual."[38]

While people are eager for a glimpse of the consecrated actors who play the roles of the heroes and heroines, most see the great scenes only from a distance.[39] In truth, it matters little if the audience can hear the actors or see their faces, although today amplification, electricity, and flare torches enhance the performance. For the crowd, these *līlās* serve as living tableaux of a story they all know by heart. The familiarity of the story, the iconic representation of the actors, the power of the imagination, and the landscape of their own neighborhoods—all join to re-create the drama of the *Rāmāyana* anew.

In the late 1980s, however, a new *rāmlīlā* was brought into thousands of villages and homes through the powerful outreach of television. Viewers all over India were able to watch the popular weekly series on the *Rāmāyana*, put to film by producer Rāmānand Sāgar. Every Sunday morning from January 25, 1987, to July 31, 1988, Indians followed the action, becoming familiar with something quite new in the repertoire of the *rāmlīlā*. They had *darshan* close-up. They could see the facial expressions of Rāma, Sītā, and Lakshmana, gaining an intimacy, immediacy, and human sympathy not possible in the large outdoor *rāmlīlās*. Many are the stories of television sets decked with garlands of marigolds for the weekly *darshan* of Shrī Rāma. The actors in the drama, especially Arun Govil, who played the role of Rāma, were greeted even in their everyday lives as partial *avatāras*.[40]

In this television drama, Rāmānand Sāgar created essentially a new telling of the epic with its own now-national authority. While the story line, on the whole, follows Vālmīki's *Rāmāyana*, the rolling credits for each episode mention the many regional variations. From time to time, songs from Tulsī's *Rāmcharitmānas* break into and enhance the sequence of events. This *līlā* is transformed by a new medium, complete with the special-effects pyrotechnics of divine weapons and the faces of Dasharatha and Kaikeyī, Sītā and Lakshmana, and above all, the god-king Rāma. In the end, Rāmānand Sāgar rises into the sky on a lotus flower, a New Age Vālmīki.

It is unquestionably the case that for millions of people, the television *Rāmāyana* lifted the saga to an immediate level of consciousness, described by one national magazine as "*Rāmāyana* Fever." *Bhakti* for Lord Rāma and affection for his Ayodhyā home were no doubt turned to effective use by the rising Hindu nationalist movement. In their rise to power, the Vishva Hindu Parishad and its political party, the Bhāratīya Janatā Party, set their sites on reclaiming the Rāma Janmasthān, Rāma's birthplace in Ayodhyā, as the movement's symbolic focus. As we have seen, the *Rāmāyana* is a powerful story and one that is written not only in the hearts of people, but on the landscape of India. The political uses of this story and its powerful landscape seized public attention in the late 1980s and 1990s, and we cannot conclude our view of the landscape of the *Rāmāyana* without reflecting on this sobering fact.

Writing of the *Rāmāyana*'s political uses, Sheldon Pollock laments, "It

seems incomprehensible that a divisive contemporary political discourse
is so accessible to, or may be shaped by, what is commonly viewed as a
narrative of the divine presence and care for the world."[41] He traces the
long history of "the relationship between *Rāmāyana* and political symbology,"[42] looking carefully through literary and inscriptional evidence
at the ways in which the model of Rāma as divine king is increasingly
utilized in the political sphere. This was especially salient beginning in
the twelfth century, when the *Rāmāyana*'s imaginary world polarized
by threatening *rākshasas* could also be called into play as Hindu cultures encountered, for the first time, the powerful forces of the Central
Asian and Turkic "other."[43] Only a few steps farther on the historical
timeline do we encounter one of the great modern *rāmlīlās* of the political sphere—the October 1990 journey of Bhāratīya Janatā Party chief
L. K. Advani as Rāma, crossing India by Toyota-truck chariot, bow in
hand, stopping in one village after another as his *yātrā* made its way from
Somnāth to Ayodhyā.

AYODHYĀ AND RĀMA'S JANMABHŪMI

There is no place in India where it is more important to remember that
a *tīrtha* is not a temple than in the little town of Ayodhyā, said to be
the birthplace and ancient capital of Lord Rāma. Here what has come
to be called the temple-mosque controversy has been fanned to flames
by Hindu communal groups, as bricks and mortar became the subject and symbol of intense and highly politicized Hindu nationalism.
The building, for more than four hundred years a mosque, was called
the Babri Masjid by Muslims, a sixteenth-century mosque named for
the Mughal Emperor Babur, who came to India in 1526. The inscription
from 1528 notes that the mosque was built by Mir Baqi at the command of King Babur to be "a descending place of the angels" with the
prayer that "it will remain an everlasting bounty."[44] Hindus called it the
Rāmjanmasthān, "Rāma's Birthplace," claiming that on that site stood a
temple dedicated to Lord Rāma on the very site of his birth, the columns
of the temple having been put to reuse in the building of the mosque.
Today there is neither mosque nor temple, but a wasteland. On December 6, 1992, Hindu nationalist proponents of Rāma's Birthplace tore the

450-year-old mosque down. On that day, well-organized activists and supporters of the B.J.P.—the Vishva Hindu Parishad, the R.S.S., and the Bajrang Dāl—broke through flimsy security lines, scaled the walls of the old mosque, and began breaking the surface of the dome with staves and pikes. By the end of the day, the mosque was rubble, and weeks of communal violence erupted in India and Pakistan.

In 1981, when I first visited Ayodhyā, it was a sleepy pilgrimage town where pilgrims bathed in the morning by the banks of the Sarayū River, a tributary of the Gangā, said to have its source at Lake Mānasa, a Himalayan lake produced from the mind (manas) of Lord Brahmā. Pilgrims on the riverbank were making the offering of a cow, holding a cow's tail and offering marigolds and vessels of milk into the river, all with the proper ministrations of the priests. The pilgrims would then set off to visit the sacred sites of the town, including the ancient temple of Shiva nearby, said to be the chief protector of Ayodhyā, and a multitude of sites of little architectural distinction associated with Rāma. I have already noted that they would find the liveliest temple by far to be the Hanumān Garhī, Hanumān's Fort, built on high ground up a long flight of steps crowded with alms-seekers. The most beautiful would perhaps be the Kanaka Bhavan, the Golden Palace, a temple-palace with a large congregational hall and an altar bearing white marble images of the royal couple with Lakshmana and Hanumān. It is this place that comes to vibrant action at the time of Rāmnavamī, the observance of Rāma's birth, when thousands of pilgrims are said to gather to watch the priest place a coconut in the cradle of Rāma.

Among the sleepiest sites in Ayodhyā then was the place called Rāmjanmabhūmī, "Rāma's Birthplace." Because of disputed claims in the mid–nineteenth century, the British had effectively fenced the site off. At the time of India's independence in 1947, a status-quo protection of holy places as of that year was put in place. In 1949, however, on the night of December 22, Hindu advocates insisted that Rāma's image "appeared" in the mosque, drawing on language we have seen commonly used to speak of the spontaneous manifestation of God's presence. According to police records, at least by some accounts, the images had been placed there that night by a group of Hindus who broke the lock on the gate and put Rāma's image in the mosque. However, in the many decades since that December night in 1949, no reversal of the placement of these images had been ordered. The gate of the fenced-in area was locked, and the site made largely off-limits to both Muslims and Hindus.

When I visited, the worship of small white marble images of Rāma and his entourage, along with that of Rāma's mother Kaushalyā, still took place in the hall of the mosque called the Babri Masjid, although it was open only for restricted hours. A sign posted outside in English noted the following: "Sri Ram Birth Place. The offering to Lord Ram in the temple encircled with the iron bar is under the management of receiver appointed by the court. You are requested to donate on the donation box fixed by the receiver on the closed iron gate." Outside the compound gate, fenced and locked most of the time, two old men sat under a canopy shielding them from the sun, chanting "*Sītā Rām, Sītā Rām, Jaya Jaya Sītā Rām.*" The signage propped up next to them indicated that they were participating in a day-and-night perpetual chanting campaign for the liberation of Rāma's Birthplace. In an adjacent structure, a doorway led down a staircase to the basement shrine called Sītā's Kitchen, a long, rectangular room attended by a brahmin priest who knew the story well. "Here Sītā had her kitchen," he said, pointing to the small hearth enclosed with an altar rail. "And when Sītā and Rām were married, Mother Annapurnā came from Kāshī to cook for them." Annapurnā, of course, is the Goddess of Plenteous Food, the consort of Shiva in Vārānasī.

More than twenty years later, I visited Ayodhyā once again. It was winter in 2004, and the town was still quiet, but much changed. Police blockades and cordons were everywhere. There were very few pilgrims, since even today the great pilgrimage season is at the annual Rāmnavamī festival in April–May, when pilgrims circumambulate the entire sacred zone of Ayodhyā in the *panchakroshī yātrā*, demonstrating with their feet that the *tīrtha* of Ayodhyā comprises much more than any single temple. The riverbank was still an active bathing place, even in the cold of January. Hanumān Garhī was still vibrant with visitors and alms-seekers. But the contested mosque was missing, and the designated site of Rāma's birth was essentially a blue plastic tent, part of an entire site that was covered with a vast series of blue plastic tarps. One could approach this site only by passing through a metal detector, into a long, serpentine fenced path, leading back and forth toward the large tented area spread with tarps. Once there, one could view the trenches, said to be archaeological trenches revealing the foundations of the old temple. Finally, there was a place where one could stop for the *darshan* of the Baby Rāma, Rām Lālā as they called him, a small image of Rāma as a child, an image of recent origin placed in his special part of the tent. It was, to be sure, a dismal scene. My guide, who was proud to have participated in the events of December 6, 1992, visually surveyed with some satisfaction the ground where the mosque had stood. He did not know what had happened to Sītā's Kitchen.

In the market, however, were not only the old penny-*māhātmyas* telling the tale of Ayodhyā's greatness, but new pamphlets, like the one simply called *Ayodhyā Karsewa, 6 December, 1992. Karsewa* means the "service of action," but here the meaning of *seva/sewa* is an extraordinary distortion: The term is used to refer to the service of the participants in destroying the structure of the mosque. This small booklet of color photos depicts a crowd surging through narrow lanes toward the mosque, young men with orange headbands breaking through the fence and clambering to the top of the three domes of the mosque, waving victoriously. Of course, in the confrontation with police that followed, some of those involved in this action were killed. The photos also depict the dead, garlanded and surrounded by a circle of men. The dead are explicitly called *shahids*, martyrs, adopting the Urdu and Arabic term for Muslim martyrs. Indeed, the narrow street leading to the mosque-temple site was called Shahid Galli, the Lane of Martyrs.

In profusion in the bazaars were also the polychrome pictures of the new Rāma Temple designed and planned for the site, with a muscular Lord Rāma astride the fine temple, bow drawn. Video CDs were on sale, too, with festive pilgrims walking along in slow motion, singing the lilting melodies "We are coming to Ayodhyā, coming to Ayodhyā to build Rāma's Temple." A VCD intended as a take-home video *māhātmya* eulogized the events of December 6, 1992, including graphic footage of the destruction of the mosque and of the *shahids*, whose bloodstained bodies were meant to be evidence of their sacrifice for the cause.

Thousands of pages of testimony, dozens of scholarly articles and books, and hundreds of newspaper articles and editorials have been written on this dispute and on the mayhem of December 6, 1992, and its aftermath. The new Hindu nationalists of the Vishva Hindu Parishad and its political party, the B.J.P., have contended that on this very site

Mir Baqi razed a Hindu temple in the sixteenth century and constructed a mosque, using some of the columns of the temple itself. This would not have been entirely unusual at the time, but did it happen here? And was this temple dedicated to Rāma's birth? The archaeologists whose trenches are there under the blue tarps attested there was a temple there. Other Indian historians and archaeologists, both Muslim and Hindu, have contended that the textual and archaeological evidence for a temple at that site is very slim, even nonexistent. An archaeologist from the University of Allahabad wrote frankly in summarizing his findings, "There is not a single piece of evidence for the existence of a temple of brick, stone, or both."[45]

Slimmer still is the evidence that this or any single place in Ayodhyā was, in fact or faith, the birthplace of Rāma. Those who have studied the *Ayodhyā Māhātmyas* in the Purānas find no textual evidence for any important site related to Rāma's birth before the sixteenth century.[46] In addition, the duplication of a single site in multiple places is here, as in other *tīrthas,* a common pattern. As Professor Ram Sharan Sharma put it in 1989, "I have been there. There are at least 15–16 *mandirs,* the *pūjarīs* of which claim that their temple is the real birthplace of Rāma."[47] This is a general observation with which I would concur from my own early visit to Ayodhyā in 1981. The duplication of such claimants to the "birthplace" is common, and not engaged in a spirit of rivalry, but in the distinctively Hindu tradition of multiplicity: Any place that is truly important is important enough to be duplicated and sited in multiple places.

As we conclude our study of the landscape of Hindu India, with its many networks of *tīrthas,* we recognize just how volatile and powerful the links to sacred places can be and how readily they can be deployed in a context far removed from the practices and patterns of pilgrimage that have been in place for centuries. The politicization of Ayodhyā brought archaeologists and historians, judges and swamis, political parties and prime ministers into the fray. From 1986 on, when a judge ordered the lock on the iron gate removed, the mosque-temple controversy seemed to gather energy with each year, generating passion and anger on all sides, leading many to wonder what was left of the democratic secular consensus of India's constitution. It led others to wonder what was left of the religious values and ethical vision of the *Rāmāyana.*

By 1991, a political-religious campaign was well under way to consecrate bricks in towns and villages across India and bring them to Ayodhyā for the building of a new temple for Rāma. Bringing bricks to Ayodhyā became its own kind of pilgrimage, and the term *yātrā* was commonly used for these journeys. The bricks and mortar became what the Bhāratīya Janatā Party described as a "national issue," although it is clear that by "national" they referred to a Hindu nation, no matter how broadly they defined its meaning. The Janmasthān, as the B.J.P. said in its 1991 election manifesto, is "a symbol of the vindication of our cultural heritage and our national self-respect." They concluded, "Hence the party is committed to build Srī Rāma Mandir at Janmasthān by relocating the super-imposed mosque with due respect."[48] The bricks were now part of the platform of a political party. That same year, the historian S. Gopal wrote, "It is a sad irony that those who claim to be followers of the same religion as Gandhi, should now, forsaking the majesty of the faith proclaimed for all time in the Upanishads and in the teachings of the *bhaktas*, be primarily concerned with collecting and transporting bricks in order to construct a temple on the site of a mosque they plan to demolish."[49] In 1992, as we know, the mosque was demolished. Far from this creating animosity toward the B.J.P., its leader, Atal Behari Bajpai, was elected prime minister in 1996. By the 1998 election, the party still maintained its platform position: "The BJP is committed to facilitate the construction of a magnificent Sri Rāma Mandir at Rāmjanmasthān in Ayodhyā where a makeshift temple already exists. Sri Rāma lies at the core of Indian consciousness. The BJP will explore all consensual, legal and constitutional means to facilitate the construction of the Srī Rāma Mandir at Ayodhyā."[50] The plan drawn up for the temple featured that new, now familiar, icon of a muscular Rāma, bow drawn back, standing astride a beautiful temple.

In its election manifestos, the B.J.P. also described its commitment to "one nation, one people, one culture." That culture, they said, is unified by the principle of Hindutva, which always constitutes "the identity of our ancient nation—Bharatvarsha." "Hindutva," they said, "is a unifying principle which alone can preserve the unity and integrity of our nation."[51] The very term "Hindutva" was inseparable from V. D. Savarkar's writing bearing that name, in which he made clear that "a Hindu is one who takes the land of Bhārata as fatherland and holy land." Savarkar was not particularly interested in either temples or religion and would surely have found a temple-centered campaign distasteful, but his term "Hindutva," "Hinduness," grew legs and traveled widely.

A. N. Noorani, in introducing his vast compendium of sources on the modern temple-mosque dispute over the birthplace of Rāma, writes, "The entire country is Rāmjanmabhūmi." What he means is that the birthplace of Rāma, as an ideal warrior and beloved lord, is much larger than any mere place he may have been born in Ayodhyā. R. K. Dasgupta, a historian from Calcutta University, expressed the astonishment of many at the virulent turn of events that brought down the mosque. "Where was Rāmachandra born?" he writes. "I confess I never asked myself this question about the hero of the *Rāmāyana* before the demolition of the Babri Masjid on 6 December 1992. . . . There is no archaeological record showing the existence of a Rāma temple on Rāmjanmabhūmī, which is evidently an invention of Sangh Parivar historiography. Researchers in ancient Indian history, in India and abroad, have established that the Rāma legend is a part of Indian mythology, the character in Vālmīki's great epic having no historical basis."[52] He would perhaps agree that the competing archaeological evidence and historical research that consumes many years and pages of this controversy is all quite beside the point if one grants the point that Rāma and the great story of his journey are not at all within the realm of what we ordinarily think of as "history."

To say one thinks of Rāma in mythic rather than historical terms does not diminish his importance, but amplifies it. It is to speak of a story that is profoundly important in Hindu culture, not because it factually happened in this place or that, but because it goes on taking place in the lives of people for whom it is meaningful and in the tales and travels of Hindu pilgrims. In Hindu terms, after all, Rāma is said to have lived in the Treta Yuga, a period of time in Hindu cosmology well over a million years ago, quite beyond the reach of what is normally investigated as history. He was born, as all India's great heroes were, by supernatural intervention. In his case, it was the sacrifice of his father, the childless king Dasharatha, that generated the gift of a supernatural puddinglike substance called *payasa* that was then consumed by his mother Kaushalyā. Myths are those great and greatest of stories, stories we never really hear for the first time because they are part of the structure of our culture and the subsoil of our consciousness. The effort to historicize Rāma by battling over a birthplace astonished and perplexed many Hindus like Dasgupta. The legend of Rāma, told in Vālmīki's *Rāmāyana* and in many regional *Rāmāyana*s, is far too deeply and widely embedded in Indian consciousness to be either affirmed or destabilized by a bricks-and-mortar controversy in late-twentieth-century Ayodhyā.

The issues raised here are critical and have to do with the very nature of religious and historical consciousness, and the relation of the power of myth to the so-called facts of history. How does one search for the "historical" figure of Rāma, whose story is deeply embedded in the Indian imagination? This is the story of the prince who lost his kingdom on the eve of his coronation, who was sent into exile in the forest, who lost his beloved wife Sītā, carried off by a *rākshasa*. Indeed, he lost everything but his fervent adherence to dharma, to righteousness. This myth has moved through many centuries and many communities. It has extended its influence throughout India and beyond India into wider Southeast Asia. As Amartya Sen writes in introducing the *Rāmāyana*, "The great thing about this classic book is not the conformity it is allegedly trying to achieve—religious or even literary—but the creative diversity it allows and encourages, which has had profoundly constructive effects across a huge part of the world."[53] Its power has never needed to be bolstered by the DNA of the archaeological or historical record. Myths are "real" and "true" in quite another way: They are true stories by which cultures pattern their distinctive values and by which people live their lives. The characters, narratives, and dilemmas of the *Rāmāyana* are far too significant for Hindu consciousness to be reduced to narrow claims of those who chant, *Hum mandir vahīn banāyenge*, "We will build the temple at that very place!"

There are many controversies piled high here. The controversy over Rāma's birthplace became in one sense a temple-mosque and, as such, a Hindu-Muslim controversy. It sparked the worst communal violence since the violence of partition in 1947. And, as Sheldon Pollock has provocatively demonstrated, Rāma's cosmic competition with the *rākshasas*, his bow ever drawn against them, has been appropriated by those who see that bow drawn against a thousand years of Turkic, Central Asian, and now Muslim *rākshasas* whose culture has challenged that of Hindu India.[54] For many, however, the broader controversy is between proponents of Hindutva and defenders of India's secular traditions. Even before the fateful events of December 6, 1992, the historian Mushirul Hasan had written, "No other issue since India's independence has generated such violent passions, led to such widespread riots, gripped the people with panic, fear, and anger, and threatened to destroy the democratic, secular consensus envisaged by the architects of the Indian constitution."[55]

For our part, this is also a controversy that has cast into high relief the many issues with which we have grappled in this book. It is a controversy between those who live in and through the resonant and symbolic myths of their tradition and those who render these same great myths as literal and pedestrian. In the *tīrthas* of the pilgrim's India, the power of myth is embedded in land and landscape, to be sure. As we have seen repeatedly, pilgrims seek out countless places that are made significant by the mythic events that "took place" there. For the pilgrim, the *tīrthas* and *dhāms* are places that do indeed provide a special access to the divine. That is why pilgrims go on their journeys. But *tīrthas* and *dhāms* are not buildings. They are not temples. And in one after another of these places we find that the place itself is circumambulated, a place comprising dozens if not hundreds of temples and shrines, *ghāts* and bathing pools. Such a place is Ayodhyā.

10

A Pilgrim's India Today

India's modern revolutions are many. In transportation, communications, and technology, India has accelerated into new worlds of speed and connectivity. Even in the years since I began working on this book—virtually three decades ago—the global connections that were then impossible have now become almost routine. The trusty old rail system has become more extensive, though still plagued by delays. Even so, there are now online reservations and information sites, and I can find out that the Kāshī Vishvanāth Express from Delhi to Vārānasī is running an hour later by checking my iPhone. The service of national and regional airlines has grown exponentially, with half a dozen new airlines launching operations since 2000. As for highways, the much-touted Golden Quadrilateral project links Delhi, Kolkata, Chennai, and Mumbai with 3,625 miles of six-lane highways.

Along with transport, technology has catapulted India into a new era. Mobile phone use in India is growing faster than anywhere else in the world, with some six million new users signed up every month in 2007.[1] By 2010, this figure had grown to some fifteen million new users each month. Vendors send vans with cell phone connectivity for sale into the rural villages of India, rightly deemed to be a ready market for the millions who were bypassed by the old landlines. By 2010, it was estimated that there were more than 600 million cell phone subscribers.[2] And not surprisingly, there is also an explosion in the number of Internet users, growing from some 1.4 million in 1998 to 42 million in 2007 to 71 million in 2009.[3] Some see India as the capital of the technology revolution—both in Bangalore and in its satellite in the Silicon Valley of California.

Those of us who have seen these revolutions march through the past decades have reason to be astonished. When I first studied at Banāras Hindu University as a student in 1965, any long-distance phone call had to be booked at the university post office. My one call home to Montana at Christmastime was a broken line of static punctuated by "Love you," "Merry Christmas," and "Can you hear me?" shouted from both ends. By the time I was roaming India doing pilgrimage research in the mid-1980s, there was satellite connectivity. More or less clear connections and calls were actually possible, though infrequent and expensive. By the late 1990s, I could sit atop the steps of Asi Ghāt in Banāras, at the telephone owned by a woman who ran a tea shop, and make one of those satellite calls, a startling and frankly jarring connection of voice to voice from the Gangā's riverfront to my mother's home in Montana. And then came the mobile revolution, as people the world over began communicating with one another while walking in the streets, sitting in cafés, or resting on a park bench.

It should not surprise us that the revolutions in transportation and communications have stimulated an even greater flow of pilgrimage traffic. Far from fading with the onrush of modern technology, pilgrimage has gained new energies. The Internet provides access to websites for Tirupati or Vaishno Devī, where one can make a booking for *pūjās* and special *darshans* and make a reservation in a *dharmashālā*. If one is simply unable to make the trip, one can listen to the chanting of the morning *suprabhātam* in the Tirupati temple and there are connections for online *darshan* and donation. Pilgrims can browse the Internet for the best deals on the *chār dhām yātrā* in the Himalayas or pilgrimage packages to seemingly countless destinations, from Badrīnāth in the mountains to Rāmeshvara in the far south of Tamil Nādu.

Tracking pilgrim traffic is surely impossible in *tīrthas* like Kāshī or Ujjain, for these are cities with their own swirling traffic and a near-constant flow of local worshippers as well as pilgrims. But in places where the pilgrimage is more contained, such as at the hilltop temples of Vaishno Devī in Kashmir or Shri Venkateshvara at Tirupati, all indications are that the number of pilgrims is growing significantly. As we have seen, the Tirumala Tirupati Devasthānams estimates that fifty thousand people a day stand in line for *darshan* of Lord Venkateshvara.[4] At Vaishno Devī, records are carefully kept and published on the Internet on a daily and cumulative basis. On one day—August 18, 2010—for example, 26,111 pilgrims made the journey. The growth in the pilgrimage has been remarkable over the years, from 1,396,000 in 1986 to 8,235,000 in 2009. To give us a sense of the magnitude of this pilgrimage, this means that the entire population of the five boroughs of New York City would climb the mountain and make their way through the narrow cave-passageway of the goddess during the course of a year! The website offers the following explanation: "The increase in the Yatra has been possible due to the efficient and pilgrim oriented management of the Shrine Board."[5]

A particular pilgrimage, like the Amarnāth Yātrā in Kashmir, can also be monitored for numbers, since it is necessary for pilgrims to register for the *yātrā* with the Amarnāth Shrine Board. In 2010, more than fifteen thousand pilgrims started out on the trail to Amarnāth on the very first day of the forty-five-day season. The season includes the full summer month of Shrāvana (July–August), especially holy for the worship of Shiva. The pilgrims string out along a mountainous trail leading to the high cave containing the ice *linga*. Beginning in 2007, the numbers began to exceed half a million pilgrims who made the long journey to Amarnāth, and this despite the restrictions and the violence that had marred the pilgrimage because of political and communal tensions in Kashmir.

Tourism, of course, is a growing phenomenon the world over. In the countries of Europe, where pilgrimage was once a major reason for people to travel, tourism has almost replaced the sacred journey. However, there are a few places, like Lourdes in France or the road through southern France to St. James of Compostela in northern Spain, where pilgrimage is a growing present-day phenomenon. Nothing in the world, however, begins to match the extensiveness or intensity of pilgrimage travel in India. While Hindu pilgrimages may sometimes include stops at palaces, government buildings, or old temple monuments, there is an important distinction between tourism and pilgrimage. Tourism may take us to "see the sights," but pilgrimage takes us for *darshan*, the "beholding" of a sacred image or a sacred place. Ela Bhatt, founder of the Self Employed Women's Association (SEWA) in Ahmedabad, once described to me the first-ever *yātrā* that the women of SEWA took, as soon as they were able to save just enough money to take the first trip of their hardworking lives. It was not a trip to Mumbai or any glossy tourist destination, but a *tīrthayātrā* by bus through Rajasthan to Krishna's Vrindāvan, and its participants included both Hindu and Muslim women.

TĪRTHAS AND THE ECONOMY OF NATURE

In addition to its communications revolution and its burgeoning pilgrimage traffic, India is also home to hundreds of environmental groups concerned with climate change, wastewater recycling, hydropower, and industrial waste. How does all this pilgrimage traffic relate to the concerns for the environment? Bathing in rivers, clambering to hilltop shrines, crouching into caves too low to stand in, circling sacred hills, winding along mountain trails into the snowy peaks, searching seacoasts for signs of Krishna, and treasuring the stones of Govardhan as Krishna's manifestations—all this sets a context of devotion that is in intimate relation with the world of nature. With such a profound sense of natural hierophany, it is all the more startling to see the ways in which climate change, pollution, and industrial development have had a devastating impact in India. Yet, on the whole, reverence for the ways in which the divine saturates the world of material nature has not yet led to a widespread cultural and religious resistance to environmental degradation.

The pilgrimage to Sabarimala in Kerala gives dramatic testimony to both the increase in pilgrimage travel in the past few decades and the devastating effect this has on the environment. Only thirty years ago, the number of Sabarimala pilgrims was an estimated fifty thousand during the two months of the pilgrimage season in January and February. Today, well over ten million pilgrims throng the temple each year during the months and days it is open. This almost unimaginable flow of pilgrims has had an extraordinary impact on the forest area surrounding the shrine, as well as on the wildlife so closely associated with Lord Ayyappa. The Pampā River is polluted with human waste, plastic bags, and water bottles. Rajan Gurukkal of the School of Social Sciences at Mahatma Gandhi University in Kottayam said, "The authorities must find out some mechanism to regulate the alarming increase in the number of pilgrims. Sabarimala is not only an environmental but also a social disaster."[6] Those who propose planning that will protect the ecosystem and the forests, such as the Clean Sabarimala Project of the Eco Pilgrimage Trust, have encountered the competing priorities of those who would develop temple facilities to accommodate more and more people.

We have discussed the uses and abuses of India's rivers, like the Pampā in Kerala, that suffer from the pollution of pilgrimage. The great waterways and sacred rivers of India have become the repositories of waste and sewage, agricultural and industrial pollution. They have been altered and have had their courses changed by damming and irrigation projects. Despite all the issues deemed vital to Hindu life taken up by the forces of the new Hindu nationalism, the rivers seem not to have become a significant part of the agenda. How would one weigh the symbolic importance of building a temple in Ayodhyā against the importance of protecting the great "mother rivers," abused by heedless design and human carelessness? After all, India's rivers immediately affect the daily lives of millions of people. Nowhere else on earth are the banks of rivers stair-stepped with bathing *ghāts* to bring the devoted into the flowing waters to bathe. One would expect this might mean a much higher level of public and political consciousness about the purity of rivers than in other countries where rivers do not bear such daily ritual expectations. But the combined forces of government will, environmentalism, and religious leadership have not yet coalesced to make this a top priority. Governmental efforts and bureaucracy have been criticized by environmental and religious leaders alike, but more rare is the critique levied at the most politically engaged Hindu leadership. The late Swami Chidānanda of the Divine Life Society in Rishikesh, however, put the critique of his fellow Hindus forcefully: "At that time [of the conflict in Ayodhyā] there was so much passion generated in one day. From the Himalayas to Kanyakumari, from Arunachal and Meghalaya to the Punjab, they carried this passion. Why don't they have this much passion for saving the Gangā and for the movement to save other rivers for the next generations?"[7]

Climate change has also had an impact on some pilgrimage places. The Chorabari glacier, some 12,800 feet above sea level in the steep glacial cirque above Kedārnāth, has been retreating year after year and is now the focus of intensive research to determine just how fast the glacier is melting. In the three years between 2004 and 2007, the snout of the glacier retreated some ninety feet, and it is now being studied carefully by glaciologists.[8] The retreat and thinning of the Chorabari glacier does not necessarily affect pilgrimage traffic to this high Himalayan shrine, but it does presage short-term flooding and long-term effects on the water supply, since the river that emerges from this glacier is one of several tributaries of the Gaṅgā. This and other Himalayan rivers supply water to a region where more than one-sixth of the world's population lives. The deterioration of these mountain rivers is potentially a serious problem for the plains of India.

In the Kashmir Himalayas, where all those hundreds of thousands of pilgrims trek to Amarnāth, the "Immortal Lord," there is also evidence of global warming. The pilgrim destination is a mountain cave at 13,500 feet, where they seek the *darshan* of Shiva, manifest as an ice *linga*. It was there, they say, that Shiva revealed the teachings of immortality to Pārvatī. The twelve-foot-high ice stalagmite, which long was said to wax and wane with the moon's cycle, melted completely in 2004 and in several subsequent years, according to the chief executive office of the Shrī Amarnāth Shrine Board. Warmer weather, plus the sheer presence of so many pilgrims with their body heat, meant that the ice manifestation of Shiva had disappeared by early July, when the shrine "officially" opened. The major pilgrimage takes place during the month of Shrāvana, in July and August. Press reports indicated some pilgrims were disappointed not to have *darshan* of the actual ice *linga*, while others were apparently not fazed by the ice melt, perhaps reflecting the wide understanding that the forms themselves are symbolic, pointing to, but not fully encapsulating, the divine reality. In any case, the ice forms representing both Pārvatī and Ganesha are still visible. Who knows how the Amarnāth *yātrā* will be affected by the shrinking ice in years to come?

The sense that the natural environment is an interconnected whole is well established in Hindu thought. As Kapila Vatsyayana writes, "The consciousness of the connections between the mountains and the oceans, the forests and the rivers, the deserts and the marshlands has been responsible for a large body of literature which has conceived of the land as a large, coherent unity with plurality and interdependence."[9] That interdependence, of course, also includes human beings, but the critical linkages between cultural practices, including pilgrimage practices, and environmental degradation are not yet strong. This is a large and growing area of concern, both for scholars and activists.

CREATING A LANDSCAPE

This has been an investigation of the pilgrim's India that begins on the ground, in the dense multiplicity of particular places, with the thick description of the pilgrim landscape. This landscape constitutes its own kind of primary text, a topographical text. At times, to be sure, the reader has been frustrated and perhaps overwhelmed by the mention of yet another local shrine and its connections to yet another place, god, or story. Suffice it to say that this dip into a sometimes-unwelcome level of detail gives us but a glimpse of what is truly a profusely storied landscape. It is the so-called tip of the iceberg. The topographical text tells us that here Hanumān was born, here he picked up Rāma and Lakshmana and carried them on his shoulders, here his tail lay heavy across the path and could not be moved, even by Bhīma, the strongman of the Pāndavas. The topographical text tells us of hillocks in Rajasthan or Karnataka where Devī slew Mahisha, of trails through the Himalayas that link the five manifestations of Shiva as Kedāra. At Kumbhakonam in Tamil Nadu, where the world was re-created from the clay pot filled with the four Vedas and the nectar of life, the topographical text points us to the place where Shiva shot the arrow breaking the pot, the places where the nectar from the pot flowed in five directions creating the Panchakrosha, the place where the rim of the pot fell into pieces, the place where the rest of the pot remained. Even in a single place, the topographical text tells us almost more than we can absorb.

And if we move to the Purānic texts, the Sanskrit and vernacular *māhātmyas*, we are likely to be even more profoundly overwhelmed, as I was, by the sheer volume of detail. Before beginning this project, I had already been tested on the major *māhātmyas* of Kāshī that detail hundreds of sites in their clusters and relations to one another in the topography of this one ancient city. In working on this unwieldy project, I gradually learned to inspect the trees and view the forest at the same time, a skill that became an urgent necessity as I turned to the whole of the *Skanda Purāna* and its prolixity of geographic and mythological detail. For example, up and down the Narmadā River, hundreds of shrines are noted, one after another. Even at a single place like Omkāreshvara, there are sub-*tīrthas* by the score. At Tirupati, there are stories that relate the significance of this place not only in this Kali Yuga, but in previous world ages as well.

So the point is pressed upon us from both context and text: The Hindu landscape is linked elaborately to the stories and deeds of the gods and heroes and their encounters with ordinary men and women. Some are the great stories known in one variation or another far and wide, like the legends of the *Rāmāyana*. Some are more regional or even local. Some are compelling and others seem to be just plain bizarre. All in all, however, we have learned that the landscape of India is a storied landscape—thickly so, intensely so.

We have seen also that the parts of the landscape, like the stories, are connected to one another. They are systematized and patterned. The *tīrthas* of Kāshī are seen as circling the city in larger and larger circles constituting a vast geographical mandala, while the *tīrthas* of Purī are imagined to array themselves as a conch, curling across the landscape by the sea. Rarely does a *tīrtha* stand alone, but rather it is grouped with others in pairs, threesomes, fours, fives, sixes, sevens, tens, and twelves. Each group constitutes a set and, as such, creates its own landscape through its imagined connections, even if the pilgrims rarely think about visiting each part of the set. Often, as we have seen, the connections are explicitly made to link the sacred sites of one part of India to another, re-creating the sites of Kāshī, for example, in the landscape of Maharashtra or more explicitly in the sacred sites of the city of Kolhāpūr.[10]

The linking of places one to another creates a landscape, a sense of locale or region, that is more complex than a single place. A landscape is differentiated, but at the same time the places that compose it are related. A landscape casts the mind's eye from place to place and embraces what is between. Two, three, four, or five places have a framing function, establishing borders and the distance between, composing and revealing. By linking together the twelve *jyotirlingas,* an imagined landscape is composed. By linking the three goddesses of Vindhyavāsinī, a local landscape is articulated. And by linking the three goddesses—Mīnākshī in Madurai, Vishālākshī in Kāshī, and Kāmākshī in Assam—a force field extending from south India to farthest northeast India is imagined. When places are linked one to another, patterned and displayed together, a landscape emerges.

For many in the European and American West, the term "landscape" is immediately associated with the painting of landscapes, a tradition in European art only since the sixteenth century. A landscape painting is, on the face of it, an apprehension of nature, observed and framed, painted or, more recently, photographed. Creating and framing a "landscape" is to a great extent the product of the vision and mind of the artist. What is the focal point? What is included and excluded in the frame? Where is the horizon? Clearly, "landscape" as a genre of painting does not merely represent or portray, but creates and composes. In doing this, the artist also participates in the shaping of regional, political, and cultural identities. In his book *Landscape and Power,* W. J. T. Mitchell broadens his investigation of landscape from a genre of painting to a medium of cultural expression, "a vast network of cultural codes," in which the composition of earth, stone, water, river, and sky signal cultural meanings and values.[11]

Thinking about the Hindu cultures of India, we note that there was no indigenous Hindu tradition of landscape representation or painting at least until the Persian and Indo-Muslim schools of painting began to take a Hindu focus. Even then, the focal point of Pahari and Rajasthani painting is not landscape as such, but the activity of the gods, set in a painted landscape: Krishna and Rādhā on a bed of leaves in the blossoming groves of springtime, Krishna lifting Mount Govardhan and holding it aloft as an umbrella, or Shiva and Pārvatī, seated by the fire, their tent of animal skins pitched high in the Himalayas. In some schools of painting, the hairline detail of leaves and blossoms, feathers and eyelashes, is astounding. In other schools of painting, the contextual surround that might constitute a "landscape" is elided altogether into a series of abstract blocks of blue, orange, or yellow—focusing the eye solely on the gods. But nowhere is landscape painted as such, simply to evoke the elements of the natural world.

However, the cultural practice of landscape, what Mitchell calls landscape as a "verb," is deeply rooted in Hindu pilgrimage traditions. It is here that the land is filled with encoded meanings and long traditions of cultural memory. The Himalayas are never mountains alone, but inhabited by the gods and filled with the lore of the Pāndavas. The hill over there is a piece of the Himalayas dropped here by Indra. The rivers that stream out of the mountains are filled not only with waters, but with myths of their divine descent and with the milk of mother cows.

We are reminded, once again, of Simon Schama's insight that "before it can ever be a repose for the senses, landscape is the work of the mind. Its scenery is built up as much from the strata of memory as from layers of rock."[12] Landscape, he observes, is a creation of culture, even the parts of the landscape we imagine to be most free of culture, beyond the pale of settlement, like the wilderness. We have seen how vividly this is so in India, where forest and wilderness are richly figured with cultural meanings and become the very heartland of India's great epics. The forest is not just there, out there, but identified by cultural markers and alive with fears and fantasies.

In a landscape, as on a map, particular places, with their names and stories, are linked together. We have seen that they are linked, in one way, by the set or group to which they belong, or by a wonderful story. For example, in the high hills of Maharashtra two of the Pāndava brothers wanted to perform a sacrifice, but they had no water and knocked over the water pot of a meditating ascetic. The water began running down the mountain, becoming the upper tributaries of the Karha River. The ascetic was aroused from his meditation and chased after the Pāndavas. Anne Feldhaus tells the tale: "With the furious ascetic hot on their heels, the two brothers ran downstream along the route that the water was taking. Each time the ascetic came too close, they would toss a grain of rice behind them. The grain of rice would turn into a Sivalinga, and the ascetic would stop to worship it. Thus were founded the Siva temples of the many villages along the upper reaches of the Karha river."[13] It is a tale, Feldhaus tells us, about the founding of a region of Maharashtra, a region that is linked by the running waters of the Karha River, by the running of the Pāndavas, and by the Shiva temples they established along the way. It is one of countless stories that compose the linked places of a landscape.

Landscape is composed not only by the overlay of narrative, but also by the footsteps of pilgrims. As they set out from home and village on a journey, their footsteps link the places where they begin to the destinations they seek. They leave their village in Maharashtra to walk with the palanquin of the local saint on the pilgrimage to Pandharpūr. They leave home in Andhra Pradesh to carry the ashes of their beloved father to the holy delta where the rivers meet at Prayāga. They set forth from Delhi to visit the holy sites of Krishna in Braj. They leave from Jaipur to visit the great temples and *tīrthas* of Tamil Nadu. They leave from Chennai to offer prayers and vows to Lord Bālājī at Tirupati for recovery from a critical illness. They leave from Mumbai to travel down coastal Karnataka to Shiva's shrine at Gokarna. Every day, pilgrims by the hundreds of thousands crisscross India on their way to somewhere, near or far. The landscape interlaced with their footsteps is part and parcel of the cumulative knowledge passed on as culture. It is cultural knowledge embedded in the day-to-day life of society. And culture, of course, is always in the making, always being composed once again, in a new context, with each new journey.

SPACE AND PLACE IN THE DIVINE ECONOMY

As we think about the significance of this pilgrim's landscape, there is an important theological perspective that emerges. Many cultural geographers have distinguished between "space" and "place." In general, space is homogeneous and open to the horizon; it is unmarked and neutral. It extends from the familiar to the beyond and often links the two. Wide-open spaces mean freedom and the lack of constraint. The most common Sanskrit term for space is *ākāsha*, which means "sky" in one sense, or the open space that extends between earth and heaven, as far up as the blue extends. It is space unlimited, the totality and fullness of space. "Transcendence" is the word that comes readily to mind.

Place, on the other hand, is particular and differentiated; it is named, bordered, and inhabited. Yi-Fu Tuan puts it succinctly in *Space and Place in the Perspective of Experience:*

> Open space has no trodden paths and signposts. It has no fixed pattern of established human meaning; it is like a blank sheet on which meaning may be imposed. Enclosed and humanized space is place. Compared to space, place is a calm center of established values. Human beings require both space and place. Human lives are a dialectical movement between shelter and venture, attachment and freedom. In open space one can become intensely aware of place; and in the solitude of a sheltered place the vastness of space beyond acquires a haunting presence.[14]

There are many terms that probe the terrain of "place" in the robust and resonant Sanskrit lexicon. *Desha* refers to a geographical place, a country, home, or region. If *ākāsha* is infinite, *desha* is finite and specific, with a particular character and culture.[15] It is related to the term for the directions. A *desha* is, indeed, a movable but always particular pivot of the four directions. The particularity of place is important, and whenever a ritual act is performed, as we have seen, the statement of intention called *sankalpa* begins with a statement of *desha-kala*, mentioning the specific place where one stands and the specific time it is right now. The term *kshetra* designates a field, a region, and again is a place with specific qualities. Often a very significant sacred place is called a *kshetra*, extending over a larger area than any one of its sacred features. The term *dhām* refers to a dwelling place, an abode, and in the sacred context it is one of the dwellings of the divine, as we have seen with the *chār dhām*, the four abodes at India's compass points. A *dhām* is an earthly, but also heavenly, place. This scope is also included in the term *loka*, meaning "world" in multiple senses, from the world of earth to the worlds of heaven, from the geographical world to the community of people, the populace. All these terms, with their many nuances, signify place as particular, familiar, named, and storied. By contrast, space is wide, expansive, and ultimately ungraspable. More than any other term, it is the term *tīrtha* that signals the linkage of place and space.

In the pilgrim's India, we encounter over and over the powerful conception of a god who fills and exceeds the span of space and is simultaneously fully present in this very place. This is a religious view in which the divine, though utterly transcendent and ultimately ungraspable by human mind and speech, takes form in the very world in which we live— in rocks and hillocks, in rivers and pools, in consecrated images and in spontaneous manifestations. God is vast, yet God is here. Shiva's *linga* of light is unfathomable, but it is here in this rocky outcropping, in these hills, in this temple, in this earthen *linga*. Vishnu's reclining body contains the seeds of the entire universe, yet he may be glimpsed here on this island in the Kāverī River, on these hills that are formed from the serpent Shesha. Devī's circle of muscular arms hold the weapons and emblems of all the gods, and when she slew the demon Mahisha, she stood right here in Karnataka, in Kashmir, in the hills of the Vindhyas.

This theological understanding of divine reality can be glimpsed in the ancient *Rig Veda* hymn to Purusha—the vast but embodied reality, the immeasurable one who fills space and extends ten fingers beyond space, who extends beyond human understanding and is simultaneously expressed in detail in the places of the measured world. The divine has spun from its very being the world of what we call "nature" and therefore can be discovered almost anywhere, depending on the quality of human apprehension. Here in this place the divine reality descends, as rivers descend from the heavens. Here the supreme god spontaneously bursts forth from the earth in a luminous hierophany. Here god's image attaches firmly to the earth and will not let go. Here the very bones and sinews of the body of the divine reality are laid out on the earth, and their circuitry provides the paths for the circulation of pilgrims.

The particularity of the sacred, the differentiation of the multitude of places in which sacred presence is apprehended, and yet the affirmation of the everywhere of the sacred—this is the particular genius of the theology given expression in the landscape of India. No one says it better than the poet-saints of south India, who relentlessly praise the supreme lord who is right here where the rivers meet, right here where the herons wade, right here where the hillock rises, right here where the palms sway over the estuary, right here where the mango blossoms are fragrant. The places they praise are different. The taste of the lord is different in each one. But each one is a "beloved place," and each one enables the pilgrim soul to catch a glimpse of the vast reality of god.

Of course, the divine presence can be created ritually, consecrated with prayers, with showers of water and mantras, and this is done wherever an image of one of the gods, what Vaishnavas call an "image-incarnation," is installed and made accessible for worship in a temple. But we have in the landscape of *tīrthas* a somewhat different realization: that the sacred may be found "in the rough," so to speak. As we have seen in our exploration of India's *tīrthas*, the image contained within the sanctum of the temple is often quite subsidiary to the hills above it or the river that flows by its door. While the temple can certainly become a *tīrtha*, the *tīrtha* is much more profound than the structure of a temple. To mistake a temple of bricks and mortar for a *tīrtha* is, then, a kind of idolatry, a religious vision that has restricted its eye to the narrow and lost the vision of the vast.

Religious vision in this worldview, then, is oriented to both the vastness of space and the specificity of place. The *linga* of light cannot be fathomed, even by the gods, but it can be created here on the banks of the Narmadā River, on a sunny afternoon, with a lump of clay, worshipped with a single grain of rice, and then committed to the river to dissolve into the water.

THE TĪRTHAS OF THE HEART

When Lakshmīdhara wrote his compendium of *tīrthas* in the twelfth century, he seemed to emphasize, at the outset, that real *tīrthas* are not the places alone, or the sacred waters alone. The real *tīrthas* are truth, charity, patience, self-control, celibacy, and wisdom—these are the *tīrthas* of the heart in which one must bathe. He quotes from the *Brahmā Purāna:* If merely going to a *tīrtha* is enough to purify, then the fish in the Gangā and the birds who roost in the temple towers would be instantly purified. Perhaps of greater concern than fishes and birds to Lakshmīdhara's patrons, the Gāhadāvala kings were the miscreants who took the garb of pilgrims and came to the *tīrthas* as fugitives from justice. Would they also be purified?

There is certainly a tension between the power of the place itself and the importance of a "right heart within," and this tension is perpetually part of the discourse of pilgrimage in India.[16] The *māhātmyas* sometimes go to great extents to emphasize the sheer power of place. They tell us that even if the worst sinner and miscreant is touched accidentally by a drop of Gangā water splashed from the river, or even if the thief trips over a Shiva *linga* while running off with the booty of a robbery, he gains a measure of sanctification. Indeed, the unaccountable purification bestowed by the holy places is one of the favorite themes of the *māhātmyas* that extol these places with soaring praise. Even if a pilgrim performs rites on the Gangā out of greed, cunning, or egotism, he may go to heaven. But the truly efficacious pilgrimage is one that combines the ritual journey with true faith. "The one who always bathes in earthly *tīrthas* as well as in the *tīrthas* of the heart reaches the supreme goal!"

Lakshmīdhara concludes his work with a final chapter on the Great Pilgrimage, the *Mahāpatha*, the journey that follows the "Great Path" into the Himalayas, as the Pāndavas did at the end of their lives. As death approaches, this is their final pilgrimage, a steady climb on that great path toward heaven. One by one, they fall along the way, until only Yudhisthira is left at the entrance to heaven. It is here that he famously demonstrates the virtues that are the *tīrthas* of the heart: He rejects the world of heaven if he cannot bring the dog, his faithful and devoted companion along the way.

If life itself is a journey, the final leg of that journey has special importance, and many people yearn to go on pilgrimage to a *dhām* or a *tīrtha* as they approach the end.

The perpetual pilgrims of India are the *sannyāsīs*, the ascetics who, presumably, have lived fully through the generative phases of life—having done their work and enjoyed their families, having seen children and grandchildren. Then they have "cast off" from settled society, indeed they have ritually died to that life, in order to live a life of renunciation. *Sannyāsīs* are the ones who have detached themselves from place, from the village or town from which they came. They move among the holy places. As the monk Agehananda Bharati put it, these *sannyāsīs* and *sādhus* "are patrons at those places, not clients."[17] They cluster at the crossings, the *tīrthas,* especially during the great *melās,* but they come not as the lay pilgrim, with the goal of *darshan* or their own spiritual benefit. In an ideal world, they give embodied evidence of a spiritual goal that crosses beyond birth and death, beyond the world of "getting and keeping" that typifies settled earthly life.

A pilgrim setting off from home at any stage of life becomes a kind of temporary *sannyāsī,* having set forth from the security of family and village with only the bundle one can carry. Especially in pre-modern times, the *tīrthayātrā* was not a journey with a certain date of return. It was fraught with the uncertainties, discomforts, and dangers of the road. Pilgrims also direct themselves toward a goal, a crossing, that takes them, at least temporarily, out of the day-to-day world of getting and keeping. Seeking out the crossing is especially profound for the elderly, who are looking inevitably toward the final crossing.

We began this journey in Kāshī, often said to be preeminent among those places where one who has come to the end of this life can find liberation, crossing over to the far shore of immortality. As Shiva shows his beloved city to the goddess Pārvatī, he compares the city to a ferry boat, exclaiming:

Look dear! Look at Kāshī, a boat stretched out for the crossing . . .
a boat not of wood and iron, but the light of illumination for all the
people it ferries across the sea of life.

And yet, in exploring the sacred geography of India more widely, we have learned that one might board this boat for the great crossing-beyond at any of the seven *tīrthas* of India said to be *mokshadāyaka*, "bestowers of liberation." But even more—the claim to a crossing inheres in the very notion of a *tīrtha*. While the *tīrtha* may ferry one over the trials and tribulations of earthly life, the *tīrtha* is finally a ferry to help one cross over from the entanglement of repeated birth and death to the freedom of liberation. One just might board that boat anywhere. Taking a pilgrim journey to a distant place may be a necessary discipline, but not because the nearby place is not also a crossing. *Tīrthas* are plentiful—where the rivers meet, where the hill rises, where the temple flag waves. The south Indian poet Dasimayya writes that for the one who is truly awake to the reality of Shiva, "his own front yard is the true Banāras." And the *tīrtha* just might be closer still. Lalla, a fourteenth-century devotional poet from Kashmir, wrote: "I, Lalla, went out far in search of Shiva, the omnipresent lord; having wandered, I found him in my own body, sitting in his house."[18]

Acknowledgments

This book has emerged over many thousands of miles and in the company of many thousands of people. The road and the people have taught me not only what is in this book, but most of what I know about the religious life of India. The long train trips, the midnight crowds on station platforms and in waiting rooms, the bumpy bus trips standing up, the terrifying road trips up and down mountainsides stitched with hairpin turns, and the blessed time on foot, on the trail—this was my life in India for more than a decade of research on this project. My destination was usually a major pilgrimage site where I would spend hours, crowded shoulder to shoulder in the airless inner sanctum of some of India's greatest and least-known temples. What I found was always much more than the major temple; it was the surrounding sacred geography that set these places in a map of reference that spanned regions and even the entire land of India.

The early years of my research in the 1980s were undertaken before the digital revolution, a fact that now seems quite astonishing. My work was driven by the sheer curiosity of a scholar who knew something of the vast textual resources in Sanskrit and Hindi on the places of Hindu pilgrimage and wondered what these places were like today. There was no *darshan* to be had without actually going there. For this I am grateful. What and whom might one actually find in the hills above the Krishnā River where Shiva's great Shrī Shaila temple is set? What would be there at the headwaters of the Kāverī? Today, there is a profusion of websites that would offer a glimpse of the sights and even sounds of the *tīrthas*. But then, the experience and the surprise of the *tīrtha* was still reserved for those who came in person and on foot.

I want to thank the wonderful colleagues and friends who have encouraged me along the way of what was always an impossible project.

In the early years, when I would return to Delhi every three or four weeks to write and plot the next leg of my journey, I was received and revived by Veena and Ranen Das, by T. N. and Uma Madan, and by Devaki and Lakshmi Jain. In Vārānasī, Bettina Baumer and Rana P. B. Singh would help me think about what I was doing, and in Vrindāvan, it was Shrīvatsa Goswāmī, who knew everything about Braj and who, with Sandhyā, always extended hospitality. In Paris, it was Charlotte Vaudeville, whose work has always been an inspiration to me. And in Cambridge, it was my friend Jack Hawley, whose work continues to set the high-water mark for those of us in Hindu studies. Jack and his wife, Laura Shapiro, have always provided literary sensibilities, levity, and love—the necessities of life, especially for academics.

Students of many years, now colleagues in our field, have also helped me in many aspects of this research, including Robert Hueckstedt, Anne Monius, Jim Laine, Rachel McDermott, and Rajam Raghunāthan, along with the many teaching assistants who enthusiastically helped to teach my Harvard Core Course, "Hindu Myth, Image, and Pilgrimage." Prabhavati Reddy did her own doctoral research on the Shrī Shaila temple, and Tamara Lanaghan wrote her thesis on the sacred center of Kolhāpūr in Maharashtra. Luke Whitmore took the course and set out to write a superb Emory doctoral thesis on Kedārnāth, and Deonnie Moodie, one of the most recent teaching assistants, is currently at work on Kālī Ghāt in Calcutta. To all of you, a heartfelt thank-you!

During the years I have been at work on this project, some of my colleagues have published studies that have been enormously useful to me, many of them regional studies that have helped me think about the wider issues of India's sacred geography. This has been one of the blessed benefits of the long arc of this project. I have learned so much from the work of Anne Feldhaus on the rivers and landscapes of Maharashtra, William Sax on the ritual landscape of the Himalayas, Jack Hawley, David Haberman, and Alan Entwistle on Braj, Hans Bakker and Peter Van der Veer on Ayodhyā, and James Lochtefeld on Hardvār.

I was funded for this work by a Fulbright Senior Research Award and, later, a Fulbright Faculty Fellowship, a Guggenheim Fellowship, an American Institute of Indian Studies summer award, and the Harvard South Asia Initiative, and I am grateful for the patience they all have shown in awaiting the completion of this book.

There are many reasons a project takes so long to complete. One of them is the mountain of books, pamphlets, maps, and notes still stacked in my library study, always reminding me how much remained to do. They are still there, and that is just a fact of life with a project of this scope. Beyond that, life, illness, and death intervened. I was launching a semester of sabbatical research when my father died back home in Montana. After more than a month at home, it was hard to resume, pack up again, and return to the field. I was able to do this only in the company of Dorothy Austin, my partner of decades, who joined me to travel into Orissa and Bengal; and then Kathryn Walker, a beloved friend, who brought sleeping bags and tins of tuna for a long trip to Gangotrī. Then my own illness intervened, and I decided to turn for a time to a book of a more theological nature, *Encountering God: A Spiritual Journey from Bozeman to Banaras* (1993).

Politics also intervened, with the rise of a form of Hindu nationalism I found deeply disheartening, as Ayodhyā and all India were rocked with violence after the destruction of the Babri Masjid in December 1992. The subsequent years seemed to leverage many of these same issues of sacred lore and sacred space into a newly empowered confrontational Hindu extremism that steamed on through the 1990s. As a result, the past twenty years has also given us a range of scholarly reflection on Hindu nationalism and secularism, for which I am very grateful. Dozens of books from this period have given me fresh perspectives on the kind of work I have been doing and have enabled me to see its place in the understanding of India today.

Meanwhile, the global movements of history have intervened, as well, with the immigration to the United States of millions of South Asians who have established Hindu, Sikh, Muslim, and Jain communities in America. In 1992, I launched the Pluralism Project to map and interpret this new religious reality here at home. Our CD-ROM, *On Common Ground: World Religions in America* (1997, 2002), and my book *A New Religious America* (2001) have taken a new look at our own country in this era. Here, too, I have had another vantage point from which to view the patterning of Hindu sacred geography, as communities in the United States replicate the temples and *tīrthas* of India.

All the while through these years, I have returned to India as often as possible, keeping this project in heart and mind, returning to the

Narmadā River, Māgha Melā in Prayāga, Ayodhyā, and Vārānasī. And all the while I have also written lectures, articles, and book chapters that have come into this work in another form. My first essay on the Gangā appeared as "Gangā: The Goddess in Hindu Sacred Geography" in *The Divine Consort: Radha and the Goddesses of India* (Hawley and Wulff, 1982). An early version of some of the Rāma material appeared as "Following Rāma, Worshipping Siva" in *Devotion Divine, Bhakti Traditions from the Regions of India* (Eck, 1992), and "The Imagined Landscape: Patterns in the Construction of Hindu Sacred Geography" was part of *Tradition, Pluralism, and Identity: In Honour of T. N. Madan* (Das, 1999).

In bringing this project to completion, I want to thank all the wonderful people in Lowell House, the Pluralism Project, the Study of Religion, and the Sanskrit Department who have given me support and forbearance while I spent time at my desk. I want to thank my agent, Jill Kneerim, and my superb editor at Crown Publishers, Trace Murphy, along with his assistant, Annie Chagnot, for their patience and skill in handling a complicated manuscript. Here at Harvard, C. Scott Walker, a digital cartography specialist, did all the groundwork on the maps. And I want especially to thank my assistant, Zachary Ugolnik, who is an inveterate pilgrim himself and, at the same time, a painstaking scholar whose assistance in the preparation of this manuscript has been invaluable.

A project of this length carries with it the longevity of love. My mother, Dorothy Eck, has lived through the entire journey with me, reading drafts of chapters I would bring with me on every vacation—whether home to Bozeman or Ovando in Montana or to our family homestead on the Olympic peninsula in Washington. My life's beloved, Dorothy Austin, has also lived with me through the days, years, and decades of this book project, from its first summer in Tirupati to its last summer in Touisset, on Mount Hope Bay. Dorothy means "gift of God," and to these two Dorothys I dedicate this book in heartfelt thanks.

GLOSSARY

Agastya: Legendary sage, credited with bringing Vedic dharma from the north to the south.

Agni: Vedic fire god; the sacrificial fire itself.

ākāsha: Sky, the open space that extends between earth and heaven.

alvārs: Tamil poet-saints (sixth to tenth centuries) whose songs of devotion are widely known and loved.

Amarakantaka: Shrine at the headwaters of the Narmadā River.

amrita: Nectar of immortality.

ānanda: Bliss, happiness. The sublime bliss of oneness with Brahman.

Ananta: Endless. The name of the coiled serpent on which Vishnu rests in between aeons of time.

anda: Egg. The unitary whole from which all creation emerges.

Annapūrnā: Goddess of "Plenteous Food," Shiva's consort; especially in Vārānasī.

āratī: The circling of oil-lamps before the divine image; used also to describe the entire sequence of honor offerings made to the deity.

artha: "Wealth, power, purpose"; one of the four *purushārthas*, the aims of life.

Arunāchala: Dawn Mountain, place of pilgrimage associated with Shiva's *linga* of light and, more recently, with the sage Rāmana Mahārshi.

āshram: Forest retreat, dwelling place of sages, yogis, and their students.

āshrama: Stage of life, traditionally four: student, householder, forest-dweller, and renouncer.

ashvamedha: Vedic horse sacrifice; a rite of fertility and creation, performed also at the consecration of a king.

asura: Beings that oppose and compete with the gods (*suras* or *devas*). Demons, but not always wicked.

ātman: Essence of life, identical with Brahman and refers to that essence within the person.

Aurangzeb (1618–1707): Emperor of Mughal Dynasty, known for emerging Muslim conservative orthodoxy.

avatāra: The "descent" of a deity; an incarnation, especially of Vishnu.

Ayodhyā: One of the seven cities of liberation; traditional birthplace and capital of Rāma, as such, the focus of late-twentieth-century communal politics.

Ayyappa: A local hero-deity of Sabarimala, Kerala, created from the union of Vishnu and Shiva.

Badrīnāth: Himalayan pilgrimage place, where Vishnu as Badarī Nārāyana is honored. One of the four *dhāms* of all India and also of the Himalayas.

Bālājī: Popular name for Vishnu as Shri Venkateshvara, honored at the hilltop shrine of Tirupati.

Ban Yātrā: Also Vana Yātrā, the pilgrimage through the groves and forests of Krishna's homeland in Braj, in north India.

Bhagavad Gītā: The "Song of the Lord," Krishna's teaching and revelation to the warrior Arjuna that forms part of the sixth book of the *Mahābhārata.*

Bhāgavata Purāna: One of the eighteen major Purānas, its tenth section being one of the most extensive sources for the life and lore of Krishna.

Bhagīratha: King of ancient Kosala whose austerities brought the River Gangā from heaven to earth. Thus, one of her names is Bhāgīrathī.

Bhairava: Strong and fearsome manifestation of Shiva, also honored on his own as protector.

bhakti: Devotion to god, the love of the worshipper for a personal god, whether understood to be a form of Vishnu, Shiva, the Goddess, or the formless one.

Bhārat, Bhārata: Land of India, named for an ancient king, Bharata—not to be confused with Bhārata, the brother of Rāma.

Bhārat Mātā: Mother India, the motherland.

Bhīma: One of the five Pāndava brothers of *Mahābhārata* fame. Great in size, appetite, and temper.

Bhīmashankar: A Shiva shrine and *jyotirlinga* in Maharashtra at the source of the east-flowing Bhīma River.

bhuvana kosha: "Dictionary of the world" or "Atlas of the World"; texts in the epics and Purānas that describe the whole cosmos, including the cultural geography of the land of India.

bilva leaves: Three-petaled leaves of the bilva or bael tree associated with Shiva and used in Shiva's worship.

Brahmā: Creator god, having four heads, one to look in each direction. Brahmā has no independent cult but is expecially honored at Pushkara in Rajasthan.

Brahman: Essence of life; the supreme, transcendent One; the reality, source of all being and knowing.

Brāhmana: Name of the priestly and ritual texts attached to the Veda.

brahmin: The priestly class or a member of the priestly class, charged with learning, teaching, and performing rites and sacrifices.

Braj: Area around Mathurā and Vrindāvan in north India sacred to the life and lore of Krishna.

chār dhām: "Four abodes" where the divine dwells, most widely construed as the compass points of India: Badrīnāth (N), Rāmeshvara (S), Dvārakā (W), and Purī (E); other fourfold pilgrimages also have this name.

Chitrakūt/Chitrakūta: Forested area and present-day pilgrimage center where Rāma, Sītā, and Lakshmana are said to have spent part of their forest exile; hermitage of Atri and other sages.

Daksha: Creator demigod, father of Satī, who insulted Shiva by not inviting him to a great sacrifice.

dāna: Ritual gift, often a charitable donation.

dargah: Memorial tomb-shrine of a Sufi saint or martyr.

darshan: In ritual and pilgrimage, the "auspicious sight" of the deity; also a "point of view," or a school of philosophy.

Dasharatha: King of Ayodhyā, father of Rāma.

desha: Place, a country, home, or region.

deva: A god, deity.

Devakī: Mother of Krishna, wife of Vasudeva.

devī: A goddess; refers to the thousands of local goddesses as well as to the consorts of the great gods and the Great Goddess, called Devī or Mahādevī.

Devī Bhāgavata Purāna: The Purāna with the most extensive treatment of the lore and theology of the Goddess, usually considered an Upapurāna, not one of the major eighteen Purānas.

dhām: "Abode, dwelling" of God. A sacred place where the divine is said to dwell.

dharma: Duty, law, righteousness; religious duties, especially rites; in more modern usage, religion.

dharmashālā: A rest house or hostel that caters to pilgrims.

dhoti: A traditional men's garment, consisting of a single piece of unstitched cloth worn around the waist.

digvijaya: Literally, "victory over the four directions," whether the king's military circumambulation of the kingdom or a spiritual leader's tour of India, as in Shankara's *digvijaya.*

Draupadī: Daughter of King Drupada of Panchāla and the wife of the five Pāndava brothers who accompanies them in their forest exile.

Durgā: "Hard to Reach"; one of the primary names of the Devī as consort of Shiva. Powerful with weapons in her multiple hands.

Dvārakā: Sacred city and last capital of Krishna in west India, on the Arabian Sea. One of the four *dhāms.*

dvīpa: Island, referring to ordinary islands and the ring-shaped islands that encircle the world.

gana: attendant of Shiva.

Ganesha: Lord of *ganas,* the remover of obstacles, the keeper of the thresholds of space and time, honored at the doorway and at the outset of any venture.

Gangā: Sacred river of north India; rising at Gangotrī; honored as a goddess.

Gangā Sāgara: Place of pilgrimage where the Gangā meets the sea in the Bay of Bengal.

garbha: Embryo, the egg, the unitary seed from which all creation emerges in the imaginative vision of the Vedas.

garbha griha: Inner chamber or "womb chamber" of a temple, where the image of the deity dwells.

Gaurī: The "white" goddess, name of Pārvatī.

Gayā: Sacred site in north India famous for *shrāddha* rites for the dead.

ghāt: Landing place or bank along a river or coast.

Girnār: Mountain sacred to Jains and Hindus in Saurashtra, Gujarat.

Godāvarī: Sacred river of the Deccan in central India, rising in the Western Ghāts and flowing east.

Gokarna: Sacred site, *linga* of Shiva, along the western coast of India.

Gomukh: "Cow's mouth," where a river takes its rise; the most famous Gomukh is where the Gangā emerges from the lip of a Himalayan glacier.

gopī: Milkmaid or herdswoman, especially one of the girls who shares the living legend of Lord Krishna and participates in the great circle dance in Braj.

gopura: Temple tower or superstructure, situated in south Indian temples above the gateways to the temple complex.

Govardhan: Holy hill lifted by Krishna to protect the village folk and their cows from the pelting rain of Indra; the site of the cult of an ancient local cowherd deity.

Gupta: North Indian empire from the fourth to sixth century C.E.

guru: Teacher, spiritual guide.

Guruvāyūr: Shrine dedicated to Lord Krishna in Kerala; famous for healing.

Hanumān: Monkey hero, faithful servant of Rāma, who helped Rāma retrieve Sītā from captivity in Lankā; worshipped today in his own right as focus of a vigorous cult.

Hardvār: Sacred city of pilgrimage, located where the Gangā enters the plains of India. Site of one of the four *kumbha melās*.

Himalaya: Mountain range spanning north India, literally the "abode of snows." Personified as the husband of Menā and father of Pārvatī.

Hindustan: Persian name for South Asia, literally "the land of the Indus [Sindhu] River."

Hindutva: Literally, "Hinduness," popularized by V. D. Savarkar in pamphlet of the same name (1923); describes a Hindu as one who holds India as both "holy land" and "fatherland."

Hiranyagarbha: Golden Embryo, Golden Egg; the unitary source of all the complexity of creation.

Hsuan Tsang: Seventh-century Chinese monk who traveled to India to collect the sacred Buddhist scriptures.

Indra: Vedic warrior god, wielder of the thunderbolt, and drinker of the intoxicating *somā*; in later times, a directional guardian (East).

ishtadevatā: "Chosen deity"; the understanding and image of the divine that each worshipper holds to the heart in his or her devotion.

īshvara: Lord; refers to the personal Lord; used in compound with other names, it refers to a particular manifestation of Shiva, such as Vishveshvara, the "Lord of All."

Jagannāth/Jagannātha: "Lord of the Universe"; name of Krishna as he dwells in Purī, Orissa. Also, name of a seventeenth-century poet, author of the *"Gangā Laharī."*

Jambudvīpa: Rose Apple Island; in Indic cosmology, the world we live in, a lotus-shaped island with four petal-continents, centered at Mount Meru, located in the middle of an expanding universe of surrounding seas and ring-shaped islands.

jnāna: Wisdom, transforming knowledge.

jyotirlinga: *"Linga* of light," the manifestation of Shiva as an unspeakably brilliant and fathomless column of light.

Kailāsa: Himalayan peak located in what is today Tibet; destination of Buddhist and Hindu pilgrims; for Hindus, the mountain abode of Lord Shiva.

Kāla: Time, death, and destiny.

Kālī: "Black Goddess," both mother of life and fearsome weapon-bearer; sometimes the *shakti* of Shiva, sometimes the supreme Mahādevī, unattached to any male deity.

Kālidāsa: "Servant of Kālī," Sanskrit poet and author of some of India's finest literature; said to have lived in Ujjain in about the fourth century C.E.

Kāma: God of passion; India's Cupid, who arouses lovers with his flower arrows; one of the four *purushārthas,* the aims of life, here the pursuit of passion or pleasure.

Kāmākshī: "Love-Eyed Goddess" whose most famous shrine is Kāmākhyā, in Assam; also dwells prominently in Kānchī in Tamil Nadu.

Kamsa: King of Mathurā who tries repeatedly to kill the child Krishna, born to be his nemesis.

Kānchī: One of the seven sacred cities of India, situated in the Tamil south, embracing major Vaishnava and Shaiva temples.

Kanyākumārī: "Virgin Goddess" at the tip of southern India, protecting and blessing; her name popularized in British times as Cape Comorin.

karma: An act, and its results, which will be manifest in time.

karma bhūmi: Literally, the "land of action"; Bhārata, where action can produce results and lead to freedom.

Kārttikeya: Deity, "Son of the Krittikās," also known as Skanda, Murugan, or Kumāra, the hero son of Shiva.

Kāshī: Popular and ancient name for Banāras, the luminous, the "City of Light," from *kash,* "to shine."

Kāverī: Sacred river of south India, rising in the hills of Karnataka and flowing south and east across Tamil Nadu.

Kedāra, Kedārnāth: Shrine and area sacred to Shiva, located in the Himalayas in the state that is now Uttarākhand; one of the northern *chār dhām;* one of Shiva's *jyotirlingas.*

khanda: A section of land (as in Kedāra Khanda) or of a literary work (as in *Kāshī Khanda,* a lengthy section of the *Skanda Purāna*). Related, kānda, also means section or chapter.

Kolhāpūr: Temple city on the bank of the Panchgangā River in Maharashtra, sacred to Mahālakshmī, the Goddess.

Krishna: Ancient cowherd god; hero and adviser in the *Mahābhārata* war; playful lover of the milkmaids in his rural homeland near Mathurā; *avatāra* of Vishnu, but honored as supreme in his own right.

Krittikās: The Pleiades, the six stars who are the mothers of Shiva's son, Kārttikeya.

krosha: Unit of measurement, about two miles.

kshatriya: Member of the warrior or noble class; more broadly, those who rule the land and protect the people.

kshetra: Field, land; pilgrimage place that comprises an entire area.

kshetrapāla: Guardian or protector of a place.

kumbha: Round water pot, sometimes consecrated to represent the Devī.

Kumbhakonam: Temple town along the Kāverī River in Tamil Nadu; site of the great bathing tank and Mahāmaham bathing festival.

Kumbha Melā: Great pilgrimage fair and bathing festival held once every twelve years at Prayāga, today's Allahabad.

kumkum: Red powder used decoratively in personal adornment or in ritual.

kund: A pool, especially a pool for ritual bathing, either clay-banked or with steps for access to the water.

Kūrma: The tortoise *avatāra* of Vishnu; the name of one of the Purānas.

Kurukshetra: Sacred site in north India, capital of the legendary King Kuru; the battlefield of the great war described in the *Mahābhārata*.

Lakshmana: Brother of Rāma who accompanied the hero during his forest exile.

Lakshmī: Goddess who embodies auspiciousness, wealth, and fortune; consort of Vishnu.

Lakshmīdhara: The chief minister of the Gāhadavāla King Govindachandra in the twelfth century; scholar of dharma and compiler of the *Tīrthavivechana Kānda*.

Lankā: The island capital of Rāvana in the *Rāmāyana;* identified today with the island of Sri Lanka.

līlā: Play, both as a human and divine activity.

līlāsthalas: In the landscape of Braj, the "places of play," the sites of Krishna's playful and loving relations with the villagers and milkmaids.

linga: The "sign" or "emblem" of Shiva and the primary icon of Shiva worship.

loka: World, in a geographical or spatial sense; includes the meanings of both "space" and "light," thus, the illumined world, the world that shines forth.

Lokāloka: Literally, "world-unworld"—an infinitely distant mountain range at the edge of the universe beyond which there is no light at all.

Madurai: Temple city in southern Tamil Nadu famous for the Goddess Mīnākshī and Shiva Sundareshvara.

māhātmya: The "glorification" or "praise" of a deity, a place, a ritual; the eulogistic literature containing such praises.

Maheshvara: "Great Lord," Shiva.

Mahisha: The bull demon, defeated by the Goddess Durgā, actually a bull water-buffalo.

Mānasa: The lake, sometimes called Mānasarovar, at the foot of Mount Kailāsa.

Mandākinī: One of the high tributaries of the River Gangā, rising near Kedārnāth and joining with the Alakanandā at Rudra Prayāg.

mandala: Circle; a circular diagram, the schematic and symbolic map of the sacred universe.

Manikarnikā: One of the primary *tīrthas* of Banāras, the cremation ground.

mantra: A sacred formula or utterance, a prayer.

matha: A monastery.

Mathurā: One of the seven sacred cities of liberation, located in central north India on the Yamunā River; early center of Buddhism; famous as the birthplace of Krishna.

Matsya: The fish *avatāra* of Vishnu; the name of one of the Purānas.

Maurya: Fourth- to second-century B.C.E. Indian empire, its most famous emperor being Ashoka, who became a great patron of Buddhism.

māyā: Illusion, the illusory quality of the transitory world of "names and forms"; the mistaken perception of the world as permanent.

melā: A fair, especially a religious fair or bathing festival to which people often come great distances on pilgrimage.

moksha: Liberation, freedom from the cycle of birth and death.

Mount Meru: The symbolic mountain at the center of the lotus-shaped world and its surrounding universe.

mudrā: In both visual arts and dance, a hand gesture to convey particular meanings.

mukti: Liberation, *moksha.*

mukut: A crown, a silver or brass cap, placed upon the Shiva *linga* at special times of worship.

mūrti: Form, likeness; the consecrated image of the deity as a focus for *darshan.*

nāga: Serpent; serpent deity, associated with pools and streams; co-opted by all the great deities in their rise to supremacy.

Nārada: Celestial sage; busybody of the sages who instigates many a plot and drama.

Narasimha: Man-lion *avatāra* of Vishnu, slays demon who can be killed by "neither man nor beast."

Nārāyana: "Dweller on the Waters," a name for Vishnu.

Narmadā: Great river of central India, rising at Amarakantaka and flowing west to the Arabian Sea; river of countless riverside shrines, including Omkāreshvara, and circumambulated by pilgrims.

Nāsik: Site of Simhasta Kumbha Melā on the River Godāvarī; famous of old as hermitage where Rāma, Sītā, and Lakshmana lived during their exile.

nishkala: Literally, "without parts," referring to the fractionless, indescribable, transcendent Shiva; contrast to *sakala,* "with parts," visible and comprehensible.

nirguna: Literally, "without attributes," referring to Brahman, to which no qualities, attributes, or adjectives may be ascribed; contrast to *saguna,* "with attributes," able to be described.

nirvāna: The extinguishing of earthly attachments and desires, freedom from rebirth; used by both Hindus and Buddhists to describe the highest spiritual goal.

nivritti: Returning to oneness, cessation, repose; opposite of *pravritti,* spinning forth, evolving.

Om: Also *Aum.* The sacred syllable, regarded as the supreme mantra, the seed and source of all wisdom.

Omkāreshvara: Shrine of Shiva on an island in the Narmadā River; one of the *jyotirlingas* of Shiva.

Padma Purāna: One of the eighteen Mahāpurānas; contains extensive sections on cosmology, geography, and the lore of pilgrimage places.

panchakroshī: "Five *kroshas,*" a circular pilgrimage with a radius of about five kroshas, or ten miles. The circular pilgrimage route around Kāshī, but also a popular designation for a fivefold pilgrimage.

pandā: A brahmin priest catering especially to the needs of pilgrims.

Pāndavas: The five brothers, sons of King Pandu, including Yudhisthira, Bhīma, and Arjuna, whose epic battle with their cousins, the Kauravas, is told in the *Mahābhārata.*

Pandharpūr: Prominent pilgrimage city of Lord Vithobā, a form of Krishna, on the Bhīma River in Maharashtra.

Parashurāma: Rāma with the Ax, an *avatāra* of Vishnu, his father a brahmin, his mother a *kshatriya;* renowned for many exploits in the epics and Purānas; forced the sea to retreat from the Konkan coast of India, now called Parashurāma Kshetra.

pārthiva linga: An "earthen *linga,*" the simplest pinch of clay into which the presence of Shiva is invoked.

Pārvatī: "Daughter of the Mountain;" Goddess consort of Shiva who won the ascetic lord as her husband by austerities.

pinda: Rice ball, shaped ritually to constitute part of a new, subtle, spiritual body represented in death rites.

pītha: Seat, bench; the locus of goddess worship, as in the 108 *shākta pīthas* found all over India.

Prabhāsa: Sacred site and *jyotirlinga* of Shiva on the coast of Saurashtra in Gujarat; also called Somnāth.

pradakshina: Circumambulation; honoring by walking around, keeping the object of honor to one's right.

Prajāpati: Lord of Creatures, referring to the Vedic Purusha, to the creator, and sometimes to Brahmā as creator.

prakriti: Nature, material substance, always dynamic and living, not inert; female complement of *purusha,* spirit, male energy.

pralaya: Universal dissolution after one of the vast aeons of time called a *kalpa,* or a day of Brahmā.

prāna: Breath, both the spiritual breath of a person and the breath of a deity established in an image.

prasād: Divine grace; in worship, the food offered to the deity and returned, consecrated.

pravritti: Flowing forth, active manifestation, arising; complement to *nivritti,* returning, cessation.

Prayāg/Prayāga: "Place of sacrifice," a *tīrtha* at the confluence of the Gangā, Yamunā, and mythical Sarasvatī Rivers; duplicated widely in sacred geography; most prominent Prayāga is today's Allahabad.

Prithivī: Earth, living and dynamic; Prithvī Sukta is the Vedic Hymn to the Earth.

pūjā: Worship, ordinarily including the presentation of honor offerings (*upachāras*) to the deity.

pūjārī: Brahmin priest responsible for worship in a temple.

punya: Goodness, a good or meritorious act.

Purāna: One of the collections of "ancient stories" that preserve traditions of cosmology, myth, legend, and ritual practice.

Purī: The sacred city of Krishna-Jagannātha in Orissa, on the Bay of Bengal.

pūrnimā: Full-moon day of the Hindu lunar calendar.

purushārtha: Aim of human life, of which there are traditionally four: *kāma* (pleasure), *artha* (wealth and power), *dharma* (righteous action), and *moksha* (liberation).

Pushkara: "Lotus Pool"; site sacred to Brahmā in present-day Rajasthan.

Pushti Mārg: "Path of Grace," a sect of devotion to Krishna.

Rādhā: The beloved of Krishna whose relation to Krishna is understood as emblematic of human-divine love.

rākshasa: One of the categories of mostly ferocious night-haunting beings referred to as demons, at enmity with the gods, disrupters of sacrifice.

Rāma: Virtuous king, eldest son of Dasharatha and hero of the epic *Rāmāyana;* an *avatāra* of Vishnu, honored and loved in his own right.

Rāmānanda: Fifteenth-century devotee who gave life to a new wave of devotionalism in north India.

Rāmānuja: Eleventh-century south Indian thinker who gave a philosophical foundation to the Vaishnava devotional movement known as Shrīvaishnavism.

Rāmāyana: The Hindu epic celebrating the legend and deeds of Rāma; Vālmīki's Sanskrit epic or one of the many vernacular epics.

Rāmcharitmānas: Hindi *Rāmāyana,* "Holy Lake of the Deeds of Rāma," composed in the sixteenth century by Tulsīdās in Vārānasī.

Rāmeshvara: Sacred site on the coast of Tamil Nadu where Rāma is said to have worshipped Shiva and built a bridge to Lanka to retrieve Sītā from her imprisonment by Rāvana; *jyotirlinga* of Shiva.

Rāmjanmabhūmi: Site honored as birthplace of Rāma in Ayodhyā.

rāmlīlā: Pageant or play enacting scenes from the *Rāmāyana* drama of Lord Rāma.

rāslīlā: High point of the cycle of Krishna *līlās,* enacting the circle dance in which Krishna multiplies himself to dance at night with the *gopīs.*

Ratha Yātrā: Chariot Pilgrimage in which the divine image is taken from the temple sanctum for procession in the streets; especially famous in Purī, when Krishna Jagannātha is pulled in huge chariots.

Rāvana: The ten-headed king of Lanka, part rākshasa and part brahmin, devotee of Shiva, who kidnapped Sītā and was vanquished by Rāma.

Rig Veda: The most important collection of Vedic hymns, forming the nucleus of the scriptures considered to be revealed (*shruti*).

rishi: Inspired seers whose wisdom and insight are represented in the *Rig Veda.*

Rudra: Vedic god related to the power of storm; later identified with Shiva.

rudrāksha: Literally, the "Eye of Shiva"; the large, bumpy brown berries or seeds used for rosaries.

sādhu: A "holy man," generally an ascetic as well.

Sagara: Ancient king of the Ikshvaku sun dynasty whose 60,000 sons were burned by the fury of an angry ascetic; his descendant brought the Gangā from heaven to earth to give life to the dead sons.

saguna: "With qualities"—referring to a divine reality that is describable, with attributes and adjectives; contrasts with *nirguna.*

sakala: "With parts"—referring to an understanding of Shiva that is describable, with faces and parts; contrasts with *nishkala.*

samsāra: Passage, flow, the world of change; the ceaseless round of birth, death, and rebirth.

sangam: Confluence of rivers.

sankalpa: Vow of intent taken at the outset of any ritual activity.

sannyāsī: Renouncer who has "cast off" worldly attachments for a life of contemplation and asceticism, the last of the four stages of Hindu life.

Sarasvatī: Goddess of learning and arts; sacred river of ancient India, now disappeared, said to be present in many confluences of two rivers as an invisible third.

Satī: Consort of Shiva who committed suicide because of her father Daksha's insult to Shiva, reborn as Pārvatī.

Shaiva: Pertaining to the cultus of Shiva; a worshipper of Shiva.

Shākta: Pertaining to the cultus of Shakti, the Goddess; a worshipper of the Devī.

shakti: Divine energy, power; term applied to the Goddess, either alone or as the consort of one of the male deities.

Shankara: A name of Shiva; an eighth- to ninth-century teacher (*āchārya*); principal exponent of the non-dualist philosophy called Advaita.

shāstra: Teaching; sacred treatise or body of learning, such as the *dharmashāstra*, the "Teachings About Dharma."

shikhara: Spire of a temple, literally the "peak"; a mountain peak.

Shilappadhikaram: Tamil literary epic of Ilango Adigal, dating to the fifth or sixth century C.E.

Shiva: The "Auspicious"; many-powered deity, both creator and destroyer, who, along with Vishnu and Devī, is widely worshipped as the Supreme.

Shivarātri: "Night of Shiva," every month, the fourteenth of the waning fortnight; the year's greatest Mahāshivarātri is in either the winter month of Māgha or Phālguna.

shrāddha: Rites for the dead performed after cremation to nourish the deceased for passage to the world of the ancestors.

Shrī: "Good Fortune," the name of a goddess, the consort of Vishnu, along with Bhū; an honorific title.

shringāra: The decoration and adornment of a divine image, whether a *linga* or an image of one of the other deities.

Shrīrangam Temple: Great temple of Vishnu as Ranganātha on an island in the Kāverī River in the city of Tiruchirappalli.

Shrī Shaila: Shaiva shrine, one of the *jyotirlingas,* on the banks of the Krishna River in northern Andhra Pradesh.

shukla: The waxing fortnight (*paksha*) of the lunar month.

shūdra: The fourth of the four classes, traditionally servants.

Simhāchalam: Holy hill of Narasimha near the coastal city of Vishakhapatanam in Andhra Pradesh.

Sindhu: The Sanskrit name of the Indus River.

sindūr: Powder made from red lead, used for anointing the images of deities and the foreheads of worshippers.

Sītā: Daughter of King Janaka, faithful wife of Rāma, kidnapped by Rāvana and recovered by Rāma with the aid of Hanumān.

Skanda: The God of War, son of Shiva and Pārvatī; said to have been raised by six foster mothers, the Krittikās.

Skanda Purāna: The most extensive of the eighteen major Purānas, its seven parts organized around the major *tīrthas* of India.

soma: Divine intoxicating nectar pressed, pounded, and strained from plants in Vedic ritual; identified with *amrita*, the nectar of immortality.

Somanātha/Somnāth: Shrine of Shiva, a *jyotirlinga,* on the coast of Saurashtra in Gujarat; also known as Prabhāsa in Sanskrit literature.

srishti: Creation, the act of creation; literally, the "pouring forth," as a spider puts forth a web from its body.

stūpa: A Buddhist monument, shaped like a dome, where the earthly relics of the Buddha are honored.

svarūpa: God's "own form"—not an image created by human hands, but a natural self-manifestation of the divine.

svayambhū: Self-manifest, describes certain *lingas* and images that are said to be uncreated, to have appeared of their own accord.

Tantra: An esoteric religious movement that emerged after the Gupta period, emphasizing the union of opposites, especially symbolized by male and female.

tapas: Heat; especially the heat generated by ascetic practice, believed to be creative, like the brooding heat of a mother hen.

tarpana: Regular ritual offerings for the deceased; literally "satisfaction," for the rites give satisfaction to the departed.

tejas: Lustrous brilliance, the power of the gods.

Tilak, B. G.: 1856–1920, nationalist leader of the Indian National Congress and advocate of Swaraj, self-rule; aroused resistance to British rule in his native Maharashtra through the use of Hindu issues and symbols.

tīrtha: Ford, crossing place, both literally and symbolically; a place of pilgrimage, bathing place.

tīrthayātrā: The journey (*yātrā*) to a sacred place; pilgrimage.

Tirupati: Pilgrim town and hilltop temple of Shrī Venkateshvara in what is now Andhra Pradesh; one of India's most popular pilgrimage sites.

Trivandrum/Tiruvananthapuram: Modern and thriving city in Kerala whose name, Abode of the Infinite Lord, derives from its most ancient and famous temple, Padmanābhaswamy, where Lord Vishnu reclines on Ananta, the Endless.

trivenī: Literally, the "triple braid," referring to the confluence of three rivers, flowing together, as at Prayāga.

Tryambaka: Three-Eyed Shiva; name of the *jyotirlinga* in the hills of the Western Ghāts near Nāsik.

tulsī: Sacred basil plant (*Ocimum tenuiflorum*) offered in worship, used ceremonially in countless ways; a goddess consort of Krishna.

Tulsīdās: Sixteenth-to-seventeenth-century devotee of Rāma and author of the Hindi (Avadhi) version of the *Rāmāyana,* beloved in north India as the *Rāmcharitmānas.*

Upanishad: One of the speculative teachings attached to the Vedas; source of spiritual wisdom, philosophy.

Vaidyanāth: Temple town and *jyotirlinga* of Shiva in Deogarh, now in the state of Jharkhand; popularly called Baidyanāth.

Vaishnava: Pertaining to the cultus of Vishnu; a worshipper of Vishnu.

Vaishno Devī: Popular mountaintop temple to the Goddess, located near Katra in Jammu and Kashmir.

vaishya: Third of the four classes, traditionally merchants and farmers.

Vālmīki: The first poet and legendary sage to whom the epic *Rāmāyana* is ascribed.

Vāmana: Dwarf *avatāra* of Vishnu, who was granted the land he could cover in three steps and then grew to cosmic size to stride through the earth and heavens.

vana: Forest; woods where ascetics and sages have their hermitages.

vanavāsa: The forest-dwelling years of Rāma, Sīta, and Lakshmana.

Varāha: Boar *avatāra* of Vishnu, who dove deep into the sea of chaos and rescued Prithivī, the Earth, setting her once again upon the surface of the waters.

Vārānasī: Name of Banāras, the city on the Gangā between the Varana and the Asī Rivers.

varna: The four classes of Hindu society: *brahmin, kshatriya, vaishya, shūdra.*

Vāyu: Wind; as deity, the guardian of the northwest.

Veda: Wisdom, knowing. The sacred literature considered to be "heard" or "revealed" (*shruti*).

Venkateshvara: Deity, considered to be a form of Vishnu, resident at the famous pilgrimage temple of Tirupati.

Vibhīshana: Righteous brother of Rāvana who tried to dissuade him from war with Rāma and eventually joined Rāma's side in the war.

Vindhyāchal: The hill shrine of Vindhyavāsinī Devī near Mirzapur in Uttar Pradesh.

viraha: Love in separation; longing love for an absent lover.

visarjana: Sending forth; either the committal of ashes to the river after death rites or bidding farewell to the temporary presence of the divine in an image, following worship.

Vishnu: "The Pervader," known for the three giant steps with which he claimed the whole universe; along with Shiva and Devī, widely worshipped as the Supreme Lord.

vrata: A vow; religious observances done in fulfillment of a vow.

Vrindāvan: Village in Braj where Krishna lived out his boyhood; pilgrimage town north of Mathurā today.

yajna: Sacrifice, especially the Vedic sacrifice.

yaksha, yakshī: Divinity of ancient India; associated with trees, pools, and vegetative abundance.

Yamunā: Sacred river of north India, rising at Yamunotrī, skirting Delhi, Vrindāvan, Mathurā, Agra, and joining the Gangā at Prayāga.

yantra: A "device" for harnessing the mind in meditation or worship. A diagram, usually of geometric interlocking triangles and circles.

yoni: Emblem of female creativity; female generative organ; the "seat" in which a *linga* is established.

Yudhisthira: Eldest of the five Pāndava brothers, son of Draupadī, fathered by Dharma, and thus the righteous one of the brothers.

yuga: The "ages" of the world, four in number: *krita, treta, dvāpara,* and *kali;* the first being the perfect age of the beginnings, the last being this age of strife—our age.

BIBLIOGRAPHY

TEXT TRANSLATIONS CITED THROUGHOUT

The Agni Purāna. Edited by J. L. Shastri. Translated by N. Gangadharan, 2 vols. Ancient Indian Tradition and Mythology, Vols. 27–28. Delhi: Motilal Banarsidass, 1985.

Bhāgavata Purāna. Krishna: The Beautiful Legend of God (Srimad Bhāgavata Purāna, Book X). Translated by Edwin Bryant. New York: Penguin Books, 2003.

Bhāgavata Purāna. The Srīmad-Bhāgavatam. Translated by J. M. Sanyal, 2 vols. New Delhi: Munshiram Manoharlal, 1973.

The Brahmā Purāna. Edited by G. P. Bhatt. Translated by N. A. Deshpande. 4 vols. Ancient Indian Tradition and Mythology, Vols. 33–36. Delhi: Motilal Banarsidass, 1984.

The Brahmānda Purāna. Edited by J. L. Shastri. Translated by G. V. Tagare. 5 vols. Ancient Indian Tradition and Mythology, Vols. 22–26. Delhi: Motilal Banarsidass, 1984.

The Devī Bhāgavata Purāna. The Srimad Devī Bhāgawatam. Translated by Swami Vijnanananda. New Delhi: Munshiram Manoharlal, 1977.

The Devī Māhātmya. Encountering the Goddess: A Translation of the Devī-Māhātmya and a Study of its Interpretation. Translation and study by Thomas Coburn. Albany: State University of New York Press, 1991.

The Garuda Purāna. Edited by J. L. Shastri. Translated by a Board of Scholars. Ancient Indian Tradition and Mythology, Vol. 12. Delhi: Motilal Banarsidass, 1978.

Harivamsha. Translated by Manmatha Nath Dutt. Calcutta: H. C. Dutt, Elysium Press, 1897.

The Hymns of the Rig Veda. Translated by Ralph T. H. Griffith. Edited by J. L. Shastri. 1889. Delhi: Motilal Banarsidass, 1973.

The Kālikā Purāna: Sanskrit Text, Introduction, and Translation in English, 3 vols. Translated by Biswanarayan Sahstril. Delhi: Nag Publishers, 1991.

The Kurma Purāna, with English Translation. Edited by A. S. Gupta. Translated by A. Bhattacharya, et al. Varanasi: All India Kashiraj Trust, 1972.

The Linga Purāna. Edited by J. L. Shastri. Translated by a Board of Scholars. 2 vols. Ancient Indian Tradition and Mythology, Vols. 5–6. Delhi: Motilal Banarsidass, 1973.

The Mārkandeya Purāna. Translated by F. Eden Pargiter. 1904. Delhi: Indological Book House, 1969.

The Matsya Purānam. Edited by Jamna Das Akhtar. Notes by B. C. Majumdar, et al. The Sacred Books of the Aryans Series, Vol. 1. Delhi: Oriental Publishers, 1972.

The Nārada Purāna. Edited by J. L. Shastri. Translated by G. V. Tagare. 5 vols. Ancient Indian Tradition and Mythology, Vols. 15–19. Delhi: Motilal Banarsidass, 1980–1982.

The Padma Purāna. Edited by G. P. Bhatt. Translated by N. A. Deshpande. 10 vols. Ancient Indian Tradition and Mythology, Vols. 39–48. Delhi: Motilal Banarsidass, 1988–92.

A Prose English Translation of the Mahābhārata (Translated Literally from the Original Sanskrit Text). 18 vols. in 3. Translated by Manmatha Nath Dutt. Calcutta: M. N. Dutt, 1895–1903.

The Rāmāyana. Srīmad Vālmīkī-Rāmāyana (with Sanskrit text and English translation). 3 vols. Gorakhpur: The Gita Press, 1969.

The Siva Purāna. Edited by Arnold Kunst and J. L. Shastri. Translated by a Board of Scholars. 4 vols. Ancient Indian Tradition and Mythology, Vols. 1–4. Delhi: Motilal Banarsidass, 1970.

The Skanda Purāna. Edited by G. P. Bhatt. Translated by G. V. Tagare. 19 vols. Ancient Indian Tradition and Mythology, Vols. 49–58. Delhi: Motilal Banarsidass, 1992.

The Thirteen Principal Upanishads. Translated by Robert Ernest Hume. 1877. Second edition, revised. London: Oxford University Press, 1931.

The Vāmana Purāna, with English Translation. Edited by A. S. Gupta. Translated by S. M. Mukhopadhyaya, et al. Varanasi: All India Kashiraj Trust, 1968.

The Varāha Purāna. Edited by J. L. Shastri. Translated by S. V. Iyer. 2 vols. Ancient Indian Tradition and Mythology, Vols. 31–32. Delhi: Motilal Banarsidass, 1985.

The Vāyu Purana. Edited by G. P. Bhatt. Translated by G. V. Tagare, 2 vols. Ancient Indian Tradition and Mythology, Vols. 37–38. Delhi: Motilal Banarsidass, 1987.

The Vishnu Purāna: A System of Hindu Mythology & Tradition. Translated from Sanskrit by H. H. Wilson. Introduction by R. C. Hazra. Calcutta: Punthi Pustak, 1972.

OTHER SANSKRIT SOURCES AND TRANSLATIONS
(LISTED ALPHABETICALLY BY TITLE)

Bhāmini Vilāsa by Jagannātha. Edited by Lakshman Ramachandra Vaidya. Bombay: Bhārati Press, 1887.

Brajbhaktivilāsam by Shrī Nārāyana Bhatta Goswāmī. Sanskrit with Hindi translation. Bombay: Baba Krishnadas, n.d.

Gangā Laharī by Jagannātha (Sanskrit edition with Marathi verse translation). Bombay: Bharati, 1887.

Hymns of the Atharva Veda. Translated by Maurice Bloomfield. Oxford: Sacred Books of the East, vol. 42, 1897.

Hymns of the Atharva Veda. Translated by Ralph T. H. Griffith, 2 vols. Varanasi: Chowkhamba Sanskrit Series, 1968.

Krityakalpataru by Lakshmīdhara. Edited by K. V. Rangaswami Aiyangar. Baroda: Oriental Research Institute, 1942.

Kumārasambhava by Kālidāsa. Edited and translated by M. R. Kale. Delhi: Motilal Banarsidass, 1967.

Mahābhārata. Edited by Vishnu S. Sukthankar (and others). 19 vols. Poona: Bhandarkar Oriental Research Institute, 1933–59.

Meghaduta, The Cloud Messenger by Kālidāsa. Translated by Daniel H. H. Ingalls. In "Kālidāsa and the Attitudes of the Golden Age," *Journal of the American Oriental Society* 96, no. 1 (January–March) 1976.

Meghaduta of Kālidāsa with the Commentary (Samjivanī) of Mallinātha. Edited and translated by M. R. Kale. Delhi: Motilal Banarsidass, 1969.

Narayaneeyam by Meppathur Narayana Bhattatiri. Translated by Swami Tapasyananda. Madras: Sri Ramakrisha Math, 1976.

Nityakarma Vidhi tatha Devpuja Paddhati. Varanasi: Thakurdas Sureka Cairiti Phand, 1966.

The Raghuvamsa of Kālidāsa with the Commentary of Mallinātha. Edited by G. R. Nandargikar. 4th ed. Delhi: Motilal Banarsidass, 1971.

The Rāmāyana of Vālmīki. Vol I. Translated by Robert Goldman. Princeton: Princeton University Press, 1984.

The Rāmāyana of Vālmīki. Translated by Makhan Lal Sen. Delhi: Munshiram Manoharlal, 1978.

Saundaryalaharī of Sankarācārya. Translated by V. K. Subramanian. Delhi: Motilal Banarsidass, 1977.

Srī Narmadāstaka Satika. Japalpur: Ramji Pustak Bhandar, n.d.

Skanda Purāna. Gurumandala Granthamalaya No. XX, 5 vols. Calcutta: 1960–1965.

The Srīmad-Bhāgvatam of Krishna-Dwaipāyana Vyāsa. Translated from Sanskrit by J. M. Sanyal. 2 vols. Second Edition. New Delhi: Munshiram Manoharlal Publishers, 1973.

Srīmad Bhāgavata Mahāpurāna (with Sanskrit text and English translation). Translated into English by L. Goswami. 2 vols. Gorakhpur: Gita Press, 1971.

Srī Venkatesa Purāna. Compiled by B. S. Ananda. Madras: Lotus Publishing, 1980.

Svayam Vyakta Kshetra. Madras: Sri Vadapalani Offset Printers, n.d.

Tīrthavivecana Kandam by Laksmidhara. Vol. III of the *Krityakalpataru.* Edited by K. V. Rangaswami Aiyangar. Gaekwad's Oriental Series, Volume XCVIII. Baroda: Oriental Institute, 1942.

Tristhalīsetu, The Bridge to the Three Holy Cities. Edited and translated by Richard Salomon. Delhi: Motilal Banarsidass, 1985.

The Vedic Experience, Mantramanjari. Edited and translated by Raimundo Panikkar and others. Berkeley: University of California Press, 1977.

HINDI SOURCES (LISTED ALPHABETICALLY BY TITLE)

Adya Jyotirlinga Tryambakeshvara by Tryambakashāstrī N. Pātankar. Nasik: Tryambakeshvara, n.d.

Amarakantak Māhātmya Evam Shrī Narmadā Māhātmya. Jabalpur: Ashok Pustak Bhandar, n.d.

Badrīnārāyan Māhātmya. Badrinath: Tin Murti Prakashan, n.d.

Bhagavān Shrī Rādhāmādhava ke Charanon me Samarpit. Hapur: Modi Bhavan, Shrī Radhamadhava Sankirtan Mandal, n.d.

Bhārat Darshan: Chāron Dhām Saptapurī Yātrā by Abhimanyu Chakradharī. Haridvar: Pustak Vikreta, n.d.

Brihat Srīcitrakūta Māhātmyam by Ramakalhan Saran. Lucknow: Tejakumar Press, 1971.

Chāron Dhām Māhātma. Hardwar: Harbhajan Singh and Sons, n.d.

Gangāsāgar Melā by Tarundev Mahāchārya. Calcutta: Firm K.L.M. Limited, 1978.

Hanumān Chālīsā by B. I. Kapur. New Delhi: Trimurti Publications, 1974.

Hanumān Garhi kā Itihās aur Māhātmya by Ramgopal Pandey. Ayodhyā: Candramaul Pustak Bandar, n.d.

Hinduo ke Vrat, Parva, aur Tyauhar by Rampratap Tripathi. Allahabad: Lokbharati Prakashan, 1971.

Jyotirlinga Mahimā by Ram Kishan Jayasaval. Baravah: Rajahansa Prakashan, n.d.

Kalyān Shakti Ank. Vol. 9. No. 1. Gorakhpur: The Gita Press, 1934.

Kalyān Shivānk. Vol. 8, No. 1. Gorakhpur: The Gita Press, 1933.

Kalyān Tīrthānk. Vol. 31, no. 1. Gorakhpur: The Gitā Press, 1957.

Kedār Badrī Yātrā Darshan by Nautiyal Shivananda. Lucknow: Sulabh Prakashan, 1986.

Narmadā Kalpāvalī by Swami Omkara Giri. Rishikesh: Muktikund Vivek Ashram, n.d.

Nitya Karma Vidhi. Bareli: Samskriti Samsthan, 1977.

Omkāresvara Māhātmya by Ram Kishan Jayasaval. Badavah, M. P.: Rajhansa Prakashan, n.d.

Purāno me Gangā by Rampratap Tripathi. Prayag: Hindi Sahitya Sammelan, 1952.

The Rāmāyana of Tulasidāsa. Translated by F. S. Growse. Delhi: Motilal Banarsidass, 1978.

Shrī Amarakantaka Māhātmya evam Narmadā Māhātmyā. Jabalpur: Ashok Pustak Bhandar, n.d.

Shrī Manasā Devī Mahātma: Kathā Itihās. Hardwar: B. S. Pramindar Prakashan, n.d.

Shrī Nāthdvārā by Narayan Lal Sharma. Udaipur: Goyal Brothers, n.d.

Tapobhūmī Badarī Vana by Prem Ballabh Dimbarī. Joshimath: Messrs. Ballabh Brothers, 1962.

Tapobhūmi Uttarākhand by Mahidhara Sharma. Badrinath: Mahidhara Sharma and Sons, 2000.

Tapobhūmi Uttarākhand by Swami Shivānanda Sarasvati. Haridvar: Harbhajan Singh and Sons, n.d.

Ujjayinī Darshan by Suryanarayan Vyas. Gwalior: Government Regional Press, 1957.

Uttarākhand kī Yātrā by Govinda Das, et. al. Gorakhpur: Gita Press, samvat 2019.

Vaidyanāth Darshan by Shri Shanti Prasad Sringari. Vaidyanath, Bihar: Navayug Sahitya Mandir, 1978.

Vaishnavī Siddha Pītha by Jagadish Chandra Shastri. Jammu: Shastri Prakashan, n.d.

Vrihat Shrī Chitrakūt Māhātmyam. Lucknow: Tejakumār Press, 1971.

OTHER SOURCES (LISTED ALPHABETICALLY BY AUTHOR)

Agarwal, A. P., ed. *Garhwal: "The Dev Bhoomi."* New Delhi: Nest and Wings, 1988.

Agrawal, V. S. *India: A Nation.* Vārānasī: Prithivi Prakashan, 1983.

Aiyar, P. V. Jagadisa. *South Indian Shrines.* Photographs by Ajay Khullar. Calcutta: Rupa and Co., 2000.

Alley, Kelly D. *On the Banks of the Gangā: When Wastewater Meets a Sacred River.* Ann Arbor: University of Michigan Press, 2002.

Alter, Stephen. *Sacred Waters: A Pilgrimage Up the Ganges River to the Source of Hindu Culture.* New York: Harcourt, 2001.

Ambalal, Amit. *Krishna as Shrinathji.* Ahmedabad: Mapin Publishing, 1987.

Anderson, Benedict. *Imagined Communities.* London: Verso, 1983.

Annamayya. *God on the Hill: Temple Poems from Tirupati*. Translated from Telugu by Velcheru Narayana Rao and David Shulman. Oxford: Oxford University Press, 2005.

Ayyangar, S. Satyamurthi. *Lord Ranganātha*. Srirangam, Tiruchi: Arulmiku Ranganathaswami Devasthānam, 1981.

Babb, L. A., and S. Wadley, eds. *Media and the Transformation of Religion in South Asia*. Philadelphia: University of Pennsylvania Press, 1995.

Bakker, Hans. *Ayodhyā*. Groningen: Egbert Forsten, 1986.

Bakker, Hans, ed. *The History of Sacred Places in India as Reflected in Traditional Literature*. Panels of the Seventh World Sanskrit Conference, Vol III. Leiden: E. J. Brill, 1990.

Barz, Richard. *The Bhakti Sect of Vallabhacharya*. Faridabad: Thomas Press, 1976.

Bayi, Gouri Lakshmi. *Sree Padmanabha Swamy Temple*. Bombay: Bharatiya Vidya Bhavan, 1995.

Bayly, C. A. *Origins of Nationality in South Asia*. New Delhi: Oxford University Press, 1998.

Bedi, Rahul K., and Subramaniam Swamy. *Kailas and Manasarovar, After 22 Years*. New Delhi: Allied Publishers Pvt. Limited, 1984.

Bhabha, Homi K. *The Location of Culture*. London: Routledge, 1984.

Bharadwaj, Monisha, and Nitish Bharadwaj. *A Pilgrimage to Kailash-Manasarovar*. Mumbai: India Book House, 2002.

Bharati, Agehananda. "Pilgrimage in the Indian Tradition." *History of Religions* 3, no. 1 (1963): 135–167.

Bhardwaj, Surinder Mohan. *Hindu Places of Pilgrimage in India*. Berkeley: University of California Press, 1973.

Bhatt, Chetan. *Hindu Nationalism: Origins, Ideologies, and Modern Myths*. Oxford: Berg, 2001.

Bhattacharya, Tarunadeva. *Gangāsāgara Melā*. Calcutta: K.L.M. Limited, 1974.

Bhattacharyya, N. N. *History of the Sākta Religion*. New Delhi: Munshiram Manoharlal, 1974.

———. *Indian Mother Goddess*. Calcutta: Indian Studies Past and Present, 1971.

Biardeau, Madelaine. *"Narasimha, Mythe et Culte"* in *Purushartha*. Paris: Centre d'Etudes de l'Inde et de l'Asie du Sud, 1975.

Bonazzoli, Giorgio. "Devīlinga." *Purāna* 20, no. 1 (1978): 121–130.

———. "Prayāga and Its Kumbha Mela." *Purāna* 19, no. 1 (1977): 81–179.

Bose, Sugata, and Ayesha Jalal. *Modern South Asia: History, Culture, Political Economy*, second edition. New York: Routledge, 2004.

Brown, Mackenzie. *The Triumph of the Goddess*. Albany: SUNY Press, 1990.

Brown, Peter. *The Cult of the Saints: Its Rise and Function in Late Christianity*. Chicago: University of Chicago Press, 1981.

Brown, W. Norman. "The Creation Myth of the Rig Veda." *Journal of the American Oriental Society* 62, no. 2 (1942): 85–98.

Bryant, Edwin F., ed. *Krishna: A Sourcebook*. New York: Oxford University Press, 2007.

Carman, John B. *The Theology of Rāmānuja*. New Haven: Yale University Press, 1974.

Carman, John B., and Vasudha Narayanan. *The Tamil Veda*. Chicago: University of Chicago Press, 1989.

Cassirer, Ernst. *The Philosophy of Symbolic Forms*, 2 vols. New Haven: Yale University Press, 1955.

Chapple, Christopher, and Mary Evelyn Tucker, eds. *Hinduism and Ecology: The Intersection of Earth, Sky, and Water*. Cambridge: Center for the Study of World Religions, 2000.

Chatterjee, Partha. *Empire and Nation, Selected Essays*. New York: Columbia University Press, 2010.

Chaudhuri, N. M. "The Cult of Vana-Durgā, A Tree-Deity." *Journal of the Royal Asiatic Society of Bengal*, Letters 11, no. 22 (1915): 75–84.

Clothey, Fred W. *The Many Faces of Murukan: The History and Meaning of a South Indian God*. The Hague: Mouton Publishers, 1978.

———. "Pilgrimage Centers in the Tamil Cultus of Murukan." *Journal of the American Academy of Religion* 40 (March 1972): 79–85.

Coburn, Thomas. *Devī Māhātmya: The Crystallization of the Goddess Tradition*. Delhi: Motilal Banarsidass, 1984.

Coomaraswamy, Ananda. *Yakshas*. New Delhi: Munshiram Manoharlal, 1971.

Cunningham, Alexander. *The Ancient Geography of India*. London: Trübner, 1871. Reprint, Vārānasī: Bhartiya Publishing House, 1975.

Daniel, E. Valentine. *Fluid Signs: Being a Person the Tamil Way*. Berkeley: University of California Press, 1984.

Darian, Steven G. *The Ganges in Myth and History*. Honolulu: University Press of Hawaii, 1978.

Das, Veena. *Structure and Cognition: Aspects of Hindu Caste and Ritual*. Delhi: Oxford University Press, 1982.

Das, Veena, Dipankar Gupta, and Patricia Uberoi. *Tradition, Pluralism, and Identity: In Honor of T. N. Madan*. New Delhi: Sage Publications, 1999.

Dave, J. H. *Immortal India*, 4 vols. 1st ed., 1961. 2nd ed., Bombay: Bhāratiya Vidya Bhavan, 1970.

Davis, Richard. *Ritual in an Oscillating Universe*. Princeton: Princeton University Press, 1991.

De, S. K. *Early History of the Vaisnava Faith and Movement in Bengal*. Calcutta: Firma K. L. Mukhopadhyaya, 1961.

Dhammika, S. *The Edicts of King Ashoka, An English Rendering*. S. Kandy, Sri Lanka: Buddhist Publication Society, 1993. File accessible at *www.buddha net.net/pdf_file/edicts-asoka6.pdf*.

Dimock, Edward C. "The Goddess of Snakes in Medieval Bengali Literature." *History of Religions* 1 (winter 1962): 307–21.

Doniger, Wendy. *Asceticism and Eroticism in the Mythology of Siva*. London: Oxford University Press, 1973.

———. *Hindu Myths*. Baltimore: Penguin Books, 1975.

———. *Other Peoples' Myths*. Chicago: University of Chicago Press, 1995.

———. *Women, Androgynes, and Other Mythical Beasts*. Chicago: University of Chicago Press, 1980.

Dube, Bechan. *Geographical Concepts in Ancient India*. Foreword by R. L. Singh. Varanasi: National Geographical Society of India, 1967.

Dubey, D. P. *Prayāga, Site of the Kumbha Mela*. New Delhi: Aryan Books International, 2001.

Dubey, D. P., ed. *Pilgrimage Studies: The Power of Sacred Places*. Muirabad, Allahabad: Society of Pilgrimage Studies, 2000.

———. "Kumbha Mela: Origin and Historicity of India's Greatest Pilgrimage Fair." *The National Geographic Journal of India* 33, no. 4 (December 1987): 469–92.

———. "Māghamela at Prayāga." *Purāna* 30, no. 1 (January 1988): 60–68.

Dubois, Abbe. *Hindu Manners, Customs, and Ceremonies*. 3rd ed. Oxford: Oxford University Press, 1906.

Dutt, Sukumar. *Problem of Indian Nationality*. Calcutta: University of Calcutta Press, 1926.

Eaton, Richard M. "Temple Desecration and Indo-Muslim States." *Journal of Islamic Studies* 11, no. 3 (2000): 283–319.

Eck, Diana L. *Banaras, City of Light*. New York: Alfred A. Knopf, 1982.

———. *Darsan: Seeing the Divine Image in India*. 3rd ed., New York: Columbia University Press, 1998.

———. "The Dynamics of Indian Symbolism." In *The Other Side of God*, edited by Peter Berger. New York: Doubleday, 1981: 157–81.

———. "India's *Tīrthas:* Crossings in Sacred Geography." *History of Religions* 20, no. 4 (May 1981): 323–44.

Elder, J. W., ed. *Chapters in Indian Civilization*, Vol. I. Dubuque: Kendall/Hunt Publishing Company, 1970.

Eliade, Mircea. *Yoga, Immortality and Freedom*. 1958. Reprint, 3rd ed., Princeton: Princeton University Press, 1973.

Entwistle, Alan. *Braj, Center of Krishna Pilgrimage*. Groningen: Egbert Forsten, 1987.

Erikson, Erik. *Toys and Reasons*. New York: Norton, 1977.

Erndl, Kathleen M. *Victory to the Mother: The Hindu Goddess of Northwest India in Myth, Ritual, and Symbol*. New York: Oxford University Press, 1993.

Eschmann, A., H. Kulke, and G. C. Tripathi, eds. *The Cult of Jagannath and the Regional Tradition of Orissa*. New Delhi: Manohar, 1978.

Feldhaus, Anne. *Connected Places: Region, Pilgrimage, and Geographical Imagination in India*. New York: Palgrave Macmillan, 2003.

———. *Water and Womanhood: Religious Meanings of Rivers in Maharashtra.* New York: Oxford University Press, 1995.

Fleming, Benjamin J. "Mapping Sacred Geography in Medieval India: The Case of the Twelve *Jyotirlingas.*" *International Journal of Hindu Studies* 13, no. 1 (2009): 51–58.

Fonia, K. S. *Uttarākhand: Garhwal Himalayas.* Revised by Iris Turner. Dehra Dun: Asian Journals, 1977.

———. *Uttarākhand: The Land of Jungles, Temples, and Snows.* New Delhi: Lancers Books, 1987.

Fox, Robin Lane. *The Search for Alexander.* Boston: Little, Brown and Co., 1980.

Fuller, C. J. "The Divine Couple's Relationship in a South Indian Temple: Mīnākshī and Sundareshvara at Madurai." *History of Religions* 19, no. 4 (1982): 321–48.

Gaenszle, Martin, and Jörg Gengnagel, eds. *Visualizing Space in Banaras: Images, Maps, and the Practice of Representation.* Wiesbaden: Harrassowitz Verlag, 2006.

Gangadharan, N. "The *Linga*—Origin of Its Concept and Worship." *Purāna* 20, no. 1 (1978): 87–92.

Ganhar, J. N. *Jammu Shrines and Pilgrimages.* New Delhi: Ganhar Publications, 1973.

Gledhill, Ruth, and Jeremy Page. "Can the Monkey God Save Rāma's Underwater Bridge," in *TimesOnLine,* March 27, 2007. Accessed on August 1, 2010, at *www.timesonline.co.uk.*

Glucklich, Ariel. *Climbing Chamundi Hill.* San Francisco: HarperCollins, 2003.

———. *The Strides of Vishnu: Hindu Culture in Historical Perspective.* New York: Oxford University Press, 2008.

Gold, Ann Grodzins. *Fruitful Journeys: The Ways of Rajasthani Pilgrims.* Berkeley: University of California Press, 1988.

Gonda, Jan. *Aspects of Early Visnuism.* Delhi: Motilal Banarsidass, 1969.

———. *The Meaning of the Sanskrit Term Dhāman.* Amsterdam: N.V. Noord-Hollandsche Uitgevers Maatschappij, 1976.

Gopal, Lallanji, and D. P. Dubey, eds. *Pilgrimage Studies: Text and Context: Śrī Phalāhārī Bābā Commemoration Volume.* Allahabad: The Society of Pilgrimage Studies, 1990.

Gopal, S. ed. *Anatomy of a Confrontation: The Babri Masjid-Ramjanmabhumi Issue.* New Delhi: Penguin Books, 1991.

Gopal, S. (ed.). *Selected Works of Jawaharlal Nehru,* Vol. XVII. New Delhi: Orient Longman, 1972.

Goswami, Srivatsa. *Celebrating Krishna.* Vrindaban: Sri Caitanya Prema Samsthana, 2001.

Govindacharya, B., U. P. Upadhyaya, and M. Upadhyaya. *Udupi: Past and Present.* Udupi: Sri Pejavar Mutt, 1984.

Granoff, Phyllis, and Koichi Shinohara. *Pilgrims, Patrons, and Place: Localizing Sanctity in Asian Religions*. Vancouver: University of British Columbia Press, 2003.

Gutschow, Niels. *Benares: The Sacred Landscape of Vārānasī*. Stuttgart: Edition Axel Menges, 2006.

Haberman, David. *Journey Through the Twelve Forests*. New York: Oxford University Press, 1994.

———. *River of Love in an Age of Pollution*. Berkeley: University of California Press, 2006.

Hamilton, H. C., trans. *The Geography of Strabo*, 3 vols. London: George Bell & Sons, 1887.

Hardy, Friedhelm. *Viraha Bhakti*. Oxford: Oxford University Press, 1983.

———. "Ideology and Cultural Contexts of the Srivaisnava Temple." *Indian Economic and Social History Review* 14, no. 1 (1977): 119–151.

Harman, William P. *The Sacred Marriage of a Hindu Goddess*. Bloomington: Indiana University Press, 1989.

Hart, George L. *The Poems of Ancient Tamil*. Berkeley: University of California Press, 1975.

Hawley, John S., and Donna Wulff, eds. *The Divine Consort: Rādhā and the Goddesses of India*. Berkeley: Berkeley Religious Studies Series, 1982.

Hawley, John S., and Srivatsa Goswami. *At Play with Krishna: Pilgrimage Dramas from Brindavan*. Princeton: Princeton University Press, 1981.

Hay, Stephen, ed. *Sources of Indian Tradition*, Vol. II. 2nd ed. New York: Columbia University Press, 1988.

Hazra, R. C. *Studies in the Purānic Records on Hindu Rites and Customs*. Dacca: University of Dacca, 1936.

Hiltebeitel, Alf. *The Cult of Draupadi*. Chicago: University of Chicago Press, 1988.

Inden, Ronald. *Imagining India*. Oxford: Blackwell Publishers, 1990.

Ingalls, Daniel H. H. "Kālidāsa and the Attitudes of the Golden Age." *Journal of the American Oriental Society* 96, no. 1 (Jan.–Mar. 1976): 15–26.

International India Centre Quarterly 28, no. 1 (Winter 2000–Spring 2001), "The Human Landscape."

International India Centre Quarterly 29, nos. 3 & 4 (Winter 2002–Spring 2003), "A National Culture?"

International India Centre Quarterly 30, nos. 3 & 4 (Winter 2003–Spring 2004), "Journeys: Heroes, Pilgrims, Explorers."

Jaffrelot, Christophe (ed.). *Hindu Nationalism: A Reader*. Princeton: Princeton University Press, 2007.

Jaiswal, Suvira. *The Origin and Development of Vaisnavism*. New Delhi: Munshiram Manoharlal, 1981.

Jalal, Ayesha. *Self and Sovereignty: Individual and Community in South Asia since 1850*. London: Routledge, 2000.

Jayapal, Pramila. *Pilgrimage: One Woman's Return to a Changing India*. New Delhi: Penguin Books, 2000.

Jha, Sadan. "The Life and Times of Bhārat Mātā." *Manushi*, issue 142 (August 2004). Accessed online at *www.indiatogether.org/manushi/issue142/bharat.htm* on August 10, 2010.

Justice, Christopher. *Dying the Good Death*. Albany: State University of New York Press, 1997.

Kane, P. V. *History of Dharmashāstra*, Vol. IV. Poona: Bhandarkar Oriental Research Institute, 1973.

Kapur, Anuradha. *Actors, Pilgrims, Kings, and Gods: The Ramlila at Ramnagar*. Calcutta: Seagull Books, 1990.

Kaviraj, Sudipta. *The Imaginary Institution of India: Politics and Ideas*. New York: Columbia University Press, 2010.

Keshavadās, Sadguru Sant. *Lord Pānduranga and His Minstrels*. Bombay: Bharatiya Vidya Bhavan, 1977.

Khilani, Sunil. *The Idea of India*. New York: Farrar, Straus and Giroux, 1997.

Kinsley, David. *Tantric Visions of the Divine Feminine: The Ten Mahāvidyās*. Berkeley: University of California Press, 1997.

Kooij, K. R. van. *Worship of the Goddess according to the Kālīkapurana*. Leiden: E. J. Brill, 1972.

Kramrisch, Stella. *The Hindu Temple*, 2 vols. Calcutta: University of Calcutta, 1946.

Lanaghan, Tamara. *Transforming the Seat of the Goddess into Vishnu's Place: The Complex Layering of Theologies in the* Karavira Māhātmya. Ph.D. Thesis, Harvard University, 2006.

Law, B. C. *Geographical Aspect of Kālidāsa's Works*. Delhi: Bharatiya Publishing House, 1976.

———. *Historical Geography of Ancient India*. Paris: Societe Asiatique de Paris, 1954.

———. *India as Described in Early Texts of Buddhism and Jainism*. New Delhi: Bharatiya Publishing House, 1980.

———. *Mountains and Rivers of India*. Calcutta: National Committee for Geography, 1968.

Legge, James. *A Record of Buddhistic Kingdoms, Being an Account by the Chinese Monk Fa-Hien of His Travels in India and Ceylon (A.D. 399–414) in Search of the Buddhist Books of Discipline*. New York: Dover Publications, 1965.

Leshnik, L. S., and G. D. Sontheimer, eds. *Pastoralists and Nomads in South Asia*. Wiesbaden: O. Harrassowitz, 1975.

Lochtefeld, James G. *God's Gateway: Identity and Meaning in a Hindu Pilgrimage Place*. New York: Oxford University Press, 2010.

———. *Haridwara, Haradwara, Gangādwara: The Construction of Identity and Meaning in a Hindu Pilgrimage Place*. Ann Arbor: University Microfilms International, 1992.

Low, Alaine, and Soraya Tremayne, eds. *Women as Sacred Custodians of the Earth? Women, Spirituality and the Environment*. New York; Oxford: Berghahn Books, 2001.

Ludden, David. *Contesting the Nation*. Philadelphia: University of Pennsylvania Press, 1996.

Ludden, David, ed. *Making India Hindu: Religion, Community, and the Politics of Democracy in India*. Delhi: Oxford University Press, 1996.

Maclean, Kama. *Pilgrimage and Power: The Kumbh Mela in Allahabad 1765–1954*. New York: Oxford University Press, 2008.

Macleod, Norman. *Days in North India*. Philadelphia: J. B. Lippincott & Co., 1870.

Madan, T. N., ed. *Religion in India*. Delhi: Oxford University Press, 1991.

Mandal, D. *Ayodhyā: Archaeology After Demolition*. New Delhi: Orient Longman, 1993.

Mate, M. S. *Temples and Legends of Maharashtra*. Bombay: Bharatiya Vidya Bhavan, 1970.

Maury, Curt. *Folk Origins of Indian Art*. New York: Columbia University Press, 1969.

Maw, Geoffrey Waring. *Narmadā, The Life of a River*. Edited by Marjorie Sykes. Hoshangabad: Friends Rural Centre, 1991.

McCrindle, J. W. *Ancient India as Described by Megasthenes and Arrian*. Calcutta: Checkervertty, Chatterjee, & Co., Ltd., 1926.

McDermott, R. A., and V. S. Naravane. *The Spirit of Modern India*. New York: Thomas Y. Crowell Company, 1974.

McDermott, R. F., and Jeffrey Kripal, eds. *Encountering Kālī: In the Margins, At the Center, In the West*. Berkeley: University of California Press, 2003.

Mehtrotra, Rahul, and Sharada Dwivedi. *Banganga: Sacred Tank on Malabar Hill*. Bombay: Eminence Designs Pvt. Ltd., 2006.

Michell, George, and Vasundhara Filliozat, eds. *Splendours of the Vijayanagara Empire*. Hampi, New Delhi: Marg Publications, 1981.

Mills, Margaret A., Peter Claus, and Sarah Diamond, eds. *South Asian Folklore: An Encyclopedia*. New York: Routledge, 2003.

Mishra, D. P. *The Search for Lanka*. Delhi: Agam Kāla Prakashan, 1985.

Mittal, Sushil, and Gene Thursby, eds. *The Hindu World*. New York: Routledge, 2004.

Mookerji, Radhakumud. *The Fundamental Unity of India*. London; New York: Longmans, Green and Co., 1914.

———. *Nationalism in Hindu Culture*. London: Theosophical Publishing House, 1921.

Morinis, E. Alan. *Pilgrimage in the Hindu Tradition: A Case Study of West Bengal*. Delhi: Oxford University Press, 1984.

Munshi, K. M. *Somanātha, The Shrine Eternal*. Bombay: Bharatiya Vidya Bhavan, 1976.

Nagarajan, K. *Cauveri from Source to Sea*. New Delhi: Arnold-Heinemann, 1975.

Nambiar, K. Damodaran. "The *Nārada Purāna*: A Critical Study." *Purāna* 15, no. 2, supplement (1973): 1–56.

Narasimhacharya, M. *History of the Cult of Narasimha in Andhra Pradesh*. Hyderabad: Sri Malola Grantha Mala, 1989.

Narayan, R. K. *The Emerald Route*. Sketches by R. K. Laxman. Mysore: Indian Thought Publications, 1977.

Nehru, Jawaharlal. *The Discovery of India*. New York: Anchor Books, 1959.

Nelson, Lance E., ed. *Purifying the Earthly Body of God: Religion and Ecology in Hindu India*. Albany: State University of New York Press, 1998.

Newby, Eric, and Raghubir Singh. *Gangā: Sacred River of India*. Hong Kong: The Perennial Press, 1972.

Noorani, A. G., ed. *The Babri Masjid Question, 1528–2003: "A Matter of National Honour,"* 2 vols. New Delhi: Tulika Books, 2003.

Oppert, Gustav. *On the Original Inhabitants of Bhāratavarsa or India*. 1893. Reprint. Delhi: Oriental Publishers, 1972.

Pal, B. C. *The Soul of India*. Calcutta: Choudhury and Choudhury, 1911. 4th ed. Calcutta: Yugayatri Prakashak Limited, 1958.

Pandey, Raj Bali. *Vārānasī: The Heart of Hinduism*. Vārānasī: Orient Publishers, 1969.

Pandey, Syama Narayana. *Geographical Horizon of the Mahābhārata*. Varanasi: Oriental Publishers, 1980.

Parashar, Utpal. "Gangā Pollution Reaches Alarming Levels." *Hindustan Times*, June 5, 2007.

Paul, Rana Satya, ed. *Our Northern Borders*. New Delhi: The Book Times Company, 1963.

Peterson, Indira V. *Poems to Siva: The Hymns of the Tamil Saints*. Princeton: Princeton University Press, 1989.

———. "Singing of a Place: Pilgrimage as Metaphor and Motif in the Tevaram Songs of the Tamil Saivite Saints." *Journal of the American Oriental Society* 102, no. 1 (1982): 69–90.

Petievich, Carla, ed. *The Expanding Landscape: South Asians and the Diaspora*. New Delhi: Manohar, 1999.

Pilgrim's Guide to Rameswaram and Dhanushkodi. Rameshwaran: Sri Ramanathasvami Temple, 1977.

Pillai, N. Vanamamalai. *Temples of the Setu and Rameswaram*. 1st Indian ed. Delhi: Kunj Publishing House, 1982.

Pintchman, Tracy. *The Rise of the Goddess in the Hindu Tradition*. Albany: State University of New York Press, 1994.

———, ed. *Seeking Mahādevī: Constructing the Identities of the Hindu Great Goddess*. Albany: State University of New York Press, 2001.

Pollock, Sheldon. *The Language of the Gods in the World of Men: Sanskrit, Culture, and Power in Premodern India*. Berkeley: University of California Press, 2006.

Potts, Rowena. "'When the Difference Between Us Was Erased, I Saw You Everywhere': Shared Identities at a Sufi Shrine in Banāras." A.B. Honors Thesis, Harvard University, 2006.

Ramaswamy, Sumathi. *The Goddess and the Nation: Mapping Mother India.* Durham: Duke University Press, 2010.

Ramesan, N. *Temples and Legends of Andhra Pradesh.* Bombay: Bharatiya Vidya Bhavan, 1988.

Rao, Chalapati, and Gudlavalleti Venkata. *Sri Venkatāchala, Its Glory.* Vijayawada: Metro Printers, 1983.

Rao, S. R. *The Lost City of Dvārakā.* New Delhi: Aditya Prakashan, 1999.

Rao, Vasudeva. *Living Traditions in Contemporary Contexts: The Madhva Matha of Udupi.* New Delhi: Orient Longman Private Limited, 2002.

Ray, Rajat Kanta. *The Felt Community.* New Delhi: Oxford University Press, 2003.

Reddy, Prabhavati. *Reconstructing the Mandala Symbolism of Siva's Lotus Land: Srisailam's Place in Religious India.* Ph.D. Thesis, Harvard University Department of Sanskrit and Indian Studies, 2000.

Redfield, Robert. "Societies and Cultures as Natural Systems." *The Journal of the Royal Anthropological Institute of Great Britain and Ireland* 85 (1955): 19–32.

Richman, Paula. *Many Rāmāyanas: The Diversity of a Narrative Tradition in South Asia.* Berkeley: University of California Press, 1991.

Sachau, Edward C., ed. *Alberuni's India: An Account of the Religion, Philosophy, Literature, Geography, Chronology, Astronomy, Customs, Laws and Astrology of India About A.D. 1030.* Delhi: S. Chand & Co., 1964.

Samanta, Suchitra. "The 'Self-Animal' and Divine Digestion: Goat Sacrifice to the Goddess Kali in Bengal." *Journal of Asian Studies* 53, no. 3 (1994): 779–803.

Sankalia, H. D. "The Ur (original) Rāmāyana of Archaeology and the Rāmāyana." In *Indologen-Tagung 1971.* Weisbaden: Steiner, 1973: 151–60.

Sankaran, R. *My Kasi-Badari Yatra: A Travel Sketch.* Coimbatore: Badarikasram, 1984.

Sastri, H. Krishna. *South Indian Images of Gods and Goddesses.* Madras: Government Press, 1916.

Satyamurti, T. *The Nataraja Temple: History, Art, and Architecture.* New Delhi: Classical Publications, 1978.

Savarkar, V. D. *Hindutva, Who Is a Hindu?* Bombay: Veer Savarkar Prakashan, Fifth Edition, 1969.

Sax, William. *Mountain Goddess: Gender and Politics in a Himalayan Pilgrimage.* New York: Oxford University Press, 1991.

Schama, Simon. *Landscape and Memory.* New York: Random House, 1995.

Sengupta, Somini. "Glaciers in Retreat." *The New York Times*, sec. D1 and D4. July 17, 2007.

Seth, Pepita. *Heaven on Earth: The Universe of Kerala's Guruvayur Temple.* New Delhi: Niyogi Books, 2009.

Sharma, Jyotirmaya. *Hindutva: Exploring the Idea of Hindu Nationalism.* New Delhi: Penguin Group, 2003.

Shaw, Miranda. *Passionate Enlightenment: Women in Tantric Buddhism.* Ph.D. Thesis, Harvard University, 1992. Published in revised form by Princeton University Press, 1995.

Shivaram, Choodie. "Court Decree Retires Tirupati Temple's Hereditary Priests." *Hinduism Today,* June 1996.

Shukla-Bhatt, Neelima. "Somnāth, The 'Shrine Eternal'? Perceptions and Appropriations of a Temple," unpublished manuscript, 2001.

Shulman, David. *Tamil Temple Myths.* Princeton: Princeton University Press, 1980.

Sircar, D. C. *Sakta Pīthas.* Banaras: Motilal Banarsidass, 1950.

Singh, N. *The Call of Uttarkhand.* Hardwar: Randhir Book Sales, n.d.

Singh, Rana P.B., ed. *The Spirit and Power of Place: Human Environment and Sacrality, Essays Dedicated to Yi-Fu Tuan.* Vārānasī: National Geographical Society of India, 1993.

Sitapati, P. *Sri Venkateswara: The Lord of the Seven Hills.* Bombay: Bharatiya Vidya Bhavan, 1972.

Skandanandan. *Arunāchala, The Holy Hill.* Madras: Weldun Press, 1980.

Soifer, Deborah A. *The Myths of Narasimha and Vāmana: Two Avatars in Cosmological Perspective.* Albany: State University of New York Press, 1991.

Sopher, David E. "The Message of Place in Hindu Pilgrimage." *The National Geographical Journal of India* 33 (December 1987): 353–69.

Srinivas, M. N. *Religion and Society Amongst the Coorgs of South India.* Oxford: The Clarendon Press, 1952.

Stietencron, Heinrich Von. *Gangā and Yamunā.* Weisbaden: Otto Harassowitz, 1972.

Stille, Alexander. "The Ganges' Next Life." *The New Yorker,* January 19, 1998.

Stoddard, Robert H., and Alan Morinis. *Sacred Places, Sacred Spaces: The Geography of Pilgrimages.* Baton Rouge, LA: Geoscience Publications, Department of Geography and Anthropology, Louisiana State University, 1997.

Strachey, Sir John. *India.* London: Kegan, Paul, Trench & Co., 1888.

Subhan, John A. *Sufism: Its Saints and Shrines.* Lucknow: The Lucknow Publishing House, 1960.

Subramanyam, K. N., trans. *The Anklet Story, Silappadhikaaram of Ilango Adigal.* Delhi: Agam Prakashan, 1977.

Sundaram, Dr. K. *The Simhachalam Temple.* 2nd ed. Simhachalam: Simhachalam Devasthanam, 1984.

Tagore, Rabindranāth. *Nationalism.* New Delhi: Rupa & Co., 2002.

Thapar, Romila. *Somanātha: The Many Voices of a History*. New Delhi: Penguin Books, 2004.

Tiwari, J. N. *Goddess Cults in Ancient India*. Introduction by A. L. Basham. Delhi: Sundeep Prakashan, 1985.

————. "Studies in Goddess Cults in Northern India, with Special Reference to the First Seven Centuries A.D." Ph.D. Thesis, Australian National University, 1971.

Troll, Christian, ed. *Muslim Shrines in India*. New York: Oxford University Press, 1989.

Tucci, G. "Travels of Tibetan Pilgrims in the Swat Valley." In *Opera Minora*, Vol. 2, Universita do Roma Studi Orientali Publlicati a Cura della suola Orientale, Vol. 6. Rome: Dott. Giovanni Bardi Editore, 1971.

Tuan, Yi-Fu. *Space and Place: The Perspective of Experience*. Minneapolis: University of Minnesota Press, 1977.

Turner, Victor. "The Center Out There: Pilgrim's Goal." *History of Religions* 12, no. 3 (1973).

Turner, Victor, and Edith Turner. *Image and Pilgrimage in Christian Culture*. New York: Columbia University Press, 1978.

Udupi: An Introduction. Udupi: Sri Krishnapur Mutt, 1995.

Van der Veer, Peter. *Gods on Earth*. London: The Athlone Press, 1988.

————. *Religious Nationalism: Hindus and Muslims in India*. Berkeley: University of California Press, 1994.

Vaidyanathan, K. R. *Sri Krishna: The Lord of Guruvayur*. 1977. Reprint. Bombay: Bharatiya Vidya Bhavan, 1992.

————. *Pilgrimage to Sabari*. Bombay: Bharatiya Vidya Bhavan, 1978.

————. *Temples and Legends of Kerala*. Bombay: Bharatiya Vidya Bhavan, 1982.

Vatsyayan, Kapila, ed. *Kalātattvakosa: A Lexicon of Fundamental Concepts of the Indian Arts.*, Vols. 1 and 2. New Delhi: Indira Gandhi National Centre for the Arts, 1992.

————. *Prakrti: The Integral Vision*, Vols. 1–5. New Delhi: Indira Gandhi National Centre for the Arts, 1995.

Vaudeville, Charlotte. "Braj Lost and Found." *Indo-Iranian Journal* 18 (1976): 195–213.

————. "The Govardhan Myth in Northern India." *Indo-Iranian Journal* 22 (1980): 1–45.

Vidyarthi, L. P. *The Sacred Complex in Hindu Gaya*. Bombay: Asia Publishing House, 1961.

Vidyarthi, L. P., and Makhan Jha. *Symposium on the Sacred Complex in India*. Ranchi: Bihar Council of Social and Cultural Research, 1974.

Vogel, J. P. *Indian Serpent Lore*. Varanasi: Prithivi Prakashan, 1972.

Wangu, Madhu Bazaz. *The Cult of Khir Bhavānī: Study, Analysis, and Interpretation of a Kashmiri Goddess*. Ph.D. Thesis, University of Pittsburgh, 1988.

Whitmore, Luke. *In Pursuit of Maheshvara: Understanding Kedarnath as Place and as Tirtha*. Ph.D. Thesis, Emory University Graduate Division of Religion, 2010.

Williams, Joanna, ed. *Kaladarsana: American Studies in the Art of India*. New Delhi: Oxford and IBH Publishing Co., 1981.

Wink, Andre. *Al-Hind, The Making of the Indo-Islamic World*, Vol. 2. Leiden: Brill, 1997.

Yang, Faxian, and Yang Xuanshi. *Travels of Fah-Hian and Sung-Yun, Buddhist Pilgrims from China to India (400 A.D. and 518 A.D.)*. Translated from the Chinese by Samuel Beal. London: Trubner and Co., 1869.

Young, Katherine K. *Beloved Places: The Correlation of Topography and Theology in the Srivaisnava Tradition of South India*. Ph.D. Thesis, McGill University, 1978.

Younger, Paul. *The Home of Dancing Sivan: The Traditions of the Hindu Temple in Citamparam*. New York: Oxford University Press, 1995.

———. "Singing the Tamil Hymnbook in the Tradition of Rāmānujā: The Ady-ayanutsava Festival in Srirankam." *History of Religions* 21, no. 3 (February 1982): 272–93.

Zimmer, Heinrich. *The Art of Indian Asia*. Princeton: Princeton University Press, 1968.

NOTES

CHAPTER 1: A SACRED GEOGRAPHY, AN IMAGINED LANDSCAPE

1. Norman Macleod, *Days in North India* (Philadelphia: J.B. Lippincott & Co., 1870), p. 20.

2. Banāras is also known officially by the name Vārānasī, the city that is bordered by the Varana River on the north and the Asi River on the south, stretching out along the Gangā between the confluence of these two rivers.

3. Here also, according to myth, Shiva became hidden (*gupta*) when he ran away from the Pāndavas, who were climbing into the sacred sites of Kedār Khand in order to rid themselves of the sin of killing members of their own family in the great war of the *Mahābhārata*. Shiva did not want to be approached by them for expiation, so he turned into a bull and dove into the earth. The Five Kedārs of this area correspond to the parts of his anatomy. See Kedārnāth in Chapter 5.

4. This kind of Purānic exaggeration is called *arthavāda*, language spoken or composed for a purpose (*artha*), which is, of course, to get you to go there and partake of the great benefits to be had.

5. Rajat Kanta Ray, *The Felt Community: Commonality and Mentality Before the Emergence of Indian Nationalism* (New Delhi: Oxford University Press, 2003).

6. Sheldon Pollock, *The Language of the Gods in the World of Men: Sanskrit, Culture, and Power in Premodern India* (Berkeley: University of California Press, 2006). Pollock sees the rise of this Sanskrit cosmopolis extending through the first millennium and developing through the use of Sanskrit not only for religious and ritual purposes, but for what we might anachronistically call "secular" and "political" purposes.

7. *Tīrtha* belongs to a whole family of Indo-European cognates that are the great words of passage and pilgrimage in the West as well: through, *durch*, and *trans*, as prepositions, and all of the many passage words related to them, which in English alone include "thoroughfare," "transition," "transformation," "transport," and "transcend."

8. See Diana L. Eck, "India's *Tīrthas:* Crossings in Sacred Geography," *History of Religions* 20, no. 4 (1981). This is a more detailed treatment of this subject.

9. All Upanishads references are to Robert Ernest Hume, tr. *The Thirteen Principal Upanishads* (London: Oxford University Press, 1921).

10. *Mahābhārata,*, III.82.14–17. My translation.

11.   C. L. Goswami, trans., *Srīmad Bhāgavata Mahāpurāna*, with Sanskrit text and English translation (Gorakhpur: Gita Press, 1971), 1.13.10.

12.   For the *mānasatīrthas*, see *Mahābhārata*, XIII.108, 2–21. This passage is quoted at the outset of the *Tīrthavivecana Kānda* of Lakshmīdhara. See K. V. Rangaswami Aiyangar, ed., *Tīrthavivecana Kānda* (Baroda: Oriental Institute, 1942), Gaekwad's Oriental Series vol. 98, pp. 6–8. The Kāshī Khanda of the *Skanda Purāna* (6.31–45) and the Uttara Khanda of the *Padma Purāna* (237.11–28) repeat the *Mahābhārata* version almost verbatim, as does the Ayodhyā Māhātmya of the *Skanda Purāna*.

13.   *Skanda Purāna*, Kāshī Khanda (Calcutta: Gurumandala Granthamalaya 20, vol. 4, 1961), 6.45. My trans. See also *Mahābhārata* XIII.108.19.

14.   Wendy Doniger, *Other People's Myths* (Chicago: University of Chicago Press, 1995), p. 31.

15.   Simon Schama, *Landscape and Memory* (New York: Random House, 1995), pp. 6–7.

16.   Iravati Karve, "On the Road: A Maharashtrian Pilgrimage," *Journal of Asian Studies* 22, no. 1 (November 1962): 22.

17.   Anne Feldhaus, *Connected Places: Region, Pilgrimage, and Geographic Imagination in India* (New York: Palgrave Macmillan, 2003), p. 215.

18.   Ibid., p. 220.

19.   E. Valentine Daniel, *Fluid Signs: Being a Person in the Tamil Way* (Berkeley: University of California Press, 1984), p. 266. Daniel's account and interpretation of this pilgrimage occupies most of Chapter 7.

20.   Fifty million is the astonishing figure commonly repeated in both the official and media websites that give accounts of Sabarimala, and all accounts indicate the yearly growth of the pilgrimage. For example, "Sabarimala: The Faith in Spate," by well-known journalist K. A. Shaji (*www.boloji.com/society/115.htm*). I will discuss the environmental impact of this in my final chapter.

21.   K. V. Rangaswami Aiyangar, ed., *Tīrthavivecana Kanda*, by Lakshmīdhara, vol. III of the *Krityakalpataru*, Gaekwad's Oriental Series, Volume XCVIII (Baroda: Oriental Institute, 1942), Introduction, p. ix.

22.   Matthew Edney, *Mapping an Empire: The Geographical Construction of British India, 1765–1843* (Chicago: University of Chicago Press, 1997), p. 1.

23.   Ibid., p. 25.

24.   See Chapter 4, "The Gangā and the Rivers of India." For versions of the story of the Gangā's descent, see *Rāmāyana* 1:38–44; *Mahābhārata* III.105–109; *Bhāgavata Purāna* 9.8–9; *Brahmavaivarta Purāna*, Prakrti Khanda 10; *Devī Bhāgavata Purāna* 9.11; and *Skanda Purāna*, Kāshī Khanda 30. K. Damodaran Nambiar lists many others in "The *Nārada Purāna*: A Critical Study," *Purāna* 15, no. 2, supplement (1973): 1–56.

25.   The comparison to mother cow's milk and mother's milk is made in *Rig Veda* X.9 and X.75, for instance, and Indra's role in forging the channels of the rivers is noted in *Rig Veda* X.47 and X.49.

26.   The myth is told twice at the beginning of the *Siva Purāna*: I.5–12; II.1.6–9. See also *Linga Purāna* 17.17–21; *Kūrma Purāna* I.25.62–111; II.31.1–31; *Skanda Purāna* I.3.1.1–2; I.3.1.6; I.3.2.9–15; VII.3.34; *Vāyu Purāna* I. 55.1–68. The *jyotirlingas* are discussed at length in Chapter 5.

27. For the latter see Alf Hiltebeitel, *The Cult of Draupadi* (Chicago: University of Chicago Press, 1988), pp. 66–67.

28. The term *asura* does not really mean "demon," though it is often and conveniently translated as such, and I often do so myself. The *asuras* are anti-gods, the oppositional forces whose struggle against the gods provides the dynamism that fuels the activity of the universe.

29. This is referred to as the *ātmalinga* and is located within the compound of the Mahābaleshvara Temple.

30. Yi-Fu Tuan, *Space and Place: The Perspective of Experience* (Minneapolis: University of Minnesota Press, 1977), p. 89ff.

31. *Mahābhārata* XIII.108–16.

32. Diana L. Eck, "The Dynamics of Indian Symbolism," in Peter Berger, ed., *The Other Side of God* (New York: Doubleday, 1981), contains a fuller explication of this organic ontology.

33. The myth of Daksha's *yajna* is found in the *Siva Purāna*, where it occupies the entirety of section II of the Rudra Samhitā. It includes many elements also found in shorter compass in the *Linga Purāna* (I.99–100); the *Bhāgavata Purāna* (IV.2–7); the *Skanda Purāna* (I.1.1–5); the *Vāyu Purāna* (I.30); and the *Padma Purāna* (I.5–11). This telling, complete with body parts, is found in the *Devī Bhāgavata Purāna* (VII.30) and the *Kālikā Purāna* (15–18).

34. D. C. Sircar, *Sakta Pīthas* (Banaras: Motilal Banarsidass, 1950, 1973).

35. Radhakumud Mookerji, *Nationalism in Hindu Culture* (London: Theosophical Publishing House, 1921), p. 39.

36. The province of Bengal was divided administratively by the British under Viceroy Curzon in 1905, but the decision raised a political firestorm, gave rise to a spirit of Bengali nationalism, and was reversed in 1911.

37. Jan Gonda, *The Meaning of the Sanskrit Term Dhāman* (Amsterdam: N.V. Noord-Hollandsche Uitgevers Maatschappij, 1976), p. 19ff. He speaks of a *dhāman* as the "'location,' of a *numen*, of divine power, of a deity, i.e., not only or merely a 'holder' or 'receptacle' of divine power, a place, being or phenomenon in which a divinity sets or locates itself, functions or manifests itself, or displays its power, or where its 'presence' is experienced, but also a particular way of presenting or revealing itself, of locating or 'projecting' a mode of its nature and essence, a hypostasis or refraction in which it is believed to be active." He notes that the suffix "man" denotes some "power concept" as in *numen, karman, bhuman*—a locative power. He further explores the close relation of *naman* and *dhāman*, name and place. Gonda compares this to the Hebrew sense of God's "glory" as present in the temple. God's name dwells in a place. "On this place I put my name." (Deut. 12:5, I Kings 9:3.)

38. See Gonda's discussion, for instance, of *Rig Veda* 10.45.2: "We know thy *dhāmani*, O Agni, distributed in many places." (Gonda, p. 24ff.)

39. In some of the many mythic versions of the origins of Rāmeshvara, the *linga* is established by Rāma and his party before crossing the "bridge" to Lanka. See Chapter 9 on Rāmeshvara.

40. There are, of course, other forms of what has been called *digvijaya*, the "conquering of the four directions." For example, four *pīthas* are said to have been established by Shankarachārya in his tour around India. The *mathas*, or monas-

teries, correspond to the four directions: Dvārakā in the west; Jyoshīmatha near Badrīnāth in the north; Purī in the east; and Sringeri (as well as Kānchīpuram) in the south. As A. K. Shastri puts it in his book *A History of Sringeri*, "The idea of establishing these *mathas* in four different corners of India was to bring about national integration which Sankara perhaps had then in his mind." (Dharwad: Karnatak University, 1982, p. 4.) See Chapter 2 for more on circling the land.

41. For instance, N. Singh, in the introduction to *The Call of Uttarkhand* (Hardwar: Randhir Book Sales, n.d.).

42. *Chāron Dhām Mahātma* (Hardwar: Harbhajan Singh and Sons, n.d.), p 12.

43. Ann Grodzins Gold, *Fruitful Journeys: The Ways of Rajasthani Pilgrims* (Berkeley: University of California Press, 1988), p. 36.

44. Fred W. Clothey, "Pilgrimage Centers in the Tamil Cultus of Murukan," *Journal of the American Academy of Religion* 40: 87.

45. *Mukti-sthalas* of Karnataka are Kollur, Udupi, Gokarna, Subramanya, Kumbasi, Kodeshvara, Shankaranārāyana.

46. Feldhaus, *Connected Places*, p. 144.

47. Ibid., p. 146.

48. Ambā is a common name for the "mother" goddess in western India. Gorakhnāth is a yogi/ascetic who is also seen as a manifestation of Lord Shiva. Dattātreya is a deity popular in western India. He is said to be the son of the sage Atri and his wife Anasūyā and is also understood to be born of the union of Shiva, Vishnu, and Brahmā. Mahākālī is the "Great Kālī," a fierce form of the goddess.

49. S. Dhammika, *The Edicts of King Ashoka* (Kandy, Sri Lanka: Buddhist Publication Society, 1993).

50. According to some legends, Parashurāma the great warrior who was also a Brahmin, gave away the entire earth as a gift to a king. Then, having nowhere to live, he had to reclaim land from the sea.

Chapter 2: "What Is India?"

1. Mushirul Hasan, "The Myth of Unity: Colonial and National Narratives," in David Ludden, ed., *Contesting the Nation: Religion, Community, and the Politics of Democracy in India* (Philadelphia: University of Pennsylvania Press, 1996), p. 204.

2. Jawaharlal Nehru, *The Discovery of India* (New York: Anchor, 1959), p. 27.

3. Sunil Khilani, *The Idea of India* (New York: Farrar, Straus and Giroux, 1997), p. 194.

4. Sir John Strachey, *India* (London: Kegan, Paul, Trench & Co., 1888), p. 2.

5. Ludden, *Contesting the Nation*, p. 6.

6. The "river hymns" of the *Rig Veda* are numerous. See *Rig Veda* X.64 and X.75, for instance. For the mythology of the slaying of Vritra and the loosing of waters, see I.32, I. 34, I. 35, II.12, II. 28, VIII. 24, X. 43, VI. 61, VII. 95, VII. 96. See also Chapter 4, "The Gangā and the Rivers of India."

7. Radhakumud Mookerji, *Nationalism in Hindu Culture* (London: Theosophical Publishing House, 1921), p. 52. Mookerji was known first for his maritime history of Indian shipping. These lectures on nationalism in Hindu culture were delivered at Mysore University in 1920 and developed ideas from an earlier work, *The Fundamental Unity of India* (1914).

8. Ibid., p. 53.

9. For an exhaustive study of mapmaking by the British East India Company in British India, see Matthew Edney, *Mapping an Empire: The Geographical Construction of British India 1765–1843* (Chicago: University of Chicago Press, 1997).

10. Sumathi Ramaswamy, *The Goddess and the Nation: Mapping Mother India* (Durham: Duke University Press, 2010).

11. Ernst Cassirer, *The Philosophy of Symbolic Forms*, vol. 2 (New Haven: Yale University Press, 1955), pp. 84–85.

12. The two epics, the *Mahābhārata* and the *Rāmāyana*, took shape in the period between 500 B.C.E. and 200 C.E., the story of the *Rāmāyana* likely being older, as it is told within the frame of the *Mahābhārata*. The Purānas emerged in the following thousand years and were in the constant process of expansion, gathering additions and appendices until virtually the twentieth century.

13. Sheldon Pollock, *The Language of the Gods in the World of Men: Sanskrit, Culture, and Power in Premodern India* (Berkeley: University of California Press, 2006), p. 191.

14. Ibid., p. 197.

15. B. C. Law, *Historical Geography of Ancient India* (Paris: Societe Asiatique de Paris, 1954), p. 2.

16. "Sanskritization" is a term coined by the anthropologist M. N. Srinivas to suggest the ways in which castes raise their relative status by the adoption of practices from higher caste groups. He first developed the usage in his book *Religion and Society Amongst the Coorgs of South India* (Oxford: The Clarendon Press, 1952).

17. Pollock, *Language of the Gods*, makes the general argument throughout that this Sanskrit cosmopolis emerges through the centuries of the first millennium of the common era.

18. Ayesha Jalal, *Self and Sovereignty: Individual and Community in South Asia since 1850* (London: Routledge, 2000). Throughout the book, Jalal brings to the fore the "territorial aspects" of Muslim identity in South Asia.

19. Rowena Potts, "When the Difference Between Us Was Erased, I Saw You Everywhere: Shared Identities at a Sufi Shrine in Banāras," Harvard University A. B. honors thesis, 2006 (Cambridge, MA: Harvard University Archives).

20. Ashokan edict, in *The Edicts of King Ashoka, An English Rendering* by S. Dhammika (Kandy, Sri Lanka: Buddhist Publication Society, 1993), accessed electronically at *www.buddhanet.net/pdf_file/edicts-asoka6.pdf* (June 28, 2010).

21. Pollock notes that Kālidāsa's account seems to be modeled on the inscriptional record of the mid-fourth-century Allahabad pillar of Samudragupta describing the "geo-political" vision of his domain. Pollock, *Language of the Gods*, pp. 239–41.

22. Alexander Cunningham, *The Ancient Geography of India* (1871, reprinted Vārānasī: Bhartiya Publishing House, 1975), pp. 1–3. He cites *Strabo's Geographia* ii.1.6. The account later reached Eratosthenes, who described the quadrilateral rhomboid shape of India.

23. Sir John Strachey, *India* (London: Kegan, Paul, Trench & Co., 1888), p. 2.

24. Ibid., p. 3.

25. Ibid., pp. 5–6.

26. Ibid., p. 8.

27. *Agni Purāna* 118.1; *Brahmā Purāna* 19.1; *Vāyu Purāna* 45.75–77; *Vishnu Purāna* II.3.1. In Mahābhārata VI:9 Sanjaya describes this whole land to Dhritarāshtra.

28. Pollock, *Language of the Gods*, p. 193.

29. Ibid.

30. E. J. Rapson, ed. The Cambridge History of India (1922). Accessed online: *www.third-millennium-library.com/readinghall/UniversalHistory/INDIA/ Cambridge/I/Chapter_I.html.*

31. Mookerji, *Nationalism in Hindu Culture*, p. 33.

32. Jawaharlal Nehru, *The Discovery of India* (New York: Anchor Books, 1959), p. 27.

33. Historical Division of the Ministry of External Affairs, "Himalayan Frontiers," in Rana Satya Paul, ed., *Our Northern Borders* (New Delhi: The Book Times Company, 1963), pp. 19–25.

34. Jawaharlal Nehru, "Last Will and Testament," quoted by Eric Newby in Newby and Raghubir Singh, *Gangā: Sacred River of India* (Hong Kong: The Perennial Press, 1972), p. 9.

35. Robin Lane Fox, *The Search for Alexander* (Boston: Little, Brown and Co., 1980), pp. 327–28.

36. Cunningham, pp. 1–3.

37. Ibid., pp. 1–2.

38. The sources quoted by Cunningham include Megasthenes, Eratosthenes, Strabo, and Pliny. See Cunningham, pp. 1–3. Interestingly, even where the estimates of the distances differ, the "India" the historians are attempting to measure is the same.

39. Megasthenes as quoted in J. W. McCrindle, *Ancient India as Described by Megasthenes and Arrian* (Calcutta: Checkervertty, Chatterjee, & Co., Ltd., 1926), p. 43. From pp. 43 to 51 there are various fragments cited giving the extent of India in *stadia*.

40. Cunningham, *Ancient Geography*, pp. 2–3.

41. See Diana L. Eck, "India's *Tīrthas*—Crossings in Sacred Geography," *History of Religions* 20, no. 4 (May 1981): 323–44.

42. This section of the *Mahābhārata* in Book III, the Vana Parva, is said to be a late part of the epic in which various aspects of *dharma*, religion and practice, are surveyed. The "Tīrtha Yātrā Parva" begins in Chapter 80 of the Vana Parva and continues through Chapter 157.

43. *Mahābhārata* III.81–90.

44. *Mahābhārata* III.82.20–40.

45. Pulastya's description of the *tīrthas* is in *Mahābhārata* III.82.20 to III.85.111. See S. Bhardwaj, *Hindu Places of Pilgrimage in India* (Berkeley: University of California Press, 1973), which includes a chapter on the pilgrimage circuits of the *Mahābhārata* and a map on "The Grand Pilgrimage of India According to the *Mahābhārata*."

46. Dhaumya's description of the *tīrthas* is in *Mahābhārata* III.87.1–III.90.34. We must imagine our pilgrim party to be somewhere in the land of the Kurus in central north India. To the east are the Naimisha Forest, the Gangā and Yamunā Rivers with the confluence at Prayāga, the Gomatī River, Gayā, and

the Kaushītakī River of Bengal. Included in the "south" is everything south of the Payoshnī River, including the Yamunā, the Bhīmarathī, the Venī, and the Krishnā Rivers, and the Tamraparnī River of the far south. No mention is made here of Kanyā Tīrtha, however. Inexplicably, the "south" also includes Saurashtra, the great western peninsula of India, which is, indeed, considerably south of the Kuru country, but would more plausibly have been classified under the *tīrthas* of the west. The western region has its own integrity, however, extending from the Narmadā River north and west through the *tīrtha* of Ujjain, called Avantī, still famous as one of the great pilgrimage cities of India today. It extends as far as Pushkara, the Lotus Pond. The "north" begins with the Sarasvatī and Drishadvatī Rivers and extends north to Gangādvāra and Kanakhala, approximately where Hardvār is today. There, following the course of the Gangā toward its source, one enters the Himalayan foothills. One of its tributaries, the Alakanandā, streams through the country famous in the *Mahābhārata* and famous still today, as Badarī Vishāla or Badrīnāth.

47. The journey of the Pāndavas begins with *Mahābhārata* III.91.1, and the long narrative includes a number of the kinds of stories they would have heard along the way: the taming of the pride of the Vindhya Mountains, which had grown up to block the course of the sun; the birth of the sons of King Sagara, the disappearance of Sagara's sacrificial horse, and the incineration of the sons of Sagara; the sage Bhagīratha and the descent of the Gangā; and many other tales. The description of the journey continues intermittently, stopping for narration of various myths along the way. In III.140 they finally reach the mountains and begin the ascent to Kailāsa and Badarī Vishāla.

48. For example, they travel from the mouth of the Gangā to Orissa in but a breath: "O Janamejaya, thereupon the Pāndavas started from the Kaushikī [river] and went, one after the other, to all the sacred shrines. O King, going to the sea where the Ganges mingles with it, he performed the sacred ceremony of a plunge in the centre of the five hundred rivers. O descendant of Bharata, that ruler of earth, the hero, accompanied by his brothers then went along the shore of the ocean to the land of the Kalingas." (*Mahābhārata* III.114.1–3.)

49. For a detailed, regional explication of this principle, see Anne Feldhaus, "The Algebra of Place," Chapter 5 in *Connected Places: Regional, Pilgrimage, and Geographical Imagination in India* (New York: Palgrave Macmillan, 2003).

50. See P. V. Kane, *History of Dharmashāstra*, Vol. IV (Poona: Bhandarkar Oriental Research Institute, 1973).

51. See Stella Kramrisch, *The Hindu Temple*, 2 vols. (Calcutta: University of Calcutta, 1946). This north Indian *nagara* style is discussed in volume I, pp. 175, 251, 286–90.

52. Anne Feldhaus, p. 187. The text she cites is the *Sūtrapāth*, a text of aphorisms by Cakradhar.

53. Ibid., p. 5.

54. K. N. Subramanyam, tr., *The Anklet Story, Silappadhikaaram of Ilango Adigal* (Delhi: Agam Prakashan, 1977), p. 33. See also pp. 33–39.

55. Ibid., p. 45.

56. Ibid.

57. Ibid., p. 87.

58. Ibid., p. 158.

59. See, for example, the work of David Shulman, *Tamil Temple Myths* (Princeton: Princeton University Press, 1980), which is built around the exploration of the *sthala purānas* in Tamil literature.

60. Indira V. Peterson, "Singing of a Place: Pilgrimage as Metaphor and Motif in the Tevaram Songs of the Tamil Saivite Saints," *Journal of the American Oriental Society* 102, no. 1 (1982): 72.

61. Ibid., p. 83. Shiva is, of course, the one who carries the skull, dwells in Kailāsa, carries the trident, rides the bull, and as Ardhanārīshvara, shares his body with the goddess.

62. *Kumārasambhava* 1.1, in M. R. Kale, ed. and trans., *Kumārasambhava* (Delhi: Motilal Banarsidass, 1967).

63. Kālidāsa, *Raghuvamsha* IV. 51. See G. R. Nandargikar, ed., *The Raghuvamsa of Kālidāsa with the Commentary of Mallinātha* (Delhi: Motilal Banarsidass, 1971).

64. *Meghadūta, The Cloud Messenger,* pp. 30–31, as translated by Daniel H. H. Ingalls, in "Kālidāsa and the Attitudes of the Golden Age," *Journal of the American Oriental Society* 96, no. 1 (January–March 1976): 20.

65. *Raghuvamsha* II.42, III.49; XVIII.24; VIII.33; VI.34.

66. *Raghuvamsha* V.8, VIII.95; XVIII.31.

67. *Raghuvamsha* XIII.58, VIII.95.

68. Early Buddhist texts of the Pali Canon also give us a great deal of information about India's geography, even though it is primarily incidental to their matters of concern. The towns and parks and forests of the area of north India called Majjhimadesha or Madhyadesha, the "Middle Country," are described. This Middle Country, described in both Brahmanical and Buddhist literature, roughly corresponds to the Gangetic plain south of the Himalayas and extending east as far as Banāras or, for Buddhists, Bodh Gayā, the place of the Buddha's enlightenment in what is now Bihar. The four places of Buddhist pilgrimage, as enunciated in the Pali Canon, are Kapilavastu, where the Buddha was born; Bodh Gayā, where he attained enlightenment; Sārnāth, near Banāras, where he preached his first sermon, thus "turning the wheel of the dharma," and Kushinārā, where he died. There is no attempt, for instance, to describe the whole of the land or its shape, although the term "Jambudvīpa" is used as a name for the "island" of the known world corresponding roughly to India.

69. Cited from a footnote, Fah-kai-lih-to, by Samuel Beal, ed., *Travels of Fah-Hian and Sung-Yun, Buddhists Pilgrims from China to India* (London: Trubner and Co., 1869), p. 36.

70. James Legge, *A Record of Buddhistic Kingdoms, Being an Account by the Chinese Monk Fa-Hien of His Travels in India and Ceylon (A.D. 399–414) in Search of the Buddhist Books of Discipline* (New York: Dover Publications, 1965).

71. Ibid., p. 29.

72. Ibid., pp. 87–88.

73. Cunningham, *Ancient Geography,* p. 10.

74. The Tungabhadrā, with Anegundi on the north bank, sounds much like the

Kishkindhā of the *Rāmāyana* as instantiated in "place" today at the temple site of Hampī in Karnataka.

75. Bhatta Lakshmīdhara, *Krityakalpataru,* K. V. Rangaswami Aiyangar, ed. (Baroda: Oriental Research Institute, 1942).

76. The *nibandhakāras* include Vācaspati Mishra in the fifteenth century, whose *Smriti Chintāmani* includes the *Tīrtha Chintāmani;* Narayana Bhatta in the sixteenth century, whose *Tristhalīsetu* gathers together information on Kāshī, Prayāga, and Gayā; and Mitra Mishra in the seventeenth century, whose *Vīramitrodaya* includes a volume on the *tīrthas,* the *Tīrtha Prakāsha.*

77. K. V. Rangaswami Aiyangar, ed., *Krityakalpataru* (Baroda: Oriental Research Institute, 1942), editor's introduction, pp. li–liii.

78. Ibid., p. xcii.

79. Andre Wink, *Al-Hind, The Making of the Indo-Islamic World*, Vol. II (Leiden: Brill, 1997), p. 330.

80. Ibid., p. 331.

81. Ibid.

82. Ibid., p. 327.

83. Richard Eaton, "Temple Desecration and Indo-Muslim States," *Journal of Islamic Studies* 11, no. 3 (2000), p. 289.

84. Ibid., p. 294.

85. Wink, *Al-Hind,* p. 294. Also see p. 323ff.

86. Eaton, "Temple Desecration," p. 290.

87. Iqtidar Husain Siddiqui, "The Early Chishti *Dargahs,*" in Christian Troll, ed., *Muslim Shrines in India* (New York: Oxford University Press, 1989), p. 18.

88. *http://blog.taragana.com/n/hindu-or-muslim-they-are-flocking-to-ajmer-sufi-shrine-letter-from-ajmer-91447/,* accessed July 22, 2009.

89. Tahir Mahmood, "The *Dargah* of Sayyid Salar Mas'ud Ghazi in Bahraich: Legend, Tradition, and Reality," in Troll, pp. 46–47.

90. As Iqtidar Siddiqui put it, "For Hindus, and often for new converts to Islam whose conversion was partial, the *dargah* was a substitute for the idol." (Troll, p. 7.)

91. Iqtidar Siddiqui, "Early Chishti *Dargahs,*" p. 21.

92. Some Qawwali singers of Delhi happened to sing a curious verse as the refrain of their song before Emperor Jahangir:

> Each nation has its right road of faith and its shrine.
> I've set up my shrine on the path of him with the cocked cap.

When Jahangir asked the meaning of this, an old courtier explained that the poet Amir Khusrau had composed this by putting together a dialogue he had enjoyed with his Pir. "One day Shaikh Nizamuddin Auliya had put his cap on the side of his head and was sitting on a terraced roof by the bank of the Jumna, awaiting the devotions of the Hindus. Turning to his disciple who had just arrived, the saint asked, 'Do you see this crowd?' Then he recited the line: 'Each race has its right road of faith and its shrine' (*Har quam rast rahay, dinay was qiblighay*). The poet replied immediately, 'I've set my shrine in the direction of him with the cocked cap.' This was the origin of the popular rhyme that impressed Akbar's son and successor three centuries later." Rajat Kanta Ray, *The Felt Community: Com-*

monality and Mentality Before the Emergence of Indian Nationalism (New Delhi: Oxford University Press, 2003), pp. 131–32.

93. From *Tarikh-i-Salatin-i-Afaghana*, cited in Rajat Kanta Ray, *Felt Community*, p. 162.

94. Ayesha Jalal, *Self and Sovreignty*, p. 10.

95. "The idea of the central realm of Hindustan was six centuries old when the British troops dispatched by Lord Wellesley under the command of Lord Lake rode into the Red Fort at Shahjahanabad in 1803. For native and foreigner alike, this was one land and its political headquarters were located in the Lal Qila built by Shah Jahan." Rajat Kanta Ray, *Felt Community*, p. 165.

96. Edney, *Mapping an Empire*, p. 9.

97. Rajat Kanta Ray, *Felt Community*, p. 5.

98. Swami Vivekananda, "The Future of India," in *The Complete Works of Swami Vivekananda*, vol. 3, *Lectures from Colombo to Almora*, *http://en.wikisource.org/wiki/The_Complete_Works_of_Swami_Vivekananda/Volume_3/Lectures_from_Colombo_to_Almora/The_Future_of_India*, accessed June 28, 2010.

99. Stanley A. Wolpert, *Tilak and Gokhale, Revolution and Reform in the Making of Modern India* (Berkeley: University of California Press, 1961), p. 135.

100. Sabyasachi Bhattacharya, *Vande Mātaram: The Biography of a Song* (New Delhi: Penguin Books, 2003), pp. 100–101. This version has been translated by Aurobindo Ghose, November 20, 1909.

101. B. C. Pal, *Soul of India* (Calcutta: Yugayatri Prakashak Limited, 1958), pp. 102–03.

102. Ibid., pp. 107–10, 135.

103. Ibid., p. 136.

104. Ibid., pp. 133–34.

105. V. D. Savarkar, *Hindutva, Who Is a Hindu?* Fifth edition (Bombay: Veer Savarkar Prakashan, 1969), p. 32.

106. Ibid., p. 82.

107. Ibid., p. 125.

108. Ibid., p. 91.

109. Ibid., pp. 5, 46, 82, 140–41.

110. Ibid., p. 133.

111. Lise McKean, "Bhārat Mata: Mother India and Her Militant Matriots," in John S. Hawley and Donna M. Wulff, eds., *Devi: Goddesses of India* (Delhi: Motilal Banarsidass, 1998), p. 263.

112. Ramaswamy, *Goddess and the Nation*, p. 166.

113. Ibid., p. 75. Her entire book is devoted to the explication of this goddess-map confluence that begins in the early twentieth century and becomes increasingly powerful with the popularization of print images.

114. Sadan Jha, "The Life and Times of Bhārat Mātā," *Manushi*, issue 142, August 2004, *www.indiatogether.org/manushi/issue142/bharat.htm*.

115. *Atharva Veda* XII.1. These translations are from Raimundo Panikkar, ed., *The Vedic Experience, Mantramanjari* (Berkeley: University of California Press, 1977).

116. V. S. Agrawal, *India—A Nation* (Varanasi: Prithivi Prakashan, 1983), p. 50.

117. Ibid., p. 3.

118. Ibid.
119. Mookerji, *Nationalism in Hindu Culture,* p. 13.
120. Ibid., p. 10.
121. Rabindranāth Tagore, *Nationalism* (New Delhi: Rupa & Co., 2002), p. 55.
122. Ibid., pp. 110–111.

CHAPTER 3: ROSE APPLE ISLAND: INDIA IN THE LOTUS OF THE WORLD

1. *Mahābhārata,* M. N. Dutt, trans., Bhīshma Parva, ch. 1–3. Hereafter VI. 1–3
2. *Mahābhārata,* VI. 4–12.
3. The *jambu* is said to be classified as *Eugenia jambolana* or *Syzygium samarangense,* commonly called the rose apple or sometimes a Malabar plum. It is native to south and southeast Asia and part of the myrtle family.
4. *Rig Veda* X.121.1. My trans.
5. *Atharva Veda* IV.2.8. Ralph T. H. Griffith, trans. *The Hymns of the Atharva Veda,* 2 vols. (Varanasi: Chowkhamba Sanskrit Series, 1968), p. 133.
6. *Shatapatha Brāhmana* XI.1.6. See Julius Eggeling, tr., *Satapatha Brāhmana, The Sacred Books of the East,* vols. XII, XXVI, XLI, XLIII, XLIV (Oxford: The Clarendon Press, 1882–1900).
7. Chandogya Upanishad 3.19.1–2. See Robert Ernest Hume, *The Thirteen Principal Upanishads* (London: Oxford University Press, 1921).
8. *Aitareya Upanishad* 1.4. My translation.
9. *Matsya Purāna* 167–68.
10. *Matsya Purāna* 167–71. The most accessible version of this myth in English is in Heinrich Zimmer, *Myths and Symbols in Indian Art and Civilization* (Princeton: Princeton University Press, 1946), pp. 35–53. A brilliant article on this subject is Wendy Doniger O'Flaherty, "Inside and Outside the Mouth of God: The Boundary Between Myth and Reality," *Daedalus* 109, no. 2 (1980): 93–125.
11. Betty Heimann, *Facets of Indian Thought* (London: George Allen and Unwin, Ltd., 1964), p. 20.
12. Mircea Eliade, "Methodological Remarks on the Study of Religious Symbolism," in Mircea Eliade and Joseph M. Kitagawa, eds., *The History of Religions, Essays in Methodology* (Chicago: University of Chicago Press, 1959), p. 98.
13. Ibid., p. 99.
14. W. Kirfel, *Die Kosmographie der Inder* (Bonn: K. Schroeder, 1920), pp. 56–57. Kirfel provides a useful list of the variants in accounts of the ring-continents. The largest group, including most of the Purānas, follows the accounts of islands and seas which I will describe here in the text. A second group, including the *Matsya Purāna* and *Varāha Purāna* and one of the *Bhavishya Purāna* accounts, and a third group including the *Mahābhārata* and *Padma Purāna* accounts, order and name the islands and seas slightly differently, although the general notion remains the same. S. M Ali, *The Geography of the Purānas* (New Delhi: People's Publishing House, 1966), also reviews the many cosmological schemes of the Purānas, relying most heavily on the most complete of them, that in the *Vāyu Purāna.* His interest is also in relating the descriptive geography of the Purānas to the lands and regions of the known world.

15. *Matsya Purāna* 122.79.
16. *Vāmana Purāna* 11.31.
17. *Vishnu Purāna* II.3.28.
18. *Bhagavāta Purāna* V.20.
19. The account here generally follows Kirfel's Group I, but the Puranic accounts I have used here are given more precisely than in Kirfel's citation: *Agni Purāna* 108.1–2 and 119 entire; *Bhāgavata Purāna* V.20; *Brahmā Purāna* I.18. *Brahmavaivarta Purāna* I.7; *Devī Bhāgavata Purāna* VIII.4, VIII.12–14; *Garuda Purāna* I.54.4–7, I.56; *Kūrma Purāna* I.43.1–6 and 26, I.47–48; *Linga Purāna* I.46, I.53.1–35; *Mārkandeya Purāna* 54.5–7; *Nārada Purāna* I.3.41–45; *Vāmana Purāna* 11.30–43; *Vāyu Purāna* 49; *Vishnu Purāna* II.2; II.4.
20. See Jan Gonda, *Loka—World and Heaven in the Veda* (Amsterdam: Noord-Hollandsche U.M., 1966).
21. *Kūrma Purāna* I.48.14.
22. For a typical account of the progression outward through the islands see the *Vishnu Purāna* II.4. Here we are taken through the seven divisions, the seven rivers, and the mountains of Plaksha, then Shālmali, Kusha, Krauncha, Shāka, Pushkara. Each is named for its distinctive tree; each has seven sacred rivers and seven mountains separating its regions. Each has caste divisions, though the castes are known by different names.
23. *Vishnu Purāna* II.4.
24. *Bhāgavata Purāna* V.20.35.
25. There are many sources for the geography of Jambudvīpa, a significant fact in itself, for this conception of Rose Apple Island is one that is contained, virtually without fail, in all the Purānas. In most of these accounts the seven *varshas* and the fourfold divisions of the lotus petals are meshed together, sometimes in garbled fashion, but more often in an orderly worldview. See: *Agni Purāna* 108; *Bhāgavata Purāna* V.16–19; *Brahmā Purāna* I.16–17; *Devī Bhāgavata Purāna* VIII.5–7; *Garuda Purāna* I.54–55; *Linga Purāna* I.48–49; *Kūrma Purāna* I.43–44; *Mahābhārata* VI.7; *Mārkandeya Purāna* 54–55; *Matsya Purāna* 113; *Vāmana Purāna* 13; *Vāyu Purāna* I.34; *Vishnu Purāna* II.2. (A few sources also see the world as ninefold: *Bhāgavata Purāna* V.16–19; *Devī Bhāgavata Purāna* VIII.5; *Linga Purāna* I.49; *Mārkandeya Purāna* 56. In this view the center zone is at Meru, with three zones to the north, three to the south, and one each to the east and west.
26. *Vāyu Purāna* I.34.46.
27. For the four rivers, see: *Bhāgavata Purāna* V.17.5–9; *Kūrma Purāna* I.44.28–33; *Linga Purāna* I.52.4–12a; *Mārkandeya Purāna* 56; *Vāyu Purāna* I.42; *Vishnu Purāna* II.2. *Devī Bhāgavata Purāna* VIII.6 says the four are the Arunoda to the east, the Jambu to the south, the rivers of honey called Madhu Dhara to the west, and the milk rivers called Kamadugh to the north.
28. See the work of Max Moerman on Japanese Buddhist pilgrimage maps used to travel, either by foot or in the mind's eye, to the sacred sites of the Buddha in India.
29. S. M. Ali, *Geography of the Purānas*, pp. 50–52.
30. Mount Vipula in the west; Mount Supārshva in the north; Mount Mandara in

the east; and Mount Gandhamādana in the south. The four buttress mountains that flank Meru are mentioned as follows: *Agni Purāna* 108.11–13; *Bhāgavata Purāna* V.16.7–12, where they are called *avashtambha giri; Brahmā Purāna* I.16. 18–24; *Linga Purāna* I.49.25b–27; *Kūrma Purāna* I.43.14–15; *Mārkandeya Purāna* 54.19–20; *Matsya Purāna* 113.45; *Vāyu Purāna* I.35.10–17; *Vishnu Purāna* II.2.16–17.

31. *Bhāgavata Purāna* V.16.19–24; *Brahmā Purāna* I.16.25–26, *Mārkandeya Purāna* 54.

32. For extensive explications of the fourfoldness of the cosmos, see *Agni Purāna* 108.11–18; *Brahmā Purāna* I.16.18–62; *Bhāgavata Purāna* V.16.7–29; *Devī Bhāgavata Purāna* VIII.5–7; *Kūrma Purāna* I.43.14–23; *Linga Purāna* I.49. 25b–37; *Mārkandeya Purāna* 54; *Matsya Purāna* 113.13–16, 37–38; *Vāyu Purāna* I.35.17–47; *Vishnu Purāna* II.2.

33. The sevenfold description is contained in virtually all of the passages on fourfold cosmology cited above. More specifically, see: *Agni Purāna* 108.5–10; *Bhāgavata Purāna* V.16.1–7; *Brahmā Purāna* I.16–18; *Kūrma Purāna* I.43.9–14; *Linga Purāna* I.49.3–11; *Mahābhārata* VI.7.2–8,50; *Mārkandeya Purāna* 54.; *Matsya Purāna* 113.7–23; *Vāyu Purāna* I.34.13–14, 23–31; *Vishnu Purāna* II.2.10–15. The sevenfold view and the fourfold view are almost always interwoven in the standard accounts of Rose Apple Island. Indeed, they are imaginatively compatible. Since the middle zone of the circle, Ilāvrita, is the widest, stretching across the entire diameter of the world, it includes the eastern and western petals of the lotus-world. The northern and southern petals are, roughly, divided laterally into three zones each. Thus the fourfold structure, based on directionality from Mount Meru, is easily superimposed on the sevenfold structure, which sees the world in its latitudes. Several Purānic accounts make the natural step from this sevenfold world and speak of Jambudvīpa as consisting of nine zones. Ilāvrita is square in the middle; Ketumāla and Bhadrāshva are respectively west and east; three zones lie to the north and three to the south. (This is in the *Bhāgavata Purāna* V.16.6; the *Linga Purāna* I.48.34–5, 49; the *Mārkandeya Purāna* 57; and the *Vāyu Purāna* 34.9, for example.) The most appealing version carries this vision a step further and sees all the zones as leafing out from Meru, in the four directions and the four intermediate directions. These eight, together with Ilāvrita, are the "nine holy and pleasant continents." (*Vāmana Purāna* 13.6; *Garuda Purāna* I.55.1–3).

34. The substances of the various mountains are described in *Linga Purāna* I.49. 18–20; *Mahābhārata* VI.6.3–5; *Matsya Purāna* 113.11–17; *Vāyu Purāna* I.34.14–21.

35. For the sevenfold division of the Gangā, see *Mahābhārata* VI.6.48–51; *Matsya Purāna* 121.38–42; *Vāyu Purāna* I.47.26–59.

36. The classic treatment is Guiseppe Tucci, *Stupa: Art, Architectonics, and Symbolism* (New Delhi: Aditya Prakashan, 1988).

37. The measurements of Meru are given as follows: *Agni Purāna* 108.3–4; *Bhāgavata Purāna* V.16.7; *Brahmā Purāna* I.16.14–15; *Garuda Purāna* I.54.7–8; *Linga Purāna* I.48.1–7; *Kūrma Purāna* I.43.6–8; *Mahābhārata* VI.6.10–11; *Mārkandeya Purāna* 54.15–16; *Matsya Purāna* 113.40; *Vāyu Purāna* I.34.49–53.

38. For example, *Bhāgavata Purāna* V.21–23; *Devī Bhāgavata Purāna* VIII.15; *Garuda Purāna* I.58; *Linga Purāna* I.54; *Matsya Purāna* 124; *Vishnu Purāna* II.8.

39. *Bhāgavata Purāna* V.23.

40. *Devī Bhāgavata Purāna* VIII.15.

41. That Meru is gold: *Agni Purāna* 108.9; *Bhāgavata Purāna* V.16.7; *Kūrma Purāna* I.43.6; *Linga Purāna* I.48.4, 8; *Mahābhārata* VI.6.10; *Mārkandeya Purāna* 54.15; *Matsya Purāna* 113.4, 20, 37, 39; *Vāyu Purāna* I.34.15, 36.

42. *Linga Purāna* I.48.4.

43. The four *varnas* of Meru are given: *Linga Purāna* I.48.8; *Mārkandeya Purāna* 54.16–17; *Matsya Purāna* 113.12–16, 37–38; *Vāyu Purāna* I.34.16–19, 47–48.

44. *Agni Purāna* 108.22–23; *Bhāgavata Purāna* V.16.7–8; *Brahmā Purāna* I.16.15, 45–46; *Garuda Purāna* I.54.9; *Kūrma Purāna* I.43.8; I.44.34–35; *Vāmana Purāna* 11.32; *Vāyu Purāna* I.34.37; *Vishnu Purāna* II.2.38.

45. The twenty filament mountains are noted in *Bhāgavata Purāna* V.16.26; *Brahmā Purāna* I.16.32–39; *Devī Bhāgavata Purāna* VIII.6.31–32; *Kūrma Purāna* I.43.26–34; *Vishnu Purāna* II.2.25–29.

46. In the east is Indra's city, the famous Amarāvatī. In the southeast is the city of Agni; in the south, the city of Yama; in the southwest, Nirriti; in the west, Varuna; in the northwest, Vāyu; in the north, Kubera; and in the northeast, Ishāna. For the city of Brahmā and the gods, see *Agni Purāna* 108.18; *Bhāgavata Purāna* V.16.28–29; *Brahmā Purāna* I.16.36b–38a; *Devī Bhāgavata Purāna* VIII.7. 15; *Kūrma Purāna* I.44.1–26; *Linga Purāna* I.48.9–28; *Mahābhārata* VI.7.16ff; and *Mārkandeya Purāna* 54.17b–18.

47. *Linga Purāna* I.48.

48. *Kūrma Purāna* I.44.5.

49. *Vishnu Purāna* II.2.31–33. Other sources for the Gangā's descent upon Meru include *Agni Purāna* 108.19–21; *Bhāgavata Purāna* V.17.4–9; *Brahmā Purāna* I.16.38–43; *Devī Bhāgavata Purāna* VIII.7; *Kūrma Purāna* I.44.28–33; *Mārkandeya Purāna* 56. 1–18; *Vāyu Purāna* I.42.

50. *Mahābhārata* II.3; *Agni Purāna* 118.1; *Brahmā Purāna* I.17.1; *Vāyu Purāna* I.45.75–77; *Vishnu Purāna* II.3.1.

51. *Mārkandeya Purāna* 58–59; also *Mahābhārata* VI.6.39; *Matsya Purāna* 113.32.

52. *Matsya Purāna* 114.10; *Vāyu Purāna* I.45.81.

53. The descriptions of Bhārata in the world-atlas sections of the various Purānas are closely related, as the German Indologist Wilibald Kirfel has elaborately demonstrated.

54. B.C. Law, *Historical Geography of Ancient India* (Paris: Societe Asiatique de Paris, 1954), p. 1.

55. The mountain ranges of India are enumerated in *Agni Purāna* 118. 2b–3a; *Garuda Purāna* I.55.7b–8; *Kūrma Purāna* I.45.22; *Mārkandeya Purāna* 57.11–12; *Matsya Purāna* 114. 17–18; *Vāyu Purāna* I.45.88; *Vishnu Purāna* II.3.3; *Vāmana Purāna* 13.14–18.

56. All rivers are holy, as cited, for instance, in the *Mārkandeya Purāna* 57.31; the *Matysa Purāna* 114.33; and the *Vāyu Purāna* I.45.108. As for listing of rivers and their sources, see *Agni Purāna* 118.7–8; *Bhāgavata Purāna* V.19.16–18; *Devī Bhāgavata Purāna* VIII.11; *Garuda Purāna* I.55.8b–11; *Kūrma Purāna* I.45.27–

38; *Mārkandeya Purāna* 57.16–30; *Matsya Purāna* 114.20–32; *Vāmana Purāna* 13.19–33; *Vāyu Purāna* I.45.94–108.

57. The breadth of the land between the Kiratas in the east and the Yavanas in the west is given precise measurement. See *Agni Purāna* 118.6; *Garuda Purāna* I.55.6–7a; *Linga Purāna* I.52.29; *Mārkandeya Purāna* 57.8–9; *Matsya Purāna* 114.11–12; *Vāmana Purāna* 13.11–12; *Vishnu Purāna* II.3.8–9.

58. This particular description is of Bhadrāshva, from the *Mārkandeya Purāna* 56.19–26, 59–60. The idealization of the other *varshas* is common, however. See *Devī Bhāgavata Purāna* VIII.7; *Matsya Purāna* 113.48–77; *Linga Purāna* I.52; *Vishnu Purāna* II.2, 4; *Kūrma Purāna* I.45; *Bhāgavata Purāna* V.18–19.

59. In *Bhāgavata Purāna* V.19 the gods say that the holy land of Bhārata is superior to their own lands; *Brahmā Purāna* 19.4–5, 23–27; *Devī Bhāgavata Purāna* VIII.11; *Kūrma Purāna* I.45.20–21; *Linga Purāna* I.52.25–26; *Mārkandeya Purāna* 57.1–4; *Matsya Purāna* 114.6–7, 59–86; *Nārada Purāna* I.3.46–52; *Vāyu Purāna* I.45.73–77; *Vishnu Purāna* II.3. 22–27.

60. *Mārkandeya Purāna* 55.21–23.

61. A paraphrase of *Vishnu Purāna* II.3.22.

Chapter 4: The Gangā and the Rivers of India

1. Jagannātha, *Gangā Laharī* (Bombay: Bharati, 1887). Sanskrit edition with Marathi verse translation. My English translation.

2. *Rig Veda* X.75.

3. These rites are especially associated with the days marked as the times of the river's descent from heaven to earth, Gangā Dasharā, the tenth day of the bright fortnight of the summer month of Jyeshthā.

4. Jagannātha, *Gangā Laharī*, my translation.

5. This is one of innumerable stories that explain how the Gangā gets rid of all the sins left in her by the countless bathers. According to some, the Gangā comes to Kāshī or to Prayāga to bathe. According to others, the Gangā goes periodically to the Narmadā River to bathe.

6. In Hindi, "*Sarasvatī nadī kā udgam sthān. Yah Sarasvatī nadī kā gomukha tīrtha hai. Yahā par pūjan karne tathā godān karne se akshaya punyā ki prapti hoti hai.*"

7. Rampratap Tripathi, *Hinduo ke Vrat, Parva, aur Tyauhar* (Allahabad: Lokbhāratī Prakāsan, 1971), p. 86.

8. See W. Norman Brown, "The Creation Myth of the Rig Veda," *Journal of the American Oriental Society* 62, no. 2 (1942): 85–98. See also, for example, *Rig Veda* 1.32, 2.12.

9. *Rig Veda* 7.49.3. Varuna is one of the high gods of Vedic myth, the all-knowing, the just, the seer of the deeds of people.

10. Ibid., 10.75.4.

11. Ibid., 10.9.2.

12. *Bhāgavata Purāna* 5.17; *Devī Bhāgavata Purāna* 8.7. Sculpture depicts this myth as well. C. Sivaramamurti, in *Gangā* (New Delhi: Orient Longman, 1976), includes two plates (figures 1 and 2) from twelfth-century Mysore in which Brahmā is shown pouring the Gangā water pot upon Vāmana-Vishnu's upraised foot.

13. *Kūrma Purāna* 1.44; *Brahmavaivarta Purāna, Krishnajanma Khanda* 34; *Bhāgavata Purāna* 5.17; *Visnu Purāna* 2.2.8.

14. For versions of the story, see *Rāmāyana* 1.38–44; *Mahābhārata* III.104–9; *Bhāgavata Purāna* 9.8–9; *Brahmavaivarta Purāna*, Prakrti Khanda 10; *Devībhāgavata Purāna* 9.11; and *Skanda Purāna*, Kāshi Khanda 30. In *Mahābhārata* and other versions, the story immediately preceding this is that of Agastya drinking the ocean dry, which is one of the reasons the Gangā comes, i.e., to replenish the waters of the ocean. Damodaran Nambiar lists many others in "The *Nārada Purāna:* A Critical Study," *Purāna* 15, no. 2, supplement (1973): 1–56.

15. "Srī Gangāshtaka," verse 1, in *Nityakarma Vidhi tathā Devpūjā Paddhati* (Vārānasī: Thakurdas Sureka Cairiti Phand, 1966).

16. For other elaborations of the Agni-Soma polarity and resolution, see Wendy Doniger O'Flaherty, *Asceticism and Eroticism in the Mythology of Siva* (London: Oxford University Press, 1973), pp. 286–92.

17. This is a common statement of praise. See, for example, the *Matsya Purāna* 106.54. See also the *Brihannāradīya Purāna* 6.27, cited in Rampratap Tripathi, *Purānon me Gangā* (Prayag: Hindi Sahitya Sammelan, 1952), p. 33. Tripathi cites all the Gangā *māhātmyas* but makes the text of the *Brihannāradīya Purāna* available here. Missing from this enumeration of hard-to-reach *tīrthas* of the Gangā, however, is the very source of the Gangā in the high Himalayas, where we started. Perhaps it was so difficult to reach that it was accessible only to the most inveterate of sādhus.

18. James G. Lochtefeld, *Haridwara, Haradwara, Gangādwara: The Construction of Identity and Meaning in a Hindu Pilgrimage Place* (Ann Arbor: University Microfilms International, 1992). This Columbia University Ph.D. thesis is a rich and important study of the city and its *melās*. The thesis has been revised and published as *God's Gateway: Identity and Meaning in a Hindu Pilgrimage Place* (New York: Oxford University Press, 2010).

19. www.nytimes.com/2010/04/15/world/asia/15india.html.

20. *Rig Veda* X.75 (*khila*, supplementary verse).

21. Gopal Raghunath Nandargikar, ed., *The Raghuvamsa of Kālidāsa with the Commentary of Mallinātha* (Delhi: Motilal Banarsidass, 1971), XIII.54–7.

22. The cycle of *tīrthas* described in the *Mahābhārata* concludes at Prayāga (Tīrtha Yātrā Parva 85.69–85) with the description of this important place between the two rivers where the gods themselves offer sacrifice.

23. D. P. Dubey, *Prayāga, Site of the Kumbha Mela* (New Delhi: Aryan Books International, 2001). Chapter 2, "Sacred Geography," has the map of the mandalas of Prayāg. See *Matysa Purāna*, Prayāga Māhātmya, 103–112.

24. *Matysa Purāna* 103–112, the Prayāga Māhātmya.

25. Ibid., 104.5.

26. *Padma Purāna*, Uttara Khanda 23.14. See also G. Bonazzoli, "Prayāga and Its Kumbhamelā," *Purāna* XIX, no. 1 (1977): 11–12.

27. K. Nagarajan, *Cauveri from Source to Sea* (New Delhi: Arnold-Heinemann, 1975), p. 36.

28. *Ujjain Sacitra Māhātmya*, p. 13; *Skanda Purāna*, Avantikā Māhātmya 54.

29. *Kalyān Tīrthānk* 31, no. 1 (Gorakpur: Gita Press, 1957), p. 418.

30. Mircea Eliade, *Yoga, Immortality and Freedom* (Princeton: Princeton University Press, 1958, 1973), pp. 236–41.

31. See C. Sivaramamurti, *Gangā* (New Delhi: Orient Longman Limited, 1976), pp. 2, 4.

32. J. H. Dave, *Immortal India,* vol. II, 2nd ed. (Bombay: Bhāratīya Vidya Bhavan, 1970), p. 11.

33. *Skanda Purāna,* Revā Khanda 9.46–47.

34. Ibid., 9.52.

35. Ibid., 227.6–9.

36. Other holy days at Gangā Sāgara include the *pūrnimā,* or full moon days, of the spring month of Vaishākha, the summer month of Āshādha, and the fall month of Kārtika, as well as on Jyeshtha Shukla Dashamī, the day said to mark the Gangā's divine descent from heaven to earth.

37. For a classic discussion of this, see E. Washburn Hopkins, "The Sacred Rivers of India," in David Gordon and George Foot Moore, eds., *Studies in the History of Religions Presented to C. H. Toy* (New York: Macmillan, 1912), pp. 213–29.

38. Tarunadeva Bhattacharya, *Gangāsāgara Melā* (Calcutta: Farma ke L. M. Limited,1974), p. 47.

39. D. P. Dubey, "Māghamela at Prayāga," *Purāna* 30, no. 1 (January 1988), p. 61.

40. *Mahābhārata* XIII.26.36. Also cited in *Tristhalisetu* 32.

41. Dubey, "Māghamela at Prayāga," p. 67.

42. See *Padma Purāna* VI.i.127.147, as cited in *Tīrthachintāmani* 21, *Tristhalīsetu* 31, *Tīrthaprakāsha* 333.

43. *Matsya Purāna* 107.7, S. C. Vasu et al., trans. (Delhi: Oriental Publishers, 1972).

44. Cited in the *Tristhalīsetu* 9.6. See Giorgio Bonazzoli, "Prayāga and Its Kumbha Melā," *Purāna* XIX, No 1, January 1977, for a discussion of the textual problems associated with such citations from the *Padma* and other Purānas.

45. Today as well, the discipline of living throughout the month of Māgha at the *Triveni* is called Kalpavās: The routine is to stay here throughout the month of Māgha, living on the bank of the river, eating once a day, and bathing three times a day. The fruit of this is great. "Whatever you want," so they say.

46. Kama Maclean, *Pilgrimage and Power: The Kumbh Mela in Allahabad 1765–1954* (New York: Oxford University Press, 2008), p. 16.

47. D. P. Dubey reviews the texts in which the common story of the churning of the ocean and the god's seizure of the *amrita* is told. None contains reference to the fourfold splashing upon earth. See D. P. Dubey, "Kumbha Melā: Origin and Historicity of India's Greatest Pilgrimage Fair," in *National Geographic Journal of India* 33, no. 4 (December 1987): 472–73.

48. *Mahābhārata* XIII.26.49.

49. In Nāsik, it is said, "bathing in the Godāvarī when Jupiter is in Leo [the time of the Simhāstha Melā], is equal to bathing in the Jāhnavī Gangā." (*Tristhalīsetu* 130.35.) At Ujjain, the Shiprā River is homologized to the Gangā because it is *uttaravāhinī,* "north-flowing," in the direction of the Gangā and its source, just as the Gangā is *uttaravāhinī* at Kāshī.

50. D. P. Dubey, "Kumbha Melā," 469–92.

510	Notes

51. Ibid., pp. 476–80, gives the various astrological reckonings, upon which there is not, incidentally, universal agreement. The most recent *melās* at Prayāga were in 1989 and 2001. At Hardvār, there were *melās* in 1986, 1998, and 2010. At Ujjain, the *melās* were held in 1992 and 2004. At Nāsik, there was a *melā* in 1992 and subsequently in 2003.

52. It is also said here that Lord Rāma came to Kumbhakonam on his way to retrieve Sītā from the clutches of Rāvana and worshipped Shiva as Kāshī Vishvanātha.

53. The thousand names of the Gangā are in the Kāshī Khanda of the *Skanda Purāna* IV.i.29.

54. *Skanda Purāna* Kāshī Khanda IV.i. 27.30, 37, 107–9; and 133–34. *Skanda Purāna* IV.1.

55. Ibid., IV.i.27.17–21; IV.i.28.28–29.

56. See, for example, the *Mārkandeya Purāna* 57.30; the *Bhāgavata Purāna* V.20; the *Vāmana Purāna* 13.33.

57. For a discussion of what I have termed "spatial transposition," see my *Banaras, City of Light* (New York: Alfred A. Knopf, 1982), pp. 39–42, 283–94.

58. James Preston, *The Cult of the Goddess: Social and Religious Change in a Hindu Temple* (New Delhi: Vikas, 1980), p. 243.

59. Raj Bali Pandey, *Vārānasī: The Heart of Hinduism* (Vārānasī: Orient Publishers, 1969), p. 30.

60. Rampratap Tripathi, *Purāno me Gangā* (Prayag: Hindi Sahitya Sammelan, 1952), p. *jha*.

61. Not surprisingly, this image of Shiva and the spurting Gangā has become a popular motif for civic fountains in northern India, such as the one seen today at Hardvār.

62. *Skanda Purāna*, Kāshī Khanda IV.i.28.84.

63. Tripathi, *Purāno me Gangā*, p. 95.

64. Jagannātha, *Gangā Laharī*, as per endnote 1.

65. *Kumārasambhava*, "The Birth of Kumāra," by Kālidāsa tells the tale of the marriage of Shiva and Pārvatī from which the son will be born to defeat Tāraka. The demon Tāraka had a boon that he could not be killed by any but the son of Shiva. Convinced that the ascetic Shiva would never bear a son, Tāraka thought he was safe.

66. *Mahābhārata* I.96–100 describes her marriage to Shantanu and the birth of their children, the Vasus, and of Bhīshma. Gangā gave birth to seven children fathered by Shantanu, and she threw each of them in the river to drown at birth. She realized what Shantanu did not: that they were divine Vasus, who had been cursed to take human form and would be released from the curse only after their human birth. Shantanu persuaded her to spare the eighth child, Bhīshma. *Mahābhārata* XIII.168.18–27 tells of Gangā's lament at the death of Bhīshma.

67. *Mahābhārata* XIII.26.50.

68. *Padma Purāna*, Srishthi Khanda 60.35.

69. The legend, which is well known, at least among the traditionally educated of Kāshī, has several variants. Lakshman Ramachandra Vaidya related something of Jagannātha's poems in *The Bhāmini Vilāsa* (Bombay: Bhārati Press, 1887).

70. These summarize some of the sentiments of the *Gangā Laharī*, verses 13, 28, 29, and 45.

71. *Gangā Laharī*, verse 24, my translation.

72. *Skanda Purāna*, Kāshī Khanda IV.i.28.85 and 87, my translation.

73. See the summary of this discussion provided by P. V. Kane in *History of Dharmashāstra*, vol. IV, pp. 603–14; 608–9 is the specific discussion of the suicide prohibition.

74. See Christopher Justice, *Dying the Good Death* (Albany: State University of New York Press, 1997). He looks carefully at Kāshī Lābh Mukti Bhavan and other hospices, documenting the stories of those who come to die in Kāshī and analyzing just what constitutes a "good death."

75. Anne Feldhaus, *Connected Places: Region, Pilgrimage, and Geographical Imagination in India* (New York: Palgrave Macmillan, 2003), p. 18. This book constitutes a rich body of research on the significance of rivers in the shaping of identity—within Maharashtra and elsewhere.

76. The seven are mentioned as a group in *Rig Veda* I.32.12, I.34.8, I.35.8, II.12.12, IV.28.1, VIII.24, and X.75. Other hymns praise the waters and rivers generally, such as X.47 and X.49.

77. See Pargiter, *Mārkandeya Purāna*, p. 369 n. and *Mahābhārata* 11.30.15, as cited by B. C. Law in *Mountains and Rivers of India* (Calcutta: National Committee for Geography, 1968), p. 4.

78. The "clan mountains" are related to a particular country or clan: the Mahendra Mountains to the Kalingas, the Vindhyas to the forest people of central India, the Malaya Mountains of the south to the Pāndyas, and so forth. The rivers then are named in relation to the seven clan mountains and listed according to the mountain range in which they have their headwaters. There are those that rise in the Riksa Mountains of east central India, such as the westward-flowing Narmadā and the eastward-flowing Mahānadī. There are those that rise in the Sahya Mountains of the Western Ghāts, such as the Godāvarī and, farther south, the Bhīmarathī in Maharashtra, the Krishnā and Venī Rivers of Andhra Pradesh and Karnataka, and, still farther south, the Kāverī, which rises in the Coorg country of the southern Sahyas and flows east through southern Karnataka and Tamil Nadu.

79. See *Kalyān Tīrthānk* 31, no. 1 (Gorakhpur: The Gita Press, 1957), for a listing of the seven rivers. Some contemporary formulations preserve the Sarasvatī instead of the Krishnā, as in the invocation of rivers in ritual found in the *Nitya Karma Vidhi* (Bareli: Samskriti Samsthan, 1977), p. 56: "*Gange ca Yamune caiva Godāvarī Sarasvatī; Narmade Sindhu Kāverī jale'smin samnidhim kuru.*"

80. David Haberman, *River of Love in an Age of Pollution: The Yamuna River of Northern India* (Berkeley: University of California Press, 2006). This is the most significant work in English on the River Yamunā. His work has included long stretches of research in Vrindāvan, on the banks of the Yamunā, and several trips along the river's course from Yamunotrī to Prayāga. His study brings the religious significance of the river together with the environmental degradation that has affected both the Gangā and the Yamunā. This is a work of importance for scholars of religion, students of India, and those concerned with the health of rivers worldwide.

81. See, for example, the *Matsya Purāna* 186.8–12.
82. In Jabalpur, I met an artist who had done the circumambulation in stages, taking his vacation every year to walk a stretch of the river. His unusual medium was bright and intricate collage, the pieces made from the cut-up colors of old *National Geographic* magazines, which this artist prized. His images of the Narmadā, however, were not the glossy photos from the *National Geographic,* but the artistic renderings made by cutting up those photos!
83. The parameters can be glimpsed by looking at the websites of the Narmadā Valley Development Authority (*www.nvda.in/index.php*) and that of the Friends of River Narmadā (*www.narmada.org/*). The BBC summary of the controversy in 2000 gives the early history (*http://news.bbc.co.uk/2/hi/south_asia/1026355.stm*).
84. *Matysa Purāna* 194.43–44.
85. Omkārānanda Giri, *Shri Narmadā Pradakshinā* (Delhi: Radha Press, 2002). This is a posthumous publication of a booklet Swami Omkārānanda had written decades earlier.
86. Ibid., p. 11.
87. *Skanda Purāna*, Revā Khanda, V.iii 9, 56.
88. Ibid., V.iii.4–5.
89. Ibid., V.iii.5.31, ff.
90. *Shrī Narmadāshtaka Shatika* (Japalpur: Ramji Pustak Bhandar, n.d.). The story is basically that of the Revā Khanda of the *Skanda Purāna.*
91. *Amarakantaka Māhātmya evam Shri Narmadā Māhātmya* (Jabalpur: Ashok Pustak Bhandar, n.d.).
92. Swami Omkārānanda Giri, *Narmadā Kalpāvalī* (Rishikesh: Muktikund Vivek Ashram, n.d).
93. *Mahābhārata* III.85.9.
94. I have left this legend in the words of a remarkable explorer of the Narmadā, Geoffrey Waring Maw, an English Quaker who lived by the banks of the river for forty years and spent a number of years during World War II, when he could not return to England at all, on vacation at Omkāreshvara, one of the most important pilgrimage sites along the river. His essays have been gathered together and edited by one of his successors at the Quaker community in Hoshangabad, Marjorie Sykes. The book, *Narmadā, The Life of a River* (Hoshangabad: Friends Rural Centre, 1991), is one of the few English-language books on the subject of this river.
95. *Brahmā Purāna* 78.77.
96. References to the river as Gautamī and the story of her descent are found in the *Brahmā Purāna* 74–76, the *Nāradīya Purāna* II.72.11–12, and the *Varāha Purāna* I.71.32–38.
97. In addition to the Puranic texts, Anne Feldhaus has a thorough discussion of the descent of the Godāvarī in her book *Water and Womanhood: Religious Meanings of Rivers in Maharashtra* (New York: Oxford University Press, 1995), pp. 24–26.
98. *Shri Godā Māhātmya* (Nāsik: Bagul Agencies, n.d.).
99. Anne Feldhaus, *Water and Womanhood,* p. 29.
100. Ibid., p. 34.
101. I presented a still-unpublished paper on the Gangā and the Ekātmata Yagna at

the American Academy of Religion in 1983. Lisa McKean has written on this initial pilgrimage "rite" of the Vishva Hindu Parishad as part of the context of the building of the Bhārat Mātā Temple in Hardvār. See Lisa McKean, "Bhārat Mātā: Mother India and Her Militant Matriots," in J. S. Hawley and D. M. Wulff, eds., *Devi: Goddesses of India* (Berkeley: University of California Press, 1996), pp. 255–57.

102. "Road to Revival," *India Today,* November 30, 1983, pp. 34–36.

103. Rampratap Tripathi, *Purānon me Gangā,* p. *jha.*

104. Kelly Alley, "Separate Domains: Hinduism, Politics, Environmental Pollution," in Christopher Chapple and Mary Evelyn Tucker, eds., *Hinduism and Ecology* (Cambridge: Center for the Study of World Religions, 2000), p. 377.

105. Utpal Parashar, "Gangā Pollution Reaches Alarming Levels," *Hindustan Times,* June 5, 2007.

106. David Haberman, *River of Love in an Age of Pollution* (Berkeley: University of California Press, 2006), p. 76. The entire chapter entitled "River of Death" is a distressing litany of the extent of Yamunā's pollution.

107. Nita Bhalla, "India's Rivers Dying Due to Sewage, Say Activists," *Hindustan Times,* June 14, 2007.

108. Kelly D. Alley, "Idioms of Degeneracy: Assessing Gangā's Purity and Pollution," in Lance E. Nelson, ed., *Purifying the Earthly Body of God: Religion and Ecology in Hindu India* (Albany: State University of New York Press, 1998), p. 308. Alley's impressive book on the subject is *On the Banks of the Gangā: When Wastewater Meets a Sacred River* (Ann Arbor: University of Michigan Press, 2002).

109. Kelly Alley, "Separate Domains," p. 377.

110. Alexander Stille, "The Ganges' Next Life," *New Yorker,* January 19, 1998, p. 63.

111. Ibid., pp. 65–67.

112. Haberman, p. 187.

113. Ibid., p. 190–91.

114. Ibid., p. 184.

CHAPTER 5: SHIVA'S LIGHT IN THE LAND OF INDIA

1. Mahākāla is a temple-in-progress, like all the living temples of India. Returning to Mahākāla in the winter of 2004, after more than a decade, the wall bearing these painted images and this inscription had been knocked down in a massive renovation project in preparation for the 2004 Simhastha Melā, when as many as six million pilgrims crowded into this temple city for the *darshan* of Mahākāla and a holy bath in the River Shiprā.

2. See Benjamin J. Fleming, "Mapping Sacred Geography in Medieval India: The Case of the Twelve *Jyotirlingas,*" *International Journal of Hindu Studies* 13, no. 1: 53–54.

3. Fleming, p. 52.

4. Indira Viswanathan Peterson, *Poems to Siva: The Hymns of the Tamil Saints* (Princeton: Princeton University Press, 1989), p. 112. This poem is attributed to the sixth- to seventh-century poet-saint Appar and is from the *Tevaram,* the collected hymns of the Tamil Shaiva tradition.

5.   The most extensive telling is the *Siva Purāna,* Rudrasamhita II.26–43. See also the *Mahābhārata* XII.283–85, the *Kurma Purāna* I.13, the *Linga Purāna* I.99–100, the *Bhāgavata Purāna* IV.2–7, and the *Skanda Purāna* I.1.1–5 for a sampling of the Shiva-oriented myth. In none of these versions is the dismemberment of Satī alluded to.

6.   Here it occupies the entirety of Section II of the Rudra Samhita. It includes many of the elements of the tale as found in shorter compass in the *Linga Purāna* (I.99–100), the *Bhāgavata Purāna* (IV. 2–7), the *Skanda Purāna* (I.1.1–5), the *Vayu Purāna* 30, and the *Padma Purāna* I.5–11.

7.   *Siva Purāna,* Rudrasamhita II.11–14.

8.   Ibid., Rudrasamhita II. 17–25.

9.   The name Satī eventually becomes synonymous with the faithful wife and, not incidentally, the name attached to wives who are immolated in the funeral pyres of their husbands.

10.   In the most ancient tradition it was the gods themselves, not Daksha, who excluded Rudra from a portion of the sacrifice. Rudra had pursued and pierced Prajāpati, in the form of an antelope, with his arrow. (*Shatapatha Brāhmana* I.210.) Since Prajāpati, the creator, *is* the sacrifice, it seems that Rudra has attacked the sacrifice once before. In that myth, the arrow extracted from the sacrifice, Prajāpati, had a tiny morsel of the sacrifice upon it. Offered to Bhaga, it burned his eyes. Offered to Pusan, it knocked out his teeth. In our present myth, Vīrabhadra taunts the gods, including Vishnu, by saying, "Come, I will give you something to offer as an oblation in the fire," meaning "I will cut you to pieces and you can offer yourselves." The gods stand and fight for a moment, but even Vishnu is knocked unconscious by Vīrabhadra. Finally, the gods flee. The sacrifice itself assumes the form of a deer, like Prajāpati of old, and flees. It is killed or beheaded, in some versions by Shiva himself, but in this version by Vīrabhadra. Pusan's teeth are knocked out and Bhaga's eyes are pulled out—seemingly incidental facts that link this myth to the ancient Vedic and Brahmanic legend of Rudra's piercing of the incestuous Prajāpati.

11.   The pilgrimage itself continues undeterred by the political turmoil of Kashmir, even though at times pilgrims have been victims of violence. More serious, of course, is the toll global warming has taken on the ice *linga.* See Chapter 10, "A Pilgrim's India Today."

12.   A *krosha* is about two miles. The notion of something being five *kroshas,* however, is also an esoteric one, the creature of five *kroshas* being the human, with five layers of being from the most material to the most subtle.

13.   H. V. Steitencron, "The Advent of Visnuism in Orissa," in A. Eschmann et al., *The Cult of Jagannath and the Regional Tradition of Orissa* (Delhi: Manoharlal, 1978), p. 29.

14.   Peterson, *Poems to Siva,* pp. 172–76.

15.   Ibid., pp. 139–40.

16.   Ibid., p. 261.

17.   *Siva Purāna,* Vidyesvarasamhita 6–12; Rudrasamhitā I.6–9. See also *Linga Purāna* 17.17–21; *Kūrma Purāna* I.25.62–111, II.31.1–31; *Skanda Purāna* I.3.1.1–2, I.3.1–6, I.3.2.9–15, VII.3.34, *Vāyu Purāna* I.55.1–68.

18. This is the version of the myth as found in the *Siva Purāna,* Rudrasamhitā I.6–9.
19. See *Kūrma Purāna* II.31.1–31.
20. See, for example, the *Siva Purāna,* Vidyesvarasamhitā 7–8 and the *Skanda Purāna* I.1.6.
21. *Kūrma Purāna* I.25.62–111.
22. The myth of Shiva's destruction of the Triple City may be found in the *Mahābhārata* VIII.33–5; the *Matsya Purāna* 129–30, 187–88; the *Bhāgavata Purāna* VII.10, and the *Siva Purāna,* Rudrasamhitā 5.1–10.
23. See, for example, the *Siva Purāna,* Kotirudrasamhitā 12, the *Skanda Purāna* I.1.6, the *Kūrma Purāna* II.37.53–39, and the *Vāmana Purāna* 6.58–93; 22–23. While the myth of Shiva's naked begging and subsequent "castration" is common enough, it is not always related to the *linga* of fire. One instance in which the castrated *linga* becomes fire is in the *Siva Purāna,* Kotirudrasamhitā 12, although here the fire is the uncontrolled fire of destruction and the *linga* is not called a *jyotirlinga.* In other versions (e.g., the *Vāmana Purāna* 6) Shiva simply disappears when the sages castrate him. Immediately they realize their mistaken perception. In most of these castration myths, it is clear that confusing Shiva's phallus with Shiva's *linga* is a dangerous mistake. What the sages thought was the phallus of the naked Shiva turned out to be a world-spanning fire, which destroys all created things.
24. As the universe begins to go up in flames, the gods and sages in desperation ask Lord Brahmā what to do. He tells them to make an eight-petaled lotus and propitiate the goddess Pārvatī to come and place her *yoni* there so that Shiva will become stable. And so she does. The fiery *linga* of Shiva and the *yoni* of Pārvatī are united in that place. Shiva's incandescence is brought under control in union with Pārvatī. Near the ancient temple town called Jāgeshvar in the Kumaon Himalayas is the little temple of Dandeshvar, where the seven *rishis* are said to have lived in the Cedar Forest, the *dāruvana,* with their wives. There the story is well known and is told in a penny-pamphlet as the story of that very place: "When the wives of the *rishis* went to the hilltop to collect grass, they saw the beautiful yogi Shiva. They became entranced and did not return even at nightfall. The sages were furious when they discovered the scene and cursed Shiva's *linga* to fall off. The *linga* did fall off, but it became fire, burning out of control. It seared and shook the world with its force, and only when Pārvatī placed herself on the earth to join with Shiva did that fiery *linga* come under control." It was here at Dandeshvar that the *linga* joined the *yoni* of Pārvatī, they say. It was here that the *linga* as we know it was first worshipped as the emblem of Shiva. So is the story told in the local lore of Jageshvar.
25. *Vāmana Purāna,* Saromāhātmya 1.
26. *Siva Purāna,* Vidyeshvarasamhitā 5.10b–12a.
27. Ibid., Vidyeshvarasamhitā 9.
28. Ibid., Vidyeshvarasamhitā 9.9–10.
29. According to the calendar observed largely in the north, which puts the full moon at the end of the month, Mahāshivarātri is on the 14th of the dark fortnight of Phālguna. The *Siva Purāna* itself places Mahāshivarātri in Mārgashīrsha (15–16), but this is not common today.

30. *Siva Purāna*, Vidyeshvarasamhitā 9.19.

31. Abbé Dubois, *Hindu Manners, Customs, and Ceremonies*, 3rd ed. (Oxford: Oxford University Press, 1906), pp. 628, 631.

32. *Linga Purāna* I.19.5.

33. *Kūrma Purāna* II.10.1 The wider meaning of *linga* as "characteristic mark" or "image" is discussed by Giorgio Bonazzoli in an article surprisingly entitled "Devīlinga," in *Purāna* XX, no. 1 (1978): 121–30. In the same issue see N. Gangadharan, "The *Linga*—Origin of Its Concept and Worship," pp. 87–92.

34. Even in that temple, Shiva also dwells as the *ākāsh linga*, the *linga* made of the element of space.

35. *Siva Purāna*, Vidyeshvarasamhitā 16.107.

36. For a discussion of the five faces and activities see Richard Davis, *Ritual in an Oscillating Universe* (Princeton: Princeton University Press, 1991), especially Chapter 2, "Oscillation in the Ritual Universe."

37. The legends of the origins of the twelve *jyotirlingas* are found in *Siva Purāna* Kotirudrasamhitā 14–33.

38. *Siva Purāna*, Kotirudrasamhitā 20–21.

39. *Siva Purāna*, Kotirudrasamhitā I.1.9, 15–16.

40. Ram Kishan Jayasaval, *Omkāresvara Māhātmya* (Badavah, M.P.: Rajhansa Prakashan, n.d.).

41. Most of the twelve are mentioned in the *Skanda Purāna* I.1.7.28–34. The standard authority for the twelve, however, is the *Siva Purāna*, where they are listed (Satarudrasamhitā 2–4 and Kotirudrasamhitā 1.21–24) and their individual myths and *māhātmyas* are presented (Kotirudrasamhitā 14–33). In addition to innumerable Hindi pamphlets, we have the religious encyclopedias, *Shivānk* (Gorakhpur: Kalyan Gita Press, 1933), pp. 545–61, and *Tirthānk* (Gorakhpur: Kalyan Gita Press, 1957), pp. 163–479.

42. *Siva Purāna*, Kotirudrasamhitā 1.21–24.

43. Those in the east include a great many well-known temples, *tīrthas*, and *lingas*— Avimukteshvara in Kāshī, Brahmeshvara in Prayāga, Nāgesha in Ayodhyā, Vaidyanāth in Bihar, Bhuvanesha in Orissa, and Sangamesha where the Gangā meets the sea. Those in the "south" begin with Mattagajendranāth in Chitrakūt, which is not really very far south and include shrines of Shiva on the banks of the Narmadā River, especially Nandikeshvara. On the whole, however, the "south" does not extend beyond the Narmadā. The *lingas* of the west, however, feature Gokarna, which is on the western coast of India, in coastal Karnataka, where Shiva is said to dwell as Mahābala. The Gokarna Temple has been well known from the time of the *Mahābhārata* to the present. Finally, the *lingas* of the north begin with Pashupatinātha in what is today Nepal (Nayapāla) and include Kedāreshvara and Muktinātha, both in the Himalayas. *Siva Purāna*, Kotirudrasamhitā 2–11.

44. Ramkishan Jayasval, *Jyotirlinga Mahimā* (Baravah: Rajahamsa Prakashan, n.d.), p. 2.

45. *Siva Purāna*, Vidyesvarasamhitā 6–10. In the *Siva Purāna*, Kotirudrasamhitā 22, the attributeless One creates Shiva, with attributes, who then splits into Shiva and Shakti, male and female, *purusha* and *prakriti*.

46. The relation of the ancient Avimukteshvara to Vishveshvara is complex and is

discussed in Diana L. Eck, *Banāras, City of Light* (New York: Alfred A. Knopf, 1983), pp. 129–36, and also in Fleming, "Mapping Sacred Geography," pp. 56–58.

47. For an overview of this history of destruction and accommodation, see Eck, *Banāras*, pp. 83–89, 120–35.

48. See, for example, the *Skanda Purāna* IV.26.67.

49. For a discussion of the *panchakroshi yātrā*, see Eck, *Banāras*, pp. 41–42, 320–21, 350–53.

50. The work of Hans Bakker on the early *Skanda Purāna* is important in this regard, drawing on the Vārānasimāhātmyam of the *Skanda Purāna* and noting the presence of a twelve-*linga yātrā* or pilgrimage in Vārānasi. This may be as early as the sixth century. The *lingas* are referred to as *svayambhū* and are the most important in Vārānasī. The names do not overlap with the great sanctuaries later given the name of *jyotirlingas*. See Fleming, "Mapping Sacred Geography," pp. 58–62.

51. Niels Gutschow, *Benares: The Sacred Landscape of Vārānasī* (Stuttgart: Axel Menges, 2006), pp. 113–79.

52. "We demand that the Muslim community of India recognizes the rights of Hindu society to these three shrines: Kāshī Vishvanāth in Vārānasī, Krishna-Janmabhoomi in Mathurā, and Rām-Janmabhoomi in Ayodhyā." See the Vishva Hindu Parishad website manifesto: The Great Evidence of Shrī Ram Janmabhoomi Mandir, *www.vhorg/englishsite/e.Special_Movements/dRanjanam bhumi%20Muti/greatevidence.htm*.

53. India's great oceanside shrines include Dvārakā, at the farthest west point of the Saurashtra Peninsula, some one hundred miles from Somnāth; Jagannātha Purī, on the coast of the Bay of Bengal, all the way across India to the east; Rāmeshvara, in south Tamil Nadu; Kanyākumārī at the tip of south India; and Gokarna in coastal Karnataka.

54. *Siva Purāna*, Kotirudrasamhitā 14; *Mahābhārata*, IX.35.37–82; *Vāmana Purāna* 41.4; 57.51–53; *Agni Purāna* 109.10–11, 116.22–24.

55. Romila Thapar, *Somanātha: The Many Voices of a History* (New Delhi: Penguin Books, 2004), Chapter 3, "The Turko-Persian Narratives"; K. M. Munshi, *Somnāth: the Shrine Eternal* (Bombay: Bharatiya Vidya Bhavan, 1976) pp. 37–43, 137–44.

56. Al-Biruni's *India*, edited by Edward C. Sachau (Delhi: S. Chand & Co., 1964), p. 22.

57. Romila Thapar's book *Somanātha: The Many Voices of a History* is a careful exploration of the ways in which the history of Somnāth has been written and utilized. However, the signal narrative of Hindu trauma and Muslim plunder seems not to have captured a major place in the histories and inscriptions of the next several centuries in Gujarat.

58. Here K. M. Munshi's *Somnāth: The Shrine Eternal*, as cited above, becomes the standard account of the destruction and rising of Somnāth.

59. Munshi, *Somnāth*, pp. 83–84.

60. Thapar, *Somanātha*, pp. 81–84; Munshi, *Somnāth*, pp. 145–51.

61. Thapar, *Somanātha*, p. 96.

62. Munshi, *Somnāth*, pp. 170–71.

63. Thapar, *Somanātha*, pp. 198–99, citing S. Gopal, *Selected Works of Jawaharlal Nehru* XVI, no. 1: 559.

64. William Sax, *Mountain Goddess: Gender and Politics in a Himalayan Pilgrimage* (New York: Oxford University Press, 1991), p. 7.

65. Neelima Shukla-Bhatt, "Somnāth, The 'Shrine Eternal'? Perceptions and Appropriations of a Temple," unpublished manuscript, 2001.

66. The story of Pārvatī's penance and the marriage of Shiva and Pārvatī is told extensively in the *Siva Purāna*, Rudrasamhita III.25.63 ff.

67. *Siva Purāna*, Kotirudrasamhita 19.

68. Luke Whitmore, *In Pursuit of Maheshvara* (Atlanta: Emory University Ph.D. Thesis, 2010), p. 294.

69. *Siva Purānā*, Kotirudrasamhita 19.18, 22, 24–5. Verse 18 uses the phrase *bhāratibhih prajābhih* to refer to the "people of India."

70. The languages in which local pilgrimage pamphlets and temple *māhātmyas* may be found is quite often an indicator of the catchment area from which pilgrimage clientele are coming.

71. *Skanda Purāna*, Brahmā Khanda (Setu Māhātmya) 50.113b–116.

72. *www.rameswaramtemple.org/worshiped.php*. This is on the "pooja" page of the official website.

73. *Siva Purāna*, Kotirudrasamhita 31. The *Padma Purāna*, Shrishtikānda 38, agrees in the establishing of the *linga* before the battle in Lanka.

74. *Skanda Purāna*, Brahmākānda, Setumāhātmya III.1.

75. *Skanda Purāna*, Brahmākānda, Setumāhātmya 44–46. This is the version told in the most popular local *māhātmya* pamphlet, *Pilgrim's Guide to Rameswaram and Dhanushkodi*, Rameshwaram: Sri Ramanathasvami Temple, 1977.

76. See Chapter 9 and Diana L. Eck, "Following Rāma, Worshipping Shiva," in D. L. Eck and Mallison, ed., *Devotion Divine: Bhakti Traditions from the Regions of India* (Groningen: Egbert Forsten, 1991).

77. Daniel H. H. Ingalls, "Kālidāsa and the Attitudes of the Golden Age," *Journal of the American Oriental Society* 96, no. 1 (January–March 1976), p. 20.

78. See Chapter 4, "The Gangā and the Rivers of India," where the myth of the churning of the sea is discussed in relation to the great Kumbha Melā at Allahabad. A smaller pilgrimage, called the Simhastha, takes place here at Ujjain. Even so, the twelve days of the 2004 Simhastha attracted an estimated twenty million pilgrims.

79. As we have seen in Chapter 4, "The Gangā and the Rivers of India," the four places that were blessed with *amrita* are Hardvār, Prayāga, Ujjain, and Nāsik, each of which has a great bathing festival at twelve-year intervals.

80. *Siva Purāna*, Kotirudrasamhita 16.

81. *Siva Purāna*, Kotirudrasamhita 17. The story ends with the appearance of the monkey-lord Hanumān, who tells the assembled citizens of Ujjain of the glory of Shiva and explains that, in the future, Lord Vishnu will be born among the cowherds as Krishna.

82. *Siva Purāna*, Kotirudrasamhita 16.49.

83. For an example of the controversy, a report on the impact on the temple of the Omkāreshwar Dam puts it this way: "One of the adverse downstream impacts of large dams is a significant increase in river bank erosion, especially in the area immediately below the dam as silt deposits are held back, flow patterns

change and sudden releases of water create flooding conditions. The erosion and potential collapse of the river banks poses a serious problem for the town of Omkāreshwar and will endanger the long-term stability of many of its temples, which are situated directly on the perimeter of the island. Although the environmental clearance letter for the project mentions the necessity of protection measures for Omkāreshwar Temple, it is not at all clear how the project authorities will be able to mitigate and deal with the above-named impacts." See Heffa Schucking (Urgewald), Kyoko Ishida, and Yuki Tanabe (JACSES), "The Omkāreshwar Dam in India: Closing Doors on People's Futures," *www.jacses. org/sdap/omkare/Omkareshwar-Briefing.pdf*, accessed June 22, 2010.

84.   One might be tempted to say that the Kāverī here is named after the River Kāverī of south India, another of the seven sacred rivers of India. There are many Purānic traditions, however, that speak of the confluence of the Narmadā and the Kāverī and lead us to believe that the name Kāverī is perhaps as ancient at this spot along the Narmadā as it is in the south. See, for example, *Matsya Purāna* 189.

85.   *Siva Purāna*, Kotiradrasamhitā 18.

86.   Ram Kishan Jayasaval, *Omkāreshvara Māhātmya* (M.P.: Rajhansa Prakashan, n.d.), p. 9.

87.   Here, as at Rāmeshvara, there are really two *lingas*. The first is the earthen *linga*, now alternatively called Parameshvara, the Supreme Lord; Amaleshvara, the Pure Lord; and Amareshvara, the Eternal Lord. The second is the *linga* of the sacred mantra *Om*, which is called *pranava*. This is Omkāreshvara itself.

88.   The most prominent and important of the five peaks is Brahmāgiri. The other peaks go by the names of Shiva's *avatāras:* Vāmadeva, Aghora, Īshana, and Tatpurusha. *Sri Tryambaka Kshetra Darshana* 7–8.

89.   The other major claimant to Vaidyanāth is at Parali in Maharashtra. The site of Nāgeshvara is also contested, with claimants in Gujarat near Dvārakā, in Maharashtra, and in Uttarakhand near Almora, where the temple of Jāgeshvara is located.

90.   Like any major temple, this is the abode of not simply one deity, but a whole cosmos of gods. Here, in particular, are numerous *devīs*, their colloquial names being Tripura Sudarī, Mā Durgā, Pārvatī, Jagat Jananī Mā, Mā Manasā, Mā Sarasvatī, Mā Bagalā, Mahālakshmī, Tārā, Mā Bhuvaneshvarī, Mā Kālī, Annapūrnā, and Jāhnavī Gangā. In addition, there is the usual host of Kāla Bhairava, Kubera, Hanumān, Kārttikeya, Ganesha, Brahmā, and Lakshmī Nārāyan.

91.   James Lochtefeld, *God's Gateway: Identity and Meaning in a Hindu Pilgrimage Place* (New York: Oxford University Press, 2010), pp. 189–95. Here Lochtefeld has a wonderful account of this practice called the *kanvar* pilgrimage, after the bamboo poles to which vessels of Gangā water are attached.

92.   Anne Feldhaus, *Connected Places: Region, Pilgrimage, and Geographical Imagination in India* (New York: Palgrave Macmillan, 2003), pp. 47, 67. Interestingly, her research confirms that this pilgrimage, like many, is growing in popularity. In the nineteenth century, records indicate that some 50,000 people might have participated. In the 1990s, this was 500,000.

93.   The core of this story is *Siva Purana*, Kotirudrasamhita 28.

94. *Skanda Purāna* and other *māhātmyas*. Exactly where Mount Krauncha was is not quite clear. There are many claimants. But in the context of the Shrī Shaila traditions it is clearly identified as this mountain, also called Shrī Mountain or Shrī Shaila, in what is today northern Andhra Pradesh. *Siva Purana*, Kotirudrasamhita 15.

95. In some versions, it is Shiva and Pārvatī's home in Kāshī that Skanda abandons for the south. See Kāshī Khanda 25.22 and 32.163ff. The most authoritative work on Skanda in this period is P. K. Agrawala, *Skanda-Kārttikeya: A Study in the Origin and Development* (Varanasi: Banaras Hindu University, 1967).

96. Abhinavagupta, *Tantraloka*, as cited in M. N. Chakravarty, "The Pentadic Universe in the Shaivagamas," in Bettina Baumer, ed., *Prakrti: The Integral Vision*, vol. 3 (New Delhi: Indira Gandhi National Center for the Arts, 1995), p. 28.

97. This is the same island that contains the great temple of Shrīrangam, dedicated to Vishnu.

98. The whole of the Arunāchala Māhātmya of the *Skanda Purāna* is devoted to the mountain as *jyotirlinga*. See the *Skanda Purāna* I. iii. Part 1, ch. 1–2; ch. 6; I. iii. Part 2, ch. 9–15.

99. *Siva Purāna*, Vidyeshvarasamhitā 9.21.

100. *Skanda Purāna* I. iii. Part 1, ch. 5.24.

101. *Skanda Purāna* I. iii. Part 1, ch. 2.32.

102. *Skanda Purāna* I. iii. Part 1, ch. 7.3.

103. Indira Viswanāthan Peterson, *Poems to Siva: The Hymns of the Tamil Saints* (Princeton: Princeton University Press, 1989), p. 170.

104. Skandanandan, *Arunāchala, The Holy Hill* (Madras: Weldun Press, 1980), p. 7.

105. "Sri Arunāchala Ashtakam," verse 2. See *Five Hymns to Arunāchala* (Tiruvannamalai: Sri Ramanasrama, 1971).

CHAPTER 6: SHAKTI, THE DISTRIBUTION OF THE BODY OF THE GODDESS

1. Cynthia Ann Humes wrote her Ph.D. dissertation on *The Text and Temple of the Great Goddess: The Devī-Māhātmya and the Vindhyācal Temple of Mirzapur* (University of Iowa, 1990). Her article on the subject, "Vindhyavāsinī: Local Goddess, Yet Great Goddess," is in J. S. Hawley and D. M. Wulff, eds., *Devī: Goddesses of India* (Berkeley: University of California Press, 1996), pp. 49–76.

2. *Mahābhārata*, IV.6.16; *Devī Māhātmya* 2–3, which is *Mārkandeya Purāna* 82–3. The Great Goddess who slew Mahisha speaks of her many appearances, including her eventual appearance as the goddess of the Vindhya to be born in the womb of Yashodā, who will again slay the demons Shumbha and Nishumbha. (*Devī Māhātmya* 11, *Mārkandeya Purāna* 91.36–40.)

3. *Mahābhārata*, IV.6.

4. Ibid., IV.1–5; *Devī Māhātmya* 11.37–39. The myths of Vindhyāchal are also found in *Kalyān, Tīrthānk* (Gorakhpur: Gītā Press, 1957), pp. 138–39.

5. *Devībhāgavata Purāna* III.6.18b–19.

6. Shankarācārya, *Saundaryalaharī*, V. K. Subramanian, trans. (Delhi: Motilal Banarsidass, 1977), verse 1.

7. *Devī Bhāgavata Purāna* VII.29.

8. Suchitra Samanta, "The 'Self-Animal' and Divine Digestion: Goat Sacrifice to the Goddess Kālī in Bengal," *Journal of Asian Studies* 53, no. 3 (August 1994): 789.

9. Sanjukta Gupta, "The Domestication of a Goddess: Carana-tīrtha Kālighāt, the Mahāpīṭha of Kālī," in Rachel Fell McDermott and Jeffrey Kripal, eds., *Encountering Kālī: In the Margins, At the Center, In the West* (Berkeley: University of California Press, 2003), pp. 72–73.

10. "That which is surrendered as gift in *bali* comprises the sacrificer's demonic or animal-like qualities. This is paradoxical at first glance, but, as an offering of those dimensions of the Hindu self that are most susceptible to material and sensory attraction and therefore most 'bound,' these are the aspects of himself that require a special effort to transcend and transform." Samanta, "The 'Self-Animal,'" p. 799.

11. Samanta, "The 'Self-Animal,'" p. 782.

12. See Edward C. Dimock, "The Goddess of Snakes in Medieval Bengali Literature," *History of Religions,* winter 1962, pp. 307–21, and N. M. Chaudhuri, "The Cult of Vana-Durgā, a Tree-Deity," Letters, *Journal of the Royal Asiatic Society of Bengal* XI, no. 22 (1915): 75–84.

13. *Vāyu Purāṇa* 9.82–98, cited in J. N. Tiwari, *Goddess Cults in Ancient India* (Delhi: Sundeep Prakashan, 1985), p. 15.

14. See, for instance, the *Skanda Purāṇa* I.2.27–30. In the *Vāmana Purāṇa,* Pārvatī hears Shiva referring to her as Kālī, because she is dark. In this case, she is offended and does penance to become light skinned. (*Vāmana Purāṇa* 25–29.)

15. See Wendy Doniger O'Flaherty, *Hindu Myths* (Baltimore: Penguin Books, 1975), pp. 251–62, and notes. When she becomes dark, Pārvatī establishes the *linga* in Kānchī as part of her penance. See the *Skanda Purāṇa* I.3.3; David Shulman, *Tamil Temple Myths* (Princeton: Princeton University Press, 1980), pp. 171–74. In the *Devī Māhātmya* V.87–88 (also *Devī Bhāgavata Purāṇa* V.23.1–5), the luminous Ambikā, or Kausikā, emerges from Pārvatī's body, and Pārvatī becomes the dark Kālikā.

16. Wendy Doniger O'Flaherty speaks of the "goddesses of the breast" and the "goddesses of the tooth" in *Women, Androgynes, and Other Mythical Beasts* (Chicago: University of Chicago Press, 1980), pp. 90–91, 117. Charlotte Vaudeville distinguishes between the "luminous" and "tenebrous" goddesses in "Krishna-Gopāla, Rādha, and the Great Goddess," in J. S. Hawley and D. Wulff, eds., *The Divine Consort: Rādhā and the Goddesses of India* (Berkeley: University of California Press, 1982). David Shulman distinguishes between the brides and the virgins/ mistresses in *Tamil Temple Myths,* Chapter IV.

17. Shulman, *Tamil Temple Myths,* pp. 211–23.

18. The study of the *Devī Māhātmya* has been undertaken by Thomas Coburn in *Devī Māhātmya: The Crystallization of the Goddess Tradition* (Delhi: Motilal Banarsidass, 1984); of the *Devī Bhāgavata Purāṇa* by Mackenzie Brown in *The Triumph of the Goddess* (Albany: SUNY Press, 1990); and of the rise of the goddess traditions by Tracy Pintchman in *The Rise of the Goddess in the Hindu Tradition* (Albany: SUNY Press, 1994).

19. *Devī Bhāgavata Purāṇa* I.8.31–51; I.16.1–15; III.6.14–85; III.9.38–9. Many other passages build upon this theme, which runs profusely through this *Purāṇa.* See also the *Kālikā Purāṇa* 66.55.7.

20. See Diana L. Eck, "India's Tīrthas: 'Crossings' in Sacred Geography," *History of Religions* 20, no. 1 (1981): 323–44.

21. My colleague Michael Witzel, the expert on these matters, has confirmed this, with the caveat that the term does occur in the *Grihya Sūtras,* in that case as the "stool" or "seat" of a student.

22. See H. Krishna Sastri, *South Indian Images of Gods and Goddesses* (Madras: Government Press, 1916), pp. 72–73.

23. The cult of *yakshas* and *yakshīs* or *yakshinīs* is discussed in the classic work by Ananda Coomaraswamy, *Yakshas* (New Delhi: Munshiram Manoharlal, 1971). They are powerful, but not really gods; rather, they are the *genii loci* and guardians of places, and they constituted the primary focus of religiousness in non-Aryan India. As such they have both fearful and beneficent qualities. *Yakshas* are often stout, associated with wealth (as is Kubera, for instance), and, later, the stocky upholders of pillars. As strong guardian spirits, they are propitiated for help. Their *yakshi* counterparts also stand as guardians and their life energy is suggested by the ways in which they are depicted with arms wrapped around trees.

24. *Devī Māhātmya* XI.3; *Mārkandeya Purāna* 91.3.

25. See N. N. Bhattacharyya, *Indian Mother Goddess* (Calcutta: Indian Studies Past and Present, 1971), pp. 15–17.

26. Raimundo Panikkar, tr., *The Vedic Experience, Mantra-manjarī* (Berkeley: University of California Press, 1977) pp. 123–29.

27. *Mahābhārata* III.230.16.

28. N. M. Chaudhuri, "The Cult of Vana-Durgā."

29. N. N. Bhattacharya, *Indian Mother Goddess* (Calcutta: R.D. Press, 1971), p. 32.

30. Akshaya Tritīya falls on the third day of the bright half (*shuklapaksha*) of the spring month of Vaishākha. It is a day on which acts of worship, penance, or prayer become "imperishable," *akshaya.* In other words, their positive effects are permanent and will not diminish.

31. *Devī Māhātmya* 11.44–45; *Mārkandeya Purāna* 91.43–44.

32. See Curt Maury, *Folk Origins of Indian Art* (New York: Columbia University Press, 1969), Chapter 8; Heinrich Zimmer, *The Art of Indian Asia* (Princeton: Princeton University Press, 1968), vol. I, Chapter VI.

33. See Gustav Oppert, *On the Original Inhabitants of Bhāratavarsa or India* (Delhi: Oriental Publishers, 1972, reprint of 1893), p. 58. He cites a text called the *Gramadevatāpratistha* on this point. David Shulman's work nearly a century later revisits these local *devīs,* in *Tamil Temple Myths.*

34. Oppert, *On the Original Inhabitants,* pp. 457–64.

35. Ann Gold, *Fruitful Journeys: The Ways of the Rajasthani Pilgrims* (Berkeley: University of California Press, 1988).

36. William Sax, in *The Mountain Goddess* (New York: Oxford University Press, 1991), has documented the great pilgrimage of the Goddess through the mountains of Uttarakhand. In Maharashtra, Anne Feldhaus, in *Connected Places: Region, Pilgrimage, and Geographical Imagination in India* (New York: Palgrave Macmillan, 2003), has documented the complex sisterly relations of seven local *devīs,* and the ritual processions that link them.

37. See Diana L. Eck, *Banāras, City of Light* (New York: Alfred A. Knopf, 1982), pp. 157–74.

38. She is called the *adhishthātrī devī*, literally the "founding goddess."

39. She is called *kshetrādīshvarī*, literally the "first goddess of this territory." See H. V. Stietencron, "The Advent of Visnuism in Orissa," in A. Eschmann, H. Kulke, and G. C. Tripathi, eds., *The Cult of Jagannath and the Regional Tradition of Orissa* (Delhi: Manohar, 1978), pp. 26–27.

40. Shulman sets the Kānchīpuram myth in the context of the theme of "surviving the flood," found in many temple myths. See *Tamil Temple Myths*, pp. 55–63, 138–39.

41. William P. Harman, *The Sacred Marriage of a Hindu Goddess* (Bloomington: Indiana University Press, 1989), p. 45.

42. Ibid., pp. 46–50.

43. See C. J. Fuller, "The Divine Couple's Relationship in a South Indian Temple: Mīnākshī and Sundareshvara at Madurai," *History of Religions* 19, no. 4 (1982): 321–48.

44. Shulman, *Tamil Temple Myths*, pp. 114–18.

45. See Kathleen M. Erndl's wonderful study, *Victory to the Mother: The Hindu Goddess of Northwest India in Myth, Ritual, and Symbol* (New York: Oxford University Press, 1993).

46. For an account of Vaishno Devi, see Mark Edwin Rohe, "Ambiguous and Definitive: The Greatness of Goddess Vaisno Devi," in Tracy Pintchman, ed., *Seeking Mahādevī: Constructing the Identities of the Hindu Great Goddesses* (New York: SUNY Press, 2001), pp. 55–76.

47. Rāvana's father was a Brāhmin sage named Vishrava, although his mother was a Daitya and in the lineage of anti-gods or demons.

48. As cited in J. N. Tiwari, *Goddess Cults in Ancient India*, pp. 18–19. The hymn, the "Arya Stava," is said to be an "apocryphal" part of the *Harivamsa*.

49. *Devī Māhātmya* 1.56–57; *Mārkandeya Purāna* 81.56–57.

50. *Devī Māhātmya*, 4.10–11; *Mārkandeya Purāna* 84.10–11.

51. *Devī Māhātmya*, 11.2–3; *Mārkandeya Purāna* 91.2–3.

52. *Devī Bhāgavata Purāna* IX.1.

53. *Devī Bhāgavata Purāna* III.3–4.

54. J. N. Tiwari, *Goddess Cults in Ancient India*, pp. 1–15.

55. For the range of traditions associated with the *shākta pīthas*, see D. C. Sircar, *Sākta Pīthas* (Banaras: Motilal Banarsidass 1950, 1973).

56. The dates of these Purānas are uncertain, but it would be accurate to call them "late." According to the work of V. Raghavan, the *Kālikā Purāna* must be dated no earlier than the eighth century and no later than the eleventh. V. Raghavan, "The Kālikā (Upa) Purāna," *Journal of Oriental Research*, XII, part IV (1938): 331–60.

57. *Devī Bhāgavata Purāna* VII.33.

58. See Diana L. Eck "The Dynamics of Indian Symbolism," in Peter Berger, ed., *The Other Side of God* (New York: Anchor, 1981). Division as a form of universalization has a place in other traditions of sacrifice as well.

59. Peter Brown, *The Cult of the Saints: Its Rise and Function in Late Christianity* (Chicago: University of Chicago Press, 1981), p. 96.

60. *Matsya Purāna* Chapter XIII.10–59.

61. *Vāmana Purāna* Chapter 4–6. Shiva's affliction with grief is 6.28–44.

62. *Devī Bhāgavata Purāna* VII.30.22–23. The tale here also indicates that it was really Satī who was insulted, as her own father lost control of himself and made advances to her, intoxicated by the fragrance of a garland he placed on her marital bed. Out of devotion to dharma and because of the insult her father had given Shiva, she left her body.

63. *Devī Bhāgavata Purāna* VII.30.39–102.

64. The Purāna is filled with *shākta* lore from the area of Bengal and Assam. Since it is cited by Laksmīdhara in his twelfth-century compendium, it would be an earlier text than the *Devī Bhāgavata Purāna*. See V. Raghavan, "The Kālikā (Upa) Purāna," *Journal of Oriental Research* XII, part IV (1938): 331–60.

65. Cited in Sircar, *Sākta Pīthas*, p. 12.

66. I am grateful to Miranda Shaw, whose Harvard Ph.D. thesis *Passionate Enlightenment* (1992) mentions the importance of Uddiyāna as "land of the *dākinīs*." For evidence of the continuing importance of Uddiyāna, she cites G. Tucci, "Travels of Tibetan Pilgrims in the Swat Valley," in *Opera Minora* 2; Universita do Roma Studi Orientali Publicati a Cura della suola Orientale, Vol. 6 (Roma: Dott. Giovanni Bardi Editore), 1971, pp. 369–70.

67. Odra, where Katyāyanī dwells with Jagannātha in the west; Jalashaila, where Candī dwells with Mahādeva in the north; Pūrnashaila, where Pūrneshvarī dwells with Mahānātha in the south, and Kāmarūpa, where Kāmeshvarī and Kāmeshvara dwell, in the east. Sircar, *Sākta Pithas,* pp. 12–13.

68. In the south, however, it would be more accurate to say not that the place claims the myth, but that the myth claims the place. It is less clear, at least to me, how much the places of the south claim the myth. Great *devīs* of the south, such as Kanyākumārī and Kāmākshī, are included in the listing of fifty-one *pīthas*. Once one gets much farther south than Shrī Shaila, however, the avid consciousness of belonging to the *pītha* mythology dims. The myth is northern, probably northeastern, in origin. It has cast its net south, but most of the *pīthas* enumerated are in the north. In the south, the primary stories told of the origins of Kanyākumārī or Kāmākshī, for example, do not include the distribution of Satī.

69. The seven are usually these: Vaishno Devī in Jammu, Nainā Devī in the Kangra district and also at Nainital, Chintapūrnī in Himachal Pradesh, Jvālāmukhī in the Kangra district, Kāngrevālī in the town of Kangra, Mansā Devī in the Kangra district and also at Hardvār, and Chāmundā Devī in the Kangra district. For a study of these, see Kathleen Erndl, *Victory to the Mother* (New York: Oxford University Press, 1992), pp. 37–60.

70. K. R. van Kooij, trans., *Worship of the Goddess According to the Kālikāpurāna* (Leiden: E. J. Brill, 1972), pp. 136–37, citing the *Kālikā Purāna* 60.41–42.

71. Ibid., pp. 136–37 and *Kālikā Purāna* 64.72.

72. See K. R. Vaidyanathan, *Temples and Legends of Kerala* (Bombay: Bharatiya Vida Bhavan, 1982).

73. Sarah Caldwell, "Bhagavatī Rituals of Kerala," in Margaret A. Mills, Peter Claus,

and Sarah Diamond, eds., *South Asian Folklore: An Encyclopedia* (New York: Routledge, 2003), p. 58.

74. As translated by Sri Aurobindo in R. A. McDermott and V. S. Naravane, eds., *The Spirit of Modern India* (New York: Thomas Y. Crowell Company, 1974), pp. 264–66.

75. B. C. Pal, *The Soul of India* (Calcutta: Yugayatri Prakashak Limited, 1958), p. 103.

76. Ibid., pp. 133–34.

77. Lise McKean, "Bhārat Mātā: Mother India and Her Militant Matriots," in J. S. Hawley and D. M. Wulff, eds., *Devi: Goddesses of India* (Berkeley: University of California Press, 1996). In this chapter, McKean also traces the connections of Swami Satyamitranand Giri to the Vishva Hindu Parishad and the Rāshtrīya Swayamsevak Sangh.

Chapter 7: Vishnu, Endless and Descending

1. See *The Temple of Sree Padmanābhaswamy* (Trivandrum: Bhavana Printers, 1984) and K. R. Vaidyanathan, *Temples and Legends of Kerala* (Bombay: Bharatiya Vidya Bhavan, 1982). The *Bhāgavata Purāna* 10.79 mentions that Balarāma visited "Syanandūrapuram" in the course of his pilgrimage, also a reference to this place.

2. This notion that three-quarters of the divine is beyond our ken is present in the Purusha Sūkta (*Rig Veda* 10.90) as well as in the *Rig Veda* I.64.45–46, where it refers to speech, three-quarters of which is transcendent, and only one-quarter our human speech.

3. Among the thousand names of Vishnu are Ambhonidhi and Apamnidhi, both of which mean the "abode of waters," the ocean. See the *Mahābhārata* XIII.149, as quoted in Jan Gonda, *Aspects of Early Visnuism* (Delhi: Motilal Banarsidass, 1969), p. 15. He is also called Toyātman, "whose self or nature is water." The *Laws of Manu* indicate that the waters are called *nāras*, because they are the offspring of *nara:* "He, desiring to produce beings of many kinds from his own body, first with a thought created the waters, and placed his seed in them. That [seed] became a golden egg, in brilliancy equal to the sun; in that [egg] he himself was born as Brahmā, the progenitor of the whole world. The waters are called *narah*, [for] the waters are indeed the offspring of Nara; as they were his first residence [*ayana*], he thence is named Nārāyana." Georg Bühler, ed., tr., *The Laws of Manu* [Sacred Books of the East, Vol. XXV] (New York: Dover Publications, 1969), 1.8.10. Later we read, "When that divine one wakes, then this world stirs; when he slumbers tranquilly, then the universe sinks to sleep." (1.52.)

4. Nammālvār, *Tiruvaimoli* 1.5.8, and 1.1.7, as quoted in John B. Carman and Vasudha Narayanan, *The Tamil Veda* (Chicago: University of Chicago Press, 1989), pp. 163 and 161.

5. See, for example, the *Vishnu Purāna* II.5.

6. *Nārada Purāna* 2.81–3.

7. See Narayanan and Carman, *The Tamil Veda*, on the emanations or *vyūhas* of Vishnu.

8. They are called *ukantarulinanilankal*, a land graciously, pleasingly desired. In

Tamil they are also called *tiruppati,* and in Sanskrit *divyadesha.* See Katherine K. Young, *Beloved Places* (uṇkantarulinanilankal): *The Correlation of Topography and Theology in the Srivaisnava Tradition of South India* (Montreal, Quebec: McGill University, 1978).

9.   Ibid., Chapter 1.

10. Young notes the images of the geyser, the light in darkness, the refreshing oasis in the desert as common to suggest the nature of these beloved places. Ibid., pp. 23–24.

11. Ibid., pp. 78–79.

12. Friedhelm Hardy, "Ideology and Cultural Contexts of the Srivaisnava Temple," *Indian Economic, Social History Review* XIV, no. i (1977): 119–51.

13. Shrīrangam is called Arankan in the texts, Tirupati is called Venkatam, Kānchī is Kacci, and Melcote is Tirunārāyanapuram.

14. Kurunkuti is south of Tirunelvelli, approaching the tip of south India, and Kotti-yur is between Madurai and Pudukkotai. One hundred and six of the 108 Beloved Places, or *Divya Deshas,* have been mapped on Google Maps; the remaining two are celestial, including Vaikuntha, "Heaven."

15. The Gita Press Hindi encyclopedia volume on *tīrthas,* the *Tirthānk,* compares the standard 108 of the Shrīvaishnava tradition with another list of 108, in the *Brahmā Purāna,* which it finds to be of north Indian origin and including places such as Purī, Shrīkūrmam, and Simhāchalam in the east as well.

16. Young, *Beloved Places,* p. 266.

17. K. N. Subramanyam, tr., *The Anklet Story, Silappadhikaaram of Ilango Adigal* (Delhi: Agam Prakashan, 1977), p. 45. The dating of the epic is as early as the third century, according to some Tamil scholars, and as late as the tenth, according to others. George Hart dates the epic to about the sixth century. See the introduction to the above volume, and George Hart, *The Poems of Ancient Tamil* (Berkeley: University of California Press, 1975), for dating discussions.

18. Friedhelm Hardy, *Viraha Bhakti* (Oxford: Oxford University Press, 1983), p. 260.

19. There are, to be sure, other places of spontaneous divine manifestation as well. This tradition includes places such as the Naimisha Forest in northern India, the holy places of Krishna in Braj, the *tīrtha* of Badrīnāth in the Himalayas, the lotus pool called Pushkara in Rajasthan, and the hill-shrines of Venkateshvara and Tiruvannāmalai in the south. *Svayam Vyakta Kshetra* (Madras: Sri Vadapalani Offset Printers, n.d).

20. V. N. Hari Rao, *The Srirangam Temple,* quoted in Young, *Beloved Places,* p. 111.

21. The story is told in the *Rāmāyana* (Yuddha Khanda 128.90; Uttara Khanda 39.14; 108.27–30) as well as in the *Padma Purāna,* the *Matsya Purāna,* the *Garuda Purāna,* and the *Brahmānda Purāna.* As with many temples, there is not only a foundation myth, there is also a rediscovery myth. Here the ancient temple and sanctuary are said to have been flooded by the Kāverī for a time and discovered again some years later when the king named Kili heard a parrot reciting the Purānic verse declaring this to be the temple of Shrīrangam. Neither King Dharma Varman nor King Kili is historical, in the sense that there are no records or inscriptions bearing their names. The temple's earliest inscriptions date to the tenth century during the Chola reign.

22. Paul Younger describes the festivals of Shrīrangam in two articles, "Singing the Tamil Hymnbook in the Tradition of Rāmānuja: The 'Adhyayanotsava' Festival in Srirankam," in *History of Religions* Vol. 21, No. 3 (Feb. 1982), pp. 272–293; and "Srirankam: Days of Wandering and Romance with Lord Rankanatan: The Pankuni Festival in SrirankamTemple, South India," in *Modern Asian Studies,* Vol. 16, No. 4 (1982), pp. 623–656.

23. B. S. Anandha, compiler, *Sri Venkatesa Purāna* (Madras: Lotus Publishing, 1980), p. 9, and P. Sitapati, *Sri Venkateswara: The Lord of the Seven Hills* (Bombay: Bharatiya Vidya Bhavan, 1972), pp. 26–27.

24. There continues to be a ritual relationship between Kolhāpūr in Maharashtra and Tirupati. See the Ph.D. thesis of Tamara Lanaghan, *Transforming the Seat of the Goddess into Vishnu's Place: The Complex Layering of Theologies in the Karavira Māhātmya* (Harvard University, 2006).

25. From the panoply of Purānic tales, this is one the temple itself has adopted. An extended version of this one is to be found on the T. T. Devasthānams website as the story of the marriage of Vishnu (Shrīnivāsa) to Padmāvatī, *www.tirumala. org/maintemple_legends.htm.*

26. One commentator puts it this way: "There are differences of opinion whether the deity at Tirumala is Vishnu, Siva, Sakti or Skanda. Suffice it to say that the various forms, according to Hinduism, point to the Supreme Brahman and hence it is pointless to extend this debate as each devotee beholds his Ishtadevata in the idol and worships the deity as the Kaliyuga Varada who answers the prayers of all devotees." Chalapati Rao and Gudlavalleti Venkata, *Sri Venkatāchala, Its Glory* (Vijayawada, India: Metro Printers, 1983), p. 234.

27. The tonsure centers at Tirupati understandably yield tons of hair, much of which is then sold for the making of wigs. Several times I have received inquiries from Orthodox Jewish communities, concerned that the hair used in the wigs Orthodox women wear has been offered in temples to "idols." My response has been to clarify the fact that the hair is not offered in the temple or ever presented in the temple, since hair cuttings would be considered a form of pollution in the sacred precincts. The hair is not offered to the Lord at all, but the person who has submitted to tonsure presents himself or herself before the Lord in the temple.

28. Choodie Shivaram, "Court Decree Retires Tirupati Temple's Hereditary Priests," *Hinduism Today,* June 1996.

29. Ralph T. H. Griffiths, trans., *The Hymns of the Rig Veda* (Delhi: Motilal Banarsidass, 1973), I.154.1.

30. In some versions of the myth, his third step is placed on the head of Bali, who bows in submission. The "demons," whether called *asuras, daityas,* or *dānavas* in the Sanskrit vocabulary, are not "evil." They are characterized primarily by their opposition to the gods, and the competition of *devas* and *asuras* drives the drama of the created world.

31. *Taittirīya Samhitā* 2.4.12.3, as cited in Gonda, *Aspects of Early Visnuism,* p. 55.

32. See, for example, the etymologies of the *Linga Purāna* 70.97 and the *Vāyu Purāna* 5.36.

33. *Mahābhārata* 12.48.88. Also discussed in Gonda, *Aspects of Early Visnuism,* p. 64.

34. *Rig Veda* I.155.5.

35. Ibid., I.154.2–3.

36. Ralph T. H. Griffiths, tr. *Texts of the White Yajurveda,* Book V. 38, 41.

37. Gonda, *Aspects of Early Visnuism,* p. 2.

38. Gayā is very near the ancient Buddhist place called Buddha Gayā or Bodh Gayā, where the Buddha is said to have seen through into the true nature of reality and become awakened, enlightened. Both Bodh Gayā and Gayā are important pilgrimage places even today for the Buddhist and Hindu traditions respectively.

39. *Rig Veda* I.22.17. Aurnavābha's mention of these three places as the three steps of Vishnu is recorded by Yāska (Nirukta 12.19). See the *Vāyu Purāna* part II, p. 910, footnote and Appendix C of Suvira Jaiswal, *The Origin and Development of Vaisnavism* (Delhi: Munshiram Manoharlal, 1981).

40. *Vāyu Purāna* II.44.64–65. The story of Gayāsura is contained in Vayu II.44. See also L. P. Vidyarthi, *The Sacred Complex in Hindu Gaya* (Bombay: Asia Publishing House, 1961), Appendix I. A *krosha* is about 2.2 miles, and the idea that a *tīrtha* extends for five *kroshas* is one that is widely duplicated, beginning with the famous *panchakroshī* pilgrimage that circles the mandala of Kāshī, seen schematically as a circle with a radius of five *kroshas.*

41. We should note, however, that even before it came to signal divine descents of Vishnu, the term *avatāra* was likely first used by Buddhists, to describe the descent of those who, like Siddhārtha, took birth on earth to become fully awakened Buddhas.

42. Cited in John B. Carman, *The Theology of Rāmānuja* (New Haven: Yale University Press, 1974), p. 237.

43. Bhagavad Gītā 4.7–8.

44. *Cintāmani Dhāma* (Los Angeles: Bhaktivedanta Book Trust, n.d.), p. 1.

45. Jaiswal, *The Origin and Development,* p. 136.

46. *Vishnu Purāna* I.16–20.

47. *Bhāgavata Purāna* VII.8.

48. Dr. K. Sundaram, *The Simhachalam Temple,* 2nd ed. (Simhachalam: Simhachalam Devasthanam, June 1984). On pp. 44 ff. he summarizes the *Sthala Purānas* and their historical context.

49. It is called the *snāpana bera.* The icons of the temple are as follows: the *mula bera* (main image), the *snāpana bera* (bathing image, used for water offerings and for daily bathing, since the sandal-paste covering of the *mula bera* does not permit this form of worship); the *utsava bera,* used for processions; the *kautuka bera,* used for festivals; the *shayana bera,* which is put regularly to sleep; and the *bali bera,* said to be used for the pacification of spirits.

50. Sundaram, *The Simhachalam Temple.* To summarize some of the history from this excellent study, this area is part of the area known in the fifth century B.C.E. as Kalinga. It is mentioned in the *Mahābhārata.* In the fifth century, the Gangā kings began to rule here, a rule that extended to the fourteenth century. In the eleventh century, there was an alliance between the Gangās and the Cholas of the south. In the late eleventh century (1087), there was the first inscription here, recording the donation to Simhāchalam by a merchant named Penugonda. There is subsequently a Tamil inscription in 1099. In all, there are thirty-seven inscriptions from the last quarter of the eleventh century (p. 67). In the twelfth

century, the great king of this dynasty was Anantavarma Choda Gangā, the same king who was involved in building Purī farther north. During his rule, Vaishnavism was patronized. The first Gangā ruler to have left an inscription at Simhāchalam was Anagabhima, in the thirteenth century. Later that century he was followed by Narasimha I, known also as Narasimha Deva, who was responsible for building the seaside Sūrya Temple at Konārak and who carried on a "wholesale renovation of the temple" at Simhāchalam (p. 19). Later kings spoke of themselves as "worshippers of the lotus feet of Simhādrinātha." Krishnaraya of the Vijayanagara kingdom came here in the sixteenth century. It was really in the period from the thirteenth to sixteenth centuries that Simhāchalam slowly became a popular *kshetra* (pp. 15–18, 67–69).

51. Sundaram, *The Simhachalam Temple*, p. 49.

52. Madelaine Biardeau, "*Narasimha, Mythe et Culte,*" in *Purushārtha* (Paris: Centre d'Etudes de l'Inde et de l'Asie du Sud, 1975), p. 53.

53. The *sthala purāna* of Simhāchalam speaks of four important Narasimha sanctuaries: Ahobilam, Kritasaucham, Harapāpam, and Simhāchalam. The location of Kritasaucham and Harapāpam is not known. Other hilltop shrines of Narasimha include Dharmapurī along the Godāvarī River; Yadavādri in Mysore State (Yadagiri), where, at Melcote, there is a meditating Narasimha; and Vedādri (near Korukonda, East Godāvarī District in Andhra), where Narasimha is with Lakshmi.

54. Madelaine Biardeau, "*Narasimha,*" and J. N. Banerjea, *The Development of Hindu Iconography* (New Delhi: Mushiram Manoharlal, 1974), pp. 416–17.

55. A. Eschmann, "The Vaishnava Typology of Hinduization and the Origin of Jagannātha," in Eschmann, Kulke, and Tripathi, eds., *The Cult of Jagannath and the Regional Tradition of Orissa* (Delhi: Manohar, 1978), p. 101.

56. *Shri Chārodhām Yātrā,* p. 5.

57. See *Mahābhārata,* XII.344–45.

58. The stories of the five rocks of Badrīnāth are told in the *Skanda Purāna* II.iii.3–4.

59. Prabhāsa is the Purānic name for Somnāth, one of the *lingas* of light on the coast of Gujarat; Pushkara is the *tīrtha* of Brahmā in Rajasthan; Gayā is renowned for death rites in what is today Uttar Pradesh; the Naimisha Forest is famous for the stories of the *Mahābhārata,* many of which took place there; and of course Kurukshetra is the *tīrtha* that became famous as the battlefield of the *Mahābhārata,* also called the Field of Dharma.

60. *Skanda Purāna,* II.iii.7.1–11.

61. *Skanda Purāna,* II.iii.6.9–42.

62. *Shri Badrī-Kedār Mahātmya* (Hardwar: Harbhajan Singh and Sons, n.d.), p. 11.

63. *Mahābhārata* III.40.1.

64. Fortunately, Pandu had another wife, Kunti, who had the book of procreating without sex, only by focusing her mind on one of the gods, which is how she gave birth to the sons of Pandu, the Pāndavas.

65. *Skanda Purāna* II.iii.1 is Shiva's review of the many *tīrthas.* This last passage is 1.60–63.

66. *Skanda Purāna* II.iii.2.1–15.

67. A. P. Agarwal, ed., *Garhwal: Dev Bhoomi* (New Delhi: Nest and Wings, 1988), p. 138.

Chapter 8: The Land and Story of Krishna

1. Krishna's Birth-Eighth, referring to the "eighth day" of the waning-moon fortnight of the month of Bhādrapada, when Krishna is said to have been born.

2. The most famous telling of the Krishna legend is in the *Bhāgavata Purāna* 10. A recent and widely available translation has been done by Edwin Bryant, *Krishna: The Beautiful Legend of God* (London: Penguin Books, 2003). The birth story is 10. Chapters 3–5. All subsequent Book 10 and 11 *Bhāgavata Purāna* references are to this translation.

3. Balarāma is often identified with the cosmic serpent Shesha, who upholds the Lord, his resting place in the vast sea of time. Here in Braj, there are many associations between Balarāma and the *naga* deities. Balarāma is known here as Dauji. His is one of the four temples of Braj said to have been established by Krishna's own grandson, Vajranābh.

4. Bryant, *Krishna: The Beautiful Legend* 10.3.13, 14, 17.

5. *Bhāgavata Purāna* 10.4.13.

6. For those interested in the slaughter of innocents here and its possible relation to the similar events attending the story of King Herod and the birth of Jesus, see John S. Hawley in association with Srivatsa Goswāmī, *At Play with Krishna* (Princeton: Princeton University Press, 1981), pp. 56–58.

7. Alan Entwistle, in his detailed book *Braj, Center of Krishna Pilgrimage* (Groningen: Egbert Forsten, 1987), refers to the Sanskrit etymology: *vrajanti gavo yasmin iti vrajah*, the "land in which the cows roam," that is Vraja. It refers to the area "ten kilometers east and south of Mathurā and nearly fifty to the west and north." The Yamunā River runs through the eastern part, while Govardhan is in the west. "Both Vraja and Gokula are used to refer to the encampment or settlement of cowherds of which Nanda was the headman," p. 28.

8. Ibid., p. 71.

9. Shiva G. Bajpai, "Mathurā: Trade Routes, Commerce, and Communication Patterns, from the Post-Mauryan Period to the End of the Kushāna Period," in Doris M. Srinivasan, ed., *Mathurā, The Cultural Heritage* (New Delhi: American Institute of Indian Studies, 1989), p. 45.

10. Frederic S. Growse, *Mathura: A District Memoir* (Northwest Provinces and Oudh Government Press, 1883), p. 34. Here Growse cites Abdullah, who lived at the time of Jahangir, and who wrote in his *Tarikh-i-daudi* a passage referring to Sikander Lodi that has become well known in iconoclastic records: "He was so zealous a Mussalman that he utterly destroyed many places of worship of the infidels and left not a single vestige remaining of them. He entirely ruined the shrines of Mathura, that mine of heathenism, and turned their principal temples into *saraes* and colleges. Their stone-images were given to butchers to serve them as meat-weight and all the Hindus in Mathura were strictly prohibited from shaving their heads and beards and performing their ablutions. He thus put an end to all the idolatrous rites of the infidels there."

11. Francois Bernier, *Travels in the Mogul Empire,* vol. I, Irving Brock, tr. (London: William Pickering, 1826), p. 323.

12. Richard M. Eaton, "Temple Desecration and Indo-Muslim States," *Journal of Islamic Studies* 11, no. 3 (2000): 283–319. In this article, Eaton demonstrates that the extent of temple desecration by Muslim rulers has been greatly exaggerated. While indeed temple destruction occurred, it was selective and aimed primarily at the state deities "to delegitimize and extirpate defeated Indian ruling houses." (289) In the case of the destruction of the Keshava Deva Temple, he sees it as a response to the rebellion of the Jāts, whose leaders had been patronized by the Mughals (307).

13. *Bhagavān Shrī Rādhāmādhava ke Charanon me Samarpit* (Hapur: Modi Bhavan: Shrī Rādhāmādhava Sankirtan Mandal, n.d.), p. 25.

14. Ayodhyā, Mathurā, Māyā (Hardvār), Kāshī, Kānchī, Avantikā (Ujjain), Purī Dvārāvatī—these are the *mokshadayaka* cities. Really these are arguably eight, since Purī in the east and Dvārāvatī in the west constitute the east-west directional axis of India. Purī Dvārāvatī can also mean "the city (*purī*) of Dvārakā."

15. Doris Srinivasan, "Early Krishna Icons: The Case at Mathurā," in Joanna Williams, ed., *Kaladarsana: American Studies in the Art of India* (Leiden: Brill, 1981), p. 130. She argues in this piece that Mathurā was unexceptional in its early depiction of the scenes, or *līlās*, of Krishna's lore and indeed produced less impressive pieces than might be found in other parts of north India and in Karnataka. The major themes of vanquishing Kāliya and Keshi are found in the first five centuries C.E. and, a bit later, Krishna lifting Govardhan.

16. Doris Srinivasan, *Mathurā, The Cultural Heritage*, p. 390, "Vaisnava Art and Iconography at Mathurā."

17. Charlotte Vaudeville, "The Cowherd God in Ancient India," in L. S. Leshnik and G. D. Sontheimer, eds., *Pastoralists and Nomads in South Asia* (Weisbaden: Otto Harrassowitz), 1975.

18. Charlotte Vaudeville, "Braj Lost and Found," *Indo-Iranian Journal* 18 (1976), p. 204.

19. David Haberman, *Journey Through the Twelve Forests* (New York: Oxford University Press, 1994), p. 91. The prayer offered is recounted from his experience on the pilgrimage, but he also cites the *Varaha Purāna*, Mathurā Māhātmya 158.63.

20. Entwistle, *Braj*, p. 30. According to some, the lotus folds in upon Vrindāban at night, enclosing the place where Krishna and Rādhā meet in their intimacy.

21. *Harivamsha*, Manmatha Nath Dutt, trans. (Calcutta: H. C. Dass, Elysium Press, 1897), LX.17–30.

22. *Bhāgavata Purāna* 10.7.35–37a.

23. *Bhāgavata Purāna* 10.8.32–44.

24. This kind of affection is called *sākhya bhāva*, the love between dear friends, the term for "friend" being *sakhya*. In the case of a female, it is the *sakhī* who is the confidante and friend.

25. Entwistle, *Braj*, p. 59.

26. Entwistle, *Braj*, p. 60, cites Nārāyana Bhatta's *Vraja Bhakti Vilāsa* 5.1.

27. From Charlotte Vaudeville's translation of the "Sri Nāthjī Prakatya kī Varta," of Sri Harirāyjī (1590–1715), included in "The Govardhan Myth in Northern India," *Indo-Iranian Journal* 22 (1980), p. 19. This text elaborates the four *dhāms*

to five *dhāms,* substituting Ranganātha in Tiruchirappalli in the south for what is ordinarily Rāmeshvara, and concludes: "A man of good disposition, having performed a pilgrimage to the four Nāthas, if he omits to visit Devadaman, all his pilgrimages are fruitless. But if he only visits Sri Nātha Devadaman on the Govardhana mountain, he obtains the fruit of the pilgrimage to all the four Nāthas in this world."

28. *Bhāgavata Purāna* 10.24–25.

29. Vaudeville, "The Cowherd God."

30. *Harivamsha* LXXI.2, 9, 10, 12. Also cited in Vaudeville, "The Govardhan Myth," p. 4.

31. *Vishnu Purāna* 10. In H. H. Wilson's translation, "Accordingly, the inhabitants of Vraja worshipped the mountain, presenting to it curds, and milk, and flesh; and they fed hundreds and thousands of Brahmans, and many other guests who came (to the ceremony), even as Krishna had enjoined: and, when they had made their offerings, they circumambulated the cows and the bulls, that bellowed as loud as roaring clouds. Upon the summit of Govardhana, Krishna presented himself, saying 'I am the mountain,' and partook of much food presented by the Gopas; whilst, in his own form as Krishna, he ascended the hill, along with the cowherds, and worshipped his other self."

32. Hawley and Goswami, *At Play with Krishna,* p. 34.

33. *Bhāgavata Purāna* 10.16.

34. Hawley and Goswami, *At Play with Krishna,* pp. 35–36.

35. Ibid., p. 36.

36. *Bhāgavata Purāna* 10.29.35.

37. *Bhāgavata Purāna* 10.33.3.

38. This is one of the four old Shiva temples said to have been established in time immemorial by Vajranābh, Krishna's great-grandson. Also called Gopeshvara.

39. Haberman, *Journey Through the Twelve,* p. 23.

40. Growse, *Mathura,* p. 80.

41. *Bhāgavata Purāna* 10.47–49–51.

42. *Skanda Purāna,* Vaishnava Khanda 6.

43. The Krishna temples are, according to Haberman, Govindadev in Vrindāvan, Keshavadev in Mathurā, Haridev in Govardhan, and Baladev in Dauji. The Shiva temples were Gopīshvar in Vrindāvan, Bhuteshvar in Mathurā, Chakreshvar in Govardhan, and Kāmeshvar in Kamaban. (Haberman, *Journey Through the Twelve,* p. 53.)

44. Vallabha was also called Vallabhāchārya, the "āchārya" added to honor his status as a teacher. See Richard Barz, *The Bhakti Sect of Vallabhāchārya* (Faridabad: Thomas Press, 1976).

45. From Vaudeville, tr., "Srī Nāthjī Prakatya," p. 24.

46. Srivatsa Goswāmī, *Celebrating Krishna* (Vrindāvan: Srī Caitanya Prema Samsthāna, 2001), p. 32.

47. Haberman, *Journey Through the Twelve,* p. 64.

48. Ibid.

49. Goswāmī, *Celebrating Krishna,* p. 54.

50. Vaudeville, "Braj Lost and Found," pp. 195–213.

51. For the brief account of Nārāyana Bhatta's life from which I have drawn, see Haberman, *Journey Through the Twelve,* pp. 56–63.

52. Goswāmī, *Celebrating Krishna,* p. 87.

53. Vaudeville, "Braj Lost and Found," p. 199.

54. Ibid., p. 212.

55. Haberman, *Journey Through the Twelve,* pp. 25–26.

56. For further information, see Amit Ambalal, *Krishna as Shrīnāthjī* (Ahmedabad: Mapin Publishing, 1987), p. 26ff., for Hariyālī Amāvasyā and other yearly celebrations in the calendar.

57. See plates in Stuart Cary Welch, ed., *Gods, Kings, and Tigers: The Art of Kotah* (Cambridge: Prestel Publishers, 1997).

58. Growse, *Mathura,* p. 130, confirms, "In anticipation of Aurangzeb's raid, the ancient image of Kesava Deva was removed by Rana Raj Singh of Mewar, and was set up on the spot where, as they journeyed, the wheels of the chariot sank in the deep sand and refused to be extricated. It happened to be an obscure little village, then called Siarh. . . . 22 miles north-east of Udaypur."

59. Vitthalnāth-jī joined Shrīnāth-jī in Nāthdvāra. Dvārakādhīsh-jī from Mathurā came to Kankroli in Rajasthan. Gokulnāth-jī, Gokulchandrama-jī, and Madanamohan-jī all remained in Braj, while Bālakrishna-jī went to Surat in Gujarat. There are other *svarūpas* that are not among the first eight, but still have local prominence, such as Nātvarlāl-jī in Amhedabad and Mukundaray-jī in Vārānasī.

60. Erik Erikson, *Toys and Reasons* (New York: W.W. Norton & Co., 1977), p. 113.

61. Vraj in Pennsylvania has replicated features of the sacred landscape of Braj in India. It began in the 1980s with farmlands and a few existing buildings. In the late 1990s, the large temple was dedicated. There are other Pushti Mārg communities in the United States as well, including those in Sayreville, New Jersey, and in Chicago.

62. The description of Dvārāvatī is elaborated in the *Harivamsha.*

63. *Bhāgavata Purāna* 11.6.29–30.

64. *Bhāgavata Purāna* 11.30.

65. The story of the battle at the seaside is told in the *Mahābhārata* 16.3 and *Bhāgavata Purāna* 11.30.

66. *Bhāgavata Purāna* 11.30.47.

67. Cited prolifically as coming from Book 16 of the *Mahābhārata,* called the Mausala Parva. This short book, the sixteenth of eighteen books of the epic, describes the devastation wrought in Dvārakā, but despite the fact that this passage is so widely cited, I can find no precise reference in the Mausala Parva. It is a paraphrase of Mausala Parva 5.8–10 and 7.41–42, which describe the sharks and alligators that now swim in the flooded streets of Dvārakā. Close, but not as beautiful and evocative as the quoted passage.

68. S. R. Rao, *The Lost City of Dvārakā* (New Delhi: Aditya Prakashan), 1999.

69. The submerging of a seacoast town, even several times over, is a fact perhaps not so incomprehensible today in an era that has become well acquainted with the force of the tsunami.

70. K. R. Vaidyanāthan, *Sri Krishna: The Lord of Guruvayur* (Bombay: Bharatiya Vidya Bhavan, 1974), p. 2.

71. B. Govindacharya, U. P. Upadhyaya, and M. Upadhyaya, *Udupi Past and Present* (Udupi: Sri Pejavar Mutt, 1984). Sanskrit verse and translations of what are said to be "certain stanzas handed down through oral tradition," pp. 17–21.

72. Bannaje Govindacharya, *Madhvacharya, Life and Teachings* (Udupi: Paryayotsava Samiti, 1984), pp. 43–44.

73. Madhva (1238–1317) was a philosopher who espoused the view that the Supreme Reality and the individual soul are not identical (as in Advaita, non-dualism), but are distinct, and the soul's relation with the divine is one of dependence.

74. There is an excellent study of the *mathas* of Udupi by Vasudeva Rao, *Living Traditions in Contemporary Contexts: The Madhva Matha of Udupi* (New Delhi: Orient Longman Private Limited, 2002).

75. Govindacharya et al., *Udipi Past and Present,* p. 25.

76. The story is told as popularly communicated by K. R. Vaidyanāthan in *Sri Krishna, the Lord of Guruvayur* (Bombay: Bharatiya Vidya Bhavan, 1974), p. 11. A spectacular book with photographs and texts of Guruvāyur has been published as well. See Pepita Seth, *Heaven on Earth: The Universe of Kerala's Guruvayur Temple* (New Delhi: Niyogi Books: 2009).

77. For a translation of the work, see M. P. Bhattatiri, *Narayaneeyam,* Swami Tapasyananda, tr. (Madras: Sri Ramakrishnamath, 1982).

78. Indeed, in 2007, the son of Kerala's home minister, Vayalar Ravi, whose mother is a Christian, went to Guruvāyūr to have the first-feeding ceremonies for his son. The temple authorities responded by ordering purification ceremonies for the temple. Public debate was heated on both sides. The temple authorities insisted that if there is any question of religious identity, applicants are referred to the Arya Samāj society in nearby Kozhikode. In 1988, I made the point to temple authorities that it was especially ironic to ask that the Arya Samāj proclaim one's fitness to enter a temple for the *darshan* of the deity, since deity worship is one of the aspects of the Hindu tradition explicitly rejected by the Arya Samāj, since the time of Dayandanda Sarasvati. Interestingly, the author of the book *Heaven on Earth: The Universe of Kerala's Guruvayur Temple,* Pepita Seth, writes in her introduction that she is English and grew up on a farm in Suffolk. After her first visit to Kerala, she writes, "Kerala reached right inside me and rearranged how I looked at life." (P. 8.)

79. G. C. Tripathi, "Jagannātha, the Ageless Deity of India," in A. Eschmann and H. Kulke, eds., *The Cult of Jagannath and the Regional Tradition of Orissa* (New Delhi: Manohar, 1978), p. 481.

80. H. von Steitencron, "Advent of Vishnuism in Orissa," in Eschmann and Kulke, *The Cult of Jagannath,* p. 5.

81. Anncharlotte Eschmann, "The Vaisnava Typology of Hinduization," in Eschmann and Kulke, *The Cult of Jagannatha,* pp. 112–13.

82. For a full description of this rite, see C. G. Tripathi, "Navakalevara," in Eschmann and Kulke, *The Cult of Jagannath,* Chapter XIII, pp. 223–64.

83. G. C. Tripathi sums up the Navakalevara in his final paragraph: "The different rites of the Navakalevara ceremony are a nice example of the superimposition

of the Brahmanic Hinduism on a cult which was purely tribal in origin. The presence of the Daitas, who are avowedly of tribal origin, everywhere in this ceremony and the important part that they play in this ceremony is an irrefutable proof to this effect. Though *Vanayāga* in itself is a phenomenon belonging to the Brahmanic tradition ... it is they (Daitas) who fell the tree, bring it to the Temple and fashion the images. The Brāhmins are not allowed even to enter the Nirmānamandapa. They are neither allowed to see nor to touch the unfinished wooden images, not even for the sake of consecration. The Nyāsadaru which they consecrate for 15 days and which serves as a lid to close the cavity in the torso of the statues is a weak consolation for the Brahmanic ritual and clearly exhibits its secondary character. In the same manner, they are kept away from knowing the 'life-substance' of the Deities and it seems that they have had to struggle hard to get hold of the statues at least on the last day, just before the end of the whole ceremony, in order to make a small stroke in the eyes of Jagannātha and others," p. 264.

CHAPTER 9: FOLLOWING RĀMA: THE *RĀMĀYANA* ON THE LANDSCAPE OF INDIA

1. Paula Richman's edited volume, *Many Rāmāyanas: The Diversity of a Narrative Tradition in South Asia* (Berkeley: University of California Press, 1991), details the range and wealth of the *Rāmāyana* traditions.

2. A. K. Rāmanujan, "Three Hundred Rāmāyanas," in Richman, *Many Rāmāyanas*, p. 45.

3. See Sheldon Pollock's Introduction to *The Rāmāyana, Book 3, The Forest* (New York: University of New York Press, Clay Sanskrit Library editions, 2008), pp. 26–28. Pollock discusses the king as deity in the form of a man, an ancient motif and one that the *Rāmāyana* renews in its narrative of the godlike king Rāma. Pollock speaks of an "extraordinary synthesis here of the numinous and the human."

4. The distinction between the *vana* and the *aranya* seems to be that between the proximate and often lovely "woods" and the farther and often alien "wilderness." See Anne Feldhaus, "The Image of the Forest in the *Māhātmyas* of the Rivers of the Deccan," in Hans Bakker, ed., *The History of Sacred Places in India as Reflected in Traditional Literature* (Leiden: E. J. Brill, 1990), pp. 90–102. In time, as she notes, both terms are used almost interchangeably. One major section of the *Rāmāyana* is called the Aranya Kanda, while in the *Mahābhārata* it is called the Vana Parva. It is not clear that there is a distinction here.

5. W. D. P. Hill, tr., *The Holy Lake of the Acts of Rāma, a Translation of Tulasī Dās's Rāmacharitamānasa* (Bombay: Oxford University Press, 1952), p. 207.

6. M. V. Kibe, *Indian Historical Quarterly* (1928), pp. 694–702; *Journal of the Bhandarkar Oriental Research Institute* XVII (1936), pp. 371–84. See also H. D. Sankalia, "The Ur (original) *Rāmāyana* of Archaeology and the *Rāmāyana*," in *Indologen-Tagung* (Weisbaden, 1971).

7. D. P. Mishra, *The Search for Lankā* (Delhi: Agam Kāla Prakashan, 1985).

8. Even before the mosque-temple controversies of the 1980s and 1990s, there were significant studies by two Dutch scholars. Hans Bakker, in *Ayodhyā* (Groningen: Egbert Forsten, 1986), deals primarily with the *māhātmyas* of Ayodhyā, and Peter Van der Veer, in *Gods on Earth* (London: The Athlone Press, 1988), looks closely at religious specialists in the life of Ayodhyā as a pilgrimage center.

9. Bakker, *Ayodhyā*, pp. 65–66.

10. Ibid., 151.

11. Van der Veer, *Gods on Earth*, p. 17.

12. Bakker, *Ayodhyā*, pp. 95 and 150.

13. Van der Veer, *Gods on Earth*, p. 18.

14. Ramgopal Pandey, "Sharad," *Hanumān garhī kā itihās aur māhātmya* (Ayodhyā: Candramaul Pustak Bandar, n.d.), p. 2.

15. Bakker, *Ayodhyā*, p. 145 n. Even in the eighteenth century there was strife between Shaiva and Vaishnava *sannyāsīs* over the possession of *tīrthas* and sanctuaries in Ayodhyā. Such strife is also mentioned in the *Hanumān garhī kā itihās aur māhātmya*.

16. *Hanumān garhī kā itihās aur māhātmya*, pp. 2–3.

17. F. S. Growse, tr., *The Rāmāyana of Tulasīdāsā* (Delhi: Motilal Banarsidass, 1978), pp. 304–5. In Vālmīki's *Rāmayana*, the arrival in Chitrakūt is to be found in II (Ayodhyakanda) 56.

18. *Siva Purāna*, Kotirudrasamhitā 3.1.

19. Kalyān Vol. 31, No. 1 (Gorakhpur: The Gita Press, 1957), *Tīrthānk*, p. 121.

20. *Siva Purāna*, Kotirudrasamhitā 3–4.

21. Rāmakalhan Saran, *Brihat Srīcitrakūta Māhātmyam* (Lucknow: Tejakumar Press, 1971).

22. Tulsīdās, *Gitāvalī*, pp. 179–88.

23. The Dandakāranya is said to extend across central India, sometimes described as the area between the Narmadā and Godāvarī Rivers, although the Narmadā receives no mention in the *Rāmāyana* until the search parties fan out in the four directions from Kishkindhā to search for Sītā.

24. *Rāmāyana* III.11.21ff. See Srīmad Vālmīki's *Rāmāyana*, 3 vols. (Gorakhpur: The Gita Press, 1969).

25. *Tarpana* is a rite of remembrance for the deceased. It means "satisfaction" and is done with water and other offerings to satisfy the *pitrs*, the ancestors.

26. Mate, *Temples and Legends of Maharashtra* (Bombay: Bharatiya Vidya Bhavan, 1970), pp. 62–63, 75–80. The story of the goddess taking on Sītā's form and presenting herself before Rāma is also told at the beginning of the *Rāmcharitmānas*.

27. Growse, *The Rāmāyana of Tulasīdāsa*, p. 476.

28. Shabarī is said to have been a disciple of a great sage. When he died, she asked to join him in death, but he insisted that she stay on earth until Lord Rāma came to the ashram, which she did.

29. R. S. D. Sen, *The Bengali Ramayanas* (Calcutta: Calcutta University Press, 1920), pp. 46–47.

30. Tulsīdās, *Dohāvalī*, poem 12. Cited in B. I. Kapur, *Hanumān Chālīsā* (New Delhi: Trimurti Publications, 1974), p. 43.

31. George Michell and Vasundhara Filliozat, eds., *Splendours of the Vijayanagara Empire: Hampi* (New Delhi: Marg Publications, 1981), p. 133. They remark that virtually all of the pre-Vijayanagara shrines there are Shaiva (p. 77).

32. Kusum Vyas, founder of Esha Vasyam, a Hindu environmental group based in the United States, in Ruth Gledhill and Jeremy Page, "Can the Monkey God Save Rāma's Underwater Bridge?" in *TimesOnLine*, March 27, 2007. The Save Ram Setu campaign has its website at *http://ramsethu.org/indexmore.html*, accessed 8/06/10.

33. *Adhyātma Rāmāyana*, Yuddha Kanda 4. It is also a source for the tradition that the proper worship of Rāmeshvara should be to begin at Kāshī and bring water from the Gangā to honor the *linga* at Rāmeshvara.

34. *Siva Purāna*, Kotirudrasamhitā 31. The *Padma Purāna*, Shrishtikānda 38, agrees in the establishing of the *linga* before building the bridge to Lankā.

35. *Skanda Purāna*, Brahmakhanda, Setumāhātmya 44–46. This is the version told in the most popular local *māhātmya* pamphlet, *Pilgrim's Guide to Rameswaram and Dhanushkodi* (Rameswaram: Sri Rāmanāthasvami Temple, 1977).

36. There are many specific *tīrthas* at Rāmeshvara associated with such penitence. At Brahmā Kund, Lord Brahmā was released from the sin of lying about the sovereignty of Shiva. At Shiva Tīrtha, Shiva was released from the sin of cutting off one of Brahmā's five heads. At Rāma Tīrtha, Yudhisthira was cleansed of the falsehood he told during the great war at Kurukshetra.

37. Makhan Lal Sen, tr., *The Rāmāyana of Vālmīki*, Yuddhakanda LXXXVI pp. 565–66. This is Sen's paraphrase of the very last chapter of the Yuddhakanda, Book 6 of the *Rāmāyana*.

38. Anuradha Kapur, *Actors, Pilgrims, Kings, and Gods: The Ramlila at Ramnagar* (Calcutta: Seagull Books, 1990), pp. 12–13, 23.

39. The quick glimpse in this context is referred to as a *jhanki*, beholding for just a brief moment. One might think of it as a quick *darshan*. The term *jhanki* is often used, for instance, for the glimpse of Shiva rendered by painting one of his faces or moods on the shaft of the *linga*.

40. Phillip Lutgendorf, "All in the Raghu Family," in L. A. Babb and S. Wadley, eds., *Media and the Transformation of Religion in South Asia* (Philadelphia: University of Pennsylvania Press, 1995), details some of the many cultural phenomena associated with the televised *Rāmāyana*.

41. Sheldon Pollock, "Ramayana and Political Imagination in India," *Journal of Asian Studies* 52, no. 2 (May 1993), p. 262.

42. Ibid.

43. Ibid., pp. 273–83.

44. Cited from *Epigraphica Indica* (1965), pp. 58–62, in R. S. Sharma, M. Athar Ali, D. N. Jha, and Suraj Bhan, "Rāmjanmabhūmi-Babri Masjid: A Historians' Report to the Nation," in A. J. Noorani, ed., *The Babri Masjid Question, 1528–2003: "A Matter of National Honour"* (Delhi: Tulika Books, 2003), pp. 39–40.

45. D. Mandal, *Ayodhyā: Archaeology After Demolition* (New Delhi: Orient Longman, 1993), p. 57.

46. "Ramjanmabhumi-Babri Masjid: A Historian's Report," in *Noorani* I (2003): 45.

47. Noorani, *The Babri Masjid Question*, vol. I, p. xviii.
48. Ibid., vol. II, p. 161.
49. S. Gopal, ed., *Anatomy of a Confrontation: The Babri Masjid–Ramjanmabhumi Issue* (New Delhi: Penguin Books, 1991), p. 15.
50. Noorani, *The Babri Masjid Question*, vol. II, "The BJP's 1998 Election Manifesto," p. 161.
51. Ibid., p. 160.
52. Ibid., vol. I, "R. K. Dasgupta on Rāma as a Political Tool," p. 20.
53. Amartya Sen, Foreword to Robert Goldman, tr., *Rāmāyana* Book I, Boyhood (New York: New York University Press, Clay Sanskrit Library, 2009), p. x.
54. Pollock, "Ramayana and Political Imagination," p. 273.
55. Mushirul Hasan, "Competing Symbols and Shared Codes: Inter-Community Relations in Modern India," in S. Gopal, *Anatomy of a Confrontation* (New Delhi: Penguin Books, 1991), p. 100.

CHAPTER 10: A PILGRIM'S INDIA TODAY

1. Heather Timmons, "For the Rural Poor, Cell Phones Come Calling," *International Herald Tribune,* May 6, 2007, www.iht.com/articles/2007/05/06/business/wireless07.1-44394.php.
2. Akansha Sinha, "TRAI Kicks Off QoS for Mobile Money," November 25, 2010, *http://voicendata.ciol.com/content/news/110112501.asp.* "India is the world's fastest-growing mobile market and adds 15 to 20 million new cellular users every month. The country, with a population of over 1.2 billion, already has over 600 million mobile connections."
3. Reported by the Business Knowledge Resource online at Bus.Gov for the week ending April 10, 2010, *http://business.gov.in/news_analysis.php?bid =380&Search=&popup_container=.* Such statistics are available on an ongoing basis from the website of the Internet and Mobile Association of India, *www. iamai.in/.*
4. *www.tirumala.org/darshan.htm*, accessed August 18, 2010.
5. *www.maavaishnodevi.org/help_desk_ystats.asp*, accessed August 18, 2010.
6. Quoted in K. A. Shaji, "Sabarimala: The Faith in Spate," *www.boloji.com/ society/115.htm*, accessed August 18, 2010. See also the website of the Clean Sabarimala Project, *http://cleansabarimala.com.*
7. Kelly D. Alley, "Separate Domains: Hinduism, Politics, and Environmental Pollution," in Christopher Chapple and Mary E. Tucker, eds., *Hinduism and Ecology* (Cambridge, MA: Harvard University Press, 2000), p. 375.
8. Somini Sengupta, "Glaciers in Retreat," *New York Times,* July 17, 2007, pp. D1, D4.
9. Kapila Vatsyayana, "Plural Cultures, Monolithic Structures," in *India International Centre Quarterly*, vol. 29, nos. 3, 4, Winter 2002 and Spring 2003, p. 97. Kapila Vatsyayana is also the general editor of the five-volume *Prakrti: The Integral Vision*, which explores the vision of arts and nature in the deep structures of Indian culture.

10. Tamara Lanaghan, *Transforming the Seat of the Goddess into Vishnu's Place: The Complex Layering of Theologies in the Karavīra Māhātmya*. Harvard University Ph. D. Thesis (Cambridge: Harvard University Archives, 2006).

11. W.J.T. Mitchell, ed., *Landscape and Power* (Chicago: University of Chicago Press, 2002), p. 13.

12. Simon Schama, *Landscape and Memory* (New York: Random House, 1995), pp. 6–7.

13. Feldhaus, *Connected Places*, p. 17.

14. Yi-Fu Tuan, *Space and Place: The Perspective of Experience* (Minneapolis: University of Minnesota Press, 1977), p. 54.

15. Sheldon Pollock in *The Language of the Gods in the World of Men* sees *desh* as signaling the vernacular in the binary of the universalizing Sanskrit cosmopolis and the vernacular space and literature of regions, and he points to the theorization of this understanding of *desh* in Sanskrit literature itself.

16. K. V. Rangaswami Aiyangar, "Introduction" to Lakshmīdhara, *Tīrthavivecana-Kāṇḍa*, pp. xxxiii–xxxvii.

17. Agehananda Bharati, "Pilgrimage Sites and Indian Civilization," in Joseph P. Elder, ed., *Chapters in Indian Civilization*, p. 90.

18. V. Raghavan, *The Great Integrators: The Saint-Singers of India* (Delhi: Government of India, 1966), p. 124.

INDEX